THE OLD SCHOOL TIE

BY THE SAME AUTHOR

NOVELS
One Foot in the Clouds
Chameleon
The Office

NOVELS FOR CHILDREN
Jane's Adventures in and out of The Book
Jane's Adventures on the Island of Peeg
Jane's Adventures in a Balloon

NONFICTION
The Unnatural History of the Nanny

THE OLD SCHOOL TIE

The Phenomenon of the English Public School

JONATHAN GATHORNE-HARDY

THE VIKING PRESS
New York

Copyright © Jonathan Gathorne-Hardy, 1977
All rights reserved
Published in 1978 by The Viking Press
625 Madison Avenue, New York, N.Y. 10022

LIBRARY OF CONGRESS CATALOGING IN PUBLICATION DATA

Gathorne-Hardy, Jonathan.
The old school tie.
Bibliography: p.
Includes index.
1.   Education—England—History.   2.   Education—
Great Britain—History.   3.   Public schools, Endowed
(Great Britain)—History.   I.   Title.
LA631.G37   1978   373.2′22   78-1780
ISBN 0-670-52316-X

Printed in the United States of America

Set in Bembo

Published in England under the title
The Public School Phenomenon, 597-1977.

For Rachel

ACKNOWLEDGMENTS

In response to a request for information about any sort of public school in a number of newspapers and magazines, and after some small paragraphs of editorial publicity, I received nearly six hundred letters, many of which resulted in considerable correspondence. These letters were of enormous help in providing illustrations, suggesting themes or areas of exploration, or reinforcing or modifying conclusions I had already come to. I am extremely grateful to everyone who wrote to me, but, at the risk of being invidious, I should like especially to thank Julia McSwiney, Mr. J. E. H. Blackie, the editor of *The History of Bradfield College*, which approaches publication as I write, and Mr. R. L. Arrowsmith, whose *History of Charterhouse Registers, 1769-1872* has recently appeared.

I owe an equal debt of gratitude to the many people who allowed me to interview them, often for several hours. These are also too numerous to mention, though, where they did not request anonymity (many of them did), they occasionally surface by name at some point in the narrative. I should also like to thank the headmasters and headmistresses, the staff and pupils of the twenty schools I visited for their generosity with time, their interest and help, and their good humour—all of which made this part of my research by far the most enjoyable.

A number of other people assisted me during the course of the book. I would like to thank Diana Summers, who helped with some research; Jenny Scott, who typed huge chunks of the manuscript and achieved miracles of decipherment with the hieroglyphics which pass as my handwriting. My thanks are due to Hodder and Stoughton and Viking Penguin Inc. of New York for the financial generosity which gave me the time to write; and to Juliet Brightmore for her skill and industry in collecting the illustrations. Five people read the typescript. I would like to thank Diana Baring, Stephanie Darnill, Rivers Scott and Alan D. Williams for the enormous labour involved and for the many valuable comments and changes that resulted from them. In particular I should like to thank Dr. John Rae, the Headmaster of Westminster, whose encouragement came before the book was finished, and whose intelligent and pointed questions and expert knowledge did much to remove the many errors. Any that still remain almost certainly do so through my obstinacy in the face of advice from these five.

I must also formally acknowledge the following authors, publishers and agents for the permission, often after payment, sometimes very large payment, to quote from the books whose copyright they control: Hart Publishing Company Inc., for extracts from *Summerhill: A Radical Approach to Child Rearing* by A. S. Neill, Copyright © 1960 Hart Publishing Company; John Murray Ltd., for some verses from *Summoned by Bells* by John Betjeman; David Higham Associates Ltd., for extracts from *The Collapse of British Power* by Correlli Barnett, published by Eyre Methuen; The Hogarth Press, for extracts from *Olivia by Olivia* by Dorothy Bussy; Constable and Co. Ltd., for extracts from *Some People* by Harold Nicolson; Curtis Brown Ltd., for extracts from *Lord Dismiss Us* by Michael Campbell, and G. P. Putnam's Sons for use of the same material in America; A. M. Heath and Co. Ltd., for extracts from the essays *Boys' Weeklies* and *Such, Such Were the Joys* by George Orwell; Alan Ross Ltd., for extracts from *Flannelled Fool: A Slice of Life in the Thirties* by T. C. Worsley; A. P. Watt and Son Ltd., for extracts from *Goodbye to All That* by Robert Graves, published by Cassell and Co. Ltd., and to Doubleday and Co. Inc. for use of the same material in America; André Deutsch Ltd., for extracts from the 1938 edition of *Enemies of Promise* by Cyril Connolly, copyright by the Estate of Cyril Connolly, and to Deborah Rogers Ltd. for use of the same material in America; to Eric Glass Ltd., for extracts from *Escape from the Shadows* by Robin Maugham, published by Hodder and Stoughton; to Philip Toynbee, for extracts from his book *Friends Apart;* Barrie and Jenkins, for extracts from *Clubland Heroes* by Richard Usborne, and to A. D. Peters and Co. Ltd., for use of the same material in America; Geoffrey Bles Ltd., for extracts from *The Loom of Youth* by Alec Waugh; The Hamlyn Publishing Group, for extracts from *My Early Life* by Winston Churchill; Peter Newbolt, for extracts from *Vitai Lampada* and *Clifton Chapel* by Henry Newbolt.

For tables, graphs, etc., I acknowledge the following: Thomas Nelson and Sons Ltd., for use in Appendixes E, F, G, and L, of tables and figures from *The Rise of the Public Schools* by T. W. Bamford; Faber and Faber Ltd., for the use of figures from *The Public Schools and the Future* by J. C. Dancy; the Longman Group Ltd., for the use on p. 453 of the table from *The Public Schools: A Factual Survey* by Graham Kalton; Professor John Honey, for the table in Appendix C taken from his book *Tom Brown's Universe* published by Millington; A. D. Peters and Co. Ltd. and Stein and Day, for the tables on pp. 449 and 452, from *The New Anatomy of Britain* by Anthony Sampson, Copyright © 1971 by Anthony Sampson; Professor Geoffrey Best, for the figures on p. 448 from his essay in *The Victorian Public School* published by Gill and Macmillan.

CONTENTS

ILLUSTRATIONS

ACKNOWLEDGMENTS

1 The Mansell Collection
2 Mary Evans Picture Library
3 Radio Times Hulton Picture Library
4 Elliot and Fry Ltd.
5 University Library, Bristol
6 Fox
7 Christ's Hospital
8 Henry Grant Photo Library
9 Longman Group Ltd.
10 Camera Press Ltd.
11 Robin Maugham
12 Philip Toynbee
13 Noel Blakiston
14 Sport and General
15 Coventry City Library

SCOTLAND

NEWCASTLE

DURHAM

ST. BEES

ISLE
OF
MAN

KING WILLIAM'S
Castletown

SEDBERGH

AMPLEFORTH

GIGGLESWICK
Settle

ROSSALL
Fleetwood

STONYHURST
Whalley

ST. PETER'S
York

LEEDS

Crosby

MANCHESTER

KING'S
Chester

WORKSOP

DENSTONE &
ABBOTSHOLME
Uttoxeter
SHREWSBURY

REPTON
Derby

NOTTINGHAM HIGH

GRESHAM'S
Holt

OAKHAM &
UPPINGHAM
Rutland

NORWICH

KING EDWARD'S
Birmingham

OUNDLE
Peterborough

BROMSGROVE

RUGBY

WARWICK

KING'S
Ely

KING'S &
ROYAL GRAMMAR
Worcester

WELLINGBOROUGH
Northampton

PERSE &
THE LEYS
Cambridge

FRAMLINGHAM

SUMMERHILL
Leiston

MALVERN

BLOXHAM
Banbury

BEDFORD

BISHOP'S STORTFORD

CHELTENHAM &
CHELTENHAM LADIES

STOWE
Buckingham

FELSTED
Dunmow

MONMOUTH

RENDCOMB
Cirencester

MAGDALEN
Oxford

BERKHAMSTED

ST. ALBANS

WESTONBIRT
Tetbury

RADLEY &
ABINGDON

WYCOMBE
ABBEY

HAILEYBURY

ALDENHAM
Elstree

CLIFTON &
BRISTOL

ST. MARY'S
Calne

MARLBOROUGH

BRADFIELD

ETON

KING'S
Rochester

DOWNE HOUSE
Cold Ash

LEIGHTON PARK
Reading

DOWNSIDE &
KINGSWOOD
Bath

WELLINGTON
Crowthorne

FRENSHAM HEIGHTS
Farnham

SEVENOAKS

TONBRIDGE

BENENDEN

KING'S
Canterbury

TAUNTON

CRANBOURNE CHASE
Tisbury

CHARTERHOUSE
Godalming

CRANLEIGH

WINCHESTER

BLUNDELL'S
Tiverton

SHERBORNE

GODOLPHIN
Salisbury

BEDALES
Petersfield

CHRIST'S
HOSPITAL
Horsham

ARDINGLY
Haywards Heath

HURSTPIERPOINT

CLAYESMORE &
BRYANSTON
Blandford

CANFORD
Wimbourne

LANCING

BRIGHTON
ROEDEAN
ST. MARY'S HALL

DARTINGTON
Totnes

WALES

Where the name of the school is the same as
the name of a town, the latter is left out.

0   50 Miles

0   50 Km

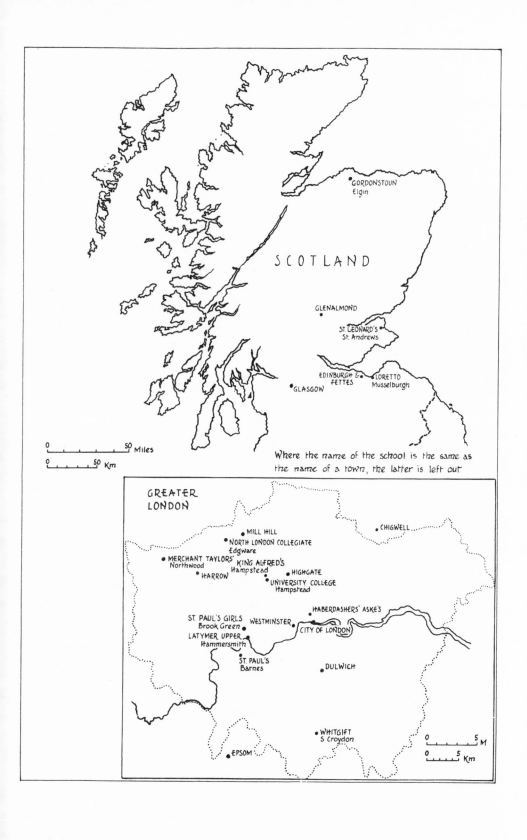

GORDONSTOUN
Elgin

SCOTLAND

GLENALMOND

ST. LEONARD'S
St. Andrews

EDINBURGH &
FETTES

•GLASGOW

LORETTO
Musselburgh

0 _____ 50 Miles

0 _____ 50 Km

Where the name of the school is the same as
the name of a town, the latter is left out

GREATER
LONDON

• MILL HILL

CHIGWELL

• NORTH LONDON COLLEGIATE
Edgware

• MERCHANT TAYLORS'
Northwood

KING ALFRED'S
Hampstead

• HARROW

• HIGHGATE

• UNIVERSITY COLLEGE
Hampstead

HABERDASHERS' ASKE'S

ST. PAUL'S GIRLS
Brook Green

WESTMINSTER

LATYMER UPPER
Hammersmith

CITY OF LONDON

ST. PAUL'S
Barnes

• DULWICH

• WHITGIFT
S Croydon

0 _____ 5 M

0 _____ 5 Km

• EPSOM

CHAPTER 1

Introductory

The introverted society thus created provided an experience from which many public school boys never recovered, and the boarding system has been blamed for most of their subsequent failings—their veneration for authority, their obsession with tradition, their frustrated sex lives.

Anthony Sampson, *The New Anatomy of Britain*

With this book I complete a study begun some years ago with *The Unnatural History of the Nanny.*

There is no need to read the first book in order to follow the second; although a number of things in it—the aspects of child psychology looked at, an explanation of some odd sides to Victorian sexuality are examples— add force and depth to certain areas we shall deal with here. But the two books are completely independent.

The book about nannies was easier to write than this one. In discussing systems of upbringing in early childhood you will inevitably discuss the sort of adult produced, and by extension discuss, or reveal, the sort of adult you think should be produced; in discussing systems of education you are doing that too, but you are also dealing with types of society. People are in rough agreement about the qualities desirable in a person, the ends of upbringing (security, ability to love, responsibility, etc.), though they may differ as to means (more or less discipline and so on); but as to the sort of society we should live in, no one is agreed either on ends or means.

Hardly anyone had written about nannies before. Here dozens, even hundreds of scholars, biographers and autobiographers have trod the ground bare. See us as we shuffle into the history class and slump at our desks: Gardner B., Leach A. F., Hollis C., Mack E. C., Bamford T. W.— an excellent effort, Bamford, though never be afraid to speculate a little; all right, Gathorne-Hardy, wipe that smile off your face, there's no substitute for sound scholarship; Trelawny-Ross A. H., D'E. Firth J., West J. M., Dancy J., Rodgers J., Blunden E., Lamb G. F., . . . a motley crew, and there are many more. I doubt if you've heard of many of us and almost certainly not of our books. The public schools have yet to find their Gibbon.

I am not he. Yet oddly enough this book is in one way unique; it is the only complete history. (Gardner, who makes the same claim, has not written a complete history; or it is complete only in the sense that he has put in a whole lot of schools everyone else has had the sense to leave out.) No other book that I can find—certainly not Gardner—deals with girls' public schools and progressive schools. No other book takes the story up to today; at around 1920 loyalty and fear of libel shrink the general histories into vague mumblings, those of individual schools into catalogues of swimming pools built.

I am conscious of failure. I have far too little about girls' schools (there *is* very little), Catholic schools, Scottish schools and day schools—but the last is because I am less interested in them. Where so many have burrowed, I could hardly hope to find anything new. The quotation from Anthony Sampson I put at the head of the chapter is the intelligent man's *idée reçue* about the 19th-century and early-20th-century public schools. I cannot quarrel with it; yet the precise truth is infinitely more complex and contradictory, and, at the depths where these complexities and contradictions start to emerge, often fascinating, sometimes sinister and strange.

There is the difficulty of accuracy and the impossibility of finding the truth. Every school is different for everyone in it, different at different moments for the same person. And covering so much wider an area and so much vaster an extent of time than anyone else means that in any one sphere someone in the classroom—and many outside—know far more than I do. I must often be wrong in detail, though I suspect that from my view high above the whole field I may sometimes gain a new perspective. At any rate, it is from that general distance that I write.

A number of things will emerge. I quite often stray from the strict definition of my subject and look at schools which no decent person would dream of describing as a public school. This may irritate some people, particularly in the classroom (actually, there is no *strict* definition of public schools, though it will become clear what they are). But, just as a study of the lunatic may give one valuable insights into the sane, so we can often learn a good deal from studying the often bizarre institutions, and the wild figures who ran them, which hover from time to time on the fringes of our field. In the same way, what happens in other closed communities—battleships, prisons, monasteries—can help to explain what goes on in public schools, particularly what began to go on from about 1850 onwards.

There is today what one could describe as a school of radical egalitarian history. Eric Hobsbawm, who is of this school, wrote recently that capital exploitation, and any society based on it, was bad at the time, left a bad legacy, and that the historian should unequivocally condemn it. The true task of the historian was to investigate the working people, the lower classes; and that their quality of life was how a civilisation should be judged, their attitudes and concerns were what constituted its history. If that is true, then is not the examination we are about to embark on, an examination of what must surely be only a slim wafer of upper-class and often distasteful privilege, a waste of time? I hope an answer to this will emerge too.

There is, however, bound to be much that many people will find distasteful. The cruelty of boy to boy, of master to boy, the almost unbelievable savagery, sometimes overtly sadistic, of the beatings in certain periods, the initiation rites, primitive in their content and in their effect—all this is disturbing.

And class. A friend of mine attacked me for being a snob because I wrote about nannies; which is as absurd as saying I was an astronaut if I wrote about space or a criminal if I wrote about crime. I am not a snob, nor are these books snobbish—indeed, I doubt that it is any longer possible to be snobbish in that strange English-class way now. At least it is difficult. But anyone who writes about England in the 19th century or early 20th century—in fact about any period of our social history, but particularly then—has to deal with class. Those who are made uneasy by the subject—through guilt or rage—will just have to bite on the bullet; or rather bite on a whole magazine of bullets.

And finally sex. Here is a quotation from an article about Waziristan which appeared in *The Wall Street Journal*:

> Drinks are served by Geba Kahn, first mess sergeant, who has been serving in the mess since 1910. At eighty-seven, he must be one of the oldest soldiers anywhere.
>
> The visitor asks Geba Kahn what the British officers used to do here in the evenings half a century ago.
>
> "Play bridge, sir," says Geba Kahn.
>
> "Oh, tell him what else," one of the Pakistani officers says.
>
> "Sodomy, sir," Geba Kahn replies.

I have felt compelled to go fairly fully, though I hope with care and discretion, into certain sexual aspects of public schools, partly because it is another area which my peers in the classroom have unaccountably neglected, but also because a good deal of what I have to suggest is still relevant today—and not just to public schools.

I wrote the book and read for it as I went along, at each stage discovering new aspects which altered my direction and modified or even changed what had gone before. In particular it was not until I had reached the very end that I read a number of books of anthropology to try to see how people of other cultures brought up their adolescents. What I read then threw quite dramatic light on certain cardinal aspects of the entire work; I have put what I found at the end so that the reader can also experience that sudden clarification as the perspective abruptly shifts.

But before we reach that moment there is a long, often arduous, always, I hope, interesting and sometimes very exciting journey ahead. Let us cast ourselves back, back well over a thousand years, and set off in search of that extraordinary and powerful institution—the English public school.

CHAPTER 2

Early History I: The Primitive Skeleton of Public Schools

Older than the House of Commons, older than the Universities, older than the Lord Mayor, older than the House of Lords, older even than the throne or the nation itself.
A. F. Leach, *Schools of Medieval England*

The snobbery of public schools about their age is absurd—but not surprising. They are the oldest institutions we have. A. F. Leach, trembling into an ecstasy of veneration and excitement at the head of the chapter, was writing about St. Peter's, York Minster, founded by St. Paulinus in AD 625. He subsequently admitted that King's School, Canterbury, founded around AD 598 when St. Augustine established the Cathedral, was older. One thousand three hundred and eighty-nine years ago—"older than the nation itself".

When Christianity first came to Britain, it brought with it services, prayers and songs that were all in Latin. Whenever a cathedral, monastery or even large church was built, therefore, they were almost invariably accompanied by schools. These were of two sorts (often combined): a song school to teach choristers to sing, and schools to teach Latin for the services. For this reason the last were called grammar schools. Thus from the start we can see two fundamental influences whose last remote tremors can still be detected today. The first of these derives from the fact that they were not just associated with the Church; the identification was far closer. They were almost a part of the Church. The first teachers were secular clergy, that is clergy who had taken vows of chastity, obedience and so on, but who worked in the world and not in a monastic order. Some early headmasters even had the power to excommunicate, and this continued into the 14th century.

But the major purpose of the schools was to provide recruits for the new Church. And so close was the association, so strong the tradition, that the later public schools were still churning out deans and canons and bishops in dozens. The route to a bishopric via a headmastership was common right up to the 20th century.

The main subject—and this is the second fundamental influence—was Latin. "The Art and Science of Grammar", as Alcuin describes it at St. Peter's, York. But, although the Latin bias is crucial, from the start certain schools had a surprisingly wide curriculum. At St. Peter's again, whose documents survive, they were taught rhetoric, law, music, Latin verse ("to run over the ridges of Parnassus with lyric feet"), astronomy, natural history, mathematics and, of course, the Scriptures.

We can learn something from the pupils. Practically all histories of this subject say that "Public schools were founded to provide education for the poor"; they then seize the chance of some glib sarcasm and point out how they "ended by being anything but public and being reserved—with trifling exceptions—for the very rich."

This does not seem to me to be historically accurate. We have just seen that the main purpose of the grammar schools was to provide recruits for the new Church. True, it was the poor who were taught. But this was not out of charity, but because, until the Church grew powerful, there was no incentive to learn. The training, such as it was, of the rich and noble took place in their own houses, or those of their peers. Therefore the poor had to be recruited. This, at any rate, is the inference I draw from two scanty but crucial accounts in the early centuries: "Whatever youths he saw of remarkable intelligence, he got hold of them", it was said of Albert, Headmaster of St. Peter's. And King's, Canterbury expelled them if they were "not of native genius, but fools . . . [lest] like drones they consume the bees' honey".

The cleverest poor boys were seized to fuel the Church. No doubt they were easily persuaded. Life in those early centres, primitive as it would be, was probably preferable to that of the very poor. As the centuries passed this did, in fact, become an adjunct to the charitable activities of the Church: as education became a method of advancement this charity gained in weight. The origin was not charitable. This correction to the received view may seem trifling, but it is significant; it shows in operation for almost the first time that process, so common with the schools and so vital to grasp, whereby anything that persisted gained, by that fact alone, the momentum of tradition. Frequently what persisted was ridiculous or unpleasant. Sometimes it was beneficial. The idea that the poor should be educated free continued strongly into the 17th century, and was still feebly alive in the 19th century.

Finally, it seems possible that the practice of taking children into schools very young was established now. Early services were largely sung, and it was therefore necessary to have a number of boys whose voices had not broken. The earlier they were taken, the more easily they could be trained and the longer the Church would have the use of them. But since they couldn't sing absolutely non-stop, all day, the custom grew up of giving them an elementary education which they would go on to complete at the grammar school. Thus was set the first division into lower and upper school, from which eventually evolved prep school and public school.

Peering back through the immense stretch of thirteen centuries it is almost impossible to discover what life was like in those tiny communities growing up in the first religious centres. Occasionally a law or a complaint survives. Little else. No doubt conditions were hard. The great gateway of St. Albans School, founded in the 10th century near the Abbey, was built in 1361 to house the pupils. It was strong enough and uncomfortable enough to be used as a prison in 1553, a rôle it repeated in the Napoleonic wars. As much as for defence, this strength was probably designed to prevent the pupils running away—a frequent complaint in later centuries. Lessons would begin at dawn to save candles, and all day the air would be filled with the drone of repetition. Because of the shortage of books, learning meant learning by heart; a concept that easily ignored the invention of printing and survives today. Discipline and life were rough. In 1309 the scholars were forbidden to carry arms inside or outside St. Albans. People who did not hesitate to beat small babies, would hardly scruple over boys or youths. Alcuin gratefully describes how his school brought him to man's estate "with whippings of fatherly discipline".

But how much is missing, how many subjects which will soon pre-occupy us and let us flesh out the bare outlines have left no trace. Sex, for example, which for one over-lengthy and feverish period is to sweep the public schools like a medieval plague, raging unchecked in the dormitories, changing rooms and studies, now torturing, now delighting, dictating the contents of sermons, the forms of social life, the minutiæ of discipline, influencing the curriculum, the sport, even the very architecture, this great theme has vanished almost without trace. But I have dwelt on the few early facts at some length because, extraordinary as it may seem, they contain the essential seeds from which, with the inevitability of an embryo following the dictates of its genes, the entire structure of the future grammar, and finally, public schools was ultimately to grow.

1 The growth of fee-paying; origins of boarding and houses

During the early Middle Ages the spread of Christianity, the growth in importance and power of the Church, meant the spread and growth of the grammar schools. As time passed their functions broadened. The general picture during this period is that the very poor, particularly the country poor, the villein, only received education in very rare circumstances; the nobleman's son and the very rich (with exceptions to be discussed) were still educated in the houses of other noblemen and had a very different training. The schools now provided for the nascent middle class, giving them a clerical training for a clerical class to transact the nation's business.

In the 14th and 15th centuries the Church and its institutions began the decline which was to lead to—or to excuse—the dissolution of the monasteries at the beginning of the 16th century. We now see wealthy individuals, the Crown and soon liveried companies, taking on the task hitherto performed by the Church. In 1382, for instance, William of Wykeham founded Winchester, and we may note three things: the earlier recruiting of the poor is in the process of becoming a charitable obligation. For this reason it is specified that the scholars must be poor. The school still has a strongly religious function (its warden could hear confessions and grant absolution); it trains choristers to sing and scholars for holy orders. At the same time self-interest begins to play a part in the foundations. Wykeham made provision that some founder's kin should be included among the scholars. Fairly soon and for a number of years the scholars included practically no one else.

By the 15th century the schools had grown sufficiently in prestige for their founding and standing to be a matter of competition. Certainly, there is something competitive in Henry VI's assumption that Eton, which he founded in 1442, would "excel all other grammar schools . . . and be called the lady, mother and mistress of all other grammar schools", an assumption which a good many people, in subsequent centuries, have found maddening. Eton, at its start, combined religion and the founder's self-interest in a way that was becoming typical, in that a large part of its function was to sing masses for Henry and his father.

To provide a continuity of education—but more particularly for continuity of self-interest—the founders during these centuries and often later founded colleges at the universities and (or) provided substantial scholarships at them. Eton and King's College, Cambridge, Westminster and Christ Church, Oxford and Trinity College, Cambridge, Merchant Taylors' and St. John's College, Oxford, are examples among dozens. This is a significant development in that it was to provide an important strand in what one can call public school incest—a spiritual and psychological phenomenon (in 18th-century Eton a more or less physical one as well) which, deep into the 20th century, dictated, among a good many other things, the ferocity of their resistance to change.

The 16th century is usually presented as the golden age of grammar-school foundation, with Henry VIII, the poet prince, Renaissance scholar and great educationalist, leading the way. This is partly true; in part it is the reverse of the truth. The break with Rome and the dissolution of the monasteries meant that education would disappear unless a new basis for it could be found. In fact a great deal did disappear. Henry destroyed far more than he created and for a long time after him, it seems, there were fewer schools than there had been before. In Elizabeth's reign the Speaker of the House of Commons said there were "at least 400 wanting, which before this reign had been".

Nevertheless, this appalling situation did produce a great deal of activity. Throughout the century the Crown endowed new grammar schools—or much more usually used monastic and Church (or Catholic) property to re-endow old ones. Henry VIII with King's School, Canterbury, Mary and Philip re-endowing St. Peter's, York, Edward VI with Sherborne in 1550, Elizabeth with Westminster—dozens of schools were re-started at this time (which is why a good many schools have "King's" or "Queen's" in their name).

But the main thrust for new foundations comes from the liveried companies; this is the great age of merchant schools, like Oundle, Blundell's, Gresham's, Tonbridge. More rarely, wealthy individuals founded schools, like Sir John Port, who started Repton. They founded them for their souls, their children, the poor—and sometimes just to preserve their names. Edward Alleyn, who founded Dulwich, said that if the headmaster could not be of his family then he should at least be called Alleyn. They somehow kept this up for 238 years, until 1857.

Preservation of their souls and the education of their families—two stronger motives can scarcely be imagined. No wonder founders provided money to finance their schools: Tonbridge, for instance, was given land round St. Pancras by the Skinners' Company. It would be tedious to give details of these endowments, except to note that they were numerous and, in individual cases (Eton, Winchester), large—particularly when added to over the centuries—and that they alone can sometimes explain the growth of a foundation into a "Great School".

To ensure the permanence of such important aims, the proper use of so much money, the founders drew up statutes. These were the contract and legal conditions of endowment; they had the sanction of the law and were enforced in the courts (at colossal expense). Various supervisory bodies— provosts, wardens, elected fellows, governors—were set up to perform certain religious functions and see to the proper disposal of the income.

The statutes did more than this. They took whatever customs prevailed at the time and enshrined them: the practice of teaching the poor, what was taught and when, the numbers taught and so on. If they were new foundations they imitated existing ones. The statutes of St. Paul's were frequently imitated. Thus traditions became law and change was entombed.

The statutes, ignorant of inflation, fixed the schoolmasters' salaries at rates which invariably and rapidly became ridiculous: Bromsgrove in the mid–16th century, for example, fixed at seven pounds per annum. But when, after the Reformation, the custom of saying masses declined, the fact that they were so fixed allowed the fellows to pocket the money provided for masses. That this money was also meant to provide for the pupils and masters, they totally ignored. By 1635 the scholars of Eton were complaining of starvation.

These two facts alone made the taking of fee-paying pupils inevitable.

But it is clear that, once it was found they were willing to come, they would have been taken anyway. The history from the 14th century on is that of the extent to which the rich took over the schools entirely.

Let me illustrate these developments. Already by 1286 all but sixteen poor scholars at St. Albans are to "pay fees to aforesaid master according to ancient custom". By 1442 when Eton was founded even the scholars could be fairly well off. "No one having a yearly income of more than five marks [£3.30p] shall be eligible." At the age of fifteen a scholar had to swear he had no more than this. But in fact five marks allowed in the son of a substantial middle-class family. It was a bar only to the wealthy aristocrats. These could come in, if they wished, as commensales or fee-payers. The statutes allowed for twenty.

By the 16th century the fee-payers are outnumbering the poor. In 1540 Provost Lupton of Eton left in his will a bequest to seventy scholars and 100 Oppidans (Oppidans because the fee-paying pupils came from outside but lived *in* the town). The division of Eton has remained the same ever since: seventy scholars, called "Collegers" who live in College; and the rest of the school, called "Oppidans" who live in houses around the town. Shrewsbury assumed at its foundation around 1560 a balance of 523 fee-payers, while there were 277 free Oppidani (in this case Oppidani because they came *from* the local town). Before long the Oppidani are paying fees too. By the 17th century fee-payers are either assumed openly—as at Bury in 1625, where the founder, the Reverend Henry Bury, wrote: "My intent and meaning is not to debar the Master and Usher from that common privilege in all free Scholes of receiving Presents, Benevolences, Gratuities, etc."—or else lip-service is payed to the tradition of educating the poor and then instantly ignored.

Although masters at smaller schools were badly off, and often actually poor, at large schools, by the 18th century, they could become extremely rich. At Eton, in 1730, the headmaster's salary was sixty-two pounds a year; but there was an unofficial entrance fee of four guineas for the upper school (noblemen double); and every boy gave a tip when he left. In 1763 the headmaster got £411 in tips alone—say £6,000. The headmaster of Blundell's is said to have amassed £60,000 in a twenty-three-year reign—a marvellous sum.

In general then (there are exceptions), by the end of the 18th century the grammar schools that survived did so partly as a result of their endowments, but to a greater extent as a result of fee-paying pupils; the wealthier the pupils, the wealthier the school, the better it survived. The final flowering of this development, its identification with class, took place in the 19th century, but at any stage it is a development of enormous importance. It was to have three effects on the public schools.

The first is cultural. It is possible to argue, as we shall see when we look at other cultures, that a major function of education can be to pass on a society's *mores*, its customs and values, as well as its fund of accumulated knowledge. If this is so, it is ridiculous to criticise this form of educational system for being conservative. That is its point. It is not there to lead society; indeed it cannot by its nature lead. It must wait until the culture has finally coalesced on one moral issue or another; it will then see that the decision is passed on. It is as absurd to expect innovation from an educational system with this purpose as it would be to expect the Oxford Dictionary to introduce new words.

This does not mean that education has to perform this function. The French public (State) system today does not do so. But if it is going to perform it, then what more sensitive mechanism could be devised than to make the educational system directly dependent on the culture financially? And it is surely significant that there is also in France today another very large sector (some seventeen per cent of the whole) which does perform this cultural function (teaching the Catholic religion) and that this sector is fee-paying. Conversely, one could argue that if a fee-paying system of education evolves, sooner or later it will take on this culture-transmitting rôle. In the case of the public schools, except in a hazy way, it was later.

Secondly, it gave the schools great and independent power. The present Headmaster of University College School (UCS) put it to me as the crucial difference between the private and State system. "We go to the wall if we don't produce results. If we start getting deplorable results, we soon empty. A State school goes on *however* inefficient." No doubt. But in past centuries the reverse was true. Provided those who paid the fees were indifferent, public schools could be as brutal, as inefficient, as licentious, as out-of-date as they liked, despite storms of public and government criticism which would have felled a church or destroyed a political party. Most of their decisive moves to change were made because they realised their clients wanted it. A perfectly tenable case can be made that the reforms carried out by Dr. Arnold at Rugby in the 1820s and 30s were panic reactions to falling numbers.

And thirdly, the fee-paying system brought about—or gave the decisive boost to—the move to boarding. Since this makes the public schools unique among world educational systems (with qualifications I shall make later) and since we shall find that it is the ultimate root of their extraordinary power, we must look a little closer at this development.

It is possible that there was an impetus to boarding from the very start. By their nature religious communities tend to cut themselves off, and the 8th-century description of Albert with his pupils at St. Peter's, York—he "fed them, cherished them"—suggests boarding. Common kindness and common sense would have made such provision for poor boys likely. Also, the monopoly that the Church had on education meant that there were for many centuries very few schools. As a result, when education became more sought after, it was at first necessary, then customary, to travel far to get it. Nor, as far as the rich were concerned, would there be any emotional anxiety about this. They had long sent their children away at the age of seven or eight to be educated in other people's houses.

By 1442 Eton shows both processes established. From the start pupils came from as far away as Devon and Lincoln and they boarded in the town. This was partly because the buildings were not finished, but the practice was known at other schools. At Winchester it had existed long enough for the town lodgers to be given a name—Street Commoners— and already outnumber the scholars.

Thereafter the development is continuous, the financial element clear. Sometimes it salved the consciences of the governors to allow fee-payers, provided they did not come from the local town. More usually they were a straight method of making money. The Headmaster of Bromsgrove, with his miserable seven pounds a year, was allowed to take "Tablers" to eat at his table. They slept in his attic.

At first it was more usual to board about the town near the school. Most of the 300 Repton boys did this in 1621. By the end of the Civil War a regularised lodging system had developed at Eton, with the lodging houses run by Dames or male lodging-house keepers called Dominies. By the early 18th century there were ten Dames' houses and three Dominies, with a good number of pupils scattered haphazardly. The rate at which scattered lodgings developed into a scattered house system differed enormously. By the mid-17th century Winchester masters were running houses for profit; at Westminster in 1733 it was still Dames who did this. Gibbon's aunt, Mrs. Porter, set up a boarding house and he lived there. At Eton, masters had boys lodging for profit from 1798, and from 1800 on, partly for disciplinary reasons, but largely to make more money, they slowly took the place of Dames and Dominies. Similarly at Harrow: in 1770 there were a lot of Dames' houses; in 1818 these were abolished and during the 1820s and 30s masters took over the lucrative trade.

By the early 19th century the large and successful grammar schools, except where specifically for day pupils, were almost entirely boarding; the smaller schools had a proportion of boarders, sometimes large, sometimes just six boys living in the headmaster's house. But one can note that it was still a fairly loose haphazard system, various, flexible.

The fact of boarding, and more particularly the house system which developed out of it, was so important to the later public schools that certain writers have treated it as an inspired invention. At the end of the 19th century and beginning of the 20th century house spirit was, after religious faith, the most important spiritual reality to a good many otherwise rational people. For some it replaced religious faith itself. In the 1914–1918 war we will find people dying for their public school houses—for School House, Cock House, B House, Mr. Lyttleton's House. Today I found a number of teachers (particularly at girls' schools) saying that in the boarding house the public schools had created the ideal substitute-family unit. This is rubbish, of course. Whoever heard of a family unit with sixty children and one parent? The house system is an interesting one from which derive certain conclusions but, like boarding itself, it was an accident. It arose as a result of those economic and historical pressures I have outlined, and once those pressures had vanished it was retained by the public schools, used by them and, like so much else in their history, justified by them for reasons, often excellent, sometimes absurd, which had nothing to do with its formation.

2 *Classical tradition, methods of teaching, age taught, prep schools*

There are two final bones, as it were, to add to the primitive skeleton of the public schools.

The first of these is the teaching of Latin (and later the classics). The essence of the situation is clear. Until the early 16th century the Latin that was taught was the contemporary and international language used for practical purposes. It was the tool by which clerks could earn their living, as practical as engineering in a technical college; it was the single avenue by which ambitious men could enter the two careers open to them—the law and the Church. It was a simple Latin—dog Latin.

During the 16th century two things happened. The Renaissance brought about the re-discovery of classical authors and classical Latin. This was too difficult for most ordinary men and at once started a move towards the vernacular, a move much re-inforced by the Reformation. The break with Rome led to a desire to separate the Church and England from the past and from the Continent. First the Church and soon the State were using English. At the start of the 16th century Thomas More wrote *Utopia* in Latin, Erasmus was sending letters so alive they are all being re-published today; at the start of the 17th century Walter Raleigh wrote his *History of the World* in English. Latin had become a dead, or almost dead, language. The 17th century finished it off. This was England's spring: Shakespeare, Jonson, Donne, Hobbes, Burton, Jeremy Taylor. Picking almost at random, one can collect a corpus of literature—great and curious—before the 18th century to rival anything in the world. The same with science. The Royal Society had been established since 1660. Newton was alive, Harvey had discovered the circulation of the blood; in this century came the barometer, the telescope, the microscope, exploration—the whole world was opening before England. In the 18th century this practical and scientific genius was to bring industrial power, industrial power which was itself to finance, and then become fuelled by, a huge Empire, movements themselves reflected in works of enormous philosophic and intellectual power—Adam Smith, Bentham, John Stuart Mill.

These intellectual developments—indeed *all* intellectual developments

—were almost entirely ignored by the grammar schools. At around 1520 they became rooted to the spot, some of them scarcely to budge till the 20th century. Indeed, traces of the Latin and Greek Ice Age can still be detected: Winchester didn't have a proper English department till the 1960s; Eton still has more classics masters than she needs or wants.

Certainly, at all times one can find individual schools with a wider curriculum; Uppingham in 1587 also taught Italian, Spanish, logic, arithmetic, geometry, music and natural philosophy (science). Christ's Hospital had a fairly wide curriculum in the 17th century, which is one reason Blue Coat schools were set up around the country. And in nearly all schools something else was taught—even if it were only "Good manners" (often included in the statutes). But by far the greater number—and surely the picture is well known—taught Latin and sometimes Greek (and Hebrew) and virtually nothing else. Sleath, a 19th-century headmaster of St. Paul's—endowed, with its curriculum on statute in 1509—said to a questioning parent in 1837: "At St. Paul's we teach nothing but the classics, nothing but Latin and Greek. If you want your son to learn anything else you must have him taught at home, and for this purpose we give three half-holidays a week."

Nor was there anything inspiring in "the classics". It is clear from a study of late-17th-century text books and from personal accounts that for the majority it was the sheerest drudgery: grammar, parsing (explaining each part in a sentence grammatically), construing (translating) and learning by heart huge chunks of *Iliad, Aeneid,* etc. And this was because a true classical education—not just the reading, translating and appreciating the classical authors, but composing Greek and Latin verse—is beyond most people; the art of versifying is a sort of trick, a knack. Indeed this is probably one reason, the need to try to teach classics to everyone indiscriminately, for the endless and ferocious beating.

One result of this ridiculous concentration was that Englishmen did not learn English. Cowper said that scarcely one in fifty who went through Eton or Westminster could speak or write it fluently. That the same is probably true of other schools is shown by the extraordinary variety in spelling, punctuation and use of words which continued well into the 19th century.

Why did this state of affairs persist so absurdly? A number of reasons are usually given. For one thing, as Lord Eldon showed in 1790, it was actually illegal for grammar schools to teach new subjects. It was not made legal until 1840. More important (because the schools had long shown they could ignore the statutes if money was involved), the parents did not mind. Had they done so they could have sent their children to one of a number of private schools which appeared in the 18th century to supply this need—Cheam School in Surrey, for instance, which almost forbade the classics and taught English instead, with arithmetic, geometry,

geography, drawing and dancing. But these schools seldom lasted because
they ran out of clients.* Amongst the upper classes there was a robust
attitude to education. "I don't know why there is all this fuss about
education," wrote Lord Melbourne to Queen Victoria. "None of the
Paget family can read or write and they do well enough." The Paget
family included several statesmen and a field marshal. Finally, there were
the schoolmasters. They were all classicists. It was their life and their
livelihood. Why should they criticise the first and jeopardise the second?
Besides, it was the tradition. The schools had already been teaching Latin
in one form or another for well over 1,000 years. Why change? Tradition
alone was enough for most parents and teachers.

However there are more subtle, complex and also interesting reasons for
the persistence of, and concentration on, the classics during this period.

It is important to remember, first, how exciting the Renaissance was;
the 16th century was a voyage of discovery into a strange world of new
ideas, new truths, new works of art. And it was open to any good scholar.
It posed a challenge to the schools. It was rather as though today the
problems and excitements of quasars and pulsars and black holes were
accessible to any good sixth form willing to study physics and astronomy.
This challenge was sharpened by the Reformation. Once their religious
function—the saying of masses—was gone the schools had a choice:
either they could continue mere grammar schools, or they could become
real centres of learning. Many took this latter course and held to it, at least
into the 18th century: St. Paul's, Winchester, Westminster, Shrewsbury
(especially later), Eton after Henry Saville. But it was not just these larger
schools. Good scholars could be found all over the country. Even Dr.
Johnson, it will be remembered, tried to teach. And it should be stressed
here, now that they are unfashionable, that for those able to benefit from
them the classics can provide a broad, as well as deep, education. Not just
the richness of a great literature, the study of a long and varied history and,
once Greek is included, mathematics and philosophy and drama, but also
logic, discrimination, a love of language and its precise, witty and subtle
use and interpretation, a whole range of intellectual disciplines and qualities, ways of thinking which go beyond subjects and can be brought to
bear on any of them.

Such benefits were open to relatively few, those intellectually gifted or
with the knack; but that did not matter. The world, England, London,

---

*It was to distinguish themselves from the private schools that the term "public"
school evolved during the 18th century to describe the leading old grammar foundations.
They were public in that they were not privately owned but incorporated under statute at
law. The use of the term was never consistent during the 18th century and it was not really
until the latter part of the 19th century that it became general. The new foundations and
revived old grammar schools of this period called themselves "public schools" in imitation
of the old leading grammar schools in order to gain something of their *cachet*.

was very small—a handful of poets, critics, writers, thinkers, some aristocratic, some not, but nearly all steeped in the classics. And it was they, heirs to the Renaissance, who shaped English culture during the 17th century, and even more in the 18th century, as far as possible in the classical mould. The subjects of paintings and poetry and history were classical; the buildings imitated those of Rome and Greece, the statues wore togas and wreaths; the terms of reference, the examples in news-papers, magazines or politicians' speeches were classical; that rolling 18th-century prose, the prose of Gibbon and Johnson, followed the periods of Latin prose, just as a whole school of 18th-century philosophy followed Plato. The classical past was not just revered. The 18th century had, in contemplating it, a feeling of safety, safety in its ideals, its achievements, its discipline; the past had in some way the secret of eternal life, eternal values. By drawing the essence of classicism across the centuries, by as it were pickling the present in the past, both would survive. We get, therefore, a curious phenomenon: the preservation of a whole way of life in the present by transfusing it with the indestructible safety of an adored past.

This aspect of 18th-century civilisation was far more apparent than the scientific or industrial revolutions, particularly to the schoolmasters and scholars who, at a remove, helped to bring it about. To them, it was a great deal more "contemporary" to teach classics than, say, science or maths.

This for the minority; but the majority gained even from the rudi-mentary classics that could be lashed into them. During the late 17th and 18th centuries, when most people were uneducated, an easy way to separate those who were educated was to have them speak Latin. If Latin, however imperfectly known, then became an essential qualification for the most desirable jobs in the land, and if Latin could only be obtained by being bought, then the rich could obtain those jobs just because they were rich. The possession of the classics became a rude but definite class distinction.

For all these reasons classics remained dominant. And, apart from the first diminutive appearance of class, a tiny note as yet hardly audible in the orchestra, we might observe two other nascent themes: the idea that, as far as scholarship went, the schools were only concerned with an able few; and the idea that academic qualification, however irrelevant, somehow fitted people for jobs outside.

Finally, how were the boys taught, for how long and at what age?

The class sizes, always crammed into one room, from the 16th century until well into the 19th century, would have made a modern comprehen-sive master first blench—then flee. At Sherborne in the 16th century the headmaster took the top three forms, the usher the bottom three; there were in all 144 boys, say seventy in each. In 1561 at Shrewsbury three masters tried to control 266 boys. Keate's classes at Eton in the early 19th century were often 200 strong. At the same time, numbers fluctuated wildly. Schools could drop hundreds in a year or two. Repton had 300 boys at the end of the 17th century; then "only a few ragged boys" by 1705. Charterhouse slumped from 480 in 1825 to 137 by 1832. Thus it was almost impossible to engage new masters. Large classes and few masters further help to explain the violent discipline, the teaching of so few subjects and the inefficiency of the teaching. It was still going on at Totnes Grammar School at the end of the 19th century. Professor Dawkins, a friend of Corvo, said to John Betjeman: "You sat round a huge hall. Your education depended on whether or not the master reached you. Sometimes he did not reach you for months."

Yet even in this chaotic system the seeds of one successful way of making boys work had already been discovered. That was competition—the public recognition and reward for success at work (and punishment for failure). Most histories credit Dr. Butler of Shrewsbury (Headmaster, 1798–1836) with discovering exams. In fact, they were a regular part of the curriculum at St. Gregory's (later Downside), at Douai in France as early as 1721.

The early history, incidentally, of these Catholic schools—Ampleforth, Downside and Stonyhurst—is intensely dramatic, almost melodramatic. Forced by anti-Catholic laws to set up in France at the end of the 16th century, their isolation abroad seems to have led to a concentration on their task far superior to that common in England. A boy called Langley, who was also at Charterhouse, said the teaching was far better at Douai. The subtle and ingenious monks had not only discovered the spur of regular examinations, but the use of separate classrooms and what we call "streaming". "The scholars," said Langley, writing home, "are divided according to their different abilities and capacities into several classes, and over each class presides a proper master." Being abroad they were all confined in neatly disciplined dormitories, avoiding the hurly-burly of many outside boarders. Discipline (long a feature, this, of Catholic schools) was fierce. Whether or not Butler copied examinations from them, Eton and Harrow copied him; thus they spread through the public school system and by 1842 are reported general.

Schoolboys spent most of their life at school. Holidays were twenty or thirty days a year: twenty at Manchester Grammar in the 16th century; thirty at Sherborne in the 16th century and 17th century; thirty at Eton in the mid-18th century. But the picture of unremitting toil which this gives is misleading. These holidays were in the summer when the boys went home, and this divided the year in half (halves for terms is still used in some schools). But, in fact, the school year had for long (probably always) been divided in three by religious festivals: at Christmas, Easter (or sometimes at the end of May), and in summer, usually around St. Bartholomew's Day (end of August) or St. Michael's Day (end of September).

They had holidays at each break; typically two weeks at Easter, and twenty or thirty days at Christmas. But because of the dangers and difficulties of travel—unless they lived close or were very influential—the boys did not go home at all three. As travel grew easier during the 19th century, the half-yearly return home gave way to the tri-partite divisions which had in fact always ruled the school year. (Travel was actually growing easier, in England at any rate, at the end of the 18th century. The slow spread of the three yearly holiday probably also had something to do with the attitude to children.)

Nor does this complete the picture. Not for nothing is the word holiday derived from holy days. Saints' days sprinkle the calendar and school was continually mitigated. Even without this it was not too arduous. At Eton in 1766 one worked about four hours a day, but Tuesday was free, and Thursday and Saturday half days; it is clear, from the unpublished "Journal" of Minet, a boy at Winchester in 1818, that the same pattern obtained there—as much as five and a half hours a day were spent swimming, duck shooting and playing cricket.

Finally, the age at which boys (and later girls) went to school. On the whole it is true to say that the effect of the same experience in childhood and youth is directly dependent on, and relative to, the age at which that experience takes place. To be removed from home at seven as opposed to eleven, to be beaten at ten instead of seventeen, are more overwhelming experiences, have greater effects, by precisely that factor alone. One would not have thought it necessary to emphasise this today. Yet I think of several masters (I think of one in particular) who said to me: "I never beat for serious offences, and I beat them young—ten to fourteen, like puppies." It was clear he thought they *were* puppies.

Of course, this can be qualified. There are experiences possible at sixteen—adolescent sexual attraction and love, appreciation of poetry— which can scarcely be undergone at all at seven. But the essential qualification is in the other direction. An important concept of behavioural psychology is that of re-inforcement. That is, the effect of a powerful experience in early life can be quite small, even negligible, if single; the effect seems to increase geometrically with the number of times (and when and how forcibly) it is repeated.

It is clear that, from the earliest times, English children were sent away to board at a very young age. Eight is usual, though at Dulwich in 1707 some were infants of three and four. In fact boys arrived and left at all ages. At the end of the 16th century Archdeacon Johnson's son left Uppingham for Oxford at thirteen. At Eton an 18th-century list shows Thomas Thackery Junior aged six, a John Ashton arriving at seventeen; Bronfield goes to university at fifteen, while Lord Lumley is still lounging around at twenty. Insofar as re-inforcement goes during this period, it was total. That is to say, the small boys were at the same schools as the older ones. And it continued total as preparatory schools appeared. The origins of these are not precise. Writing of Westminster in 1835, Southey said: "Preparatory schools, which were not heard of fifty years ago, have annihilated the under school." They developed only slowly from around 1770, because until well into the 19th century the lower schools of public schools were taking children of seven and eight. Their real growth is from 1860 onwards.

CHAPTER 3

Early History II, to 1820: The Brutal and Permissive Ages

From Powles I went, to Aeton sent
To learn straightways the Latin phraise;
Where fiftie-three stripes given to me
At once had.
For fault but small, or none at all,
It came to parse thus beat I was:
See, Udall, see, the mercy of thee
To mee, poore lad.

Thomas Tusser

We now leave the skeleton of the early public schools; it is time to add some flesh—to look at the faces of those in them, to try to imagine what their lives were like.

As the years pass, the dim figures from earlier centuries—Albert, Alcuin—are replaced by sharper portraits, the colours harsh, even crude. In the 16th century, and for long after, standards in the schools were modest, and even then frequently not reached. The statutes of Felsted stated only that masters should not be "drunkards, whore-hunters, or lewd in living". And almost without exception they were violent floggers.

Nicholas Udall, the Headmaster of Eton from 1534–43 and the figure Thomas Tusser reproaches in his curious and sometimes moving autobiography from which I quote above, was notorious for the savagery of his beatings. It was he who beat poor Thomas Tusser—fifty-three blows for a little boy. Nor were these beatings gentle. Cook, High Master of St. Paul's in the 16th century, beat John Sandeson so hard that he bore seven scars on his backside for the rest of his life. At Eton in 1560 the assistants at a beating were known as the "holders down". There was often blood. The instruments of torture were savage too. A mid–17th-century account recommends "a good sharp birchen rod and free from knots, for willow wands are insufferable". At Charterhouse a hundred or so years later (but many other schools had this) a five-foot bunch of birch switches were fastened at the handle end and "armed with buds as big as thorns, renewed after six strokes for fresh excoriation". For a number of years, Winchester tried long, strong, flexible apple branches secured in the grooves of a heavy two-foot handle. Finally they decided birch was more painful. No wonder there are frequent records of boys running away in terror of the lash.

Udall was notorious for more than beating. His sexual behaviour with his boys was flagrant, continuous and open, and in 1543 exposed him to blackmail. Two pupils, Cheney and Hoorde, were caught stealing silver images and plate from college. It seems likely that they threatened to expose Udall's sexual indulgence unless let off, and he called their bluff. At any event, they accused him of the grossest sexual misdemeanours, and implicated him in the robbery. The whole case was examined by the Privy Council, mindful that a law had just been passed making the extreme homosexual offence—buggery—punishable by death. Udall was cleared of the theft and found guilty of everything else. However, as Hollis notes in his account, headmasters are rarely hanged; particularly perhaps headmasters of Eton. The sentence was commuted to imprisonment.

One might note two things about the case. The fuss and the use of the Privy Council is to some extent an indication of the growing importance of Eton. But it is more expressive of Henry VIII's money troubles. The monasteries were dissolved partly on the grounds of their lascivious and scandalous behaviour; how much more monstrous was Udall's exploitation of his rôle as guardian of the young—and in an institution still regarded as very close to the Church. It is likely that had Henry VIII not died in 1547 Eton would have been dissolved. The second point is that Udall was subsequently released and went on to become Headmaster of Westminster. Then, and for the next 270 odd years, such monstrous behaviour was, in fact, little regarded.

During the 17th century Eton, at least, went through a temporary improvement. For a while beating was not the automatic and invariable punishment, as it was under Udall and would be under Keate. Statutes were drawn up saying when beatings should be given—for breaking bounds, going to ale houses, etc. At this time, the 1660s, smoking was made compulsory because it was thought to be a prophylactic against the plague. Thomas Hearne in his diaries describes Tom Rogers telling him that "he was never so much whipped in his life as he was one morning for not smoking".

But in general, the violence continues unabated, unmitigated, almost jovial. One trouble with beating as a method of punishment is that it frequently gives pleasure to the master, and that pleasure can be overtly sexual. Sometimes it seemed the only thing that kept them alive. Richard Roberts (St. Paul's 1769–1814) was scarcely more alive than his bust, "except when plying the cane; and on such occasions he was wonderfully active, as if inspired by new life . . .". But, although many of the effects of beating, its disadvantages (and advantages) as a disciplinary tool, will emerge as we progress, I want to reserve a fuller discussion of that particular side, the sexual side, until the 19th century. It is then that a peculiar relish enters the descriptions, the involvement becomes deeper and more emotional, and also spreads out through the community, so that the whole school becomes caught up, gripped by an excitement which is horrified, morbid and delighted all at once; at the same time the frenzies of the master, beating "in a white heat", often seem more personal and somehow sinister.

You do not find this in the 17th and 18th centuries. The atmosphere is brutal, certainly; but it is more open, less loaded. There was Gill of St. Paul's (1608–35), who seemed to believe in a sort of divine right of beating. He would beat Old Paulines when they came down and misbehaved and once, when a stone came through the classroom window, rushed in a fury out into the street, seized the nearest passer-by, a Sir John D (John Aubrey tells the story), and beat him so severely he never dared go near the school again without an armed guard.

The power of masters was in these respects absolute. One reads again and again of coarse brutes able to do all but kill their pupils (and sometimes that too); men like Boyer of Christ's Hospital, who simply whipped and punched to relieve his feelings. "I have known him double his knotty fist," wrote Charles Lamb in a famous description, "at a poor trembling child (the maternal milk hardly dry upon its lips) with a 'Sirrah, do you presume to set your wits at me?'."

How could it go on so long, why did the parents tolerate it, why was it allowed?

The reasons are well known. We have already seen the continuing contribution of huge classes, low-calibre masters, the intolerable boredom of the classics. More important was the attitude to children. Children were the fruit of original sin, they were defective adults whose sin was to be beaten out of them. And it followed that, until this had happened, they were scarcely company for adults. Parents didn't on the whole seem to care what treatment they received provided they kept out of the way. This is another explanation of the huge stretch of time they spent away from home, even when roads began to improve. (It also explains why in the 18th and early 19th centuries running away was the worst crime; sexual offences are scarcely mentioned.) But the principal reason was the age: sailors were frequently lashed to death, men were hanged for trifling offences and died of trifling diseases, the rich were cruel to the poor, and equally cruel to their own children. Schoolmasters were expected to be brutal; just how brutal is shown, paradoxically, by the legal limits designed to prevent their excesses. Burn's *Justice of the Peace* in the late 18th century has this:

> Where a schoolmaster, in correcting his scholar, happens to occasion his death, if in such correction he is so barbarous as to exceed all bounds of moderation, he is at least guilty of manslaughter; and if he makes use of an instrument improper for correction, as an iron bar or sword, or if he kick him to the ground, and then stamp on his belly, and kill him, he is guilty of murder.

Nor were alternatives experimented with to any large extent. There were impositions of extra work and enforced roll calls; Christ's Hospital tried solitary confinement. Here is Lamb again:

> The sight of a boy in fetters, upon the day of my putting on the blue clothes, was not exactly fitted to assuage the natural terrors of initiation. . . . I was told he had *run away*. This was the punishment for the first offence. As a novice, I was taken soon after to see the dungeons. These were little square Bedlam cells where a boy could just lie at his length upon straw and a blanket—a mattress, I think, was afterwards substituted—with a peep of light let in askance from a prison orifice at top, barely enough to read by. Here the poor boy was locked in by himself all day, without sight of any but the porter who brought him his bread and water—who *might not speak to him*—or of the beadle, who came twice a week to call him out to receive his periodical chastisement and here he was shut by himself *of nights*, out of reach of any sound.

This was the punishment for the second offence. For the third, you were thrashed from the school.

But in this particular respect, as far as I can tell, Christ's was unique (and only in this respect. Although it was a school for the poor, it remains typical of contemporary grammar schools in all other ways). On the whole, savage and uncontrolled beating remained the chief method of disciplining boys, and we must look at one final exemplar of its practice, partly because he is the most celebrated, and partly because he is revealing about two fundamental aspects of these early centuries.

1 Dr. Keate of Eton—the flogger

Dr. Keate became Headmaster of Eton in 1809, at a difficult period. Discipline was slack; although the school was barnacled now with many absurd traditions and practices Goodall, the provost, thought it perfect. It was incapable of improvement and he therefore allowed no change. Many of the boys thought that Benjamin Drury, another lower master, should have been appointed and the mutterings of rebellion started in the huge classes the moment Keate took over. Nor was he helped by his other masters. Drury himself was a heavy-drinking ruffian, who frequently played truant. There was another who took opium and habitually appeared drugged and incoherent. There was Bethell, who was said to have made only two comments in his entire career. One was when a boy translated

"*Postes aeratos*" as "brazen gates". "Yes," said Bethell, "that's right. Probably so called because they were made of brass."

Things were difficult, and there are further qualifications to be made about Keate; but despite these the general picture of his disciplinary methods is astounding.

He was a fantastic figure: five-foot tall, strong as a bull, and equipped, under a high cocked hat like Napoleon, with enormous shaggy red eyebrows, great angry tufts, so long that he used them like arms or hands when he wished to point at something. His temper was terrifying: he would get "so inflamed in the face, and foamed and spurted from the mouth" so ferociously that it was like someone in a fit. At these times his voice became a furious quack; and quacking, foaming, snarling, he tried to thrash Eton into submission.

There are many stories about him, a good many no doubt, as with any legendary master, exaggerations. There were the candidates for confirmation whose names were sent up to him on a long strip of paper resembling the "bill" on which wrong-doers' names were usually written. When, seeing the familiar signs of preparation, the candidates nervously explained the purpose of their visit, Keate flew into a rage at an excuse "not only false but irreverent". He flogged the lot.

Yet, even without exaggerations, the well-authenticated accounts are so extraordinary that it is difficult to see, as Hollis remarks, how any sane man could have supposed they would effect their purpose. This is particularly true of the mass executions. (It is significant how naturally the language of capital punishment attaches itself to beating.) Over May and June 1810 the boys of the lower fifth gradually built up the practice of rushing to their places in chapel at the last moment. Keate imposed an extra five-o'clock absence (roll call) during holiday afternoons. No one turned up. Keate decided to birch all hundred of them. He did so in public, in front of anyone who cared to watch, and in front of those about to be beaten. Before long, angered or excited by the sight of their friends being flogged, the audience began to stamp and shout. Soon they began to throw eggs at Keate; his task of flogging, while also dodging and sloshing about in burst eggs, became not only ludicrous but impossible. He had to send out for the assistant masters to patrol with birches while he beat the final eighty-odd boys.

As well as dozens of individual floggings, there are many massed scenes like this. They are a measure, incidentally, of Keate's strength. Suppose each boy had six strokes the lower fifth alone meant 600 blows (and often he beat the entire fifth and sixth). Take a walking stick now and try beating your bed 600 times as hard as you can. When Dr. Heath birched seventy boys at Eton in 1796 (ten cuts each) he had to go to bed for a week with strained ligaments and muscles.

Keate reigned until 1834. His features and form were indelibly imprinted upon the minds of the little boys he had so terrified. It was said that for the rest of his life, any Etonian could draw the famous and ferocious silhouette. Many years afterwards Alexander Kinglake, the traveller and historian, was in Cairo and was called over by a charcoal gazer in the street who said that, for money, his boy would describe any person he cared to name. At once Kinglake said "Keate". There was a long pause while the boy stared into the quivering fire, then at last, to King-lake's delight, he said: "I see a fair girl, with golden hair, blue eyes, pallid face, rosy lips."

What was the effect, in general terms, of all this beating? The most common reaction to being beaten is rage, resentment and the desire for revenge. Sometimes this was exacted. Usher Rose, at Merchant Taylors' in the 1780s, was a fiend, and one Old Boy returned and publicly flogged him in the cloisters to wipe out old scores. The next day, when another usher attempted to beat someone, the pupils rushed him and broke his canes.

But the aggression is usually transferred. It will become noticeable through this history that in a school where there is a lot of beating (and particularly in one where the boys beat a lot) there is also a lot of bullying. The reason was put succinctly by a ten-year-old to Bertrand Russell; "The bigs hit me, so I hit the smalls; that's fair." In the same way, although the rebellions of the late 18th and early 19th centuries were not directly inspired by beating, they were a fruit of that climate of aggression. Violence as a solution is one lesson beating teaches.

Next, beating obsessed the schools and those connected with them in a way that is now incredible. George III's principal, almost only topic with the Eton boys he saw at Windsor was their most recent flogging. In 1792 Robert Southey produced a magazine called *The Flagellant*. Its fifth number proved "flogging was invented solely by the malice of the devil". Hook—Headmaster of Westminster—expelled him. When we look at the schoolboy literature of the early 20th century we will find floggings provide the juiciest illustrations, the climax to chapters.

Yet, in contradistinction to this, the more usual overt reaction to beating is stoical, humorous or unconcerned. This does not necessarily mean that deeper reactions have not been transferred or dealt with in other ways, but one should recognise the response. When the brutal Boyer died, Cole-ridge, who had been much beaten by him, wrote to Lamb: "Poor J.B.! May all his faults be forgiven; and may he be wafted to bliss by little cherub boys, all heads and wings, with no *bottoms* to reproach his sublunary infirmities." In fact the affection for an apparently brutal master often seems excessive—not sexual exactly, so much as fawning, the dog that licks the hand that beats it. Psychoanalytic theory postulates that a child who is beaten by a parent cannot tolerate the hatred he feels for one he loves so much and who is so necessary to him. He therefore represses the rage and covers it with a show of love. This is no doubt psychoanalytically sound, and may indeed cover a few instances. Yet it does not quite seem to fit some of the examples I have in mind.

Corporal punishment inflicted continually and arbitrarily ceases to be a punishment and becomes a way of life. It encourages the brave to braggadocio, the coward to cringe and flee; as a method of discipline during these centuries it was virtually useless. Roberts, the St. Paul's master whose last days were made sprightly by beating, was notorious for lack of order. The noise from Keate's classes was continuous and deafening, so that passers-by would stop and listen in wonder. Not four months after he had birched the entire lower fifth for loitering on the way into chapel, they had taken instead to yelling at the tops of their voices as they sat down.

But a way of life can say something about the attitudes of those who live it. Hollis says the significance of such behaviour is that it shows a fundamental difference in how boys and masters expected each other to behave. Today, even in the worst comprehensive, it is impossible to imagine rebellion and chaos on such a scale, with wholesale yelling and disobedience the normal and inevitable condition of teaching and living.

This is true, of course, but the nature of the difference is more subtle. Once again, and this is the first fundamental aspect of 18th-century school life he demonstrates, Keate is an example. The details need not over concern us. A popular boy called Munro had, quite rightly, to be expelled. His case was taken up by the lower and middle fifth who, when absence was called, all bellowed "Munro, Munro, Munro" at the tops of their voices. Keate imposed extra absence, which a hundred boys skipped, planning also to refuse the inevitable flogging. Keate would hardly dare sack a hundred boys, one-quarter of the school. He didn't. Nothing happened. Then, in the middle of the night, the assistant masters poured out and silently seized, by ones and twos, the culprits from their houses and lodgings. Their cries were muffled and they were brought before the Doctor. The ferocious figure, with huge eyebrows and foaming mouth, was a great deal more terrifying at night and faced alone. Only two did not submit to a flogging, and they gave way next day.

But the significance of the story lies in its end. Next day, Monday, Keate crossed Long Walk. Upon his appearance, a vast crowd of boys, including most of his victims, turned out and cheered him. The point is, it was a sort of game: the boys playing not to get caught, the masters to catch. If the boys were outwitted in an ingenious way, they cheered. Paradoxically, savagery which brutalised generally and terrified or enraged individually was not as a system unpopular, just as Keate was not unpopular. Nor was the system, since in essence a game, even meant to deter. Almost all the anecdotes about Keate are of boys deliberately disobeying in situations where, if caught , the punishment was certain.

They hoped to trick or frighten Keate, or otherwise escape. Flogging meant they'd lost that match. And there were rules on their side too. One day, as often, Keate was being pelted with books, and someone threw a stone at him. "I hope boys," he said, "I have not deserved that." The boys agreed, and cheered him.

There is distance in this attitude. Levity. Detachment. Although the level of activity is different, the attitude itself is perhaps not after all so far removed from one you would find in a good many comprehensives today.

2 Surroundings, life. Random themes: sex, traditions, public school incest

All institutions, except to a very small number of people (those from unhappy homes, those holding exceptionally exalted and privileged positions within the institution), are by their nature in varying degrees unpleasant. The lack of privacy, the bad food (only the French can cook good food for more than ten), the discipline, the impersonality, the frequent absence or difficulty of love, the inevitable presence of unpleasant people, all mean institutions are just more or less endurable. We can compare them, at worst, to a concentration camp; at best to a don's life in a college at Oxford.

Early accounts are fairly rare. A description of five-o'clock rising at Eton in the 16th century; another at Westminster—huge draughty chambers, near glassless windows, wooden beds, water from the pump. An impression of intense cold. In smaller grammar schools (like Bramley in the 17th century) ten or so boys huddled under the rafters in the headmaster's attic, rats running over their knees at night, and waking with snow blown in on them in winter. Many schools were dominated by the towns that pressed in on them. Here is James Matthews at Merchant Taylors' in London around 1816. It is night, the scene is Dickensian, with the boys free to roam the dark, gloomy, yet also thrilling streets, "Where I might have been seen wandering, without my hat like the little ragamuffin I was, or running up Suffolk Lane on a dark night in my bed gown, in my capacity of fag, after having been lowered from the bedroom window in a sheet . . .".

Food was usually unpleasant and, no doubt to save money, sparse. At Christ's Hospital in 1678 it was water gruel with currants at noon, cheese at night, varied with porridge and cheese. But they did have meat—mutton or beef—four times a week. This had stopped by Lamb's time. In fact in nearly all schools, pupils were expected to provide a large part of their diet themselves. No midday meal was provided at Merchant Taylors' till 1870. In 1817, "some went to the chophouses which still existed in the neighbourhood . . . I, myself [Matthews] went to the bar at Cannon Street Station, where I had a glass of stout and an Abernethy biscuit." Tuck boxes, tuck shops, the scent of frying sausages floating down the corridors of Greyfriars, had their origins in a tradition where if they hadn't fed themselves schoolboys would have starved.

It is during these centuries (the 16th, 17th and 18th) that, picking almost at random, we can discern a number of major themes appearing or, alternatively, note that they are significant by their absence. The attitude to sex remains extremely casual and natural. Homosexuality is hardly referred to at all—though no doubt it was common enough. Certainly some of the phraseology is rather suggestive: "tart" for favourite at 17th-century Winchester, for example; and at many schools boys shared beds until quite old. Eton founding statutes stopped this at fourteen; but Westminster in 1560 stated that they must sleep two to a bed, and at Harrow the scholars slept together in beds till 1805. We have seen Udall move straight from prison for buggery to a headmastership. To a considerable degree, however, the boys gained their experience in the rumbustious, immoral, whore-ridden world of the towns the schools were set in. At Tonbridge in 1562 the boarding keepers had to inform the master if their charges were "lewdly occupied". These lewd occupations were almost certainly wenching, drinking and gaming. Gaming is mentioned specifically and a letter of May 27th, 1690, talks of Westminster boys openly "handing about young women in the streets". On the whole these were sexually permissive centuries. In the early 19th century Eton ran a sixth-form brothel, and Lord Hinchingbrooke's being served with a bastardy order by a woman in Windsor was regarded as no more serious than missing an absence. He was given ten strokes of the cane.

Cowper sums the situation up. Notoriously unhappy at Westminster, it was the immorality of the boys he wrote about, not the brutality or bullying or fagging:

> Would you your son should be a sot or dunce,
> Lascivious, headstrong, or all these at once. . . .
> Train him in public with a mob of boys,
> Childish in mischief only and in noise,
> Else of mannish growth, and five in ten
> In infidelity and lewdness, men.
> There shall he learn, ere sixteen winters old,
> That authors are most useful pawned or sold;
> That pedantry is all that schools impart,
> But taverns teach the knowledge of the heart;
> There waiter Dick with Bacchanalian lays
> Shall win his heart, and have his drunken praise,
> His counsellor and bosom-friend shall prove,
> And some street-pacing harlot his first love.

It is now that traditions arise—and congeal. Some songs date from the 18th century; like that mournful plaint which has been Winchester's school song for many years and which, far from praising the school, doesn't even mention it.

> Domum, domum, dulce domum,
> Domum, domum, dulce domum,
> Dulce, dulce, dulce domum,
> Dulce domum reconemus!

How poignant that third line—"Sweet, sweet, sweet home". Yet this embryonic development is important. Music, songs, are extraordinarily powerful forces for arousing emotions; songs preserve experience, then enrich it with nostalgia and finally fire it with passion. Miners and football crowds sing songs to express (and bring about) their brotherhood; but miners march on strike singing, football crowds sing their teams to victory, tribes and armies go to war inflamed by music and song. And by the end of the 19th century we shall find the public schools bound together by a common body of song in which, though not obvious, all these factors were implicit. (Most individual school songs, like those at Harrow, date from the 17th century.)

Traditions, started for whatever reason, continued for centuries, long after the reason had vanished. In 1395 all Winchester boys had their heads shaved, no doubt for religious reasons. They were still having their heads shaved in 1695 for no reason at all. Schools took traditions from each other—the long dormitory at Westminster was set at right angles to the Abbey, and the whole school was taught there till 1884. At the Abbey end, the apse was in the form of a shell and the form taught there was called the Shell. This was copied by Harrow, Charterhouse and later Wellington, and other schools (today the modern "shell" shape can be moved by button and reveals a stage). The Greaze—where Westminster boys fight violently for bits of pancake tossed from a large frying pan over a bar by the school chef—is mentioned in the 18th century, but is probably the remnant of some ancient Shrove-tide custom. It continues today. The tradition of preserving traditions became a tradition.

There are a number of reasons for this, but one is certainly public school inbreeding. That boys from public schools who wish to teach should go to university and then return to teach at public schools is almost inevitable—what else, after all, are they to do? And that they should remain in the same school all their lives is also not surprising. Solicitors remain in the same offices all their lives, doctors in the same practice, engineers in the same firm. But the difference is that other professions are not nearly so involving or cutting off as teaching in a boarding school was for many hundreds of years, and to an extent still is. The experience is single in a peculiar way—from the age of eight till death in the same sort of environment, the same problems, often the same people.

In the 19th century, headmasters, at least, sometimes moved from school to school. This acted as a conforming, unifying force on the schools themselves, but provided some alteration of experience. In the 17th century and more particularly 18th century it was not so much inbreeding as public school incest. Take Stephan Sleech, appointed provost of Eton in 1746. Sleech's father had been an Eton fellow. His widowed mother married the headmaster, Newborough. His sister married a lower master, Weston. A scholar of Eton himself, he married the daughter of Stephan Upman, another Eton fellow. One daughter married Charles Hawtrey, elected to King's in 1707 and from whom the later headmaster and provost was descended. His son married a sister of Cooke, the provost of King's and his own brother-in-law. These Eton masters and fellows (and the picture can be paralleled in other schools) were as isolated and restricted in surroundings and experience as the inhabitants of Tristan da Cunha and just as inbred. One wonders if their peculiarities—often to become extremely marked—need any other explanation than genetic. Men like Sleech were not going to put an end to a tradition of nutting on May 10th, say, just because it had been going for 200 years.

The sort of ways in which Old Boys helped each other—certainly inevitable and natural, but later to become a significant theme—occasionally appear now. The circumstances could be dramatic. In 17th-century Westminster a curtain hung between lower and upper schools and a small boy once tore it down by mistake. To save him from a savage beating, William Wake offered to take the blame. Many years later, says Addison telling the story, Wake was implicated in a Royalist rising in Wiltshire. He was captured, imprisoned and put on trial for his life. The judge, on hearing his name, suddenly leant forward and asked if he had been at Westminster. When he heard that he had, he realised that here was the person who had saved him from a flogging as a boy. He managed to secure a reprieve for him. And as the period progresses there is evidence of a fairly mild continuing interest in their old schools by boys who had been there. In 1816 Charles Fox Townshend started a debating society at Eton in a house belonging to a Mrs. Hatton who had originally kept a "sock" or tuck shop, the Latin name for which is *Popina*. Some years later, when his society, Pop, looked like foundering, he wrote in protest. There are one or two rudimentary Old Boy groups. At Felsted, under Simon Lydiatt, Old Boys met in 1707 for their annual service and feast. But there is nothing to resemble the tight-knit far-flung societies of later years: the post-school obsession that haunted many boys until they died.

Nevertheless, it was clearly understood by the early 19th century that to send a boy to certain schools was a sensible way to introduce him to friends who would be influential in the future. Gladstone was sent to Eton with this in mind and with this effect. He got to know Canning's son, also Gerald Wellesley, Lord Lincoln and other grand friends. However, this is an effect of the rise to dominance during this period of some nine or so of the old grammar schools. To trace and explain each individual rise would be a complex and lengthy task. In the 16th, 17th and into the 18th century Westminster, for instance, rose to a position above all other schools including Eton. This was in general due to its central position (four of the major schools were in London), its patronage by royalty (especially Charles II) and in particular by the reign, during the difficult 17th century, of Dr. Busby. This resilient and adroit man, like most great headmasters then, a savage beater, ruled for fifty-seven years, and raised Westminster to a pitch it was not to reach again until today. Even more lengthy, though more amusing, would be to trace the fifty times as numerous collapses—of schools like St. Peter's, Sedbergh, Warwick, The Perse and many others—though one might note that the fall, as the rise, often began with the headmaster. Sedbergh, for instance, at the start of the 18th century was a flourishing northern grammar school. Then in 1742 William Broxholme became headmaster. He hated schools and boys, became a recluse and shut himself up in his room refusing to see anyone. His successor, William Bateman, was a fine scholar but could not control his pupils. They used to pull his nose. Numbers plummeted. I think it is enough if you hold this picture in your mind: during the 15th and 16th centuries some 800 grammar schools had been set up in England. By the 1820s and 30s only about a hundred had effectively survived the temptations and corruptions of time. Of these, some ten per cent—Eton, Winchester, Westminster (but coasting now, actually in decline), Rugby, Charterhouse, Harrow, St. Paul's, Merchant Taylors'—had become pre-eminent, the great schools. Of the rest, some had remained almost equally successful—see Dr. Samuel Butler's furious letter in 1820 when Shrewsbury was not included in the Charity Commissioners' special list (after which Shrewsbury becomes a great school, completing the nine). Some were in a state of almost total disintegration. To anticipate a little, Sedbergh, under George Henry Day, had reached a new low. He sacked all the boarders in his house "for the simple reason", wrote the school historian, "that they made his life unbearable". He had a habit of slinking about against walls or fences. It became a village school with four or five boys in boarding houses. The Charity Commissioner who visited it in the 1860s, though hardened to extremes of dilapidation, wrote: "As to Sedbergh, I despair of putting it into any class at all. In its present state it simply cumbers the ground."

But this beginning of school snobbery, classes of schools, was in itself partly the product of another movement—the growth of class dominance and class consciousness in English society. The annexation of first some, then all the public schools by the upper and middle classes was for two hundred years or so one of the fundamental sources of their power; if the schools are destroyed, or fall in ruin, this past annexation will be the cause of that too. Class, with all its peculiar and peculiarly English ramifications, absurdities, injustices and indignities, must be another major theme of this book.

3 Class

We have seen how the schools have been gradually dominated by fee-payers. Their domination in class terms is a separate though allied process (in the long term the two developments made each other inevitable). It is best seen at Eton. Eton is not typical exactly, because class domination happened earlier at Eton and more completely. But at Eton the process is naked.

A nobleman first died at Eton in 1521. By this time it was still a slight oddity for the landed gentry to send their sons there. During the 17th century it took in gentry and aristocracy increasingly. The first school list is found in 1678, when there are a good number of peers, and the Oppidans are mostly Cavalier. But there are also local Windsor tradesmen. In the early 18th century the register shows parents to include a baker, bookseller, brick master, cheesemonger, feltmonger, grocer, innkeeper, tobacconist, mercer, stagecoach-builder, etc. Noblemen are charged double. But between 1753 and 1790 there were only thirty-eight entrants of tradesmen class out of a total of 3,000. These shifts in entrance were mirrored by shifts in attitude. In 1750 lists in upper school appear with noblemen in order of rank—dukes' sons, earls' sons, baronets, etc., then commoners. In 1770 titles in the school list are printed in red. By the early 19th century noblemen had a number of (to us) extremely offensive privileges—special clothes, special seats, a licence to arrogance.

The change shows in the attitude towards masters. In general, at all schools, these were of lower social standing than their pupils until the mid-19th century. Provosts were usually of a higher class, and the appointment of Craddock, in 1681, caused surprise because he was a grocer's son. But surprise was all it caused. In 1765 Dr. Foster became headmaster. He was the son of a Windsor tradesman and began his rule by mistaking (he was astigmatic) a large black sow lurking near Long Walk for a boy. "Come here, you Colleger," he called imperiously several times; behaviour that was greeted with ridicule. "A natural mistake," writes Hollis (to whose excellent book I am indebted), and argues that there must have been other defects to merit such treatment. There were, though the mistake seems only fairly natural to me. But it is clear from other incidents that Dr. Foster's class was the major cause of the insolence to which he was subject.

A final, but significant twist to this process was the bias towards politics. Political power in the 18th century still lay in the hands of the aristocratic landowners and land-owning gentry. Any school which attracted this group, as Eton was now doing, would inevitably therefore soon start to have politicians amongst its Old Boys. St. John (Viscount Bolingbroke),

Wyndham, Walpole and Townshend were all at Eton under New-borough, the usher in 1689. And once started, the process would continue. Politicians who had been there would send their sons who, since politics then and for many years were predominantly a matter of influence and connection, would themselves become politicians or draw benefits from the world of power. Those ambitious for their children would send them to schools where they could make these connections. Walpole *et al.* were followed by Pitt, Bute, North, the Foxes, Canning. And a second process flowed naturally from this. Newborough was finally appointed Bishop of Exeter by his old pupil Walpole. What better way of expressing gratitude to an old master than by promoting him; and if not gratitude but repressed rage was the real motive, what better way of demonstrating your final superiority? The great schools became a recognised avenue of advance-ment via successful pupils; and since the schools were still intimately entwined with the Church, it was there that the headmasters advanced.

Similar if not so spectacularly snobbish developments took place at other schools. Mid–18th–century form lists at Westminster are fairly democratic still. In 1746, for instance, the fourth form includes three peers, generals', parsons' and doctors' sons, and twelve sons of local Londoners. But by the end of the century mounting fees were driving these out.

Analysis of school lists for the 1830s shows that Eton and Harrow were fairly similar, serving the aristocracy, landed gentry, and with one in ten from the professions (doctors, lawyers, etc.). Harrow has more clergy than Eton, Rugby has more clergy than Harrow.

And it is now that the venom of class consciousness begins to appear—tinged with fear and sharpened by spite. The phrase "working class" used pejoratively dates from the 1830s. The schools felt they could be openly contemptuous. When the Brougham Committee asked Winchester in 1818 why there were so many rich boys at a school meant for the poor, the school replied that the boys were really very poor. Indeed they had no money at all. It was their parents who were rich.

The reason for this is plain. By the early 19th century the industrial revolution, the expansion of trade, had begun to produce newly rich in significant numbers. There is a natural tendency for those who have just made money to join the company and ape the manners of those who have always had it—and to despise those they have left. In England this was enormously re-inforced by the fact that the newly rich appeared at a time when the wealth-owning classes—the landed gentry and the aristocracy—still held all political power. There were sound practical reasons for joining them.

There was also an idealistic reason for admiring the aristocracy. England had just won a great victory over France; and France had just destroyed her aristocracy. The continuance of England's aristocracy therefore became the mark of the differences between the two countries, the symbol of that victory.

The avenues by which the newly rich families could join the upper classes were already—and became increasingly and soon almost solely—the public schools.

The privileged classes were not stupid. They warmly welcomed the better-educated and more amusing members of the rising rich—and these graces could be obtained from the schools. But to a coarse manufacturer they—and lesser arts—seemed impossibly difficult. An 18th–century nobleman could sit quite safely on the same bench as a tradesman's boy. They were different beings. But a manufacturer's son was almost the same, with uncouth accent and odd table manners. How could his father hope he could ever change into a gentleman if he was jammed up against a lot of common tradesmen? It was middle-class fear of contamination, as much as anything, which solidified the class system.

And by 1820–30 there was already something to change to—the upper classes had already gone far to evolve distinctive ways of speaking, dressing, ways of holding their knives and forks, styles of writing letters and so on. Jane Austen is full of such niceties. This, too, is a natural tendency and can be partly explained by the ways we form our identity; but it so happens that public schools—boarding communities where everyone is in full view of everyone else—are peculiarly conducive to codifying, elaborating, intensifying and enforcing these aspects of behaviour. And the rising middle classes wanted them codified and elaborated: a code could be learnt; the more they were set off from their old associates, the more ways they had of showing kinship with their new ones. (And, in the end, the more likely they were to keep their new money. If anyone can marry anyone, then clearly in time accumulated wealth will spread. But if you can only marry—or only want to marry—and transmit money among a limited number then fewer share and all are richer. Class distinction which evolved for a number of quite different reasons [to join the group with political power for instance] ended by preserving the wealth of a class and became vital to keep for that reason alone.)

We may note two final, fundamental points. The obvious difference between the landed gentleman and the manufacturer was that the second earned his money, the first inherited it. Paradoxically, therefore, the ambitious merchant or industrialist, while he exalted work, had to value idleness as the supreme mark of status. A gentleman does not need to work.

This is absolutely crucial to a number of British class attitudes. It underpins the idea of the amateur. It explains the attitude to science, industry and many aspects of business. It is a strand in the very curious attitude to intellectual endeavour the public schools developed. And it lasted well into the 20th century. Popular literature demonstrates this. No Wodehouse hero works. In Wodehouse's books, money grows on aunts. The same is true of heroes in Dornford Yates (or Agatha Christie, or Buchan, or any number of examples).

Lastly, the power and wealth of the aristocracy and land-owning gentry in the 18th century derived ultimately from the practice of giving land in return for military service. Its roots, however altered and buried, were feudal. The class deference of the 19th century and early 20th century had, at its heart, the hierarchical deference of a fighting machine.

4 Games

One last theme significant, not by its absence, but by the lack of emphasis placed on it, is games.

Schoolboys have always played games and minute traces echo down the centuries, like Christopher Robson being given "six yerkes with a byrchen rod on the buttocks" in 1466 for kicking a football into the Minster at York. Many games were invented to fit into the physical pecularities of school buildings or available patches of ground: examples are the game of fives from the buttresses of Abbey Walls, a Tonbridge version of football using the gutters on their gravel pitch, and the Eton wall game. Because of the youth of many pupils we read of marbles, hoops and hobby-horses. In the late 18th century there were two developments. The excitement of matches (still within the school) was from weighting—that is the 1st fifteen against the next thirty, or, as in *Tom Brown's Schooldays*, the sixty boys of one house against the rest of the school. These "Bigside" matches were really battles; furious encounters without rules and without mercy, where bones were often broken and blood poured into the mud. (It was these ghastly scrimmages which Wellington—a lonely and withdrawn boy— wisely avoided. Like Ferdinand the Bull he preferred to play in the gardens of the Manor House where he boarded. He loathed his two and a half years at Eton and left in 1783. He did not go back for thirty-four years. When he saw the boarding-house garden he said: "I really believe I owe my spirit of enterprise to the tricks I used to play here.") These dis-organised routs were eventually to evolve into rugby and Association Football. Traces of them remain in Eton football, and the Winchester "Hot", during one of which a boy had his neck broken some fifteen years ago.

At the end of the 18th century roads had sufficiently improved for schools to start playing each other. The first recorded cricket match was that between Westminster and Eton in 1796, but there had probably been earlier ones because there was a Westminsters versus Old Etonians in 1768. The first Eton and Harrow match was in 1805. Byron played for Harrow and scored seven in his first innings and two in his second. Eton won easily and Byron went out and got drunk.

Games during the 18th century and early 19th century were extremely popular and much time was spent on them. Minet's "Journal" is full of cricket scores (one part of the school playing another part) and shows that Winchester boys could spend half the day on sport. But the point is that it was entirely left to them. It was not part of school life, and matches and rowing races were always being banned. Games were not played to keep fit or to instil "virtues" like team spirit or to occupy and therefore discipline boys or to sublimate sexual energy. They were played purely for pleasure.

5 Kind masters, good teachers

Extravagant, outrageous or violent behaviour is remembered where ordinary doings vanish. There are twenty stories about Keate to one about his gentle predecessor Dr. Goodall, whose "pleasant joyousness . . . beamed and overflowed in his face".

Yet there were always men who realised that boys can learn without being beaten. John Holmes, who introduced French into Gresham's in the 16th century, wrote: "Schoolboys are expected to be led, soothed and entic'd to their studies [not by] force or harsh discipline drove, as in Days of Yore."

There are instances of kindness even in the most brutal centuries and toughest schools. Bagshawe, Busby's irritable under-master at Westminster, was blamed for teaching boys in his own room. "The school," he answered, "was so raw, and the weather so extremely cold, that I did provide a fire for my scholars in an out-room, and taught them there for an houre only in the Morning; which if it be a crime, then Compassion, Care and Charity are Criminal; and I am glad that I am proved Guilty of them."

Furthermore, it was perfectly clear to a good many masters that boys will behave as well or better without savage floggings. John Nicholl was long remembered at Westminster for his mild, early–18th-century reign and for how well-behaved and prosperous the school was under him. Barnard at Eton in 1754 was witty, sarcastic, elegant—and caneless. "The Pitt of masters," said Horace Walpole. "Boys who would have been hardened by the infliction of punishment trembled at his rebuke."

But it is Keate who furnishes another corrective. Where beating is the standard and accepted punishment, virtually the only punishment, a schoolmaster is not necessarily cruel because he beats. It is important to remember this now, and throughout the 19th century. Keate was in fact an extremely kind and merry man. He frequently gave supper parties for his boys, and used to ask them back to his house to play French cricket with his wife. There are dozens of stories of his individual kindnesses and help.

Keate was also—and this is the second fundamental aspect of 18th- and early–19th–century school life which he demonstrates—an extra-ordinary teacher. Gladstone long remembered the brilliance and stimula-tion of his "Play", a special class he took alone for the most advanced of the sixth form. And though, as we noted earlier, good teaching was confined to relatively few, it could, within its limits, be very good indeed. It is important to emphasise this because, though it complicates the picture, it redresses an imbalance. It was always important to have a certain number of good scholars. Busby used to concentrate on small boys who looked young so that people would marvel at a master who could produce such prodigies so soon. Butler at Shrewsbury, Gabell at Winchester—and there are a number of others—were inspired classical teachers. But the learning was wider. Wharton, at Winchester, was a minor poet of distinction. Parr was an interesting and widely read man, who used to make his pupils translate *The Spectator*. To be "up" to these men was a genuinely educative experience.

There were also other ways of learning. At Eton, and to a much lesser extent at other of the great schools, it was the custom for wealthy boys to bring their own tutors (there were a good number at Westminster). And a good deal of knowledge was simply picked up. Without any compulsory games, and not much work, intelligent boys learnt a great deal in talking to each other and to sympathetic masters. Byron is an example. He read, so he said, "Huge amounts of History, Biographies (Charles V, Caesar, Sallust, Marlborough, Eugene, Bonaparte . . .), all the British poets, French (Rousseau), dozens of English and French philoso-phers, 4,000 novels." Not everyone believed him. "Certainly he did *not* read these books," commented his friend Hobhouse. But later he wrote more cautiously, "As Lord Byron says he read these volumes I am inclined to believe the fact, but it is certain he never gave any sign of this know-ledge afterwards." Do any of us? Certainly the Letters, now appearing in Marchand's marvellous edition, are those of a well-read man.

And Byron demonstrates a further qualification. The schoolmaster before Arnold is usually represented as remote from his pupils; indifferent to the screams from the dormitories, unconcerned with their lives, their characters, their morals; indeed with anything outside the classroom and frequently not with much other than discipline inside it. There is a good deal of truth in this. But once again, the precise picture is more complex.

When Byron aged thirteen, arrived at Harrow in 1801 Dr. Drury, who had been headmaster since 1785, was immediately sensitive to the fiery yet delicate temperament of the young lord. On the first day he took him into his study and tried to draw him out. "I soon found that a wild mountain colt had been submitted to my management. But there was mind in his eye. . . . His manner and his temper soon convinced me that he might be led by a silken string to a point, rather than by a cable—on that principle I acted." He was extremely patient with Byron. He put him in his son's house and several times intervened on Byron's behalf when Henry Drury and Byron did not get on well. Finally he moved Byron to another house.

These examples of concern could be multiplied, but there is one more—an oddity—which should be included. In the 19th century the evangelical movement started by John Wesley in the century before was to have an overpowering effect on the public schools—as on Victorian England generally. Strangely enough in 1748 he had started to run a public school of his own. It sounds absolutely frightful.

Kingswood School was begun to educate young dissenting ministers and in a number of exaggerated respects it did, in fact, presage certain features of the later-19th-century public schools. Wesley pointed out that most schools were in big towns. Children met other children and were, of course, instantly corrupted. He therefore set his school out in the wilds. He confidently expected that he could destroy every trace of original sin by his methods. The essence of these was total control. Boys were taken at eight, and then not allowed to go away from school, even for a single day, until they left. The ratio of staff to boys was one to five; this ensured that they were never out of sight of a master for a single instant, especially during the dangerous masturbating hours of night. There were no games or recreation of any sort "for", as Wesley wrote in his account of the school, "as we have no play-days (the school being taught every day in the year but Sunday), so neither do we allow any time for play on any day." They got up at four in the morning, winter and summer, and lived almost entirely on a diet of porridge and water gruel.

The Plain Account of Kingswood School is reticent as to the results of these methods. Some pupils died. In 1767—"To Doctor's Bill, £1.3.9; to coffin, shroud, etc., 19s." Whenever Wesley went away there were mass outbreaks of weeping, howling and shrieking. Wesley was always delighted to hear of these and put them down to visitations from God.

Only one moment of anything like relief occurs in twenty years of gloom. In 1757 Wesley appointed one of his converts as housekeeper. She was a sluttish but attractive young woman who had first married a cork-cutter, then an Italian and then, the other two still being alive, an Irish sailor. Mrs. Wesley hated her. She thought her "flippant, giddy" and was intensely jealous. The housekeeper's effect on the crushed boys, since the *Plain Account* does not go into it, can only be imagined.

This is an incident; indeed good teaching and kindly masters were incidents, too, though very much more numerous. Public schools invariably mirror their age, they do not lead it. It was a brutal age and in many ways a corrupt one and so were its schools.

6 Corruption, rebellion

The cause of corruption is greed for money. We have seen how in the 18th century the Headmaster of Blundell's amassed £60,000 from fees over twenty years.(That is around a million pounds at today's value.)Clearly the temptation to cut back on staff was severe. There were other temptations. The fellows and staff could seize the income from endowments for themselves, and this was general among grammar schools. The pressure here would be to cut down on pupils. Most masters and headmasters were clerics; this meant they had parishes and benefices to attend to and so neglected their schools. The schools had sometimes been founded partly to provide jobs in perpetuity for the founder's family. Giggleswick, started in 1512, employed the Carr family for 250 years. There was still a George Carr as usher in 1755. This, public school incest, and the low opinion in which the profession was held, meant the calibre of staff was generally appalling.

It was these forces which steadily reduced the 600 schools to an effective rump of a hundred, many of them in advanced decay. The process is well documented. Berkhamstead, founded in 1523, to teach some 144 boys, came under Forsan who, no doubt pocketing the endowments, turned boys away "in a passion". Numbers sank to ten. In 1727 at Stamford School they complained that in six years as headmaster Mr. Hammes had frequently absented himself and when he did turn up only worked two hours a day. Numbers went from eighty to five. And so it continues. The Perse School was founded in 1618 for a hundred scholars. By 1816 the fellows have whittled the scholars down to fifteen and are paying themselves £840 a year. In the mid–18th century Bromsgrove was the largest school in the Midlands after Rugby. In 1818 the headmaster, the Hon. Rev. Joseph Fell, was accused of spending nine consecutive days in a public house. He couldn't even cope with the twelve remaining pupils. (Drink is often a factor.)

The French Revolution occurred not just because the *Ancien Régime* was harsh, unfair, tyrannical and bankrupt but because it was also inefficient. This last was essential because it meant that revolution was possible.Exactly the same was true of the public schools, and at the end of the 18th and beginning of the 19th century, due to the corruption and inefficiency of the vast majority of the masters running them, they were rocked by a series of rebellions and violent revolutionary disturbances which, viewed from the (in comparison) pale and insipid calm of today's roughest comprehensive, appear quite astounding.

Sometimes the revolts were against the harsh conditions. This was the cause of violence at Eton in 1783. The boys joined the assistant masters, who were also in revolt at the time. When Dr. Davis, the headmaster, appeared to quell them, they rushed him. Pursued by hordes of yelling boys, he just managed to race into the Provost's Lodge. The boys then proceeded to break every window in the school. They invaded the headmaster's chambers, tore up all his papers, smashed all his furniture and burnt chunks off that hated symbol and weapon of authority, the flogging block. Order was finally restored and the boys sent home to cool down. There was a similar explosion at Winchester in 1793, partly because the old commoners were shut up all day, partly because all the scholars were to be beaten.

Another reason for rebellion was boys supporting a popular master. This was the cause of two uprisings at Harrow, one organised by Byron in 1805. His fondness for Dr. Drury led him to support a third Drury, Mark, for new headmaster when the Doctor retired. George Butler was appointed. Led by Byron, the boys dragged the headmaster's desk into the middle of school and burnt it. They then planned to blow the whole place up, and actually got as far as laying a trail of gunpowder down a passage below the school. But the idea was abandoned when they realised they would have destroyed all the signatures carved on the walls of the hall.

It should also be remembered that riots and mob violence were common at the end of the 18th century. The diary of Smith, a master at Westminster at this time, is full of them, and he more or less accepted permanent violence in the school. Furthermore, as the gentry increasingly took over the schools, they were to that extent invaded by people whose future in no way depended on what they learnt or how they behaved.

But it is clear that the French Revolution or the thinkers associated with it were the major factor. There were practically no rebellions before Rousseau; after the Revolution they gradually died away.

Campbell, a master at Westminster, wrote in 1815 that the school was getting easier to control. "It may seem ridiculous but the French Revolution and the rights of man &etc., caused this imitation. We always act second-hand scenes among men." (Just so, did masters today describe to me how much easier life had become since the end of the 1960s.) The Harrow boys in 1771 wrote an address to sustain their support of Dr. Parr which rings with the democratic spirit: "As most of us are independent of the foundation [i.e. they were fee-payers], we presume our inclinations ought to have some weight in the determination of your choice . . . a school cannot be supported when every individual is disaffected towards the master; neither will the disregarded wishes of the members want opportunities in showing their resentment." Many other examples of this influence could be given (every single major school had one or more rebellions). Here is a last one. In 1794 Rugby was ruled by a savage man called Henry Ingles, known as "The Black Tiger". One day he flogged a boy violently for firing a pistol in the yard of his boarding house. At once revolt broke out to "assert the Rights of Boys". Windows were smashed, and Ingles ordered the fifth and sixth forms to pay. Now the whole school

rose. A vast pile of desks and benches was made in the close, Ingles's library
was piled on top and the whole heap fired. Ingles called on a battalion of
soldiers in the town for help. The boys retreated and reformed in defensive
positions, but it was while a JP was reading the riot act that another force
of soldiers crept up on their rear and they were taken. The Black Tiger
exacted ferocious revenge; many were expelled and many more flogged.

They all ended like this; no headmaster lost his head. And in another,
paradoxical, aspect the little school revolutions differed from their great
instigator; where the French was a result of excessive tyranny, the school
rebellions can be seen as an expression of excessive, indeed anarchic,
liberty. It will have become obvious already that in many respects boys in
these centuries had extraordinary freedom. Before we finally plunge into
the turmoils of the 1820s and beyond, it is this freedom I want to examine
in three crucial areas.

7 Boy freedom

"Boys . . . roamed the countryside, tippled ale and, when they were not
roasting fags, roasted snared pheasants over open fires." So Evelyn Waugh,
and the gay picture is not much exaggerated. As it is again today (the
price of drugs, like all commodities, having soared), drink was a problem.
At Eton, late in the 17th century, "the scholars had frequently bottles of
wine drawn up to their windows in baskets (tho' they were locked in)."
Long Chamber at Eton became legendary in the 18th century. Feasts of
food were smuggled in, poached from Windsor. Once (the story is
possibly apocryphal, though the first report, by H. J. C. Blake, reads like
an eye-witness's) a sow was kept on the roof until she had farrowed and
produced suckling pigs. "Wild revelry and fun and the rollicking freedom
of that land of misrule," wrote Edward Thring describing it in 1835.
"Drunkenness and dissipation," noted another 19th-century commentator,
"sank deep into the social life of Harrow during the first forty years of the
century."

Minet's "Journal" of 1818–1820 portrays a delightful life, with hours of
free time spent swimming, duck shooting, playing cricket—and drinking.
Here are the last two entries.

> Thurs. May 25th, 1820: "Sat up all night with 3 other fellows swigging wine
> and playing cards. We had 3 bottles and a fine ham. Shirked chapel next
> morning. We had about 2 hours' sleep and I was told I looked very unwell
> next morning, I felt very sleepy. Meredith was much worse than I; after
> breakfast I was very well."
> Sat. 27th: "All our room overslept themselves, so we shirked chapel, got off
> the roll being shirked down."

This tradition of freedom began to be expressed architecturally. Dr.

James built the first row of studies at Rugby in 1784. They could be locked from the inside (which they certainly can't be now). A number of other schools did the same. At Eton at the start of the 19th century the Oppidans were given their own rooms in the masters' houses. Shelley had a room in the house of Dr. Bethell. He used to wire the door handle and gave that slow-witted man violent electric shocks when he called.

As a result of this freedom these loose societies generated far less loyalty than did those that came later. This will become significant when we consider the public schools as total societies. Just how loose—the extent of that disloyalty—was not I think properly appreciated up till now, and I am indebted to Mr. Arrowsmith's *History of Charterhouse Registers, 1769-1872* (recently published) for this insight. There is no reason to suppose that Charterhouse was anything but typical and it is clear, especially in the fifty years after 1769, that the mobility between schools was extraordinary. There were dozens of boys from St. Paul's, Merchant Taylors', Westminster, Harrow, and many other schools at Charterhouse during the period; and equal numbers of Carthusians left to join these other schools. There were seventy Carthusians at Eton in the period, and similar numbers of Etonians coming to Charterhouse. It was also by no means unknown for a boy to come to a school for a period, leave on some pretext or other (usually warlike) and then return to complete his schooling. An example out of several is Thomas Humberston. He was born on May 17th, 1780, entered Charterhouse as a scholar July 1792, left to be commissioned in the 78th and fought in Flanders till January 1795, when he returned to school where he stayed till 1796.

Loyalty, such as it was, was to a master more than a school, and it was very common for a new headmaster to bring pupils from his old school. Dr. Elder brought ten boys from Durham to Charterhouse when he came in 1853 and there are many other instances. Both these customs—the bringing of boys and inter-school mobility—declined sharply from about 1850 onwards and had virtually disappeared by the end of the 19th century.

A reflection of this freedom and looseness can be found in the relationship between the masters. I said in connection with discipline that the power of the headmaster was absolute. In this context it was true; in other ways it was severely curtailed. The old pattern had been a senior school taught by the senior master, and a junior school taught by an autonomous junior master or usher (that this had been the usher's rôle for a long time is clear, though Bamford for some reason seems to doubt it, from Malin's "Consuetudinarium" in the 16th century). The savage Boyer, with his great knotted fists, shared Christ's Hospital with the Reverend Matt Field. Field spent most of his time away from school and his pupils were as free as birds. These empty scholars poured upon Boyer and naturally caused a lot of extra work; but he did not interfere since "the province was not his own". This independence lasted well into the 19th century. The attitude is reflected in the position of assistant masters (Keate, for instance, had to "ask them in" to help with discipline). Often headmasters were not called this, but the Schoolmaster, the Master; Arnold in *Tom Brown's Schooldays* is the Doctor.

8 Boy cruelty, boy rule; origins of fagging and prefects

But this freedom is more parallel to than caused by boy freedom (though that, in its turn, naturally considerably curtailed the field where the masters could exercise power). But boy freedom had a further profound result. If you leave a lot of boys to their own devices, in a brutal age, themselves brutalised by rude surroundings and rendered aggressive by violent discipline and often harsh childhoods, you will get bullying. You get it sufficiently without all these. The bullying in these centuries was inevitable, continuous and fiendish.

Here is Southey writing of a friend of his at late-18th-century Charterhouse: "He was taken from Charterhouse . . . because he was almost literally killed there by the devilish cruelty of the boys; they used to lay him before the fire till he was scorched, and shut him in a trunk with sawdust till he had nearly expired with suffocation. The Charterhouse at that time was a sort of hell upon earth for the younger boys."

There are horrific accounts from all centuries, but it is clear the 18th and early 19th centuries marked a climax. Boys killed each other. There is a 1730 inscription in the churchyard at Eton: "Edward Cockburn, only son of Archibald Cockburn Esq., of the island of Antigua in America, who unfortunately lost his life by an accidental stab with a penknife from one of his fellows." The chapel register more realistically lists him as "murdered by Thomas Dalton, his Schoolfellow".

In such a jungle, physical strength and courage were naturally admired. This is the age of great school champions, battling with bare fists for thirty rounds surrounded by cheering supporters in "The Close". These too could end in tragedy. In 1825 little Ashley Cooper, a slight boy but of indomitable courage, was pitted against a much larger boy, Woods. Although it soon became clear that the contest was unequal, his supporters (particularly his two elder brothers) cheered him on. Little Ashley fought with desperate bravery, but began to fall, battered into unconsciousness. Whenever this happened, as it did more and more frequently, he was revived with brandy. He lasted two hours, fighting sixty rounds, before he collapsed and could not be roused. He was carried back to his tutor, Knapps. The tutor was out and no one told him. Six hours later a doctor came, but Ashley had sunk into a coma from which he never recovered.

From bullying grew fagging and the prefect system. The big boys forced the smaller ones to be their slaves, beating them up if they refused or did their jobs badly. Accounts begin in the mid-17th century, though it is virtually certain the practice started long before. At Winchester in 1668 there is a complaint "that Inferiors are many times forced to make beds of Prefects, and likewise to supply them with ink, paper, and such-like implements . . .". At Westminster by 1690 the older boys

> esteeme it a privilege [to send] Gentlemen's sons on their errands, to fetch them strong drink, buttered ale, cakes, custards and tarts etc. to the Schoole doore; and not onely to fetch, but to pay for them too; and if they refuse to goe, they are abused and beaten with ropes ends, and sometimes with sticks and cudgells; not onely to bruises and bloodshed, but often to wounds, and scarrs, that remaine all the daies of their life.

Masters left boys to themselves. The effect of time on accidentally growing powers of this sort is to sanctify them and to give them formal titles, rituals, forms. By the beginning of the 19th century fagging was universal and had become institutionalised in this way, and was often a system of full time slavery. Eton, 1824:

> The condition of a junior colleger's life at that period was very hard indeed. The practice of fagging had become an organised system of brutality, and cruelty. I was frequently kept up until one or two o'clock in the morning, waiting on my masters at upper and indulging every sort of bullying at their hands. I have been beaten on my palms with the back of a brush, or struck on both sides of my face, because I had not closed the shutter near my masters bed tight enough or because in making his bed I had left the seam of the lower sheet uppermost.

A similar development took place over prefects. Anyone who has been at a school knows that a cruel pupil is more to be feared than a cruel master. This is because pupils spend more time with each other than they do with masters, and therefore a cruel boy (or girl) has far more opportunity to do harm (and often fewer scruples) than a master. From this simple and obvious fact about bullying, much derives. Boy rule as a result is always more effective than rule by master, and from early on we find hard-pressed masters attempting to enlist the help of senior boys. By the 16th century they are on the statutes. Westminster, 1560: "At five o'clock, one of the chamber praepositors (to be four in number) shall intone *Surgite* [get up]. . . . Then each shall take any dust or dirt, to be swept up afterwards into a heap by four boys appointed by the monitor." Some of these early monitors could—or did—beat (as at Westminster), some were officially supposed only to report offences, as at Eton, Winchester and Harrow, where they were to inform on instances of "uncaring, fighting, filthiness and wantoness of speech".

By the end of the 18th century and beginning of the 19th the prefect system was virtually universal; it too had become formalised, the punishment meted out was usually a beating, and it, along with so much else, was

often brutalised in the way with which we are now familiar. "The oppres-
sions of these young brutes," wrote Lamb about Christ's Hospital, "are
heart-sickening to call to recollection. I have been called out of my bed,
and waked for the purpose, in the coldest winter nights—and this not once
but night after night—in my shirt, to receive the discipline of the leather
thong, with eleven other sufferers."

Prefects and monitors had changed from accusers to magistrates and
executioners—if they had not been those from the start. In fact, so much
had beating become a monitorial privilege that when it was withdrawn, as
at Harrow after Byron, they rebelled. Most of the rebellions of this time
were led by the prefects, and this is the measure of how much they were in
fact on the side of authority.

All these developments—boy freedom, boy cruelty, the power of the
prefect, and all the wildness and terror these provoked—are seen at their
most appalling, and can be best, and finally, exemplified by Eton during
the late 18th and early 19th centuries.

For over a century, the horrors (and, to some, fierce joys) of Long
Chamber echoed in English history. This barn-like room, where fifty-two
scholars slept, was 172 feet long and fifteen feet high, it was unheated until
1784 when two fireplaces were put in; the windows were broken and in
winter snow drifted in and covered their beds. It was filthy, stinking of
corrupting rats' corpses, ordure and urine. A parody on Gray's ode written
in 1798 begins:

> We chambers three, ye foul abodes
> Which filth and bedsteads line
> Where every instant adds fresh loads
> To Cloacina's shrine.

There were not enough of the large oaken beds four feet six inches
across, in which the boys slept together for sex or huddled close for
warmth, and some had to sleep on the floor. There was nowhere to wash,
except a sloppy shelf for the sixth. In 1834 a report stated "that the
inmates of a workhouse or a gaol are better fed and lodged than the
scholars of Eton".

But it is at night that the accounts read like descriptions of hell out of
Dostoevski. Then great fires were lit, so great sometimes that they
threatened to destroy the ancient building, sending monstrous shadows
dancing up the walls. Rats poured out of the walls and floors to feed on the
filth, at which the fags would give chase, stuff them into socks and smash
them against the beds. Their numbers can be gauged by the fact that in
1858 two cartloads of rats' bones were taken from beneath the floorboards.
Scenes of the coarsest and most flagrant orgiastic indulgence took place, of
a sort that participants (or victims) could later barely bring themselves to

describe. Charles Simeon, an earnest evangelical preacher, said he would be tempted to murder his son, rather than let him see in college the sights that he had seen. The larger boys, inflamed by drink, could become demons. Bedsteads were crowded round the fires and lower boys (no more than nine or ten sometimes) would be beaten, scorching, from side to side by the upper boys. Or a cord would be tied to a toe and they would be rushed up and down the room. They would be tossed in blankets. One boy, hurled high into the air, fell head first onto a bedpost and was completely scalped. And no one came to see what went on. No one else ever lived in the building. They were locked in at eight and left alone till morning. Their shrieks of pain and terror, their moans of pleasure, went alike unheard.

It is hardly surprising that Long Chamber became a grisly legend. Many parents refused to let their sons become collegers till the last possible moment. If they survived (not all did) it became evidence of remarkable toughness. A Dr. Oakes was applying to an insurance company in 1826 and mentioned in passing that "he had slept in Long Chamber for eight years". At that the chairman of the board interrupted: "We needn't ask Dr. Oakes any more questions."

But pain and terror were not confined to collegers. Bullying was rife in the boarding houses—and outside them. When Shelley went to Eton, aged twelve in 1804, he rapidly stood out as non-conformist. He stayed aloof and refused to be menial. He refused to fag for his fag-master Matthews. His appearance was notable: lanky and delicate, feminine. They soon discovered his rages, when he would lash out with open hands "like a girl in boy's clothes". It is not very surprising that he soon became a target for the whole school. The results were horrific:

He was known as Mad Shelley [wrote a boy a year below him], and many a cruel torture was practised upon him for his moody and singular exclusiveness. Shelley was my senior; and I, in common with others, deemed [him] as one ranging between madness and folly . . . conscious . . . of being the reverse of what the many deemed him—stung by the injustice of imputed madness, by the cruelty, if he were mad, of taunting the afflicted, his rage became boundless. Like Tarso's jailor, his heartless tyrants all but raised up the demon which they said was in him. I have seen him surrounded, booted, baited like a maddened bull—and at this distance of time I seem to hear ringing in my ears that cry with which Shelley was wont to utter in his paroxysms of revengeful anger.

On winter evenings there was a game called "nailing" played in the dim cloisters waiting to go into the upper school for supper. A heavy, muddy football was kicked rapidly through the crowd and then directed with ferocious violence at one agreed target. This target was frequently Shelley.

The mob had endless diversions:

The particular name of some particular boy would be sounded by one, taken up by another and another, until hundreds echoed and echoed the name. . . . The Shelley! Shelley! Shelley! which was thundered in the cloisters was but too often accompanied by practical jokes—such as knocking his books from under his arm, seizing them as he stooped to recover them, pulling and tearing his clothes, or pointing with the finger, as one Neapolitan maddens another. The result was, as stated, a paroxysm of anger which made his eyes flash like a tiger's, his cheek grow pale as death, his limbs quiver, and his hair stand on end.

Once, tormented into a delirium, he struck out violently and involuntarily with a penknife so that it pierced right through the hand of one of his torturers, pinning him to a desk. And this went on for *four years*, until at long last he reached the relative civilisation of the Remove and the sixth form.

What effects did it have? Indeed what effects did the primitive public school system have as a whole? Can we make any generalised comments about their freedom, brutality and anarchy?

The experiences in early childhood that result from certain patterns of upbringing are, to a degree, predictable in their effects. Continual severance from love, for example, or its absence, the death or cruelty of a loved figure, will usually produce a person who is insecure, someone who will later have difficulty with love relationships. Or violence inflicted in childhood will produce violence later, or, repressed, fear, insecurity and guilt. But by the time people go to public schools their characters are largely formed; the effects therefore are enormously more varied, the reactions as different as the different people reacting. Statements that public schools "caused" this or that general effect become far more difficult to make and over large areas impossible.

If at a universal level one has to be extremely tentative and careful, it is often possible at a personal one to be more sure. Richard Holmes, whose excellent account of Shelley I have been closely following, discerns a number of both long and short term effects that Eton had on him. The disturbances began to manifest themselves at once. Shelley began to wander the gardens of his house, Field Place, in disguise, spending whole nights locked in Warnham Church, applying for work as a gamekeeper's boy and speaking with a heavy Sussex accent. His mischievousness became more and more violent and uncontrollable. Now the nightmares, which had begun at his prep school, Syon House, grew worse. These torments of the night, visions and sleepwalking when he re-lived the school hell of his early youth, were to last the rest of his life.

The sense of betrayal was overwhelming. How could they have sent him away to such torture? Fear of rejection became central to his emotional life. And, as a result of his two schools, he gradually transformed his childhood into a time of extreme oppression, putting his father,

William of Wykeham,
Founder of Winchester
College. An engraving from
the picture in Hall.

Seal of Louth Grammar
School.

Dr. Richard Busby of
Westminster, at the start of
his fifty-seven-year reign as
headmaster.

The Upper Classroom at Westminster in 1858. The whole school was
taught here from its start until 1884. Note the "shell" at the far end.

The Lower School at Eton. This is the oldest schoolroom in Britain still in constant use.

though most of the evidence is to the contrary, in the rôle of tyrant.

Eton produced other and equally permanent effects. Fear became an element entwined in his character: fear of society *en masse*, fear of enforced solitude, fear of himself. The instinctive violence of the penknife incident was to recur in similar acts; his imagination was often furiously aggressive, a side which drove Claire Clairmont into hysterics and crowded his verse with ghosts and furies. He found it difficult to accept that streak of induced or, if latent, roused viciousness. These conflicts, planted at the centre of his personality, meant that it became fundamentally unstable and volatile. All this may be plausibly laid at the door of Eton and prep school acting on the temperament nurtured at Field Place.

Nonetheless, despite what I said earlier, public schools were already having more general effects then, and were to have many more later. These must be treated with caution, but there are a number of social patterns, peculiarities of attitude and character, the formation of some of our fundamental institutions, values and standards accepted right down through our society, which can hardly be understood without, at the very least, reference to the public schools.

Shelley remembered his time at Eton with an intensity of anger and expressions of horror he brought to nothing else. But from it he also derived his dislike of violence, his swift generosity to those in distress; these years produced his loathing of tyranny in any form, and his instinctive and marvellously sympathetic hatred of authority. And this recurs again and again, in various forms. Throughout the 19th and 20th centuries the public schools are to be accused of producing crushed, conventional, class-conscious philistines eagerly deferring to authority: and they are to be rightly accused. But dislike and defiance of authority, the refusal to be crushed, the deliberately unconventional, the elaborately bohemian are equally strong, if numerically fewer, elements in the British upper and middle classes. When class becomes an issue, often the most persuasive writers (Orwell of Eton) or the most effective politicians (Gaitskell of Winchester, Benn of Westminster) against class privilege come from the very class it is hoped to destroy. All countries share these phenomena, but in Britain their strength and persistence are largely due to the violence of the revulsion against things—class arrogance, tyrannical authority, attempts to impose conventions and so on—experienced for so long, so intensely, when so young.

A few more general points must be made about these aspects of the 16th, 17th and 18th centuries.

It is easy enough to skim lightly through accounts of bullying and beating, mildly titivated perhaps but essentially untouched. Yet remember yourself when small or think of your son now. Imagine that at this very moment, while you are reading, you are suddenly seized, dragged out and flung over a stairwell tied at the ankle to a sheet; or that someone ten foot tall and strong as a horse smashes you in the face so that you lose two teeth, or every night, in deepest winter, forces you to warm his icy sheets until, when he comes to sleep, he pulls you out and sends you to your own freezing bed. And that this is to go on for three or four years.

Similarly, imagine that you have just heard that your son's or nephew's headmaster has been absent nine days in a pub. The drunken and licentious behaviour of the pupils shocked even that permissive age, and articles, as in *The Gentlemen's Magazine* of 1798, complained of the appalling state of sexual morality. We may later smile at the almost insane moral fervour of some 19th–century reforming headmasters, but the savage brutality, anarchy, drunkenness and so on which they had to deal with were real and appallingly difficult problems.

Another point is that though as we have seen this boy freedom and boy rule grew up accidentally, and though there was virtually nothing the masters could do about it, once there, it was accepted and justified. Freedom and independence, allowing boys to choose in areas unconnected with the classroom, meant that they would grow up free and independent, tough, able to choose and decide for themselves. It became a perfectly explicit educational theory. In an essay on education in 1804, W. Barrow wrote: "Were it not for the dormitory at Westminster and the quarter-deck of a man of war, we should soon be a nation of macaronies." One of the complaints against Gabell at Winchester in 1818 was that he had abandoned "the English Method"—masters trusting boys, and the boys having self-government under prefects—for "the French Method", where the boys were not trusted and government was by the masters.

This of course echoes one of the most prevalent views of education current today. The trouble was that the psychology was primitive and faulty. It was supposed that to bring a boy up in tough conditions made him strong, whereas in practice such brutal conditions imposed so young led far more often to insecurity and fear. Certainly, boys exceptionally strong in the first place survived quite well; far more were crushed. And this too was fairly well recognised. For this reason vast numbers of boys were educated at home. Gladstone said that to send a boy who was not strong to a public school was "madness". And Lord Chatham stated he "scarce observed a boy who was not cowed for life at Eton".

Finally, during the 19th century a curious development took place. The various freedoms and practices we have been discussing proved too strong for reform. They were therefore taken over in their entirety and became the public school underworld, the "informal system" which even today obsesses sociologists. So in fact that whole structure of fags, bullying, prefect justice, monitorial whoppings, studies, feasts and illicit escapades which is unique to boys' public schools (girls' schools don't have it, nor do foreign schools or State schools) and which furnishes two-thirds of the material of their literature, was not a 19th–century growth but was a relic from the 17th and 18th centuries, imported whole and then explicitly condoned provided it remained more or less out of sight. It became an integral and adored part of the system, just as important later as games and "team spirit" and the classical tradition.

9 *Conclusion*

What conclusions can we draw from this sketchy survey? Let me try to summarise. The first schools were founded in the 6th and 7th centuries as adjuncts of the new Church, to provide clerics and also choristers for the cathedrals. We traced various interrelated processes which had culminated by the 1830s: the move to fee-paying and away from educating the poor (though only after some centuries had educating the poor become an obligation); the growth of boarding of one sort or another; the teaching of Latin first as a living, later as a dead language through the classics. We saw the emergence of various themes, some conspicuous by their lack of emphasis—sex, games; some by their growing emphasis—class, the peculiarities of tradition, public school incest, food, school songs, the loose loyalties of pupils towards and movement among the schools. The picture is not always simple: colossal classes, poor teachers, a combination of violent discipline and total disorder, must be balanced by inspired teachers, gentle masters, and a high standard of scholarship among the few. As the Church ceased to be a force in founding schools—ending in the dissolution of the monasteries when a good many schools disappeared—we saw the Crown, wealthy individuals and the livery companies take on the task of foundation, creating some 800 schools by the end of the 16th century. We followed circumstances of rising brutality, corruption and inefficiency from the late 17th century to the early 19th century, climaxing in a series of tempestuous rebellions. During this time while some nine or ten schools emerged as pre-eminent, and another ninety or so survived in all gradations of health and decay, approximately 700 slowly collapsed. Finally, sufficiently close to need no summary, we examined some of the strange and often horrifying phenomena of boy freedom, boy cruelty and boy rule, and their implications for the future.

The long flight over thirteen centuries is over. It is now time to look at that future. The public schools are about to enter the most extraordinary period of their history.

CHAPTER 4

Public School Reform and the Victorian Moral Climate: The New Sexual Traditions

Desmond knew that there were beasts in the Manor. Had you forced from him an expression approaching, let us say, definiteness, he would have admitted that beasts lurked in every house in every school in the kingdom. You must keep out of their way (and ways)—that was all. And he knew also that too many beasts break a house as they break a regiment or a nation. . . .

Horace Annesley Vachell, *The Hill*

In the complexities and confusions of the 19th century, the difficulties caused by the different ways and rates and reasons the public schools changed, the contradictions that arise because every school at any moment is different for everyone in it, three broad movements can be discerned. The first is the move to reform the schools. The second is the spectacular growth, both in numbers at and in numbers of schools. And the third, and in some ways the most interesting, is the ever-increasing concentration of the schools: the concentration within themselves—the intensity with which they pursued their aims, imposed their disciplines and aroused the love (and loathing) of those in them; and also their concentration together, the extent to which they became a system, and the force this system, permeating down to the most remote and unlikely areas of our society, exerted on the country as a whole.

1 The move to reform

The reaction to the brutality, inefficiency, corruption and immorality with which we have become familiar was a surprisingly long time coming. This was partly upper-class complacency, and partly the French Revolution. The French Revolution terrified English rulers. All reform—political, educational, social—seemed revolutionary. Most was delayed for thirty years. By 1816, however, criticism (especially of the great schools) was becoming furious. It was typical of the new age that this should be in "the press"—particularly in the *Edinburgh Review* and *The Quarterly Review*. They criticised the teaching, the hours of play, the indiscipline.

"The system of fagging," wrote the *Edinburgh Review*, "the only regular institution of slave labour enforced by brute violence which now exists on these islands." Of Eton floggings it wrote with disgust that they were "an operation performed on the naked back by the headmaster himself, who is always a gentleman of great abilities and acquirements and sometimes of high dignity in the Church".

Between 1816 and 1818 the Brougham Committee, a committee of the House of Commons, studied and severely criticised the great schools. Since all the schools were technically charities, endowed by statute in perpetuity to provide education to certain stated groups, they came under the Charity Commissioners. In 1816, therefore, these Commissioners started a bumbling eighteen-year journey through the other surviving grammar schools; every now and again sounds of muffled criticism emerged as a result of their wanderings.

Reforming governments, like that of Lord Liverpool, became possible again; in 1832 the Whigs passed the Reform Bill. There was also a rising interest in education, and at this time the first grants of public money were voted to this end by Parliament. (It is significant, too, that the first stirrings of a real girls' education start in the 1830s.)

But as well as these developments, at a much deeper level in the social magma, two great movements, of much more moment to the public schools, were steadily accelerating. The first was the continued growth of England's wealth and power. The improving energy of the Victorians was partly a spiritual and mental counterpart of their material success. Since improvement was so clearly evident and possible physically, it was possible in all departments of life. But, far more important, material success led to a vast increase in the middle classes. There is always a difficulty of definition with the middle classes. For our present purposes, we need only note that the numbers of those able and eager (for the class reasons we have already studied among many other reasons) to pay for a public school education grew continually throughout the 19th century. (The following figures give an idea of the numbers involved. Between 1800 and 1860 the professions of law and medicine doubled to 40,000; the clergy rose from approximately 7,000 in 1827 to 16,000. The *average* family had seven children, and everyone who was able to got married.) The 19th-century headmasters were perfectly aware of this. Woodard, the founder of Lancing, Hurstpierpoint and other schools spoke of the "new army of the middle classes". Time and again we will see a Thring or a Pears running into heavy debt, gambling over buildings and staff, certain that if they got the mix right, they'd get the pupils—and succeeding. The growth of the public schools is, at one level, a straightforward response to market forces.

But in the late 1820s and 30s, at the very moment when this great new market was making itself felt, numbers at many of the great schools began to collapse. At Eton they fell from 627 in 1833 to 444 in 1835; Charter-house 489 in 1825 to 137 in 1832; Harrow 295 in 1816 to 128 in 1828; Rugby had 300 pupils in 1821; in 1827 it only had 123. This was partly due to a temporary slump in the 1830s; but it was largely because the scanda-lous reputation and behaviour of the schools ran directly counter to the second great movement now reaching its climax: the spread of evangelical religion.

The essence of the religious revival started by Wesley and Whitehead in the 18th century was feeling—feeling whipped up by passionate open-air sermons to thousands—mob passion. The feeling whipped up was guilt. Guilt over personal sin, sin which was to be conquered in desperate personal battles; sin which, since it was human, was also social, and which had therefore to be conquered in society too. One of the most extra-ordinary and significant phenomena of this period is how this evangelical fervour and guilt swept first through the old 17th-century non-conformist sects, then the Catholic sections of the English Church, the Church of England itself, until finally, by the middle of the century, it had become a generalised social force dominating every department of private and public life.

> No one will ever understand Victorian England [wrote R. C. K. Ensor in 1966], who does not appreciate that among highly civilised countries . . . it was one of the most religious that the world has ever known. Moreover its particular type of Christianity laid a direct emphasis on conduct . . . it became after Queen Victoria's marriage practically the religion of the Court, and gripped all ranks and conditions of society . . . nothing is more remarkable than the way evangelicalism in the broader sense overleaped sectarian barriers and pervaded men of all creeds.

It is this spiritual element becoming dominant at precisely the same moment as did that fairly gross materialism which also characterises the age (and in part becoming dominant because of that materialism, in conscious opposition to it) which caused the tension, the conflict (and often the hypocrisy) which make the Victorian period so fascinating to study.

In 1827 there appeared on the school scene one man acutely sensitive to all these different social currents and pressures, a man of passionate intensity, mesmeric personality, iron will and fierce energy. That man was Thomas Arnold.

2 Thomas Arnold

Ever since Lytton Strachey there has been some rather mild controversy about Arnold: to what extent was he an innovator, the inventor of houses, prefects, organised games, of the idea that the main concern of public schools was with "Character"? There is a good modern biography by T. W. Bamford, though on the whole he and other writers have tended to follow Strachey's denigrating line. "By introducing morals and religion into his scheme of education," wrote Strachey, "he altered the whole atmosphere of public school life. . . . After Dr. Arnold no public school could venture to ignore the virtues of respectability." No one, at any rate, doubts the depth of Arnold's religious fervour. He used to break down and weep openly in front of the whole school at the story of the Passion. He was obsessed by sin, inherited original sin, and that deep urge to sin which we all feel. In particular, boys feel it. In a letter of June 20th, 1830, he wrote of his life ". . . it has all the interest of a great game of chess, with living creatures for pawns and pieces, and your adversary, in plain English, the Devil. . . . It is quite surprising to see the wickedness of young boys. . . ." He saw his life as a constant battle against sinning boys. But everyone's life was a battle against the sin inside them. And this is where— it is a rather complex idea—boys can show "manly spirit". Boys are "manly" insofar as they are valiantly engaged in the battle against sin; the effort of this deep struggle should show on the face. Arnold fought too. "That ashy paleness and that awful frown were almost always the expression . . . of deep, ineffable scorn and indignation at the sight of vice and sin," wrote his contemporary biographer Stanley. He fought with sermons:

> . . . the tall valiant form [wrote Thomas Hughes], the kindling eye, the voice, now soft as the low notes of a flute, now clear and stirring as the call of the light infantry bugle . . . the long lines of the young faces, rising tier above tier down the whole length of the chapel. . . . We listened, as all boys in their moods will listen (ay, and men, too, for the matter of that) to a man whom we felt to be, with all his heart and soul and strength, striving against whatever was mean and unmanly and unrighteous in our little world.

And he flogged. At first he had hoped that fierce moral exhortation would be enough. It was not. The tides of sin had to be beaten back. In 1832, he thought he caught a boy, March, lying. "In a passion", he laid on him eighteen strokes. In the event, he found he'd been mistaken. He apologised in front of the whole school and humbly to March himself. But the significance of the story is not so much Arnold's scrupulousness: it is that phrase "in a passion". Laziness, lying, deceit, breaking bounds, cribbing, were seen by Arnold, and the headmasters who followed him, as *grave sins*. How different this is from the 18th-century attitude. It is engaged. Lashing was not just justified as helping to save a boy's soul, it was something evil, a sin, they were lashing. The step to someone evil is small. There is no suggestion that Arnold was even remotely sadistic, but one can see how much closer to the heart flogging would be to men who felt like that; there can be little doubt that with some Victorian (and later) headmasters other, less relevant organs were involved.

It was not just a personal crusade; it was a national one. Although himself a radical, Arnold was terrified at the effect radical hopes might have on the lower classes. He was haunted by visions of mob violence, chaos, revolution. Nor were his fears all that foolish. In 1830 Thomas Attwood addressed ever-growing crowds of workers demanding parliamentary reform: 70,000 at Birmingham, 80,000, then 150,000. There were meetings of a million threatened in London. Arnold was literally kept awake at night, thinking about it.

His solution was simple: religion, the Church. This was the force that would unify (and pacify) the country, and since they would naturally be led by the upper classes it was essential these should be truly religious too. This then was the main purpose of a public school. "It is *not* necessary that this should be a school of 300 or 100, or fifty boys; but it *is* necessary that it should be a school of Christian gentlemen."

And Arnold appeared to be successful. Dr. Moberly, Headmaster of Winchester, asked for his opinion by Stanley after Arnold had died, wrote a famous passage, which Stanley quoted, in which he said Dr. Arnold was the first headmaster to try to effect such moral improvement and that he was very successful. "It soon began to be a matter of observation to us at the university that his pupils brought quite a different character with them to Oxford than that which we knew elsewhere . . . manly-minded, conscious of duty and obligation . . . influence for good . . ." etc.

There are other aspects of Arnold about which most commentators agree. The central issue of the 1830s was discipline. Arnold knew perfectly well from his experience at public schools (he was at Westminster till 1807 and then at Winchester) that half the battle was to get the boy leaders, the prefects, on his side. They were the prime targets of his moral fervour; in personal terms he scarcely knew the rest of the school. Indeed, to such a degree did he concentrate on his senior boys in the sixth form that it is a perfectly plausible view that he was really the teacher of a small school which he recruited from the rest of Rugby. As with the sixth, his prefects, so with houses. He invented neither, but he concentrated on both. "Every house was thus to be [Stanley again] as it were an epitome of the whole school . . . every master was to have, as he used to say, 'each a horse of his own to ride'." And Arnold began to unify the school, to draw it together. He raised the status of teachers by raising their salaries to £1,500 a year (see Appendix A). This meant that while they remained clerics—a profession, Arnold noted, which certainly couldn't ensure virtue but was at least an insurance against gross vice—they did not need to have benefices. They could concentrate on the school. He consulted them regularly and, on the whole, would not implement a policy if the vote of his staff went against him. He interfered directly in discipline: dogs and guns were forbidden, bounds made stricter, fights had to take place in the Close, in view of the Doctor's house and therefore became less dangerous.

His character was complex. He had a formidable will: "We have heard it regretted [*Edinburgh Review*, 1845] that a man who should have been in his proper place swaying all the Russias, or sitting on the throne of the Antonines, should have been thrown away on the hopeless task of reclaiming a public school." He was one of the first to insist that a head-master should have complete independence from his governors. People spoke of his fascination, his almost hypnotic power. He was also a gentle man: *Tom Brown's Schooldays* first finds him modelling a boat for his children. He had a profound instinct for his work. Here are some things he said: a headmaster should leave after fifteen years or when "you feel no emotion on receiving a new boy". "A teacher should always be eager to experiment and to find out new things"; only by continually learning could he retain his interest. "I enjoyed [1831], and do enjoy, the society of youth of seventeen or eighteen, for they are all alive in limbs and spirits at least. . . ." Yet he did not, in fact, approve of public schools. As a task, his headmastership often bored him and he longed for the holidays. He was a radical in religion and politics. Indeed, his reputation outside was far more due to the fierce stance he took in the controversies of the time than to what he did at Rugby. His position as headmaster just made those stands seem the more outrageous.

But to return to Arnold's influence on the public schools. The contribu-tions I have outlined are those left by Strachey after his demolition work on the towering figure Arnold had become by the end of the century. But now Bamford and others would demolish still more. For one thing, his effect on Rugby itself, in religious terms, appears to have been enormously exaggerated. Bamford cites an analysis of every single boy under him at school which proves that he clearly did not effect a moral revolution. The idea of such an analysis makes one boggle somewhat (Bamford does not say who did it or how); but such results are hardly surprising. Certainly, examples of reformed youth are rare enough to stand out when they appear. There was Spencer Thornton, swept by religious zeal in 1829. Every moment of his spare time was spent visiting the sick or preaching to his schoolmates. He hurried from the school service in chapel in order to be in time for a second sermon at the parish church. "I would stand to that man, cap in hand," said Arnold. Or there was Arthur Stanley himself, a sort of saint. He rose so swiftly through the school that he was exempt from fagging within six months, and, preoccupied with manly struggles, an ethereal character, simply did not notice the bullying and the bawdi-ness. He baffled his contemporaries and was treated with "a deference, unparalleled in those rough days in the history of Rugby". After Arnold, there were eight headmasters till the end of the century and, so far from being set, the religious course of the school fluctuated accordingly.

Nor did he have any particular effect on the other schools or head-masters of his time. His contemporary headmasters had, after all, long become fixed in their own views. Some schools—Charterhouse and Westminster are examples—continued much the same as before; and these, out of tune with the times, declined. But a good many other schools were equally responsive to the evangelical spirit. Langley, Arnold's contemporary at Harrow, went on to become an archbishop. When Samuel Butler left Shrewsbury to become Bishop of Lichfield in 1836 he made a typically Arnoldian speech to his successors "to labour faithfully, zealously and happily in their calling, training those who are confided to their care in the principles of the religion and sound learning, and endeavouring to make them good Christians, good scholars and honourable and useful members of society. Amen!" It was a typical Arnoldian speech, but it was Butler's own. That is the point. These schools were reforming independently. "The truth is," said Charles Wordsworth of Winchester, plainly nettled by Arnold's reputation, "there was a general awakening, which in many instances, as with us at Winchester, partook decidedly of a Church character, such as Arnold's teaching and example, however excellent in their way, had little or no tendency to create." As for Moberly's famous letter, he had in fact never been to Rugby. Nor did he know a large number of Rugbeians. What he had known was Stanley at Oxford, so intense, so "manly", so good (and so well connected). When Stanley wrote to him years later and asked him for his opinion of Arnold and Rugby, what he was really asking for, as Bamford points out, was Moberly's opinion of Stanley—and this was what he got.

In other important spheres Arnold was inactive or even reactionary. It is perhaps anachronistic to expect him to share our feelings about class distinctions and inequalities; but here too he was utterly with the head-masters of his time. Class was where the money was. Apart from the "gross vice" reasons, he employed clergy because that was the easiest way to give an appearance of class to the staff. Bamford cannot understand why he abolished the lower school. The probable reason is the obvious one. By doing so he effectively prevented lower-class local people entering the school since they couldn't reach a high enough standard to pass into the upper forms—unless they paid for outside schooling. A law case decision said he was wrong. Arnold ignored it. There is fringe evidence that, had he lived, he might have introduced science; in fact he abolished science classes in 1837 and, aside from a little French and maths, confirmed the classics in the concrete in which they were already set. As for games, Arnold is irrelevant to their development. They bored him. In *Tom Brown* he watches a football match—still boy-organised on 18th-century mob-rout lines—for a brief half hour; at the end of the book he cannot be bothered to wait for "Tom Brown's last match" (cricket this time, against "the Marylebone men"). He escapes thankfully to the Lake

District. Finally, even the bullying remained atrocious. (One of my correspondents, Julia McSwiney, told me that her father was there fifteen years after Arnold, in the early 1870s, leaving at nineteen with a moustache. There were still ferocious boxing matches with bare fists, and the bullying and general roughness were such that it was universally accepted that you just wouldn't send someone there who wasn't tough. They would be educated at home.) This, along with other disciplinary matters, he scarcely touched. In fact there was no noticeable change of "tone" at Rugby under Arnold. "Tone", that marvellous Victorian word, typically vague, where the implication is that a school is somehow like a bell (a church bell) which can be made to ring "pure", ring "true" when impurities, flaws, gross alloys are removed—a *manly* bell.

Now, these further reductions of Arnold are narrowly true, though at places they can be challenged. Religion may have fluctuated at Rugby after Arnold, but it was, because of him, irreversibly a religiously oriented school (it still is). All his successors were devout clergymen. Two of them—Tait and Temple—became Archbishops of Canterbury. Temple was in some ways like Arnold. He paraded his religious passion and sobbed openly when flogging. Percival of the Knees was fanatically moral—that Percival who went on from Rugby to Clifton and insisted that boys playing football should wear trousers down to and tightened at the calf lest they should become inflamed at the sight of one another's knees.

But I think, in fact, that such a reductive view is rather trivial. It misses the point of Arnold over two extremely important areas. Arnold was not so much concerned with a boy's character as with his soul; if he could save him morally he would save his soul. But once you concern yourself with a boy's morals, you are bound to concern yourself with his life outside narrow school lessons; his conduct generally. So Tom Brown finds that the Doctor has given him Arthur, a weakling, which gives him "manliness" (that is, leads him to fight sin on Arthur's behalf) and so "steadies" him. The more you concern yourself with a boy's life outside school, the more you need to supervise and control it. And the more complete your control becomes, the more you, as a teacher, take the place of the parents and, in turn, the wider the implication of character training becomes, leading to still greater degrees of control.

School as a place to train character—a totally new concept so far—was what came to distinguish the English public school from all other Western school systems. It is what amazed and impressed foreigners—and amazes them still. That terrific growth of concentration (and its effects) will be one of our main studies. Both derive directly, if implicitly, from Arnold's Rugby. (In a rudimentary way they are explicit. We have seen Arnold restrict bounds. One reason he was against public schools was that, since school became the family for most of the year, he himself too much replaced the father. It "loosened the affections". This was why—the soul bias again—he refused to take any boy whose father disagreed strongly with his religious views.)

It could be argued that these developments were implicit in the evangelical fervour of which Arnold, but other headmasters, too, was an exponent. But, and this brings us to the second significant area, it is correctly derived from Arnold alone because people *thought* it came from Arnold.

In all great new religious, social, political or philosophical movements there is an apparently irresistible need to personalise: it makes events, or ideas, more dramatic; they become easier to remember, more human, simpler; above all a single figure can become the authority for what his followers do. The general influence, and therefore general significance, of these men is frequently just as much due to what they are supposed to have said or done as it is to what they actually did. Rousseau *is* freedom, Freud, psychoanalysis, Einstein, modern physics, Marx is communism. And Arnold and Rugby are "the public school system".

There were additional reasons for Arnold to gain this position. First, he was a "great" headmaster in a particular sense. He was, in his time, a national figure; his fame started there. And his national reputation was confirmed by having a son, Matthew Arnold, with an equal or greater fame. Temple and Benson were influential as headmasters and are remembered, if at all, as men, because they became archbishops. For the rest—the Thrings, the Warres, the Butlers, Mosses, Harpers—have you ever heard of them? Remove them from the exaggerating gaze (and memories) of the tiny subjects in their tiny kingdoms, make them step from under the huge magnifying glass of their schools—and how they dwindle. A sign of this is how very few biographies of "great" headmasters there are.

Second, two highly influential books were written about Arnold. Stanley—whose love for his old headmaster became, as he noted himself with misgivings, almost idolatrous—published his *Life and Correspondence* in 1844, two years after Arnold died. Here, if parents, pupils and other masters needed one, was a gospel to turn to. And turn they did. By 1845 it had raced through six editions. By 1881, when John Murray took over from the publishers, B. Fellowes, it had reached twelve editions, and it continued to sell heavily into the 20th century. Stanley was the architect of Arnold's legend. Here houses, prefects, school spirit, the idea that he was the first and only seriously influential reformer, are developed, then enshrined. I have already quoted from him. Here he is again, with an example of the subtle way he developed his case. First, he takes part of Dr. Hawkins' famous testimonial before Arnold was appointed: "If Mr. Arnold were elected to the headmastership of Rugby, he would change the face of education all through the public schools of England." Next, he uses this "would" as a buttress to his argument that this was what Arnold did. Stanley's experiences at Rugby were the most important in his life. He therefore assumed, by extension, they were the most important in Arnold's life, and, by a yet further extension, they were of some intrinsic, almost cosmic importance.

The second book was *Tom Brown's Schooldays* by Thomas Hughes. In a recent essay from *The Victorian Public School*, Patrick Scott has conclusively shown that the true interpretation of this book is as a moral tale, in which Tom grows, through experiences at Rugby, to man's stature, aware of moral right and wrong and determined to uphold the former. This was why Hughes wrote the book, and he followed it up with *Tom at Oxford* where the message is totally clear. The bullying, the games, the "boy culture" pranks at the beginning of *Tom Brown* are all relatively short incidents put in, as Hughes said, as "plums" to lead the reader to the moral heart.

No doubt this analysis is all accurate. But to my mind it makes the same mistake as concentrating on what Arnold "really" did. The significance of *Tom Brown* is quite different.

It, too, was enormously successful. Published in 1857, it had run through five editions—11,000 copies—by November of the same year. By 1862 it had sold 28,000 copies, and fifty-two editions by 1892, when other firms started to bring it out. It is still in print. And it was praised for its realism— it was not only thought to be true but to be a picture of what a "great" public school should be like. And the realism all those readers enjoyed is found precisely in those plums the book is "really" not about. That is because all the literary energy of the book is in those passages. Here is a description of the football game at the start of the book—an old-fashioned weighted match—sixty against 300—which gives us, incidentally, a clear vision of what those horrible great routs must have been like.

"Then the two sides close, and you can see nothing for minutes but a swaying crowd of boys. . . ." There are pitched fights, sudden piercing dramas, breaks, feints; heroes appear:

> The school leaders rush back, shouting, "Look out in goal!" and strain every nerve to catch him, but they are after the fleetest foot in Rugby. There they go straight for the school goal-post, quarters scattering before them. . . . Is there no one to meet Crew? Yes, look at little East! The ball is equal distance between the two, and they rush together, the young man of seventeen and the boy of twelve, and kick it at the same moment. Crew passes on without a stagger; East is hurled forward by the shock, and plunges on his shoulder as if he would bury himself in the ground, but the ball rises straight into the air, and falls behind Crew's back, while the "bravoes" of the School-house attest the pluckiest charge of all that hard-fought day.

It is very exciting, and throughout the book Hughes uses games for drama, to develop confrontations, build heroes, etc. But the significance is clear. The apparent concentration on games, due entirely to their intrinsic excitement and the vivacity of Hughes's prose, allowed later schools to say these had been a major element in Arnold's Rugby.

The same is true of many later facets. The feasting and rampaging continue, but are contained, within the school. It does not matter whether Arnold actually achieved any significant increase in piety. It is enough that he was thought to have done so. Though it is obviously rubbish, Hughes says at one point that by the end of Arnold's reign it was common for all the boys to kneel by their beds and say their prayers each night. Fagging, house spirit, team spirit (Brooke: "Why did we beat 'em? . . . It's because we've got more reliance on one another, more of a house feeling, more fellowship than the School can have . . ."), the idea that justice and its administration should be left to the prefects and sixth form: all this is embodied in Hughes's book. *Tom Brown's Schooldays* marks an important step, and was an important agent, in the wholesale take-over of the 18th-century boy culture and its enshrinement—since allowed by Dr. Arnold—underground.

As a result of these two books, the need for an idol, his own exertions, and his reputation, Dr. Arnold had, by the end of the century, become transfigured. It is impossible to open a book on education written at this time and not see his name. He was used to justify anything and everything —or nothing.

". . . That pioneer of English public school education, Dr. Arnold," says the headmaster in *George Brown's Schooldays* by Bruce Marshall (about Glenalmond in 1916), "who was among the first to see that although our Saviour taught us to turn the other cheek He did not mean that we were not to tackle our man low." In terms of effect and influence, his reputation should be returned to something a great deal closer to what it was before Strachey's reappraisal than the rather mingy deference it has been allowed ever since.

The last element in Arnold's apotheosis, but a very concrete expression of his influence, was the appearance of apostles. Certain susceptible members of the sixth were fired by the enormous power of his concentration with an overt missionary zeal; and this idea that the school was a mission continued after his death. From Rugby, they streamed across the country: Hart to Sedbergh, Phillpotts to Bedford, Vaughan to Harrow, Percival to Clifton, Potts to Fettes, A. G. Butler to Haileybury, Cotton to Marlborough; the word also went to Monkton Combe, Felsted and Lancing.

It is necessary, in order to introduce a preliminary examination of another new 19th-century theme, to turn briefly to the career of one of these missionaries—C. J. Vaughan of Harrow.

3 *Vaughan of Harrow—the canker at the heart of the rose*

Until very recently (when the private diaries of J. A. Symonds were discovered and used by Phyllis Grosskurth in her biography of him, a brilliant account which I follow), C. J. Vaughan was regarded as one of the leading Victorian headmasters. He was, for a start, intensely ambitious. At twenty-six, he applied for and nearly got the headmastership of Rugby. He was only twenty-eight when he seized Harrow, an even greater plum. Indeed, the only inexplicable thing about his career was why he suddenly resigned from the school fifteen years later, in 1859. It looked as though the task of reform had almost broken him, or as if, like Napoleon, hesitancy had begun to interrupt his drive and ambition. In 1863 he was offered a bishopric. He accepted; then abruptly, a week later, resigned. Another explanation was that, a deeply religious man, he wished to curb his over-riding ambition. This is the line taken by the *Dictionary of National Biography* today, where it speaks of "a severe struggle with his ambition" but "his determination had been taken". Not until 1879, presumably having conquered these fires, did he allow himself the modest success of Dean of Llandaff.

If the first explanation, exhaustion, was the true one, certainly Harrow, in 1844, was a daunting task. It was notorious for drunkenness. Yet here again, the view was that Vaughan was triumphantly successful. Sir Charles Dalrymple wrote: "Vaughan was, in every sense, the restorer of Harrow. He re-created the school, and he ranks among the great headmasters of the century." Bounds were enforced, discipline became firm; as for drunkenness, he stamped it out. In fighting evil he had an iron control and imperturbability. Once he contrived to read prayers while a boy writhed in an epileptic fit at his feet. And, as a result, as a headmaster he passed the acid test—when he arrived there were only sixty boys; when he left, 469. But not for nothing had he been one of Arnold's principal favourites, showing such promise that the Dean of Peterborough warned him not to "throw himself away" on Harrow. His main object was to deepen the spiritual life of the school; and he did this with incessant services. J. A. Symonds complained in a letter to his parents that "four services and three sermons" on a hot summer's day were "too much". He was an inspired, terrifying sermon orator, with a passionate voice and flashing eye. Sir Charles Bruce, Governor of Mauritius, still trembled forty years later at the memory of one of Vaughan's sermons: "Cast forth that evil person from among you." Yet one might note a peculiarity. On several occasions, he seems, unconsciously, to have expressed his own inner torments and struggles in the sermons; not that that made them any the less effective.

In manner he was cold, secretive, contained. One of his weapons was a savage sarcasm, always particularly wounding to boys. At the same time, he had a sense of humour. A boy called Dodd was sent to him for punishment. Vaughan started to write down his name, then stopped. "Do you spell it with one *d* or two?"

"Three, Sir," replied the boy.

Vaughan burst out laughing and sent him away without flogging him. "I could no more have punished that boy," he said later, "than I could have flown. Nobody before ever gave me such a lesson in spelling."

Only one thing seemed out of place in this reformed Harrow of the late 1840s and early 50s; occasionally rumours leaked out of sexual irregularities. Examination has shown that "irregularities" was something of an understatement. In fact, Symonds's diaries and other sources have shown that the school at this time was, sexually speaking, an adolescent boy's jungle; a jungle where lust and brute strength raged completely unrestrained. Every good-looking boy was given and addressed by a female name; he was regarded either as public property—in which case he was frequently compelled into (often public) acts of incredible obscenity— or else taken over and became the "bitch" of an elder boy. Lust could turn to loathing or sadism. Symonds noted one sensual-mouthed boy whose lovers, all monitors, turned against him; they used to kick and spit and throw books at him. Symonds himself, delicate and sensitive, had numerous advances made at him which he managed to repulse, and eventually he was left alone.

It seemed that here, too, Vaughan made every effort to stamp out the vice. One day a note was caught being passed between two boys. It was given to Vaughan. At once, the whole school was summoned. Sir Charles Dalrymple, naturally not revealing the cause of the occasion, describes the almost incredible, thrilling tension. "The stillness was phenomenal, and the impression produced by the words, addressed to the school generally, and to the culprits in particular, cannot be exaggerated." Vaughan read the letter aloud, and then banned the sending of such letters. He banned the use of female names. The offenders were both flogged.

Yet at this very moment—and it was certainly not for the first time— Vaughan was in the grip of a devastating physical passion which he was completely unable to control. In January 1851, a lively, superficial, good-looking boy called Alfred Pretor, a friend of Symonds, sent him a letter (which Symonds kept) telling him that he was having an affair with their headmaster. Symonds simply did not believe him. It seemed inconceivable. However, Pretor was able to show him a number of passionate love letters Vaughan had written to him. Symonds was stunned. That it was true was bad enough, but with a boy as superficial as Pretor, and Vaughan, a man in charge of nearly 500 other boys. . . . And to these feelings were added disgust. He had to sit beside Vaughan and read aloud his essays on the very sofa where he knew acts of love had occurred. Now, when Vaughan reached out casually and stroked his thigh, he shrank away. Before, he would not have noticed the subtle if familiar gesture. And these feelings were complicated by a growing awareness of his own homosexuality. He became infatuated with a handsome boy himself, and eventually, to gain contact, stole his hymn book from chapel. But he was too frightened and excited to speak to him. Another night he nearly succumbed when a boy made advances to him in his bedroom.

Symonds did not mention the incident to anyone for eight years. At seventeen, he left Harrow and "Dr. Vaughan's malign influence" as he now felt it, and went to Oxford. But he brooded upon it incessantly, his guilt over his own desires transferred to guilt about not revealing Vaughan's; then self-sympathy, envy even, transferring itself as well. Finally, in 1859, the pressure became too much. One day, on a reading party at Whitby, he blurted out the whole story while walking on the cliffs with John Conington, the Corpus Professor of Latin. Conington, who liked Symonds and was interested in him, was absolutely appalled. He read Pretor's letter and said that Symonds should tell his father what he had told him. Now, Symonds's inner conflict became acute. Later, as Frances Haskell put it, to be "driven to the verge of madness out of hatred for the chastity to which he had been expected to conform in Victorian England", his sympathy with Vaughan must have been strong. He also felt guilty about violating Pretor's confidence. At the same time he felt Vaughan could only encourage the vice at Harrow, and perhaps deprave boys who might otherwise remain normal. Besides, he had already set things in train. He told his father.

Gradually, the great engine of Victorian moral outrage began to move. Dr. Symonds—with considerable relish, one can't help feeling—had no hesitation. His duty was clear. He wrote to Dr. Vaughan to say he had learnt of his behaviour with the boy Pretor. There would be no public exposure, on one condition: he must resign at once. The unfortunate Vaughan hurried to Clifton, to Symonds's house. There was a long confrontation, of which no details remain. In the end, Vaughan agreed; he had to resign. But four days later his wife Catherine arrived from Harrow (ironically enough she was the sister of Arthur Stanley of Rugby). She flung herself on her knees, weeping and begging for pity. She had known of her husband's little weakness but it had never interfered with the running of the school. Dr. Symonds was deeply moved by the sufferings of this unhappy woman at his feet, not less because she was the daughter of the Bishop of Norwich and sister of the then Professor of Ecclesiastical History at Oxford, shortly to be Dean of Westminster. But he remained rock-like. Vaughan must go.

Now things moved into top gear. There were two urgent considerations: first, how to arrange the headmaster's resignation with some show of justification; second, how to stop the scandal exploding publicly. Pretor had continued to boast and it was already known to a few people. Stanley and Hugh Pearson (afterwards Dean of Windsor) acted for

Vaughan. Correspondence flowed. Professor Conington was kept privy to all moves and deliberations. Moral imperatives guided each step.

The first was fairly simple. On September 16th Vaughan sent a circular to all the parents: "I have resolved after much deliberation, to take that opportunity of relieving myself from the long pressure of these heavy duties and anxious responsibilities which are inseparable from such an office, even under the most favourable circumstances." And thus, amidst a series of speeches, dinners and formal farewells, he left. He preserved his iron self-control until the end. Only in his last sermon did he seem to speak. Two emotion-charged passages appear to be directed straight at the two Symondses, who together had brought him crashing. The sermon was called "Yet once more". First, he aims at the father:

> How am I to utter these last words, *Finally, brethren, farewell* I know not. I would fain postpone them; but until when? How can I sever myself, even in imagination, from this place? . . . Three months ago it seemed to be possible: the clearest and most decisive judgment dictated it: but today it is hard to execute.

Next, he turned to the son:

> Some of you lately left us: they can tell you something, but not all, of what presses upon me today. They had scarcely been mixed up as I have been with the permanent life of this place. They had another home all the time. Their gladdest associations were with that other home all the time: and when they left this place, they had life all before them. Some are going now, with me: yet even they can know but a portion of my parting. . . .

Thus, in public, he revealed the anguish which otherwise he kept deeply hidden. And now the mystery of the second resignation is explained. Dr. Symonds had told Vaughan he must never hold any high position in the Church. Perhaps, after four years, Vaughan thought, he would relent. At any rate, in 1863, he accepted Lord Palmerston's offer of the Bishopric of Rochester. The moment he heard the news, Dr. Symonds dashed off a telegram: Vaughan must resign immediately or there would be complete public exposure. So Vaughan resigned again. For sixteen years he occupied the, for him, humble position of Vicar of Doncaster. Not until Dr. Symonds died did he dare stir, and become Dean of Llandaff.

That the scandal should have been suppressed until this day is almost incredible. Indeed, as I have said, there were leaks from Pretor's boasting, which he bitterly regretted. (He was also furious about Symonds's part in the affair and never spoke to him again.) Hugh Pearson, one of the intermediaries, said that after the second resignation people suspected something must be up. In fact Bishop Samuel Wilberforce came and asked what it was. Pearson refused to say anything. Wilberforce lost his temper and said he would never speak to him again if he did not tell him. Pearson remained silent. A little later Wilberforce came to him in triumph and said he'd heard the whole story from a lady sitting next to him at a dinner party.

But, essentially, the secret was kept. Everyone contributed. R. E. Prothero's collection of Stanley's correspondence gives no letters between him and Vaughan during this period, as though at this crisis they had abruptly stopped writing to each other. Horatio Brown, Symonds's biographer and literary executor, simply suppressed his friend's memoirs and passed over the entire Harrow period and its aftermath with the words "The autobiography of the Harrow period is not copious". When he died, Vaughan had all his papers destroyed and ordered that no life of him was to be written.

What Vaughan felt no one knows, least of all his contemporaries. That rigid self-control, that secrecy, kept him hidden. "In truth there was no art to find the construction of Vaughan's mind either in his face or his voice," wrote L. A. Tollemache. "His mother-in-law, Mrs. Stanley, told my father that she herself did not understand why he first accepted and then declined Lord Palmerston's offer of a bishopric." Yet the feelings of this proud and autocratic man must have been intense. Few falls have been as swift, as catastrophic and as complete. He was at the height of his powers, only forty-one; within three months, for an event which had taken place eight years before, he had vanished into total obscurity. He was clearly destined for high position in the Church, perhaps the highest; and he was still ambitious for it, as his first and instant acceptance of the bishop's mitre shows. What bitterness and fury can he have felt when he was yet again forced to humble himself? And not just afterwards, what did he feel at the time when, a religious man, he inveighed against and severely punished the very vice in which he was himself indulging? These feelings he did, at least, express, and once more it was in that curious public communing with himself in one of the sermons he gave in front of the whole school, a sermon on the loneliness of sin:

And if such be the loneliness of repentance [he mused aloud], what must be the loneliness of remorse, which is repentance without God, without Christ, and therefore without hope; the sense of sin unconfessed and unforsaken, only felt as a weight, a burden, and a danger. If repentance is loneliness, remorse is desolation. Repentance makes us lonely towards man; remorse makes us desolate towards God. That is indeed to be alone, when . . . not only earth is iron, but also heaven brass. From such loneliness may God in His mercy save us all through His son Jesus Christ.

There is tragedy here. And there is often something tragic in the situation of the homosexual schoolmaster (or schoolmistress). As a profession it naturally attracts more of a certain type of homosexual than any other except the armed forces. It provides, among much else, a useful and satisfying rôle for the homosexual who is barred by his inclination from having children but still wants them. If, as most do, the homosexual resists the all too numerous temptations, he leads a life of sometimes acute frustration; if he gives way to them, the secrecy is squalid, discovery leads to outrage and ruin. Yet these men are not bad schoolmasters. On the contrary—just as homosexual officers in the war were found to be unusually conscientious in looking after their men and exceptionally brave, in order to win love and admiration, so homosexual schoolmasters are often outstanding. Cory at Eton was one such. Bamford seems to think that Vaughan's sexual behaviour vitiates all his achievements. It does not. They remain considerable. There will be other examples through the book. One thing I might note : this situation is common to all schools; but public schools, because they were single sexed, boarding and increasingly enclosed and isolated in a peculiar way, intensified it. They intensify it still.

As for the Victorian school scene in general, the case of Vaughan shows what a long way we have come since Udall was elevated to Westminster after imprisonment for buggery. But it is a clear-cut case. The response would no doubt be much the same today. To discover (and so discuss) the full flavour of the Victorian schoolmaster's obsession with sex and sin— and thereby to see just how appalling the Vaughan case must have been to those involved—it is necessary to look elsewhere. The most vivid picture, if a slightly hysterical one, appears in a book called *Eric, or Little by Little* by Frederick W. Farrar, published in 1858.

4 Eric, or Little by Little

The novel is the hectic tale of how Eric—so beautiful, strong and manly— goes to Roslyn School and falls "little by little" into a great mire of sin.

Good and Evil are successively personalised. At first Ball is evil; while Russell presents "that most noble of all noble spectacles—one so rare that many think it impossible—this spectacle of an honourable, pure-hearted, happy boy . . . ever growing in wisdom, and stature and favour with God". He it is that Eric first follows. He resists cribbing. He works hard. But then comes the first tiny step. Afraid of being thought a coward, he writes out a crib for others to use. "Ah Eric," said Russell, "they will ask you to do worse things if you yield so easily."

Next—little by little—he laughs in church because a grasshopper gets into a lady's hat. It seems harmless enough but—*it is in church*. So comes the first flogging from Dr. Rowlands. Eric flings himself on his bed; ". . . he felt something hard at his heart, and, as he prayed neither for help nor forgiveness, it was pride and rebellion, not penitence, that made him miserable."

And so Farrar moves to the great Victorian lesson, which is the book's *raison d'être*. These boyish sins may seem small but they are not. Sin led to sin, small to greater, until a lad was by degrees crushed in a great net of ever-increasing sinfulness so that the smallest and most childish sin was, because of where it led, as important as some heinous crime. And also all these sins—small and large—were like some violently pleasurable and irresistible torrent; this is because they were connected, by the net, to that most terrible and delicious of all the sins and so partook of its nature. The language becomes sexual, orgasmic:

> We are not worst at once; the cause of evil
> Begins so slowly, and from such slight source
> An infant's hand might stop the breach into day,
> But let the stream grow wider, and Philosophy—
> Ay, and Religion too—may strive in vain
> To stem the headlong current.

It is no accident that Ball now comes to the fore. Eric dislikes him; indeed he makes all the boys feel uneasy, but Ball "had tasted more largely of the tree of the knowledge of evil than any other boy". This knowledge fascinates them:

"Ye shall be as gods, knowing good and evil," such was the temptation which assailed the other boys in dormitory No. 7; and Eric among the number. Ball [Freudian name] was the tempter. Secretly, gradually, he dropped into their too willing ears the poison of his immorality. In brief, this boy was cursed with a degraded and corrupting mind.

And now Farrar, agitated and appalled by what he is to recount and yet impelled to recount it, cannot contain his feelings. He springs into the narrative himself:

I hurry over a part of my subject inconceivably painful; I hurry over it, but if I am to perform my self-imposed duty of what school life *sometimes* is, I must not pass it by altogether.
    The first time that Eric heard indecent words in dormitory No. 7, he was shocked beyond bound or measure. Dark though it was, he felt himself blushing scarlet to the roots of his hair, and then growing pale again, while a hot dew was left upon his forehead. Ball was the speaker. . . .

Will Eric stop this first and, by Farrar's reaction, appallingly deep plunge into the filth?

Now, Eric, now or never! Life and death, ruin and salvation, corruption and purity, are perhaps in the balance together, and the scale of your destiny may hang on a single word of yours. Speak out, boy!

But Eric, after half an hour "in an agony of struggle with himself", does not stand firm. So comes the first great fall. But fall into what? What are these dreadful things Ball is saying and, from the passion of Farrar's cry, leading the boys to do? He never tells us. The mire gets deeper, blacker, more terrible—but no hint as to its concrete nature is given.Or at most, there is one very obscure hint.

A little later, Russell says that the worst of these things, the dreadful "It" is "more than blackguardly, it is deadly . . . my father said it was the most fatal curse which could ever become rife in a public school". And he reminds Eric that Dr. Rowlands had warned them against "It" in his sermon on Kibroth-Hathaavah. Now Kibroth-Hathaavah occurs in Numbers and is the place where those who have lusted are buried. So the sin is sexual, and we know at once it must be masturbation. Nothing else could arouse such eloquence, nor that particular form of eloquence. And indeed Kibroth-Hathaavah sets Farrar off with thrilling horror:

> Kibroth-Hathaavah! Many and many a young Englishman has perished there! Many and many a happy English boy, the jewel of his mother's heart—brave, beautiful and strong—lies buried there. Very pale their shadows rise before us—the shadows of our young brothers who have sinned and suffered. From the sea and the sod, from foreign graves and English churchyards, they start up and throng around us in the paleness of their fall. May every school-boy who reads this page be warned by the warning of their wasted hands from that burning marle of passion where they found nothing but shame and ruin, polluted affections, and an early grave.

Here then is the familiar and terrible Victorian warning—masturbation means death. But it must have been baffling for many of his young readers.

One thing it is not, oddly, is anything to do with friendships between older and younger boys. This is not exactly encouraged by Farrar, but certainly not condemned. Eric is "taken up" by Upton, "a fine sturdy fellow of eighteen". Later he himself takes up a bewitching dark-eyed younger boy called Wildney. True, they both lead Eric astray, but in a mild way; not into the burning marle of passion of Kibroth-Hathaavah.

So the book continues, a moral cliff-hanger—will he fall?—and also a moral tug-of-war, the forces of good (Mr. Rose, Montagu and Russell) fighting fiercely, and each plunge deeper, followed by a desperate struggle to get back. The contest is fairly equal until in a chapter called "The Silver Cord Is Broken", where Farrar reaches mad heights of sentimentality, Russell dies.

"The Silver Cord" had bound Eric to virtue; with Russell gone, Mr. Rose and Montagu become very prominent. But Ball has gone too, and now, in his place, a devil enters, big, burly, low-browed Brigson—the very spirit of masturbation. And, as befits such a spirit, the language takes on that combination of orgasmic violence and obfuscating vagueness with which we are becoming familiar:

> Never did some of the Roslyn boys, to their dying day, forget the deep, intolerable, unfathomable flood of moral turpitude and iniquity which he bore with him in a flood, which seemed so irresistible that the influence of such boys as Owen and Montagu to stay its onrush seemed as futile as the weight of a feather to bar the fury of a mountain stream. . . . [Soon Eric] was swept away in the broadening tide of degeneracy and sin.

He neglects his work, takes to drink, is shunned by his friends, loses his temper with Mr. Rose and breaks his cane, goes on an escapade to pinch some pigeons from a rival house, neglects his brother; but, as before, little by little, each time drawing back, Mr. Rose and Montagu fighting for his soul, until finally he staggers into assembly too drunk to stand.

For such an enormity, he is expelled. This brings him to his senses. He persuades Dr. Rowlands to let him off. His repentance is complete. Gradually, he starts to climb back.

But it is too late. The sins that you commit take on a life of their own. He is pursued by them, blackmailed, and finally accused of a theft he hasn't done. The point really is that the wages of sin is death and so the only fit atonement Eric can make is to die. And this he does. He runs away to sea, has a terrible time, and comes back so weakened that when he returns to his aunt and uncle, though he appears to recover (and by any medical logic certainly should) "the Trevors soon become aware of the painful fact that he was sinking to the grave, and had come home only to die".

In his last moments he is virtually sanctified. "Every trace of recklessness and arrogance had passed away; every stain of passion had been removed; every particle of hardness had been calcined in the flame of trial." And, as one might have guessed. Mr. Rose sums up his life as no failure since it served as a warning to others.

"The kind of book which Dr. Arnold might have written," said Hugh Kingsmill, "had he taken to drink." And it is true that it was plainly written in a state of extreme agitation; Farrar's involvement is palpable. But it is not as literature that I want to comment on it (though it has a strong narrative drive and is rather effective at a melodramatic, tear-inducing level), but as a guide to certain aspects of Victorian and Edwardian public school behaviour.

Social historians usually disapprove of using novels as source material, and certainly they should be used with great care; but in certain important respects they are particularly relevant to a study of public school life. For one thing nearly all the best ones are autobiographical; the writers took great pains to make them accurate. Arnold Lunn took copious notes all the while he was at Harrow and from them wrote *The Harrovians* in 1913. Even when they are inaccurate—and clearly as an exact description of the preoccupations of a public school Farrar's is quite ludicrous—they tell us something. Indeed, it is often in their unconscious assumptions that novels tell us most. Thus we learn something from the innumerable cold baths and violent exercise that Buchan's heroes take; or from the way a Dornford Yates hero will automatically know the home secretary or the prime minister. The fact is, school literature is minor literature, good third rate: at this level books show the *idées reçues*, the accepted, the *mores* of their period. It is the exactness with which they do this that marks their success. Great literature can change its time and so outlast it; minor literature embodies it and therefore passes with it.

Finally, we are still in the period when new schools and new pupils were appearing very fast. *Eric*, like *Tom Brown*, was read as a guide; both as to what a school should be like, and as to what it would be like and how to behave when you got there. From its appearance in 1858, it too went into many editions. Writing in 1903, after his father's death, Farrar's son said that thousands of people had written to him confessing "with gratitude that the reading of *Eric* had marked a turning point in their lives . . .". Farrar himself was a formative influence; he became a schoolmaster at Harrow, Headmaster of Marlborough, and later canon and finally Archdeacon of Westminster. His gaunt anxious features still look down from the walls of the last two schools.

5 The new sexual traditions

The central sin in *Eric*, when the anguished prose swells and becomes red-hot, is sexual; and the specific sexual sin is masturbation. The revival of sexual sin in Victorian times was another result of evangelical religion (though it has a much more ancient history). Various other factors exacerbated the situation. Up to 1914, and indeed for long after, the drive to material wealth meant that men married later and later in order, the fathers insisting, to keep wives in the manner to which they were "accustomed". Novel after novel pictures the man in love but unable to afford marriage. As a result many men passed years of their lives in severe sexual frustration. The Victorians quite literally invented on no evidence whatever a number of sexual diseases. Here Dr. William Acton (completely typical) diagnoses the symptoms of masturbation:

> The frame is stunted and weak, the muscles undeveloped, the eye is sunken and heavy, the complexion is sallow, pasty or covered with spots of acne, the hands are damp and cold, and the skin moist. . . . His intellect has become sluggish and enfeebled and if his habits are persisted in, he may end a drivelling idiot . . . self-indulgence, long pursued, tends ultimately, if carried far enough, to early death or self-destruction.

Here, coldly scientific, is the clinical description of those buried on Kibroth-Hathaavah. And, of course, of all places, a public school was bound to be the one where the conflict between instinct and these confused and desperate forces of repression became most acute. Here suspicious, often extremely frustrated men (themselves, as we have seen, sometimes just as tempted) tried to control sexual appetites which were at their height. To give one example, according to Kinsey, twenty-two point three per cent of fifteen- to sixteen-year-old boys have, or require, at least one orgasm a day; while two or three or more orgasms a night, or over a single evening, are not at all uncommon. These two forces met head on.

The resulting obsession with masturbation throughout this period seems, today, fantastic. Sermons were devoted to it, boys and masters prayed earnestly to be free from it, boys were taken aside and compelled to confess to it. And the battle began early with terrible warnings from prep school masters. Cyril Connolly describes (this about 1916) how he was told the world was full of appalling temptations, particularly for Etonians. He was to report anyone who tried to get into bed with him, and avoid anyone older. "Above all, not to 'play with ourselves'. There was an old boy from St. Wulfric's who became so self-intoxicated that when he got to Oxford he had put, in a fit of remorse, his head under a train. That miserable youth, I afterwards learnt, had attended all the private schools in England."

And this situation continued with unabated vigour in many schools almost until today. Canon Farrar went to King William's College on the Isle of Man in the 1840s. John Hughes Games went there a hundred years later. So strong, still, was the injunction against masturbating that all trouser pockets had to be sewn up as a bar to pleasure-seeking fingers. There were continuous spot inspections by the prefects. If one finger could be got in, one stroke of the cane; if two, two strokes; if the whole libidinous hand could be thrust in then you got a sound thrashing. And sex as a disease continued. T. C. Worsley's housemaster at Marlborough in the 1920s said, "You might find some white matter exuding from your private parts, Worsley. Don't worry about it. It's only a sort of disease like measles."

Indeed, quite strong traces of this cruel and damaging taboo can still be found today. An informant at Catholic Belmont Abbey in 1951-3 described the anguish of guilt over masturbation, the desperate seeking of a lenient confessor. Only comparatively recently—with Roth's *Portnoy's Complaint* and Brian Alldiss's *The Hand-Reared Boy*—could it be made the major theme of a novel.

Nor are the medical textbooks wholly free yet. In the 1960s J. A. Hadfield wrote a popular paperback *Childhood and Adolescence*. This book is "a classic", it is still widely read and, I suppose, widely believed. Yet it is clear that J. A. Hadfield is extremely screwed up about masturbation.

Certainly he admits that there is no physical harm in it, Oh no; but it is harmful if "excessive" and the harm is psychological. Having thus opened the gates wide to disapproval, Hadfield says "excessive" masturbation can cause frigidity in marriage because a girl gets used to having her clitoris stimulated which she won't get in marriage (why not?); he says that it encourages self-love and later the ex-masturbator will only seek self-gratification; he uses words like "excessive indulgence", "attempt at control". Yet what does he mean by "excessive"? What is his evidence for all this "harm"?

I make no apology for turning to Kinsey again at this point; Hadfield's purposefully vague and menacing view is still prevalent, as I found, in some public schools, particularly girls' schools, and in prep schools; it is still found in books of advice written for adolescents. Kinsey's two reports have, in essentials, neither been challenged nor superseded (though some reservations have been expressed about the report on the Human Female); and our two cultures were, and are, sufficiently similar for Kinsey's findings to remain relevant.

By fifteen, ninety-five per cent of all boys were sexually active. He found that concepts like "normal" or "excessive" just did not apply. The variety was too great (particularly with girls). There were people who masturbated twenty or thirty times a week, and people who did so two or three times a year, and all gradations in between. Certainly there were males who had experimented to see how many orgasms they could have. But when their physiologic capability had been reached, they could no longer get an erection and that was that. They felt fatigue and some local pain; and since it was unsatisfactory did not repeat the experience.

Nor was there any evidence of psychological or physical harm, or that it had any effect on future sexual relationships. In fact the evidence was clear that boys and girls who had masturbated freely subsequently led more balanced sexual lives. Harm was caused, but only where guilt and anxiety were induced by people like Hadfield. Indeed Kinsey specifically singles out the use of the word "excessive" as not only unscientific but particularly disturbing since undefined.

Just as terrible to Victorian schoolmasters—perhaps even more terrible —was the problem of homosexual contacts. It obsessed E. W. Benson, the first Headmaster of Wellington (1850s). He devoted hours to the problem of putting wire entanglements along the tops of the dormitory cubicles. The danger hour was when they were going to bed and lovers might slip away together. Benson issued detailed orders to prevent this:

> While they are undressing, steward and matron to walk up and down in the middle of the dormitory and report any boy who goes out of his own dormitory to another. . . . Doors of cubicles, as at Eton, to be incapable of fastening on inside, but may be locked on outside, every door to be commanded by a master key.

In these sexual concentration camps, lavatories were another danger area. Thus we find that in many schools they were built with half doors, or no doors, sometimes with no walls at all. At one school they were on display, rows of closets, to a wide arc of countryside and building. (Is this the reason, incidentally, why the lavatory in England—the one place, above all others, that should be warm—is still the coldest place in the house? From the desire to drive people out?)

Conan Doyle, at Stonyhurst in 1871, wrote that boys were never allowed to be alone together for a single instant. Masters accompanied boys on walks, at games, and at night patrolled the dormitories sniffing and peering. As a result, says Conan Doyle, "the immorality which is rife in public schools was at a minimum". (One might note that because boys had to suppress and repress very strong instincts, violent fantasies were generated—they could imagine a place "rife" with sex and sin. And these fantasies would be enacted. Repression thus brought into existence the very acts it was designed to prevent.) It is no accident that the great growth of prep schools is from 1860 on, when it seemed imperative to remove from the lustful hands of eighteen-year-olds the lovely little boys of nine and ten.

In fact the public school code which now developed regarded any sexual experience whatsoever as wicked, dangerous and disgusting. Censorship was heavy. Most headmasters banned all modern novels. Arnold specified Dickens and "Yellow novels", translations from Dumas, etc., which used to sell at railway stations. And this continued—and still continues. In the 1920s and 30s D. H. Lawrence was banned; Bedales withdrew A. S. Neill from their shelves in 1937; Henry Miller was widely banned. Pornography (particularly magazines) is still often banned—but the modern equivalent is the banning of films like *Last Tango in Paris* or *Last Exit to Brooklyn*. Talk about sex, called "smut", also became a crime. And this, too, continued for so long that some masters developed curious powers to combat it. Here is Kurt Hahn, in many ways a reactionary and ludicrous figure, showing T. C. Worsley round Gordonstoun in the late 1930s:

> The first crack in my enthusiasm appeared early on when, two or three days after term had started, he was showing me over the school, which had been converted from a castle. We were going through the classrooms when, in one, he suddenly stopped, gripped my arm, raised his nostrils in the air, and then, in his marked German accent, he solemnly pronounced: "Somevon has been talking dirt in this room. I can smell it."

As for experiences with girls . . . when Benson heard that three Wellington boys had had a servant girl in the holidays ("one of them contracted a shameful disease") he sacked the lot. He was resolutely supported by the Headmasters of Eton, Harrow and Winchester.

One should be careful not to exaggerate the effects of this repression. The fear of masturbation, like the fear of hell, could be lived with. Boys are strong, growing, full of energy and curiosity. The evidence of this both contradicts the rubbish adults tell them—no one actually became a drivelling idiot, noses did not fall off—and supplies endless distractions. Though they may believe the rubbish, it can be contemplated without bothering. Also, the hysterical attempts at repression frequently produced precisely the opposite effect. To forbid something can be to make it desirable and delightful; since sex is already desirable and delightful it became doubly so. Boys from public schools were often obsessed with sex to an exaggerated degree; and so one gets, in contradiction, the figure of Victorian defiance, of private immorality and cynical indulgence, a figure which continues to be quite common among the English upper classes throughout our period.

But the weight of repression was both extended to far removed fields and much increased by the vagueness and confusion with which the Victorians surrounded the subject. The muddle was both practical and verbal. Practical because at nearly every point Victorian/Edwardian sexual morality directly contradicted fundamental appetite and experience: no one should masturbate, yet everyone masturbated; they should all be drivelling idiots, yet no one was; homosexual attraction was a sin, yet it was "rife", unstoppable, even among distinguished headmasters. . . . And the contradiction is expressed most exactly in the key, if fuzzy (or rather, key because fuzzy) concept of manliness. Manly meant to crush sin, but the worst sin was sex; therefore manly meant to curb all sex, that is all that made you a man. Manly meant to be un-manly.

No wonder an archetype emerged—the great, gown-billowing headmaster who hadn't the faintest idea what it was about at all. Here is Warre, Headmaster of Eton 1884–1905, Provost 1909–18: "When he sailed into a room, with his head thrown back and crunching stride, with flowing gown and very broad silk band round his middle, he seemed hardly mortal in his bigness. His voice, too, was tremendous, it came out of the depths of him and vibrated . . .". Warre was described as in a state of "massive confusion" about sex; when it was mentioned he became paralysed with embarrassment.

As a result Victorians couldn't mention the subject. Stanley (how he must have loathed the Vaughan business) "shrank from the coarseness and vice that stains school life". He fled to purity, invoking it for the thousandth time in a sermon a week before he died. "Purity from all that defiles and stains the soul—filthy thoughts, filthy actions, filthy words— we know what they are without an attempt to describe them. . . ." When they did make the attempt, a huge often luridly coloured cloud of euphemisms descends. When one examines the crimes in *Eric*, they nearly all turn out to be virtually peccadillos—breaking bounds, taking some pigeons belonging to another house. Partly, as we have seen, it is the enmeshing nature of sin that gives to each tiny one its vast significance: "To God, boy's sins were not trifling." But also it is because the central sin is too hideous to be mentioned by name. It requires a special language, and this language—of stains and torrents and depths of black turpitude, of sin "unbaring" as Farrar puts it almost phallically at one moment, "without a blush, its hideous ugliness"—spreads out, takes hold of the peccadillos and transforms them; the little sins are infected by the greater, written about in the greater sin's exalted language, and so take on its colour and significance.

It was in this ever intensifying but extremely confusing moral climate that, from 1830 on, the last great period of public school growth took place.

CHAPTER 5

The Growth of the Public Schools: First Steps to Concentration

I must pull myself together: it was only a question of being careful: if one was terribly careful one could succeed in being exactly the same. My whole energy during the terms that followed was concentrated on achieving uniformity.

Harold Nicolson, *Some People*

The public schools fused steadily into the single system we know today out of three groups: first, the "great" schools; second, some revivified old endowed grammar schools and third, new Victorian foundations. By the end of the century, if one accepts a rather strict definition of public school, approximately half were from old foundations ("great" and old grammar), and half newly formed (see Appendix C). The second guideline to grasp is that the years of maximum intensity were from 1840 to 1870; activity remained high until 1900, and then the entire movement virtually stopped.

1 The old endowed grammar schools

We have noted already that some hundred or so of the old endowed grammar schools survived the ravages of corruption sufficiently to continue sending boys to university. The aim of an ambitious master was to get one of these and turn it into a public school. It was a Herculean task. The schools were small, parochial, with restricted entry; the powerful governors, helped by the statutes, were used to the large schoolroom and single master (perhaps with usher) system. They had to be persuaded to gamble money on buildings and classrooms and equipment; the school had to be expanded until it was large, expensive, getting people to board from all over the country. Many of the schools had only survived the ravages by the skin of their teeth. Take Repton. At one point it had one pupil. By 1854 the numbers had crept up to fifty. Then arrived Repton's "great" headmaster, Dr. Pears:

When Pears first visited the school [says the school history], in order to survey the scene of his future labours and triumphs, he was for a moment totally overwhelmed by the desolate prospect which the studies in the hall offered. He sat at a table with his head sunk upon his hands, in the attitude of a man appalled by the magnitude of the task he had set himself.

It was a feeling that many of those pioneering headmasters must have had (it is one I often have writing about them). Yet they set to with incredible energy. Dr. Pears centralised: building proper boarding houses round the Priory, building new, small classrooms, building a chapel. When Edward Thring arrived at Uppingham in 1853 he found twenty-eight boys in a small grammar school. Once again, building and centralising held the clue. Over-riding his timid governors, accumulating huge debts, classrooms, dormitories, a concert hall, all shot up; but so did numbers, slowly at first, then spectacularly: from twenty-eight to forty in the first year; in 1861 to 171; in 1863 to 200. By 1868 there were 310. And there Thring kept it, turning boys away.

There is Mitchinson arriving at King's School, Canterbury, in 1859, to find fifty boys, and only twelve boarders. He transformed it, as Harper transformed Sherborne; this is the time of Empire builders, and there are many examples. It continued till the end of the century. Even Sedbergh, which we left "cumbering the ground", finally got airborne towards the end of the century. Hart achieved this, or at least completed the elevation begun by his predecessor Heppenstall. He could not teach, so turned Sedbergh into a ghastly little Rugby, a stance it retained for many years. "Character more than scholarship was the aim of his teaching"; the teaching itself was to be a duty not a pleasure. The boys, trapped in the austere bleakness of the Yorkshire Dales, went for runs in the howling wind and enforced swims in the freezing rapids and icy pools of the Rivers Rowthey and Lune.

What strikes one most about the early men is their vigour and ambition. Partly it is youth: Mitchinson was twenty-five, Harper twenty-nine, Dr. Butler of Shrewsbury twenty-four, Kennedy thirty-one, Moss twenty-four, both Arnold and Vaughan, as we have seen, were very young men. But there is some extra quality of drive and ambition. When it was objected that John Percival (Percival of the Knees) was unmarried and too young to be appointed Headmaster of Clifton he replied forcefully that the first would be remedied in a few months, the second in a few years. He was married eight weeks later. He was tall, masterful, completely arbitrary, and with fearsome driving power: "Like an inspired demonic conductor of an orchestra," wrote T. E. Brown, "he has lashed us into Bacchic fury—wind and strings and voice—forte, forte, FORTIS-SIMO. . . ." The combination at this time offered by schools of a religiously biased vocation, the exercise of naked power and the amassing of considerable wealth seemed to attract young men with ambitions peculiarly suited to their task and to release the very essence of Victorian energy.

These transformers of the old grammar schools were also much helped by the Endowed Schools Bill of 1869, but to understand the significance of this it is necessary to turn for a moment to the great schools in the 1840s and 50s.

2 The great schools. The Clarendon Commission, the Taunton Commission

The task of these first reforming headmasters, as we have seen with Vaughan, Arnold, Wordsworth of Winchester and Moberly, was to hew some sort of shape out of the tangle of debauchery, tradition and violence they had inherited from the 18th and early 19th centuries. In 1844 Dr. Hawtrey and the Provost Hodgson (who had suffered there) finally destroyed the Long Chamber at Eton. They divided it into cubicles to sleep fifteen boys, and the rest were given bed-sitting rooms in what are still called New Buildings (opened in 1846). Classes were made smaller. Hawtrey himself took twenty from the sixth form and twelve Liberty (boys below the sixth) and taught them separately; the rest of the upper school was split into smaller divisions and a master assigned to each. There was a minuscule extension to the curriculum—three maths lessons a week from 1851. Private tutors were abolished. By 1844 numbers were back to 777. The same sort of thing went on (rather late) at Shrewsbury, particularly as here Dr. Kennedy had begun to break away from the old learning and reciting methods of teaching. And all these masters were followed by others who built on their work: Warre and Hornby consolidated Hawtrey, Ridding built on Moberly at Winchester, Moss (a great beater) took over at Shrewsbury. These men—principally because they had to control the vast numbers the reforms engendered—were overwhelming and autocratic to a degree. (Warre may have been massively confused about sex. Nothing else confused him.)

But not all the great schools reformed—tradition and debauchery could be too strong. Westminster, squashed by the foul growth of Victorian London, did nothing. By 1841, numbers had shrunk to sixty-seven. Charterhouse, for the same reason, had dropped to around 120 in the 1860s. And despite the reforms we have noted, abuses remained in the other schools. As the Victorians gradually grew more humanitarian the continued violence of the discipline seemed more and more horrible. The papers took up cases. And after the middle of the century, the curriculum became increasingly ludicrous. Above all, none of the schools did anything decisive about the endowment scandal. In 1860 the warden and fellows at Winchester still gobbled up half the college revenues—eight times that

A Wykehamist at his "scob". A "scob" was the double-lidded box in which college boys at Winchester kept their property, and which could also serve as a desk.

Dr. Edward Hawtrey, Keate's successor: Headmaster 1834–52.

Dr. Keate, legendary Headmaster of Eton 1809–34.

"Black Monday", or the departure for school. A late-18th-century print.

Home at the end of term. A scene—probably of Winchester boys—of 1836.

spent on the staff. It was this that absolutely enraged people, and in 1860 the press, particularly *The Westminster Review*, began to contain scathing and lengthy comment. In 1861 the *Edinburgh Review* exploded. It was, ended an article furious throughout, absolutely scandalous that at Eton "enormous revenues willed by an English king for the promotion of education amongst the upper and middle classes of this country, should . . . be illegally diverted from their original destination into the pockets of a small number of individuals who are not entitled to them". It was, as Bamford notes, tantamount to accusing the mentors of cabinet ministers of living by embezzlement.

As a result, the Clarendon Commission was set up in 1861 to investigate the great schools. (In fact, as well as the Nine—Eton, Winchester, Westminster, Charterhouse, St. Paul's, Merchant Taylors', Harrow, Rugby, Shrewsbury—it also examined "several great schools recently founded in England: Marlborough, Cheltenham and Wellington".) Immediately, huge abuses sprang into the light. Here is some dialogue from the first day at Eton.

Lord Clarendon (summarising an illegal position already glaringly clear): And the fines on renewal of leases during the last twenty years amount to £127,000?
Mr. Batchelor (the Registrar of Eton): Yes.
C.: And that amount of fines has been divided during the last twenty years among the provosts and fellows?
R.: Yes.
C.: The provost taking two shares to each fellow's one?
R.: Yes, that has been so.
C.: And it has appeared to the provost and fellows that there is nothing contrary to the statutes in their so doing?
R.: No.

Their only defence—the only defence of all the great schools as similar scandals were unearthed—was that it had all been going on for centuries. The fellows, fat on illegal money, watched paralysed with horror as it slipped away from them. "But the law of the land," as J. D'E. Firth writes, "on whose letter they had relied for hundreds of years to cheat the children and starve the ushers, now turned its bleak face against the exploiters themselves. They might whimper and snarl like old dogs driven off a juicy and familiar bone, but their teeth were drawn."

The Clarendon Commission suggested other reforms, in the organisation of governing bodies and the curriculum. It made specific suggestions. After its report on Charterhouse, for instance, the school pulled itself together and moved to Godalming. Before long numbers had risen to 500. But in particular, by its very existence, the Commission drew attention to the other endowed grammar schools. If the great, why not the lesser?—

particularly as there were abuses here too, and it was from here important new public schools were rapidly appearing. In 1864, the Taunton Commission was set up to examine and report on these much more numerous institutions.

This was a mammoth Victorian investigation of incredible scrupulousness, skill and industry. Hundreds of inspectors covered the country, spending years at their task. In a sense they uncovered chaos; Sedbergh cumbering the ground, thirty-eight schools in Yorkshire and Durham alone, still with endowments and claiming to provide a classical education, which in fact had *no* pupils. But from this chaos they emerged with an extremely interesting general solution. Though often individually quite small, in total the sum of endowment money was colossal. If all these endowments were put together and redistributed on a national scale, they could form the financial core of a great new national system of secondary education. The Commission drew up detailed plans for this: the control to be central, via Parliament, a national exam system, regular inspection, a modern curriculum including science. But more than this, the system was to be for everyone, from every class: those too poor to pay would be educated free, those who could afford to pay would do so, augmenting the merged endowments. For a moment the heart leaps. Supposing this had been done, just supposing those bastions of class and privilege, the new public schools, had been swept ruthlessly away into a national and classless system, and that proper secondary education for everyone had started to come thirty years before (much less sweepingly) it did—how different our country might have been. That neglect of science (and later industry) by the public schools, which writers like Correlli Barnett regard as so damaging, might never have happened; that inequitable educational disadvantaging of the poor, those rigid class divisions and inequalities which continued so long (and continue now)—all this might have been changed. And it was possible. The proposals were put to Parliament in an Endowed Schools Bill. What happened?

The conclusion of the Taunton Commission hit the public school world like a bombshell. Although they were specifically excluded, many of the Great Nine spoke against it. Those affected rose in fury at the prospect of their lives' achievements being snatched from them. Thring could scarcely contain himself: "How ridiculous it will seem in years to come . . . a lot of squires . . . promiscuous evidence . . . intricate professional question . . .". Benson at Wellington (new foundations were to be included) was even angrier. He fired off letters to every pillar in the establishment—Gladstone, Forster, the Archbishop of Canterbury, etc. But they were not all against it. Temple of Rugby, even though excluded, thought this wrong. The Nine should be included in such a national system. He was pitiless to Benson from whom, like everyone else, he had received letters. He wrote back that, far from having a good claim to exemption, "Wellington had less claim that most other places". Less than Newbury Grammar School? Than Ipswich? Than little Nothing-on-the-Marsh? It was the end of a long friendship.

In the face of danger, men combine: thus families form tribes, tribes join up and enclose territories, these become nations which absorb other nations, forge empires, alliances and wage wars. So with the public schools. It was Mitchinson of King's School, Canterbury, who saw the dangers of disunity. In February 1869 he wrote to Thring and suggested that the headmasters of the endowed schools should meet together to discuss their attitude to the proposed legislation. Thring, although appalled by the coming bill, was extremely reluctant to attend: for one thing he was doubtful about the calibre of his fellow headmasters. What sort of *class* would they be? Mitchinson got Daniel Harper of Sherborne to back him up and, again at Mitchinson's suggestion, the first meeting took place in the Freemasons' Tavern in London. Twenty-six headmasters attended—schools like Bromsgrove, Tunbridge, Felsted, Repton, etc.—and to his delight Thring found that, as far as class went, they could scarcely be better. "A very superior set of men," he noted, an expression of relief which has been used by Alicia Percival for the title of an excellent book to which I am indebted.

So began the Headmasters' Conference. It was Mitchinson's idea, but Thring—stimulated to oratory by so many Superior Men (though practically anything could stimulate him to oratory)—soon took over.

In fact, there was no need for the conference. Furious behind-the-scenes lobbying (not yet fully researched) completely castrated the bill of its radical elements. But, as the Endowed Schools Bill of 1869 finally emerged, it helped these new headmasters. It set up Education Commissions with powers to introduce the reforms they thought necessary; on the whole they were quite willing to think the same things necessary as Thring, Pears, Mitchinson and the other Very Superior Men. That is, cutting the numbers and powers of the governors, opening the schools to unrestricted national entry, and generally setting aside the statutes wherever they interfered with the creation of a proper public school.

But the significance of the conference lies elsewhere. Although, practically, it was now quite unnecessary, Thring had become intoxicated. Excitedly, he suggested they all meet every year. The start was shaky. Only twelve headmasters came to the December meeting at Uppingham. There were arguments about whether to include "the Nine". "I most certainly object to being tied to the chariot wheels of the great schools," said Mitchinson. However, when they met at Sherborne in 1870, thirty-five headmasters attended; in 1871 fifty. By 1874 Eton and Harrow had joined and soon, in the most tactful way, the great schools dominated the conference.

So the elders met, and so the tribes were unified into a nation. I shall go

further into this outer concentration of the public schools, the way they
became a system of essentially identical elements, later on; but clearly the
Headmasters' Conference was an extremely important factor. From the
start they discussed and advised each other on discipline, the pronunciation
of Latin, on the value of school magazines, of games, of how to combat
"the moral problem" and so on. Schools copied schools and, though
minor differences were naturally tolerated, if anything too outrageous
were being attempted—"A word in your ear, Headmaster . . .". The
conference was—and is—like a club (members are invited to join by name,
not school), and capable of all the powerful if subtle suasion such places
are famous for. It was also somewhere for a new school to aim at and
provided standards by which that aim could be realised. It became the
tuning fork to test "tone". And the conference was a great help in fighting
the outside world, of giving moral support, say, to a young headmaster
resolutely resisting an attempt to cut down the classics in 1885. Each new
member became, as Dr. G. Baron put it in *Some Aspects of the Headmaster's
Tradition*, "a member of a well-organised body of vigorous and active
men who . . . constantly voiced their disapproval of any infringement of
their authority and their autonomy".

One group of schools at whom the conference naturally looked closely
—whose "tone" was carefully judged—was that of the new foundations.

3 The new foundations

The new foundations—in common with the freshly stimulated old ones—
were reacting to the growing market of boys and the Victorian evangelical
spirit. But within this framework, although a single school was seldom
influenced by one alone, three particular responses can be discerned.

The first is specialisation. Once you get a big and rather amorphous
market, which the middle classes increasingly became as they grew larger
and larger, one way of making money is to concentrate on particular
sections of it sufficiently numerous to provide good profits. This now
began to happen with the schools. Marlborough, founded in 1843, aimed
particularly at clergymen's sons (they are still offered what are now
completely inadequate financial inducements); University College School
(1830) was started for more enlightened parents (often Jewish) who
shared the ideals of Bentham and John Stuart Mill; Epsom was founded
for doctors' sons in 1855. Certain areas of middle-class interest were too
large to let any one or two schools predominate. The Empire is one.
Although Haileybury was founded by the East India Company (and
always retained a strong Imperial bias), nearly all the public schools were
involved. By the 1870s, 80s and 90s most of them had special courses for
those entering the Colonial Service. The same is true of the army. This
was the one sort of "work" the English aristocracy (and therefore by

imitation the rest of the upper classes) felt would not demean their younger sons; partly this was in deference to their feudal origins; partly because "work" was almost the last thing to be encountered in the Victorian army. As with Imperial Service, during the last quarter of the century most schools developed "Army" and "Modern" sides. One might note, however, that Eton, Harrow, Wellington, Clifton, Cheltenham and Marlborough were particularly busy here.

Sometimes the method of cashing in on the market became so integral that it determined the classification and type of the school. This was true of the proprietary schools, common in the middle of the century. Here people bought a share and could then nominate a boy to the school (if they failed to do this, the right often passed to the governors). Cheltenham and Marlborough are examples of this (a share at Marlborough cost fifty pounds); but similar joint-stock type arrangements were made at Rossall, Epsom, Clifton, Haileybury and other schools.

The last force behind the new foundations was politico–religious. Many men shared Arnold's panic that without a Christian education civilisation would collapse—but they directed their attention to the growing middle class. The most passionate among the men moved in this way was Canon Woodard. "Somehow or other we must get possession of the middle classes," he wrote, ". . . and how can we so well do this as through public schools. . . . Education without religion is, in itself, a pure evil . . . [making] Communists and Red Republicans . . . unless the Church, therefore, gets possession of this class at whatever cost, we shall reap the fruits . . . of an universal deluge. . . ."

Clearly, it was imminent. Woodard's solution, a man of dynamic energy and high Anglican persuasion, was total: nothing less than cover England with public schools. He divided the country into areas and planned three schools in each, graded on class lines; top, middle and bottom, the profits from the top going to help finance the bottom. Lancing was founded in 1848, followed by Hurstpierpoint (1849), Ardingly (1858); later came Bloxham, Denstone, Ellesmere and Worksop and other schools of various sorts. Lancing was to be the centre of this empire, which is why it has a school chapel the size of a cathedral. Unfortunately in his haste to stem the deluge, Woodard fudged his classes; the top schools got some gentry, but the lower schools were often just for small traders. As a result the Woodard schools were rather looked down on—tone was a bit shaky and so on—and it took some time before they became recognised public schools.

All schools, not just new foundations, were obviously helped by the rapid spread of the railways from 1824 onwards. But new foundations could choose their sites and many of them, like Cranleigh and Wellington, chose as though by divination places suitable for termini. Marlborough was deliberately built near Swindon. There is sometimes a suggestion that the railways were the decisive factor in public school growth; this seems unlikely. It is clear from the 17th and 18th centuries that boys who wanted an education would travel vast distances. The railways were simply an important part of the general quickening. One thing they did bring about, however, was the division of the school year into three terms, though the slowness with which this took place showed how long the 18th century persisted (or was copied): Mill Hill, to give some examples, abandoned "halves" in 1855, Oundle did so in 1867, Sherborne in 1872, Marlborough in 1873.

This also completes the general picture of public school development during the 19th century; the final large block is added if we try to get some idea of number. This is not as easy as it sounds. As the century proceeds, the struggle to be "recognised" as a public school became quite fierce; it is echoed by the historians now, who are almost as snobbish about who they let into their books as the Headmasters' Conference or *Public Schools Year Books* were about who they would allow in then. Bearing in mind, then, that what follow are the lowest possible figures, let us initially follow Bamford. These are his criteria for 1865: they must be expensive enough to exclude the lower classes and lower-middle class; the education must be based on the classics; they should have a national reputation and recruit from all over Britain; they should be principally boarding. On this basis he allows the great schools (nine), a further nine recently revitalised old grammar schools, and sixteen new foundations—that is thirty-four public schools. These taught 7,500 boarders out of a total receiving a classical education (from the many other little grammar schools) at this time of 25,210. (The first *Public Schools Year Book* in 1889 lists thirty-six schools. See Appendix B.) By 1902 the controversy has become even more tedious because the Headmasters' Conference had become rather indiscriminate. However, Professor J. R. de S. Honey of the University of Rhodesia has recently done a very thorough study and has come to the conclusion that by that time there existed a public school community of sixty-four schools (see Appendix C). These were teaching approximately 20,000 pupils. We will not go far wrong if we imagine this 1902 community as having grown steadily from something around twenty-five schools and 7,000 odd pupils in 1865.

4 The great Marlborough Rebellion

It is now time to start finding out what went on—and why—in these rapidly growing public schools. I think the best way into this exploration is via the last, and most shattering, of the school rebellions. This took place at Marlborough in 1851.

A number of factors combined to produce the explosion. (I base what follows on the account of the school historian, Bradley. Some feeble tinkering with this recently has done nothing to alter the general validity of his account.) First, in its eagerness to attract numbers, Marlborough set its fees far too low. As a result clergymen's sons poured in: 200 in 1843, 400 by 1846, 500 by 1848. This was too fast. These "new" foundations were not new in any educational sense; they embodied no new ideas or theory. They simply copied what was current at the time. And in the early 1840s, although the idea of small forms was gradually spreading, the Keate situation was still common. Marlborough adopted it (partly, too, owing to shortage of money), and nine forms were packed into the huge upper school. This seething mass was continually agitated by ferocious beatings, the cruelty and violence seen by all. The masters would openly thrash until screams of pain had been elicited. It was noted that the canes at Marl-borough in 1847 were "weapons of hideous length and terrible circum-ference". In one case, the master lost control of himself completely and eventually, owing to the heroism of the victim, had to give up exhausted. The boy was carried to the sick room where the school doctor, Dr. Fergus, had to use pincers to extract strips of shirt from his lacerated back. At the same time, it was becoming clear to the public schools that discipline, difficult enough anyway, was impossible if boys were scattered in lodgings and houses round the local town. At Marlborough, concentration was physical: they slept in large dormitories (this was also so that some, at least, of the profits gained by the masters from the houses should accrue to the school). They all ate together in one large dining room. (The effect on the food was catastrophic; and, revolting as it was, there was hardly any of it. Boys were ravaged by hunger. Anyone who asked for more was caned.) And the first new buildings were just extensions to the original house. Some of these (they are pleasant buildings) were planned by the man who went on to design the prison at Wormwood Scrubs. And, though one might note parenthetically that school architects often went on to design prisons, churches and so on not because there is any connec-tion between them but because they are all institutional buildings, in this case the conjunction is apt. The Marlborough boys were in prison.

It was an extremely inefficient prison. Where it needed some academic Cromwell, the school had the Reverend Mr. Wilkinson. He was a quiet, scholarly, gentle man, who—despite some, in my view, unconvincing attempts to rehabilitate him recently—was totally ill-equipped to govern Marlborough. The other masters, apart from their ferocity in class, were inexperienced and too terrified to venture out among the boys when not inside it. (There was, too, a certain conflict: boys should be confined and disciplined; at the same time "tradition" dictated boy freedom.) As a result boys freely escaped and used to invade the town, where they got drunk and infuriated the inhabitants, particularly the miller, who waged war on them. The culprits were seldom discovered, and each time the entire school was punished. From 1846 to 1850 almost all their privileges were removed, one by one . By 1851 Marlborough was like France in 1789 in all, this time, but ideology. Years of savage, unjust but also inefficient tyranny were about to be overthrown. Events took place in two steps. There was an initial and very violent eruption one evening in late October, which rapidly led to chaos. By November 1st Mr. Wilkinson had been forced to capitulate and the school appeared to calm down. In fact, as in all revolutions, once the tyranny begins to make concessions, events move ever faster and become ever more extreme.

November 5th was still a day of popular licence in England at that time, a day of Liberty. In complete secrecy, and with great swiftness, Marlborough prepared itself. Meetings were held late at night,and councils and revolutionary committees set up. Some were to co-ordinate the uprising, others to buy provisions, yet others to lay in arms. Fireworks of any sort were expressly forbidden. Now, over 1,000 squibs and crackers were concealed in hidden dumps; a large but unspecified amount of heavy artillery was also purchased, huge unstable rockets, gunpowder. As the time grew close, the school became electric with concealed excitement. The explosion had been fixed for five o'clock on November 5th, 1851.

"Punctually at that hour," says an eye-witness, then a small boy huddling with some friends over a grating near the chapel wall, "we saw a rocket shoot up into the sky from the centre of the court, and knew that the revolution had begun." It was to rage for a week.

On the signal, the school appeared to blow up. The court became ablaze with fireworks, and fireworks shot from every building. Mr. Wilkinson, rushing out in a state of extreme agitation, had a bottle full of gunpowder exploded behind his back and rushed back. The other masters were equally powerless. Chaos reigned all night. The long corridors of B House echoed to ceaseless detonations. For two days the college reeked of gunpowder and smoke drifted through the smashed windows and broken doors. The authorities were paralysed.

On the third day, a feeble attempt was made to restore order. Making a sortie, the masters seized five boys from the throng and these were expelled. Unfortunately, one of the boys, a prefect, was "the most popular boy in the school". Now the revolution was driven to new heights. His expulsion seemed quite unfair—why him? As he drove through the gates, the entire school, 500 strong, roused to a fury only clergymen's sons can reach, surged after him following his fly up the streets, shouting and cheering with wild enthusiasm. The people in the town caught the excitement. They too poured from the shops and houses and joined the uprising. Eye-witnesses say that feelings of grief, resentment and excitement ran so high that tears streamed down the cheeks of the older boys.

As the "tumultuous throng" stormed back towards the school, their old enemy, the miller, was unfortunate enough to ride into them on his speckle-bellied pony. At once, amidst a cacophony of jeering and shouting, he was hauled from his mount and thrown to the ground.

At the end of the week Mr. Wilkinson was forced into total surrender. The school was called together and asked their terms. They demanded back every single privilege that had been taken from them over the past four years; this was granted immediately. Mr. Wilkinson's own conditions were pathetic: peace, an apology, and a collection of ten pounds to cover damage costing thousands.

Thus ended the great Marlborough Rebellion, the last of any consequence in a public school (the very last was at Haileybury in the Boer War). There were sporadic outbreaks in December, but then the half ended.

At the beginning of 1852 Mr. Wilkinson resigned and retired thankfully to the small village of Market Lavington in Wiltshire and the life of a country parson for which he was well suited. Dr. Cotton, a Rugbeian and a redoubtable one, arrived to tame Marlborough.

5 Towards concentration: headmaster dictators, the rise of the house

Two important lessons can be learnt from this incident. In the first place, from 1850 on (and to an extent before) we can trace the same physical concentration in other schools as took place at Marlborough. They gather themselves together: boys are crammed into dormitories, teaching is done more and more in small classrooms, "houses" as often as not are in the same building. Or when separate, as close to the main complex as possible, bounds and rules and walls cut the school off from its surroundings. This is a complex process to follow because it took place in so many different ways and at such different times; but I have analysed the physical growth of fifteen schools over this period (roughly 1840–1900) and the pattern is clear. At Tonbridge, for instance, in 1863, instead of boarding houses, a whole new wing is built; expanding numbers bring the same response at Sherborne in 1853 and 1860; not until 1880 does Oundle start getting small classrooms; at Bradfield the boys are eating together by 1883. These examples could be continued indefinitely. In London such concentration was naturally particularly difficult to achieve and in the end all but Westminster moved: St. Paul's in 1884, Charterhouse in 1872, Christ's Hospital in 1902, Merchant Taylors' at last in 1933. Again, though there is an even stronger reason for this, it is noticeable how the new foundations —as Wesley's school had been—were set in large houses, cut off by great oceans of land from the outside world. The concentration both accompanied and demanded the rise of autocratic headmasters. This is the age of dictators. "The Headmaster should have uncontrolled power," advised the Public School Commission in 1864, "of selecting and dismissing assistant masters; of regulating the arrangement of the school in classes or divisions; the hours of school work. . . ." Wickham, the Headmaster of Wellington in 1893, had raised the salary of two masters to £700 and £550. Soon after, his successor Bertram Pollock (1893–1916) arrived and considered the rises ridiculous. He immediately slashed them to £250 and £200— back to what was about average for an assistant master in a large school around 1900. Pollock openly despised and bullied his staff. "If all the staff resigned today," he said to one of them, "I could easily supply their places tomorrow."

Total power, a captive audience desperate to please—it is not surprising that amusing "mannerisms", eccentricities cultivated in response to years of sycophantic applause (an occupational disease of schoolmasters) now flourish. Bradley raced pigeons. Any chance visitor would be given a basket of them on leaving and told to release them at Didcot or Exeter. They could develop the most bizarre traits and no one dared laugh. Braythwaite, the second Headmaster of Lancing, was for a lengthy period "afflicted with some extraordinary form of indigestion which caused him suddenly to produce appalling belches. I [it is Dr. Plummer writing] have never heard anything like them. They were terrific, and absolutely uncontrollable. Even when he got his hand to his mouth in time, it was blown away by the explosion." Lancing used to receive these eruptions in complete silence. Weird *Alice in Wonderland* figures totter into view. "At frequent intervals," writes the historian of Hurstpierpoint, describing the school during the 1850s in an account which is mostly rather flat,

the two staffs of Shoreham and Hurst [Hurstpierpoint] used to meet together for a joint conference. The Reverend Frederick Mertens had no sense of taste or smell, and Pennell, one of the Hurst masters, was almost blind. Mertens was bending down low over his food to scrutinise it (his method of testing food owing to his defective sense of taste), and Pennell, dimly seeing Mertens' clerical collar almost on the table, mistook it for the rim of his teacup and proceeded to pour milk down Mertens' neck.

As the century progressed, some of the empires of these dictators, eccentric or not, grew very large. A big school of 800 or so is like a great liner, a little army with hosts of camp followers: tons of coal and food are consumed, millions of gallons of water. An idea can be obtained by looking at a public school today (1976). Cheltenham Ladies' College, with 850 pupils, has a turnover of £1½ million a year. Food costs £85,000; the rates are £20,000; coal, gas and electricity £45,000; they employ 420 people. In Victorian times there would have been many more servants, and these too became part of the empire; matrons and dames revelling in the gossip, porters, handymen and estate workers chuckling when the school won a match.

Paradoxically, it was the very size of these empires which began to diminish the power of their rulers. "A headmaster is only the headmaster of the boys he knows," said Edward Thring. "If he does not know the boys, the master who does is their headmaster—and his also." This is quite true, and as a result he restricted Uppingham to about 330. Yet I do not see how someone in any realistic sense can "know" 330 people. As numbers grew, the controllable unit became the house. Frequently, as at Winchester in the 1860s, and Shrewsbury, indeed many schools, they were owned by the housemaster, who chose the pupils and finally sold the house to his successor. And even if not actually owned, exactly the same developments towards concentration and autonomy took place in the houses which we have seen in the schools. By the end of the century the houses were often little kingdoms of their own. Housemasters did not have to retire or give up their houses at any particular time; they lingered on for years, looming obstructions in the path of a headmaster, resisting change. When Preston went to Malvern as headmaster in 1914, he was the youngest member of the staff and was faced with housemasters who had been there thirty or thirty-five years.

But if, by the end of the century, there were curbs to the autocracy of the 1840s, 50s and 60s to the power of men like Vaughan, Mitchinson or Percival, the crucial development was the concentration of the public schools, as isolated communities, in upon themselves. From this much else, perhaps all else, flows.

I have noted how few "great" headmasters were great men in any national sense (there is no reason why they should have been); but frequently, cut off, they seem figures of simplicity, foolishness even, with concepts of purity and good conduct absurdly out of touch with reality. It was precisely this isolation from the world that allowed men like Farrar or Thring (and hundreds since then) to work themselves so often into acute states of moral excitement over trivialities. And from the 1860s and 70s until very recently this isolation surrounded their pupils too like a mist. "The outer world" (Michael Campbell was writing in his perceptive novel *Lord Dismiss Us* of St. Columba's, Radley's sister school, in the late 1940s, but the comment is timeless and universal) "was occupied, so it was said, but blank as Mars as far as they were concerned." It used to be noted how vulnerable public school pupils looked when they ventured, blinking, into the glare of the outside world, how clean and innocent and young; especially when they were travelling to away matches in white. And a great many of what later came to be considered elements in the public school spirit (and, by extension, elements in the British upper- and middle-class character) are in fact perfectly normal and understandable responses to living in small enclosed communities. There will be numerous examples of this. Here is one. Gordon Carruthers in *The Loom of Youth* has just played a great innings:

"It was splendid! You ought to be a certainty for your Colt's cap." "The Bull" was fearfully bucked.

"Oh, I don't know, it was not so very much." In his heart of hearts Gordon was pretty certain he would get his cap; but it would never do to show what he thought.

In enclosed communities strong feelings are contagious and can easily become upsetting; they must therefore be suppressed. The same is true of prisons and mental hospitals; feelings are contained in the first by locking inmates in separate cells and in the second by drugs. In public schools the code was self-imposed. But schools also raise a series of goals at which all aim and for which there can, therefore, be intense competition. It follows that the most upsetting expression of emotion is boasting. Modesty, the denying or understating of achievement, the concealment of feeling are not the results of English hypocrisies but developments evolved at public schools in the interests of general peace.

But, at any rate, as far as the staff were concerned, the most immediate result of this concentration—and this is another lesson we learn from Marlborough—was the way it exacerbated the problem of discipline. When boys were free there was strictly speaking no solution because there was no problem. They were their own masters. Caged, a solution became imperative. From now on, discipline obsessed public school masters as much as sex.

6 Discipline: beating and its effects

"Corporal punishment has at the same time greatly diminished; flogging, which twenty or thirty years ago was resorted to as a matter of course for the most trifling offences, is now in general used sparingly and applied only to serious ones." The quotation is from the Earl of Clarendon's Commission in the 1860s. From now until the 1970s there will be a succession of identical statements. And it is true—decade by decade, stroke by stroke—boys were beaten less. Evidence of increasing public intolerance to schoolmasterly brutality is shown, as we have already seen, by the way cases now got into the papers which before would have been ignored. When Arnold gave the boy March eighteen strokes it was unfavourably reported; there was similar criticism when Thring gave a ferocious beating to some boys who had missed a train and were back late from the Easter holidays. "If he did not train their minds," said Punch, "he made them mind their trains." There was a celebrated case with the Headmaster of Shrewsbury, Moss, where questions were asked in the House.

Yet how painfully slow the change was. In Arnold's time sixty strokes with an ash plant were still allowed. (Not till 1866 did an Act of Parliament limit to forty-eight the number of lashes which could be given to a seaman for any one offence.) The weapons, as at Marlborough, remain for years horrifying to read about: at Arnold's Rugby the canes were weighted with lead; other schools used "knotted blackthorn sticks" or thongs. At Stonyhurst in 1871 the "Tolley" was a piece of solid rubber the size and thickness of a big boot sole. Struck with this, as Conan Doyle, who received many beatings to "break" him, describes, the hand would change colour and swell up hugely. The usual punishment was eighteen blows, nine to a hand. Eighteen to one hand was the limit of human endurance.

But every school of that time, every public school boy until the end of the century, could produce similar accounts. Masters lost control of themselves and, in a frenzy, would reduce a naked back to pulp, spattering themselves with blood. One boy spent a whole night with his friend, easing the shirt off his back and pulling out "at least a dozen pieces of birch-rod, which had penetrated deep into the flesh". The case that got Moss of Shrewsbury into trouble was when he gave a boy eighty-eight strokes of the birch in 1874. (Moss reigned for forty years; when he retired he went to live in a village called Much Birch.) As in some primitive state, these tyrants would issue general pardons, the gaols would empty. "Sat. June 6th 1846. About 2 o'clock a son and heir was added to the Doctor's [Kennedy of Shrewsbury] family. Bells rung. The Doctor graciously announced an amnesty of penals and punishments of all sorts." Beatings could be almost as upsetting to watch as to undergo. Here is the traveller Brinsley Richards:

> I never quite believed the stories I heard until I actually saw a boy flogged, and I can never forget the impression which the sight produced on me. . . . Several dozen fellows clambered upon forms and desks to see Neville corrected, and I got a front place, my heart thumping and seeming to make great leaps within me. Next moment, when he knelt on the step of the block and when the lower master inflicted upon his person six cuts that sounded like the splashings of so many buckets of water, I turned almost faint.

Nor was there much use of, or experiment in, alternatives. In 1850 Mill Hill employed solitary confinement with bread and water. Extra work and lines were given; there are legendary statistics here too. Young Cathcart of Wellington amassed 1,500 lines in a week. Such gigantic impositions could only be cleared by a flogging. The final punishment was expulsion, usually for sexual crimes.

As the century progresses the lessening of brutality is noticeable—just. We have left Busby and Keate behind. One of the great floggers, especially in a "white heat", would have killed a boy with eighty-eight lashes. We will see the gradual deepening of concern and skill with men like Cory of Eton or Sanderson of Oundle. After 1900 there are experiments in different methods of discipline. But up till then—and deep into the 20th century—flogging was still the universal punishment; there were still many examples of violence and pain.

One might note some reappearances. Boys take revenge. J. M. Wilson went to King William's College in 1848 when he was twelve. As a new boy he was mercilessly bullied in the great cold draughty attic dormitory. Once, in a frenzy of fear, he kicked out at the master's door as he was being carried past it on the way to his torture.

> . . . The fellow instantly dropped me; out rushed the master—this was not Hollis but an Irishman, O'Reilly—with the never-failing cane. He asked no questions but simply thrashed me till I roared.
>
> It may add to the picture if I describe my revenge. He generally came to bed more or less drunk on Saturday night. Relying on this, two of us, stealthily crept into his room. He was sound asleep with a stocking round his neck. We put all his clothes into a footpan, and from every vessel in the room poured their contents into his boots and the footpan and retreated. We heard no more of it.

Revenge by Ordure.

There were suicides. There is the appalling case of twelve-year-old William Gibbs at Christ's Hospital in 1877. After a caning for gross insolence to the gym master and then, having run away to his sister, a public flogging, he became too terrified to return to school. He was forced back by his father and locked into a room to await his fate. "He looked defiant," said the master. "He looked as if he did not care much what happened." How much Gibbs cared can be gauged from the fact that two hours later he was found dangling by a cord from the window, strangled to death. There was a public outcry, with letters to *The Times*. The report resulting from a Home Office inquiry was vague and whitewashing. William Gibbs is not even mentioned in the various histories of the school.

Death in Victorian schools was extremely common, particularly in the first twenty years of the reign. This was partly due to poor sanitation, the primitive state of medicine and the prevalence of disease. Usually it was the young who died because they were weakest; and those harrowing deaths in *Eric* or *Tom Brown's School Days* and other school books, though put in for drama and moral effect, were based on reality. George Melly at Rugby in 1844–8: ". . . one half-year, death laid his hand heavily upon us: one of the youngest, a child in years, and of infantine purity in his life, was snatched away from us." The boy had confessed on his deathbed to tearing a leaf from another boy's book. When the story spread about "serious thoughts filled all the household". There were also deaths from accidents, from drowning or exposure (as in *Eric*), falling from windows and so on. Again, because they are weaker and less experienced, these too tended to happen to younger boys. A number of recent studies in the United States (reported in the *New Scientist* of November 9th, 1972) suggest strongly that a good many accidental deaths and injuries among children under twelve are in fact suicides or suicide attempts. In 1,100 cases of child poisoning studied by Dr. Robert Litman at the Los Angeles Suicide Prevention Center, twenty-eight per cent were found to be suicide attempts, and forty-eight per cent suicide "gestures", to draw attention to ill-treatment, loneliness, unhappiness and so on. A factor is that children of this age often don't appreciate the finality of death. They think of it like sleep (to which it is often compared, particularly in Victorian literature). "Even though a child may be trying to kill himself," says Dr. Larry Dizmang of Johns Hopkins University, "he doesn't realise it is permanent."

It should be remembered that the beatings and violence I have described were administered as much, or more, to small boys as to big ones. They were beaten continually at the prep schools, which were formed in dozens from 1860 onwards. "They might as well have had me educated at a brothel for flagellants," said Stephen Spender of his early–20th–century prep school. These places, and the lower forms of public schools, might have been specifically designed to produce unhappiness, loneliness and ill-treatment. One cannot, of course, be certain (just as there are no reliable statistics of deaths, which were always instantly hushed up), but it seems likely that a good many of them were in fact deliberate responses to frightening and unpleasant circumstances.

It would be tempting to assign to public schools some responsibility for those very brothels mentioned by Spender. This is the great age of *le vice anglais*, with an immense attendant literature, where lords and marquises, moaning with pleasure, are birched by fantasy-exaggerated nannies or enraged schoolmasters. I dealt at some length with this in my earlier volume, *The Unnatural History of the Nanny* (and received as a result some highly over-stimulated letters). My conclusion was this: "The more I read the more it seemed to me that no one really understood flagellation. The explanations were either inadequate, contradictory or absurd. But whatever the truth, I reluctantly came to one conclusion; the nanny could not be held responsible." Nor can the public schools. The most one can say is that if anyone had a tendency to get sexual pleasure from beating or being beaten, then for many years public schools were ideal places in which to discover the fact. In this sense, they no doubt performed a small service.

And beating contributed a particular quality—terrified, violent, excited, even exhilarated—to that mental atmosphere which was a conse-quence of the physical concentration, a psychic atmosphere the constitu-ents and intensity of which it is essential we should appreciate. Beating bound boys together. They showed off their wounds. "Marks are half the glory of being beaten. A boy shows them to everyone he can and hopes they'll help to make him popular and they usually do." So the anonymous author of *Sixteen—A Diary of the Teens by a Boy*. But the bond was closer. Sometimes it almost resembles the feeling which sweeps prisons at the moment of execution. It will have been noticeable how the language of judicial death is always explicit in beating. In *The Hill*, a novel about Harrow *circa* 1905, the fourth-form room is called "The place of execution", the chapter on flogging is called "Decapitation". The "splashing" Richards heard as the cane struck naked flesh was subconsciously the sound of blood. The connection between death and sex; it may not be possible to pin it down precisely but flogging in public schools set deep currents moving.

Robin Denniston remembered a beating at Westminster in 1944. All disciplinary dramas can produce a sense of purging; none so effectively as a thrashing. Those sitting round watching, those being beaten, those beating and, by extension, the whole school or house, share this excitement. The beating releases the excitement, provides the climax, rids the community of very powerful tensions. The beaten boy is in a sense a scapegoat, a willing victim. He returns to receive praise. The corporate emotion after a beating is like that after an orgasm; perhaps like the release, going even further back, of having done a shit in a nappy when very small. And since all members of the community shared these deep subconscious feelings, they were drawn very close together.

Finally, from 1850 onwards, on the whole the system worked. Discipline was restored and, however they seethed within, the tribes appeared to be conquered. As the century continued, a number of factors contributed to this ever-tightening grip.

7 *The drive to conform*

It is clearly easier to control a lot of boys if you can consider them, or better still force them, to be the same. Control can then be blanket: the same disciplines, the same curriculum, the same games imposed on everyone. From the 1840s and 50s onward we see the schools, at widely differing times, stumbling upon the same methods of enforcing uniformity.

Like prisons, monasteries and armies they discovered uniforms. A uniform does what it says—makes one form; it depersonalises you, making you easier to control and also stamping you with the image of the institution. A picture of 1824 shows the Eton Oppidans wearing gay clothes; in fact at this time the very long period of mourning for George III (who died in 1820) was creating a tradition of wearing black, which solidified into a uniform. This was exceptionally early. Mill Hill had a uniform in 1837—black or blue jackets, black trousers. In 1860 Bradley brought uniforms to Marlborough. Oundle in 1880 still has no more than straw hats. By 1900 most schools had a uniform of one sort or another.

All groups try to impose conformity. We have seen what happened to Shelley. The more closed the group, the greater the conformity; as the public schools became ever more self-concentrated, so the pressure became stronger. That is another reason why feelings must be suppressed. Nothing must stick out. In *The Hill* the Caterpillar even hides his passion for cricket. "One bottles up that sort of thing, I suppose." To a frightened new boy, recently wrenched from home, the need to conform was overwhelming. "All the boys have grub-boxes," Brown , (in Bruce Marshall's *George Brown's Schooldays*) wrote desperately. "Please, Daddy, send me a grub-box by return of post. Please, Daddy, this is really a necessity because all the other boys have grub-boxes. Please, Daddy, this is really important."

By the end of the century it was a perfectly explicit aim of the public schools to turn out a type, a socially conforming unit; most schoolmasters (not all), and then prefects, found individuality horrifying.

Harold Nicolson demonstrates this about Wellington around 1900: ". . . One ceased so completely to be an individual, to have any but a corporate identity, one was just a name, or rather a number, on the list." The chief stamp descending on Nicolson was J. D. Marstock, a splendid bone-like figure, worth a detour.

> How clean he was, how straight, how manly! How proud we were of him, how modest he was about himself! And then those eyes—those frank and honest eyes! "One can see," my tutor said, "that Marstock has never had a mean or nasty thought." It took me six years to realise that Marstock, although stuffed with opinions, had never had a thought at all.
>
> I can visualise him best as he appeared when head of the school, when captain of football. A tall figure, he seemed, in his black and orange jersey striped as a wasp. Upon his carefully oiled hair was stuck a little velvet cap with a gold tassel: he would walk away from the field, his large red hands pendant, a little mud upon his large red knees. He would pause for a moment and speak to a group of lower boys. "Yes, Marstock—no, Marstock," they would answer, and then he would smile democratically, and walk on, a slight lilt in his gait betraying that he was not unconscious of how much he was observed.

Marstock took enormous pains with Nicolson who apparently reminded him of a young cousin who had died of scarlet fever. He bent his heavy energies to get Nicolson to fit in. They have to have ink-pots. Nicolson loses his and in a panic borrows for class a "small, brass model of the Temple of Vesta". It is an inkstand rather than a pot. Returning from class carrying this ungainly object he unfortunately meets Marstock.

"What on earth," he said, "are you doing with that?" "It's an inkstand, Marstock." I held out the Temple of Vesta, down the columns of which ink had poured in shining runnels. "An inkstand," he snorted, "who but you would take an inkstand up to college? And a model of St. Paul's too! Oh why, *oh why* will you persist in being different to other people? I give you up; you simply refuse to be the same." He paused and looked at me with real perplexity in those open eyes. *"I think you must be mad,"* he concluded solemnly.

The most powerful element forcing uniformity in a group is the group itself, not the staff in charge of it. The discipline and conformity in the public schools were enormously strengthened because of the ways, official and unofficial, they were imposed by the pupils. Since the flowering of this boy system—its growth into something with the complexity of Byzantium and the formality of Versailles—was one of the chief glories of the public schools, it is necessary to understand a little of its nature.

CHAPTER 6

The Conditions of Public School Concentration

By the boys, for the boys.
The boys know best.
Leave it to them to pick the rotters out,
With that rough justice decent schoolboys know.
John Betjeman, *Summoned by Bells*

Betjeman was at Marlborough just after the First World War. When he arrived as a new boy he found, as he would have done at all public schools at this time and for several decades before, that he was enmeshed in a great web of rules:

At first there was the dread of breaking rules—
"Betjeman, you know that new boys mustn't show
Their hair below the peak of college caps:
Stand still and have your face slapped."
"Sorry, Jones."

There appeared to be sound reasons for this. Plainly discipline must be more effective the more areas of a person's life you control. At public schools, the control became total—clothes, hair, where you could move and with whom and when, when you went to bed, got up, the very language you used (see Appendix D). There were other reasons for this. Restrictions removed became privileges, rewards for good behaviour. The more restrictions, therefore, the more potential privileges. And privileges, however small can become goals, things to look forward to. When you were shut up for two-thirds of the year for five years, with a very restricted curriculum, goals were essential.

Let me give some examples. Verney, in *The Hill*, wants to look at his uncle's initials:

"Crickey! I must go and look at it."

"You can look at the panels, of course: but don't say 'Crickey!' and don't go into the next room. The fifth-form fellows have it. It would be infernal cheek."

L. P. Hartley, at Harrow at the beginning of this century, gives enormous lists of things you could be "whopped" for: leaning too far out of the window on Sunday, letting a sixth former's fire go out when "On

Boy", walking in the middle of the High Street when not a "blood" or with a "blood", etc. A little after this, at Charterhouse, "You must turn up your trousers, must not go out without your umbrella rolled. Your hat must be worn tilted forward, you must not walk more than two abreast till you reach a certain form, etc., etc." In the end, in fact immediately, recitals of these customs and traditions become very tedious.

Even more tedious would be to trace their growth through all the schools during the second half of the 19th century. We might note two things. Already numerous by 1840, developing as we saw from 18th-century boy freedom, by 1900 they are uncontrollable. Whole languages developed sometimes into vocabularies of several hundred words, which were often printed in books and had to be learnt (see Appendix D). The first two or three weeks of a new boy's term were spent feverishly learning trivia suddenly become vital. Second, though the schools developed different rules and traditions and, where these appeared, different languages (differences of which they were very proud), what strikes the observer studying them as they were then—or visiting them now—is how they are essentially the same.

Not that some differences are not interesting—or strange, depending on how you view this whole elaborate structure. Some schools developed the "blood" system. These were often members of the top games teams, usually in their third or fourth year. It was a position that could be trained for. The Caterpillar in *The Hill* "was a dandy, the understudy—as John soon discovered—of one of the 'Bloods'; a 'Junior Blood' or 'Would-be'. A tremendous authority on 'swagger', a stickler for tradition, he had been nearly three years at school." Often a blood "emerged" by being accepted by other bloods; then it was a question of behaving in the right way. Here is one at *The Loom of Youth*'s Fernhurst (Sherborne) in 1911, though accurate for fifteen years before that time. We are in the tuck shop, the place where social standing is at its clearest:

> The real blood is easily recognised. He strolls in as if he had taken a mortgage on the place, swaggers into the inner room, puts down his books on the top of the table in the right-hand corner—only the bloods sit there—and demands a cup of tea and a macaroon. . . . When he is once inside the inner shop however he immediately lets everyone know it. If he sees anyone he knows, he bawls out:
> "I say, have you prepared the stuff for Christy?"
> The person asked never has.
> "Nor have I. Rot, I call it."
> No blood is ever known to have prepared anything.
> The big man then sits down. If a friend of his is anywhere about, he flings a lump of sugar at him. When he gets up he knocks over at least one chair. He then strolls out observing the same magnificent dignity in the outer shop. No one can mistake him.

Clothes are a principal means of self-expression; hence, as we saw, uniforms. And it was therefore in dress that these minute gradations in status were expressed. Marstock waddled off the field in a tasselled cap. By 1900 all the schools had evolved often fairly elaborate clothes for the different games' teams: coloured blazers, caps with dragons stitched onto them, ties, crests, trousers, shoes. But it wasn't just games. Here is Charter-house around 1900: a new boy had no distinctions and no privileges. The second term you were allowed a knitted tie instead of a plain one. Second year—coloured socks. Third year—turned-down collars, coloured hand-kerchiefs, a coat with long lapels, etc. Fourth year—still more distinctions and privileges and you could arrange raffles. But the blood's dress was unique and peculiar: light-grey flannel trousers, butterfly collars, coats slit up the back, and the privilege of walking arm-in-arm.

All the schools were different in detail. In essentials they were all the same. Not all had the unofficial "blood" system; but in all it was a series of privileged steps, a built-in hierarchy with fags at the bottom and prefects at the top.

About fagging, not a great deal more needs to be said by way of illus-tration. The duties and organisation were infinitely varied. At Westminster in 1840 the junior boy in each dormitory tied a string to his toe and hung it out of the window. One fag, therefore, by rushing round the quad and pulling all the strings, was able to wake the whole school. At one school (Sherborne) each prefect had four fags and two prefects shared a study; that was eight servants scurrying about cooking, tidying, flirting. At another, there would be no personal fags and the fifth form or sixth form or prefects would just bellow Boy! Fag! Doul! Junior! Election! or what-ever the particular school cry was. But in general one can say fagging became less strenuous, less "a full time slavery", as the century progressed. There are aspects of fagging—the part it played in vertical integration in a school, for instance, or the love relationships between fag and master (does the American expression "faggot" for homosexual come from fag?)—which I shall deal with later.

1 The prefect hierarchy and prefect justice

Schools were either ruled by their sixth forms, from which heads of houses and school were appointed (as at Rugby), or else by various houses and school prefect systems, or by a combination of both. Once again, the differences in organisation were (and are) considerable. They were (and are) seldom significant. Take Eton. Pop, the society we saw start in 1816 as a debating society, fairly soon took over monitorial duties. By the second half of the century, its position was fixed. Cyril Connolly, who was there in 1917, has given a succinct account in his book *Enemies of Promise*.

The whole school ruled in theory by sixth form and the captain of school, was governed by Pop or the Eton Society, an oligarchy of two dozen boys who, except for two or three ex-officio members, were self-elected and could wear coloured waistcoats, stick-up collars, etc. and cane boys from any house. . . .

This system makes Eton the most democratic of schools where all the prefects except the sixth form (who are only powerful in college) are self-elected. The boys get the government they deserve.

One should add to this, perhaps, the Library system—which was in effect a series of little Pops, copy of the big Pop, in each house (in college called Chamber Pop).

Much is made of this system (and was already being made in 1854; Hollis, in his book, regards it as one of the foundations of Eton's uniqueness), particularly of its democracy. But it is not democratic. The rulers elect themselves; they are not elected by the ruled. As Connolly says, it is an oligarchy. And here the difference is more apparent than real. In all schools where the prefects or monitors were appointed, it was done in consultation with the other prefects. On the whole, no house or headmaster would appoint someone of whom they disapproved; usually, he accepted their advice. In practice, therefore, all public school prefect systems tended to be in varying degrees self-perpetuating oligarchies, although usually disguised by a master's veto or rôle of suggestion (just as at Eton housemasters and headmaster do in fact fairly tactfully oversee the various elections).

This was the more so because of the degree—and here is the first significant element common to all systems—to which justice and its administration was left to these prefect, Pop, monitorial or whatever you call them bodies. The degree to which they were left alone in this one area becomes striking at the end of the 19th and beginning of the 20th centuries. At Marlborough, when the head of the house came to report that it was on fire, the housemaster roared, "That part of the house is your department not mine." In books like *The Loom* or *The Harrovians* it is always the sixth or prefects who administer discipline; the masters are not mentioned. "Christy believed in leaving his house entirely to his prefects. It was a good way of avoiding responsibility. . . ." Discipline was usually administered collectively; that is, several members of the governing body were present to discuss the case, asking questions and so on, to give an appearance of justice to what was in fact an arraignment, and then lounged about while punishment was delivered.

We saw this idea of prefect justice begin to evolve out of the 18th century in Arnold's time. Now the element of bribery—in return for privilege and freedom you must support the disciplinary aims of the school—becomes explicit. In *The Hill*, Warde is the good new housemaster.

"It is your duty to help me."

"I beg your pardon, sir," Lovell replied, "I have never considered it my duty as a sixth form boy to play the usher."

"Nor did I; but you ought to work in parallel lines with us. You accepted the privileges of the sixth."

The second significant factor all systems had in common was this. Although a good master and responsible prefects would clearly try to see that these boy tyrannies were not too tyrannical, a system of such independence gave many opportunities for abuse. These were often seized; they were aggravated by the methods of punishment. You no doubt noticed the almost Japanese humiliation in Betjeman's poem of having your face slapped which developed at Marlborough; more usually it was a thrashing.

Sometimes cases reached the papers, as for instance did the case of Platt and Stewart in 1854 at Harrow. Both were schoolboys, and the unnecessarily severe beating (thirty-one blows, requiring medical attention) that Platt gave Stewart reached *The Times*. Examples could be multiplied indefinitely. It is perhaps enough to note that, as with beating generally, the actual violence seems to have declined somewhat as the century went on—doctors are called less often, Parliament is no longer involved. (Palmerston wrote to Dr. Vaughan over Platt and Stewart.) But around 1900 and for decades afterwards many public schools, especially for the first two years, were nightmares of beating at the hands of bullying prefects.

Cyril Connolly found that the little boy in charge of chamber could beat him with a rubber tube. Chamber Pop could beat him. Practically everyone seemed able to beat him—and did.

> The captain of the school, Marjoribanks, who afterwards committed suicide, was a passionate beater like his bloody-minded successors Wrougham and Cliffe . . . in one satisfactory evening Majoribanks had beaten all the lower half of college. Thirty-five of us suffered. Another time we were all flogged because a boy dropped a sponge out of a window which hit a master, or we would be beaten for "generality" which meant no specific charge except that of being "generally uppish". . . . We knelt on the chair, bottoms outwards, and gripped the bottom bar with our hands, stretching towards it over the back. Looking round under the chair we could see a monster rushing towards us with a cane in his hand, his face upside down and distorted—the frowning mask of the captain of the school or the hideous little Wrougham. The pain was acute. When it was over some other member of sixth form would say "Good night"—it was wiser to answer.

These boys were able to exercise power over the destinies and well-being of others on a scale they were never to attain again. No prime minister, said Churchill, no field marshal had the personal power available to a prefect or captain of school. At one Jesuit school prefects were called Senators and Emperors of the East and West (the names of their houses). At Rugby they were really minor members of the staff. So we find emerging another English archetype—the frustrated benevolent dictator. School stories and English autobiographies are full of the sadness felt when, after the last day of the last term, this power vanishes away. When Tom Brown returns to Rugby to mourn the death of Dr. Arnold, he is about to chase the town boys off the cricket ground when, "'Psshaw! they won't remember me. They've got more right there than I,' he muttered. And the thought that his sceptre had departed, and his mark was wearing out came home to him for the first time, and bitterly enough." This is one reason— to preserve for their Old Boys the memory of their power—that the walls and the halls of so many public schools are plastered, like an Aztec settlement or an Egyptian tomb, with the names and achievements of the departed.

The rule about public schools is that they never initiate (except educationally): they imitate, then intensify and finally entomb. So it was here. Victorian and Edwardian social life was very like public school life. It was rigidly conventional, and organised in minutely graded steps of social rank. Public schools initiated adolescents into a world of trivial rules, and precisely the same sort of trivial rules—what clothes to wear at Ascot, at breakfast, at funerals, playing cricket; how to address, or leave your card on, a peer, a woman, a bishop; how to seat people at dinner. And—in addition to canalising competitiveness and ensuring discipline—because progress up the public school hierarchical ladder was in many instances automatic, it taught all its pupils their places in the social hierarchy: at the top. They were expected to lead. This was quite explicit. When Dr. Vaughan replied to Palmerston, who had expressed doubts about the fagging system, he explained that it was not just a method of keeping discipline, but also of "inculcating a system of organised rank" and was therefore essential as a "memento of monitorial authority". Every headmaster would have agreed.

Public schools intensified this type of social system quite simply because of the age at which, and the pressure with which, they impressed it. In the small, increasingly enclosed communities, apart from one or two trifling pursuits like passing exams, there was really nothing else for them to do but get and maintain the little psychological and actual territories symbolised by colours, caps, ties, third-year, fourth-year and prefectorial privileges. They pursued them fiercely and, as we have seen, the privileges were ferociously enforced. Now, a number of public school boys, equating the position of fags with that of the lower classes, reacted violently against the class system; others learnt the need for delicacy and tact when exercising power. But it seems plausible to suggest that many others were enraged by their treatment when small, took their revenge later on their own fags and, gaining a taste for proud order-giving power, still fuelled by inner resentment, continued to exercise it for the rest of their lives on the lower classes with that particular arrogance and conceit which was quite often a characteristic of upper-class behaviour.

Just as the classical and Church traditions from which the schools grew carried with a heavy momentum on through the 19th century and into the 20th century, so the rigid disciplines, the Saint-Simon-like elaboration of privileges, carried right through the first half of the 20th century. It will have been noticeable that I have been able to take illustrations from 1905 and 1917. In one case, from 1940. This was not because examples did not exist earlier. They did, though they were naturally fewer in 1850 when there were fewer schools and the developments we have discussed were only just becoming elaborate and general. The later examples seemed to me written with more point. But the significance is that they were relevant. These developments of the second half of the 19th century will continue to concern us almost till today. (In 1966 Graham Kalton's survey carried out for the Headmasters' Conference showed that three out of five boarding schools still had some form of fagging.) Though my choice of 1900 is arbitrary (I could as well have chosen 1914), I choose 1900 because it is then that the first signs of a reaction began, the tiny start of a titanic battle which was to rage for sixty years.

It is fascinating to see how deeply the idea of prefect justice entered the national consciousness. One can trace this by looking at the popular litera- . ture, in particular the Bulldog Drummond books by Sapper, the Berry books by Dornford Yates and the works of Buchan. (Any comment I make or quote at any time on these books, incidentally, can be assumed to come from Richard Usborne's brilliant study, *Clubland Heroes*.)

The heroes of these books all went to public schools—in Yates to Harrow around 1900, in Buchan to Eton. And, just as they had fags at school, these prefect heroes all have personal servants who do everything for them: bone their shoes, iron their newspapers, even die for them sometimes as Standish's man (a Buchan hero) poor Stanhope did, killed in mistake for his master—and then quickly burnt to a crisp by Standish to confuse the villains further. But, now grown-up, they had "no fags to show off to or rotters to punish for letting down the tone of the schools. Now there were crooks and robbers and rotters to punish, sometimes for the good of England, sometimes just because they were crooks, rotters or foreigners." They punish with the same zest they once caned. Sapper's heroes never wonder if they have the right, say,

to torture a dago bar-tender in Valparaiso (because he was a white-slaver) or hang a Hebrew jewel robber (because he tried to paw an English girl). Drummond, though gone fairly berserk at the time, had no qualms or regrets afterwards about transfixing a Russian revolutionary, in peace time, to the wall of an Essex mansion with the Russian's own bayonet. The Russian had tried to murder Drummond's wife. That was enough.

The assumption is the same as that behind prefect justice, that upper-class Englishmen have the right to take the law into their own hands and kill where once they caned. It was an assumption based on countless bullyings and canings in the prefect room, and the killings were countless too. (Usborne does not try to count how many times Bulldog Drummond kills. I tried, and gave up. But it was already clear that effectively he was a mass murderer.)

Now this idea—that the hero has the right to take justice into his own hands—has been of immense influence, if at a popular level. It is the *sine qua non* of the thriller writers, the direct lineal descendants of Buchan, Yates and Sapper. From them came Mickey Spillane, Leslie Charteris, Ian Fleming, *et al*, a *genre* so enormous, especially in the United States, that it is only necessary to draw attention to it. From them, in turn, developed the thriller series on film and television, the invisible men, the Callans and Kojaks who now dominate the evenings of continents.

But it operates at a fantasy level. That is, these prefect heroes and their descendants allow us to play out our desires for revenge, or sadistic wishes to bully, in imagination. It is possible, though I don't want to press this too far, that the idea had a more profound influence on our destiny. Clearly, if you unconsciously believe that as an upper-class Englishman you have the right and the ability to administer justice on your own, then, if you find yourself precisely in that position governing an Empire, your task will be that much easier. There are a number of explanations for the way the British took their Empire for granted, the way in which they believed it was their "right" to govern it; but this should be one. And the reverse, as it were, is even more interesting. The principle behind the public school method was that of the gradual evolution towards power and privilege: a fourth-year man had more than a third-year man, a fifth-year man still more and a sixth-year man had most of all. Finally, inevitably, came the ultimate freedom—you left school. And though there is no doubt that the public school boys who went out to govern the Colonies never thought for a moment we would give them up—C. A. Vlieland of the Malayan Civil Service wrote to Correlli Barnett:"Naturally we believed whole-heartedly in . . . the permanence of the British Empire"—nevertheless there was at the heart of the system which had trained them and their rulers the idea that anyone over whom you had authority would one day have authority themselves, that ultimately you were training them for the time they would be free.

The common judgment is that because the entire structure developed from the need to impose discipline what had happened to the public schools by 1900 was that means had become ends. This is to miss the point.

It was recognised from 1840 to 1850 onwards that deference for a hierarchical society, the ability and desire to lead, an appreciation of the nice gradations of social form were all-important goals for a public school to give its pupils. It is quite possible to view the whole prefect-privilege structure as a method evolved to do this. That is why school books of the period were quite right to make the operation of this structure central to their picture. And it was exported. When Plumtree was founded in Rhodesia in 1900, there was no nonsense about waiting for traditions to grow up. A master called Hammond sailed out from Winchester and slapped them on entire—fagging, colours, prefect justice, monitorial beatings, everything.

And in fact, in this respect, Plumtree was like other Victorian schools. Much of the structure was deliberately copied, taken from books or, more usually, imposed by the headmaster and based on his old school. (It was common for masters to bring senior boys from other schools to help them do this. Cotton did so at Marlborough, and as late as the 1920s it was done at Stowe and Canford.) But there is one area in this field of boy discipline where similar rituals seem to have grown up spontaneously.

Ceremonies initiating people into institutions serve a number of purposes, some of which dictate that they should be violent, or at least unpleasant. Testing courage and establishing pecking order is one. The pack initially rejects. Neill noticed that at Summerhill every new entrant had to endure three months' unconscious hatred from all the other pupils. They were jealous of this person with whom they had to share the approval of Neill and other hero figures. They therefore regressed to the equivalent family situation where the new baby is hated for having the mother's love. The initiation ceremonies were ritualistic to express (and so dissolve) those feelings and contain them. The institution also seems to feel the need to impress its power and authority (whether this be official or unofficial) on the newcomer.

Certainly in many public schools these ceremonies were often both violent and very unpleasant. At Winchester in the 1840s a new boy was asked if he had any tin gloves. When he said no, the other boys would take a blazing stick from the chamber fire, blow it out, and while the boy was held, draw the red hot stick from each knuckle down to the wrist and do several strokes across. It left a grid of massed blisters—the "tin glove". At Marlborough in 1870 the initiation was to be tossed in a blanket over the stair well in "A" House. This was continued till a boy missed the blanket and fell to his death. As the century continued, it does seem that here, as in other ways, public schools became more humanitarian, though I have many examples of very rough handling continuing. At Marlborough again, in the 1920s, though your life was no longer at risk, you had to crawl along a red hot radiator singing "Clementine" and at the end "take a face", that is have your face slapped. (I can see now the face of the man as he told me this, plump and amiable, suddenly contorting with fury as he remembered it. "The upper classes were *not* pampered," he said fiercely. "We were treated with the ferocity of a concentration camp.")

But by far the most common form of initiation evolved along with the rules and privileges and made use of them. The essence is the new boy being tested in front of prefects or sometimes a larger group; sometimes books are thrown at him or he is beaten if wrong, sometimes he has to sing a song as well; sometimes the ritual has contracted back into a song only. I have a great many examples of this, mostly from 1860 on. One will suffice. Here is Robert Graves writing in *Goodbye to all That* about Charterhouse in 1910.

> "It's Jones' turn now," said a voice. "He's the little brute that hacked me in run-about today. We must set him some tight questions!"
>
> "I say, Jones, what's the colour of the housemaster—I mean what's the name of the housemaster of the house, whose colours are black and white? One, two, three. . . ."
>
> "Mr. Girdlestone," my voice quivered in the darkness.
>
> "He evidently knows the simpler colours. We'll muddle him. What are the colours of the Clubs to which Block Houses belong? One, two, three, four. . . ."

Of course, in the end he is counted out. "You'll come to my 'cube' at seven tomorrow morning. See?"

Not all schools had these initiation ceremonies. Some had them for a period, or a few houses had them, then they stopped. But they are a further ingredient in that concentration which we are now studying in depth, which, where they were similar, served, by making the schools similar, to draw them together into something we can accurately, around 1900–1914, call a "system".

2 Class

In our preliminary discussion of this subject we saw that during the first thirty years of the 19th century, broadly speaking, three things were happening: there was a steady growth in the number of the middle class, these for a number of reasons (not least because political power still resided there) sought to assimilate the manners and customs of the classes above them, and the public schools increasingly became the avenue of this assimilation. It will come as no surprise to learn that during the remainder of the century all these processes became very much more widespread, more intense and more complicated.

Class becomes overt and stated. Bradfield was founded in 1850 to educate the sons of gentlemen. So was Cheltenham. Brighton, started in 1847, followed Cheltenham, the secretary having sent them a quick-potted philosophy: "Had we admitted tradesmen in any instance, we must have done so almost without limit, and in the confined circle of shops in Cheltenham we should have had the sons of gentlemen shaking hands with schoolfellows behind the counter." Hollis says that it was "monstrous" of Eton to assume by 1850 that everyone there was a gentleman. Leaving aside that Eton assumed that long before 1850, I do not see it in this particular instance as monstrous. Victorian snobbery is so extreme that it often passes beyond the monstrous; it becomes ludicrous. But, from the schools' point of view, it was sound commercial sense—you had to advertise to your market that you'd got what they wanted. It didn't, of course, mean you really only accepted gentlemen's sons. That would debar two-thirds of your market. "I want you, Sir," said a prospective parent to Haig-Brown of Charterhouse at a later date, "to assure me that the boys who come to your school are the sons of gentlemen." "Well, they always leave gentlemen," said Haig-Brown.

Class distinctions even appear, and are thereby re-enforced, in exam papers. Here are some questions from the 1850s. "If a servant receives £3.10s for 20 weeks' service, how many weeks ought he to remain in his place for 12 guineas?" "If a gentleman be taxed £37.0s.10d at 7d in the £ what is his rental?" "If a person gives 5 guineas for his lodging for the month of July at 20d a night, what sum will be returned to him?" Someone who paid 20d a night could be nothing more than a "person"; he could not possibly be a gentleman. It is an odd source for such information. The distinction is made clear in many sums.

How essential class was to the success of a public school in market terms can be seen in the case of Wellington. When the duke died in 1852, his family, looking forward to vast sums from public subscription, planned a bronze statue for every single town in the country. But they were over-ruled by the Court, particularly by the Prince Consort. Albert had had a marvellous idea, a huge new school to provide "free education of orphan children of Indigent and Meritorious Officers of the Army". The family was appalled. The idea would appeal to nobody; it was also, well, in some way, extremely common. They were right about it not appealing. Despite huge publicity, 100,000 letters, and a compulsory levy of one day's pay on the whole army, only £105,000 was collected. A desperate second appeal raised £6,000. Plans were ruthlessly cut back. The education of girls chopped. When the building was finished, there was only £29,000 left for endowment. Education could no longer be free. Wellington, even in this modified version of Albert's early plan, would almost certainly have failed.

It was saved by the first headmaster, E. W. Benson. Completely ignoring the Court he saw at once the only solution was to create a great public school, skimming where the cream was thickest. This he did, and when he retired the gratitude of the family was touching. The second duke, somewhat inarticulate, couldn't somehow get the nub of his feelings into his farewell speech. After it, he drew Benson aside and struggled to express the simple, almost crude, but powerful feelings held by the Wellingtons.

> I and my family hoped that there would be a fine monument set up. . . . And you can fancy what our feelings were when we found that it was . . . a charity school . . . where scrubly little orphans could be maintained and educated. . . . But you have made the college what it is—one of the finest public schools in England—and I and my family are more than content at the result. There [digging Benson hard in the ribs with his elbow] that's what I meant to have said. . . . But Lord, when I stood up to speak, it all ran out at my heels.

Perhaps it's as well it did. Even in the 1850s "scrubly little orphans" might have irritated some people. By the end of the century snobbery at Wellington (among other schools) had become farcical. In 1898 the governors of the school, in total, comprised two princes, three dukes, three earls, three bishops, six knights and a former prime minister.

It was not all a matter of farce. In the 18th century, although Englishmen were extremely conscious of rank, they also had a perfectly sound respect for themselves as individuals. Because someone was of a higher rank it did not mean he was a better person. "The Englishman . . .," wrote Dr. Johnson, "was born without a master; and looks not on any man, however dignified by lace or titles, as deriving from nature any claims to his respect or inheriting any qualities superior to his own." It is the fact that during the later 19th and early 20th centuries English class consciousness in some respects and among a good number of people came much closer to what we today call racism that made is so odious.

We can see it take place in religion, where morality became layered like the classes and you got worse as you went down. Henry Hayman wrote in 1858, "I will venture to say that there is little of that honourable love of truth, which distinguishes English public school boys, to be found in the homes of the lower classes." But it was more than this. In *The Hill*, when Scaife gets very drunk, "One is reminded," said the Caterpillar, "that the poor Demon is the son of a Liverpool merchant, bred in or somewhere about the docks." On another occasion Scaife loses his temper because defeated. Caesar, another boy, just smiles "with the tact of his race". It was in fact a question of upper-class breeding; the upper classes inherited qualities just as their horses inherited fine fetlocks or a good wind. And the reverse was true—the inheriting of poor qualities, moral defects. When Consuelo Vanderbilt married the Duke of Marlborough in the 1880s one of the first things she did was to stop them giving the huge quantities of left-over food to the locals all chucked together, as for pigs.

Yet these racist strands were muddled and complicated in the same way as the Victorian views about sex were muddled and made complex by other considerations. Class was breeding, yet we saw earlier that you could almost catch lower classness like a disease, and that this was a factor in the physical isolation of public schools. This continued. As they were threatened by the encroaching populace, Eton and Harrow scurried to buy large amounts of land at vast expense. In the fourteen years after 1885 Harrow bought 220 acres for £90,000. As far as the new schools went, there was a corollary to this. In the same way it could be caught, lower classness could be cured. The right school worked. But since the aim was to join the aristocracy and the landed gentry, and since the symbol of these was the country house, public schools set themselves amidst parks and woods, in the largest houses possible. By going to a public school in a country house you not only absorbed something of the country-house way of life, it was almost as though you had been born in one. Thus there was an inter-action—class consciousness led to the country house which cut the public schools off and intensified class feeling.

In fact, public schools intensified the various manifestations of class and elaborated them in a way with which we are now becoming familiar.

Take accent. Differences between people are very much increased if there is something physical to identify them with. In England accent has been to class what colour is to race. The public schools have often been blamed for this; indeed the accent of the English upper classes is sometimes called the public school accent. But, as we have seen, the public schools initiate nothing. Accent as a distinguishing feature began hundreds of years before, with the emergence in the 15th century of the Court and capital in London. This dialect, that of London and Cambridge and Oxford, was originally South-East Midland but, becoming a "social speech", it developed apart from the regional variety. By the 16th century London English was regarded as the only language for a literary man or a gentleman. Sir Thomas Elyot complains that nurses teach foul pronunciation; the speech of rustics is parodied in Shakespeare; Puttenham in *The Arte of English Poesie* (1589) says that a poet should use the language of London and not about 60 miles beyond. From the 17th century on, comments which are made on accent are increasingly rare because it is unusual: Aubrey on Raleigh's Devonshire accent; Dr. Johnson's "Poonch" for punch, almost all there was left of his Warwickshire; Disraeli noting in his journal the provincial accent of Peel.

Public schools elaborated this, often by introducing their own variations. After the Lyttelton boys had been at Eton for a while in the 1860s they began to draw out their As, saying "Brawss" and "glawss" instead of brass and glass. Their elder sisters told them it was common.

The intense scrutiny of communal life naturally noted accent. In *The Hill* Scaife says "ines*teem*able".

The Caterpillar drawls, "One pronounces that 'inestimable'."

"My father doesn't," said Scaife hotly, "I've heard him say, 'inesteemable'."

"No doubt," said Egerton, coldly. "How does your father pronounce it, Caesar?"

Desmond said hurriedly, "Oh—'inestimable', but what does it matter?"

And so with all the other signals—titles, addresses, country houses, occupations, from the crooked finger of Mrs. Pooter to the type of champagne at the Eton and Harrow—all the myriad of tiny but significant flags which fluttered from the tall mast of class.

The Hill is stiff with titles. Here the housemaster, Rutford, brings Lord Kinloch's mother into his dormitory.

"This is Scaife, Duchess," he said in thick rasping tones. "Scaife and Verney, let me present you to the Duchess of Trent."

He mouthed the illustrious name as if it were a large and ripe greengage.

The Duchess advanced, smiling graciously. "These"—Rutford names the other boys—"are Egerton, Lovell and—er—Duff."

Scaife, alone of those present, appreciated the order in which his schoolfellows had been named. Egerton—known as the Caterpillar—was the son of a guardsman; Lovell's father was a judge; Duff's father an obscure parson.

We might note that an analysis of schoolmasters at Eton and other schools in the 1850s shows them to have been predominantly middle-class professionals. They ascribed to the values of their upper-class pupils, whom others of their pupils wished to join, and therefore intensified them. This remained true into the 1920s and 30s.

. . . It is astonishing [noted Orwell, writing about the years around 1910] how intimately, intelligently snobbish we all were, how knowledgeable about names and addresses, how swift to detect small differences in accents and manners and the cut of clothes. . . . "How much a year has your pater got? What part of London do you live in? Is that Knightsbridge or Kensington? How many bathrooms has your house got? How many servants do your people keep? Have you got a butler? Well, then, have you got a cook? Where do you get clothes made? How many shows did you go to in the hols? How much money did you bring back with you?" etc. etc.

Such catechisms, helplessly hid through or triumphantly passed, stamped boys indelibly with the importance of wealth, class and position.

Because the flags signalling position were so numerous the picture can appear complicated.

"You going to Scotland this hols?"

"Rather! We go every year."

"My pater's got three miles of river."

"My pater's giving me a new gun for the twelfth. There's jolly good black game where we go. Get out, Smith! What are you listening for? You've never been to Scotland. I bet you don't know what a blackcock looks like."

At first sight the fashion for Scotland at the end of the 19th and start of the 20th centuries seems purely romantic, which in part it was—the scenery, the beauty and, as Orwell says, "a mixture of burns, braes, kilts, sporrans, claymores, bagpipes and the like all somehow mixed up with the invigorating effects of porridge, Protestantism and a cold climate". But there is a simpler reason. Scotland was a private paradise few could enjoy. In particular, the few (who included Queen Victoria and John Brown) had to be very rich. Nearly all snobbish fashions resolve themselves when it is realised you need money to indulge them—no matter how else they are disguised.

Yet it is over money that the muddle at the heart of Victorian and Edwardian snobbery does become complicated. We saw this muddle expressed in the contradictory ideas that breeding was hereditary and unalterable, but that it was also alterable since it was contagious—lower classness being "curable" if you went to a public school. The same contradictions appear with money.

Clearly, it was essential to possess it. At first boasted about—"I'm going up on a bob but of course my people have got tons of tin"—older boys were more adult. Neither they nor their parents mentioned money; they just assumed its massive presence in colossal bank accounts. At the same time new money, money from what was loosely termed "trade", was despised. We have seen this in the quotes about Scaife. I was brought up on a story about my great-grandmother, Lady Glasgow. The Broadwoods had come to the neighbourhood. After a while (they were extremely rich) Lady Glasgow said that although they were in "trade", they must be asked to stay. But instructions were given that absolutely no one was to mention the word "piano". That would be in extremely poor taste. The weekend went very well. Finally, the farewells came, the embraces. At last my great-grandmother went to the window and turned with uplifted arms sadly. "I'm afraid, Mrs. Broadwood, the time has come to part," she said. "Your piano's at the door." I had told this story for several years when one day someone told me he had heard it, but about a different family and a different object. Then someone else had heard it, but about yet another item. This did not make me doubt my own version. My grandmother, who told me, was extremely accurate about her mother. It just showed how widespread the ridiculous prejudice was. No doubt it was happening all the time, all over the country—Mrs. Palmer, your biscuit's at the door,

Mrs. Stevens your ink's at the door, Mrs. Crapper your water-closet is at the door.

But, and here the two sides of the contradiction jar together, the Victorians and Edwardians were ashamed of their snobbery. This comes out in the school literature. Scaife is really the hero of *The Hill*. In *Coningsby* by Disraeli, a novel about Eton, Millbank whose father is in trade is generally sneered at, especially by the hero Coningsby himself— "Why should you ask an infernal manufacturer?"—but the book ends with Coningsby and Millbank becoming best friends, almost lovers. In general, Victorian guilt about class was expressed, not by any suggestion that privilege or money should be given up—that was unthinkable—but by the idea that in return for them the upper classes had "duties" towards the lower classes. *The Hill*, a mine of unconscious social comment, exemplifies this in Fluff. His father is a duke, but is justified in this because he "works very hard at it". The entire field of Victorian charity is in part an expression of class guilt, but in fact we are moving away from public schools in exploring this area.

There were already people in the 1860s who disapproved of public school class bias. It disgusted Percival, the Headmaster of Clifton. He wanted 150 humble local boys there, paid for by the school and local subscription. Nothing happened and it was this failure to bring about "the abolition of social distinction" which made him leave.

But the contribution of the public schools to class guilt was minuscule. Their weight was all the other way. They imitated class distinctions, then elaborated and intensified them in all the ways we have observed. Another profound effect they had in this field was to enormously increase class solidarity.

This was partly an automatic and obvious result. I find an unacknowledged note on my files (I think I took it from Correlli Barnett): "The public school bond that those who have not been to one find so difficult to understand and so easy to deride." Easy to deride perhaps; why difficult to understand? People who share the intense experiences of childhood and adolescence are naturally bound together—families, friends from the same village or area of a town or city. And the point is, as I have been at pains to stress, public school boys all shared, essentially, the same experiences. Not only that, but these differences were peculiar and different, making them more alike to each other, yet more different from everyone else. And the schools were different in peculiar ways. The binding effect of youthful (indeed any) experience is increased if it is harsh and difficult. You see this with miners, or with people from notorious slums like those in Glasgow or the East End of London; you see it after wars. As we have observed, public school life at this time was extremely harsh and difficult. It also had a second dimension. Miners for many years went down the pits at fourteen or younger, but they were not separated from their families. Public school boys were, from the age of eight. Odd things happen when you do this to children. Studies of kibbutz life show clearly that, separated from their families, children become dependent on each other; a good deal of the love and loyalty they would feel for their fathers and mothers attaches itself to the peer group.

And, just as a miner's first loyalty is to the mates in his own pit, but easily spreads to other miners and then to the whole working class in general, or as kibbutzim are, of all Israelis, the most intensely patriotic—so public school boys were loyal to their schools, then to other public school boys and finally, inevitably since they all came from the same class, to their class. Nor is class comfort a small thing. It is a deep communal unreasoning emotion, when we feel, as Wyndham Lewis wrote of National Socialism, "the love and understanding of blood brothers, of one culture, children of the same traditions, whose deepest social interests, when all is said and done, are one. . . ." The distinguished psychiatrist Dr. Anthony Storr told me that he had frequently noticed with his upper-class patients how class love and loyalty, the reassurance this gave, compensated for the way they had been deprived of parental love.

Feelings of this sort are both expressed and strengthened by song. It is so with miners, with soldiers marching to war, and it was so with public schools. I do not just mean the individual school songs, though these were affecting enough, especially at Harrow, where Old Boys (Churchill among them) would return again and again to join, tears pouring down their cheeks, the great swelling surge as 500 youthful voices sang "Forty Years On", or "Willow the King" or "Fortuna Domus".

> Five hundred faces, and all so strange,
> Life in front of me—home behind,
> I felt like a waif before the wind
> Tossed on an ocean of shock and change.

> Chorus: Yet the time may come as the years go by,
> When your heart will thrill
> At the thought of the Hill,
> And the day you came so strange and shy.

But public schools had their own corpus of song, great simple stirring songs that echo down the 19th century and on deep into the 20th century. These are the splendid hymns of the Church of England, collected together in *Hymns Ancient and Modern*. Hymns bound the public schools together: Wesley's "Jesu, Lover of My Soul", Cowper's "God Moves in a Mysterious Way", perhaps best known of all, Augustus Toplady's famous "Rock of Ages Cleft for Me". "Lord Dismiss Us" comes under the section *End of Term*; for an instant it seems like a division of the religious year. Many headmasters and masters wrote hymns, and one can quite often detect hymn themes or treatments in English composers of a certain generation as thousands of public school Sundays and assemblies stir in their subconscious—in Vaughan Williams (Charterhouse) particularly, but also in Britten and Lennox Berkley (Gresham's).

It is the closeness which all this generated which helps to explain a number of things. The formation, but above all the functioning, of an élite and the whole "Old Boy net" become more understandable. It is exemplified in the popular novels. Buchan calls it the "totem", a close-knit tribal system of powerful friendship. But even the more generalised community of the upper classes can be invaluable. In a Sapper story, *The Eleventh House*, the "nondescript" man (nondescript but clearly a public school man) discovers evidence that proves the innocence of Ronald Vane, condemned to death:

> I had a vision of a woman's white face with hope too marvellous for words dawning on it: then I was back in the car driving full speed for London. Only the home secretary would do for me, and I caught him as he was dressing for dinner.
> "What on earth!" he began, as I burst past the butler into his room.
> "Sorry," I gasped. "I'm not an anarchist! Look at these two photos. Ronald Vane case."
> "Well, what is it? . . ."

The nondescript man explains to the home secretary, who says, "Good God! Good God!" and issues a reprieve for Ronald Vane on the spot. Here the hero didn't even know the home secretary. But he was part of the totem, he had the right "feel"—his accent and imperiousness alone probably got him into the house.

As I interviewed ex-public school boys, particularly older ones, as I raised old memories, I was struck again and again by the strength of this invisible bond. They seemed to know the most extraordinary and intimate details about each other—even when they had been to quite different schools—information which they would divulge at the drop of a hat: "Connolly? Oh, he didn't have an orgasm until he went to Oxford. Then it was a fellow called Longden, who I think went on to become Head-master of Wellington. . . ."

It is the nature of this bond—this curious impersonal intimacy—which explains why so many British "establishment" institutions work the way they do; by contact, by influential men talking and deciding in small groups, by word of mouth.

You can see it working in the two rather odd criteria proposed by the compilers of the first *Public Schools Year Book* in 1889. They themselves were simply "three public school men". Their guidelines had been "Does the school possess the public school spirit? Are its pupils entitled to be called public school men?" The esoteric "sensing" is typical; nuances of class can only be felt, they cannot be explained. It also introduces us to the snobbery of the schools about themselves, which in turn is a function of the degree to which they unified as a system.

3 Tradition, school snobbery

> *Sir Ninian Comber:* "We've always called Glenalmond the Eton of the North."
> *Anthony Barnes:* "Yes—and we've always called Eton the Glenalmond of the South."

Traditions are to men what instincts are to animals: a method of guiding his behaviour, in various crucial areas, instantly and without thought into the right channels. The "right" channels are those which have proved to work in the past. This is true of all societies, of all cultures, at all times; but it was especially true from the early Middle Ages up into the 19th century when our institutions and our own culture were evolving. During these centuries change was very slow. Fundamentals such as land tenure, the structure and balance of power, social needs and expectations and customs, remained much the same for generations. The likelihood was, therefore, that what had worked in the past would work in the future.

At the same time, change—change of king or government, change of agricultural methods, change of religion—often meant civil war, persecution, chaos, loss of property and even life. As a result our major institutions, our forms of government, law and education, were all largely based on the principle of enshrining precedent—that it was wisest to follow custom and tradition.

To this fundamental impulse educational systems add something peculiar to themselves. The rôle of education in anthropological terms is to pass on the accumulated knowledge, learning, morals and customs of the culture. But to have anything to pass on you must first of all preserve it. There is therefore a generalised instinct to preserve in educational systems, which operates indiscriminately and with considerable power.

These are broad principles; there were a number of particular reasons why the public schools in the second half of the 19th century were so concerned with tradition and why the traditions they preserved (or invented) were so universally the same.

The most important of these was that most of the schools were new (the rejuvenated grammar schools were in effect as new as the new foundations). In order to attract pupils they imitated the great schools. This was done quite shamelessly and openly. *The Public Schools Year Book* stated that Malvern was founded on the Winchester system. The idea was that you were sending your son to Winchester. In 1851 Mill Hill adopted, from nowhere as it were, a coat of arms—legless martlets. A little later, in 1879, they started an OB association. "The idea of an Old Boys' Club was no novelty. Other schools of importance had theirs; so naturally the question would arise of founding one for Mill Hill." Naturally. In effect, the new schools were pretending they were old. And since fagging, prefect justice and all the rest of it were what distinguished the old schools, what filled *Tom Brown* and *Eric* and *The Hill*, these were the "traditions" they adopted. And very soon they began to *feel* old:

> There's a breathless hush in the Close tonight—
> Ten to make and the match to win. . . .
>
> . . . his Captain's hand on his shoulder smote—
> "Play up! play up! and play the game!"
>
> This is the Chapel: here, my son,
> Your father thought the thoughts of youth. . . .

These famous lines were written by Henry Newbolt, not about Rugby or Harrow, but about Clifton. Clifton had been founded twenty-five years before, in 1852, the year Newbolt was born. There was no question of anyone's father thinking the thoughts of youth there when Newbolt wrote; or if there was he would be exhorting a son aged about five.

It is this, incidentally, which makes nonsense of Thring's apparently defeated but ringing call to the first meeting of The Association of Headmistresses at Uppingham in 1887. "You are fresh, and enthusiastic, and comparatively untrammelled," he cried, "whilst we are weighed down by tradition, cast like iron in the rigid moulds of the past . . . the hope of teaching lies in you." What tradition? Thring had no tradition to contend with when he arrived at Uppingham. It was a tiny, run-down grammar school with twenty-eight boys. He could, had he been so minded, have done what he liked with it. Any traditions were brought by him and imposed by him, deliberately. When he said he was "cast like iron in the rigid moulds of the past" he was boasting.

And this of course was a reason for choosing places like Uppingham in the first place. Although they had often been little more than village schools for sixty years or 150 years, their headmasters absent or drunk in pubs, they could say they were founded in 1584 or whenever it was. And, just as going to a school in a country house was like being born in one, so if your school, however technical the connection, could trace its foundation to 1584, it was rather like tracing your own lineage back there too.

These were all pressures imposed by the market. There were pressures from inside too. Masters have always pointed out, rather smugly, that boys are inherently conservative: "You may think I'm an old fogey, but I can tell you . . . " We saw that the old rebellions were often over the ending of traditions or removal of privileges. This was sometimes because they were all that made life bearable, but there is more to it than that. Boys are not so much inherently conservative as inherently insecure. They arrive at twelve or thirteen, alone, thrust out of their homes into a new and frightening environment. They are desperate to be accepted, to belong, and the most obvious way of achieving this is to learn all the rules and customs of the new institution—its traditions. It was sound psychology which made Hughes have Tom plunge, with almost feverish enthusiasm, into a great School-House match only minutes after his arrival. But if knowing traditions gives you confidence, removing them threatens that confidence. And, since you have grown up adapting to a tradition, in a subtle but definite way it becomes a part of your personality. I suddenly realised this when I was being shown round Winchester. A master—I'll call him Mr. S—was pointing their "toys" out to me. These are tiny cubicles, more like big boxes, in which the boys work. He was explaining to me how their presence had delayed the coming of studies. These had only started seven years or so ago. (I was somewhat startled to learn that this delay had been going on since 1859. Winchester is an extremely slow-changing school.) Mr. S obviously loved toys. They seemed to him an ingenious and lovable way of denying boys studies. Another master—call him Mr. K— had said toys increased work. I could see what he meant. You couldn't, as it were, do anything but work in a toy. The distance between you and your book was too small for you to look at anything else. You couldn't, said Mr. K scornfully, get away to a study and develop your personality. But it was the nature of Mr. S's emotions that interested me. He had strong fond memories of his own toy. He could see himself as a boy, squashed into it, learning forty odd years before. I realised that by destroying toys he felt he was destroying his own memories and therefore destroying a part of himself.

It was this reaction which kept so many traditions rigidly the same year after year. It operated in Old Boys. If anything was changed they rose in a body and wrote furious letters or arrived, purple in the face, at the headmaster's front door. And Old Boys had another reason. Not only did this continuance of old traditions reassure them that there had been nothing wrong with their own education; it also proved to them that the same education was being given to their children. The old school was "the same".

Nor was it just the identities of those at, or those who had been at, the school. The very identity of the school itself was involved. Although there were (and are) enormous differences between the schools in 1900— between, say, the wide differences in the houses at Eton, the lack of snobbery at UCS, the science bias developing at Oundle, the fact that Bedales was co-educational—they were all much more like each other than they were like anything else. Often they were in essentials identical. The only things that differentiated them were their traditions. Without them someone at Wellington might suddenly have started thinking he was at Cheltenham. (John Betjeman, who was at Marlborough, knows far more about Harrow and often finds himself thinking he went there.) When Charterhouse moved to Surrey, the new buildings and many of the rooms were given the names from the London school: Crown, Hall, Long Room, the Writing School. They even took great chunks of masonry with them, like the Gown-boy Arch, and stuffed them into the new school.

It was this complex of forces, acting in concert with the Headmasters Conference, *The Public Schools Year Book*, that unconscious evolution towards uniformity, the considerable mobility (particularly of head-masters) between schools, which first formed the public schools into an extremely coherent system, and then kept them like that. By 1898 there was a *Public School Magazine*, which contained news from all the schools and went out to them all. P. G. Wodehouse was Rugby correspondent. It was an outer concentration which complemented that inner concentration which has been our concern. And just as that inner concentration compounded the snobbery inherent in the Victorians' and Edwardians' class system, so the outer one abetted the snobbery between the schools. They were all conscious of inferiority to Eton. Fluff, in *The Hill* says: "You fellows know that everybody talks of Eton and Harrow—whoever heard of Harrow and Eton? People say—I've heard my eldest brother Strathfeffer say it again and again—'Eton and Harrow', just as they say 'Gentlemen and players'." I find school snobbery tedious and do not intend to go into it. But Professor de Honey has done a lot of work on it on the basis that schools would only play games with other schools they regarded as approximately their equals. (The Ivy League in the United States became, among other things, a group of East Coast colleges which played each other at football.) His results—the snob groupings of schools in 1900—can be studied in Appendix C.

4 Curriculum, work, exams

With these last two sections in mind, it becomes much easier to understand the development, or rather lack of development, in the curriculum of the public schools during the last two-thirds of the 19th century.

A cursory study of time-tables, in 1805, say, or 1820, can often give an appearance of variety—French, German, Italian, Spanish, writing, dancing, drawing, fencing. It is an illusion. These were irrelevant frills; eccentric, even mad foreigners with strange names allowed to haunt the fringes in order to counteract criticism of specialisation. They were often left on the lists long after they had stopped teaching and even after they had died—the Dead Souls of the public schools.

We have seen the true picture earlier. It remains true for the middle of the century. In 1840 anything from three-quarters to four-fifths of the time was spent on classics, forty hours a week. In 1863 staff list analyses show classic masters outnumbering the rest by seventy-five to thirty-five. The story of the next hundred years is the rate at which, the degree to which, and the particular schools and even classrooms in which this situation was broken down. The matter is rather complex and before embarking on it there is some value in looking briefly at the reasons (and defences) which made the classics able to retain this hold so long.

It will come as no shock to learn that the fact that they had been taught for over 1,200 years was a reason for continuing them. And they had a longer history still. They had been taught centuries before that, and in the same way, by rote. Augustine of Hippo was talking of friends in the 4th century who knew the whole of Virgil and Cicero by heart. The classics had the tall monuments of two great Empires behind them; the shadows of Greece and Rome stretched on into the 20th century.

Nor will it occasion surprise to be told that class played a part, an overwhelming part, in their retention. Because gentlemen were supposed to be too rich to work the criticism that practically undiluted classics did not prepare someone to earn his living became a powerful recommendation. Some slight concession to necessity the upper middle classes did allow: the navy, army, church, law and at the end of the century some of the professions (all if possible for younger sons). "Trade" was anathema; so, in this great age of science, when England was veined with railways, when the 1851 Exhibition celebrated a hundred years of industrial and scientific achievement, although they invested money in manufacture and goggled at the Exhibition they would no more have dreamt of putting their sons into manufacturing industry, or letting them learn the sciences which had given rise to it, than they would have put their daughters into brothels because they had recourse to prostitutes.

And science seemed somehow physically close to the artisan. This is shown, in reverse, by the success T. H. Huxley had with working-class audiences:

> I am, and have been any time these thirty years, a man who works with his hands—a handicraftsman. I do not mean this in any broadly metaphorical sense. . . . I really mean my words to be taken in their direct, literal and straightforward sense—in fact, if the most nimble-fingered watch-maker among you will come to my workshop, he may set me to put a watch together, and I will set him to dissect, say, a blackbeetle's nerves. I do not wish to vaunt, but I am inclined to think that I shall manage my job to his satisfaction sooner than he will do his piece to mine.

All this was absolutely explicit. Classics masters sneered openly at mathematics and modern–language masters. Here is the answer of a Rossall schoolmaster when asked by the Devonshire Committee "What departments of science are preferred by parents?" "Parents exhibit complete indifference to the whole subject, with the exception they sometimes object to their sons devoting any time at all to it." Lord Plumer at Eton himself in 1870, addressed the school in 1916: "We are often told that they taught us nothing at Eton. That may be so, but I think they taught it very well." This sounds idiotic, indeed, it is idiotic, but it is interesting because it shows how completely it was accepted that a school was not to train for a job or even in any sense meant to be academic, but there for social and all the "character" reasons.

There were practical considerations. All classical (with a little mathematics) schools were easy to run, easy to time-table. The universities gave no encouragement to science. Cambridge virtually ignored science; at Oxford only three colleges—Christ Church, Balliol and Magdalen—were mildly interested. There was therefore no incentive to teach it at the public schools, and since it was not taught at the public schools, no incentive to teach it at university.

Furthermore, as the century proceeded, the Empire became increasingly important. Of what use was science to this? It was a protected mercantilist system which required administrators—and these the public schools felt they could provide.

These are all fairly thumping reasons; but there were more interesting, more subtle ones. Classics were a part of that defence the public school masters felt they almost alone maintained against the evils of industrialisation and voracious materialism—evils which we now are in a better position to appreciate. The classics, wrote a schoolmaster in 1906, "formed the one bulwark against that purely utilitarian tendency today which deprecates any study that has no practical value."

They were even said to produce the inventiveness and resource which won the Battle of Jutland (if "won" is not too decisive a word to use about this difficult and controversial battle). In some ways the Victorians and Edwardians had very simple, concrete minds. Because for 250 years or so the classics had been the pursuit of clever men, men who had the knack of doing it, an inversion took place: since it took clever men to do it, men doing it would become clever. The mind was like a muscle, once made strong by the classics it would be able to tackle anything. But the mind is not like a muscle, it is a great deal more complex. Many people of high intelligence failed completely at the classics. Many people brilliant at the classics failed at everything else but them. Yet—to what degree have we coped with that complexity today? True, we have realised that people can be good at different things, and now provide opportunities for them to become good at them. But to an overwhelming extent these studies have no direct relation to what students will do later. It is clear that the difference between us and the Victorians is one of degree not principle; we see the mind as a more complex muscle but still a muscle. The scholarly bias to our education comes directly from the Victorian defence of the classics which their schools had started teaching centuries earlier for quite different reasons.

The second, though related, principle underlying the Victorian defence was that what you read will affect your character. If you read moral books, you will become more moral; if you read immoral books you will become immoral. The same, it might be thought common sense, supposition underlies the entire corpus of Victorian children's books and most of the adult novels. The attitude was subtle. The object of education was to train the character, to change it, to make it wiser, more civilised, more profound, more humane. Since what you read affected, *stained* as it were, your mind directly, these effects could be brought about by reading. And the most civilised, profound, powerful and subtle literature the world had known was the classical.

Temple to the Clarendon Commissioners: "The real defect of mathematics and physical science as instruments of education is that they have not any tendency to humanise. Such studies do not make a man more human, but simply more intelligent."

This idea is still strong today, though–except for F. R. Leavis and American children's book publishers–it has now largely deserted literature and attached itself to television. But the fact is, despite immense research, there is virtually no evidence that what we read (or view) does affect us in this simple and direct way. Nevertheless, there are plenty of people, probably the majority, who will say that it does. We cannot therefore very well blame the Victorians for thinking the same.

It is part of Correlli Barnett's thesis against the public schools that the retention of the classics was made possible by our victory at Waterloo. After 1815 we'd won. There was no longer any need to compete and we could afford luxuries like a moral evangelical outlook on life, and an unrealistic curriculum even more unrelated to life than it had been before. This is an interesting idea, but it can remain only that. It is impossible to prove or disprove. My own feeling is that the forces and concepts we have been uncovering were so strong they would have operated no matter what our position in the world. They certainly continue to operate today when our position is the reverse of what it was after Waterloo and has been crystal clear for thirty years.

Quite apart from our position vis-à-vis our competitors, the pressure on the schools to extend their curriculum, particularly to include science, was considerable. Both the Clarendon and Taunton Commissions urged it, the Taunton one, in 1868, saying that there should be at least one science master for 200 boys and the public schools should build laboratories. Eminent scientists like Faraday, Huxley and Darwin argued that the classics were not, in fact, capable of training the whole mind. Honours Schools in science were formed at Oxford in 1850 and Cambridge in 1851. During the 1860s the criticism that England as a nation and the upper classes as a class could not afford to ignore the power of science and its attendant technologies became common.

From the late 1860s the great ice floe of the classics began to crack. At Eton (if in rather dilettante fashion) and Rugby some science had been introduced in the 1840s. Percival left Rugby a scientist and collected a fine staff of scientists at Clifton, three of whom became Fellows of the Royal Society. Uppingham introduced science. In the mid-1850s the way into the army and the Civil Service became via competitive exams and a wide range of subjects was allowed. By the 1880s nearly all the public schools had their "Modern" and "Army" sides—teaching science, German, French, English literature, history—to cope with this.

We should note other things about this period. Throughout the 19th century, Scottish education was a great deal better than English. The Academy movement at the beginning of the century forced the independent schools—Loretto School (1827), Morrisons (1813), the Edinburgh Academy (1824) and others—to adopt wide curricula. The Argyll Commission in 1864 found that one in 250 had some form of secondary education compared to one in 1,300 in England. Hours at the Scottish independent schools were twice as long as at Eton and Winchester.

The teacher-pupil ratio altered dramatically in the 19th century. This, a function of concentration, can be demonstrated by Sherborne. When Harper came there in 1850 he found forty boys and one master—himself. When he left in 1877 there were 278 boys and eighteen masters. The result of this—combined with the steadily improving calibre of the staff which followed the growing prestige of the public schools—meant that it was statistically much more probable that any pupil would meet a gifted or congenial master. Nearly every biography or autobiography from, say, 1870 on contains a reference to the one master who made life bearable, who stimulated in this subject or that, who changed a life.

Let us take the case of Winston Churchill. Churchill is always represented as a complete dunce at school (a legend he cultivated). Indeed he is the archetypal comforter of all those bad at work. In fact this isn't so. The truth is more interesting. Churchill was not in the least stupid nor bad at work; he was only bad at classics, a very different thing.

He went to Harrow in 1888 when he was twelve, and his first lesson set the pattern for all the rest.

"You have never done any Latin before, have you?" he said.
"No, Sir."
"This is a Latin grammar." He opened it at a well-thumbed page. "You

must learn this," he said, pointing to a number of words in a frame of lines. "I will come back in half an hour and see what you know."

Behold me then on a gloomy evening, with an aching heart, seated in front of the First Declension.

Mensa	a table
Mensa	O table
Mensam	a table
Mensae	of a table
Mensae	to or for a table
Mensa	by, with or from a table

What on earth did it mean? Where was the sense in it? It seemed absolute rigmarole to me. . . . However, there is one thing I could always do: I could learn by heart. And I thereupon proceeded, as far as my private sorrows would allow, to memorise this acrostic-looking task which had been set me.

In due course the master returned.

"Have you learnt it?" he asked.

"I think I can say it, Sir," I replied; and I gabbled it off. He seemed so satisfied with this that I was emboldened to ask a question.

"What does it mean, Sir?"

"It means what it says. Mensa, a table. Mensa is a noun of the First Declension. There are five Declensions. You have learnt the singular of the First Declension."

"But," I repeated, "what does it mean?"

"Mensa means a table," he answered.

"Then why does mensa also mean O table," I enquired, "and what does O table mean?"

"Mensa, O table, is the vocative case," he replied.

"But why O table?" I persisted in genuine curiosity.

"O table—you would use that in addressing a table, in invoking a table." And then seeing he was not carrying me with him, "You would use it in speaking to a table."

"But I never do," I blurted out in honest amazement.

"If you are impertinent, you will be punished, and punished, let me tell you, very severely," was his conclusive rejoinder.

However, because he was hopeless at Latin and Greek he remained three times as long as anyone else in the bottom form. Here he learnt English endlessly and, because he had an extremely gifted and exciting master, enjoyably. "I got into my bones the essential structure of the ordinary English sentence—which is a noble thing." Thus by chance a latent gift was encouraged and the foundations set for a prose and oratorical style so powerful, so clear, so expressive that not since those classical times which meant nothing to him have a leader's words so roused a nation. Later on, still officially in the lower school, he got a sixth-form friend to do his classical exercises, while he wrote his friend's essays. The essays were commended by Welldon the headmaster. It was now that Churchill contracted the habit of dictating what he wrote, so easily and thoroughly could he manipulate English. He won a prize for learning 1,200 lines of Macaulay's *Lays of Ancient Rome*. He did well in history, arithmetic and French. So far from being a dunce, Churchill was highly intelligent and, in their terms, did well at Harrow.

And it perhaps goes without saying that the top classical scholars were very good indeed. This tradition continued. Brilliant coteries of students from the sixth form who astounded examiners and, with a good master, could create a real academic school within the frame. (Even the frame worked fairly hard, at least for the first three years.) This work was highly competitive. It is during these years that there came the enormous proliferation of often quite valuable school prizes. And from the 1880s onwards exam interest became a fever. Lists were published in the papers and scanned minutely. The intensity was just as strong as today, even if the curriculum was biased.

It is this bias which must, finally, be emphasised; the fact that these developments were cracks only. The ice floe survived.

In the first place, although the "Army" and "Modern" sides were almost universal, they were despised, regarded as refuges for the second rate. Sometimes, as at Bradfield's "Army House", they were segregated in special houses. On the whole the standard of teaching was low. With foreign languages, frill treatment continued. Bullied Europeans, with strange names like M. Bulticaz, were expected to teach any continental language just because they were foreign. In the 1870s Repton had a polyglot Pole trying to teach French, German, Italian, Spanish and dancing. Sometimes they committed suicide. Hyde-Turner's 19th-century memoir has this laconic sketch: "Wiett, the German master: small with beard and glasses. Committed suicide about 1876." And this arrogant attitude to foreign languages and foreigners went deep into the English character. Dagoes began at Calais. In the popular novels the villain is usually a foreigner trying to smash Britain—a dago, a Teuton, a Jew, a Russian. No English hero ever bothered to learn a foreign language (by which he meant French) beyond the standard of Chardanal's First French Course. *"Nous avons craché dans les oignons,"* said Drummond to everyone's delight, when his aeroplane came down in an onion field.

The low standard was reflected in the tremendous growth of "Crammers" at the end of the century. In 1870 the purchase of commissions was abolished. More and more papers loomed up to confront public school boys, and few schools seemed able to jack the boys up enough to get them through. Hence "Crammers". Churchill, a genius at English, and high in other subjects according to Harrow standards, had to go to Captain James in the Cromwell Road in the 1890s: "It was said that no one who was not a congenital idiot could avoid passing thence into the army."

(One might note that even the congenital idiot did not have to despair. Until 1908 a back door into the army was via the County Militia and Volunteers.)

The move to science was extremely piecemeal. At Eton, it ranked below drawing. In 1875 the Devonshire Commission looked at 128 public and small endowed grammar schools: "Science is only taught in sixty-three, and of these only thirteen have a laboratory, and only eighteen apparatus, often very scanty. . . ."

Finally, the teaching of classics was largely a waste of time. Despite the groups of brilliant scholars, much of the learning was still simply learning by heart. Winchester was famous for repetition—"Standing Up". They were not so much learning as training for record-breaking sessions. One boy learnt the whole of a Sophocles play without a mistake. There were incredible feats; instances of 10,000, 13,000, even 16,000 lines learnt. Then, the ridiculous task completed, the lines were forgotten in a week.

But vast numbers did not even learn lines. They learnt nothing at all. Their school lives were entirely wasted. Again and again one comes across laments like that of Lord Robert Cecil, at school in the 1880s: "When I went up to the university after twelve or fourteen years' tuition in the classical languages I was unable to read even the easiest Latin authors for pleasure . . . we were taught no English literature. . . . Nor do I remember learning any history."

The Royal Commission in 1864 noted that boys often left school knowing nothing, neither Latin nor Greek, "ignorant also of geography and of the history of his own country, unacquainted with any modern language but his own and hardly competent to write English correctly".

And even for those who did pick up a smattering of Greek and Latin—what an appalling waste of time. "Six years of solid and undiluted classics" (Repton, 1875); "The dead languages were our portion and the tradition of pedagogy saw that they remained dead"; "The drone of the master's voice"; "Twenty-seven classes a week classics—just for repetition—for seven years"—boredom, that is the overwhelming impression of these years, monumental, stifling, paralysing boredom, rising, or rather heavily settling around the end of the 19th century like the miasma which sits above a stagnant and oxygenless pool through a long hot summer.

There were, however, two things which went some way to alleviate this boredom, two powerful ingredients in the public school concentration: games and sex.

CHAPTER 7

Games and Sex

"Evidently you have a high opinion of me?"
"Yes," said John.
The quiet monosyllable, so seriously uttered, challenged Desmond's attention. He stared for a moment at John's face. . . . Blood and mud from the footer disfigured it. But the grey eyes met the blue unerringly. Desmond flushed.
"You've stuck me on a sort of pedestal. . . ."
They were opposite the Music Schools. The other Manorites had run on. For a moment they stood alone ten thousand leagues from Harrow, alone in these sublimated spaces where soul meets soul unfettered by flesh. . . ."
Horace Annesley Vachell, The Hill

"One of the great sadnesses of my life is that none of my sons is queer."
Interview with a public school mother

At first sight nothing in the extraordinary structure the public schools were creating wasp-like about themselves is so astonishing as the part games came to play in their life by the end of the century. As usual, the detailed picture is complex because the schools developed at different speeds; there is a deliberate effort to introduce school-organised games at Eton in the 1840s, while Sherborne did not play its first match till 1893. But the general picture is quite clear.

Despite Eton, games in the early 1840s were still 18th century. The Winchester "Hot" was a savage battle. Moberly, the headmaster, said, "The idle boys, I mean the boys who play cricket".

From the 1850s on, organised games begin to spread with an ever increasing swiftness and intensity. I could give dozens of examples. Here are four: 1856, games are "recognised" at Shrewsbury. 1858, Tonbridge introduces cricket colours. In the same year Cotton completes his task at Marlborough and leaves. Significantly, one of the three great achievements he hopes to find on his return is—victory over Rugby at football. Alas, it is a dream never to be realised. He became Bishop of Calcutta and one dark night slipped from the gangplank of a steamer and vanished for ever into the turbulent waters of the Hooghly. Meanwhile, a little earlier, in 1855, the Count de Montalembert is wandering around Eton researching a book on Wellington. Mishearing some legend, he rambles into a lengthy fantasy; ". . . one understands the Duke of Wellington's *mot* when, revisiting during his declining years the beauteous scenes where he had been educated, remembering the games of his youth, and finding the same precocious vigour in the descendants of his comrades, he said aloud: *'C'est ici qu'a été gagnée la bataille de Waterloo'.*"

It is during the 1860s, 70s and 80s that the schools start to become obsessional. In 1860 Rugby had one fives court. By 1879 it had nine fives courts, two pavilions, cricket pitches, a gym and swimming bath. Winchester buys enormous amounts of land for pitches in the 1870s. Ridding, the headmaster after Moberly, says, "Give me a boy who plays cricket and I can make something of him." By 1889, when the first *Public Schools Year Book* comes out, there are 215 pages given to details of the schools and this is followed by 122 pages solid with the names of players and the results of matches. And sometime before this, in 1876, Sir Edward Creasy writes *Memoirs of Eminent Etonians.* He takes Montalembert and, since playing fields did not exist in 1876 terms in 1771, puts them in. Now Wellington is pictured passing them, musing on the excellence of games, the "manly character" they nurture and suddenly saying gruffly, "There goes the stuff that won Waterloo."

By the 1890s, and for many years to come, the obsession is universal, all-embracing, and sometimes so violent that it seems a form of madness. Sherborne, the school that was to become Fernhurst in *The Loom of Youth*, may have started late, but under the Reverend Frederick Brooke Westcott it soon caught up. A cycling blue who had ridden a penny farthing against Oxford, he attended all school matches in all weathers "with a frenzied interest", running round the touch line screaming in English, Greek and Latin. If a boy could speak at the end of a match it was a sign of inadequate effort and he was beaten. A senior could seize, was expected to seize, a new boy's umbrella and beat a scrum of juniors till the umbrella broke. The local railwaymen would put fog signals on the line to welcome victorious teams and the Reverend Westcott would preach a congratulatory sermon from the pulpit.

Nor was Westcott exceptional. Rather, he was the rule. Housemasters frequently broke down and wept when their houses lost. H. H. Almond the Headmaster of Loretto, a strong games school, had in later years to be restrained by force from watching matches because it was bad for his heart. It is now, in 1889, that Sir William Fraser adds elegance to Creasy's manly playing fields and Montalembert's wit (as the present Duke has noted, it is really a Napoleonic epigram, not one of Wellington's blunt statements): "The battle of Waterloo was won on the playing fields of Eton." Thus the past is the creation of writers, and history is continually being re-written to confer authority on the present.

This, then, is the outline. It is when we begin to look at it more closely that not only does the nature of the contagion become clearer but its spread, though still odd, ceases to be astonishing. It becomes quite easy to understand.

1 *The causes and consequences of the games obsession*

In the first place games are after all very exciting. The Japanese went, as a nation, sport-mad overnight. The money, time, energy and publicity devoted to them in the world today are arguably greater than to any other single pursuit. There are sound reasons for including them among school activities. Exercise, and the habit of exercise, is good for you. Not only is sport fun, it generates confidence. If your school wins matches it can be thought of as better than another school. It is pleasant to think of oneself in a stronger, "better" school. You feel more secure, confident that it can look after and teach you better. It is a well-known phenomenon that production in factories always rises when the home team wins.

To these general considerations, the public schools in the last half of the 19th century (and for many years into the 20th century) added their own peculiar impetus. We have seen in full the problem of caged energy, the rebellion at Marlborough, the need for discipline. This was what initiated games. Hawtrey introduced boat races between the houses, built fives courts, enlarged games pitches and encouraged matches with other schools, with this specifically in mind. The day he abolished Montem in 1847, one of the oldest Eton traditions, he arranged a cricket match as a diversion. He had feared rebellion. Nothing happened. Although the one thing to come from the recent research on the Marlborough Rebellion is that Wilkinson had made some effort to introduce games, it was Cotton who used them as an organised instrument of control.

At the same time the other disciplines and restrictions we have explored in those repressive and authoritarian societies generated considerable aggression. This often expressed itself in gang behaviour, with fierce team spirit. All this aggression could find outlet in sport. Football boots at Rugby were called "navvies"; these were heavily tipped with iron and had "a thick sole, the profile of which at the toe much resembled an iron-clad". Here is Orwell on football:

> I loathed the game and since I could see no pleasure or usefulness in it, it was very difficult for me to show courage at it. Football, it seemed to me, is not really played for the pleasure of kicking a ball about, but is a species of fighting. The lovers of football are large, boisterous, knobbly boys who are good at knocking down and trampling on slightly smaller boys. That was the pattern of school life—a continuous triumph of the strong over the weak. Virtue consisted in winning. . . .

Games are healthy, they are the test and the enjoyment of skills, they are exercises in co-operation; but principally they are canalised aggression. The prime object of playing a game is to win it. In a good many primitive tribes there are ritualised "games" where spears are taken on shields or turned away by other spears. We civilise it and call it cricket. Cricket is a sophisticated form of primitive combat by missile. It is important to emphasise this rather obvious point for the sake of future discussions.

There was a second impulse. Arnold, as we saw, was chiefly concerned with a boy's soul and therefore with his moral character. Soul was saved, character proved, in the fight against sin. A boy should fight manfully against sin, the effects of the struggle marking the face. He was to be "manly". Now this is an abstract, fairly complex concept, particularly for adolescents. How much easier and more exciting to judge such things in the simple, concrete world of games. Now character showed up in action: bravery in the face of the scrums, humility under your captain. And there was reverse pressure. The evangelical spirit meant that everything— prefects, the classics, fagging, games—needed an ethical justification. Between 1850 and 1890 games gradually took over entirely the whole nebulous area of "character", "manliness" and "tone".

By 1867 the *Marlburian* could write, ". . . a truly chivalrous football player . . . was never yet guilty of lying, or deceit, or meanness, whether of word or action." Games, when they involved some form of self-denying diet, were praised for the opportunity of self-abnegation. Above all, team spirit, an almost mystical submerging of self for the good of a little games "community", appeared to become all important (clearly discipline and drive to uniformity were also factors here). "The Bull" in *The Loom of Youth*: "If we are going to turn out good sides we must be in dead earnest the whole time. You imagine you are loyal to Fernhurst. My old sides followed me implicitly. I loved them, and they loved me. We worked together for Fernhurst; now, are you doing your best for Fernhurst?" Even losing lost its sting: ". . . tho' we got the worst of it, yet the spirit displayed by the losers was a most encouraging sight . . .", November 13th, 1883, Marlborough College House Report. Gradually, from a discipline, a diversion, games became a religion. Here is the fictional Glenalmond *circa* 1916:

> "Most excellent, Brown Quartus, you play like an angel, if angels play cricket and sometimes I am inclined to think that they do, for cricket is the nearest thing to poetry and religion except poetry and religion," the headmaster said. "And I think it is a matter for national pride that England should have kept this one game for herself and her Colonies, this—this prayer of a game whose movements, silences and slownesses so rhyme the monks' old sentry-go in the chancel."

Just as the classics trained your mind for anything, games trained mind, character and body for anything. It trained you for war—or at least the straightforward notion that a lad who'd had a good rugger training was well on the way to commanding troops certainly appealed to a good many soldiers and most schoolmasters—and this was often the reason for

the weakness of many School Corps before the 1914 war. Colonel
O'Callaghan-Westropp, a military member of the Royal Commission on
the Militia and Volunteers (1904): "I will put it this way. Situations may
arise in a good cricket or football team requiring a quick decision,
perhaps a shade quicker than a company commander with his line of
skirmishers in the field." If you'll believe that, as Wellington said, you'll
believe anything.

Because the point is—how true is all this? I do not mean how extensive
was this games domination; that is indisputable. But in general, do games
help "train" your character, make you braver, or more honest, fit you for
leadership in war or business? In particular, what affect did the emphasis
on team spirit have on those who submitted to it? I stress this because it is a
strong supporting argument for the "case" against the 19th-century and
early–20th–century public schools, particularly as mounted by Correlli
Barnett, that the continued preaching of team spirit gradually made this
more important than winning. The incentive to individual effort and
ambition was removed. This spread out; it no longer became "good
form" for individuals to strive for conspicuous success in any sphere of
life. Nationally, a "great" defeat, Dunkirk say, became more important
than a victory. Cricket, its "fair play", impressed the importance of
conforming to laws and accepted ways of behaviour. A "wrong" stroke
which hit the boundary was somehow less admirable than an elegant
late-cut which missed the ball.

In general terms, games probably have some effect on a person's
character—particularly as they affect one's playing of games. One will
learn to concentrate on a ball better, learn to stick out on the left wing and
wait for a pass, learn the discipline of hard training. Clearly these are of
some relevance to life later; but in my view the relevance is marginal.
Because you tackle your man "honestly", "cleanly", in full view of an
umpire, does not mean you will necessarily be honest or "clean" in
business or in married life. If you are conscientious and hard-working in
the outfield you may be extremely lazy in an office. The spheres are quite
different. Or take the example of warfare again, where even today a
conjunction might be supposed. In fact, the relation between games and
warfare is not nearly close enough to make the first any sort of training for
the other. You can be a brave fullback; it does not mean you will be brave
under fire. It is the difference between a few bruises and death. As a straight
road to physical health, games are no doubt useful to a soldier; one can
hardly dispute this. But there seems little evidence that German or French
officers got out of breath quicker than British in the 1914 war. They
seemed to have attained fitness, somehow or other, without playing
rugger. With the games mystique we are seeing that same *simplicimus* at
work which made Greek and Latin a total training for the mind.

With the practical effect of team spirit I would go further. Correlli

Barnett's view is the received one, and at first sight it seems obvious. But let us look closer.

As games reached their zenith around 1900–1910, so did the English cult of the amateur. Here Mansell in *The Loom* boasts about the house: "We are not going to set ourselves to win some rotten gym cup or house fives; we haven't time for that. We are amateurs. We play the hardest footer and the keenest cricket of all the houses, and that's where we stop. . . . We aren't pros who train the whole year round; we are amateurs."

The English amateur cult is usually represented as a class phenomenon. A "professional" was one who did it for money. Therefore he had to work for a living, therefore he was not a gentleman. Now this certainly came to underpin the idea of the amateur much later on. But at its inception the "professional" sportsmen were virtually non-existent; they were confined to a few jockeys and prize fighters (not relevant here) and to the (often ex-army) figures employed by the public schools. It was not until the 1920s and 30s that they existed in any amount, and required, therefore, to be set off in class terms, just as it was not until the sons of "trade" became numerous that they became defended against.

If we look carefully at Mansell's statement we see that pros are not people who are paid, but those "who train the whole year round". Mansell's men will win without really trying, just because they are so good. That is the force behind amateur. If you can win without trying, the supposition is that if you really tried you could be fantastic. It is a way of boasting. The entire English cult of the amateur has at its root the childish boasting and desire to impress which came from living in an open community of boys.

It is in this light we must examine team spirit. A major reason for the success of games, as I suggested, was the appalling boredom of the classics. Compared to them, games were at least concrete, explicable, alive, fun. They also embodied, in its most intense form, the intoxicating glory of school success. Here is *The Loom* again:

It is inevitable that the end of the summer term should be overhung with an atmosphere of sadness. . . . But for all that those last days are not without their own particular glory. Rome must have been very wonderful during the last week of Sulla's consulship. And in the passing of Meredith there was something essentially splendid. . . .

It takes place on the cricket field.

The house had only two wickets in hand, and still wanted over eighty runs to avoid an innings defeat. But Meredith was still in. It had been a great innings. He had gone in first with Mansell and watched wicket after wicket fall, while he had gone on playing the same brilliant game. Every stroke was the signal of a roar from the pavilion. The whole house was looking on. It was a fitting end to a dazzling career. It was like his life, reckless and magnificent. At last he mis-hit a half-volley and was caught in the deep for seventy-two.

As he left the wicket the whole house surged forward in front of the pavilion, and formed up in two lines, leaving a gangway. Amid tremendous applause Meredith ran between them. The cheering was deafening.

There are two points to note about this description: first it is about the success of an individual. And this is true of all accounts of games, whether factual in school magazines or in fiction; it is the boy who scores the magnificent try, gets a hundred, crashes home the goal, who is singled out. The captain of the boats at Eton in 1880 is "the most important boy in the school". And the whole history of games and athletics is precisely this, a succession of heroes: W. G. Grace, Don Bradman, Viv Richards, Pele, George Best. . . . These get the fame and applause and it was the same at public schools. The second point is that it is the description of a battle and a victory. I stressed the aggressive element in games and this remained true as well. It was victories that lights were put on lines for, and for which pulpits boomed; house magazines went wild, and novels reached their climaxes at victories—not defeats. It is quite absurd to say that team spirit replaced either individual effort or the desire to win.

What team spirit did, apart from provide some palliation for defeat, was to create a cloak under which individual achievement could seem less glaring and therefore less upsetting. Just as "amateur" was actually a form of boasting, so team spirit was a ritual way of showing and so containing, and therefore at the same time allowing full expression of, the ambitious individual's intense need to express aggression and achieve success.

The enormously powerful effect of games during this period can be seen in several other developments.

Solid fanatical figures evolved, one-dimensional, stripped of all but the simplest motivations. Men like T. C. G. Sandford at Marlborough before the 1914 war. He had been a schoolboy athlete there "who early learned how to train others . . . and became", as his obituary in the February 1943 *Marlburian* put it, "a very successful and rather terrific captain of house and school". He returned almost immediately as a master and, "a prodigy of physical energy", dedicated every second of the next thirty odd years to games. His house became a harsh little spartan state within the school, dominating it athletically, and with training so intense that Ulric Nisbet, who was there five years, never even had time to get out into the marvellous Wiltshire countryside to see Avebury, Silbury or Savernake Forest— all within twenty minutes of the gates. Every afternoon was devoted to games, and all Sunday, except for time-wasting breaks for chapel. Only in the worst conditions did T.C.G.S.'s house wear overcoats. When very occasionally released from their own games to watch a school match they could always be recognised on the touch line, shivering in football kit.

And these Thurber-like characters, strong of arm but with innocent uncomprehending brows which would knit fiercely over the simplest academic problem, hired purely as games coaches, had somehow to be fitted into the teaching staff. They filled the despised Army and Modern sides. There was Gower at Cranleigh, an ex-Welsh International "of meagre—indeed non-existent scholastic attainments". Raymond Mortimer, at Malvern in 1909, can remember one such teaching him maths. He rapidly understood the subject far better than his master.

By 1900–1914 the public schools, as far as the majority of their pupils were concerned, had really ceased to be academic institutions. "A great many people think of the public schools," J. H. Simpson, a Rugby master, wrote in 1900, "when they think of them at all, as being primarily places where boys learn to play games . . . the popular impression is in this matter broadly true." Great games figures were allowed to linger on for terms at school, on the grounds of what they "contributed". And naturally it made no difference if you were no good at games or disliked them. You watched them. They ceased even to have the justification of exercise. Memoir after memoir, corroborated in interview after interview, speaks of hours and hours and hours and hours watching games, while being dragooned by some obsessed and incoherent master, like Mr. Buller in *The Loom*: "As the school lined up behind their line, 'The Bull' strode behind them. 'What are you doing? Put some life into your game. Buck up, all of you; it is a filthy show. Guts!'"

It is hardly surprising that the fires of games enthusiasm, blown upon with such intensity and for so long, spread far beyond the confines of the public schools. Narrowly at first. The parents and Old Boys came to watch matches and soon the great occasions—the Eton and Harrow, the Regatta at Henley, Westminster v. Eton—became vast social celebrations of games and class, huge tribal gatherings reported in endless detail by the press. By 1863 the Eton and Harrow drew carriages five or six deep round Lord's, with 10,000 spectators. Just how far the Eton and Harrow moved from a competition can be seen from the fact that between 1819 and 1938 Harrow did not win a match. They finally won in 1939. The scenes were, obviously enough, "unprecedented".

In 1863 the rules of Association Football (in essence, no hands) were codified nationally at Charterhouse and in 1880 an old Carthusian side won the FA Cup. In 1871 public school Old Boys founded the Rugby Football Union. First across the whole of Britain, and down through the classes, next the Empire, finally the world. As public schools were set up in South Africa, Australia, India and New Zealand they took their games passion with them. Sometimes strange transformations occurred. At a Jesuit school in Feldkirch, Austria, where Conan Doyle went for a year, they played football on stilts. This is not the place to describe or explain the extraordinary enslavement which sport has gradually—but particularly in the last thirty years—cast right across the globe: from the Russian, Spanish, Italian, German and South American footballers, through the cricketers of India, Australia, the West Indies and South Africa, to the athletes of the US and Japan. . . . The point does not need labouring. Games are the greatest, indeed only, common denominator in the world today. There are other factors, other influences and, with athletics, provisos, but, incredible as it may seem, the essential seeds from which this world-blanketing growth has come can be located precisely in those tiny 19th-century boy communities which we are studying. It is true that, quantitatively at any rate, Britain's most significant contribution to the world at the present is not parliamentary democracy but the football, cricket and athletics invented by its public schools.

The automatic assumption that the upper-class Englishman should be a games player, and virtually nothing else, shows up in the popular literature. In Sapper's *Bulldog Drummond* books it is naked. Jim Maitland is famous "in three Continents" as a big game shot, and has been Amateur Heavyweight Boxing Champion of England. Drummond himself had been a sprinter and a boxer, and was still a Free Forresters Cricketer. "Tiny" Carteret had been capped seventeen times at rugger for England. Their weekdays were filled with playing or watching cricket or rugger; the weekends in country houses, shooting, fishing, golfing and playing more cricket. "Their rooms," says Usborne, "in Clarges Street, Half-Moon Street or Brook Street, were littered with cricket bags, golf-bags and gun cases; the walls were hung with boxing gloves, fencing foils and photographs of team groups from schooldays onwards." And because they are still schoolboys, they form easily into teams, with team spirit and captains. Maitland captained his team; Standish his, unless he was on Drummond's team. The captain got total obedience and loyalty, despite fearful wounds with lead piping or horsewhip. In *The Female of the Species* there are even colours (in the form of cufflinks). They are awarded to Joe Dixon who gets dragged into the plot and fights a good clean fight.

There are two final aspects of this "athleticism", the hideous word coined to describe the phenomenon. If the major rôle of a school is to teach games (and to create "character" through games) the academic goals, indeed all intellectual and artistic values of any sort, are likely to suffer. And that meant that anyone who wanted to pursue intellectual activities or was any good at them would suffer too. There were forces working towards this in the public schools in any case. The classics were so boring, their mastery so much a special skill, that most people were instinctively irritated at anyone good at them. It was unfair. Again, those who spend a lot of time working have, inevitably, to cut themselves off from the community—thus appearing to express a dislike of the community. The community resents this (unless, which was emphatically not the case at this time, a tenet of the community is to respect the individual *more* than itself). Time spent on games, on the other hand, is by its nature communal. And although success in other fields is for the fame of the community, games success is more obvious, more dramatic and more frequent. Lastly, the public schools took a fairly high proportion of stupid boys. This is said to be a result of Thring. My own view of Thring's influence in all fields is that it has been considerably exaggerated. The schools accepted lazy and stupid boys before him, and continued, with no noticeable rise, after him. It was simply a sizeable slice of their market. But it was another reason for the rise of games and another force towards the despising of intellectual and academic achievement.

As a result of these inherent tendencies this last aspect appears early. "'For I take it,' cries Old Brooke, in *Tom Brown*, 'that we're all in earnest about beating the school whatever else we care about. I know I'd sooner win Three School-house matches running than get the Balliol Scholarship any day!' (Frantic cheers.)"

The advent of the games obsession meant that esteem for academic and intellectual endeavour was, except for a tiny minority, almost entirely obliterated. Leonard Woolf, at St Paul's from 1893 to 1899, wrote: "Use of the mind, intellectual curiosity, mental originality, interest in 'work', enjoyment of books or anything connected with the arts, all such things, if detected, were violently condemned and persecuted." This theme appears again and again. Here is *The Loom*:

> The house was getting fed up with Simonds. It's all very well working in moderation for scholarships, but when it came to allowing games to suffer through it, it was getting serious. Private inclination cannot stand in the way of the real business of life. And no one would hesitate to own that he had come to Fernhurst merely to play footer.

There is always a degree of tension in a school between staff and pupils— the one rules, the other is ruled. Games were traditionally the sphere of boys, work the concern of masters; one might therefore expect the despising of work to be simply an expression of this tension. But in this instance many, perhaps most, of the masters supported the games ethos. "This attitude was not confined to the boys," wrote Leonard Woolf; "it was shared and encouraged by all the masters." "Hearty Y [William Plomer, Rugby, 1914] with his mania for cold baths and early morning runs and his habit of speaking of 'a slab of poetry'."

The contempt of the country's leading educational institutions and their staff for what they were supposed to be teaching—a dominant characteristic for some fifty years—is one of the oddest developments in the public schools. In the ordinary course of events one might be inclined to temper the judgment. Those who comment are, almost by definition, writers and intellectuals. They suffered considerably in this climate. They wanted revenge—and took it (Harold Nicolson's treatment of Marstock is, at the end, feline). But so universal is the picture—confirmed unanimously in interviews, in school magazines and histories, by rugger players when they too, with halting fingers, write their lives—that one has to accept it as broadly true. It had one considerable effect.

"The public school was the nursery of British philistinism. . . . The intellectual was, as he still is widely today, disliked and despised," wrote Leonard Woolf in 1960. This philistinism was a marked feature (only now a diminishing one) of the British middle and upper classes. Since they were never taught to read good books, to think, to look at paintings or listen to music, how could they regard them as anything but ridiculous? I think it would be difficult to say that Britain, as a result, had "worse" artists or fewer writers and musicians. She did not. But they had less popular esteem and success than on the Continent. They inclined to cut themselves off, and thus the significance in social terms of third-rate novelists like Sapper, Buchan or Galsworthy is increased. (One might note that the heroes in these books are frequently asinine, like Bertie Wooster. Sapper says Bull-dog Drummond has got a brain "and that's what becomes ice cold in an emergency". But in fact he seems almost mindless, certainly not educated beyond the shell form at his public school.) But in one area the effect was more important. A potent force in Europe has been the unemployed (and often unemployable) undergraduate—intellectual, rebellious, frequently active in politics, usually on the left. Britain never developed this—though there are signs we are doing so now. Not until later in the 20th century does this become relevant, but I note it here because its base is here.

As a result of this despising of the mind we see emerge in the 1900s yet another British archetype—the disguised male intellectual, hiding beneath a bluff exterior and a low tackle. Leonard Woolf: "I was sufficiently good at games to make intelligence and hard work pass as an eccentricity instead of being chastised as vice or personal nastiness"; Sassoon with his poetry, and his leg breaks and seventy not out.

And Leonard Woolf hints here at the final aspect of games, which further explains their attraction (particularly to masters), and that is games and sex.

> I do not think I am exaggerating [writes Harold Nicolson] when I say some boys derived the impression at Wellington that intellectual prowess was in some way effeminate and that it was only by physical prowess that one could manifest or even subscribe to, that aim of "manliness" for which alone we had all, teleologically, been sent to Berkshire.

Since games had become the way to prove you were manly, and manly meant overcoming sin, and the worst sin was sex—*ergo*, games overcame sex. The connection was direct. You were tired after sex. Games tired you out. Therefore after games you could not have sex. It is *simplicimus* again, and the whole equation was clear and explicit to all Victorian and Edwardian schoolmasters. The Headmaster of United Services College: "My prophylactic against certain unclean microbes was to send the boys to bed dead tired." (The same sort of equation attached itself to cold baths: sex made you hot, cold baths made you cold, therefore . . . etc.)

Once more, the popular literature shows how completely this was assumed and how deeply it entered the middle-class consciousness. Marton is unfit in *The Return of Bulldog Drummond*: "in rotten condition . . . the type he [Drummond] utterly despised. If fit, Marton would have been big enough and strong enough for anything on two legs; as he was, one good punch and he would have split like a rotten apple." Drummond, who is of course unbelievably fit and strong, describes this strength modestly but revealingly. "Oh, I can push a fellah's face in if it's got spots and things."

I said the equation was explicit, but explicit was, as we know already from Kibroth-Hathaavah, the last thing anything to do with sex would be. The Headmaster of USC might have been combating some form of lice. We have seen before how the overtones of sex, because undefined by precise language, infected all boyish "sins". The same sort of ramification happened to the public schools here. An interesting demonstration of the sort of elaboration that could take place can be traced in Buchan. Buchan did not go to a public school. But, as new arrivals to a class or a religion often do, in some instances he absorbed and expressed upper class *mores* even more thoroughly than they did themselves.

In his books cold baths (or icy plunges in freezing tarns before breakfast) and violent exercise are essential for the health of any decent fellow. His heroes indulge in both constantly and ferociously. Buchan likes nothing better than to get them out on to a moor and make them run until they drop. There is even evidence he thought hot baths were bad. Certainly Mr. Craw in *Castle Gay* (a title Buchan could not have chosen today) finds his health and outlook improving in the specific absence of hot baths.

Exercise leads to exhaustion; but from exhaustion as a result of exercise Buchan, following the unconscious logic of *simplicimus*, marched out to worship exhaustion of all kinds. Exhaustion became an end in itself since exhaustion stops sex (and is sex). Usborne, with his usual percipience, though not, I think, aware of this exact connection, charts the way Buchan heroes are always exhausted, seeking it as an alcoholic seeks drink. Hannay three or four times manages to resolve a crisis simply by being exhausted. Almost unconscious with malaria or hunger or just the sheer distance he has run, suddenly his brain clears and he becomes simple. In this simplicity he solves the clue, spots the cipher. Adam Melfort, in *A Prince of the Captivity*, never stops running from the start of the book and finally runs himself to death in the Alps of Italy. Leithen, the main Buchan hero after Hannay, had a history of exhaustion since he won the mile at Eton.

That games and exercise could solve the "sex problem" immeasurably increased their power in the school curriculum. Schoolmasters fell upon the answer with relief. Warre, for example, suddenly saw a way out of his massive confusion. "A keen participation in athletic sports," he testified, ". . . is an antidote to luxurious and extravagant habits, to drinking and vice of all kinds."

And yet—were they right? Does exercise—or anything else—have this effect? Perhaps we should once again look closer at the nature and the strength of the great tides these courtiers of Canute thought they could turn back.

2 Sublimation and public school sexual passion

Whatever the precise degree of significance you assign to sex, few educated people today, I imagine, would deny that its importance is considerable. It is an activity which affects many other crucial areas— marriage, child-upbringing, social relationships, art, mental health, etc. It is also an instinct which is at its strongest, and yet also more readily influenced than at any time since childhood, in adolescence. Any book, therefore, which has as its subject the education and upbringing of adolescents would, one might think, be considered almost frivolous if it did not try to deal quite fully with this problem. Yet curiously enough this is true of almost every study of British public schools.

Take John Dancy, who wrote a book called *The Public Schools and the Future* in 1963. In many ways this is a highly intelligent and interesting work, remarkable for its clarity. But when dealing with the effects of segregating boys away from girls (the book is devoted entirely to boys' schools) and of the homosexual "attachments" that result, he says this is "probably" a natural phase of adolescence. Besides, it is just as common in day schools. And in any case it is perfectly all right from a long-term point of view.

It is quite clear he has made no attempt to study the subject at all, even cursorily. His evidence that such behaviour is just as common in day schools is taken—it is almost unbelievable—from *girls' day schools*. The other two hopeful assumptions are, in general, also quite untrue. Mr. Dancy, perhaps wisely for his peace of mind, makes no effort to explore them. Matters which will strongly affect the most intimate and important areas in the lives of the boys who are presumably his ultimate concern are dismissed in two and a half airy pages.

Perhaps the first thing to establish is the reality or otherwise of sublimation. This is clearly of direct relevance to the whole games mystique from the 1860s onwards. But it remains central to the public schools right up until today. By 1936, at Bedales but also at several other schools, art has replaced games. Sublimation is possible and boys should be given music, painting and drawing "without stint". Dancy talks of "the authorities making every effort to divert such emotions". I found that most public school staff vaguely believe in the value and existence of sublimation (plays are a great "outlet" today); nor is it just schools. The 1974 British cricket eleven in Australia were only allowed to sleep with their wives twenty-one times during the whole five-month-long visit. The tour was a disaster.

The idea behind sublimation is that it is possible to divert sexual energy into other, non-sexual channels in the same way as nervous energy is shunted from one part of the nervous system to another, or as electricity is switched to new paths; and these new channels are often the "higher" levels of activity like art, literature and science. (Sublimate comes from the same root as sublime.) It is a very old concept, going back, through the tormented struggles of St. Augustine, to Hebraic, Greek and even more ancient mysticisms. It was first put forward as a scientific thesis by Freud in 1938, and since him treatment has simply involved faithful acceptance and repetition of the doctrine. The grave drawback to Freud's presentation is that he merely formalised the age-old ideas. It was dogmatic and entirely without supporting evidence. It is hard not to suspect that it was in reality just a subjective expression of his own desperately sex-starved hopes.

It was this situation that Kinsey and his fellow researchers set out to remedy. Included in his enormous study were a series of carefully designed programmes to find out whether sublimation existed, its extent, the methods employed and diversions chosen, and the effects. He started with five principles (Kinsey's italics):

If sublimation is a reality, it should be possible to find individuals whose erotic responses have been reduced or eliminated, *without nervous disturbance*, as a result of an expenditure of energy in utterly non-sexual activities . . . persons of proved sexual capacity . . . whose energies are not merely dulled or suppressed.

Having decided this, he had one further problem. He could have looked among high-rating males to get persons "of proved sexual capacity", and searched out those whose activities would have been still more frequent if there was not some sublimation. Clearly, this would be rather complicated. It seemed more sensible to look at the lower-rating males and see what proportion of these low rates were the result of sublimation. He also looked at a large group of highly religious segregated males whose avowed aim was sublimation.

First, however, he turned to the lower-rating males, and at once, to his dismay, over half (52·5%) of the sample vanished. So far from having a proved capacity, he found the reverse. They had never, at any time in their history, given evidence that they were capable of anything but low rates of activity—one or two orgasms a fortnight.(I got a faint, almost subliminal feeling that Kinsey rather disapproved of low rates of activity. His high raters often seem to be lawyers or scientists of "the highest repute".) Even when they put themselves deliberately in erotic situations they were unable to respond except once in several weeks. Such fundamentally apathetic people, he found, were the ones most insistent that sublimation was a simple and fulfilling way of using sexual energies. But such inactivity was no more sublimation of sex drive than blindness or deafness are sublimations of the power to see or hear.

It would take a long time to follow his careful and painstaking analysis; but bit by bit the sample melted away until "if then one removes those who are physically incapacitated, naturally low in sexual drive, sexually unawakened in their younger years, separated from their usual sources of sexual stimulation, or timid and upset by their suppressions, there are simply no cases which remain as clear-cut examples of sublimation".

It was at this late stage Kinsey discovered his group of highly religious segregated males. It is clear he fell on them with delight. They seemed ideal: most were in their twenties (82·8%), most college trained, and they were sexually extremely restrained. "Many of these males are belligerently defensive of their sexual philosophy. Some of them are vociferous in claiming that they are perfect examples of sublimation, and many outsiders look on the group as sexually sublimated."

But once again, on examination, the evidence deteriorated and then vanished. Certainly, the incidence of pre-marital intercourse was far less than that found in the whole population (74% of the figure), but the incidences of masturbation and homosexual contact were almost identical. Furthermore, a number of psychiatrists who dared to enter the belligerent group reached the conclusion that a high proportion was extremely neurotic. Several of them were under psychiatric treatment at the time Kinsey's interviewers called.

Kinsey, with the care that characterises the report, does not go nearly as far as an Augustinian Sister of Meaux, quoted in a book published recently about nuns: "You can't sublimate it. You can't suppress it. You simply have to damn well sacrifice it." His findings neither prove that sublimation does not exist, nor that it is not possible. What they do prove is that "among the many males who have contributed to the present sample, sublimation is so subtle, or so rare, as to constitute an academic possibility rather than demonstrated actuality." How much more academic it must be now, and must have been in the past, to public school boys and girls, the majority of whom, one imagines, don't want to sublimate, don't need to, and don't know how to.

As to the effects of athletics and sports, so vast was Kinsey's sample

(12,000), that it was possible to isolate and study different groups. Those taking part in games included people of both high and low outlets, but it was plain that a lot of exercise increases the frequency of sexual performance appreciably. Victorian and Edwardian schoolmasters were actually fanning the very fires they thought they were putting out.

We saw when discussing masturbation that most (95%) of all males are sexually active by the age of fifteen. It is important to get a clear picture of just how active "active" is. The *average* number of orgasms is about five a week. But nearly a quarter (22·3%) have a good deal more, two or three a day not being uncommon. The maximum period of sexual performance is around sixteen or seventeen. Not later. But statistics obtained from pre-adolescent sexual behaviour suggest strongly that in fact peak capacity is in the early teens. For example multiple orgasm—two, three or even more over a few hours—is not unusual before fifteen. The figures for maximum performance were taken from the married group, and marriage began at sixteen. Had the figures been taken in a society where marriage began earlier, then it is probable the peak would have been in the early teens. There is also considerable evidence that most individuals would be far more active sexually if they were not restrained by convention and fear. For instance, the high-rating group contained nearly half (49.4%) of all the underworld who contributed to the study, and this sample was distinguished by continually and openly defying convention and law.

This explosively strong instinctive force was caged, therefore, during the very years it was most powerful. It could not be sublimated. It had to find expression. As a result the public school experience was overwhelmingly one of erotic and romantic passion. It is important to bring this alive, to try to feel what it was like to be an adolescent part of, contributing to, subject to that intense sexual excitement. It is the final and most significant element in the public school concentration; only when its strength and nature have been fully grasped, even, if possible, imaginatively lived, will we be able to understand fully what it was like to be in a public school and thus be in a position to appreciate some of the most profound effects of that experience.

Schools which allowed their pupils separate bed-sitting rooms—Dartington and Eton are early examples—provided easier opportunities for an active erotic life. Robin Maugham was at Eton in 1929. Here, in a description which catches the extraordinary physical vividness, freshness and sharpness of early sexual experience, is his account of his affair with Drew. Both boys are aged fourteen.

Maugham, although extremely attractive, is not popular. Nevertheless he has realised that Drew—"dark-haired and lithe, and there was an odd secretive look about his lean face and dark eyes. He was a fine athlete and a favourite of M'Tutor [the housemaster] for that reason"—has been watching him:

One winter evening after M'Tutor had made his nightly round, the door of my little room opened and Drew came in and closed it softly behind him. By the glow of the fire which we were allowed twice a week I saw that he was wearing only a dressing gown. He sat down on the chair by my small table which I used as a desk.

"I want to talk to you," he said quietly.

"Talk to me tomorrow," I whispered back. "There'll be a hell of a row if you're caught here."

"I won't get caught," Drew replied. "M'Tutor's done his rounds, and he won't come back because he's got a dinner party tonight. I saw all the cars outside."

"What do you want to talk about?" I asked.

At first Drew explains that he, Maugham, must try to be more like the other boys, use their language and slang, etc., if he wants to be more popular. But then, that winter evening:

Drew got up from the chair and came and sat at the end of my bed.

"You're still pretty green, aren't you?" he said.

"I suppose so," I answered.

"You play with yourself, of course. You toss yourself off?"

I could feel myself blushing. "Yes," I said, "sometimes."

"Have you ever done it with anyone else?"

"No."

"But someone must have tried."

I thought of Neal with his freckled face. "Yes," I answered.

"Then why didn't you do it?"

"I'm not sure, really," I said.

"I bet I know why," Drew said. "It was because you were scared. You were scared of being found out."

"Perhaps."

"But what if you were dead certain you'd *never* be found out? Then what?"

"I'm not sure."

"Do you think it's wrong?"

"People think it is."

"Not all people don't. Some people who are really intelligent go in for it. Shall I tell you a secret? Promise you'll never tell any of the others?"

He then tells Maugham of his own seduction in the last terms at his prep school, by a boy and by a master:

I was silent. Drew's story had revolted me. I wondered if it was true.

"So you see," Drew said, "there's nothing wrong with it so long as you don't get found out. And if you swear to keep it a secret, and I swear I'll never tell a soul, then—if we did it—there isn't a chance we can ever be found out."

I was silent. I could feel my heart thudding against my chest, and I was afraid. I felt I was walking in darkness near to a precipice. I knew we would both be expelled if we were found out.

The "level gaze" of Dr. Thomas Arnold.

Dr. Vaughan of Harrow, and J. A. Symonds
at Oxford at the time he precipitated the
terrible scandal.

A thrashing—by
Du Maurier.

Rough justice by
the boys—the
famous moment
when Flashman
is defeated by
Tom and East in
*Tom Brown's
Schooldays*.

"I've been mad about you ever since I first saw you," Drew said. "Quite crushed on you."

I was certain that at least this was the truth, because I could remember that each time I looked at him in prayers, he had been staring at me. But I was still frightened.

"Wait till tomorrow night," I said hesitantly. "Give me time to think about it."

But even as I spoke I knew I wanted it now. . . . The boy was sitting at the end of my bed. Suddenly he got up, and I was afraid he would go. But he didn't go. Very slowly he took off his dressing gown and threw it on the chair and stood before me naked. His shoulders were heavy, his skin was very smooth, his waist and thighs so delicate that his genitals seemed almost obscenely large.

"Please," he said.

"I promise I'll let you know in the morning."

"No," he answered. "It's got to be now."

I was silent. A coal flashed in the grate, and I saw that his whole body was taut and trembling. I could feel the power of his desire surging through the little room.

"Please," he urged. "You've got to say 'yes' now, otherwise I'll just stand here waiting all night."

I laughed because I was happy. I knew that at last something a part of me had longed for . . . was going to happen.

"All right."

Slowly and quietly he slipped into my bed and put his arms round my neck. I pressed his lithe body against me. The skin of his waist was very warm and smooth. I wanted to remain in that wonderful state of calm mixed with the most intense happiness I had ever known. But soon Drew's body began to move and he gently turned away from me, so I could caress his lean back and heavy shoulders. Then he took my hand and guided it so that presently our bodies were joined together.

Their affair, physical, passionate, the only happy moments Maugham knew, continued for two years. He had Drew whenever he could, and Drew taught him all sorts of ways in which they could satisfy each other with incredible and delicious fiery swiftness:

Drew was waiting for me one day when I came into my room. He beckoned me over to him and told me to lock the door. This was dangerous because a strict house rule forbade one to lock one's door. It was possible to jam it shut with a scout's stave, but this was not allowed and could be punished by a caning.

"Don't be a fool," I said to Drew. "Anyone might come in."

"Don't worry," said Drew. "It's all right."

And he took my right hand and put it into his pocket. But he had cut the outer seam so that my hand slipped right in and touched the flesh between his thighs.

"You do the same with your trousers, and we can always pull back our hands at a second's notice."

It was passions such as these, though not necessarily expressed or even consciously acknowledged, which seethed throughout public schools. Eyes met, desired figures were glimpsed in the distance and pursued (or fled from); at night, in the crowded dormitories, fantasies hovered thick in the darkness above the creaking beds while their physical release poured out in masturbation. They were, and are, the most sexual places in the world. C. S. Lewis, in a book *Surprised by Joy*, described how each term, but particularly at the start of the school year, new boys at Malvern were eagerly studied by the rest of the school to see who was attractive. The book was put in the library, but this passage was continually cut out by Old Malvernians, creeping in in secret, deeply ashamed. They need not have worried—the practice was universal. Sexual dramas, who was attracted to whom, were major items in school gossip. "Hunter," wrote Alec Waugh, "was rather a nonentity; his chief attraction was that he usually had the last bit of scandal at his finger tips. It was his boast that he had sufficient evidence to expel half the Fifteen and the whole Eleven." And, as they did in school life, sexual scandals provide localised climaxes to the school novels. In the early ones—disgusted climaxes, often short. *The Hill*: "Among the fifth form boys of the Manor was a big coarse-looking youth of the name Beaumont-Greene [who] . . . ran, hot foot, to anything which would yield pleasure to his body." He doesn't wash. His father is "in trade". One day, one of the young heroes, Kinlock, goes "off-colour". It transpires that Beaumont-Greene has come hot-foot and threatened him:

"Go on," said John grimly. "No, you needn't go on. I can guess what this low cad is up to."
"He said he'd be my friend, as if I'd have a great beast like that for a friend."
John goes to the beast and . . .

And so on. Beaumont-Greene is humiliated, Kinlock regains colour. In the later novels sexual dramas, ending in expulsion, are, as in *The Loom* for example, sympathetically treated.

It might be wondered what proportion of boys actually physically made love. This is impossible to answer. There has been no Kinsey of the public school. The nearest we come to him is Dr. Royston Lambert, who analysed the public schools during the 1960s in a series of painstaking and lengthy research studies. He does not go into this (at least I don't think so; the massive tomes are heavy going). He does, however, confirm one thing I'd noticed myself, and that is the way in which homosexuality was sometimes fashionable and then abruptly not among the boys of a particular school; and how schools differed in the way they accepted positive attitudes to homosexual behaviour. Why? His researchers could find no satisfactory answer. My own solution is based on ant behaviour. When an ant nest is opened, I believe, it is possible to see that rescue and repair work start at various haphazard centres and from these spread out to inspire the whole colony. These centres of energy and initiative cannot be located on a single leader ant, but rather to an area where four or five exceptionally energetic ants happen to find themselves side by side. They mutually excite each other and create, as it were, sufficient momentum of activity for it to spread outwards. So with public schools—only in the case of sexual fashion it might be five or six highly sexed boys who are prepared to defy convention, by chance arriving in the same house or in the sixth form together. They might be followed by a particularly puritan group.

This is guesswork. There can be no doubt about the phenomenon, both as regards the differences between schools and within the same school at different periods. Malvern in the 1914 war was repressed sexually; and Wellington in the 1890s had made homosexuality unfashionable. The boy disapproval of homosexuality could be terrifying and revolting. At one school in the 1950s a sixteen year-old boy was expelled for "dirty practices". The night before he left, some boys made a solution of treacle and water and gave him an enema of this with a bicycle pump. The next day he had to carry his suitcase on foot from the school to the station. The route was lined with boys hurling eggs, tomatoes and filth at him. At Sherborne in 1916, on the other hand, the bloods were expected to have other boys—". . . and look at the bloods, every one of them as fast as the devil. . . ." At Oundle in 1920, when Sanderson asked any boy who had been passing notes to stand up, half the school rose; according to Brian Inglis, at Shrewsbury around 1930, it was "done" to have love affairs and romantically to sigh over boys. I had been reading evidence which suggested that Haileybury towards the end of the 19th century had made homosexuality unfashionable. When I had to go to discuss life at the same school between 1921 and 26, I met my informant at a London club and he appeared somewhat taken aback when I arrived with folder and sheets of paper for my notes. "We're not really allowed to transact business in the club," he said. "We'll go to the Cat-nap. I don't suppose the members will notice. Keep your voice down." After we had had several large drinks, I followed him past marble pillars and leather armchairs to an area partially screened from the totally uninterested members. We spoke in low voices, and I kept my notes to a minimum—curriculum, discipline, conventions, games, the Empire. Finally, I mentioned sex; did the boys encourage it? "Oh yes, dear me, yes," the plump face glowed, the eyes darted; "there was a great deal of sex, a *great* deal. I had an enormous amount— but I wish I'd had more. You slipped someone a piece of paper—'Will you come for a walk on the heath?' If they agreed it was more or less certain they were willing. Boys always enjoyed carrying notes from A to B if they were in different houses. There wasn't much time. One had to snatch it. There was a moment between supper and prep ideal for sex. You could slip up to your study with someone whose eye you'd caught." He got pinker and pinker, tones more and more animated, the stately walls rang to his voice and we began to be the object of curious glances—"Oh yes, *masses* of sex. Make you a bugger?—certainly not. I don't think so. The most active person I knew became a tremendous womaniser. Ralf Rollball went to bed with everyone."

As far as I can judge, from interviews and reading, and allowing for differences between school and school, perhaps some twenty-five per cent had sexual relations with each other on any regular basis.* And these relations could range all the way from the passionate eroticism of Drew and Maugham to the crudest form of experiment and victimisation. At Wellington in the 1930s the vice was sensational, with young boys being virtually raped. An informant, a psychiatrist, described to me how at Bedford at about the same period there was a boy, New, whom they all used to masturbate. One day they noticed two naked wires high up in the wall, but lifting New could not quite bring him and the wires together. So they lifted him and then also took a bugle and touched one end to the wires, the other to his penis. "There was a tremendous flash and he screamed. I swear to you his penis changed colour. I can hear his screams to this day." It is not surprising that beautiful boys were often too frightened to move and spent terms cowering in their studies (compare John Dean's plea that he was too attractive to be sent to prison).

"Most good schoolmasters," said Evelyn Waugh (he was writing about J. F. Roxburgh of Stowe) ". . . are homosexual by inclination—how else could they endure their work?—but their interest is diffuse and un-acknowledged. J.F.'s passions ran deep." He adds later, "I do not think he ever gave them physical release with any of his pupils." Noel Annan, in his excellent biography of Roxburgh, comments that schoolmasters, and their motives for teaching, are more varied than that. But Waugh's state-ment contains a general truth. If a fair (but incalculable) proportion of public school masters were homosexual, on the whole they did not satisfy their inclinations on their pupils. It was not uncommon, as we have seen; but it remained the exception. Men of this sort were often instinctively encouraging to the homosexual underworld. More and more as the 20th century progresses, kindly masters, not necessarily homosexual at all, respond sympathetically to (usually by ignoring) the desperate attempts of their pupils to come to terms with a sexually intolerable situation. And even before then, during the last quarter of the 19th century, there developed a form of aesthetic, chaste homosexuality—a product of

---

*This estimate is to some extent supported by Kinsey's findings that twenty-seven per cent of all males had homosexual contacts leading to orgasm between the ages of eleven to fifteen, thirty-three per cent in their later teens.

manliness crossed with the classical curriculum—whose hero was a public school Greek boy hurling a javelin. This cult is exemplified by men like William Cory at Eton, poet of aesthetic manliness, celebrating boyish exploits on river and with rifle, and peering short-sightedly but with passion at the sports he was too blind to join.

An interesting observation on this minority group of sympathetic staff occurs in a book called *The Vanishing Adolescent* by Edgar Z. Friedenberg. He postulates a clinical type with the condition *subject homo-eroticism*. These are men who have great anxiety about heterosexual relations and therefore retain the erotic attitudes of pre-adolescence. They see young adolescent boys taking the next step of development which they were unable to take, and identify with them. The feeling of a man of this sort towards boys is tender, and often over-protective since he is by definition over-anxious. It is called *subject* homo-eroticism because, initially, it has no specific object—he loves boys generally because it is a way of loving the "boyishness" in himself, and is also a way, by identifying, of reminding himself of the time when he was last sexually "happy". He is not exactly adolescent all his life, but he is caught, sexually, in the predicament of early adolescence and escapes by loving the young men he might have become. He is often a very good teacher, because he understands adolescents (he is one), and he is ardently protective (he is protecting himself). Because he is intensely subjective, he is very good at close analysis of his own condition and all its constituents, hence he is frequently an artist (Friedenberg cites Henry James and Proust). This quality of intense self-examination is highly germane to adolescence; but it frequently produces minds which are in general highly critical, and for this reason homosexuality is least accepted by societies undergoing intense social change. Authorities in such potentially unstable societies want unquestioning obedience, not criticism. Friedenberg instances the challenge to the Greek aristocracy by the popular leaders of the time and the ensuing death of Socrates; and the rise of the middle classes in Prussia during the 19th century when homosexuality became punished by imprisonment.

I put this in because I think it illuminates a certain sort of public school master; I am not sure how true it is generally. I would not have thought Socrates was subject homo-erotic. Our society is changing very fast indeed but we are more tolerant to adolescents and homosexuals than for 140 years. But certainly it was true of Victorian and Edwardian society, and without pausing to discuss the historical validity of Friedenberg's thesis, we can end this section by re-emphasising that the overwhelming reaction of public schools and their staff, and of society in general, to anything overtly homosexual was repressive and savage to a degree. This was true of the years up to 1900 and in many instances into the 1950s and beyond.

You will remember Benson, Headmaster of Wellington in the 1850s, clambering along the tops of cubicles laying entanglements of wire. There is no need to add to the examples I gave then, but one aspect is important. From 1850 and 60 onwards junior boys began to live separately. Prep schools sprang up. And this separation was enforced within the schools; while sexual repression was a further disciplinary reason, and among the most powerful, for a rigidly controlled time-table.

> The authorities [wrote Harold Nicolson] in their desire to deprive us of all occasion for illicit intercourse deprived us of all occasion for any intercourse at all. We were not allowed to consort with boys not in our own house: a house consisted of thirty boys, whom ten at least were too old and ten too young for friendship; and thus during those four years my training in human relationships was confined to the ten boys who happened more or less to be my contemporaries. In addition, one was deprived of all initiative of action or occupation. The masters took a pride in feeling that not only did they know what any given boy should be doing at that particular moment, but they knew exactly what the said boy would be doing at three thirty p.m. six weeks hence. . . . And the vices which this system was supposed to repress flourished incessantly and universally, losing in their furtive squalor any educative value which they might otherwise have possessed.

Both these conditions, but particularly the first, continued well into the 20th century. Brian Inglis at Shrewsbury in the 1930s, Derek Verschoyle at Malvern in the 1920s (where the lavatories stood doorless)—but there is hardly a school where fear of sex did not rigidly keep the age groups apart. Acting was discouraged because it led to sex. The randy life of Charterhouse when he was there had left Roxburgh with certain inhibitions. The seats in chapel did not face each other, nor was the choir raised up; thus he hoped to discourage the exchange of ravenous glances. Betjeman would not have agreed. Seats facing in chapel were all right: "an inducement to love; a corrective to lust."

Love—there is the crucial word. Denied expression physically, their passions turned to love; and love, frequently, of the most passionate, romantic and idealised intensity. And it was not just—or even principally —the transmuting of blocked sexual passion into something the society, and therefore the individual, could find acceptable. Pace Dancy, and with some provisos later, boys of fifteen or sixteen are usually quite ready to begin relationships and love affairs with girls. No one in the centuries before the 19th was surprised that the protagonists in one of our literature's great love stories—Romeo and Juliet—were sixteen and fourteen. But at public schools they only had boys. Where twenty-five per cent had lust affairs, at the same time, and quite distinct from these, ninety per cent, in fact or fantasy, had love affairs, by which I mean romantic and, in fact if not fantasy, platonic passions. "The only thing that kept me going," said John Betjeman, "was love. I never dared touch anyone. I thought I would have gone to gaol—and hell." Where lust dramas provided localised climaxes, love is a major theme in nearly all books about these schools, and the only theme in some.

3 *Love*

The Hill is subtitled *A Romance of Friendship*. (Romantic friendships was the name given to these love relationships.) It is an account of the love of John Verney for Desmond (Caesar) and his jealousy of Scaife, whom Desmond also loves.

Quite early on John Verney is looking at himself in the mirror ("ruefully", of course). Desmond comes in. John complains about his face:

> "Your head is all right, old Jonathan. And your voice is simply beautiful." He spoke seriously, staring at John as he had stared in the speech-room when John began to sing. "I came here to tell you that I felt odd when you were singing—quite weepsy, you know. You like me, old Jonathan, don't you?"
>
> "Awfully," said John.
>
> "Why did you look at me when you sang that last verse? Did you know that you were looking at me?"
>
> "Yes."
>
> "You looked at me because—well because—bar chaff—you—liked—me?"
>
> "Yes."
>
> "You like me better than any other fellow in the school?"
>
> "Yes; better than any other fellow in the world."
>
> "Is it possible?"
>
> "I have always felt that way ever since—yes—since the first moment I saw you. . . . You smiled at me, Caesar. It warmed me through and through. I suppose when a fellow is starving he never forgets the first meal after it."
>
> "I say. Go on; this is awfully interesting."
>
> "I can remember what you wore. One of your bootlaces had burst—"
>
> "Well; I'm—"
>
> "I had a wild sort of wish to run off and buy you a new lace—"
>
> "Well of all the rum starts I—"

And so on. However odd the 1890 language, it is charged language, the language of love.

These romantic friendships were often—indeed usually—complex. They were complex, in the first place, because, as Robert Graves puts it, they were frequently "heterosexually cast"—the boy had to be a girl. Therefore he was younger (here is one explanation for the enormously long time fagging has persisted), beautiful, in another house perhaps, in need of protection; above all, the relationship had to be chaste—not just because guilt and fear dictated repression—but to preserve this central illusion. The chastity of these older/younger boy relationships—as opposed to the lust-satisfying exchanges between contemporaries—does, if one believes the vast proportion of the evidence, and I see no reason not to, seem to be true.

In this sense, then, complete obtainability was not the point—indeed it is the delicious and agonising difficulties which haunt the love stories. The great love of Cyril Connolly's life at Eton (possibly of his entire life) was Nigel—"dark hair, green eyes, yellow skin and a classic head with the wistfulness of a minor angel in a Botticelli". Connolly fell passionately, physically, spiritually—and chastely—in love with him. Nigel was one and a half years younger, so technically not allowed to be seen. This made endless subterfuges necessary—notes, signals from a distance, wonderful glances exchanged as they passed in the corridors—"the intrigues were worthy of Versailles or Yildiz". In such difficult soil, love blooms:

> At the house match I asked Nigel who he liked best in the school. Langham? "Second best." Loxley? "Fourth best," and so on. He also asked me. We realised that we had both omitted "first best" and that the only people we had not mentioned had been each other. I experienced the thrill not untinged with apprehension by which the romantic recognises reciprocated love.

These friendships, these loves were heightened—and also made more difficult—because adolescence is the time of idealism (Starbuck in *The Psychology of Religion* notes that most religious conversion takes place at sixteen): before life has thumped and battered for a few years, there seems no reason why everything should not be perfect—including love. And the changes, and so jealousies and miseries this brought about, were added to because adolescence is also a time of self-discovery:

> finding out
> What you really are. What you really feel.
> What you really are among other people.

So Eliot in *The Cocktail Party*. To find out means, among other things, to experiment with people—to love and copy first one, then another, then another.

And they were caught up, these affairs, in that general ecstasy when nature, poetry, music, youth, love, seem to unite in blurred gusts of supercharged passion—intoxicating, yearning, melancholy:

> The smell of trodden leaves beside the Kennet,
> On Sunday walks, with Swinburne in my brain,
> November showers upon the chalk dust, when it
> Would turn to streaming milk in Manton Lane
> And coming back to feel one's footsteps drag
> At smells of burning toast and cries of "Fag!"

The after-light that hangs along the hedges,
On sunward sides of them when sun is down,
The sprinkled lights about the borough's edges,
The pale green gas-lamps winking in the town,
The waiting elm boughs black against the blue
Which still to westward held a silver hue—

Alone beside the fives-courts, pacing,
Waiting for God knows what. O, stars above!
My clothes clung tight to me, my heart was racing:
Perhaps what I was waiting for was love!
And what is love? And wherefore is its shape
To do with legs and arms and waist and nape?

First tremulous desires in Autumn stillness—
Grey eyes, lips laughing at another's joke,
A rose, a cowlick—a delightful illness
That put me off my food and off my stroke,
Here, 'twixt the church tower and the chapel spire
Rang sad and deep the bells of my desire.

Thus writes Betjeman, in *Summoned by Bells*. The emotions involved could be, and often were, as powerful (more powerful) and just as adult as any that were to come later. Graves, writing *Goodbye to All That* at the age of thirty-two, still—in his satisfaction at his revenge and callous disregard for its consequences—reveals the fury of his jealousy at seventeen.

He was several times taxed with his love of a much younger boy called Dick, but always refused to give him up because he said his love was entirely moral (that is chaste), which it was. (The fact that he was allowed to go on seeing Dick says something for Charterhouse in 1910.) But one master warned him about exchanging glances with Dick in chapel. He was infuriated:

But when I was told by one of the boys that he had seen the master surreptitiously kissing Dick once, on a choir-treat or some such occasion, I went quite mad. I asked for no details or confirmation. I went to the master and told him he must resign or I would report the case to the headmaster. He already had a reputation in the school for this sort of thing, I said. Kissing boys was a criminal offence. I was morally outraged. Probably my sense of outrage concealed a murderous jealousy. I was surprised when he vigorously denied the charge; I could not guess what was going to happen next. But I said: "Well, come to the headmaster and deny it to him." He asked: "Did the boy tell you this himself?" I said "No". "Well then," he said, "I'll send for him here and he shall tell us the truth." So Dick was sent for and arrived looking very frightened, and the housemaster said menacingly: "Graves tells me that I once kissed you. Is that true?" Dick said: "Yes, it is true." So Dick was dismissed and the master collapsed, and I felt miserable. He said he would resign at the end of the term, which was quite near, on the grounds of ill-health. He even thanked me for speaking directly to him and not going to the headmaster. That was in the summer of 1914; he went into the army and was killed in the next year.

So a career was ruined, perhaps even a life lost, because of the rivalry of a boy and a master. But, more incredible even than that, Graves learnt later that Dick hadn't been kissed by the master at all. He must have lied to save Graves's face, lied in fact out of love for Graves. "It must have been some other boy," says Graves casually.

Despite the fact that the majority of these romantic friendships were chaste and although I am speaking at a different level, in a sense in contradiction to what I said earlier, the psychiatrists I have discussed the subject with all agree that unconsciously those involved wanted to give them physical expression. Whether you agree with this or not depends on your view of currently accepted psychoanalytic theory. Certainly this crucial element provides the central theme for one of the best books on public schools and their love affairs ever written—that is Michael Campbell's *Lord Dismiss Us*.

The dominant love is between Carlton, the second prefect, and Nicky Allen, a sixteen-year-old new arrival from Eton, who looks marvellous and plays marvellous cricket. Carlton falls in love with Allen, and at first does not dare to show it. After a triumphant away cricket match Allen has to sit on his knees in the bus:

> And this was ecstasy enough. Such absolute unimagined joy. He was afraid to raise his hands to hold him. No, he had laid his right hand gently on Allen's soft blue blazer. On his waist. Oh heavens . . . has he felt my hand, does he know? The black hair came out in a wave from under the back of his blue cap. His neck was brown. His beautiful shoulder-blades moved inside his blazer, as he turned at an angle to join in the talk . . . may these moments of bliss go on and on forever!

Gradually his love is revealed—and reciprocated. Notes are left in secret places. Thrilling notes: "Don't worry, I love you, I love you, I love you. N.A." Now they can have secret meetings:

> "Oh, I do love you. I love you, my darling. Don't be shy, look at me. Do you love me?"
> "Yes."
> "Do you swear?"
> "Yes."
> He leaned up and kissed Allen softly on his blushing cheek. He felt a new sweetness enter him. He felt he had become, instantly, a more tender person. He felt older, with a purpose; someone to look after, to cherish, and love, for always.

Yet this love is completely chaste. That is indeed what gives it its purity and intensity and what makes it so valuable to Carlton. Then a young master Ashley (a secondary theme is his love for Carlton) lends him his room in which to have an assignation with Allen. They meet there, kiss each other. Carlton finds he is lying on top of Allen—and has an orgasm. He is horrified, astonished and disgusted. This love had seemed quite unconnected with sex, separate from it:

> And the most appalling, unbelievable, terrible thing began to happen; and he could not stop it. He tried, but he could not stop it. And the worst part was that it was wonderful too, and yet it was awful. Thus the shame was doubled. The disgrace and horror were absolute. It was profane. It was ruin. . . . Everything, everything lovely, their whole past, was contaminated. He had sinned and profaned; as with Naylor, but this was with Nicky.

In the agony of the moment he springs apart and rejects Nicky, who is deeply wounded, and never wants—nor has—any sort of intimacy with him again.

It is unfair to single out and condense this single strand. Campbell treats it with great skill and his book is rich in other ways. But he has made explicit the dilemma which one senses quite often in the agonisingly physical descriptions, the way in which these loves were not forgotten, even in the odd timbre of certain sentences in earlier books as the subconscious vibrates: "The roaring bases and baritones of the big fellows made him shiver with a curious bitter-sweet sensation never experienced before [*The Hill*]."

At any rate it was clear from the response to his book that he had hit some note with a sledgehammer. Letters poured in, from girls in astonishment and envying the intensity of passion boys felt at school, from masters and ex-masters, agreeing with his portrayal of love, from his school, St. Columba's, saying the book had been banned. But overwhelmingly the letters were from public school boys and Old Boys saying (I have read them) how accurate it was and describing their own love affairs, or else bitterly regretting the love they could not show or had not shown. Nor was it just the humble; the great wrote too. Sir Stephen Runciman wrote, so did Ned Sherrin, Noel Coward, Christopher Isherwood; Sir Terence Rattigan wrote fourteen pages. Best of all, Dirk Bogarde suddenly arrived one day with two pink-shirted aides and a cheque for £1,500. It was to be the first of many. It was the most wonderful book he had ever read. He himself would play Ashley. Oh yes, he fully understood the main theme was Carlton and Allen. They had already taken a girls' school—it would be empty, of course, in the holidays, not a girl in sight. Campbell, embarrassed by the praise, embarrassed, if delighted, by the cheque, deprecated:

"Oh, I don't know. I don't think it's all that good. There's one book I've always thought would make a marvellous film."

"What?"

"Death in Venice."

"Never heard of it. Who's it by?"

"Thomas Mann. It's the story . . ."

While he explained, or started to explain because Dirk Bogarde soon stopped him impatiently and continued to enthuse about *Lord Dismiss Us*, Campbell saw one of the pink shirts making a note.

They left, the Rolls departed, the days, then the weeks, finally months began to pass. He rang Bogarde's office to see what progress was being made. "Oh, we're not doing that any more," it was an aide. "No, let me see, I can tell you what we are doing—wait a moment . . . it's by a fellow called Mann. . . . one moment. . . ."

But love affairs could be physical without the catastrophe Campbell depicts, as the letters elicited by the book showed clearly enough. One of the men I interviewed, as well as sexual encounters at Rugby in the 1930s, had one proper passionate love affair and went through a form of marriage in church. He and his friend continued lovers and only stopped when my informant, M, became head of his house, when the expulsion if caught would have been doubly damaging. Afterwards, his friend married and told his wife. M, however, never told his wife.

And finally there is the fact that boys of eight and nine, or thirteen and fourteen, still require a father, just as men of eighteen or young masters of twenty-three and upwards, too poor to marry, were able to respond paternally. This is the last strand, truly chaste this time but no less powerful, which wove its confusing way into that invisible but, to those involved, completely palpable net of love and lust and romanticism which draped itself suffocatingly over every public school, and does so still.

4 *Effects on homosexual inclinations, on relations with women, on marriage, on life afterwards*

What effect did it all have?

Perhaps the first thing to establish is whether or not it made boys homosexual.

Dancy started his brief grappling with this difficult subject by assuming, or hoping, that there was a period of homosexual attraction between boys even in "natural" surroundings. Clearly, if all cultures and studies showed that adolescent boys were homosexual between twelve and eighteen the problem disappears. Dancy gets some support from a number of books, particularly British books. Hadfield's *Childhood and Adolescence* (1962) is typical of this viewpoint. Between the onset of adolescence around twelve and maturity around eighteen he postulates no fewer than seven stages. Between twelve and thirteen there is the group homosexual phase where boys form gangs; between thirteen and fourteen comes the individual homosexual phase (can be a bit of mutual masturbation here); at fifteen comes the transition phase. The boy is moving to the heterosexual but has not reached it. He abandons his friend, becomes moody, may make up to his mother. At sixteen comes the first heterosexual phase—the polygamous phase. This is characterised by sexual curiosity—interest in "dirty" books, asking questions about reproduction—not sexual desire for girls themselves. There are three exceptions: those who have been stimulated too early in life and so have an unnatural interest in sexual intercourse, those who have a similar interest because they have been deprived of love and those who are constitutionally over-sexed—"But these abnormal manifestations of love," says Hadfield in his classic, "should not blind us to its natural and healthy development." Next comes the monogamous phase one. This too is not sexual, but romantic, a passionate "idealistic" phase. Finally, around eighteen, comes monogamous two and boys are ready for life.

It is odd that it should coincide so neatly with the age they leave public school. I was becoming increasingly irritated by Hadfield's croquet hoops —why on earth should the development of what is after all the most powerful and direct of all the instincts be so elaborate?—when I turned to the Preface. Here it stated that his material came from studying boarding schools—the Leytonstone Homes. At once all was clear. Hadfield was simply charting the convolutions of an instinct subjected to the same sort of artificial conditions we described earlier—and calling the convolutions "natural and healthy". Certainly they were what the instincts "naturally" did given that environment—but you might as well study monkeys in a zoo and say their "natural" sexual outlet was masturbation.

The problem begins to clear when we read American studies. Edgar Friedenberg, for instance, is a great deal more relaxed. He, too, postulates a brief period of homosexual attachment around thirteen and fourteen, due largely to shyness. This passes and from the end of fourteen and fifteen onwards boys are dating girls and experimenting with girls in various forms of relationships. In both developments, "whether anything sexual happens in the course of them is unimportant, unless someone steps in and makes it important".

It is when one looks at the question from an anthropological point of view that it becomes quite plain that these—and indeed all—phases of adolescence are socially and culturally determined. They have only local validity. In societies where the relationship between the sexes is entirely free and unrestricted from the start, there is no "natural" phase of homosexuality, no sexually inhibiting shyness. They move gradually into closer inter-sex relationships as they wish and as they grow older. This is true, for example, of the Alaskan, Samoan and Melanesian cultures. At the same time there can be a "natural" phase of homosexuality if the culture creates an environment which dictates it. The Manus of New Guinea segregate the boys from the girls when they are fifteen and homosexuality and masturbation are quite common.

When we move from there to consider whether or not public schools caused homosexuality it is much harder to be so clear cut. It is an extremely complex and still controversial subject. Believers in psychoanalytic theory would in general agree, I think, that sexual orientation occurs quite early in development, during the first five or six years and that what happens subsequently can modify or confuse the expression but not the direction of the instinct. They are not agreed as to what causes a homosexual orientation. Some would say it is altered by a traumatic early experience—rape, death of the father or mother. More would incline to the view that the relationship with the parents is crucial—typically a weak or absent father and a strong, emotional and usually physically demonstrative mother or mother-figure (with a girl it is the reverse equation) so enslaves the child that he subconsciously never dares or wants to break free. Or the mother can be an authoritative, often violent figure, with hysterical and uncertain temper; homosexuality can then be an expression of fear of the opposite sex. But there are explanations placing sexual orientation early which have nothing to do with psychoanalytic theory. It is possible that the endocrine glands are responsible and that homosexuality is a response to a particular balance of hormones. A recent study from the US has suggested that homosexuals are an altruistic strain which has become bred into society. Altruistic, because they play their part in the community (and clearly it doesn't matter if that part is "selfish"—virtually all activities to some degree help the community) without wasting time and energy breeding. Once bred in, the variation is passed on via the genes. (A difficulty with this theory, it seems to me, is that it would, by definition, fairly quickly breed itself out again.)

However, all these explanations—and they add up to a convincing case —would agree that public schools do not cause homosexuality. Old Rollball of the Haileybury interview is typical. In his book *Homosexuality*, D. J. West writes: ". . . the frequency of homosexual indulgence at school has probably more to do with the strength of the sex drive than the direction it will take in later life." Royston Lambert found no evidence that public schools caused homosexuality; only that it sensitised boys to their homosexual instincts and homosexual situations. And in this connection it is possible to argue that the schools did a service. The dilemma of the homosexual who does not discover his inclination is a sad and real one. Raymond Mortimer (Malvern, 1909) said that a potential homosexual might have been put off sex for life by the hideous crudity of public school indulgence. No doubt this was true, but I think in general they must have often alerted young men (like J. A. Symonds) to their true natures. There is not space to explore this interesting B road of English social history, but one might note parenthetically that middle-and upper-class homosexuals frequently chose lower-class partners. This was partly economic (they could be bought), partly because they were often less inhibited and so more willing, partly because their position made the activity more secret and less guilt-inducing, and partly for the same complex of reasons that their heterosexual fellows chose lower-class girls as tarts or mistresses (see Chapter 3 of *The Unnatural History of the Nanny*). But in this small area public schools were class unifying, not divisive. In the literature from 1890 to 1920 or so you can always tell if partners are not the same class; lower class ones are called "lads" (compare the way middle-class mothers today talk about "the kids" to show they are really the same as lower-class "mums").

But to return. The situation as regards homosexuality becomes rather different if one looks at what actually happens, as opposed to how theoretically homosexuality occurs and what should happen.

One thing Kinsey established beyond doubt was that the idea—which the statements "public schools create homosexuals", or "do not create homosexuals" implicitly assume—that the homosexual was in some way a third sex "fails to describe any actuality". It is true that there are those who seem to have exclusively homosexual reactions and experiences and those who have exclusively heterosexual ones; but these are relatively rare extremes at either end of an infinite and continuous gradation of experiences and reactions ranging from one end to the other. It is the same picture we found, for instance, in masturbation, where the range was from once a year to dozens of times a week. In this vast range, eighteen per cent of men have equally homosexual-heterosexual experiences between the ages of sixteen and fifty-five, that is one in six. Thirteen per cent have more homosexual experience (one in eight) and ten per cent have exclusively homosexual reactions. Although there is clearly a preponderance of heterosexually directed reactions (fifty-nine per cent as opposed to forty-one per cent equal of homosexually directed) it is similarly graded and differentiated between heterosexual and homosexual.

That is one point. The second is that the very much more widespread occurrence of homosexuality in cultures today, where it is not taboo and/or where circumstances dictate it or are propitious (the Manu and certain Arab cultures around the Mediterranean are examples) as well as its apparent normalcy in Ancient Greece, suggests that the ability to respond erotically to any stimulus, whether from the same or the opposite sex, is basic to the species. It argues that patterns of either response represent learned behaviour which depends to a considerable degree upon the *mores* of the culture in which you are raised; and that this explanation is at least equally tenable with psychological or hereditary ones.

If this is true then it is likely that what happens in adolescence—and therefore public schools—plays an important part. This was clearly borne out by Kinsey. Kinsey and his researchers correlated what happened in adolescence to the vast sample with their subsequent sexual patterns and found that, no matter what theory you accepted about homosexuality, "whether exclusively heterosexual or exclusively homosexual patterns are followed, or whether both heterosexual and homosexual outlets are utilised in his history, depends in part" upon the circumstances of adolescent experience.

It follows, therefore, that public schools are likely to be strong influences in a culture bringing about increased homosexual response. Dancy's confidence turns out once again to be misplaced. Indeed common sense would suggest that it would be extremely surprising if the intense bias we charted, operating from eight to eighteen, in an area of extreme sensitivity, had no effect whatsoever. If this were so we should be entitled to ask Dancy (and I use him only as representative of all public school masters in 1900, and most now) why public schools should have no effect here, when he confidently asserts that they have such beneficial effects in other important areas—in the inculcation of a sense of responsibility, the value of service to the community, an appreciation of cultural and academic goals and so on?

Now this tendency might not have mattered particularly had it not taken place at a time when society expected men to be heterosexual, to marry and have children, and violently condemned homosexuality. The result was that many middle-class Englishmen were put into a state of almost unique confusion, guilt, anxiety and evasion about their sexual natures. The benefits of men like Symonds discovering they were primarily homosexual were instantly extinguished because they had to suppress it. The furore over Oscar Wilde (and unfortunate successors up till today) is entirely explained by repressed guilts, fears and desires. The "Nigel" Connolly was in love with at Eton was in fact Noel Blakiston, who recently (1975) published Connolly's letters to him in a book called A Romantic Friendship. Noel Blakiston, it is clear, is anxious to establish how "normal" their relationship was since he chooses to end the book with a letter from Connolly in 1963—"and we weren't homosexual". Yet this is too simple. Connolly's subsequent love life was complex and often tortured. At twenty-six, when in love with and about to marry Jean Bakewell, he told Blakiston with his characteristic honesty and insight that "of course the trouble is I'm emotionally homosexual still". And so we come to the last of Dancy's happy-go-lucky assumptions—that the public school experience "has no apparent long-term effects".

My uncle told me a story current at Eton in the 1920s (this is an example of schoolboy "smut"):

There was a dame who lusted after one of the boys. Finally, unable to contain her desires, she drew him ravenously into a room, locked the door, pulled down her knickers, pulled up her skirt and said, "There! What do you think of that?"

"Gosh, ma'am," said the boy. "Stand still. If you wait a minute I'll run to my room, get my bat and come back and kill it."

"Not," said my Uncle Eddie, "a very popular story with women I've found."

I'm not surprised. It is a story which expresses a strong latent fear, and therefore dislike, of women. And any tendency towards this was clearly much reinforced, and often induced, by cutting off any contact with girls and women for the greater part of this sexually formative period. General Sir Ian Hamilton had been attached to the Japanese army in the Russo-Japanese war. Unveiling a Boer War Memorial in 1905 he explicitly exhorted his public school audience to follow Japanese self-sacrifice, meeting death for their country "as a bridegroom who goes to meet his bride". It was an apt simile for many of his audience's feelings towards sexual congress and marriage. Not only were women confusing and frightening; they were almost like some different species.

Years after he has left Wellington, Harold Nicolson meets J. D. Marstock, the once formidable head of school, at a public lunch:

> There was a touch of grey about the carefully combed hair, he was a little thinner, and his eyes had given up being merely open and had become just blank. But it was the same good old Marstock in his brown suit and Old Wellingtonian tie.
>
> I asked him what he was doing now . . . I asked him whether he was married. He laughed a little shyly. "No", he said, "you see it's the Wimskies." I put on a serious and condoling expression, imagining he had invented some obscure disease. "The Wimskies?" I enquired considerately. "The women, you know—I always call them that. They're all so fascinating, I can't make up my mind." I answered him that, to my mind also, women were delightful and perplexing little things.

And this development had the most curious effect on the popular writers of the period. Their heroines aren't really girls at all; they are boys. Take Buchan. Janet Raden was a great walker and "famous for her wind". She also hunted. Sandy Arbuthnot fell in love with Barbara Dasent when he saw her handle a stampede of horses at his HQ in the Olife campaign. Saskia, the Russian in *Hunting Tower*, ran so well across country that Archie Roylance cried out in admiration, "Gad! She's a miler!" At one time or another all the heroines are praised because their looks, lines, strides, manners and hips are "boyish". The same is true of Wodehouse, Sapper and many other writers.

To balance this, and in line with it, some of the heroes had feminine characteristics. Sandy Arbuthnot, for example, with "a pair of brown eyes like a pretty girl's", or Peter Pienaar with "a face as gentle as a girl's". In R. C. Sherriff's play *Journey's End*, the hero, although in the trenches, is really indistinguishable from a girl and is treated by the other characters as such.

"British upper—class males," said one of my informants, "were homosexual in everything but their sex lives." Certainly ignorance, fear or dislike of women much exaggerated the development, likely in any male-dominated society, of that pompous, cosy, boisterous Victorian and Edwardian world (which continued intact up to and beyond the 1939 war) of close male friendships blossoming in clubs and army messes, of men in clumps striding across grouse moors, in the City, booming in *The Times*, booming after dinner when the women had left; all this, too familiar to need elaboration, owes a great deal to public schools.

". . . Everything but their sex lives"—what were these really like? More particularly, what were their marriages like? Quite apart from the heterosexual-homosexual developments, which we have fully explored, Kinsey found conclusively that marital and sexual relationships between couples were profoundly influenced by the experiences of adolescence. If these years were spent in single-sex institutions, they then experienced considerable difficulty in making the necessary adjustments. "Coital adjustments of this group [upper—level college group] are frequently poor. . . . These difficulties would seem related to their late experience and tardy acceptance of heterosexual coitus." Royston Lambert found "an inability to accept girls as real and complete people, a tendency to polarise in perception of them towards the unreal goddess model . . . or machines for gratification. . . ."

It is of course impossible to prove exactly what effect this had. But *a priori* one might suppose that a society in which the men (and we will soon come to the women) were brought up so that their most intimate friend-ships formed naturally with men, where they were both guilty and confused by the homosexual elements in their make-up and had difficulty in making heterosexual adjustments, where they sometimes feared women, sometimes regarded them as goddesses and sometimes looked on them as "machines for gratification", was scarcely one conducive to profound or satisfactory married lives. At the least, one can say that those English middle— and upper—class stereotypes—the sexually cold and inhibited man, the unresponsive woman, the distant and unintimate marriage with little real contact or appreciation—all had considerable basis in truth, and that public schools played an important part in bringing them about.

At the same time, it is important not to overstate this. I remember a remark in an early Auberon Waugh novel. The boys are coming up to Oxford: "They imagined the girls would find them attractive. Everyone else always had." The girls did. Clearly a great many marriages of public school boys were as successful as marriages ever are. Adjustment may have been difficult; it was made, if late. And this introduces a general caveat which means that any generalisation about the effects of public school must always be extremely tentative. For two-thirds of the year boys were at school; but for the other one-third they were at home. The existence of the home means that any general effect is to that degree mitigated. The closeness prep and public school boys felt for each other was indeed a kibbutz-like effect; but it was a scaled down kibbutz-effect. Furthermore, the success of any relationship depends to a considerable extent upon the expectations you bring to it. I think it is probably true to say that the Victorians and Edwardians did not set such store upon sexual satisfaction as we do, and did not expect the same degree of intimacy in a marriage. They were therefore less upset by their absence.

Statements must be tentative. But they can be made. It remains true that in this important sphere the public school was an unsatisfactory way of bringing up adolescents which, though there were often exceptions, had seriously deleterious results.

Despite considerable advances in tolerance, we are still basically an anti-homosexual, pro-heterosexual, pro-marriage society today (and one, it might be added, with enormously high expectations of heterosexual relations). Most of our public schools are still single-sexed, or virtually so, still criss-crossed by the same interlocking nets of passion, attraction and affection, still producing similar, if not quite so extreme, effects to the ones we have observed. Dancy's attitude, his confidence, totally unwarranted in these crucial areas, as we have seen, that these effects don't take place is shared, if my quite extensive experience is accurate, by the vast majority of public school masters today.

There are four final points I want to make in this area. The first is no more than a suggestion. I remember when I was at Cambridge my tutor, Peter Laslett, described how the same network of homosexual love and hero-worshipping relationships used to spring up in a battleship when it was at sea. In fact these pockets of intensely joined men were general during the war—in platoon, battalion, whole armies and air forces, the entire fighting forces were knit together in this way. And this must always have been so, since women have never played a major rôle actually along-side men. It had occurred to Laslett that when wars ended and these forces broke up you got a series of emotional breaks on an unprecedented scale. It was like the ending of an enormous love affair. And, just as in human terms, the end of a love affair often leads to disturbed and erratic behaviour, so the break up of these vast love affairs could explain the destruction and disturbance which have always typified the return of troops at the end of wars. Although this can be no more than speculation, it is certainly an alternative—or additional—explanation of the behaviour of public school boys when they first get to university, usually put down to new found freedom.

Second, the segregation by age and house which Harold Nicolson wrote about, restricting the circle of acquaintance to about ten, almost universal around 1900, was one of the prime causes of that silliness and immaturity people often noted about public school boys.

Thirdly, we find in the sexual life of public schools the origin of yet more British archetypes. The English male virgin is well known. But just as there evolved T. C. G. Sandfords and men like "the Bull" in the games environment, solid and obsessed figures, extreme examples of biological specialisation, so, under the fierce if muted gaze of almost universal love and lust, beautiful boys became still more beautiful, with a bloom like that on English country-house grapes or, still not quite old enough to shave, with the down and colouring and texture of a hot-house peach (both things which are, as well, the best in the world). Nor did they always change—these *garçons fatals*. They became that familiar figure, the aging English male beauty, perfectly preserved, frequent glancer into the plate glass of shop windows, with a curious way of walking, with his feet slightly turned in, developed self-consciously years and years before when he was an object of desire.

And, finally, what afterwards? What in the head, in the memory, walking in the streets? When they parted, these men of eighteen, they gave each other photographs of themselves, lest they forget. As the boy who loves Betjeman did at Marlborough:

> Then on the final morning of the term,
> Wearing his going-away suit, which had lain
> Pressed by his mattress all the previous night,
> He came and handed me an envelope
> And went without a word. Inside I found
> The usual smiling farewell photograph.

They need not have worried. They never never forgot, and this is perhaps the most poignant thing of all, the immortality of those piercing early loves. "These are not childish things," reflected the chaplain in *Lord Dismiss Us*, "and they are not put away." Heterosexual loves in co-educational schools merge and blur with later loves, they become part of growth. There are no co-ed novels. But these homosexual loves, because they were unconsummated, because they were so different to anything that came later, were embalmed and secreted away—having to find satisfaction and expression years later in that unique English *genre*, the novel about public school. England is full of these ex-lovers who are poignant, it is true, but also infinitely sad; as when Cyril Connolly with a friend at the theatre suddenly noticed a large red-faced man with a white moustache and stared at him fixedly for several moments. Outside in the taxi going home he suddenly burst into tears, sobbing, until at last he blurted out, "At . . . school . . . he . . . used . . . to . . . smell . . . of . . . tangerines". And wept bitterly and unrestrainedly—for what? Lost youth? Lost love? Lost dreams?

CHAPTER 8

The Final Picture:
1900–1914

I'll borrow life and not grow old;
And nightingales and trees
Shall keep me, though the veins be cold,
As young as Sophocles.

And when I may no longer live,
They'll say, who know the truth,
He gave whate'er he had to give
To Freedom and to Youth.

William Cory

Correlli Barnett says the evidence is overwhelming that for most boys schooldays were happy. But a study of the authorities he cites, and many others, reveals a far more complex picture. The idealistic school novels which begin to appear from the 1880s on, the successors to *Tom Brown* and *Eric*, naturally pictured schooldays as idyllic. But it was an idyll built on an odd base; if you isolate the actual events from the later attitudes towards them, it is plain the first two years or so were often hell. From 1905 the novels begin to be mildly critical (*The Harrovians, The Loom*) and by 1930 (describing the schools from 1890 on) it has become fashionable to attack public schools. Criticism is never thereafter absent, but no matter whether the final verdict is "happy" or "unhappy", all accounts of schools up to 1910 (and long beyond in fact) retain that element—the first two years had frequent moments of extreme unpleasantness. We already know a good many ingredients of this: fagging, beating, pressures to conform, the games obsession if you were intellectual, a boring and restricted curriculum and so on. But there were other significant factors.

1 Early hell and bullying

Homesickness was a vital element; that terrible piercing loneliness of small children cast out from their homes. It is without question the most important single aspect of public school education; yet because it was the most painful it is the memory most usually repressed. But it is the unexpressed longing for the love of their mothers and nannies, the comfort and safety of home, which defines the other deprivations.

The tradition that boys fed themselves, the fact that housemasters needed to make a profit, meant food continued to be revolting, even sinful. Here is Orwell:

> On the whole I accepted Sambo's [the Headmaster's] view that a boy's appetite is a sort of morbid growth which should be kept in check as much as possible. A maxim often repeated at St. Cyprian's was that it is healthy to get up from a meal feeling as hungry as when you sat down. Only a generation earlier than this [in 1905 therefore] it had been common for school dinners to start off with a slab of unsweetened suet pudding, which, it was frankly said, "broke the boys' appetites".

But the scarcity and foulness of the food (Haileybury, 1905: "I would have starved had we been unable to buy food"), were just part, as Orwell again describes, of a general discomfort and squalor endured in far more schools than not by these cold, bruised, homesick little boys:

> . . . And the always damp towels with their cheesy smell: and, on occasional visits in the winter, the murky sea-water of the local baths, which came straight in from the beach and on which I once saw floating a human turd. And the sweaty smell of the changing room with its greasy basins, and, giving on this, the row of filthy, dilapidated lavatories which had no fastenings of any kind on the doors, so that whenever you were sitting there someone was sure to come crashing in. It is not easy for me to think of my schooldays without seeming to breathe in a whiff of something cold and evil-smelling—a sort of compound of sweaty stockings, dirty towels, faecal smells blowing along the corridors, forks with old food in between the prongs, neck-of-mutton stew, and the banging doors of the lavatories and the echoing dormitories.

Thirdly, there was bullying. It is always difficult to be certain about this. Novels and autobiographies always say things are better than in "their time"—and in a sense this is the trend. After 1840, good water made beer unnecessary; new ideas about hygiene and health reduced overcrowding, both conducive to bullying. England gradually became more humanitarian and, in the schools, there is objective evidence of this. At the beginning of the century, it was very rare for a boy to be sent to the same school as his father. By 1850 (at Rugby, but the pattern is echoed in other schools) ten per cent went to the same school, and from 1880 onwards the figure climbed to thirty per cent.

At the same time, just as you think there will never be hounding again on the scale endured by Shelley, say, you come across an incident like the buggery demonstration in the 1950s that I described. There are sufficient, and sufficiently terrible, accounts of bullying, in the 1900–1914 years to show that, especially in the first two years, it was still extremely common. Raymond Mortimer was held—as in *"If . . ."*—upside down in an unflushed lavatory bowl. Graves was hideously bullied. So was Cyril Connolly; but after two terms two things happened to him. He was given a "Chamber Pop beating", then a boy called Maynell, relenting, had a heart-to-heart: "Ugly, why are you so filthy, what's the matter with you?" After crying, Connolly made him laugh. So he discovered the power of laughter. This enabled him to join the bullies and for a year he bullied. He also discovered sarcasm, and wielded this too. They were to be potent weapons in his armoury for the rest of his life—and they introduce us, by contrast, into certain aspects of happiness at public schools which we must know about.

2 *Gossip and freedom*

I wrote earlier that the privileged classes were quite prepared to accept the rising rich provided they were well educated and amusing, and that both graces could be obtained from public schools. The idea that you can be taught to be amusing may have seemed odd, but public schools set an enormous premium on humour. Mimicking, scandalous fantasy in those places where, as Michael Campbell puts it, "ridicule was a way of life", were one method of redressing the authority of prefect or pedagogue. In closed communities (particularly adolescent ones) humour is the oil which smoothes too many close-meshed cogs, the verbal television that for a moment repels boredom. And this has gone deep into our national character. There are Americans remembered for a wisecrack or two, Frenchmen for some succinct and aphoristic summings up; only in England do we reward men with immortality because of their sense of humour—I think of Whistler, Oscar Wilde, Sydney Smith. Many of the novelists we most admire—Jane Austen, Evelyn Waugh, Anthony Powell —have really written novels of inspired gossip. The greatest biography in the language is of a conversationalist. And it is because most of our great men have been to public schools that, as Correlli Barnett notes, the "great" moments in English history are characterised by humour, irony and modesty, making them easier to undergo—though no less great—than the same moments on the Continent. The conferring of power on Churchill in May 1940 was short, friendly and amused. An Italian like Mussolini would have larded it with bombast, Hitler invested it with obedience, de Gaulle with destiny.

The essence of gossip is place—who's in, who's out, who up, who down. Public schools, quite apart from information about favourites, the social side of love, were, like the court of Louis XIV, electric with rumour, news and speculation because of the innumerable posts and privileges to be obtained. Here is Cyril Connolly, himself on occasion a conversationalist of genius, on getting into Pop:

> My only hope was to be elected as a wit. Although it was but a small section of Pop who thought me funny, they were influential. My tactics were to seem as important as I could in college, so that my Oppidan friends would not feel that I was too powerless in my own fief to deserve recognition abroad.

And—to everyone's astonishment—he gets in:

> Suddenly there was the noise of footsteps thudding up the wooden staircase of the tower. The door burst open and about twenty Pops, many of whom had never spoken to me before, with bright-coloured waistcoats, rolled umbrellas, button holes, braid and spongebag trousers, came reeling in like the College of Cardinals arriving to congratulate some pious old freak whom fate had elevated to the throne of St. Peter.

Just as the essence of gossip is place, so the essence of place is power:

> At that time Pop were the rulers of Eton, fawned on by masters and the helpless sixth form. Such was their prestige that some boys who failed to get in never recovered; one was rumoured to have procured his sister for the influential members. Besides privileges—for they could beat anyone, fag any lower boy, walk arm-in-arm, wear pretty clothes, sit in their own club and get away with minor breaches of discipline, they also possessed executive power which their members tasted, often for the only time in their lives. To elect a boy without a colour, a Colleger too, was a departure for them; it made them feel they appreciated intellectual worth and could not be accused of athleticism; they felt like the Viceroy after entertaining Gandhi. The rest of the school could not understand that a boy could be elected because he was amusing; if I got in without a colour it must be because I was a "bitch", yet by Eton standards I was too unattractive to be a "bitch"—unless my very ugliness provided for the jaded appetites of the Eton Society, the final attraction!

(Actually Connolly was not ugly at Eton. Photographs and his contemporaries recall a snubby attractiveness, something between a pug and a satyr.)

Clearly, the thrills of gossip, the exercise of wit, are better appreciated as adolescents get older; particularly as gossip requires freedom, time and privacy. After two years at school, privileges began to multiply, as we saw, and common to them all was freedom: freedom to break bounds, to stay up late, to be alone with your contemporaries. Here the study is important. All public schools had them, though in varying number. They meant that although limited freedom was the reward of conforming, once given, it was real. It was possible to be independent, at least for some of the time. And not only was independence possible, it was often encouraged.

Towards the end of the 19th century a number of intelligent masters became aware that they were part of a far too conformist system of education and did their best to rectify it.

This was true, for instance, even at that ultra-conforming school, Wellington in the 1890s, in the person of the headmaster, Dr. Pollock, whose "tall slim figure", in the words of Harold Nicolson,

> billowed in a silken gown as he glided rapidly through the cloisters, leaving behind a faint but pleasant smell of hair-wash, an impression of something rich and luxurious and mundane. I realise, of course, on looking back, that his methods, for all their subtlety, were perfectly calculated and deliberate. He knew that the system of the school had scored upon our brains deep grooves of habit which were in danger of becoming rigid: he set himself to render those grooves more flexible, to create new channels and associations in our minds.
>
> [He] appeared to devote his energies to destroying all the educational convictions which we had hitherto absorbed: he taught us that the mere avoidance of howlers was a means only and not an end: he taught us that the greater proportion of classical literature as it figured in the school curriculum was not only dull but silly: he taught us that life was more than scholarship, and literature more than books: he taught us to feel, and even to think, for ourselves. . . .

The Masai tribe finishes off the education of their adolescents by allowing them, in one glorious burst, to break every single code they have been at such pains to inculcate before. There is a tribe in Basutoland that sends its young away for six months. Their education ends on graduation day with the burning down of the school. Something of the same instinct, isolated but perceptible, now gradually begins to emerge in the public schools.

Of all activities, teaching is in one sense the least adventurous because it is the most well known. All teachers have been to school themselves for ten years or so and therefore return after university to a little world they know inside out. This can make them parochial. Auden said that a schoolmaster was the last person he'd like to sit next to at a dinner party. It will attract the timid; it will attract those low in vitality who charge themselves from the packed batteries of adolescence. "Those who can't, teach," said Shaw.

But teachers also become teachers because that is what they enjoy and are good at—the pleasures and techniques in imparting and sharing knowledge. And not only knowledge, but the encouragement of other attributes. Just because a teacher may at some level be timid and unadventurous, it does not mean he cannot appreciate and foster quite other qualities; in the same way that certain philosophers and writers, timid as men, have written books of revolutionary, even terrifying boldness. It is the ability to teach the need for adventurousness, for personal freedom, for intellectual independence and originality, the dangers of conventions and institutions, while operating within a system which in part negates all these, which has often characterised the best teachers.

3 The case of William Cory

Take William Johnson (later Cory), one of the most interesting and also tragic figures of the 19th century. Cory was a master at Eton in the 1850s, 60s and 70s. He was tall, extremely short-sighted, indeed almost blind, with a high-pitched voice "as if shouting in a very high wind", said one pupil, and possessed of incredible energy and vitality. He was first of all, as he had to be at that time, a brilliant classical teacher. "Nothing he taught could ever for a moment while he taught it, be dull," wrote Herbert Paul. "He never seemed as if he tried to be interesting, but as if he could not be anything else. That he was teaching 'dead languages' never occurred either to him or his pupils. It was the living voice that came to us." To make a subject or an idea come alive, to involve, fascinate and excite your pupils so that they pursue it on their own—good teaching is neither more nor less than this.

But Cory's range extended far beyond the classics. He makes quite clear in his writings on education that he regarded the exclusive classical curriculum as ridiculously cramping. The art was to teach everything else —science, history, English literature, the whole range of intellectual endeavour—while appearing to respect the confines. To remain in the system, yet escape it. He was an exhilarating and startling tutor. He would simulate (or feel) huge rages, stamping about the room, spouting furious jets of sarcasm. Or he would interrupt a lesson and launch suddenly into a rambling but riveting discourse upon any subject which had crossed his extraordinarily active mind. "His genius," wrote Faith Compton-Mackenzie in a recent biography, "was to make the smallest thing significant to those that had ears to hear and minds to respond. It might be a lesson in which he seemed to teach twenty things at once, and yet there was no confusion, but a blithe leaping from stone to stone in the rippling stream."

But above all it was qualities of mind and character he was interested in. Robert Rhodes James, whose account of Cory in his masterly biography of Lord Rosebery I largely follow, writes:

> In some respects he was too brilliant for his charges, since much of his deep erudition and withering jibes were lost upon them. He taught contempt for cant and despised the commonplace; anything sloppy or conventional withered at his touch; his manner was brusque and his sharp tongue made many enemies. Devoid of vanity, bitterly intolerant of the second rate, excellently versed in the vocabulary of contempt, he brought to Eton the indefinable air of the eccentric and fascinating university don.

Palmerston, in fact, suggested him for Professor of Modern History at Cambridge in 1860, but was over-ruled by the Prince Consort.

To elicit qualities of this sort—of independence, of originality, of unconventionality—requires a great deal more time and attention than is available in the classroom. Cory's lessons, if that is the word, continued in long walks or in endless lazy voyages down the Thames in summer evenings, when he impressed his fascinating personality on the intoxicated and brilliant band of his chosen pupils. And he worked, also, with a skill born of extraordinary understanding. For, as a tutor, it was Cory's intense concern and insight that are so impressive. Long before proper reports, long before Roxburgh's detailed letters (themselves exceptional in the 1920s) he was writing accounts quite remarkable for their powers of analysis.

Here is an extract from his report in 1862 on the future prime minister, Lord Rosebery:

> . . . He has in himself wonderful delicacy of mind, penetration, sympathy, flexibility, capacity for friendship—all but the tenacious resolutions of one that is to be great. . . . He is original all day long; too original to be very popular. He has more affection than tact, and quite as much antipathy as sympathy; so that he is not floating with the stream of popularity. All would come right if he were seriously engaged in a course of study, overcoming difficulties and competing with the many worthy rivals whom a great school contains.

"Cory's acuteness of judgment", writes Robert Rhodes James, ". . . is quite remarkable, for his comments could have been made with justice at any time in Rosebery's lifetime."

But, penetrating as they are, these detailed comments were made about relatively few. Cory had favourites, and it was increasingly noticed that these favourites had to be high born, brilliant and also beautiful. As well as reports, he wrote poems about them and to them, he sent them notes and gave them nicknames—like Mouse or Joab. The romantic charm of their intimate evenings on the Thames is preserved in his poetry:

> This sun, whose javelins strike and gild the wheat,
> Who gives the nectarine half an orb of bloom,
> Burns on my life no less, and beat by beat
> Shapes that grave hour when boyhood hears her doom.
>
> Oh, Thames! My memories bloom with all their flowers,
> Thy kindness sighs to me from every tree:
> Farewell! I thank thee for thy frolic hours,
> I bid thee, whilst thou flowest, think of me.

But it is clear that Cory felt for his pupils, in the enervating languor of those Thames Valley summer hours, emotions which were much more powerful than these poetic fancies. To Rosebery's mother he wrote, when the boy was ill: "He gives not only me, but many of the boys, the greatest pleasure we have. . . . He gives me more happiness than I can trust myself to speak of in writing." To Rosebery himself he wrote, "Good and dear friend, come back soon, as well as possible; for I miss you."

The age, as Rhodes James comments, allowed expressions of emotion between men that we would still find strange; but this was not then, or now, a normal letter for a schoolmaster to write to a fourteen-year-old pupil. Another, which Cory wrote the year after, is stranger still:

Midnight, Sunday, March 23rd, 1862

My dear Dalmeny [as Rosebery then was],

What is the matter?

Wood says you are not coming here any more, because I cut you.

I don't agree to that.

You cut me for *four* days.

You came here on Thursday night and I was very polite, only Mr. Day's presence prevented any ordinary conversation.

On Friday night I made reasonable overtures, stomaching my pride, which is not less than yours: only reason convinces me it must be subdued, or else I shall lose more than I can afford to lose in this dearth of sympathy.

Why could you not be civil enough to come in on Saturday, or today: I have been in the whole of both days. . . .

Cory's tongue had gained him many enemies at Eton; his teaching methods were so unorthodox that they inspired distrust and jealousy among his more conventional colleagues. If there were a scandal, he could have expected little support. Something of this sort must have happened. In 1872 he abruptly resigned all his Eton appointments and left. His departure has never been explained. It is possible that the father of one of his beautiful favourites intercepted a letter, was shocked by its tone, and reported it. It is impossible to find out. His name was instantly expunged from his textbooks, though they continued to be used for a further eighty years, and there descended one of those profound and mysterious silences which public schools, like the families they all to some extent are, let fall to protect those who belong to them. It has never been penetrated, still shrouding in safety the reputation of Eton's most brilliant master and the jealous men who got rid of him.

4 *Calibre, conditions and appointment of staff; religion*

Greatness in any sphere is rare. Cory would be exceptional in a school today; he was certainly so then. As in the 18th century, the good teacher was very much the exception. But although in such qualitative matters it is impossible to give objective figures, it is quite clear that during the last half of the 19th century and on into the 20th, the calibre slowly improved.

It would no doubt have improved a great deal faster if the conditions of employment had been better. For the top three or four schools they were excellent. In 1863, for instance, at Rugby the thirteen ordinary classical masters had over £1,000 a year, at Harrow they had slightly less, at Eton slightly more. And there were extras—generous presents from rich parents, comfortable accommodation and the like.

But for the rest, it was little better than penury. In 1850, £150–£250 was considered ample. It had barely changed, and indeed was often worse, by 1909. A writer then noted: "The majority of the public schools . . . pay their men such stipends as £105 resident or £125 non-resident . . . £180 or £200 respectively after, say, four years' service, and in some cases going on until the maximum of £250 or £300 non-resident is reached after ten years' service." If money was needed for new buildings or repairs these unhappy men, their marriages, if they were heterosexual, once again postponed, frantic from lack of sex, took a salary cut.

The result of such poverty meant that the scramble for promotion was very fierce; and the relations between the masters often correspondingly violent. When Joshua Fitch inspected Sedbergh in 1867 he found that the first and second masters (both clergymen) hadn't spoken to each other for fifteen years. In 1850 at Mill Hill, the school chaplain Mr. Crump accused another master of making love to a housekeeper. There are stories of many such battles, which suggest that A. S. Neill's experience of common-room life must often have been true. "In most schools where I have taught," he wrote, "the staff room was a little hell of intrigue, hate and jealousy." Turnover was also very high as masters gave up in despair. At the top three or four schools, on the other hand, there was hardly any turnover at all. They stayed till they dropped—forty, fifty, sixty years; at Eton John Wilder, if you include being a fellow, had been there as a man sixty-eight years. Since they had often been educated at the same school these men passed their entire lives in one institution, like monks or madmen.

For the few who lasted the course in the less important public schools, retirement was without hope. They either had to try to live on what they had saved, or else continue teaching. At the important schools, correspondingly, it was much easier to save and invest substantial sums. Headmasters of all schools were much better off. Even at a Repton, Sherborne or Bradfield, the headmaster was paid ten or twelve times the salary of any other master, and could save for old age. At the "great" schools (but not infrequently at other public schools) a headmastership remained a recognised avenue of Church preferment well into the 20th century; Bishoprics and deaneries were, if wanted, virtually inevitable.

I should perhaps say a brief word about the appointment of headmasters. This was the time when the governors of a school, usually no more than rubber stamps to approve the actions of the headmaster, had a brief moment of power. Two factors influenced them: the candidate's influence with outside notables and his family.

Influence with outside notables was proved by testimonials. These were amassed and hurled into the fray like little armies. When Henry Montagu Butler was fighting for Harrow in 1859 he had thirty-two: one signed by William Whewell and twenty-five fellows or ex-fellows of Trinity, and others from two bishops, two deans, an archdeacon, three professors, the Headmaster of Westminster, Lord Macaulay, etc., etc. Jex-Blake, in his bid for Haileybury in 1867, got together sixty-five. He had them beautifully printed and bound in book form—and then lost.

As the schools proliferated, grew in size and power, so dynasties were founded; these family networks were common in Victorian and Edwardian times—the Arnolds, Butlers, Hawtreys or Riddings (see Appendix E). When Ridding was standing for Winchester it was really pointless anyone competing: he had been born there, he was already second master, his father had been second master, the warden was a great uncle, two of the fellows were relations, and the retiring headmaster was his father-in-law. And of course candidates had to satisfy as to "tone"; every note on the huge scale from class to religious views to classical attainment to games having to ring absolutely sound. Looking into these little pools of life, unique but sharply defined environments, we see how nature tussles to adapt—again and again changing the pattern of habits here, shape there, colour, movement, voice—until finally she comes to perfection. Charles Wordsworth (Winchester) is an example of almost perfect adaptation; plumage, display, courting—everything is plum right. Let Firth describe the marvellous creature:

> Nephew of the poet, godson of the Archbishop of Canterbury, a scholar of exquisite taste and instant facility in Greek and Latin verse, disciple and friend at Christ Church of Pusey, tutor and intimate friend of Gladstone and Manning, of a personal life judged saintly by contemporaries who applied rigorous tests, among the best cricketers, oarsmen, skaters, rackets and tennis players of his day, joint founder of the University Cricket Match and Boat Race, Wordsworth brought to an assistant mastership a "background" and an assemblage of gifts surely unrivalled in public school history.

The schools remained a major avenue of Church preferment, but at the same time the closing decades of the 19th century saw the ties with the Church beginning to loosen for the first time in 1,200 years. From the 1850s laymen began to be appointed more and more frequently. By 1886, seventy-three per cent of masters in twenty-three leading schools were not clergy; by 1890, eighty per cent. (I except from this Catholic schools.

Then, as now, most masters were priests. Indoctrination was fierce and meant to last.) Headmasters, however, were nearly always clergymen. Since the number of clergymen who had been schoomasters was falling rapidly, the choice became much more restricted. As a result, the calibre of headmasters declines somewhat at the end of the century.

This loosening of the Church connection was part, of course, of a general decline in religion which becomes noticeable from 1870 on. (This is when church attendance began to drop.) Darwin, the continued rise of science and 19th-century materialism are usually the most important factors given to explain this; it is impossible to prove, but I suspect that the public schools were themselves a fourth. We saw how even a preacher of Arnold's mesmeric power had no measurable effect on his listeners. Those who followed him have been described, and their effects are measurable. It is clear that the vast majority of school preachers came from the hosts of boredom: certainly from 19th-century memoirs it is religious boredom that rises as stupefying as that exacted by the classics. "My Sunday evening feeling," wrote D'Arcy Thompson of Christ's Hospital, "of blank, cold, hungry, church-wearied, sermon-stunned, for-ever-and-for-everish despair." At Eton, in the 1840s, but also at Harrow and many other schools, not only would preachers deliver the same sermon again and again, but they "were so inaudibly delivered as to be, in some instances, little more than a dumb show". Nor did the fact that the actual physical connection of the schools with the Church start to loosen have the slightest effect on the intensity with which they continued to din her teachings into the bored and exasperated ears of their pupils. Churchill went to chapel so often and built up such a huge reserve in his religious bank he felt that, really, he had no need to go again for the rest of his life. He would quote Disraeli's maxim—"all sensible men are of the same religion"—with approval. When pressed as to the nature of that religion he would also quote Disraeli's reply: "Sensible men never say."

The result shows up clearly in Appendix F. From 1830 to 1880 the number of boys entering the Church falls steadily and steeply. The evangelical revival among schoolmasters led directly, by a paradoxical but understandable reaction, to the religious collapse of their pupils. And by 1920, while religious instruction and practice continued to be thumped into them at school, the decline in church attendance, also steady since 1870, had become so pronounced that some religious commentators said hysterically that Britain was little better than pagan. This of course is rubbish. The canons and *mores* of Britain then, and now, were unmistakably Christian. What had happened was more interesting. Growing up during an evangelical revival, as we have seen, the whole corpus of school beliefs and values whose origins and growths we have been uncovering— team spirit, house loyalty, sexual continence and fidelity, the whole orchestra of "tone" and the like—is, if sometimes in a rather muddled way, to a large extent Christian. While eroding its magical base by boredom, they supplied a new *raison d'être*, new forms and new rituals for some of its ethical standards. From 1900 onwards the real religion of most British middle- and upper-class men (followed dutifully by their wives) was their public school.

5 Empire

Public schools have often been criticised as crude agents of British Imperialism. Derek Verschoyle, for instance, in an attack centring principally on Malvern, notes that the authoritarian nature of public school upbringing was precisely that which England imposed on her Empire. This could be likened to a vast school in which pupil natives were ruled in arrogant prefect fashion, while being slowly and patronisingly trained to be prefects themselves so that they could, in a limited measure, run the schools themselves. This was not casual, says Verschoyle, it was deliberate. The public schools were deliberately formed to do just this, and in this way. Robert Birley has written that from 1800 the Empire meant a great deal more to the middle classes than is generally realised.

The picture is not totally clear, partly because little research has been done. It should be obvious from earlier chapters that the Empire had nothing to do with the founding of new public schools or rise of old ones. Quite other forces were at work. In fact from 1800 to 1850 the Empire, as a concept, is conspicuous by its absence. It hardly appears in sermons or headmasters' addresses; school novels and memoirs virtually ignore it. It appears once in *Tom Brown*—Mrs. Arnold says vaguely, "Ay, many is the brave heart now doing its work and bearing its load under the Indian sun, and in Australian farms and clearings . . ."; in *Eric* there is an equally vague suggestion of boys masturbating themselves to death in the Colonies; there is very little else. Mr. Arrowsmith, in his analysis of Charterhouse registers up to 1872, says that between ten per cent and fifteen per cent went to service this Empire in India. This is an astonishing figure. There is no reason to suppose Charterhouse was different from other schools in this respect, and if accurate it would mean the Empire was flooded with public school boys at this time. Yet it is generally agreed that, for such immense territories, the Empire was run by a relatively minute number of men. (See Heussler's *Yesterday's Rulers* and Sir Ralph Furse, *Acuparius*.) I strongly suspect that the bulk of Mr. Arrowsmith's fifteen per cent was serving India in the army and would return, not colonial administrators pure and simple, which is what I am concerned with here. If this is so, then Charterhouse falls into line with other analyses of public schools for this period (see Appendix G) when quite large numbers enter the army while, until 1850, few have jobs "overseas".

The point is that public schools did see themselves as producing leaders.

An interesting moment in the development of Rugby—1852. The ball is being carried, but the game is still, in essence, "a ghastly scrimmage".

The Procession of Boats at Eton, late 19th century. Note the elaborate uniforms.

Durham schoolboys in 1900. In this simple scene there are at least ten articles or variations of dress designating different positions in the school's hierarchies.

Before a match—Harrow.

"Of course you needn't work, Fitzmilksoppe;
but play you must and shall!"
Games: the new religion.
Du Maurier *Punch* cartoon.

A class system of élite leadership would automatically extend itself to lead anything that turned up to be led—other classes, armies, if the Victorians had landed on the moon public school boys would have appeared to lead there. The same was true of the Empire. But the system did not grow up because of the expanding needs of Empire. The difference is subtle, but important. It is a question of emphasis. Once the process had started, however, it would become more and more conscious.

A change begins around the middle of the century. As the school communities concentrated ever more intensely on those in them so they aroused ever stronger loyalties, a kind of school house patriotism. This patriotism was expressed in the same language as national patriotism. After a fight in *Tom Brown*, when the boys are wondering whether to go on later, Arthur says, "Can't tell about that—all depends on the houses. We're in the hands of our countrymen you know. Must fight for the School-house flag, if so be." And, as these mini-worlds became the whole world to those in them, so in turn the outside world was reacted to in the little world's terms—school patriotism, house patriotism, spread out, rousing national patriotism, became one with it and both, as the century progresses, grow steadily more exalted, fierce and explicit. Cory wrote proudly in his journal of a pupil "killed at Sebastopol with glory"; his own glory, and to the greater glory of Eton and England. Throughout the Second World War Churchill attended the Harrow songs, and returning from them one night he said to his son Randolph: "Listening to these boys singing all those well-remembered songs I could see myself fifty years before singing with them those tales of great deeds and of great men and wondering with intensity how I could ever do something glorious for my country."

Such moments are given the full treatment in *The Hill*, showing exactly how the schools managed to whirl school loyalty, patriotism, games, God, the Queen, the headmaster, team spirit and nostalgia into one great, intoxicating, sentimental, muddled and inflaming brew. A general arrives:

> Conviction seized the boys that a conqueror was among them. Even now, he remained the active untiring servant of Queen and Country. And he had taken time to come down to Harrow to hear the boys sing. And, dash it all! he, John, was going to sing to him!

> > "Forty years on, growing older and older,
> > Shorter in mind and in memory long,
> > Feeble of foot and rheumatic of shoulder,
> > What will it help you that once you were strong?
> > God gives us bases to guard or beleaguer,
> > Games to play out, whether earnest or fun,
> > Fights for the fearless, and goals for the eager,

Twenty and thirty and forty years on!
Follow up! Follow up! Follow up!
Till the field ring again and again,
With the tramp of the twenty-two men.
Follow up!"

As the hundreds of voices, past and present indissolubly linked together, imposed the mandate, "Follow up!" the headmaster glanced at his guest, but left unsaid the words about to be said. Tears were trickling down the cheeks of the man who, forty years before, had won his sovereign's cross—For Valour.

Despite this, I don't think it would be accurate to say that the extreme heights of patriotism reached in England—Bulldog Drummond once actually applied the word "patriot" to a Swiss for being pro-British—were caused by the public schools. Extreme patriotism was common all over Western Europe in the last decades of the 19th century. What one can say is that in England these schools were one of the chief methods of engendering patriotism and also often explain the terms of its expression and its intensity.

The effect on their attitudes towards the Empire was considerable. One of the reasons for the silence about the Empire before 1850 was snobbery. It had been appreciated since the 18th century that money could be made in the Colonies. But, of course, gentlemen don't need to make money. That is why nabobs are often the subject of some derision in the novels of the period. These class scruples remained to an extent, but were more and more blown away by gusts of patriotism. You were not going out to get rich, but for the good of your country. And so now we see more and more public school boys serving "overseas" (see again Appendix G). We have already remarked on Empire—oriented schools like Haileybury and Cheltenham. Cheltenham had a foreign–language department with a building larger than the classical department. You could learn Sanskrit and Hindustani.

And it was not just for the good of the country—it was for the good of the Empire itself. After the Indian Mutiny in 1858 it seemed clear that if we withdrew the result would be barbarism. And the great boast of the public schools was that they trained *character*. They were actually turning out men who were morally better. Material benefits, railways, schools, hospitals, Britain would of course bring—and take. But her real contribution would be moral. By the 1880s the rôle of the public schools as a body had become explicit. Here is J. E. Welldon, Churchill's headmaster:

An English headmaster, as he looks to the future of his pupils, will not forget that they are to be the citizens of the greatest Empire under heaven; ... he will inspire them with faith in the divinely ordered mission of their country and their race; he will impress upon their young minds ... that the great principles

. . . of truth, liberty, equality, and religion—are the principles which they must carry into the world; he will emphasise the fact that no principles, however splendid, can greatly or permanently affect mankind, unless they are illustrated by bright examples of personal morality.

After Harrow, Welldon went on to become Bishop of Calcutta, and took great pride in the many boys he had persuaded into Imperial administration.

The letter to Correlli Barnett I have already quoted from, written by C. A. Vlieland, once in the Malayan Civil Service, goes on: "I think we all believed in our hearts (though we should have shrunk from any such ethical and altruistic motives) that the creation of the British Empire was the best thing that ever happened to mankind."

And it is extraordinary, as Correlli Barnett says, how the concept, a public school one, spread out and how long it lasted. Even now we think that Britain exercises, has the right to exercise, a special "moral" influence on world affairs; a feeling that other powers will heed the raised hand, the frown and shaken pipe of that grave and kindly figure, the wise house-master across the sea.

It should be noted that, as far as public school influence went, the Empire was not just one big red lump. H. B. Gray, who studied this at the time, wrote:

. . . The English boy, as he emerges from the crucible of the public school laboratory, is generally a more conspicuous failure—especially at first—in these new and partially discovered Continents [Australia and Canada] than he has proved himself to be a conspicuous success in dealing with lower or more submissive races in the wilds of Africa or in the plains of India.

Considering their prefect training, this is not surprising.

With this proviso, by 1900, therefore, the situation did much more resemble that in Verschoyle's attack. But even then, and on into the 20s and 30s, class anxiety kept it muffled. "The school specialises in the preparation of boys for the ICS and the Colonial Services." Some such phrase is in many a prospectus or *Public Schools Year Book* entry; but it is tucked away.

6 The army

Wars are explained as much by the general belligerence of the country, the extent to which a populace has been excited into wanting a war and believing it to be morally right, as by the assassinations and telegrams that spark them off, or even the weighty tides of economic and political self-interest that appear to be the "fundamental" causes. We have observed the

growth of public school patriotic belligerence, seen earlier in their attitude
to foreign countries–which have quite often been put forward as a major
cause of our entry into the First World War. It is important, therefore, to
evaluate the charge. This is the subject of an essay by Geoffrey Best, the
most amusing and cogent in *The Victorian Public School*.

We are already clear that the public schools approved of the army as a
career. To the boys themselves it was a way of continuing school in a
slightly different form. In *Tom Brown*, East goes to India to join his
regiment.

"'He will make a capital officer.'

"'Ay, won't he!' said Tom, brightening.

"'No fellow could handle boys better, and I suppose soldiers are very like
boys.'"

Another glance at Appendix G will indicate how continuously popular
the army was as an occupation throughout the century; and Appendix H,
made from army lists of the Boer War, shows which schools provided
most officers and for what branches of the service.

But Best goes on to see just how helpful the schools were in bringing
this recruitment about. The avenues into the army were via the Royal
Military Academy, Sandhurst, Woolwich and, from 1909, Addiscombe.
Only at Woolwich did you need to know a little trigonometry and a little
physics to become one of the socially inferior engineers or artillery men
(Eton did not supply a single officer to either branch during the Boer
War). "There seems," writes Best, "to have been no limit to what you
didn't have to know to get into the infantry or cavalry." Nevertheless it
was a limit many public schools managed to exceed. As we have already
seen, to get into one of these institutions it was nearly always necessary to
go to a crammer first. These, far more than public schools, were the
direct and necessary educational link.

What then of the School Corps in the 1870–1900 period? Some schools
certainly had Corps of a high standard. Dr. Warre was extremely militaristic—no doubt glimpsing a further avenue out of his massive confusion—
and in the 80s and 90s Eton had a proper and efficient Volunteer Corps. At
Wellington about half the boys came from military families and would be
ploughed back into the army. The Corps here was affiliated to the
Volunteers and had a small grant. We have here, therefore, loose
connections with the War Office.

But these were exceptional. The overwhelming evidence is that up till
1900 the various Cadet Corps and Rifle Corps (sometimes interchange-
able, sometimes separate organisations) were militarily completely ineffective, with little or no direct or serious connection with the army. In
particular, they met hostility from the games side; a fatal drawback.
Loretto wouldn't have a Corps till 1910 for that reason. The Headmaster
of Westminster told the Ward Committee in 1907 that they had a Corps

but it was ineffective since "necessarily officered in the main by boys who are not very good at games, and consequently they are not so much respected". Indeed it was only when they became a branch of games, with shooting matches and large social occasions—as at Bisley or the Royal Review at Aldershot in 1887 or 1897 at Windsor—that the Corps achieved any success, and this was non-military.

But the two earlier dates are significant—1907 and 1910. Westminster is apologising, Loretto reluctantly starting a Corps. After the Boer War there comes a decisive change. And as the 1914 war draws nearer, excitement becomes frenzy. Now Corps are founded, time is given to training, special officer-training schemes are set up—schools are increasingly seen as part of the military system, their job to provide officers.

Special lecturers were despatched hot-foot from the Navy League and given all the class time they needed, albeit some of their swords lay rusty in the scabbard. "Dr. Rogerson of Merchiston . . . confined himself to the Tudor period of our history." Mr. Johnstone of Edinburgh Academy talked to Fettes about the navy between 1603 and 1780, and then to Loretto about "the various methods of fighting and manoeuvring for the windward berth".

Lord Roberts, fresh from South Africa, was a bit more up to date. He was the big gun of the National Service League and was fired repeatedly. Public school records are full of him: "Lord Roberts came to review the corps"; "Lord Roberts came to give the prizes"; "Earl Roberts came to open the Boer War Memorial". At Glenalmond, in 1906:

I look to you public school boys to set an example. Let it be your ambition to render yourself capable of becoming leaders of those others who have not your advantages . . . public school training inculcates just those qualities which are required in leaders of men. . . .

Now all of this is militaristic of course, but, as Best says, it is merely part of the movement outside. It is, with rising patriotism, another element in that anxiety about England's performance relative to her international rivals which grew steadily from 1870 on—in industry, in educational (especially scientific) efficiency, and here in military strength. It reached its height after the Boer War, which was followed by Fisher's naval reforms, and Haldane's army reforms—these indeed directly introduced the Officer Training Corps. The schools reflected this. They did no more.

Finally, Geoffrey Best turns to see if the ideas which underlay public schools inculcated militarism in any specific way. "Militarism can mean (1) the prevalence of military sentiments or ideals among a people. (2) The predominance of the military class in government and administration. (3) A tendency to regard military efficiency as a paramount interest of state."

As regards the first—the prevalence of military sentiments—the

Victorians had fairly mild cults for General Gordon and Wellington and rather enjoyed dressing up as soldiers in the Militia and Volunteers. The schools shared the feelings about the generals as far as one can tell. Their Corps activities meant that they joined in at playing soldiers—but very much on the fringes.

The second—predominance of a military class—applies neither to Britain nor to the schools.

The third—military efficiency as a paramount interest of state—became important to Britain, particularly after 1900. But no more important than to other Western nations, and much less than to some—Germany for instance. The schools reflected but did not originate this.

What then of those other public schools' goals—games, "tone", "character"? Games and war I discussed in an earlier chapter; as to "tone" and "character", they encompassed a good many things, but they were not particularly to do with intelligence. Indeed extreme intellect was distrusted. But it was this that military experts realised the army needed above all—intelligent trained men. Colonel G. F. R. Henderson, the best military writer of the time, returned to this theme in article after article, but, writes Best:

> He did not find it necessary to discuss the public schools. They simply did not come into his ideas about increasing the proportion of intelligence in the army. He had something to say about Woolwich, about Sandhurst, about Oxford and Cambridge, he even looked at crammers, but what was happening in the public schools did not seem to interest him. They seem to have been below the level at which he thought it sensible to start.

Other advanced military thinkers, Spencer Wilkinson for instance, the First Chichele Professor of Military Science at Oxford, agreed with him.

Thus Geoffrey Best concludes that on all counts—as training for and avenues into the armed forces, as regards underlying ideology, and in the character attributes they instilled—the public schools made no significant contribution to the British army; and insofar as they joined the militaristic and patriotic fervour of the years before 1914 they were only reflecting national (indeed European) emotions and not originating them.

This is a useful corrective to the crude assertion that the public schools were in some way a "cause" of the First World War. At the same time I think Best underestimates certain ingredients in the pre-1914 atmosphere. Anthropologically a function of education is to instil and pass on the *mores* of a culture, and a good way to ensure schools did this was to make them dependent on fees. That was certainly a function of the public schools and is why we found, and shall often again find, them reflecting social movements and not initiating them. But they did more than this. By now all the varied forces of public school concentration which we have built up piece by piece had combined to form probably the most powerful system of educational indoctrination since Sparta removed her sons from their families at the age of seven to train them into soldiers. The public schools reflected social movements, but then intensified them many times and twisted them in peculiar and fascinating ways. This is not the ground I would ideally have chosen to demonstrate what I mean. It might be thought that nothing could have made Britain in 1914—after virtually a hundred years of peace (sharpened by Boer War humiliation), the richest, most powerful country in the world—more bellicose than she was. Yet I think public schools did do this—not just to the middle and upper classes but right down through the social strata.

In Alec Waugh's *The Loom of Youth* it was argued, absolutely seriously, that games were entirely responsible for Britain's position in the war at that time (it was grave). Games were so important they could encompass anything, until even war itself became a game. Sapper, in his books about the war, continually refers to fighting as The Game or The Great Game. And this was universal at the time. Boys at the front wrote endless personal letters to their headmasters and housemasters, and many of these were printed in school magazines. Nearly always they use sports language to describe the action. Captain Nichols to Loretto can stand for thousands of others: "The German Flying Corps is the only part of that degraded nation's military machine which 'plays the game'." This extended right up to the generals. General Lord Horne: "It may fairly be claimed that when hostilities ended . . . we had outplayed Germany at all points of the game . . . possibly Germany was more quick to imitate methods of warfare. . . . Certainly we were slow to adopt, indeed our souls abhorred, anything unsportsmanlike." But if war is just a game then how much easier it is to whip up enthusiasm for it, how simple to transform all that yelling at the edge of football pitches, the breathless excitement of seventy-two not out, into a violent—and yet somehow safe, bloodless, deathless—desire to go out and fight.

And by 1914 that patriotic intensity, which we saw derived from, was the same as, school and house patriotism—whose fires had been continually fanned by schoolmasters—had become so exalted that it was able to make the demand which all religions must, ultimately, be able to make. When Sir Henry Newbolt's hero is to have his head cut off at dawn, it is of his school he thinks:

> He saw the school close, sunny and green,
> The runner beside, the stand by the parapet wall,
> The distant tape, and the crowd roaring between,
> His name over all.

Letter after letter from the front says how glad the writers are not to have let school or house down, how if they are to die they are proud to die for school and country. And these themes are echoed again in the school obituaries. The public school ethos had gone beyond the grave. Games too got caught up in this passionate confusion. To play well for your school meant to die well for your country. Indeed, the first imperative led to the second:

> O, safe with thy soldiers up-grown
> Is thy honour, high Queen of the Glen,
> And the battle shall seal them thine
> Glenalmond, right mother of men.

So sang the boys of that northern school.

In the bloodiest struggle of them all, one platoon of soldiers was led not by an officer carrying a sword or a revolver but by a subaltern kicking a football. Perhaps Waugh was right. There is a sense, because of the blithe, almost carefree heroism with which they went to such terrible slaughter, in which the battle of the Somme was lost on the playing fields of Sherborne.

CHAPTER 9

Some Effects of the Public Schools: The Monolith Established

The schoolboy sense of an impending doom
Which goes with news of deaths and clanging bells . . .
Doom! Shivering doom! Inexorable bells
To early school, to chapel, school again:
Compulsory constipation, hurried meals . . .
The dread of beatings! Dread of being late! . . .
John Betjeman, *Summoned by Bells*

In 1972 an attack was delivered on the Victorian and Edwardian public schools so sweeping in its extent, so devastating in its power that, reading it, one half expects those unfortunate institutions to have somehow expunged themselves from the memory of history in shame. This was in *The Collapse of British Power* by Correlli Barnett. I have mentioned it before, but it is necessary now to look closer at his attack because this brilliant book had a considerable and deserved success (it is still among the most borrowed books in the London Library); it represents something of a received view and echoes of it, for instance, can be found in Anthony Sampson's various *Anatomies of Britain*.

1 The Collapse of British Power

Let me try to summarise Correlli Barnett's argument. In 1880 Britain was the richest country in the world. She was still immensely powerful after 1918, having smashed her strongest enemy and being buttressed by strong allies. Yet in 1942, she was within four months of complete bankruptcy, totally dependent on the US for capital, raw materials, steel and armaments. This catastrophic decline in power had been entirely brought about by the British themselves. Our weakness was revealed by the war, not caused by it. Even the Empire turned out to be a liability and a danger, requiring defence and protection and not contributing, at first, anything like enough to bring this about.

What caused this decline? Failure to re-arm; pacifist politicians like Baldwin, MacDonald and Chamberlain; and the failure of the British government between the wars to remedy British industrial backwardness:

> All these are partial explanations; outward facets of an inner truth, but they do not explain, for example, *why* such a particular stamp of men as Baldwin and MacDonald, Chamberlain, Simon and Halifax, Henderson and Eden, held sway in British politics between the wars; *why* British public opinion was so pacifistic between the wars; *why* "appeasement" was so widely congenial and re-armament repugnant; *why* British governments handled international crises in the feeble and nerveless way they did; *why* the British permitted the catastrophic decline of their industrial power; *why* the Empire was allowed to remain a source of strategic weakness and danger. The answers lie deeper, in the very springs of judgment and action: in the national character itself, as it had evolved by the early 20th century. For it is character which, at grips with circumstances, governs the destinies of nations as it does of individual men. It is the key to all policies, all decisions.

And the key to Britain's national character is her public schools.

Correlli Barnett now directs his attack to three fronts, the first of which is evangelical religion. This, together with all the attendant high-flown moral afflatus which flapped about "character", "tone" and the rest, inculcated a totally unrealistic Christian "moral" outlook on politics and international affairs. It was often even wetter than this. Dr. Cyril Norwood, Headmaster of Harrow in 1928: "For what has happened in the course of the last hundred years is that the old ideals have been recaptured. The ideals of chivalry which inspired the knighthood of medieval days . . . have been combined in the tradition of English education which holds the field today. It is based upon religion; it relies largely upon games. . . ." But the privilege of such uplift in international affairs was only possible after Waterloo, when England reigned supreme. We were able to have it in the same way as the rich are able not to feel envy. By 1880 Germany and America had caught up, France was not far behind—by which time we were reluctant and unable to face competition again.

This soft pacific strain was compounded by the ridiculous public school curriculum, the classical and high academic education effectively removing the best brains from science and industry. And, except for a few boys in the sixth, the teaching was stereotyped and deadening, hours of learning by heart, with no scope for initiative or exploration.

And so he comes to the final, and perhaps the most important, of his assaults: that the public schools were above all engines to produce uniformity. They were designed to reward conformity, obedience to authority, and to crush originality and rebellion. And they had succeeded. The saving graces of the upper classes had once been their variety, individuality and spontaneity; now they were conventional, dull, self-satisfied and snobbish. And this whole slack, uncompetitive crowd of "leaders" was brought up on a games ethic where the point was not to win but to "play the game"; where team spirit was more important than team victory, and anything that was not cricket was not on. At a time of turbulent change, of an aggressive Germany, of ferocious and unscrupulous competition, of—at the end of the 19th century—intense scientific progress and speculation, the schools had become static, they took for granted their position and their Empire, thinking that both would last for ever, when the time had come to defend and change and fight.

So strong was the influence that the statesmen of the 1920s and 30s, at school in the 1880s, began to look and sound like public school headmasters—prissy, intoning, measured. Sir John Simon, foreign secretary from 1931 to 1935, "spent a successful life on earth without learning its ways, for he was unworldly, though the reverse of other-worldly. . . ." Lord Halifax, foreign secretary from 1937 to 1940 had "a meek and Christian nature".Attlee–"a senior geography master".But above all it was Baldwin, at Harrow in 1881, returning to watch the cricket, sing the songs, a revered Old Boy,who was the prime example. He was Headmaster of England more or less from 1922 to 1937, pipe-smoking, full of commonsense firmness. When dismissing the Trade Unionists at the end of the General Strike he said, "Now run along." He was a contemplative speaker, redolent of an older England, an England of apples and farms, fond of evoking moods, gently uplifting the nation. "And the favourite mood was one of sunset calm and nostalgia, in which the British nation, like an old couple in retirement enjoying the peaceful ending of the day, contemplated some sweep of English landscape and hearkened to the distant church bells."

Another result was that public school virtues were preferred in the Civil Service where much more robust ones were becoming more and more urgent. The Colonial Office's confidential *Appointments Handbook* stated that "duty and chivalry are of more account than ambition and self-seeking". H. E. Dale, in *The Higher Civil Service of Great Britain*, noted that the home Civil Service too—confronting the already formidable machines of European bureaucracy—encouraged the steady, safe, orthodox man of academic approach rather than, as one senior civil servant put it, the man of "intense energy, great driving force and devouring zeal", a type he'd only met once.

But the most serious area was that of international affairs. After the 1914 war, public school faith in good form, decency, honour between nations—even though they had just been shown to be completely worthless—became dominant in an England totally enfeebled by them. Britain made a fundamental mistake of exporting the romantic and unrealistic public school ideals into international relations, where they gave rise to appeasement, League of Nations fantasy, failure to re-arm, and the rest. The result, coupled with public school fear of competition, was disastrous. "Indeed," writes this military historian, "other characteristics fostered by Victorian education—conservatism, doctrinaire orthodoxy, rigidity, inertia and unbounded complacency—are classic attributes of an army about to suffer a catastrophic defeat."

And yet we won the war. In fact we won two wars in extraordinarily quick succession. Belatedly, Correlli Barnett returns to face this fact:

> For this was the hour, an hour too long delayed, when England returned to herself; when English policy once again spoke in broadsides instead of sermons. To the world's astonishment, the nation which had allowed itself to be represented by—which had even seen itself mirrored in—men like Baldwin, MacDonald, Henderson, Simon, Chamberlain—reverted of a sudden to its eighteenth-century character, hard as cannon.

"To the world's astonishment"; one feels Correlli Barnett's astonishment too. Because his brilliant attack—the violence of which I have in no way exaggerated—raises, by the very force and effectiveness of its argument, a new problem. If the national character had been as totally weakened as he suggests, it would have been quite incapable of responding to this challenge. It would have been incapable of responding to any challenge whatsoever. It is not enough to say, as he does, that we did it on American money, American arms, American planes. We are talking about *character*, not material things. The French army was numerically weaker than the German (ninety-four divisions against 160); but they were strong, well equipped and well trained. The Maginot Line was a superb piece of military engineering. Nor was the numerical disadvantage a straight ninety-four versus 160; the divisions were spread about. Yet we didn't collapse and the French did—one of our supposedly "ferocious" competitors, whose national "character" had not been sapped by public school education.

It is a tricky concept, "national character". I do not see how it can at one moment change and be weak to explain the policies of the 1920s and 1930s, and then at the next moment change back to its 18th-century "self". Correlli Barnett cannot have his cake and eat it.

I would like to embark on a fairly lengthy detour, at all times relevant to the public schools, and one which will illuminate and demonstrate their effects at many points, and which I think explains how and where *The Collapse of British Power* has gone wrong.

2 Total societies

In 1961 Erving Goffman wrote a book called *Asylums*. Here, although he was not the first to use the words "Total Society", he was the first to clearly define the concept. In doing so he added to it a new and extremely interesting dimension.

A "Total Society" can be defined like this: it is a place of residence which provides for all the needs of the inhabitants and where they are cut off from society for appreciable periods of time. The activities of the society are performed together, they take place under a rational plan, and they have a common goal or goals. Goffman's principal studies were done in large American mental hospitals, the Institute of Mental Health in Bethesda, and St. Elizabeths Hospital, Washington, DC; but he uses material from all the other examples he gives of total institutions: old people's homes, TB sanatoriums, prisons, concentration camps, army barracks, ships, convents, monasteries, abbeys—and British public schools.

Goffman found that total societies evolve a great many unique characteristics which are found together nowhere else; they don't all exhibit all, but they all exhibit a great many of them.

Let me give some examples. Because total societies have large numbers controlled by relatively small staff, the staff tend to think the inmates secretive and evil; at best they are always wary, ready for "mischief". Their anxiety is not allayed by the knowledge that anti-authority moves may be the result of boredom, or a move to get self-respect. Even the weak have power. An old, weak mental patient can cause a great deal of infuriating trouble just by locking his thumbs into his trouser pockets when being undressed.

Total institutions make various attacks on the self, particularly at first, in order to impose the authority of the institution. Newcomers are given derogatory status and names—"swab" in the army, "fish" in borstal. They are often not allowed to personalise their bed-spaces; Benedictine monks have to change cells once a year in case they get too attached to them. There is public exposure; in prisons nakedness on arrival, lavatories without doors. Attacks of this sort lead to fear, fear to a readiness, indeed a need to join the group: "Make the little fuckers sleep and eat together," grinned Jock MacKay, senior instructor, "and we'll have 'em drilling together, naturally" (*The Mint*, T. E. Lawrence).

Punishments are given in public. Flogging was in public on naval warships. The punishments take on the colour of the institution. In mental hospitals it was often shock therapy (as in *One Flew over the Cuckoo's Nest*). Inmates sometimes have to assist. "The patients' convulsions often resemble those of an accident victim in death agony and are accompanied by choking gasps and at times by a foaming overflow of saliva from the mouth . . . [serving] the others as a frightful spectacle of what may be done to them."

The self is attacked; it is also curtailed. Endless rules grow up controlling dress, manners, behaviour, where the inmate can walk and when, so that a member suffers endless anxiety because of what Goffman calls echelon authority—all the staff having authority over all the inmates.

But these restrictions open the way to rewards, privileges upon which the ravenous self can fall. The rewards are the removal of the restrictions and lead to co-operation.

An under-life develops; secret loyalties, secret practices engaged in just because they are illegal, and done as dangerously as possible. In Central Hospital there was an alcoholic who smuggled in vodka and then drank it in the middle of the lawn. (In schools this is complex because the under-life can provide the attacks on self which in other institutions are provided by the staff. The split is not direct and simple. The prefects or bullies sometimes assume, as it were, a second line of total institution. Prisons share this complexity.)

Special group and space loyalties spring up within the society—houses, studies, libraries.

A language develops to cover all important areas.

The most profound rebellion against a total institution is, paradoxically, evidence of the most profound involvement. All aspects of the institution have to be rebelled against, so the orientation is therefore total. (Public school sociologists, for example John Wakeford in *The Cloistered Elite*, have noticed that among reactions to school goals—acceptance, withdrawal, desire to change, intransigence, etc.—rebellion often precedes acceptance.)

The institution puts on occasional "shows" to the outside world, often to try to persuade them that it is really different from what it seems. A mental hospital will show it is "liberal"; a prison that it has good food, proper rehabilitation classes. You can often tell where an institution secretly feels uneasy by what it parades. (I was amused sometimes at the "fronts" put on by public schools. At the open day of one progressive school, a big feature was the essays of the sixth form. They were pinned on the walls for all to see. Winchester would have thought you were mad if you had suggested their sixth form stick their essays on the walls for the parents to read. But it was at Winchester that no less than five masters casually let drop the enormous success of Britten's *War Requiem* which they had mounted in collaboration with Bedales, how well they'd got on with them, etc., etc.)

The favoured inmate—the "Trusty"—will often have more power and prestige than the lowest members of the staff: the sergeant major compared to the new second lieutenant, the bo'sun on a ship.

There is a tendency for the goal or goals of the institution to grow and get out of hand. Members, staff and inmates, can completely lose their sense of proportion; soon everything is connected with the all-involving aim—"verbalised perspectives . . . come to play a central and often feverish rôle". And things are seen in different distortions peculiar to the different goals. Dr. Belkrap on mental hospitals: "In the usual case of this kind, such things as impudence, insubordination, and excessive familiarity are translated into more or less professional terms." That is, they mean you are more or less mentally ill. In a prison you are more or less of a security risk, in a monastery more or less subject to spiritual pride or other temptations, in a public school around 1900 more or less likely to lose the match or lack "character" or become exposed to "sin". Harrow around 1905:

"Oh, Caesar, you're—you're—"
"Well?"
"You're going to play bridge?"
"Yes? What of it? . . ."
"All right," said John, stiffly, but with breaking heart.

There is no need to labour the relevance of all this to our subject. The characteristics of total institutions which I have just outlined are, in every instance, the very things whose development we have been studying. And perhaps it is not all that surprising. The point is if you enclose people so that what they are in—a total institution—becomes the whole world, then you can expect that institution to start mimicking the world. It will have its own language, its own love, its own criminals. Enclosed, the passions, emotions, aggressions, needs which can normally be dissipated or satisfied in a thousand different ways can only be expressed in terms of, by means of, that little shut off world.

But this does mean we must alter our perspective slightly. We have been tending to explain some of these developments historically—by the influence of evangelical religion, say, or the way in which 18th-century boy freedom and culture persisted in the 19th century but were only allowed if out of sight thus becoming the public school "under-life". We now see that these characteristics arise in all total institutions and arise *only* in them. They arise when they become total and because they become total and for no other reason. The more "restrictive", more total an institution is the more of these characteristics does it share; the less total, the fewer (this development we shall gradually trace during the 20th century). The historical explanations are still extremely important. They explain why public schools became total institutions at all, the particular and unique form their total characteristics took, and they explain the timing and the methods by which they developed. But we can now see them not as causes but as results of—and ingredients in—that restrictive totality to which I gave the name "public school concentration".

And there is more to it than that. All total institutions show examples of adjustment in escape and defiance. They often put on plays or reviews and have magazines. (These are often allowed to be critical and satirical, even violently so. The staff can then feel how unstable and explosive the society "really" is and so justify their restrictions.) There is the *sotto voce* rebellion. Brendan Behan:

"The Warden shouted at him.

"'Right, Sir,' he shouted back. 'Be right along, Sir,' adding in a lower tone, 'you shit 'ouse.'"

Or "there is a special stance that can be taken to alleviate authority; it combines stiffness, dignity, and coolness in a particular mixture that conveys insufficient insolence to call forth immediate punishment and yet expresses that one is entirely one's own man."

The whole school "under-life" is clearly to do with this. In all total institutions, Goffman notes:

> We find that participants decline in some way to accept the official view of what they should be putting into and getting out of the organisation . . . where enthusiasm is expected, there will be apathy; where loyalty, there will be disaffection, where robustness, some kind of illness. . . . We find a multitude of homely little histories, each in its way a movement of liberty. Whenever worlds are laid on, under-lives develop.

The key words here are "whenever" and "laid on". Early progressive educationalists thought that they had only to make a school free and the evils of public school life would vanish. Many of the evils did, but other reactions often remained, and remain, the same. It doesn't matter how liberal a school is, it is still "laid on", it has not been chosen. So there appear movements of liberty. Dartington, still one of the freest of the progressive schools, certainly evidences this at times—"where enthusiasm is expected, there will be apathy. . . ."

Now the obvious reaction to all these various forms and degrees of rebellion is that they are methods of defence, ways of preserving the self in a totalitarian society. It is here that Goffman starts to go deeper than the sociologists who had come before him.

It had always been noted how individuals were formed by groups, identified with them and wilted away unless they had emotional support from them. At the same time when we observe any social group we find the same patterns of rebellion combined with the need to identify and belong (it is just easier to see the pattern in a total society). An individual seems to need the group; at the same time he seems to need to create elbow room between himself and the unit others assume he should identify with.

Goffman now elevates these two apparently contradictory movements to a central place. Perhaps these defences (the under-life) are not just a move against restrictions, nor are they a move to somewhere perfect— what a boy or girl would do if the school were "freer", say—but that they are inevitable and necessary no matter what the social unit is like.

An individual, in this view, is part self, part member of an organisation. To grow, to exist at all, he has to take up a position between identification with the organisation and opposition to it, and he retains this position by being ready, at the slightest pressure, to shift his involvement in either direction. That is to say, it is only *against something* that the self can emerge and continue to live. It is a continuous process of tension, of compromise between rebellion and conformity. Without something to belong to, to conform to, we have no stable self; but total identification means becoming the same as the unit, thus losing the self. We keep our sense of self by distancing ourselves, by criticism.

We see now how fundamental is the apparently trivial objection of schoolboys to changes in the structure of the school. "They enjoy criticising the frame and saying it is wrong," a Rugby master said to me, "but they don't want to change it." He thought it was insecurity, which, as we saw, is true. But far more is it because they do in fact define themselves by criticism; if what they are defining themselves against suddenly goes, naturally the process is more difficult. Even if they see intellectually that it should go—an old and useless tradition, fagging or whatever—they instinctively realise that the necessity to form the self is more important and prefer to keep it.

It is at this point, though we shall continue our trajectory away from him for some while, that we can glance briefly back at Correlli Barnett. It is clear that the equation restrictive, conformist, authoritarian, boring public schools equal crushed, conformist, bored, lacking drive and initiative, "sapped" public school products and therefore a "sapped" Britain is far too simple. It takes no account of the extremely varied and complex reactions which are possible to total and authoritarian institutions. The real freedom of the sixth form, the studies, the existence of men like Cory, all ensured that a good many boys survived those oppressive and unpleasant regimes with confidence, initiative, and sense of self, at least, all intact. We can now see that elements in such regimes—the conflicts and criticism they create—are actually essential ingredients in the growth to individuality.

Confirmation that this is so can be found in the book on American education—*The Vanishing Adolescent* by Edgar Friedenberg. Here he notes the necessity for conflict and disagreement, the need to take one's stand in adolescence in the process of self-definition. American schools, by blandness, by the use of subtle appeals and the use of group guilt, have managed to produce an "homogenized" society, according to Friedenberg, where conflict is reduced to a minimum. As a result, self-definition cannot take place—hence the "vanishing" adolescent. In this context he sees virtues in the public schools, however idiotic their rules and oppressive their system. "The British public school . . . made adolescence much more than an interregnum. It made it an epoch . . . its heroes became myths and in turn clichés, but the schoolboy had strong feelings about them." There were prefects who cared, who helped you and didn't, classmates you liked or were indifferent to, good masters, bad masters. The sum effect was, compared to American schools now, that "at best, they helped the adolescent make himself into a strongly characterised human being . . . they defined the context of adolescence; they gave the adolescent something to be adolescent about . . . at worst their impact made adolescence interminable and their victims permanently fixated Old Boys".

3 Old Boys—some facets of permanent adolescence

. . . Were I to deduce any system from my feelings on leaving Eton [wrote Cyril Connolly, in a seminal passage which has been echoed by Friedenberg and by every other writer on the subject] it might be called *The Theory of Permanent Adolescence*. It is the theory that the experience undergone by boys at the great public schools, their triumphs and disappointments, are so intense as to dominate their lives and to arrest their development. From these it results that the greater part of the ruling class remains adolescent, school-minded, self-conscious, cowardly, sentimental and in the last analysis homosexual. Early laurels weigh like lead and of many of the boys whom I knew at Eton, I can say that their lives are over. Those who knew them then knew them at their best and fullest; now, in their early thirties, they are haunted ruins. When we meet we look at each other, there is a pause of recognition, which gives way to a moment of guilt and fear. "I won't tell on you," our eyes say, "if you won't tell on me"—and when we do speak it is to discover peculiar evidence of this obsession.

He has met Old Etonians who have had the same experience; some dream they are back in their old rooms while their wives and children hang about outside to disgrace them.

Connolly is the philosopher/psychiatrist of the public schools. And his idea is perfectly tenable according to current psychoanalytic theory. Events which are too violent in childhood or early adolescence can fix the emotions at that stage and prevent growth. But the Old Boy state is more than this. It is not just the emotions; the entire experience seems to have been branded in. Connolly himself was haunted by it for years:

For my own part I was long dominated by impressions of school. The plopping of gas mantles in the classroom, the refrain of psalm tunes, the smell of plaster on the stairs, the walk through the fields to the bathing places or to the chapel across the cobbles of School Yard, evoked a vanished Eden of grace and security; the intimate noises of college . . .

This is the note one comes across continually—anguish, a sense of expulsion from Eton, as English boys, now men, sick with longing and nostalgia, go over those intense pains, those pleasures lost for ever, again and again. Naturally, Marstock had no room for any other memories or thoughts at all. Eight years after leaving Wellington, Nicolson meets him in Paris. They look over the bridge that crosses the Seine at the Latin Quarter and Nicolson points out to Marstock the two sphinxes at the end and tells him how

> Wilde in those last shambling years would tell how that sphinx there on the right was the only person who returned his smile. "But why," said Marstock, "the one on the right? They're both exactly the same?" I was silent at this, looking into the river and thinking vaguely of mighty poets in their misery dead. "Do you remember," said Marstock, "how after footer one would come back to the house and one would brew and read a book?" I said that I remembered very well.

Now I'm not sure that psychoanalytic theory, though it can explain emotional fixations and stuntings of various sorts, does fully account for the range and extent of this experience. Perhaps the mini-kibbutz situation, the fact that to a variable extent their school was their family, goes some way to doing so. But most childhoods, however intense, don't hang on in this way. It is as if for a good number of people, though not all by any means, the result of being confined in an extremely regimented total society at a very early age has a unique effect. For some reason the experience cannot be assimilated. Nor can it be repressed. It remains a permanent, somehow active block in the head, for ever. Certainly it is as the public school concentration was reaching its zenith that another unique feature of the Old Boy situation appears. From 1870 on the schoolboy literature, which we saw beginning with *Tom Brown* and *Eric*, becomes a flood, and continues until after the Second World War. No other country in the world has this. It is impossible to estimate the size of this literature, but it ran into many thousands of novels. John Betjeman told me that in the 1920s a massive bibliography of school books was produced by a German. Unfortunately I have been unable to trace it. These books, which filled prep and public school libraries, were enormously successful. *The Hill*, for example, was reprinted twenty-one times between 1905 and 1913; in 1905 alone it was reprinted nine times.

And these school books created wide echoes. *The Boy's Own Paper*, started in 1879, was almost entirely school stories, and was extremely popular among public school boys. Much popular literature shows this influence. For instance, G. A. Henty, at Westminster in late 1850, who wrote eighty novels dictated at a rate of 6,000 words a day, was one of the first to create the Buchan hero: manly, handsome and "with that nameless air of command", as John Carleton puts it, "which distinguishes most young men who have passed through the upper forms of a great public school". It will long have been clear from my quotations that, although Usborne called his excellent book *Clubland Heroes*, they were really public school heroes. The values, the characters, the emphasis on fitness, the attitudes, even the ways of speaking, found in the books of Sapper, Buchan and Yates are inexplicable without a knowledge of the public school ethos around 1900–1914.

I shall not bore you with an analysis of this school literature, but should perhaps just draw your attention to some highlights. The novels of Gunby Hadath, the Reverend E. E. Bradford and Desmond Coke are all worth reading, Desmond Coke in particular. He taught at Clayesmore and Shrewsbury, and can be read at the peak of his powers in books like *The Bending of the Twig* and *The Worm*. This last was his final novel and is about a boy who was no good at anything until (as in *Tom Brown*) he took over another boy and made good. All the books have beating scenes of extraordinary violence; and there are illustrations, drawn with trembling relish by A. M. Brock, of boys beating each other (see especially *The House Prefect*). He collected Rowlandsons. Another whole area is Catholic school literature, which is often even stranger than the rest. A typical example is *The Bonfire* by Anthony Brendhan. The climax in this is a boy dying of fright when he sees one of the Fathers.

Noel Annan says that the reason for all this—this nostalgia and sentimentality, this great body of glorifying literature—was gratitude. Public schools, and we shall see this especially as the 20th century advances, evolved to teach, among others, the stupid and became very good at it. And even where they failed to teach them very much academically, they gave them other assets like class confidence, manners and ways of speaking, which were of enormous use in later life. As a result they inspired gratitude. No doubt this is true, but once again it does not seem adequate to fully explain such a widespread, extraordinary and often ridiculous phenomenon.

For it is quite clear that the public for school literature was by no means confined to boys. Adults read it. *The Hill* and in particular *The Harrovians* were written specifically for adults. When *The Boy's Own Paper* celebrated its fiftieth anniversary, in 1929, the prime minister, Headmaster Baldwin himself, arrived to pay tribute to the "beloved paper of his boyhood".

The point is that, not only did they look back with longing, not only were the memories of their schooldays permanently fixed, entire and ever present, but many of them spent a great deal of time pretending that they had in fact never left. The Old Boy societies which sprang up during the last half of the 19th century grew into great networks of contact and reunion, with branches in every country of the world, magazines and newsletters, special hobbies committees, ties and badges and blazers to be worn like the uniform they had just put off, and frequent dinners, meetings, matches and jamborees of every sort. And to cater for the more extreme cases of this, there grew up a whole shadowy culture, shifting and fantasy-ridden, which hovers around the more straightforward school literature like the unhealthy emanation from a seance, a culture which had its own novelists, painters and poets and where men, entering it, could imagine they were once again at school.

Let me give some examples of this world. There is *Sixteen—A Diary of the Teens*, about a boy at school at Portlaw in 1917. It was one of a series—there had already been *Fourteen* and *Fifteen* and the work was finally brought to a close, after *Sixteen*, with *Sixteen and a half* and *Seventeen*.

I had been told that *Sixteen* was flagellant pornography, but this is not correct. True, a certain amount of it dwells on beating :

> "You wouldn't really have bummed me, would you, Turberville?" said Aske whitely.
> "Were you here when we bummed Keir?" said Turberville.
> "No, but I've heard of it."
> "Well, don't green yourself only bosens can bum you. If we want to bum a tick, we will."
> "Sorry, Fowker," said Aske with a sucky cheese.
> "You needn't bumsuck to Fowker," said Turberville, "you didn't hurt him."
> "You should have seen Keir's arse," Powlet was saying to Aske, "it was rather like blackberry and apple."

(The book is entirely in schoolboy jargon. Here, bummed = beaten; green = delude; bosens = prefects; tick = new boy; sucky = ingratiating; cheese = smile; bumsuck = toady to.)

The book is really an obsessive re-creation of school life for adults as they like to imagine they were at sixteen. Among the changing rooms, love affairs, the smells and lavatories ("Phew! No wonder there's a stink in here," said Rawson, picking up his waistcoat from the floor. "Fowker, isn't there an awful stink?") and among all the events, beating is just the most exciting. The book is shot through with strange intimations of self-love and self-pity :

> In the study was Colbert making me feel like a lamb and in the bedder was Turberville making me feel a babe. Oh, it was impos to be myself. . . . *Jan 6.* Was tired in the morning, but it's wonderful what you can stand if you have youth, health, and strength. . . . *Jan 7.* Cleaned my bike—I don't take such a pride in it as I used to do. But all the same it's an old friend and I remember my young bim [his bottom] has sat on the saddle and so the saddle is rather dear to me.

It is an odd book on several levels. It is hard to envisage that a grown man could have painstakingly set down day by day these imaginary minutiæ; it contains extraordinary and half-repressed fantasies that swell above the surface again and again—like the idea of buggering himself above; but in particular it is the density and strength with which his obsession charges the atmosphere: the dormitory at night, with its intimacy, the scuffling, the squeaking springs, the laughter and hysterics in the dark; the sleazy changing rooms, wallowing in filthy but hot water; the cold lavatories; and above all the sucky bummings by the bosens onto the tight-stretched bims of the ticks.

The painter of this culture was Henry Scott Tuke (1858–1929), who could do for boys' flesh what Renoir could do for women's. Year after year, in those unknowing days, he could exhibit at the Royal Academy or have hung in the Tate vast glowing paintings of naked boys or youths, posed on boats so that their buttocks caught the reflections of water, and no one so much as blinked. He was, I was told by one of his chief models, a man of great charm. This man, then a boy of exceptional beauty, had been taken to see Tuke at the age of sixteen by his housemaster ("Who wanted to seduce me"). "Tuke used to use," his ex-model told me, "bits of boys— here a calf, there a buttock, somewhere else a head—and create 'perfect' boys. His own lover was then aged forty, but he'd kept his figure and quite a lot of him could still be used in the paintings. Tuke also used to paint boats and clippers—but it was mostly boys."

Tuke can surprise one; the poets take your breath away. There is J. G. F. Nicholson, a schoolmaster whose books of poems were called *A Garland of Ladslove* and *The Romance of a Choirboy*. His boys used to return regularly to have photographic records kept of their growth. But my favourite is the Reverend E. E. Bradford. I've noted he also wrote school novels (usually they were stories based on school mottoes and how boys, by following them, finally triumphed in dramatic and moving circumstances); but chiefly he was a poet. Volume after volume poured from the pen of this small, innocent, apple-faced man who kept pennies for when boys came to see him: *Sonnets, Songs and Ballads, Passing the Love of Women, The Quest of Love, Lays of Love and Life* and many others.

I say innocent, and no doubt he was; yet so close to the top sometimes is the reality behind the symbols, that it is almost visible through the surface:

> *The Call*
> Eros is up and away, away!
> Eros is up and away! . . .
> Strong, self-controlled, erect and free,
> He is marching along today!
>
> He is calling aloud to the men, the men!
> He is calling aloud to the men—
> "Turn away from the wench, with her powder and paint,
> And follow the Boy, who is fair as a Saint" . . .

Sometimes the symbol comes crashing through the surface; and the result, the Reverend E. E. Bradford still unknowing, is really farce:

Frank
What led him to lay
His whole heart bare,
When nothing compelled him to?
Looking away
With a vacant stare,
He dragged all out to view!

His books were widely reviewed and widely praised, never, as far as I can judge, with the slightest hint of irony. Here is *The Westminster Review*, but it is absolutely typical, on *Passing the Love of Women*: "Friendship between man and man, and even more, the friendship between man and youth form the theme of many of Dr. Bradford's poems. He is as alive to the beauty of unsullied youth as was Plato."

Plato is the clue. There was a pretence that all this love was really the love of the classics, and that when it was pure it was a marvellous thing. The point is, of course, that the love of the classics wasn't pure in the least; classical literature is the most lascivious and openly erotic homosexual literature in the world. Knowing this, Bradford "purifies" it with the same fresh air that whips round Sedbergh and Rugby—that "fresh air" that somehow made schools "clean". (I sometimes think the very siting of their public schools had something to do with Victorian sex panic. At Roedean you're blown flat on your face.)

Is Boy-Love Greek? Far off across the seas
The warm desire of Southern men may be:
But passion freshened by a Northern breeze
Gains in male vigour and in purity.
Our yearning tenderness for boys like these
Has more in it of Christ than Socrates.

I shall quote one more of his numerous poems. It is rather long, but he has been out of print for many years and I do not suppose many people will have read him or will get a chance to do so. Also, Bradford sometimes needs length to achieve his finest effects:

At Last!
Returning from Church on a fine June night,
With a shy little fellow called Merrivale White,
I was never so startled in all my life—
The boy seemed altered quite!

Was it the magic of the woodland way,
The moon, or the scent of the new-mown hay?
I have no idea: but the fact remains—
He seemed quite changed that day.

"Look here," he began, "you are going again,
And all this visit I've waited in vain.
Are we going to be chums? You know what I mean—
    Real mates? Put me out of my pain."

"But White," I demurred, "you seemed such a kid:
I like you of course, and I always did.
But all I can say is—if you liked me,
    You kept it jolly well hid!"

"Did I?" said he. "Do you mean that you doubted
My feeling for you?" Then he frowned and pouted.
"Do you think that a boy can offer a man
    His love—and perhaps be scouted?

"Do you think that a boy—and a shy boy too—
Finds it easy to come to a man like you,
And propose to be friends—real mates for life?
    You make a mistake if you do!

"But I've done it at last." And there his voice broke:
And he slashed at the weeds with his stick as he spoke.
Then he went on fiercely, "Whatever you do,
    Don't treat what I say as a joke."

What I said or did doesn't matter a straw;
I could see there was no great need to jaw.
I suppose we behaved like a couple of fools—
    But nobody heard or saw.

I only know we were awfully late.
White's father and mother were quite in a state
Till the boy came out with a cock-and-bull tale
    That we couldn't unfasten a gate!

I shall never forget that night in June,
When the scent of the hay, or the gleam of the moon
Made a shy boy bold to break the ice—
    After all, it was none too soon.

4 How the whole country succumbed to the public school ethos

The return to Correlli Barnett begins at this precise point—with the school
literature and the influence of the public schools on popular literature
generally. Buchan, Yates, Sapper and the rest were not just popular
middle-brow best-sellers. They had mass sales—so large that it is almost

impossible now to get the cumulative figures. In the 1930s and 40s several Buchan books were made into films. Films were also made out of Sapper books, and there have been several *Tom Brown* films. Similarly, *The Boy's Own Paper* had an extensive lower-class readership, as is clear from the advertisements in it. (It was a vehicle for carrying many other public school beliefs and taboos down through the social strata. The numbers of the 1890s, for example, are full of terrifying warnings against masturbation.) Furthermore the school adventure stories proper had a far wider readership than the middle and upper classes. One difference between working-class education and that of the bourgeoisie during (roughly) the first half of the 20th century was that the latter paid. There was a further gulf between the petty bourgeoisie at "private" fee-paying little schools and various grant-aided schools, and the middle and upper classes at "posh" public schools. The petty bourgeoisie yearned for the world of quadrangles and house colours. They satisfied it by reading *The Chaps of St. Renold's* or *Play Up! The School!*

But unquestionably by far the most potent force spreading the public school ethos throughout the culture were the boys' weeklies and comics—the twopenny and penny dreadfuls—which became extremely common from the late 1890s on. George Orwell wrote a brilliant study of these in 1939. He makes a number of important points relevant to our present concern.

First he takes the comics—the early *Gem* and *Magnet*, and a little later *Modern Boy*, *Triumph*, *Champion*, *Wizard*, *Rover*, *Hotspur*, *Skipper*—and analyses their contents. It was, in *Gem* and *Magnet*, almost a hundred per cent public school adventure stories. And the stories were exactly the same as they had been in 1900. Partly this was because they had evolved a style which could be copied by an infinite number of hack writers. In case you have forgotten it—or more likely never read it—here is a short extract from *Magnet*:

"Groan!"
  "Shut up, Bunter!"
  "Groan!"
  Shutting up was not really Billy Bunter's line. He seldom shut up, though often requested to do so. On the present awful occasion the fat owl of Greyfriars was less inclined than ever to shut up. And he did not shut up! He groaned, and groaned and went on groaning. . . .
  Harry Wharton & Co. stood in a wrathy and worried group. They were landed and stranded, diddled, dished and done!

The snobbery is shameless and gross. Every school has two or three titled boys, and snobbish facts are thrust in one's face—"You are constantly reminded that Gussy is the Honourable Arthur A. D'Arcy, son of Lord

Eastwood, that Jock Blake is heir to 'broad acres', that Hurree Jamset Ram Singh (nicknamed Inky) is the Nabob of Bharripur, that Vernon-Smith's father is a millionaire." Money fantasy is rampant. Every week in *Magnet* a false school magazine reveals that "some of the fellows in the Remove get five pounds a week pocket money". Fantasy to the readers no doubt; in fact not all that far out. Churchill got three pounds a week at Harrow.

Who were these readers? They ran into hundreds of thousands, with colossal sales in every town in England. Nearly every boy who read went through a phase of reading them, which is why they give such a clear indication of what the youth of England (and so by natural extension, the adults too) were thinking from 1900 on. Orwell said that public school boys stopped reading them around twelve. But at the cheap petty-bourgeois private schools—he had taught at two—they went on reading them up to sixteen. These were the sons of small shopkeepers and little businessmen. But they had a very large lower-class sale as well. They were always on sale in the poorest parts of the town. Orwell saw a young coal miner reading them. The Pen Pals department of *Gem* shows that there were readers in every part of the Empire. The publishers expected the readers to be about the age of the heroes, fourteen; but they also had a considerable adult readership. The Admiralty regularly inserted advertisements for boys of seventeen to twenty-two. It was common for adults to say they had read *Gem* and *Magnet* for thirty years.

The intensity of interest in these comics is revealed by the correspondence columns. They are full of questions like: "Can you give me a list of the Shell and their studies?" "How much did D'Arcy's monocle cost?" "Where is St. Jim's situated? Could you tell me how to get there, as I would love to see the buildings? . . ."

It is clear that, just as certain poor black children in America today have been shown to identify with white dolls, so the vast lower-class readership became, in fantasy, the figures in these stories. And characters were provided to fit, or at least please, all types. This is true even of the most unlikely. For instance, take Gussy, the Honourable Arthur A. D'Arcy—"the swell of St. Jim's". Although he is years out of date, a masher of the 1890s—"Bai Jove, deah boy!" or "Weally, I shall be obliged to give you a feahful thwashin'!"—he is also "the monocled idiot who made good on the fields of Mons and Le Cateau. And this evident popularity goes to show how deep the snob appeal of this type is. English people are extremely fond of the titled ass who always turns up trumps in the moment of emergency."

The working classes only enter as comics, servants or semi-villains (race-course touts, etc.). Of class friction, poverty, unemployment, strikes, trade unions, there is not a single mention.

It is a mental world which Orwell sums up like this:

The year is 1910—or 1940, but it is all the same. You are at Greyfriars, a rosy-cheeked boy of fourteen in posh tailor-made clothes, sitting down to tea in your study on the Remove passage after an exciting game of football which was won by an odd goal in the last half-minute. There is a cosy fire in the study, and outside the wind is whistling. The ivy clusters thickly round the old grey stones. The King is on his throne and the pound is worth a pound. Over in Europe the comic foreigners are jabbering and gesticulating, but the grim grey battleships of the British fleet are steaming up the Channel and at the outposts of Empire the monocled Englishmen are holding the niggers at bay. Lord Manlever has just got another fiver and we are sitting down to a tremendous tea of sausages, sardines, crumpets, potted meat, jam and dough-nuts. After tea we shall sit round the study having a good laugh at Billy Bunter and discussing the teams for next week's match against Rookwood. Every-thing is safe, solid and unquestionable. Everything will be the same for ever and ever. That approximately is the atmosphere.

After the 1914 war there were new comics—the *Wizard, Rover, Hotspur, Champion*, etc. There were differences, which Orwell discusses. Only one need concern us here. The stories are not now totally public school—there are Tarzan type stories, Westerns, Foreign Legion and Science Fiction (from H. G. Wells). But the vast majority still are public school—about sixty to sixty-five per cent. And, although there are minute mitigations of absurdity the outlook is essentially the same. The same "posh" upper-class accents, the same upper–class school. Sometimes the snobbishness was worse; Orwell found one where an actual *majority* of the boys mentioned were titled.

The significance of all this is clear. There were ten of these comics, all of enormous circulation, in every town and many villages of England, read by a large proportion, probably a majority of English boys between ten and eighteen, many of whom would read nothing else again. And they all read and accepted a social system which should have been, and from 1900 on rapidly became, completely out of date. It was a system where public schools, public school morality and way of life, the inevitable success and *rightness* of the success of the public school class were not only accepted axiomatically, unquestioned, but as it were deified. The point is that the ideals, ideas, taboos and standards of the public schools—that thin wafer of privilege—had become *national* ones, they had sunk deep into the unconscious of the nation. This was especially so by the years 1900–1914; but even in 1939 over sixty per cent of the comics were devoted to the same out-of-date claptrap. Orwell thinks (this is the point of his essay) that this was a deliberate plot on the part of the then Lord Camrose of the Amalgamated Press and D. C. Thomson & Co. He points out, as evidence, that the Amalgamated Press also printed *The Financial Times* and *The Daily Telegraph*. He sees it all as a capitalist and right-wing plot, a deliberate and conscious and extremely long-term plot to subvert the whole nation—it is "obvious that the stories in the boys' weeklies are politically vetted". The aim of his essay is to advocate left-wing comics for boys, though he balks a bit at the thought of what these might be like and how they could be written. This seems to me in the highest degree unlikely. I would say there is a much simpler lesson to be learnt. The most I can see Lord Camrose doing—outside stern scrutiny of balance sheets—is saying, "Let's have good, profitable adventure stories for boys, and adventure stories for boys means public school stories, so let's give them that." And his audience, lower class and all, agreed with him. Lord Camrose had no need to subvert the nation; it had been subverted already. *That* is the real lesson.

And this spread of public school prejudices and ideals—and the idea that they dominated by right—was reinforced at many other points.

By the late 1890s football began to be commercialised, with a few players and more spectators coming from the industrial working class. But here, and of course in cricket, the intense public school training meant that public school boys were often dominant figures. Leadership in sport gave a popular dimension to the process we are analysing.

An article in the *Journal of Criminal Law and Criminology* (LXIV, 1973) has shown recently that the British borstal system—our method of disciplining junior criminals—was expressly based on the public school system, with houses, prefects, "character" ideals and so on. The same is roughly true of the approved school system, and in fact I had some very interesting correspondence from an Old Boy of one of these institutions. It is clear they shared many public school characteristics and, in the person of their headmasters, raised strong loyalties.

But the most significant area of this sort, where the public school ethos was dominant, is the grammar schools. This began early. James Prince Lee was eight years at Rugby under Arnold, then became Head of King Edward's, Birmingham, in 1838. In fact to move from a public school to the headship of a day grammar school was regarded as promotion throughout the 19th and 20th centuries (except perhaps from Eton). And there was a great deal of movement the other way. Boys from day grammar schools became masters at public schools. At the end of the 19th century there were more masters from day grammar schools at Eton, Harrow, Rugby than from all other boarding public schools, excluding the seven.

The result was that grammar schools aped the public schools. This can be clearly seen in the memoirs and autobiographies of grammar school boys. For instance H. E. Bates, who was at Kettering in the Midlands in 1916, said that he was steeped in public school stories and expected prefects, studies, sausages, etc. Their conversation was all about honour, tradition, caning, the good name of the school and so on.

There was strong two-way traffic between grammar schools and public schools, but there was movement down too. As education slowly spread from 1902 and 1907 on, both across the country, and, to use a sociologist's euphemism, through its "pattern of social stratification", it was, in the vast majority of cases, staffed and led by men who came from grammar schools.

Now the reason all this is significant is that children identify with, imitate the behaviour of and absorb the values and goals of those who teach them. This becomes absolutely clear when one studies anthropology. All cultures and all societies take great care to specify who does the teaching. You can deduce the sort of social structure they want from this. Thus, if the teaching in a tribe is done by non-family members, then the child is being eased out of the small family circle and being taught that the unit of loyalty and obedience is the wider one of the tribal clan. If he is taught by members of the family but all from the mother's side, he is being introduced into a matrilineal system, where the hierarchy, the authority and inheritance all come from the mother's family. If the teachers are from the father's side he is being trained into a patrilineal society.

But we have just seen that the entire educational system in England was what you might call public school-lineal. This fact alone is virtually enough to explain (and demonstrate) the complete acceptance of the class structure and the dominance in it of public school leaders, values and ideals. By 1900–1914 (and into the 1930s) the ethos had sunk right down through the culture, from top to bottom.

At the end of our first examination of the class system and the public schools I wrote these two sentences: "Its roots, however altered and buried, were feudal. The class deference of the 19th and early 20th centuries had, at its heart, the hierarchical deference of a fighting machine." England did not return to an 18th-century self—if we are to use such images, then it is truer to say that a much older self had been preserved quite close to the surface, indeed intensified, by the public schools. The penetration of the public school ethos explains why England rose with such complete unity, not pacific at all but extremely belligerent. It explains why its soldiers were prepared to follow callow youths into battle. But it also explains why callow youths were able to take command. In some respects the public schools produced ideal officers for an army: a majority of conformist disciplined men who were yet absolutely confident they could lead; a good number of men capable of individual dash and resource but still within the system. And a third group, impossible to number but sufficient. We have seen that the "team-spirit-equals-defeat" equation is a myth; also that the response to restrictive total institutions is not predictable. The public schools also produced men of dash, initiative, determination and extreme individuality. The First World War in particular was a public school war; the Second less so. But even in the Second the great majority of our top leaders were from public schools, and this is reflected in the war films. It was indeed precisely those qualities of individuality—

flexibility, ingenuity, the ability to disobey—that were our great advantage over the Germans. So far from explaining why we came close to defeat, the public schools are one of the reasons why we won.

At this point Correlli Barnett could protest that his book had nothing to do with fighting the war; it was a book about the collapse of British *power*. That is true—but his attack on the public schools was so absolute, his conclusions so sweeping, that they made the fighting and winning of a war—much less two—inconceivable. Since we won both wars, something must be wrong with his argument.

But in general terms, as far as our industrial efficiency and strength go, it seems obvious that the class-induced (and public school reinforced) bias against business and science, the attraction of the best brains to rarefied classical study, must have had a seriously deleterious effect. And we noted this when discussing these two aspects.

Yet to determine the degree of public school responsibility would require some skill. For example, I wonder just how suited to business are the sort of people who excel at academic classical studies. If evangelical religion had so marked an effect on our ability to be realistic in international affairs and presumably business too, why did it wait until the 1920s before really manifesting itself? It was far stronger in the schools in the 1840s and 1850s. In any case, the League of Nations idealistic movement between the wars was a European, in some respects a world, one. It is more conventional but I think more convincing to find its roots in a horrified reaction to the 1914–18 slaughter. Again, education in France at this time (1880–1910) was also extremely authoritarian, the masters distant, originality and exploration crushed in a rigid insistence on work and the work itself excessively academic. In Germany the picture is similar, though, as in England, there was some movement towards relationships between masters and boys.If so much weight is to be put on British middle- and upper-class education in relation to its rivals, then Correlli Barnett would have to show why comparable education abroad did not have the same effect.

I say all this not to deny that public schools did have profound effects in these broad spheres, only to emphasise that it is important not to exaggerate.

5 Effects on the individual: more British archetypes

I said earlier that for a number of reasons—the variety of reaction, the more profound effect of early upbringing, etc.—it was necessary to be as tentative about the effects of public schools on individuals as about their more widespread social effects. This is compounded because, while it is relatively easy to remember school life, it is very difficult to recall that of early childhood. Also people don't like admitting strong aggressive feelings towards those they loved when small. The result is that public schools are often blamed for effects which are the responsibility of fathers and mothers, or more likely, at this period, nannies. Similarly, they are often thanked for a stability really due to good nannies. I think the most sensible way is to phrase it like this—there are a good number of traits and reactions common among British people of a certain class from roughly 1870 and continuing, if with diminishing force, right on through the 1920s and 30s till today, in which, if you find they exist with marked intensity, you can be almost certain public schools are seriously implicated.

Take the quotation from *Summoned by Bells* which headed this chapter. Chivied and harried from dawn to dusk, continually kept at work they were bored by, yet rewarded for doing it, punished for not doing it—the compulsive doing of tasks became ingrained. The result is so obvious that scarcely a single social study mentions it—the English upper classes were absurdly over-conscientious. In a notebook found at his death Orwell had written this:

> It is now [1949] sixteen years since my first book was published, and about twenty-one years since I started publishing articles in the magazines. Throughout that time there has literally been not one day in which I did not feel I was idling, that I was behind with the current job, and that my total output was miserably small. Even at the periods when I was working ten hours a day on a book, or turning out four or five articles a week, I have never been able to get away from this neurotic feeling that I was wasting time. I can never get any sense of achievement out of the work that is actually in progress, because it always goes slower than I intend, and in any case I feel that a book or even an article does not exist until it is finished. But as soon as a book is finished, I begin, actually from the next day, worrying because the next one is not begun.

This is why so many of them could be sent 7,000 miles away and trusted to govern or administer or fill in ledgers. Leonard Woolf's account of his seven years' colonial administration in Ceylon is a monument to colossal conscientiousness; so are the lives of Curzon or of Morant or dozens of others.

Lives—those bells continuing to ring in the head for ever—were led by the clock. How often I arrived to find congested faces and elderly fingers drumming because I was four and a half minutes late. One man told me he had once climbed a distant and precipitous mountain in Spain, timing his arrival—although it was the first time he had climbed it—to the second.

Conscientiousness, then, was often a product of guilt and fear. Guilt is a common feature. Here is Cyril Connolly:

> Consider Jacky: playing fives with me one afternoon he said, "Damn and blast" when he missed a ball. The headmaster who was passing, heard him and told sixth form. That night he was beaten. In the excitement of the game he had forgotten to prepare his construe. Others had prepared theirs but after the

silence before boys are put on to construe, when all diversions have been tried in vain, it was he who was called upon. He was ploughed and given a "ticket", "Failed to Construe", to get signed by his tutor. He had not the courage to show it to him, forged his tutor's initials on the bottom and handed it back. By chance the two masters met, the ticket was mentioned and the fraud discovered. Within three days of the game of fives the Præposter came with the terrible summons. "Is O'Dwyer K. S. in this division? He is to go to the headmaster at a quarter to twelve." The wide doors are open which means a birching will take place. The block is put out. The boys in the sixth form are there to see the headmaster does not raise his arm above the shoulder, and an old college servant to lower his trousers and hold him down. "Call no man happy until he is dead. Next time it may be me.".

The feeling is really Greek, a consciousness of nemesis—misfortune is just round the corner. Against this feeling they developed stoicism. But it is more personal than that. The retribution, if it came, was just. For many years the children of the upper classes were told they were wicked and were beaten for it. In the 19th century, as we saw, the conviction of sin was strong and widespread. But even in the 1920s and 30s it lingered on as a vague sense of having done wrong. This was intensified because they were sent away from home so young. To a small child the only convincing reason, at a subconscious level, for being sent away like this was because they were not loved; and they were not loved because they had done wrong. I think it probable that the deep sense of guilt about their class which afflicted so many of them was compounded by this—this guilt, really, about being themselves.

It is hardly surprising that, confused by these strong guilts and corresponding resentments about their parents, family relationships were often hopeless. Brought up by nannies, sent away to school at seven, many of them hadn't the faintest idea what their parents were like. This was particularly true of fathers. The only "father" they really knew was often a strict schoolmaster, and this is what many of them therefore became. Robin Maugham was dominated and almost crushed by a terrible father. Churchill was bullied by his father. And these two were typical of many other parents through this period and into the 1920s. In an age of tough, over-disciplinarian and unsympathetic prep and public school masters, you got fathers who were the same. It was the only sort of adult male rôle they had to copy.

The effect of family lives of this sort—intensified by the prep–public school situation—need not be stressed. Equally, it should not be exaggerated. Because you don't show feelings—or only express them through acceptable channels—it does not mean you don't have them. Passions, as Racine and Mozart show, are often the stronger because they are confined and only let out according to rules. But on the whole I think the truism about the English upper classes having difficulty with both feeling and expressing emotion is accurate—even today. One odd offshoot of this is the length they will go to to avoid meeting in the streets someone they know—even someone they quite like—when they see them approaching from a distance. Go to Curzon Street or St. James's or Bond Street, emptying tracks in the jungle, it is true, but where you can still find Old Boys of sixty and more stalking warily along—it's like a game of hide-and-seek.

Given the psychology of individuals and the organisation of institutions in large societies—Parliament, business, the Civil Service or whatever—some form of "Old Boy" system is inevitable. It is true of America and France and Germany today; it is true of the Trade Unions in England now. Given the negligible spread of secondary education in Britain by 1900 it was also inevitable it should be an upper-class Old Boy system. The closer these networks are, the more they speak the same language and know about each other, the better they work. It is likely that this aspect of public schools contributed to the efficiency of the governing élite—even their love affairs were, in Disraeli's words, "a spell that [could] soften the acerbity of political warfare".

But public schools intensified this upper-class Old Boy network. There is a perfectly sound goal, as far as a school goes, of creating a sense of community. This can be exciting as well as useful. In this context games, for instance, became even more like wars than ever. They were wars against outside tribes and drew each individual tribe together. Unfortunately the idea that it requires a lot of effort to produce a sense of community is not true. It is a natural and immediate reaction. This has been shown by some recent experiments at Bristol. Numbers of people were arbitrarily split up into two groups called, for example, the Klee and Kandinsky groups. It was found that in various tests they *instantly* began to identify with and favour "their" group in relation to the other. Here is the instinctive base of rôle, comradeship, identity; but also, it seems, of aggression. This is not particularly strong personally; when aroused on behalf of "your" group it becomes many times stronger. Now it is clear how all this probably evolved for social/tribal/pack reasons; but it means that if these group ties are forced and encouraged they can easily become extremely powerful. If the group is then faced with another existing or potential group, aggression will become far stronger than is necessary; in effect, the group is preparing for war.

It seems likely that it was something of this sort that the public schools did to class feelings. The results were often odious. Harold Nicolson wrote:

I am conscious, moreover . . . of a marked distaste for those who have not benefited by a public school education. This distaste is based on no superficial prejudice; it is founded on experience. People who have not endured the restrictive shaping of an English school are apt in after life to be egocentric, formless and inconsiderate. These are irritating faults. They are inclined, also, to show off. This objectionable form of vanity is in its turn destructive of the more creative form of intelligence.

He once said, "I hate the lower classes."

There were many specific injustices suffered by the working classes during this period. But it is no accident that they were uniting at the very time the upper classes were consolidating themselves through the public schools. They too were thus generating an ever increasing, and one might think a great deal more justifiable, fury in response to the almost neurotic rage and contempt of many of those above them.

There are four other effects that are usually traced—or which I trace—back to these Victorian and Edwardian public schools.

There is the "burnt-out case". This is the phenomenon of the brilliant boy who shows something almost like academic genius and then seems to burn his talent out and who never fulfils his promise. A. S. Neill thought it usually happened to someone who had been forced too fast, and often forced to do something that didn't really interest him or her. But why does it happen, and what precisely is happening? Is it that the talents of these people are really only suited to public schools and not to life; or is it perhaps that success at school removes the drive to succeed—they have already succeeded? Or is there perhaps no such thing as "burning out"? Hadfield says a boy who tries too hard to get scholarships can be over-stretched *permanently*. But he offers no evidence. What is it exactly that gets "overstretched"? This is the muscle simile of *simplicismus* again. I suspect that in the "burnt-out" case we have a false archetype.

We showed when modifying Correlli Barnett's strictures, that the public schools of those days did not inevitably crush individuality. I do not, however, as we come to the end of this review, want in my turn to leave an exaggerated picture of this individuality. How many courageous individuals with initiative do you need to run a successful military machine? Perhaps not very many, particularly in relation to the thousands the public schools were now stamping out every year. It is obvious enough, but important to emphasise for the final picture to be accurate, that over-strong authority, too rigid imposition of conventions when young, much more normally produces over-conventional, authority-accepting human beings. This (as indeed were many of Correlli Barnett's arguments) was noted at the time.

Royston Lambert found that people will rebel at school to retain some individuality, yet readily accept all its deeper assumptions—sex guilt, class division, competitiveness, not showing emotion and the rest. And here we find the source of another archetype—the English eccentric. This is the figure who has many fringe non-conformities, often picturesque and amusing, adopted to express individuality, but who conforms to all the major social *mores*. It is a common rôle at public schools as well as afterwards.

Among numerous other cultures the dichotomy between work and play does not exist; nor is there a distinction between those two and education. In Samoa, for instance, the education is in things necessary for the life of the tribe—sweeping, child-minding, the boy digging for bait and so on. And these merge into similar adult tasks—house-building, getting food, entertaining guests. With both, leisure comes not as a reward or a relief, but is sometimes part of the work, or comes in the wide spaces between work. In the West we split these activities: work—play, job—private life. These distinctions begin at school and are easily explained by the complexity and, as it were, sheer quantity of our culture. But in the State system here, and generally on the Continent and in America, school at least corresponds to the later job situation—something done in the day and then finished. Only the public schools erected this vast sentimental edifice, lichen-encrusted.

And this brings me to my final point. The reaction against the 18th century, the excitements of the French Revolution, the return of emotion and feeling, that whole complex movement which we label "romantic" gave prominence again to a strain long inherent in the English national character. I think it is probably an ingredient of any country with a long history, able to look back upon a succession of heroes who can become the more glorious the further they recede—Nelson, Bonnie Prince Charlie, Drake, Robin Hood, King Arthur. Certainly it is a strong element in Shakespeare. In Victorian times it became particularly lush, swelling up in many extravagant growths. Chivalry returned—with Walter Scott, the Pre-Raphaelites, Tennyson. By 1877 the Reverend E. P. Roe, in *A Knight of the Nineteenth Century*, knew that all his readers would immediately appreciate that the moral redemption of a young man could be expressed in terms of a rise to knightliness. Victorian evangelical romanticism was behind Ruskin, Morris and indeed the rise of the whole Labour Party. It was strong in that nostalgic "pastoral" stream of English literature, that longing to look always to the past; and the strain is strong today with Tolkien, *Akenfield*, books about nannies and public schools.

There is something unreal about this. Indeed one of the root meanings of romance is unreal, a tale, a fantasy. (Fantasies are not necessarily unhealthy. They serve an essential psychological purpose.) Public schools involve separation from family and parents, who are therefore missed and nostalgically and romantically dreamt of. The same is true of the sexual situation. Girls (or at girls' schools, boys) are fantasised about, glorified. Even the homosexual loves, as we saw, because so much has to be suppressed, and since they often take place at a distance, through glimpses in corridors, in the head, have the same effect. Fantasy and unreality in such important areas twist the whole personality; romanticism becomes inherent. And this has shown up in recent sociological studies. Mallory Wober ends his excellent book *(English Girls' Boarding Schools)* on this note: ". . . this may often be tactfully hidden away from the public, and even from the individual's own explicit awareness. Yet boarding school is a mechanism for producing a romantic structure in the individual, however well it may often be hidden."

This element will have been obvious for some time—the Old Boy situation, the agonised nostalgia of Cyril Connolly, the songs of Harrow, the entire corpus of school literature: the public schools were romantic and sentimental to a degree. And so we come to the last public school-induced British archetype of this chapter: the bowler-hatted, stiff-collared, conventional Englishman, one whole drawer of whose office desk is stuffed with romantic poems. In Anthony Powell he puts on a dress to read them.

6 Conclusion—the Monolith is established

Within seventy-six years, between approximately 1824 and 1900, the public schools had reversed themselves. From being anarchic, ill-disciplined, loosely defined societies, uninterested in games, lax about religion, indifferent to sexual licence, with huge classes and moderately easy about class, they had become highly disciplined, concentrated into very tight, close communities, obsessed with games and every possible ramification of sexual expression, fervently religious, with small classes, and were snobbish and class conscious to an often odious extent. Almost the only respect in which they had not altered was in their intense classical bias. While they provided a certain class confidence, a confidence that their pupils should and could lead, and the useful disciplines and stability that go with self-control and conformity, they led on the whole to a far too great loss of individuality, too great a conventionality, and twisted and repressed the psyches of those at them with guilts, anxieties, Old Boy obsessions and all the other effects, both personal and national, whose intricacies we have been unravelling and which it is unnecessary to rehearse again. And they had evolved an ethos, a system of sometimes muddled values, which they had imposed upon the entire nation.

They had become a Monolith, not just each individual school—in essentials so like every other—but as a system. And many of the characteristics of the Monolith were to last for years. That is why many of the effects I have been analysing will continue to appear through the 1920s, 30s, 40s and 50s. Some of them, if considerably diluted, continue today.

The history of the next seventy-six years will be that of the breaking of the Monolith: the areas where, the degree and speed with which it altered —or was smashed—the way it happened in different schools, different houses, sometimes even in different forms in the same school, sometimes to the same master at different moments in his career.

But before we proceed to the breaking of the Monolith, we must turn to two parallel developments—neither of which was to have the slightest effect on the Monolith—both of which were to become extremely interesting and important parts of the public school system: girls' public schools and progressive public schools.

CHAPTER 10

How Girls Had to Fight for Education and What Resulted

Jane Hubbard was a splendid specimen of bronzed, strapping womanhood. Her whole appearance spoke of the open air and the great wide spaces and all that sort of thing. She was a thoroughly wholesome, manly girl, about the same age as Billie, with a strong chin and an eye that had looked leopards squarely in the face and caused them to withdraw abashed into the undergrowth, or wherever it is that leopards withdraw when abashed.

P. G. Wodehouse, *The Girl on the Boat*

There is a great deal less information about girls' public schools than there is about boys'. For one thing there are far fewer biographies, autobiographies or memoirs of women, reflecting the position they held in our society for many years. There is no entirely satisfactory general history covering the whole period; and the school histories themselves suffer, almost without exception, from one grave drawback. The authoress of the history of Roedean, Miss Dorothy E. de Zouche, was chosen by the School Council after "prolonged consideration". She was eight years a member of Founders Staff and great friends with Dame Emmeline Tanner, who reigned there for twenty-three years from 1924. Not surprisingly she "has thus approached her task with love and enthusiasm". It is a perfectly sound book, but you don't find much in the way of criticism, far less scandal. Indeed love is a keynote. Many of the loyal historians describe their work, as does Miss A. K. Clarke her own history of Cheltenham Ladies' College, as "a labour of love". Both are usually only too evident.

Nevertheless there is still quite a lot to go on, and, as usual, the early history is crucial to a number of later developments.

1 Early history

One of the most important and formative facts about girls' education is that until the middle of the 19th century it virtually didn't exist.

The Anglo-Saxon Church had laid down that everyone, regardless of sex, should be well grounded in religion. Until the 12th century there is some evidence that minute numbers of rich girls, the daughters of kings and nobles, were educated in convents, learning Latin. From 1118, after the death of Matilda, there was a decline—if something so small, becoming yet smaller, can be said to decline. The fashion of Latin-reading women went out, and even nuns in the Middle Ages were usually unable to write and were concerned with institutional housewifery. The over-all picture from then until the 18th century is of girls being virtually illiterate in any modern sense, but being brought up to get husbands and run the home —and to this end they were taught certain graces (music, singing and so on) religion, and a range of practical skills necessary to run a large household. As with boys, girls were frequently sent away to learn these skills in the households of nobles. A strong subsidiary reason for this was that they should make contacts which would eventually lead to an advantageous marriage. It should also be noted that their household position was not an inferior one. It was a position of great power. Until well into the 18th century, the upper-class wife had at her command an enormous range of those skills necessary to run a vast household which she ruled absolutely and which, in earlier centuries, she would often have to defend in a siege, directing the entire operation of a military stronghold.

Throughout these centuries there are occasional exceptions—learned abbesses, or the daughters of scholars, the freakish daughter of some duke or earl. Nobles' daughters had governesses. But it is the complete absence of any real education that forces authors dealing with this subject to expend tedious chapters on the seven or eight scholarly ladies who appear each century.

2 The 18th century: "the accomplishments", the academies

It is in the 18th century that we at last, about 1,001 years after the first boys' schools, get two faint movements towards a proper girls' education, the first superficial but influential, the second more profound but premature.

From about 1720 onwards there grew up what later came to be known as Ladies' Academies. These were boarding establishments taking fifty or sixty pupils, and by the end of the century they had become "too numerous to mention". In 1836 there were over a hundred in Brighton alone. Some were very cheap, others cost £500 a year—far more expensive than Eton at this time. They continued well into the mid-19th century, but began to decline in efficiency during the 1830s.

These schools taught a little general education—languages (French, German, Italian), a smattering of mathematics, geography (the globes); but the main thrust of their curriculum was towards the accomplishments.

The accomplishments! Dancing: "A whole train of successive masters," wrote Hannah More, "are considered as absolutely essential to its perfection. . . . There is one master to teach the Scotch steps, another to teach French dancing." There was German dancing and Italian dancing and every variety of English dancing. There was the feminine "art" of marching, taught by army sergeants. There was a French teacher to teach "behaviour"; and a sewing teacher to teach needlework. This alone occupied hours. The introduction of one book is ten pages long and, in précis-fashion, gives but an outline of the subject: tent-work, chairs and carpets, needlework, pictures of Solomon and the Queen of Sheba, cloth-work, crêpe-work, chenille-work, ribbon-work, wafer-work. . . . And women had to become—even without the faintest talent—mistresses of innumerable instruments: the spinnet, the harpsichord, the fiddle, the guitar, the harp, and also be able to sing and even compose. Maria Edgeworth worked out in 1798 that a girl learning the piano from six to eighteen gave 14,000 hours of her life to playing scales. Hours were spent at the easel—not drawing the human figure, but flowers or leaves or landscapes. They pored over miniatures. They learnt japanning, lacquering and how to perform in romantic plays and recite verse. The subject— or subjects rather—reached the same preposterous heights as classical studies in the boys' public schools, and whirling wildly from accomplishment to accomplishment to accomplishment, twirled now in a gavotte, now in the heavy folds of tent-work, now lost in the whorls of a still-life of wortleberries, the unfortunate girls must often have felt as dizzy as if they were spinning on a lathe—at which they also had to work. It was called "turning".

At the same time, and this is typical of the age, as we saw in the late-18th-century public schools, the teaching of these trifles was done in circumstances combining spartan toughness and undisciplined licence. The food was appalling—there is a description of meat pies of such incredible toughness that they could be thrown "with the greatest force up to the ceiling without breaking"—and girls were often near starvation. Conditions were cold, cramped and dirty, with children sleeping two or three to a bed. Horrendous braces, bars and clamps tried to wrench soft bodies into the right shapes. Mrs. Somerville, sent to a boarding school in 1790 aged ten, was at once clamped "in stiff stays with a steel busk in front, while, above my frock, bands drew my shoulders back till the shoulder blades met. Then a steel rod, with a semi-circle which went under the chin, was clasped to the steel busk in my stays." At the same time discipline was extremely lax. The women in charge often drank and were dominated by their rich charges. Girls were seduced and elopements from the academies were frequent. They were held up to ridicule in verse and in plays—as in Sheridan's *A Trip to Scarborough*.

Clearly all this was ludicrous. Nevertheless I think the accomplishments were probably a more important influence on girls' education than has been realised, or rather, they represented more accurately than is usually acknowledged a number of strands which were to remain significant for many years. The first is that women were weaker than men and should not therefore be presented with such intellectually taxing pursuits. The popular educationalist Mrs. Williams Ellis (1843), in a series of books, *The Women of England*, based all her themes on this: "The first thing of importance is to be content to be inferior to men—inferior in mental power in the same proportion that you are inferior in bodily strength." This whole idea—that women were different, weaker, to be both chivalrously protected and yet also despised and (secretly) feared, an idea quite alien before that time—was much intensified by the concentrated separation of male 19th-century public school education. But it also had an economic root. The explosion of the population at the end of the 18th century and throughout the 19th century, the growth of wealth which remained concentrated in relatively few hands, meant a rapid and continuing rise in the number of servants. This effectively deprived upper-class women of any serious function. They had nothing to do except be weak and ineffective, forced by lack of activity into often totally wasted lives. A second point of the accomplishments, as Dr. Gregory told his daughters at the end of the 18th century, was "to enable you to fill up, in a tolerably agreeable way, some of the many solitary hours you must necessarily pass at home".

The only function left to a woman was to get a husband. To do this serious education was unnecessary—"It is not the intellectual, but the corporal endowments that allure us," said *The London Magazine*. Indeed serious education was almost certainly fatal. Thomas Broadhurst who ran a girls' boarding school at Bath in 1808: ". . . of all objects that are disagreeable to the other sex, a pedantic female, I believe, is the most confessedly so." Women were in complete agreement. Lady Bradshaigh, a correspondent of Samuel Richardson, wrote, "I hate to hear Latin out of a woman's mouth. There is something in it, to me, masculine." Queen Victoria was more moderate. In a letter to the Princess Royal she wrote, "Education can be overdone."

From all this, two important if muddled themes emerge: the first is that, being weaker, domestic and in pursuit of men, women need a different education, suited to them and their aims. That is, women's education was to be vocational. This concept, because of its history, was, and is, quite foreign to boys' education. The second theme is that—in the accomplishments—the nature of that difference was laid down. These two themes are as important because of the reactions they forced from the 19th-century educationalists as they are in themselves.

We might note three other points. The first is that the accomplishments —with their music, their painting, their dancing, their drama—allowed a great deal of self-expression. Regardless of aptitude, said Hannah More sarcastically, they "erected the whole sex into artists". But in many respects they are the same progressive elements which public schools and comprehensive schools are so proud of today. And the attitudes they embodied did not die. The numerous small, private girls' schools which litter the south of England (and did in the 1920s and 30s), the only lately less numerous finishing schools in Switzerland, Paris and London, are direct lineal descendants of the academies. John Hunt, Headmaster of Roedean, told me of a father who sent his daughter to one of these recently: "I don't mind my girl taking one A-level as long as she doesn't look clever." Secondly, the tradition grew up that girls shouldn't read the classics except in translation. This saved them endless boredom and trouble later. Lastly, the academies, like the public schools, were methods of class advancement. They were often cheap, and the late-18th-century satirical writings are full of complaints and attacks on the scheming daughters of tradesmen and blacksmiths able to go and get the airs of a lady.

3 Bluestocking movement

On a more profound level of discussion, the 18th century also saw what can be loosely called the "Bluestocking movement". The name comes from Benjamin Stillingfleet. He was a member of a society of men and women interested in learning formed by Mrs. Elizabeth Montagu in 1750; she wore blue stockings. As far as women were concerned this society derided the "phrenzy" of the accomplishments and argued that women should have the best education then available—that is the classics (but in translation, of course). As the century progressed the thinkers became more radical. Catherine Macaulay Graham was one of these. A woman of strong will and impervious to convention—she wrote an eight-volume *History of England*, and, at forty-seven, took as second husband a youth of twenty-one—she saw that the mental inferiority women suffered from was not inherent but due to their situation and education. The solution was co-education (already common in America). Thus, in one go, both the status and education of women would be raised to that of men; it should be followed by political equality.

Catherine Graham was seized on by Mary Wollstonecraft (1759–97), who said she was the greatest woman England had ever produced. This passionate and effective prophetess for women's rights took Mrs. Graham's arguments and used them in her *Vindication of the Rights of Women* published in 1792.

The existence of Bluestocking circles—figures like Hannah More, Fanny Burney, Lady Mary Wortley Montagu—showed that it was possible to have educated women. And Mary Wollstonecraft's books—she wrote an earlier one in 1787, containing a ferocious attack on the accomplishments—caused quite a stir. Horace Walpole called her a hyena in petticoats. But, in fact, they made not the slightest practical difference to women's education. They were forerunners. The decisive moves were to be delayed until well into the next century.

4 The battle for women's education

During the first fifty years of the 19th century women's education appears to have got worse—if that were possible. The middle and upper classes became richer, had more servants, and domestic economy—which had at least given some practical edge to the academies—disappeared from the curriculum. The accomplishments grew ever more trivial.

It was the 1830s that began the change. This was the decade of political change. It also marked the great reforms in the boys' public schools. As far as women went, it started the attack on what was eventually to be the area of decisive movement—the position of the governess.

Governesses are the last—and probably the largest (in 1850 there were some 40,000 of them)—strand in women's education from approximately 1750 to 1890. Their position was humiliating and depressing to a degree. They were very badly paid; Charlotte Brontë was paid twenty pounds a year, of which twenty per cent was deducted for laundry. An advertisement in *The Times* offered twelve pounds a year for a morning governess. Half servant, half equal, they were treated with disdain and condescension. Mary Wollstonecraft's anger was fuelled by humiliations of this sort. She was once summarily dismissed when the children started to prefer her to their mother. She describes the loneliness, the sense of waste, the children treating her "with disrespect and often insolence. In the meantime life glides away and the spirits with it." There was the frustration of clever women lumbered with stupid, lazy children, which Charlotte Yonge depicts. To an eight-year-old: "Five apples and eight apples, come . . . what will they make?" "A pie," answers the child.

But, however clever these unfortunate women were, because there was virtually no women's education, they were themselves on the whole very badly educated. If they could be educated, then the education of middle- and upper-class women generally would be improved, and on this base education for all the women of England could be built. Such were the arguments, growing in intensity during the late 1820s and 1830s, of women like Harriet Martineau, Mrs. Sinclair, Mrs. Reid and others. A magazine devoted entirely to education, *The Quarterly Journal of Education*, started now. And very slowly, women began to have some success. In 1828, they were allowed to attend lectures at University College, which had been founded in 1826; also at King's. In 1843 the Governesses' Benevolent Institution was started, at first to help those who had fallen on evil days; and it was at once besieged by hordes of desperate governesses, old ones, ill ones, all broke. But in 1847 it began a series of lectures, primarily for governesses but open to any woman interested in self-improvement.

This was the breakthrough. The lectures were such a success, the attendance so enthusiastic that when a Mrs. Murray, one of Queen Victoria's ladies-in-waiting, had collected some money to found a women's college, she gave it to David Laing, the secretary of the Governesses' Benevolent Institution. In 1848 he bought a house in Harley Street and the Queen's College for Women opened.

Again, this was mainly for governesses, but any "lady" over twelve could attend. There were courses in English, theology, history, Latin, maths, modern languages, science, music, the fine arts and lessons on how to teach. The college was such a success that in 1849 Bedford College was started in Bedford Square. Both, in effect, were public schools for girls, and among the first pupils at Queen's were two future giants of women's education—Miss Buss and Miss Beale. Miss Buss (1827–94) was a woman of enormous and volatile energy. After two years at Queen's she started the North London Collegiate School for Ladies—important because it became a model for later popular secondary schools for girls. Miss Dorothea Beale (1831–1906)—who "threw herself with joy into the Queen's College lectures and examinations" (she read classics and mathematics)—joined the staff of the college and was head teacher until 1856. Then, after a short interval, she was "called" to her life's work—a pioneer girls' public school, Cheltenham Ladies' College. But before we look at these two colossi, particularly Miss Beale, we must study a figure even more important, fundamentally, than either. That is Emily Davies.

The 1850s and 60s were vintage years in the long march towards women's rights. They are the years of the Langham Place Circle, where innumerable battles were planned, victories painfully won. Among women like Harriet Martineau and Barbara Bodichon—generous, radiantly beautiful with a great coil of golden hair, but immensely determined—Emily Davies was outstanding. By 1861, although naturally still interested in all reform (women's suffrage, improved working conditions, equal rights under the law and so on), she had realised that education was the clue. And in education the most important thing was to gain women the right to higher education at university. The reason for this was two-fold: once they had gained a university education women immediately became eligible for all sorts of careers, and if they had the same careers they should have the same votes, rights and conditions as men; secondly, if they obtained the opportunities to acquire higher education then the lower—that is elementary and secondary education—would automatically rise to supply it and rise at the right standard. The logic was impeccable (even if its consequences have still not been fully realised), and in other ways Emily Davies was well suited to carry the war so deep into the men's camp. She was dainty, plump, attractive, extremely "feminine"; but she was also tough (she lived to be ninety-one), cunning, with a clear agile brain that was capable both of the broad strategic grasp and swift tactical brilliance.

All these qualities were to be tested to the full, because the opposition was often ferocious. She had to fight on two main issues. The accomplishments (here is their significance) had enshrined the two principles: first, that women were inferior, weaker, incapable of being educated. This myth she had to destroy; and it was here her opponents—imagining the argument unanswerable—attacked. So feeble were women believed to be that the strain of attaining any knowledge at all would, it was thought, drive them mad. After she had disproved that, the argument was shifted to higher education. When Emily Davies was campaigning for women to take the London BA exams, *The Saturday Review* began one of many attacks by stating that the proposal "for submitting young ladies to Local University Examinations . . . almost takes one's breath away." It ended, after concentrating on the torture of mathematics, "I believe that we should have half the young women in the country in brain fever or a lunatic asylum, if they were to make up their minds to try for it."

Emily Davies's reply was devastating in its logic, irony and humour. It was as likely, she said, "that we should have half the young *men* in the country in brain fever if they were to make up *their* minds to try for it." Besides, why should the mathematical side, say, be so tough? "Women are expected to learn something of arithmetical science, and who shall say at what point they are to stop? Why should simple equations brighten their intellects, and quadratic equations drive them into a lunatic asylum?"

The second principle enshrined by the accomplishments was that women should have a special education suited to their "station" in life. The result had been disastrous. Emily Davies realised, therefore, that equality of opportunity meant that women must take the same exams as men; scholastically they must be treated exactly the same. If this were not done, they would be fobbed off with something second best. This happened, for example, when London University instituted a special exam in 1869. Emily Davies continued to struggle until London capitulated in 1878. There is no doubt that she was right, but the idea she then introduced —that girls' education should be the same as boys'—was to be as significant in the development of girls' public schools as the fact that girls' education came so late. Its influence was not always beneficial.

It would take too long to detail her long struggle—the endless committees, lobbyings, meetings; the essays, articles and speeches. Above all the speeches, powerfully argued, witty and passionate by turn, and which she was always too astute to deliver herself. They were read by men, and so did not seem to come, as it were, from some threatening and aggressive woman. And usually she chose some respected and intelligent figure of the establishment—often educational—won by charm or logic to her side. Men like Mr. (later Sir) Joshua Fitch, Her Majesty's Inspector of Schools for Yorkshire, who read her speech at the Social Services Association in 1864. Gradually the citadels fell. In 1865 Cambridge allowed girls to sit examinations; by 1867 this was a permanent feature. In 1870 Oxford did so, following Edinburgh and Durham. But these were just examinations to test the result of secondary education, the thin end of Emily Davies's wedge. During the 1860s, and after, she hammered home the whole thing —complete higher education for women. First to let women take degrees (at Cambridge, Newnham—called Merton—opens 1871; Girton, 1869; the closing years of the 19th century see Lady Margaret Hall, St. Hugh's and other colleges at Oxford); then to get the degrees they'd proved they could get recognised as real degrees. Incredibly, Cambridge stubbornness on this point of elementary justice did not give way till 1948. Oxford had collapsed in 1920 (Emily Davies was ninety). London, as I said, in 1878. Other universities had allowed degrees at various times towards the end of the 19th century.

She had transformed the scene. It was due to her that the Endowed Schools Commission of 1864 also studied girls' schools, and thus tacitly admitted that girls had the same right to education as boys. The inquiry said that every town of over 4,000 inhabitants should have a girls' school on the lines of Miss Buss's North London Collegiate. The act which followed directly inspired two women, Maria Grey and her sister, Emily Sherriff, to set up the Girls' Public Day School Company and from this schools started up all over the country. By 1901 there were thirty-eight. They were fairly cheap—about ten to sixteen pounds a year—and provided elementary and secondary education to exam level, with a curriculum much wider than boys' schools at the time. Their success was imitated by the girls' high schools.

Even the magazines were invaded. During the first half of the 19th century they can be summarised by a regular feature in *The Ladies*, one of the most popular. The feature was called "Twitterings". There were articles on dresses, toilet, scent. One magazine devoted a whole issue to bonnets and hats. But by the 1870s they had begun to change. The April 1872 issue of *The Ladies* reported a lecture by Sophia Jex-Blake (one of the pioneers) on the Medical Education of Women. In June there was an article on the Education of Girls. A little later they began to report the results of the Cambridge Examinations for women.

There was, taken all together, a ferment of middle-class activity. And it is now, both benefiting from it and becoming part of it, that there came the first great girls' public schools, sailing out like mighty galleons onto the sea, with, first of a long line, some very intimidating women at the helm.

5 The first girls' public schools

In fact, in the interests of accuracy, we should note that there were some girls' private schools aiming at an academic education even before Queen's College and Bedford College. If one waives "Public" (it was not incorporated until 1886) Princess Helena College, founded in 1820, was one of the earliest. It taught future governesses (the daughters of dead clergy mostly), and gave an education well beyond the accomplishments— English, arithmetic, French, "sacred and profane" history, and the globes. The 1830s saw similar schools. St. Brandon's School, started in Gloucester in 1831, is one. And it is clear from the researches of Mrs. Lane, whose daughter was at the school, that St. Mary's Hall (Brighton,1836) is another. There are probably more.

These were valuable, but they were relatively small. It was in no sense a movement. It is after 1850 that things got going, partly because of the middle-class ferment I have outlined but also because of motives so far somewhat muted in the public expressions of the high-minded fighters for women's rights—money and class.

That same rich, class-obsessed middle-class market which was making boys' public schools so profitable also existed, if to a lesser degree, with girls. Its influence on girls' own public schools is as decisive on the founding as in the growth. The first resolution of Cheltenham Ladies' College, in 1854, went like this:

> That an institution for the daughters and young children of Noblemen and Gentlemen be established in Cheltenham and be entitled The Cheltenham College for the Education of Young Ladies and Children [the "Children" was quickly dropped]. The College to be established by means of one hundred shares of £10 each; the possessor of each share to have the right to nominate a pupil and to a vote at annual and special meetings.

Roedean was started specifically as a result of a serious accident a Mr. Lawrence had in 1881, which meant he was unable to support his family (he had fourteen children). Three sisters, Dorothy, Millicent and Penelope Lawrence, started a school in Wimbledon in 1885. The work was hard, the pupils slow in coming. In 1889 they decided to move to Brighton. Their aunt Fanny Martineau said, "In Brighton, all schools succeed."

It must be very exciting starting a school. There is an amusing description of a 19th-century girls' private school opening. The first few girls arrive with the term's fees jingling in their purses. The young mistresses seize the sovereigns and rush giggling and thrilled to the bank.... Penelope Lawrence was twenty-nine, Dorothy twenty-five, Millicent twenty-two. They took 25 Lewes Crescent, made the curtains and stained the floors themselves. They started with ten pupils, most of them children of friends. Four of them didn't pay anything and were just for show.

But aunt Fanny Martineau had been right. It is clear that Roedean (as it was later to be called) was a goldmine. Indeed, given the right leadership, this was true of other girls' public schools at this time. Miss Beale arrived at Cheltenham in 1858. By 1864 the press of pupils and money had forced her to buy houses in the town outside her fortress-like original building.

Yet more were bought in 1874. In 1871 she started a college for advanced education; she added a kindergarten and in 1876 started teacher training, which had grown, by 1885, into a second large college. By 1898 she was reigning over an empire, a community of girls 900 strong, where they were educated all the way from early childhood until, if they wished, they were sent out into the world to teach. Roedean too grew with marvellous swiftness. It was always expensive—the first year's fees were £126. By 1895 it was decided to move from Brighton to Rottingdean, just outside the town, and by 1897 there were 130 shareholders and a working capital of £60,000 (it remained the absolute private property of the Lawrences until 1920). The actual move, and change of name, to Roedean took place in 1899.

Similar accounts could be given of other schools during this period— 1850 to about 1910—of most rapid growth (but particularly during the last two decades, as opposed to boys' schools, many of which appeared between 1840 and 1860, as we saw): St. Leonard's came in 1877, Wycombe Abbey in 1896, by 1900 there was St. Felix at Southwold and Sherborne in Dorset, and when St. Paul's School suddenly became overwhelmed by the rise in value of its endowments at the beginning of the century, it started St. Paul's Girls' School in 1904. By 1910 there were some twenty-one girls' public schools, teaching approximately 5,000 pupils. (These figures are very rough approximations. They are derived from *The Girls' School Year Books* of the period.) Thereafter, the foundations tail away, though distinguished schools continued to be started—Westonbirt, Benenden, Cranborne Chase, etc.—and will appear as, and if, they can contribute to the story. (The middle of these, incidentally, Benenden, was started in 1923 in a house which had once belonged to my great-grandfather, and some of the principal rooms bear family names. Princess Anne went there in 1963 and I have a fantasy that she may have slept in a dormitory called Gathorne-Hardy.)

What were they like, these schools, what customs evolved, what curriculum, above all how do they compare to boys' public schools? In certain respects, of course, we would expect them to be like boys' schools —or any Victorian institution. They were part of the age. It would be a waste of time, therefore, to go over again things like the emphasis on religion (evident enough in the names), the rise of patriotism, or class feeling. Many similar developments took place. We find the same school-as-country-house equation, with the danger of men outside adding high fences to broad acres (or, in Cheltenham's case, battlements). Roedean bought eighteen acres in 1897, twenty-four in 1903 and seventy-seven in 1930—the school now sits protected by 119 acres, blasted by those cleansing surgical winds I mentioned earlier. Many such things can be taken as read. Similarly, with our knowledge of total societies, we can expect, as they grow, a certain feverishness to start entering the ideology, an increase in discipline. In early years Roedean was remarkably free, more like a family; there was no uniform and the girls could go into the town whenever they liked. By 1904 rules had become innumerable, their application incessant. Every item of clothing, including knickers, was laid down. An Old Girl said, "We had a fourteen-hour day during every bit of which we did what we were told to do." The prospectus actually said "The leisure of the pupils is carefully organised," a contradiction in terms which, along with the whole development, we are well used to. But at the same time a number of important features appeared which are unique, some of which had significant results; and a number of familiar features (that feverishness for instance) developed in unique ways for often interesting historical reasons.

6 The dictator headmistress tradition

A book was published three years ago called *Reluctant Revolutionaries—A Century of Headmistresses, 1874–1974* by Nonita Glenday and Mary Price. Actually the headmistresses were not at all reluctant nor in the slightest degree revolutionary—except in so far as it was *girls'* schools they were starting. The fact that they had not existed before and now came so suddenly, alone made them revolutionary and is the point of the title. Indeed so revolutionary was it, still, in 1874 (Miss Beale, like Miss Davies, had to get medical evidence on the strength of women's brains) that it required women of ferocious will-power and total dedication. I could give many examples. There was Lydia Rous of the Mount School—"a woman of impelling force and quick sagacious mind". But she was "frugal of speech" and so terrified her staff that an American visitor thought they were not allowed to talk. It became customary for the head to exert her personal influence down to the minutest detail in the running of the school. Here is Kate Unwin of Walthamstow Hall; she

> superintended the whole of the teaching, taking many subjects herself, from the lowest to the highest forms. Every detail of household management, all the arrangements in the garden, the poultry yard, etc. were under her immediate direction, and she found time also to supervise the plain and fancy needlework in which she so much excelled. She was, of course, responsible for the choice of books, methods of teaching, arrangement of classes, school hours and holidays and whole internal organisation, management and discipline of the school. Her care of pets will be recollected by all. . . .

The rest of the staff were regarded as inferior (this was partly because at first many of them were hardly trained and in this respect were indeed inferior to their headmistress) and were ruled with a rod of iron. In 1889 a group of young teachers had settled to read *Jane Eyre*. The headmistress appeared, looked at the book, and forbade them to read it till they were twenty-five.

Now, we have seen autocratic heads in the boys' schools. But we also saw, that, as time passed, the increase in numbers, the growth of house loyalty and autonomy, the persistence of boy freedom in the "under-life", considerably curtailed the power of the headmaster. This did not happen to nearly the same extent in girls' schools. Certainly, houses became important and numbers grew, but the tradition of tyranny—itself necessitated by, or at least the result of, the strong characters arising in this "revolutionary" situation—had set fast and continued right through the 1920s and 30s and is still discernible today. Staff were expected to live in the headmistress's house or stated lodgings. In one school, in 1925, a teacher of five years' experience consulted her head before she "shingled" her hair. They seemed, sometimes, almost more than human these women, towering over their schools, pressing upon their pupils the impact of their personalities. Here's how one pupil, in the 1920s, remembered the impression made when she first encountered one of these formidable creatures: "Miss Scotson Clark, the headmistress, was seven or eight feet high, dressed from neck to toe in black, ornamented with a frontal fin of agate buttons like very black shiny currants. She was as graceful as a dolphin."

Their power was added to by another factor. The choice before women then was either marriage or a career. If they taught (and it was one of the very few things they could do), it meant giving up marriage. And this continued almost (a qualification many people would omit) until today— the dichotomy between marriage and a career, at least; the choice of career did grow. In a comparatively recent book (1967) on girls' schools, Dr. Kathleen Ollerenshaw notes that heads made "a slightly wistful observation that . . . [they] rarely have a separate house and their life is thereby harder and much more closely wrapped up in the school." Thus teaching was, even more than in boys' schools, a vocation—or a life sentence. The energy and motivation of the headmistresses, the deference of their staff, were by that degree increased.

I was interested to observe evidence of this power when I visited girls' schools. It was not just the position of present headmistresses, or the awe in which recent figures, like Diana Reader Harris of Sherborne for instance, were still held; it was the way in which many of their past headmistresses, going right back to the beginning of the schools, still almost seemed to be alive. Let me give examples. It is difficult to get at the characters of the three Lawrences of Roedean. Miss de Zouche, calling them "The Firm", is at pains to make them seem a team. In 1894 Penelope Lawrence, the eldest, wrote to the Royal Commission, "I have my school inspected. . . ." No doubt, says Miss de Zouche, she wrote "I" and "my school" for brevity. No doubt; though "We have our school inspected" is only a little longer. In fact, it is quite clear the other two sisters were completely dominated by Penelope (known either as PL or Miss Lawrence); and she was a very dominant woman. The portrait by S. W. Orpen, painted after years of power and adulation, shows a heavy, obtruding personality, a little like Queen Victoria only more masculine—some Venetian doge, say, or Hanoverian prelate. She had a loud voice and always expected her hats to be admired. Phrases remain—the famous bidding, "Go quickly and quietly to bed". On retirement she became President of the Women's Lacrosse Association. A non-playing president, one imagines, because in fact the Orpen portrait, though the figure is large, was discreet; towards the end of her life she grew colossally fat. Many people said she was the fattest woman they had ever seen.

And this considerable figure is still clearly detectable at Roedean today. Her portrait was one of the first things I saw. Several of the staff brought her up in conversation. The first thing Mr. Hunt said to me was that it was due to the foresight of Miss Lawrence, who had built the new head-mistress's house large enough "in case a family should ever run Roedean", that he was so comfortable there. It was foresight, it is true; but in fact he was doing automatically what he had probably done dozens of times before—invoking the authority of Miss Lawrence for his presence and so making acceptable the (momentary) incongruity of this highly intelligent, comparatively young married man, with a pretty wife, being headmaster of a school which I knew from reading and interviews had been, until fairly recently, extremely conventional, extremely snobbish and in which the atmosphere had been, as someone once said of all girls' public schools, "relentlessly feminine".

Miss Lawrence was merely detectable; Miss Beale was unavoidable at Cheltenham.

From her earliest years Dorothea Beale had wanted to be a school-mistress. As a child she had created a fantasy world, into which she would retire for hours, where she was ruling a school. As often happens to people whose ambitions become explicit very young, she had a sense of destiny. It was this, together with two other characteristics, which formed the major outlines of her personality. The first was an iron self-discipline. It was said she never learnt to play. Many years later, softened by perpetual obedi-ence, a whimsical element entered. She used, somewhat to the confusion of visitors, to refer to Cheltenham as her husband. But at first, stern of face, strongly built, it was this discipline, directing a driving energy, and combined with "acuteness and business capacity and power", which pulled Cheltenham from the brink of collapse. The first principal, Miss Annie Proctor, who had come with her mother in 1854, had had a difficult time. She was not allowed full control. The town gossiped and criticised. Rows became frequent. After a while she and her mother left, taking several pupils. Others followed. When Miss Beale arrived there was no money and no prospects. In four years she had reversed the situation and had begun to create the great scholastic empire whose outline we have glanced at.

But there was another strand to her character. She not only had a sense of destiny; that destiny was divinely directed. Deeply religious, even mystical, she was aware of a strange affinity with St. Hilda, whose name she used on every possible occasion. She gave it to the college she founded at Oxford and also to her teachers' training college at Cheltenham; she dreamt of founding a religious order to embody her feelings—the Society of St. Hilda—but nothing came of it. Instead she managed a fusion between religion, Cheltenham and her mission—education. The symbol of this fusion—and its organ—was the Guild, the Association of Old Girls formed in 1883. Its two chief principles were "continued self-education and service to the community". Girls had to enshrine this in their "Guild Promises" on joining. Writers note the "graciousness", the "refinement" of the twice yearly meetings, when the Guild's "aims" were tied ever more closely to Cheltenham "aims" by "especially memorable addresses" from Miss Beale. She reserved her "wisest and deepest thought" for the Guild.

The whole thing was seen as a crusade, with Cheltenham girls forging out to change the world. The Missionary Study Circle was formed in 1896 to be a link with the Guild's overseas missionaries (it lasted until 1952). Mayfield House, at Bethnal Green, was set up to do the same sort of thing for the East End in 1889, and later another centre was put in Old Nichol Street called—what else?—St. Hilda's East. Thus the Gospel of Cheltenham was spread to the lower classes and the heathen.

On my visit to Cheltenham, Miss Beale might have died a year ago; she might even have been on holiday. Here stood her bust, there a portrait, and there its copy; I was shown her books, letters to her from the Victorian establishment—Ruskin, Jowett, the Master of Balliol, who also sent her copies of his Plato; Miss Hampshire spoke warmly of her predecessor; but above all it was in the moments between lessons when, in a dead silence which dated from the beginning of the school, a silence more awesome and more indicative of discipline than any bell, 800 girls swished in swift lines down the long, dim, tiled corridors towards the next classroom, that one seemed to sense the continuing presence of Miss Beale, standing massively to watch, or swishing swiftly too.

But, just as significant to our developing picture of these girls' schools as the power of the headmistress, was that mystic note struck by Miss Beale over the Guild. She was by no means unique. On the contrary. It is a diapason we will often hear.

7 *"Uplift" and conformity*

Because women's education came so late, because women like Emily

Davies, Miss Beale and Miss Buss had had to fight so hard for it, against fierce opposition and ridicule, they felt passionately—and quite rightly—that what they were bringing was very important. The chance for women to learn was a precious, almost holy gift. Thus an evangelical note entered the attitude to work. At Milton Mount College, in 1873, it was stated "No prizes will be given. The luxury of acquiring knowledge is its own reward." The same was true at Cheltenham—"work for work's sake". Thus it was in this direction that the feverishness grew, spreading out from work to embrace the entire school in that "uplift" which is the girls' public school version of "tone".

It naturally took in religion, indeed in a sense it was chiefly religious. But it has a special flavour which can perhaps best be caught by quotation. While Marcia Mathews, in writing the history of the Godolphin School in 1928, is tracing its physical growth, the growth of discipline and so on in the 1900s, she interjects the saving grace of uplift—because all the time Miss Jones "was caring, caring intensely that we should care, care for poetry, care for art, care for beauty, but we were not very good material on which to work. It was not till many years later, not until she had a Peggy Deansley or a Nelly Kenyan in her house, that she found someone with a real soul for Browning." The headmistress, Miss Douglas, addressed the school like this in 1919:

> I believe that, with few exceptions, there is a spirit of earnest work in the school, and a growing realisation as the girls reach higher forms that school life *must* lead on to definite service in the larger life when school days are over . . . character . . . self control . . . neat smartness . . . good taste . . . school before house . . . the spirit of reverence . . . the school spirit . . . like the watchful star in the East, waiting for the Holy Child who came at Christmas, to live the pattern-life for all God's children.

It is this attitude—cloudy, gushing, in the last resort sentimental—which allows Miss Clarke, in her history of Cheltenham, to say, with an almost audible smack of her lips, that Miss Beale's character and that of the college "flourished together in a lovely mutuality of growth". And this attitude persisted. We can see it in the pious mottos and symbolic flowers adopted by many girls' schools. In the 1920s and 30s "honour" was the great word (the motto of Roedean is in fact Honour Roedean). At Queenswood in 1938 the school was addressed like this—"Girls! You are the flower of English womanhood!" Miss M. E. Popham, Headmistress of Cheltenham from 1937 till 1953, could talk about "work as part of a growth in goodness". It is pure clergyman's talk, claptrap which seems to mean something but doesn't.

As well as influencing the power of the headmistress and the form the exaggerations of the ideology would take, the lateness with which girls' education arrived had one more effect. Since just to exist was revolutionary, girls' schools were terrified of shocking anyone. The tendency towards conventionality, strong enough in Victorian and Edwardian England, a natural tendency anyway in total institutions, was thus yet further reinforced. It could over-ride anything, even the power of the headmistress. During a lecture at Cheltenham one of the staff passed a note to Miss Beale: "PLS DNT+LGS." The response was instant. "I sat up and uncrossed the offending limbs." Conventions were the more rigid because the practice of staff staying on for years at the same school was more pronounced than for all but the most consistent employees at the boys' schools. At Cheltenham, where they were often Old Girls, they stayed for years: figures like Miss Elizabeth Sturge with her "exacting standards and exquisite integrity", or Miss Andrews and her "deep spirituality". At Roedean there were similar celebrations of thirty or forty years of service. In the first thirty-eight years more than twenty OR's returned. Miss Gulick and Mrs. Leigh were assistants to all three headmistresses from Miss Lawrence to Miss Horobin in 1947. There were "Miss Lowenstein's zestful thirty-two years"; Miss D. Batho who, after forty years of teaching divinity, had become almost divine and was ordained deaconess. Often it seems that rather authoritarian figures are picked out for admiration. Miss de Zouche is particularly keen on "Miss M. Mellanby's unique record. Specialist teacher of English and for twelve years Number Two's house-mistress, she became Governor of the Aylesbury Borstal Institution in 1935, and in 1943 Assistant Commissioner to the Head Office of the Prison Commission. Since 1951 she has been a member of the Prison Board. . . ." This tendency is particularly strong at these two schools, but analyses of other school lists show they are not exceptional. It was a tendency increased, again, because there were few other jobs for them to take. They had nowhere to escape to. And, as one teacher said to me, "In medicine you cannot be really bad at your job for long. But a teacher can be mediocre for *years*."

Often the restrictions at girls' schools were even more oppressive than at boys' public schools. Antonia White, at a convent school in 1914, describes regulations almost unbelievably minute and numerous. Every movement was controlled by bells, each graded to a particular indicative strength—to pray, to wash, to read, to walk, to sit, to sleep. There were no mirrors (vanity), little talking, hairstyle was dictated (drawn so fiercely back that the eyes became narrowed into slits), even the position in which she slept was laid down:

> At first I used to curl up in bed for warmth as I did at home but I was cured of this evil habit by an old French nun. "Supposing my child," she said gently, "that you died in the night. Would that be a becoming posture in which to meet our dear Lord?" And she taught me to lie on my back "like a Christian" with my feet thrust well down into the cold sheets and my hands crossed on my chest.

The second point that can be—rather tentatively—made here is that, as well as there being historical reasons for the extreme conformity within girls' public schools, they were also "naturally" more conformist. For one thing, there is some evidence that one of the very few genetic differences between men and women is that women are less aggressive. Certainly centuries of subjection had conditioned women to conform to whatever society demanded of them, and rendered them less able, or less willing, to rebel. The impression I get therefore, right up to today, is not so much that girls' public schools imposed their restrictions more violently than did the boys' schools—they imposed them less violently, so in this respect the girls' schools were pleasanter places in which to be—but that the restrictions were more oppressive because they appeared more universally accepted and that escape and individuality were much harder to engineer. E. Arnot Robertson, at Sherborne Girls' School in 1916, describes how when she brought sweets back one term *everyone* refused them and public opinion forced her to give them up. The atmosphere, she says, was hysterical and hypocritical: "Oh-goody-goody-we-ought-to-do-well-in-lacrosse-this-term. Hurrah-for-the-house-and-I'm-glad-I'm-not-pretty." Elizabeth Bowen, at Downe House in 1914, says that the repression of personality and individuality meant that adulthood was simply put off until they left. That is the reason for the "silliness" of girls' schools, for the teddy bears and ornaments that littered the beds (or were concealed in drawers) of young women of eighteen. At boys' schools one way to be popular, or at least gain acceptance, was to be the buffoon, or adopt some eccentricity of dress or manner. Theodora Benson, at Cheltenham, had a satchel made of matting with three blue geese stitched onto it (given her by a bishop) as opposed to the leather regulation ones; she found afterwards she was hated for it. She left at seventeen and was able to view the silliness with detached irritation—the way, for example, they not only smelt their own eggs at breakfast but passed them round for everyone to smell and pass opinions on.

As I say, I cannot prove this point about conformity. It is an impression only, if a strong one, gained from reading and interviews. But it gets some confirmation from Mallory Wober's survey. For instance, a series of questions designed to test conformity and rebellion found that the overwhelming mass of girls was conformist. Only one girl out of 750 was remotely rebellious. Similarly, one aspect of a total society which did not appear to develop properly in the twenty-three boarding schools he studied was the secret life, the sub-culture. There was little "serious illicit activity". This is borne out in the school literature of our period. The under-life is usually restricted to one "madcap".

Finally, it should not be thought that because girls may conform more easily, they therefore suffer less in restrictive societies. Once again, there are no studies of this sort for the girls' schools during the period—roughly

1850 to 1910; clearly, exact studies are no longer possible. But findings made about how girls adjust to society today probably have some relevance. The problems today are two-fold: first, adjustment in a society which is still male-orientated, second adjustment in a society where standards are confused and changing. Both are problems, but today the second is probably stronger than the first. In the period we are discussing the first was stronger than the second (though by being educated at all girls of 1900 were put in a position of some confusion—what were they being educated *for*?). All research today shows that girls have considerably more problems in adjustment than boys. This comes out strongly in *Problems of Adolescent Girls* by James Hemmings (1960), a study whose main findings have been confirmed by later research. A study by C. W. Valentine found that seventy-six per cent of the sample could recall moods of intense depression, while nearly thirty per cent had contemplated suicide.

None of the sociologists who made these surveys would commit themselves to why this is so. Sociologists seldom commit themselves to answering the questions their surveys raise. But, since the problems of changing standards and confusion are common to both sexes, it is at least possible that the reasons adolescent girls find difficulty in adjusting is, still, that they are growing up in a male-dominated world. If this is so, then the girls at public schools between 1850 and 1910 (and for years afterwards) had the problem many times magnified. That was because, over this period, a development of the utmost peculiarity slowly took place.

8 Girls as boys, games: the basic dichotomy in girls' education

Knowing the views of Victorian society about the rôles of the sexes a detached observer might have expected girls' education—since education reflects society—to have evolved from the accomplishments; a more academic, more realistic development perhaps, but something definitely "feminine". And indeed, as we shall see, the accomplishments did continue to exert a direct influence—as opposed to influence through reaction—in a number of ways.

But in certain important respects girls' education, as far as their public schools went, evolved for many years in a completely different direction—towards the masculine.

Partly this was because they were new. They only had boys' schools to turn to for example, and turn they did. Paul Lawrence went to Malvern (modelled on Winchester) and this was a considerable influence on Roedean. The houses for example are called 1, 2, 3, 4. The great school families could now find occupation for their daughters. When Cecily Ray Ash became Headmistress of Godolphin School she was steeped in the ethos of public school because her father was "Ash of Haileybury".

But far more it was an extension of that logic which had led Emily Davies and others to see that if the girls' schools were not to be relegated to second best they must, academically, have exactly the same standards as the boys' schools. They must sit the same exams and work for the same degrees. But this set in train an ideological momentum the force of which was that, if they were not to be second best, they must be like boys' schools in every single respect.

I did not know of this bizarre development until I began reading for this history. But I discovered it is fairly well known. A few random examples will perhaps be enough, therefore, to illustrate what happened.

In essentials, of course, the basic structure of the girls' public schools was plainly a copy—houses, dormitories, studies (much fewer until very recently), age segregation, the prefect system—all this was taken from boys' schools. But the imitation was very marked in two spheres: the area concerned with uniformity and restriction—discipline, house and school "spirit", clothes, etc.—as the societies became total, and games. Uniform was masculine, and often hideous. At Cheltenham this appears early; as do prefects. By 1904 Miss Beale was able to compare Cheltenham to Eton and Harrow. At a number of schools it was customary to give each other masculine nick-names—Jacko, Bob, Charlie, Tom. The Godolphin School gives a good chronological picture and can serve as an example for many schools. In 1889 this was a small old-fashioned private school with about eighteen boarders. There were few rules or restrictions and girls were free to go out, had no uniform, and a curriculum which, while it has French, German and mathematics, also has a mass of bookbinding, carpentry, domestic science, art, acting, gardening and housewifery. During the 1890s girls pour in. Houses are introduced, monitors and prefects started, and some elements of uniform—white hats with black bands and gym tunics. By 1899 Marcia Mathews is talking of house spirit and how Nelson (Nelson!) House has never won a match. Latin is on the curriculum, and two hours' "prep". "We were proud, too, of the fact that our house, and our house alone, I believe, contributed brothers to the South African War (Miss Jones's, Phyllis Frene's, Phyllis Ruddle's and my own)." Miss Jones is becoming a figure, with her rigid discipline, her obsessive punctuality and "her blazing wrath. Who does not remember her indignation at such things as scribbling on school dictionaries, at stupid slang (how she hated the word 'ripping'); how she blazed out when someone once spoke of 'filthy' sandwiches)". By 1904 there are over 200 girls. Eton collars and ties are added to the uniform. Ming Forsyth, School House, 1902–07, can talk of "its great traditions". By 1907, Gladys Adams reports: "The whole atmosphere of the school was one of keenness." When moving from place to place, they march. Skirts and regulation coats are added to the uniform. In 1910 the final articles of clothing unspecified—blouses and shoes—are regulated. One girl can refer to the others as "chaps". And Mary Alice

Douglas, the "great" headmistress who oversaw these changes, has changed in tune with them. In 1890, it is certainly a strong face, but it is a feminine one; she has long hair pulled back and piled up, a long skirt, fine bosom and a slender waist. In 1919 she is wearing collar and tie, a pin-stripe coat, a waistcoat, a skirt (or are they trousers? It is impossible to see); she has the short-cut hair, greying at the temples, and the level gaze of a successful headmaster.

The only element I have left out is games. It is here, in what might seem the most unlikely sphere, given the period, that the imitation of boys' public schools became most slavish. Yet it is precisely because it was the most unlikely sphere that an extension of Miss Davies's logic was most likely.

If one of the arguments against girls having any education was that they were too weak then, as well as proving they were not too weak, you could also take pains to make them stronger. It was less an admission of defeat than a way of reassuring nervous parents. This was the root of most early games activities at girls' schools, and it dictated their form. Often, as at Cheltenham, Godolphin and others there were not at first any real competitive games at all. There were croquet, drill, callisthenics, bowls, quoits, tobogganing. Then, in 1885, the Madame Osterberg College opened at Dartford, followed by other physical-training colleges. Specialists joined the schools. "The physical-training mistress became a power in the land."

But fairly quickly sterner disciplines were introduced. It is clear that from the start Roedean was a games-orientated school. Miss de Zouche hotly denies this "widespread belief". But certainly the prospectus gave them "special emphasis", putting physical education as the first priority and promising "two or three hours daily" of outside games (a promise they were unable to keep). It is also clear that this orientation was largely due to the prevailing fashion in boys' schools. It was introduced from them at the beginning by the Reverend E. Luce (a Double First and Double Blue), who whipped the school into a frenzy over matches and awarded medals for batting and bowling. Theresa Lawrence, another sister, "took with her his gospel of the straight bat . . . in her junior school". Miss Sharpe wrote to Miss Lawrence in the late 1890s, "You are sailing just now on a wave, because your school falls in with the popular sentiment for games and so forth. . .". St. Leonard's was also notable for prowess. The games mistress could over-rule the head. By 1900 Cheltenham had begun to capitulate; and the appointment of Miss L. M. Faithfull in 1907 was partly due to her being President of the All-England Women's Hockey Association. Women began to use sporting terms. Elizabeth Bowen remembered being criticised for doing something that was "not cricket". It was by "a friend whose brother at that time captained the Winchester eleven, and who was herself our only over-hand bowler".

Once again we can trace the process at Godolphin. There are virtually no games in 1889; the girls say to the mistress, "You name five games and we'll choose one." By 1899 hockey is compulsory and matches are being played. From then on games become more and more important. In 1900 a teacher is engaged who has a "tremendous reputation from Oxford as a Left Inner." There is "Miss Bagnell . . . generally in charge" who "did so much towards licking into shape generations of small people. She was an adept at teaching the most unlikely person to 'play the game'."

By 1910 Godolphin and most other girls' public schools were playing compulsory cricket, hockey and lacrosse, and being made to watch all these when other schools were played. They were fanatical about cups and teams, and obsessive about colours and games uniforms—tunics had to be of a precise length, hair ribbons an exact width, the tie-pin placed exactly *there* in the tie. 1900–1939 are the vintage years of the girls' team photograph. It is in this respect that they most closely resembled boys' schools and sometimes the same crazed figures appear. The Reverend Fred Brooke Westcott (Sherborne 1888–1906) organised mixed football matches with the girls' school. He would put on cycling kit and a rat-catcher's hat and join in, yelling "Run—woman—run!", belting them over the shins with his stick.

Friedenberg says that a difference between girls and boys is that girls have more common sense and a greater sense of purpose. Purposeless activity—and games have no ultimate purpose beyond themselves—does not interest them. As well as any physical difficulty, therefore, they have, according to him, a natural bias against games. That is why, however well done, a girls' game looks *unconvincing*. I don't know how true this is psychologically; though certainly the few girls' games I watched when I toured the schools did look rather unconvincing. Nor am I sure if it matters. They seemed to be enjoying themselves in a bluff sort of way. Similarly, the games cult, taken alone, of the 1900s and onward probably had some of the same effects as it did at boys' schools (not all—it did not seem to lead to the same philistinism, for instance): it wasted a great deal of time, some girls hated it, a great many more were bored by it, and some liked it. But taken with the whole attempt to make girls' public schools like boys' schools, games reinforced this; and this in turn reinforced a very much more serious contradiction which was inherent in this entire feminine educational development.

The point is quite simple. By giving women the same education as men the public schools introduced the idea that women should be able to lead the same lives as men—as Emily Davies and the earlier fighters intended. Not just introduced the idea, they made it theoretically possible. Society began to educate them like this and then loosed them into a social order which expected them—and to a large extent still expects them—to be wives, mothers, mistresses, housewives and also subservient to men. Their true potential began to be understood but remained unattainable. The mistake these earlier fighters made, a mistake which is still being made by their "Liberationist" successors today, is two-fold. First, education is the way society transmits its values, it is not an agent of social change (though many people, from Plato down to H. G. Wells and A. S. Neill have hoped it could be). Mao Tse-tung first revolutionised China, for example, then altered the educational system, not the other way about. And second, even if it were a matter of changing society, this particular freedom, like many freedoms, is fundamentally economic; to bring it about you would have to alter the economic power structure in society. We shall return to a full discussion of this problem later. I introduce it here because its roots are here.

At a less fundamental, though scarcely less important level, the fact that this problem was not resolved meant that as far as women went there was a dichotomy between education and a career and their personal life. Right through the 1920s and 30s—and to a fair extent today—a proper career meant sacrificing marriage. Miss Baker, Headmistress of Badminton (it became a public school in 1931), really believed that anything a man could do a woman could do better. She was fiercely determined her girls should have a career (Indira Gandhi went there, as did Iris Murdoch). Not to have a career meant failure. In fact, if you married you had failed; success was non-marriage, university and a career. She was an interesting woman (to digress minutely), living to an immense age and coming to resemble a brilliant tortoise. She was left-wing, vegetarian and non-denominational. Like many successful generals, she realised that her best chance of winning was to concentrate all her forces on a narrow front. Practically only Latin and French were taught.

Finally, this dichotomy also revealed itself in certain aspects of the curriculum at girls' public schools.

9 Curriculum, womanliness

The academic strand, the idea that they should have the same standard and type of education as boys, remained powerful in girls' public schools. This was particularly true of Cheltenham, and Cheltenham, as we shall see, is important because of its influence over other girls' schools.

Free of the classics, Miss Beale at first put the emphasis on history and literature. But the curriculum rapidly widened to include all the main academic subjects. Science began early, and a science wing was built in 1905. The encouragement was always towards advanced education. She entered more and more girls for university exams, and Cheltenham's own degree courses were equal to those at Oxford and Cambridge. And Cheltenham was the model for a great many other girls' public schools. Nor was this academic approach—as far as curriculum went a great deal broader than nearly all boys' schools at the same period—confined to the larger schools. At St. Brandon's School, Bristol (it has since moved to Clevedon), with ninety pupils in 1901, ten major subjects were studied and the girls worked an average of forty-three and three-quarter hours a week. There are accounts from other schools of girls being so anxious to pass exams that they would refrain from answering questions in class in case they gave information away to their competitors.

An equal stress was placed on teacher training. The early pioneers had realised the teacher was fundamental and we have seen that the entire movement began from the governess. This continued. Miss Beale's teacher-training college—a year on the theory and practice of education—was the first resident one; but Miss Buss had been active too. There were, for example, the 1878 Maria Grey Training College, and in 1885 the Cambridge Training College (later Hughes Hall).

But at the same time—and here the dichotomy begins to emerge—girls' public schools were unable to throw off the knowledge that it was girls they were educating. Partly this is because, as educational machines, they were unable to abandon completely their rôle of training their pupils to fit the society they would find when they left—and society wanted them to be women not men. But the main reason is historical. Boys' schools then (and now) were quite unperturbed that their education did not bear the faintest relevance to anything that would come later. In the same way, but directly contrary in thrust, girls' education had begun in the accomplishments with the idea that it should have some relationship to what came later and thus we get a second strand, equally strong, of girl-orientated education.

In some ways this was beneficial. Their curriculum was both broader, and broader in interesting ways—music, art, housecraft, and manual work were usually part of it, or if not, as with art at first at Roedean, an "extra" taken by most pupils. In 1905 the Association of Headmistresses helped fight Robert Morant, at that time the unusually powerful permanent secretary to the Board of Education, when he wanted to impose a rigid classics-based curriculum on girls' secondary schools. They argued that a spectrum of non-academic subjects, and recreation, was necessary for "the whole child" (a favourite word with mistresses for many years. That full-throated "whole" has a hint of the uplift diapason.)

But it also meant that academic standards could be very low. Again, this was partly the period. Miss Buss and Miss Beale concentrated on teacher training because many teachers were very bad. Nineteenth-century teaching methods were often primitive (and this means a simple list of subjects is not really very valuable ; a "wide" curriculum badly taught is of less value than a narrow one well taught). The main method (and this continued well into the 20th century) was learning by heart—reams of dates, places, names from books like Mangnall's *Questions* or Mitchell's *Catechist*.

But academic standards were much more vitiated by the knowledge that, in a more fundamental way, it was all a total waste of time. They were never going to use any of this knowledge, even if well taught, these rich middle- and upper-class girls. They were not going to have jobs but babies, husbands, houses. They would benefit a great deal more from needlework, domestic science and dancing classes—and these were all taught. Appearing, in their Eton collars, to follow Emily Davies's or Miss Beale's ambitions to be the equal of boys, hiding behind the masculine clash of hockey sticks, academically the girls at many of the public schools in fact had a pretty slack time of it. At Roedean, for example, this was clearly so. Neither of the two younger Miss Lawrences could spell, and Miss Lawrence's own subject, science, Miss de Zouche is astonished to report, was criticised by the Board of Education Inspectors in 1906 on every possible ground—syllabus, methods and standards. In 1912 the inspectors again criticised the school for its lack of work. There is no real record of the teaching staff, so little was "teaching" regarded, through the first twenty-nine years of its history.

And this element in girls' public schools persists right through the 1920s and 30s. At the Winchester School for Girls (St. Swithin's) in the 1920s— as well as compulsory games, prefects and so on—there was a whole recognised stratum of pupils which was concentrated in what one might call the "Girl's Side", learning domestic science, botany and the like. At Roedean in the 30s, bridge and wine tasting were popular subjects in the curriculum. The ideas behind it persisted as well. In 1948, in a book called *The Education of Girls*, John Newsom argued that they should have a completely different education from boys, centering in essentials of Boeuf Bourguignon. To give it depth, girls should learn the chemistry of Boeuf Bourguignon, the history of cooking, the medical details of food poisoning and the basic workings of sewage systems.

Headmistresses were despotic; but they were also women. Miss Beale's references to her "husband", Cheltenham, implies that her pupils were her children. These were despotisms tempered by sentimentality. Mary Buss took sweets with her whenever she visited her juniors. The Miss Jones who "blazed out when someone once spoke of 'filthy' sandwiches" made delicious cakes and would give sweets and other presents at birthdays. While Miss Bagnall, in the intervals between teaching them how "to play the game", would sit reading Walter Scott aloud while the girls sat in a circle round her, darning. Sometimes this could get out of hand. Miss Clarke talks a little wildly of Cheltenham "centring itself round a garden like every true family should". I can think of many better things for a family to centre itself on—a father and mother, for instance. And often the effort—from all sorts of fear—to keep their girls "children" was extremely stultifying. I have an image from St. Swithin's in 1923. However old (seventeen, eighteen, even nineteen), whenever they walked in town they always had to wear uniform, always walked in a crocodile, always had an escort—those great huge girls tramping along. . . . Yet, however retarding, they must have been comforting too, those sweets and cakes and darning while Miss Bagnall read *Ivanhoe* or *Peveril of the Peak*.

10 Class; schools as a block

The second area affected in this way was class. Apart from all the usual manifestations, where they were like boys' schools, two aspects were particularly feminine. In fiction, and in fact, the lady of the manor always had a charitable rôle—calves' foot jelly, cast-off clothes, "I'm worried about the Bumbleweed children, Jones." Like huge ladies of the manor, girls' schools duplicated this. In 1874 the prefects suggested Roedean should support, or start, a charity. In a flash of inspiration, Miss Lawrence saw that it should take the form of "giving some London waif the benefit of a fortnight by the sea". So began the Wimbledon House Mission Society which lasted until 1954. Nearly all girls' schools supported some charity or other for, as it was put at Cheltenham, "preparation for service to the community when schooldays were over". One should perhaps not sneer at these efforts. No doubt they did good. But there does seem something patronising about them, an element of acquiescing in the injustices of society by allowing its dregs to have a few easily afforded and easily given crumbs from the rich women's table. Nor was the contact particularly close. At Roedean, for instance, the children who came down from London or elsewhere were not allowed to see the girls for a week; they were kept in quarantine in case they were harbouring some fearful lower-class bug.

There is a pleasanter aspect. The excitement and revolutionary fervour of forming schools at all bound all girls' schools together. They have always been, collectively, far less snobbish than boys' schools. The Association of Headmistresses, which by 1881 had formalised into rules and procedures, is, and always has been, open to anyone—day schools, boarding schools, county schools, independent, grammar, technical, comprehensive; any secondary girls' school recognised as efficient can be member. The contacts between the State and the private system have always been closer and in 1942 the Association only defeated a resolution to abolish the private sector in education altogether by a fairly narrow margin.

This meant, of course, that when girls' secondary schools became more numerous under the Education Act of 1902, the older girls' public schools supplied the headmistresses. "The new secondary schools offered these women an opportunity," as Nonita Glenday and Mary Price put it, ". . . and they seized it eagerly." Thus there is the same permeation of the public school ethos down through the social strata on the girls' side as with the boys'—a pincer movement clamping England ever more firmly into her belief in public school virtues and values.

And, in exactly the same way as with the boys' schools, the girls' public schools themselves formed a block of essentially identical units. The block was created by imitation, of each other (often through discussion at the Association) and of the boys' schools, and because headmistresses naturally tended to model their own schools on the one they had been to or first taught at. Cheltenham and Miss Beale were particularly influential here. St. Leonard's first headmistress, Miss (later Dame) Louisa Lumsden, taught under Miss Beale at Cheltenham, Miss Mulliner of Sherborne was a Beale student, Miss Grey of St. Paul's (1904) and Miss Jane Frances Dove of Wycombe Abbey (1896) both came from St. Leonard's. By 1897 the headmistresses of over forty schools here and abroad had come from Cheltenham. Miss Beale runs not so much like a thread but a great thick hawser through the girls' public schools.

And the effects of this block upon those under it were enormously increased because they began so young. As with boys, girls were sent away to school at eight or even younger, and we get girls' preparatory schools starting up towards the end of the 19th century to supply partially trained material for the public schools. Often, as with Roedean in 1907, these were junior schools directly associated with the senior.

And I might note here a significant fact about these schools. On the whole, although there are naturally unpopular girls and cruel ones, teasing and sarcasm, girls don't seem to bully in the crude physical ways boys do. There are few accounts of bullying at girls' public schools. There are accounts of bullying at prep schools. A. S. Neill observed that girls from the age of eight to thirteen or so were just as ready to use physical force as boys and often formed gangs to facilitate this. I also noticed this in my interviews. One particularly violent school, to jump ahead chronologically, was Wickhouse in the 1940s. My informant, Kate Millbanke, described how if new girls (seven years old) were at all bumptious the dorm would wait until they were sobbing at night from homesickness and then leap on them with pillows. Her best friend, Louise Pleydell-Bouverie, was tied, as on a rack, and left hanging under her bed for hours. While one —a huge sadistic girl who had a gang—would take new girls to a hut in the wood, tie them to a post and thrash them with nettles.

The significant thing about this behaviour is that it dies away at twelve or thirteen. The reason is almost certainly that it is then that girls become fully subjected to the enormous pressure of society's expectations: girls are not "meant" to be violent physically, that is for little boys. It is part of the same pattern that made girls more conventional; a pattern which appears again in the sexual and amorous lives of adolescent girls at public schools.

CHAPTER 11

The "Crush": Sex and Love at Girls' Schools and Some Other Considerations

Miss Buss and Miss Beale
Cupid's darts do not feel.
How different from us
Miss Beale and Miss Buss.

Anon

The attitude to love and sex at girls' schools was one of violent and confused disapproval; a disapproval in which the ingredients were silence, repression, disgust and terror. This remains true right through the period until after the Second World War; in a number of schools it is substantially true today.

1 Repression and disgust

The silence is so complete that often only small indications remain of the repression. Cheltenham itself is built, from the outside, like a fortress, and the blank towering walls reveal so little that it is possible to live in the town for a lifetime and never know where the Ladies' College is. From the start it is clear that the major enemy from which the girls were to be protected was anything male. In Miss Beale's time virtually the only men allowed in were the music teachers and they were all chaperoned. No contact was allowed with Cheltenham boys' school. In the school history it gets only two brief mentions, and it does not appear in the index at all. In the 1950s there were maps to show which parts of the town were out of bounds. The red lines grow thicker and more numerous the closer they come to the boys' school until, as they reach it, they become completely solid, and the school leaps out at you, a flaming red ball, somehow the centre of a target.

The silence created considerable confusion. At St. Swithin's in the 1920s —as at many schools—the facts of menstruation were never mentioned, even amongst the girls themselves. At their periods, girls crept to the "off-games" bag and, peering round to see that no one was looking, put their names in it (keen houses ignored the event and would win matches). At Antonia White's convent, founded by the Order of the Five Wounds, lest they be fired to self-love, they were not even allowed to see their own bodies. They bathed in a large calico cloak like a bell tent. They were constantly guarded by a nun, and girls were never allowed to be alone. There had to be three.

Yet since here, and at other schools, no one ever dared say what all these precautions were about, never explained the facts of life, much less discussed masturbation or lesbian attraction or sex in any terms at all, if the silence was in any way broken the girls were completely baffled. At Sherborne in 1914 the headmistress suddenly burst out in a wild emotional address that she trusted the girls alone in the bathroom. What she trusted them about Arnot Robertson hadn't the faintest idea.

The fact is that many of the staff were extremely confused too. As late as 1970, at a convent school, circumcision was explained to the girls as scratching a small circle at the top of a male thigh. But there were also forces at work which many mistresses, even now, would find difficulty in facing. As with boys' schools, only in reverse, teaching at girls' schools attracted a considerable, but quite incalculable, number of lesbians. And just as homosexual men often fear and dislike women, so lesbians, and for the same reasons, often fear and dislike men. Again, women who entered teaching sometimes did so because they could not get married; subconsciously part of the attitude of some of them to men would include desires for revenge. Often these pioneer liberationists resented (quite understandably) the privileged and dominant position of men in society. They envied men and wanted to equal or surpass them. But there is aggression here too. All these forces help to explain the quite noticeable elements of fear, disgust and hatred towards men which girls' schools often manifest during this period. And this emotional charge further complicated, in those in whom it was present, the logical dichotomy which we have already noted: these women teachers were striving to emulate men and bring up their pupils to do the same, yet they disliked and feared men; they disliked men, but they were training girls who were going out into a society in which the goal of a woman, and so their pupils' prime aim, was to attract and serve men.

Apart from Castle Cheltenham there are dozens of illustrations of this attitude. When Nancy Spain was at Roedean in the 1930s it was discovered that at one point on the journey from Brighton to Rottingdean it was possible, from the top of a double-decker bus, to see a small part of the school grounds. The staff were instantly reduced to a state of panic. Within a week vast wooden barricades were erected to shut out the view. The inference was that men were bursting with an almost insane lust. They would catch a glimpse of a Roedean girl, go completely mad, leap off the bus and charge in to rape her. At Queenswood, in the 1930s, letters were read and pupils writing more than twice to any male were closely questioned. Books were frequently banned, as was the film *Gone With the*

Wind. No girl was allowed into another's cubicle, and all the landings were patrolled each night by staff to ensure this. In summer they changed their clothes five times a day. Uniforms frequently seemed to have been designed to make the girls unattractive. At one school the regulation grey knickers were so thick and coarse as to resemble chastity belts. Another frequent complaint, made about Sherborne in 1916, for example, is that such instruction as they did get always represented sex as something beastly in store for them.

What survived all this? To what degree did the sexual and amorous life of girls' public schools resemble that of boys' schools and equal it in intensity?

2   The "crush"—sexual patterns

The one universal phenomenon seems to have been the"crush"﹒This is the "love" which a younger girl—between eleven and, at the latest, fourteen —has for an older girl. Taking place at the onset of puberty, when interest in the opposite sex is beginning to deepen, there is clearly an element of subconscious attraction in the relationship, the older girl representing the man. The different names given by various schools demonstrate both the strength and the slight hysteria of the feelings felt towards your partner, herself unmoved—your pash, rave, keen-on, your fad. When you had a crush on someone you carried their exercise books or put sweets under their pillow—"Is there anything I can do for you?" At Roedean "friendship" was always shown by making the friend's bed (the forms love takes are traditional). A smile would make you happy for a week; you would lie awake for hours wondering if your rave would look in and say goodnight and cry if she didn't. Even these innocent liaisons were frowned on. In many schools the banning of mixing between the age groups was just as strong as it was in boys' schools. At Hatherop Castle, Mrs. Fife suddenly gave an extraordinary talk on crushes (1955)—*there were to be no more crushes.* Kate Millbanke, deeply in love with Florence Harcourt-Smith, couldn't understand why she should suddenly stop being so.

The relationship of the younger girl to the older was complicated because it was also, to a greater degree than with boys, that of a child to her mother. And this keen-on/mother was, too, a heroine—a figure copied in the natural process of growing up, a character adopted to see if any parts fitted the imitator.

By fifteen this stage had passed. The chief outlet thereafter was in fantasy —about actors and film stars, characters in novels, boys met at dances in the holidays and also about schoolmistresses. Mistresses now played a greater part, their admiration and praise taking the place of the wanted, but unobtainable, male attention. In this older version of the crush, girls fell in love with mistresses and were rivals for their favour; they also identified with them. At St. Paul's in the early 1960s there was a furore of love around a young and lovely teacher—call her Miss C—which reached fever pitch when she became engaged to the Conservative candidate. But the furore of love was not so much for Miss C, there was no jealousy; the girls were really imagining they *were* Miss C and that they were themselves therefore, 300 of them, all becoming engaged to the Conservative candidate. In the late 1930s, but far more after the war, certain daring girls' schools employed a few men on the staff; they were nearly always the focus of powerful fantasies and wildly oscillating reactions of love and loathing.

It is much harder to pin down girls' schools in this sphere than it is boys' schools; there is greater reticence, things are less definite, inchoate, the atmosphere is tense and charged—but you are not quite sure with what. To what extent, for instance, were relations physical, how common was lesbianism? To answer these questions it may be a good idea to look a little more closely at some aspects of female sexuality.

Once again, since we are concerned with what actually takes place, our best guide is probably Kinsey (1953 edition). There are areas where subsequent commentators have suggested he is unreliable, but we can try and avoid these. The fact is that no comparable survey has yet appeared. Kinsey's is once again characterised by his scrupulous and elaborate cross-checking and, interesting from our point of view, a sizeable proportion of the sample was born between 1900 and 1910, while a number were born from 1860 onwards. Our cultures are not the same (for instance in this respect the US has always been more overtly disapproving of homosexual relationships between women; we have simply pretended they did not exist); but they are similar. At the least, we will probably get a fairly accurate indication of pattern.

During the period with which we have been dealing, girls were not really supposed to have any sexual feelings at all—a supposition contradicted by the mass of inhibitions and restrictions I have outlined. By 1953 the current psychoanalytically based view of their development came from Freud's four stages: (1) narcissistic, (2) latent (just pre-adolescent), (3) homosexual, (4) finally—heterosexual. Neither view was borne out by the survey.

The first thing that emerged was that pre-adolescent sex-play was far more widespread than had been realised. Twenty-seven per cent had been aroused erotically, fourteen per cent of them to orgasm. So, far from being narcissistic or homosexual, an equal number of females recalled interest in boys as in girls (forty-eight per cent of that twenty-seven per cent who had been erotically aroused)—a significant figure since girls are usually given girls as companions. For most of the sample sexual play was restricted to a few incidents and was the result of curiosity. But because satisfaction had been learnt at so early an age they were conditioned to the acceptance of later sexual activities and to the enjoyment of them. Conversely, where punishment or strong disapproval had ensued, the effect had been marked and had "in many instances prevented the female from freely accepting sexual relationships in her adult married relationships".

Up till adolescence, the patterns of sexual activity are approximately the same for girls and boys. Thereafter they diverge quite distinctly and are markedly different in a good number of significant respects. With boys, as we saw, the onset of sexual activity is very rapid, reaching its potential height in the early teens; there is a very gradual decline from then on until, with extreme old age, it ceases altogether. With girls activity begins much more slowly, it steadily climbs to a height around the mid–thirties and then, instead of declining, remains steady up to the age of sixty and beyond. (One such lively figure was a woman of ninety responding to orgasm once a week.)

This pattern shows up clearly in masturbation. Before adolescence, girls and boys are roughly the same (in fact figures are higher in pre–adolescent girls). But after adolescence (around thirteen) girls are much less active; by fifteen, twenty per cent are masturbating, by twenty, thirty-three per cent; with boys the figures are eighty-two and ninety-two per cent, respectively. That is to say, the average adolescent girl gets on with one-fifth as much sexual activity as boys. There are two other differences; girls appear to talk about sex less frankly and openly than boys. As a result, fifty-eight per cent of girls who masturbated discovered it for themselves, while seventy-five per cent of boys learnt about it from other boys. The second is that, though on average girls' frequency is one-fifth that of boys, the differences between girls, and between girls and boys are even more extreme than the differences between boys. There were girls or women (two per cent) who were never aroused erotically at all, some who masturbated once or twice a year, and gentle gradations upwards until there were some who reached orgasm thirty times a week, or even numerous times an evening, able to have orgasms ten or twenty times an hour. And this variation, far greater than with men, continued in their patterns of heterosexual response, ranging from nothing to orgasm many times a day for long periods of years. This extreme variation also complicates the adolescent picture somewhat. Although on the whole girls make do with one-fifth as much sexual activity as boys, some girls are a great deal more active. In a situation where coition is not discouraged, therefore, you sometimes get a pattern of one girl with several partners.

As with men and boys, Kinsey found that there was no evidence masturbation caused any harm at all. The only harm came because it was against the, quite unrealistic, moral codes and caused worry and guilt. The result has often been that "some millions of females in the US . . . have had their self-assurance, their social efficiency, and their sexual adjustments in marriage needlessly damaged. . . . There is no other type of sexual activity which has worried so many women." Many psychiatrists simply move the burden by rating the activity "infantile and immature", thus fortifying old traditions with a new set of terms which appear scientific. "Many adults," notes Kinsey, "who are not immature in any realistic sense do masturbate, and there is no sense in refusing to recognise this fact."

I do not want at the moment to see if there are any reasons why men and women should be different in their rate of sexual development; but clearly it will have considerable bearing on the sort of sexual life a school, especially a boarding school (and also parents), should allow adolescents. The general picture is clear, whatever the reasons. The statistics would no doubt be somewhat different for Victorian and Edwardian England and for England today; but the pattern of slow onset and lower frequency in adolescent girls as compared to adolescent boys would undoubtedly be the same. And a similar difference appears when we turn to the last aspect in this rather brief survey that I want to look at—lesbian contacts at girls' schools.

In most primitive cultures records of male homosexuality are common, with attitudes towards it varying from acceptance to condemnation— usually variations of the latter. Records of female homosexuality are much less common. (It is possible that this rarity has something to do with the taboos of the anthropologists collecting the data; also, most of them are male.) Only in one are there records of exclusively homosexual female relationships, among the Mohave Indians of the American south-west.

But certainly female homosexuality seems to be rarer than male homosexuality in our Western culture. As far as adolescents go, between sixteen and twenty, nine per cent in Kinsey's sample had erotic contacts, of which two to three per cent led to orgasm (with boys the figures are approximately thirty-three and twenty-two per cent). This was the sphere, however, where sexual behaviour and responses were more closely related to educational background than any other. The college grade level —the nearest to our public school class—had a markedly more homosexual response (although still far below that of boys). For instance, where fifteen per cent of the whole sample were aware of strong physical attraction leading to erotic arousal towards another girl or girls, thirty-three per cent of the college groups recognised this. The reason for this seems quite simply to be the embargo placed on heterosexual relationships at college level (in 1953); which is precisely the situation we have found in the girls' public schools.

Finally, in the male we found an extremely blurred distinction between homosexual and heterosexual, with the preponderance being towards the heterosexual, certainly, but with an infinite series of gradations in between and with most men being mixed. With women there are also gradations but the weight is considerably more towards the heterosexual—in general terms twice as much as with men. For instance, less than one-third as many women were exclusively homosexual compared to men.

Once again, the statistics need be no more than indicative; but, as far as my own infinitely much smaller researches go, the pattern they reveal is accurate. The number of lesbian contacts at girls' schools was (and is), relative to boys' schools, extremely small. It certainly existed. Every school at all periods could furnish a few instances. Oddly enough, the most active example I found was a day school—St. Paul's in the early 1960s. Three quite independent sources described numerous active liaisons, both with other girls in the school and girls outside. One father discovered what was going on and rushed round in a fury to the other family:

Father A: I hold Camilla entirely responsible for Caroline's being a lesbian.

Father B: What is a lesbian?

But on the whole the ravening couples the patrolling schoolmistresses expected to stop in the corridors existed in their imaginations; if they were not indeed themselves the only candidates. At Cheltenham in 1915 a friend of Theodora Benson described the most overt way she could express her love: "It's heartless to like Patsy better than me, when you think how I filled her hot-water bottle for her every night of the winter term. I don't think Patsy would have filled her hot-water bottle for her—at least I'm sure she wouldn't have done it in quite the same way." Nearly all girls' schools seem to have had dances, usually on a Saturday, as at Downe House in 1914, and also at Roedean. It was (echo of the accomplishments) part of a girl's equipment to be able to dance. The girls danced together, if possible with their raves, or with the mistress they loved. And the fact such dances were held at all shows how much more relaxed the atmosphere was. No boys' school at the time would have dared allow such physical contact. Nor much later. At Bryanston, a supposedly advanced school, dancing classes in the early 1950s were taken by Miss Lethbridge, a beautiful creature of about twenty-seven, lithe and strong but light as a feather in the hand, and with that marvellous feminine capacity to lead while seeming to be led. But the boys certainly did not dance with each other, nor with the girls from Cranborne Chase, a school started nearby with co-educational projects in mind. Both were considered far too explosive. After she had demonstrated a quickstep, say, with a neat new reverse chassé, Miss Lethbridge would put on Victor Silvester and say in her strong voice—*Partners, boys!* And the boys would walk over to a stack of brooms leaning against the wall and shuffle round the floor with one of them held awkwardly in front.

Nevertheless, it would be a mistake to think, just because the physical expressions of love and desire were so much less at girls' schools than boys', that they were not present at all. How you fill a hot-water bottle may be a nuance—even a ludicrous one—but nuances are all-important in love. Theodora Benson describes the "raves" at Cheltenham at this time. These were passionate attachments to contemporaries, with wild scenes, furious jealousies, the employment of spies to see who talked to whom, and storms of hysterical tears. The Lawrences practically forbade any social contact between staff and pupils in order to discourage "sentimental friendships" at Roedean; "but experience suggests," says Miss de Zouche delicately, "it was not the best means to that end." It would be surprising if the atmosphere was not quite tense. After all, Kinsey's survey showed that thirty-three per cent of girls around sixteen were aware of "strong physical attraction" to each other, and this was in a non-boarding situation. There is also reason to suppose that the powerful moral disapproval in America meant that the actual figures should .be considerably higher. (Female homosexuality was illegal in forty-three states at that time, though the law was hardly ever enforced. It has never been illegal in Britain.)

3 Love

It is important, if we are to understand what it was like to be in a girls' public school, to get some impression of the atmosphere. And, just as Drew and Maugham did for boys' schools, I should like to give a similar account, though of wider application, for girls' schools. The best description, although it is written in English by an Englishwoman, is the autobiographical account of love in a French boarding school towards the end of the 19th century, Olivia *by Olivia, written by Lytton Strachey's sister Dorothy Bussy.

The school is divided into Mlle. Cara's favourites and Mlle. Julie's. It is the central topic of conversation, obsessing everyone. Nina says the moment she saw Olivia—the heroine, aged sixteen—she knew she would be a "Julie-ite". And Olivia's attraction for Mlle. Julie begins the moment she starts being noticed by her. She is indeed an intoxicating and fascinating person, capable of dominating the most select salons in Paris. "Mlle. Julie was witty. Her brilliant speech darted here and there with the agility and grace of a humming-bird. Sharp and pointed, it would transfix a victim cruelly."

Olivia becomes a favourite. They go on little trips together into Paris to the theatre, to art galleries. Capricious, gay, mysterious, Mlle. Julie allows her into the inner sanctum, the library. In this heady air, love grows swiftly. Coming back in the train in the evenings after their visits to Paris, Olivia takes to staring obsessively at Mlle. Julie, who lies back with closed eyes:

Once, as I was watching her like this, she suddenly opened her eyes and caught me. Her glance held me for a moment, and I was too fascinated to look away. Her glance was piercing, not unkind but terrifying. She was searching me. What did she see? "Come," she said at last. "Come here and sit beside me." I think she said it to get rid of my intolerable gaze. After I had obeyed, she put her hand on mine for the space of a heartbeat. I turned my eager palm to clasp it, but she withdrew it gently and sank again into her corner and her reverie.

Before long Olivia is in the grip of a total, all-embracing, passionately physical, mental and spiritual love. She and another girl, the second great favourite, are discussing what they feel for Mlle. Julie. "And tell me this, Laura," says Olivia. "Does your heart beat when you go into the room where she is? Does it stand still when you touch her hand? Does your voice dry up in your throat when you speak to her? Do you hardly dare raise your eyes to look at her, and yet not succeed in turning them away?" Laura, it seems, is not so consumed.

The book was written about events at the end of the last century. Because women had an extremely limited rôle, they accepted that love, or at least human relationships, should be the central thing in their lives. As a result, it is the occupation of the whole school. Olivia's position is discussed openly by all the other mistresses and girls. So is Mlle. Cara. It turns out that she is furiously jealous of Olivia and in fact of all Mlle. Julie's conquests. The gossip and discussion about attachments, favourites, the endless minutiae were more obsessional in girls' schools and derived from awareness that, until recently, love, the relationships between people, were their only real business.

Since love is the only means of expression, it must express other things as well as love—ambition, skill, the desire to do things. The love in the book is also a love of power, of manipulating others; it is therefore a possessive love, since you can only exert power if you possess. The other sort of love is possessive love turned on its head—the desire to serve, to be a servant to the loved one, to be possessed. The Signorina doesn't want to teach Italian; she really only wants to clean Mlle. Julie's shoes.

As the book proceeds, the feelings on both sides become more passionately physical. Olivia goes late one night to visit Mlle. Julie in the library:

I suddenly found myself kneeling before her, kissing her hands, crying out over and over again, "I love you!"—sobbing, "I love you!"

Can I remember what she said, what she did? No. Nothing. I can only remember myself kneeling beside her—the feel of her woollen dress on my cheeks, the feel of her hands, the softness and warmth of her hands under my lips, the hardness of her rings. I don't know how I left the room.

Very occasionally Mlle. Julie comes and says goodnight to her in her room. Olivia lies awake for hours waiting for her. At a dance—a dance where, whirled by one of her friends, she has a long fantasy that she is in the arms of Mlle. Julie—Julie whispers to her that she has a pretty figure and that night she looks at her *"joli corps"* in the looking glass, runs her hands over it and—"Ah!—That was more than I could bear—that excruciating thrill I had never felt before." Her jealousy—which becomes passionate too—is reserved for the physically beautiful. "No, it was not Laura I was jealous of; it was rather, for some inexplicable reason, of Cecile. Cecile was an American beauty. Tall, elegant, exquisitely dressed, with a lovely little head as perfectly finished as a Tanagra's, a dazzling skin of cream and roses, and dark, lively, empty eyes." When Mlle. Cara has an hysterical attack, it is of physical love she accuses Mlle. Julie, screaming that she goes to the girls' rooms at night, shrieking of vice, shamelessness, *viciousness*.

The vice is never mentioned. Olivia does not know what it is Mlle. Julie is being accused of, which she is being accused of since Mlle. Julie comes to her room most of all—but whatever it is she knows that she wants it passionately. And Mlle. Julie resists it. Again and again she murmurs that she loves Olivia more than she can know, but that she is trying to do what is best for them. . . . She says she'll come and say good night, then doesn't. In a final scene this resistance and what is being resisted are made explicit and shown to be lifelong:

"It has been a struggle all my life—but I have always been victorious—I was proud of my victory." And then her voice changed, broke, deepened, softened, became a murmur: "I wonder now whether defeat wouldn't have been better for us all—as well as sweeter." Another long pause. She turned now and looked at me, and smiled. "You, Olivia, will never be victorious, but if you are defeated"—how she looked at me!—"when you are defeated" —she looked at me in a way which made my heart stand still and the blood rush to my face, to my forehead, till I seemed to be wrapped in flame—then she suddenly broke off and brushed her hand across her eyes, as if brushing away some importunate vision. When I saw them again they were extinguished and lifeless.

With Drew and Maugham it was only necessary to transpose and extend their excitement to boys' schools generally; with *Olivia* we must allow a diminution to take place. But it is an element of this that we must retain if we are to have an imaginative appreciation of the difference between the two closed institutions; it is the essence of the "relentless femininity" I mentioned which one schoolmaster who had taught at both sorts of school in the 1930s tried to convey to me: "*En masse* girls and women together are worse than men. The air becomes intense, mad. All sense of humour seems to leave them. There are terrible jealousies and rivalries. They get quite out of hand. I can remember the WAAFs in the war—it was frightening."

4 Effects of girls' public schools

Girls' public schools had the same sort of effects on those in them, with differences, naturally, of emphasis and flavour, as boys' public schools; there is no need to repeat what applies to both.

As with men, Kinsey found clear evidence that adolescent sexual experiences and influences strongly affected subsequent behaviour. Apart from anything else, on purely physical grounds, long-delayed experience means that physical adjustment is a great deal harder. For instance, he found that women in his sample who had not responded to orgasm, by whatever means, before their marriage were three times less likely to do so in their first year after it. Now, as he says, orgasm is not the only end of marriage, but it is probably as reliable a guide as any to the degree of physical satisfaction obtained from it. Again, he found this and similar difficulties were a great deal more common among college-bred females than in other groups. And this, too, was due to "their tardy acceptance of heterosexual coitus". There is no reason to suppose that these considerations would not apply to public school-bred females of the past—and the present. Indeed if one adds the barricaded segregation from men and the deliberate inculcations of fear and disgust towards them, the rigid and hysterical repression of the mildest hint of sex and even friendship, the exalting of purity, chastity and ignorance, the reiteration that "sex was something beastly in store", one can suppose they would apply a great deal more forcefully.

In one respect, with the attempt to imitate boys' schools—with their ties, their games, their prefects, colours, and all the rest—they seem to a certain extent to have succeeded. During the 1920s and 30s a new type of woman came striding out of the mists around St. Leonard's and off the lacrosse and cricket pitches of Roedean, St. James's, Malvern or St. Mary's, Calne; as gauche as men in personal relationships, their hair cut short (the Eton crop), their breasts squashed flat, their clothes severe, with boys' nick-names, boyish attributes and using boys' slang, they show that by characterising their heroines as public school heroes, which we observed in the popular novelists, was not solely a wistful hangover from their own public school days. These portraits were not all that far removed from life.

We can observe, though it was somewhat less agonised and obsessive than it was with boys, the growth of that same nostalgia, that same reluctance to leave which we explained, perhaps not entirely adequately, as an effect of the replacement of home and family by a total institution from an early age and for a considerable length of time. By 1902 ex-pupils of Roedean would return to the school in large numbers for a weekend, put on the blue Djibbah (their uniform until the 1939 war), weave their hair into pigtails and pretend they had never gone away. Other schools had similar reunions, with songs and shared memories. Natasha Harris,

Godolphin School House 1907–11: "... do you remember cricket matches on hot Saturday afternoons?" Betty Pryce-Jenkin: "The autumn of 1910 was my last term. It was one of the saddest farewells, when I said goodbye to Godolphin, and closed the first chapter of my life in Sixth Special and with one coveted first eleven badge, which was for hockey."

By 1909, but particularly after the First World War, the momentum of nostalgia, the sheer number of public school girls had created a market for school literature (though, as with boys, it had a far wider readership). The writers were often Old Girls and they and their novels were too numerous and too similar to make analysis profitable (Enid Blyton contributed dozens of novels). But we might just glance at one of the most famous of them, Angela Brazil (pronounced Brazzle). She is the subject of an excellent biography by Gillian Freeman to which, together with (especially) an article by her in the *Sunday Times*, I am indebted.

What is interesting about Angela Brazil is that her obsessions are exactly the same as those we found in so much of the boys' literature (and so add yet further to our picture of these girls' institutions); a deep involvement with the remembered minutiae of school, as evidenced by the slang—"It's a sneaking rag to prig their bikkies"—and love. The books reverberate with the passions of the girls whose relationships are at the centre of the plots. "I'm falling in love with her," she (Loveday in *A Harum-Scarum Schoolgirl*) admitted to Wendy. "I was taken with her, of course, the moment I saw her, but I believe now I'm going to have it badly. If there was a peach competition she'd win at a canter."

Love ranges all the way from straightforward mothering to powerful and agonised affairs which come close, in their intensity, to that between Olivia and Mlle. Julie. The language and approach, however, are a great deal less sophisticated; sometimes incredibly so to our own sexually oriented contemporary minds.

> Regina was no ordinary girl . . . she did not want to pose as clever, and curiously enough seemed to covet most all the specially feminine character-istics which she rather conspicuously lacked. She admired Lesbia, much as a boy would, for her pretty hair, her dainty movements, and the general Celtic glamour that hung about her; she behaved, indeed, more like a youth in love than an ordinary schoolgirl chum. Her large soulful eyes would gaze at her idol during classes as if she were composing sonnets, and she haunted her round the school till the girls christened her "Lesbia's shadow".
>
> "She's queer, of course," declared Kathleen, discussing the newcomer in the cloakroom.
>
> "Yes, she's certainly queer. She never does anything in the least like anyone else," agreed Ermie Hall. *(Loyal to the School.)*

There is little doubt that the love in Angela Brazil's books was "inno-cent", in so far as it was not physical. Yet the force with which she wrote sometimes stirred uneasy echoes. In 1936, Ethel Strudwick, principal of St. Paul's, delivered an impassioned address after prayers on the first day of the autumn term. She said she would like to burn every volume of "The Works" (as their authoress called them) in the playground. And this is because, equally clearly, that force was the emotional lesbianism which drove Angela Brazil—as it must often have done her schoolmistress readers. As an adult her most intense relationship was with a schoolgirl whom, for the sake of privacy, Gillian Freeman calls Dolly. Their love was transmuted into the art of *For the School Colours*, where Dolly becomes Avelyn "instantly in love with the Lavender Lady", Lesbia Carrington, a poetess who was Angela Brazil. (She also used Lesbia Carrington as an *alter ego* in *Schoolgirl Kitty*.)

The second motive behind the books—and here she differs from most of her fellow writers—was to create a world she had longed for but never entered. Born in 1869 in Preston, Lancashire, her father was a cotton manufacturer and her mother, of Scottish and Spanish ancestry, had been brought up in Rio de Janeiro. (Odd, notes Gillian Freeman, that a girl from Rio should marry a man called Brazil.) She went first to a "dame" school, and then to a private day school in Manchester. Her schoolfriend here was Leila Longdale, the other relationship that was to last all her life (Leila was Lilian in her first book, *A Terrible Tomboy*).

Love and a fixation on a world she had never been able to enter gave her books a power few rivals could equal. Miss Strudwick would have had, by 1936, a blaze of unmanageable proportions on her hands. *The Nicest Girl in the School* alone sold 153,000 copies, and there were forty-eight other titles. During her life she sold three million books under the Blackie imprint, and there were Dutch, Polish, German, Scandinavian, American and French editions as well.

She sells still. A small Indian publishing house has just brought out three Brazil titles, including *The Madcap of the School*. Gillian Freeman quotes a scrap of typical dialogue from Chapter One:

"Jubilate! You're right, old sport! Scooterons-nous this very sec! Quick! Hurry! Stir your old bones, can't you?"
"This is top-hole!"
"What a chubby place!"

It is interesting to speculate, she writes, just what the teenagers of that socially turbulent country will make of that.

But finally, and above all, it was that whole area restricting intelligence, initiative, and personality that I would like to emphasise again. Evelyn Cheeseman, at a school at Ashford in the 1900s, remembered a mistress obsessed with "conscientiousness". She would enter the classroom at a run and say, not expecting an answer and before she even had time to look round, "Are you all conscientious?" The girls' schools, all virtually identical, themselves a unified system, with their multitudes of rules, their hierarchies of command, their repression of feeling, were both the mirror, the intensifier and the perpetuator of an authoritarian and rigid society in the same way and almost to the same extent as the boys' schools. It is the Monolith again.

The reaction began in 1889. But the progressive school revolution which started then — and which, of the three arms of public school education, was to be far the most influential as far as the outside world was concerned— had its roots far back in the 18th century.

CHAPTER 12

The Progressive School Movement

God makes all things good; man meddles with them and they become evil.
Rousseau, *Emile*

The type of education you support depends ultimately on the form of society you want. But, still more fundamental, and fundamental to both, is your view of human nature—your idea of what people are really like. Psychology is the branch of human thought that is basic to all others and precedes them. For instance, much of Plato's thought stems from his idea that human beings have natural inborn functions and capabilities—one is a carpenter, another a sailor and so on—and that men are happier and the State is best served if they perform the functions they are best at (the crucial step in his argument, of course, is that some men are better leaders). Hobbes's political philosophy derives from his assumption that the basic motive behind all action is fear. Similarly, all educational systems rest upon basic views of human nature, views which are often quite unconscious.

Behind the forms of education up till now the basic view was the Christian/Pauline one: people, but particularly children, were innately wicked owing to original sin. Education was a process, therefore, of curbing, disciplining and pruning, and finally training and guiding. As a corollary to this, knowledge was something an adult had which he had to impart, to train into the child. Schools were places of adult domination over pupils being taught set subjects.

Not only were these two assumptions—that children were not naturally good but must be taught to be so and that the method was a superior adult disciplining and training—behind nearly all education up to 1890; they are still very powerful today.

It is in following the developments, which derived from different assumptions about human nature, that we find ourselves studying the course of progressive education. It is a huge and daunting subject and, although the bibliography cites the numerous works I have read, and the text will bring out some of the people I talked to, I am particularly indebted to Professor W. A. C. Stewart's massive and comprehensive work *Progressives and Radicals in English Education, 1750–1970*. Another difficulty is that there were, and are, relatively few progressive public schools. With girls' and boys' public schools up till now (*c.* 1900–1914), while considerable differences existed, it was their similarities which were more striking and more important. The number of the schools meant it was possible to make valid generalisations and sketch broad lines of historical development. I tried to avoid concentrating on any single school, or writing a series of little potted histories—a method, in my view one of infinite tedium, other historians of this subject have sometimes adopted. I shall try to continue this, but it will sometimes be necessary to follow the stories of individual schools more than hitherto. Finally, I think it will be helpful to try to remember that there were three broad periods of development: (1) the late 18th and early 19th centuries; (2) the 1890s to 1914; (3) the 1920s and 30s.

1 Rousseau, Bentham, early experiments

The opposition to the idea that man was inherently wicked goes back almost as far as that concept itself. As early as AD 413 Pelagius was arguing with great force and brilliance against the sin-obsessed St. Augustine of Hippo. Pelagius's contention was that man's nature was fundamentally good because it had been created by God. It followed that any sin was due to the corruption of the world and the various constrictions this had imposed. Remove these constrictions and man's natural goodness would flower. Unfortunately, St. Augustine won the controversy.

But from our point of view, of incalculably greater influence was Rousseau, and in particular his novel *Émile*, published in 1762. We noted with Arnold how necessary an authority is for a movement, and Rousseau was often as important in this rôle, or as a symbol, as for what he actually said. *Emile* was translated into English immediately, with two further translations in 1763. From then until 1790 there were outbreaks of Rousseau-mania all over England. *Émile* was imitated constantly, for instance in Maria Edgeworth's *Harry and Lucy* (1778), and Thomas Day's *Sandford and Merton* (1783). This last had run through thirteen editions by 1823.

What were the ideas expressed in the book?

Émile is not really a novel, but an educational treatise in novel form. "Begin thus," opens the preface addressing teachers, "by making a more careful study of your scholars, for it is clear that you know nothing about them." Children are fundamentally *good*. They are only made bad by the ideas and disciplines imposed on them. Remove these and, being naturally good, they will spontaneously develop in the right ways.

> Let us lay it down as an uncontrovertible rule that the first impulses of nature are always right; there is no original sin in the human heart. . . . That man is truly free who desires what he is able to perform, and does what he desires.

This is my fundamental maxim. Apply it to childhood, and all the rules of education spring from it.

Now in 18th-century educational terms this was, of course, absolutely revolutionary. Since Rousseau assumed the most "natural" man must be a savage, he advocated labouring in the fields and the use of hands and exercise. Finally, because *Émile* was a novel, Émile and Sophie get married and start a life of civic virtue. The curriculum of the book is not particularly important. Nor is it precisely the fact that it made education child-centred—it had always been that (it could hardly be anything else). The point is that Rousseau made the child at that centre good. The task now became that of examining the nature of that goodness and adapting education to it.

If a child's spontaneous impulses are good then consideration must be given to individual differences. Since these are large this consideration will be reflected in the curriculum. It will also be reflected in the methods of teaching, since different people respond to different methods. It will be reflected in the discipline, since if they are not inherently wicked there should be less need for discipline. And all this will affect the pupil–teacher relationship. If children are not fundamentally bad then one considerable base for teacher domination—his rôle of eradicating evil—is removed. The two at once become more equal. (It might be thought that these two positions—that people are either fundamentally good or fundamentally bad—and gradations of them, are all that is possible. But, of course, there can be many others. For instance, the idea that people are basically motivated by money—a perfectly tenable theory—could lead to a commercial relationship between pupils and teachers. There were in fact early-19th-century schools where this happened. Discipline was largely through fines, and rewards—usually paid from the fines—were cash handouts. The teacher was a cross between a judge in a commercial court and a central bank.) But these are some of the major developments we shall be concerned with: wider curriculum, more adaptive methods of teaching, greater freedom from discipline, and more equality between teachers and pupils. These are all developments, incidentally, which can make the work of a teacher more difficult.

Rousseau had numerous successors. There was Pestalozzi, born in Zurich in 1746, upon whom his own adored mother and *Émile* seem to have had equal influence. Rousseau had said, "Look to nature". Pestalozzi did so and worked out a rather complex psychological theory of learning based on what the mind did automatically when faced with a lot of objects. He incorporated this into his system, adding to it the love and freedom he remembered from his mother and also the way in which she'd taught him by moving from the simple to the complex. He expressed all this in *How Gertrude Teaches Her Children* (1801), which has virtually nothing to do with Gertrude or her children (though one can see what he means), but is—an old convention in books of all sorts including educational ones—a series of letters to a friend.

Another figure was Fellenberg, who advocated labour as a cure for moral vice, at the same time stressing self-government and self-activity. But it would be easy to get bogged down studying these and related thinkers. It is sufficient to bear in mind that Rousseau's central statement produced at the end of the 18th century a ferment of related educational ideas—interest the pupil in his work, stress on *doing* not memorising, the sciences not classics, less authority, etc.—themselves gaining added fervour from the liberal excitements generated by the French Revolution. The major figures may have been Continental, but there were many English followers and sympathisers, particularly among the philosophical societies and radicals like William Godwin and Mary Wollstonecraft and writers like Maria and R. C. Edgeworth (*Practical Education*, 1801).

It would also not be worth our while going too deeply into the often very interesting (and quite numerous) institutions which grew up during this period to put the ideas into practice, like, for example, David Williams's Lawrence Street Academy in 1773. Two other strands we must, however, note: the first is the association from the start of progressive education with a left-wing political stance. Concern for children as individuals rather than as an age-block seems to be accompanied by concern for individuals as such and not as members of a class and so to political views designed to help the lower classes as containing the most disadvantaged individuals. Apart from the radical figures I have mentioned, Robert Owen began the Lanark Schools in 1816 to bring the educational ideas of Rousseau, Williams and Pestalozzi to the working-class children of his father-in-law's mills. They came to an end, but inspired the Co-operative Movement Schools and Rational Schools of the 1830s which were themselves related to the Chartists, Trade Unions and those first great flexings as the working class braced to fight for itself. But this connection continued. We shall find Badley of Bedales voting Labour all his life and taking lower-class pupils and children from poor parents when he could afford it; Simpson of Rendcomb and Dartington in the 1920s and 30s did the same. Other progressive schools had similar leanings. In the end they have been defeated. Partly by economic necessity; partly by some rather curious consequences of boarding about which progressive headmasters and headmistresses, in common with all their public school counterparts, seem unaware. But the left-wing bias remains. Indeed it is interesting that the State comprehensive and primary ideology in Britain today, which is in essence "Progressive" (though it owes nothing, as far as I can see, to the public school progressive movement), is on the whole a left-wing socialist one.

The second theme is that of pragmatism. England is of overwhelming importance as far as progressive education is concerned because, although some of the seminal thinkers were Continental, it is in England that their ideas were first put into practice and therefore from England, stamped indelibly with that English mode of practice, they spread all over the world.

And there is in fact, at the end of the 18th century and start of the 19th, alongside the Rousseau/Pestalozzi/Edgeworth/William stream, another stream—utilitarian, Benthamite, product of the practical common sense of a successful industrial age. Men of this sort had no particular doctrinal bent. Children were not "naturally" wicked or good—but they had noticed, as a matter of experience, that they were of differing abilities and varied inclinations. Common sense would suppose they would respond to invitations of commercial reward, or success, that they would prefer a subject to be interesting; common humanity would suggest a search for inducements other than the whip or the birch.

Such a man was William Gilpin, who started Cheam School, in Surrey, in 1752. His over-riding principle was that a school should be a microcosm of, and training ground for, society as he saw it. Thus there should be no tyranny, no arbitrary master rule, but the boys should be involved with the law and understand it. There could be no hierarchy, no fagging system, since all should be equal under the law. A code was drawn up and regularly read out. If it was transgressed, Gilpin would mete out punishment. But a boy could appeal if he felt he had been treated unjustly, and disputed cases were heard by a jury of twelve boys. If the appeal **was** successful, Gilpin paid compensation. Indeed, the whole system of punishment was largely financial, in keeping with the commercial world whose sensible but powerful motives Gilpin harnessed. The boys kept shops, trading in apples, gingerbread and cakes. There was a legalised scale of profits and if you were caught profiteering you lost your shop. The boys also had gardens, little strips of land where they grew produce for the school. They "owned" these strips, and on their departure left them in a "will". The curriculum was wide, much being learnt through these activities; Greek and Latin were unusual; the other subjects were taught in an interesting way. Geography, for example, was taught by fitting together pieces of a jigsaw map of England. In 1765 a boy wrote home saying he'd lost Flintshire and would they send a replacement.

Cheam would be interesting if it existed with these practices today (the school itself does still exist). To find it in the last half of the 18th century, when learning was being forced to get huge, and hugely boring, hunks of Latin by heart, when accounts of punishment are of a savagery to freeze the blood, when boys lived together in conditions of almost indescribable filth, anarchy and discomfort, and while Long Chamber was reaching its horrific heights of brutality, terror and debauchery, to read about this gentle and pleasant institution amongst all that, is little less than astounding. For Cheam was not some piddling experiment for eccentric left-wing cranks. William Gilpin had "a commanding person, dignified manners and a deep sonorous voice". His school was enormously successful and well known. Although the fees were reasonable (£25 p.a. and £6 extras), and the pupils not stinted, he had saved £10,000 by 1777, and retired to devote his life to drawing in an original landscape style. By 1804, when he died aged eighty, his former pupils included a prime minister (Henry Addington: at Cheam, 1762–67; Tory Prime Minister, 1801–1804), a Lord Chancellor of Ireland, two Secretaries of the Treasury and one at the War Office, as well as numerous other successful establishment figures. Cheam was irrefutable, demonstrable proof that the whole grisly public school edifice, as it was then and for long afterwards, was completely unnecessary. It was to be 200 years before such humane and, to us now, obvious developments became general.

Nor was Cheam an isolated instance at this interesting time. There were quite a number of other schools, sometimes small it is true, but remarkably enlightened. Here is one more which, like Cheam, was perfectly qualified, in size and success, to rival, for a while, the "great schools" of the period.

The Hazelwood experiment was described by its founders in a long and detailed book—*Public Education: Plans for the Government and Liberal Instruction of Boys in Large Numbers; as Practised at Hazelwood School*. The school was in fact started by Thomas Hill in 1803 and called Hill Top; but it was taken over in 1819 by his three sons Matthew, Arthur and Rowland (who later introduced the penny post) and moved to Hazelwood in Edgbaston. Rowland Hill was the driving force and it was he who designed the new school buildings. These alone were revolutionary. There were lots of classrooms, an assembly hall for 250 with a stage at one end for plays, a museum, an observatory on the roof and built-in central heating.

The school was self-governing, with the laws made by a committee of boys, and enforced by an elected court presided over by a judge. Corporal punishment, public disgrace and lines were abolished. Instead, marks were awarded for everything—work, behaviour, voluntary labour—and a boy's standing in school judged by his marks. The punishment of the court was to fine marks; extreme cases were kept in on holidays. A number of executive boys helped run the school. For example, times of silence were enforced by a Silentiary, who wore soft soundless slippers and a tall hat. He was paid a small salary raised by a tax on talkative boys.

The curriculum was wide, as one might suppose, and included shorthand. ("A good deal of time was wasted on shorthand," wrote one irritated pupil.) English was regarded as a *sine qua non* and taught by everyone; it underpinned the court and jury work, the plays, the school magazine and so on. Science was particularly important. Although there were other science pioneers (Mill Hill in 1821 and a Quaker school, Bootham, in 1828), Hazelwood had by far the best equipped-laboratories and fuller courses than anywhere else in England. They were run by Brayley, a brilliant young scientist.

The aim of the Hills was to produce "men of business", by which they meant not just commercial operators, but people able to function efficiently, independently, and decisively in any walk of life they cared to choose. In fact their ideal was really themselves; sensible and capable administrators like Rowland Hill running the Post Office, or Matthew Hill who became MP for Hull and Recorder of Birmingham. And we might note parenthetically here that the idea of himself or herself is often—perhaps always—of decisive importance to the way a head of a school conducts it. It is a peculiarly creative activity; it is nothing less than the moulding of human beings. And, as did God, the moulder often (and often unconsciously) creates in his own image—or its reverse. We have seen this before, and it has often been most interesting (or at least startling) precisely when unconscious: the exceptional sexual immorality at Harrow in the 1840s, despite a successful moral tightening in general, reflecting the secret and uncontrollable desires of Vaughan himself; the schoolmistresses trying to produce the men they would really like to have been. We shall see it with Sanderson of Oundle creating exactly the sort of atmosphere best suited to his own impulsive manner of growth and self-discovery; we shall find it with Badley of Bedales creating, in particular, the rather odd sexual attitudes which mark that school. We shall see the image in reverse (or wish-fulfilled) at Dartington, where Curry, all brain, presided in the 1930s over a freedom from inhibition, the flow of feeling, whose necessity he could grasp intellectually while lacking it himself.

But to return to Hazelwood. The Hills claimed they were not innovating but just putting into practice ideas "current for years" in education. And this, we can now see, was true. They had read the thinkers we have summarised; they were even more part of that practical Benthamite stream. For instance, the attention given to each subject was measured—just as Bentham would have measured it—by "its effect on the welfare and happiness of the individual pursuing it, and of society at large". Again, Maria Edgeworth and others had said that the motive for learning must be strong. The Hills inverted the usual practice in schools by putting fear of punishment and hope of reward and marks bottom of the scale. Love of knowledge was the most important motive, and this was aroused by making it interesting and exciting—plays, maps, models, experiments, etc.—and by success. Success, fame were the spurs. By continually re-ranking the school according to different activities (including dozens of hobbies) they made sure each boy tasted for a while the sweets of achievement.

But it is clear that in some spheres they did actually invent. Languages were taught by speaking. You learnt grammar by talking; you did not learn to talk by learning grammar. Their enormous concentration on science was unprecedented. And in their attitude to and use of success they actually anticipated the theories of the behaviourist psychologists of the last few years.

Here then, once more, is a large, extremely successful school, of a humanity, freedom and liveliness which would make it interesting today, existing at a time when the Monolith was beginning its ponderous and unstoppable growth. During the very years that Rowland Hill and his brothers were running Hazelwood, Arnold was putting his stamp on Rugby—beating "in a white heat", setting the classics in concrete, spreading an almost mad moral fervour and guilt, and starting that multiplication of disciplines which was to get so out of hand. And what makes the contrast the sharper is that Arnold was almost certainly aware of Hazelwood. It was only thirty miles away from him, in Birmingham. The school was famous. The *Plan*, a substantial volume of 390 pages, was widely reviewed, the second edition particularly in the *Edinburgh Review* of 1825. During the 1820s Arnold was extremely interested in the Society for the Diffusion of Useful Knowledge. The three Hill brothers were prominent and active members of it. Not only that, but Mrs. Fletcher, a great friend of the Arnolds, was also a close friend of Frederick Hill, the fourth brother. It is inconceivable that Arnold did not know of the Hazelwood experiments. The likelihood is he knew them intimately.

And yet he ignored them. Why?

The reason is obvious—if depressing. These schools and the ideas they expressed were totally out of tune with the main forces at work in public school education at that time. (I would exclude the Quaker schools from what follows.) By 1830 the parents were objecting, among other things, to the amount of time spent on science at Hazelwood, and Rowland Hill had to discontinue that whole side. History has many examples of ideas and experiments before their time, and the movement we have swiftly traced is to education in the late 18th century and early 19th century what the Levellers are to politics in the 17th century. In the second, the Civil War produced, as it were, a mini *zeitgeist* in which they could momentarily flourish; with the first it was that complex interaction of Rousseau, the French Revolution, the Romantic and Utilitarian movements which was vigorous during their slightly longer life.

Soon after abandoning the science side of the curriculum Rowland Hill, deeply disappointed, gave up teaching altogether. The same sort of thing happened to the other schools. Cheam had a brief renaissance under Dr. Mayo, when it was rather hysterically patronised by Lady Byron who wrote long poems to Fellenberg. But by the 1840s most of the schools had closed or, as did Cheam and Hazelwood, had become conventional again, much on the lines we know so well.

Yet this movement, though it soon sank away, had introduced deep and powerful currents of thought and experiment which continued underground. It had proved that totally different forms of education were possible and successful—forms without savage punishments, tyrannical disciplines, class-influenced hierarchical structures and narrow, leaden learning. After an interregnum of some fifty years these currents were to surface again; still in advance of their time, they were nevertheless to survive; finally, decades later and after many vicissitudes, they—or many of the ideas they embodied—were to triumph.

2 *Interregnum ; second great movement—Reddie and Abbotsholme*

The interregnum need not long detain us. The 1850s saw the growth of the Froebel movement. This in essence applied Rousseau/Pestalozzi/Fellenberg ideas to infants. The kindergarten which resulted was virtually the only mid–19th–century experiment which became permanent. Radical suggestions and experiments continued between 1850 and 1870, with figures like Barbara Bodichon (Portman Hall) and Henry Morley prominent. The only new feature they introduced was radical views about religion (William Ellis, a follower who ran the Birkbeck schools, forbade religious instruction or even reading the Bible). They also accepted co-education, but this had appeared at the end of the 18th century.

There were three reasons the progressive tide momentarily slackened. First, it was during this period that it became gradually clear that it was essential to establish a free, compulsory system of national education. By the end of the century the elementary stage of this had arrived. But this activity siphoned off much educational energy and interest of a radical sort which might otherwise have continued the work of Bodichon and Morley. Second, the Commissions of the 1860s took over, in their criticisms of the public schools, many of the progressive arguments—particularly as regards the curriculum and science. That the public schools responded like snails or not at all is not relevant. It is always hard to be radical when the government of the day seems to be so as well. Thirdly, the very size and power of the Monolith itself depressed reformers—it seemed to be ever intensifying and ever growing, indivisible, unchangeable and invincible. However it was this very fact that at last started the reaction and it is now, in 1889, that there strides onto the scene the ultimately highly eccentric but also highly influential figure of Cecil Reddie, the often neglected pioneer of the second great reform movement.

Reddie was born in London in 1858. He became an orphan at the age of twelve, and from then until he was twenty both lived and was educated at Fettes near Edinburgh. This public school therefore became all important to him and the clue to much of what occurred later lies in the intense feelings generated there. Five things stand out: the fierce discipline, the narrow classical education, his passionate sexual love for a young boy when he was senior prefect, and his repression of this love and, owing to the absence of any instruction or advice, his confusion about sexual matters generally. He left Fettes and went to Edinburgh University, where he read science. He moved on to Göttingen where, as well as developing a deep respect for certain not very pleasant aspects of the German national character, he took a doctorate in chemistry. After 1884 he came back to England and taught at Fettes for a year. But increasing irritation with aspects of the public school system drove him to Clifton. Here he was allowed to teach science for two years. Percival of the Knees had made Clifton innovatory in this respect—but Reddie was beginning to see that "reform within the old type of school would be difficult if not impossible". It suddenly occurred to him, at the age of twenty-nine, that the best way would be to found a school of his own.

Two other forces influenced Reddie. During the 1880s he read Carlyle, Ruskin, William Morris and Hyndman. In Germany he attended lectures on Karl Marx. By 1884 he was a violent socialist, with strong Ruskinian and Morris overtones about the dignity of labour. These two strands, socialism and educational reform, finally erupted in a series of fierce attacks on the public schools during 1888 under the general title *Modern Mis-education.*

Meanwhile, from 1883, a society called Fellowship of the New Life , started by Thomas Davidson, had been gaining some influence. Its general idea was that society should be improved, made cleaner and healthier and also become more egalitarian by the setting up of self-supporting communities devoted to manual work (a contemporary ring here). Society would be changed from inside by the example of these communities; the emphasis was on changing each individual in society. The message was a bit vague. Some thought too vague, and broke away to form an intellectual pressure group with more edge—the Fabian Society.

But its very vagueness drew the Fellowship to *Modern Mis-education.* Reddie attacked the things he had suffered from, the pointless discipline, the narrow curriculum; he attacked the way the public schools encouraged the lust for power and money and a contempt for manual work. Some of these themes were social and seemed to fit roughly into the Fellowship aims. Their emphasis on communities, on educating and regenerating the individual and society from inside had always indicated a school; indeed schools. At last they seemed to have found their headmaster. Unfortunately Reddie only had eighty-eight pounds, but two Fellowship friends —F. R. Muirhead and William Cassels—came in as partners with £2,000 each. The rest was put up by Fellowship member Ed Carpenter. In 1889 Abbotsholme opened in Derbyshire.

Within a few weeks, Muirhead and Cassels had left. Yet their hope that Abbotsholme would be a truly progressive school was in many senses fulfilled. The curriculum was English based, not classical, and wide—

science, art, music, French, German, with opportunities for plays and hobbies. Religion was not dogmatic and non-sectarian. Boys were not crammed for work, there were no prizes and lessons were only in the mornings. The games madness was condemned; instead much time was spent on manual labour in fields and garden, and the boys were also taught tailoring, boot making and cookery. Remembering his confusion, Reddie introduced a good deal of sex instruction. Discipline was much freer and its base was in trust and friendship between boys and masters.

Now all this was extremely exciting in 1889. And indeed throughout the 1890s Abbotsholme was a very stimulating place to be. Reddie was a man of enormous vitality and energy, with the magnetism necessary to start movements. Not only that, he regarded Abbotsholme as a crusade. People visited the school from all over the world and left, charmed and enthusiastic. Many Abbotsholme masters started their own new schools. Reddie was the father of the English progressive movement—but he was not its most influential figure nor was Abbotsholme its most influential school. From the start another, more precarious side of his character began to appear; it grew steadily more dominant until it overwhelmed both school and Reddie himself.

During the 1880s he had become more and more influenced by Carlyle. When Muirhead and Cassels arrived at the school they found to their surprise that Reddie called it a public school. He had also, it seemed overnight, abandoned any attempt to abolish class distinctions. It was to be "a school for the sons of the directing classes". The attitude of the hierarchy would be reformed; the structure would remain. He had also suddenly become passionate about the British Empire and, always stimulated by symbols, decreed that the school colours should be red, white and blue. Any attempt to remonstrate about these changes, as Muirhead and Cassels saw them, was met with fury. When they suggested that the school should be run as a triumvirate with majority decisions, Reddie instantly refused and said he would resign that day and set up elsewhere. Instead they resigned on condition he repaid their investment, which he did quite soon. When, in 1894 he finally bought the school "with the generous assistance of a friend", he went and rolled about in the grass for joy.

But this turbulence—though a presage—was as nothing compared to what would follow. Throughout the 1890s his socialism declined until by 1900 democracy was "idiotic", and he held views, politically, as violently and idiosyncratically far to the right as he had, in 1884, been far to the left. But this was only part of a more general and personal lust for power. Tall, with jet black hair, dark piercing eyes, and very expensive very strong black shoes which were polished till they blazed, he demanded total obedience. He was an autocrat who, while he believed in boys' and masters' freedom, yet crushed all opposition. Towards the end of the 1890s his behaviour became more and more odd. He was subject to manic-depressive cycles and these brought attacks of acute paranoia and increasing violence. He now started a series of shattering rows with his colleagues, culminating in colossal explosions in 1900, 1904 and 1906. In the 1900 one, when he was accused of behaving like Napoleon, five masters were summarily dismissed or fled. But it was not only masters. He quarrelled with everyone in sight: parents, boys, Old Boys, other headmasters, tradesmen, women (especially women), the aristocracy, the working classes. He began to have numerous breakdowns. The deep sexual repression now surfaced explosively too. He fulminated against women and the 1906 row was over accusations of homosexuality. A committee of parents investigated and Reddie was exonerated; but it was nineteen months before he could return to Abbotsholme. The idea of co-education had always enraged him; his opposition now became ferocious. Numbers began to plummet, but Reddie was in the grip of his obsessions; by 1913 he was delivering passionate addresses in praise of Germany.

The war [wrote a friend, G. H. Dixon] shattered Abbotsholme. . . . The numbers dropped from thirty-nine in the summer term of 1914 to twenty-two the following term. . . . The strain of the situation rapidly affected CR. . . . His temper was ungovernable. He shouted, stormed and raged. He seldom came into class without a cane. Teaching, what there was of it, was thrown completely to the winds, and instead we suffered tirades against the English, against women and against public schools. Only Germany was extolled, although at that very time German bullets were tearing old Abbotsholmians to death.

From 1919 increasingly strong efforts were made to get him to abandon his sinking school. But Reddie's fingers could not be prised from the tiller till 1927. Even then the magnetism and power which had once made him such an influence was still there. Colin Sharp, who was to replace him, lived with him for ten weeks in order to learn as much as he could. He says that every night they talked from six p.m. until two in the morning, or rather Reddie talked and he listened. And, once off his obsessions, the old man "talked with humour, decisiveness and a delicacy of sympathy and artistry which produced a gentle and deep affection". By this time—with one pupil away with a cold—there was exactly one boy left in the school.

It is a strange and in many ways a sad story. But I have told it at some length for a reason. The explosions which almost destroyed the school also scattered the masters; these started schools themselves and so, as dying plants make seed and scatter it, the species continued. One of these masters was J. H. Badley. Every single one of Badley's ideas was taken from Reddie; filched, Reddie said, and he was absolutely furious when Badley left to found Bedales. It precipitated the first of his gathering paranoiac outbursts and he made all future masters sign a pledge not to steal his ideas. Yet it is Badley who is usually cited as the founder of the English progressive movement. So much so that a major scholar of British public schools, who deals at some length with progressive schools (E. C. Mack, *The Public Schools and British Opinion since 1860*, New York, 1941) names Badley as the founder without mentioning Reddie or Abbotsholme at all. They have vanished. It is a result which Reddie would have paranoiacally expected—and raged against. Some amends are due.

3 Badley and Bedales

J. H. Badley was born in 1865, the son of a rather austere, well-off doctor and a mother who was both warm and lively and at the same time an evangelical. He was not sent away to his prep school until the (comparatively) late age of thirteen, and at fifteen he went to Rugby. Although he recognised the narrowness of the life there, he did well; he was a fine classicist and good at rugger. It does not seem to be until he went to Cambridge, in 1884, that his ideas began to change. He became a socialist and was also influenced by the ideals of William Morris about art and community life. But the direction these ideas should take, and the decisive influences were Reddie and Abbotsholme. He heard about the plans for the school when he came down in 1888, went there and was instantly fascinated by both. He was, at the age of twenty-four, one of the first masters appointed, but it is probable that from the start he had secret plans to found a school of his own. After two and a half years two typical Reddie problems were becoming acute: the first was Reddie's increasingly autocratic temperament; the second was an expression of this—Badley wanted to marry and Reddie said he couldn't. In 1893 he left and started Bedales.

All Badley's ideas—initially at any rate, their development was quite different—were taken from Reddie. For instance, the account I gave of the Abbotsholme curriculum can stand for that of Bedales. And he copied many of the early organisational details too, right down to the earth closets which enabled him to return to the soil that which had been taken from it. There were differences of emphasis, of course; Bedales talked more of co-operation; there was also no mention of "sons of directing classes". Badley's socialism remained constant all his life.

It is at this point we should perhaps note that both Abbotsholme and Bedales were in a good number of ways only relatively "progressive". In certain respects they were more like public schools of the 1890s than they were the mild régimes we saw at Cheam or Hazelwood. E. L. Grant-Watson, who went to Bedales in 1893, describes a routine that was almost brutally spartan: "Cold baths were the rule, even though we had to break the ice on the goose cans". There were runs before breakfast, the last two being swished in by a prefect with a cane. More runs in the afternoon, more swishing. The emphasis on labour was not comfortable: there were beds and butter to be made, much digging, the rougher the better, cows to be milked early on frosty mornings. The earth privies seemed inexhaustible:

> . . . Not in this, or any other occasion, did he [Badley] in the least unbend from his attitude of stern and dignified reserve. They wheeled the barrows into which Mr. Badley shovelled the excrement, and very full he would load them for small boys to wheel, for there was no pampering, no thought of weak hearts or young muscles strained to lift barrows, swimming to the brim.

Girls did not go to Bedales until 1898, and at first discipline was left to the boys. As a result, it was often harsh and the expectation of courage and stoicism made it difficult to complain. There was also bullying. Grant-Watson gives an horrendous description of a dreaded Bedales "pie". Roger Powell says that Grant-Watson had it in for Bedales. The brother of the assistant headmaster married Grant-Watson's mother and produced a Hamlet effect. But I find his descriptions are substantiated by others. Powell himself described scenes of bullying, of canes being broken by over-zealous prefects. It is clear that early Bedales was fairly tough. Mr. Moorsom was there from 1902–10. He, too, remembered the cold baths, the runs, the oceans of excrement. ("Unpleasant tasks were not actually meant to be unpleasant. So Badley put on immaculate white tennis trousers and gym shoes to help. Rather embarrassing.") He said being caned was like being "burnt alive".

One side of Badley was extremely reserved, almost cold. He was strict and he was obeyed; he neither smoked nor drank (Reddie was the only man allowed to smoke in the study): "When he came stalking with his quick, silent tread, into the classroom there was immediate silence; if there happened to be a piece of paper on the floor, he would point to it without deigning to say a word, and the boy who was nearest would hurriedly pick it up. . . ." In some ways he had been strongly influenced by Rugby, and he brought from there conceptions of "character" and "tone" which he altered, elevated indeed, by ideals of craft, high thinking, William Morris, Ruskin, and his own brand of purity—it was the public school figure transposed to another plane. Mr. Moorsom described Mr. Geoffrey Lipton:

> He personified Badley's ideal. He completely epitomised what Badley was struggling to turn out. A fine strong clean Englishman—a perfect craftsman—at the same time extremely puritanical and totally repressed. He never smoked or drank and when he joined the army and became an officer, if any of his troops swore he simply knocked them out. Needless to say he made a

disastrous marriage. He couldn't carry it through. His wife committed suicide actually in front of his house. But he was the ideal Bedales type, exactly what Badley stood for—wonderfully idealistic and great uplift. He was eventually gored to death by a bull. He lost his temper with it.

These are elements in that early Bedales and they should be remembered. I mention them to counteract a certain fuzziness that can be conjured up by the word "progressive". But it would be wrong to emphasise them; indeed the emphasis should be the other way. Badley was experimenting. Everything could change, and did. By the time Moorsom was at Bedales there was very little bullying, "pies" had gone. Nor could the prefects beat, though they could spank with a slipper. Badley's own use of the cane was so rare as to be virtually synonymous with expulsion. And all this, too, changed. Bedales next evolved a highly complex system of drills and adding up of faults; there followed, in the early 1920s, a period of no punishments at all. After this the system was one of compromise and flexibility. Now (I am talking of the mid-1920s) only Badley caned—and as usual he did so extremely rarely. And Badley found that the few school laws were much more easily accepted if they were reasonable, and if they could be questioned. He set up a "Parliament"; not a legislative body, but a place where action could be explained, grievances brought up and suggestions made. There was a feeling of being consulted.

But—as one escapes the stifling pressure of conventional public schools around 1900–1910—it is the sense of freedom that is exhilarating about Bedales. Free time was really free—the evenings, Saturday afternoons, Sundays. Grant-Watson remembers getting up at dawn, barefoot and in untidy clothes, and going to see his friend the gamekeeper. Moorsom expressed his individuality by going to church; he was thought "madly eccentric". "I wasn't particularly happy at Bedales but I should have *died* at an ordinary public school." There was also a sense of pioneering, of being engaged in an exhilarating shared endeavour which was shocking to the outside world. If things went wrong they could together put them right; if new experiments were attempted, they would be attempted in unison. Badley consulted the older boys before the school went co-educational.

Public schools formed houses and grouped closely together largely for disciplinary reasons, as we know; they became communities by accident, willy-nilly. *Thereafter*, as was their custom, they began to attribute values to this that had nothing to do with the original development. By 1900 the idea of learning community values from the public school community was implicit in all of them to a greater or lesser degree. But, from the influence of Ruskin and William Morris and other "community idealists" current in the 1880s, it was far stronger and more explicit in progressive schools. That was why the school environment should be more "realistic" and should more closely resemble the outside world. Another way of looking at this, which Badley expressed, was that the way to learn to live in the complex community of the outside world was to learn to live first in the simple community of school. It was a question of stages. There was also the idea of change. Badley said, "Every school is, consciously or not, an embodiment of social aims, and it was by making Bedales a working model of what a community should be that I thought I could do most to realise mine." At Bedales—and at many other progressive schools—the direction of change was very roughly left wing and egalitarian.

The second point is that as well as communities, the progressive reformers wanted happy communities. This was a prime concern, not a secondary consideration. Education was to do with life, not earning a living; it was more important to be happy, to lead a full life, than to pass exams. And here the Rousseauesque roots became relevant. If man is essentially good, then he should be allowed freedom to develop that goodness and so become happy. Rules must be kept at a minimum. Given time, he will develop the necessary discipline himself; indeed self-discipline is the only sort worth having, and it can *only* be self-taught. If it is imposed rigidly from outside it either forms a compulsive straightjacket of automatic rules, which the individual continues to obey unthinkingly thereafter, and requires a rigid society to continue imposing on him and others, or else it leads to a wild and rebellious reaction.

The element of "self-regulation" was to become much stronger in some of the progressive schools of the 1920s and 30s, but it is absolutely explicit in early Bedales and was due largely to the characters of the two chief masters. Badley was aloof and shy; but he was more complicated than that. He was also a brilliant class teacher, whose Latin classes were electrifying. He was an enormously kind man, always the least prone to expel, most keen to give a second chance: ". . . he did not seem to be identified with the rigorously puritanical tone that he appeared to have created." He often took children free whose parents could not afford to pay; he used to lead expeditions to Switzerland. At the same time, aware of his shyness, disliking any form of autocracy, he was able to supply what he lacked through his second master, Oswald Powell, who was extremely active in the school and frequently ran it alone for a year or more when Badley was away. Powell came from a large Victorian family and was a warm, easy, loving man. He provided essential ingredients Badley could never have supplied: he was open where Badley was inhibited, could communicate where Badley was silent, close where Badley was distant. He was the eyes and ears and hands of Badley, the heart where Badley was the brain. It seems doubtful if Badley could have carried the school alone, and it is clear that Bedales was far more a partnership than is usually acknowledged.

There is one other area where Badley's influence, initially at any rate, has been exaggerated, and that is co-education. Here, Bedales was truly revolutionary in England. (In the US and Scandinavia co-education had long been familiar and single-sex schools the exception.) When the first girls came in 1898, the strangeness of the idea can be gauged from the ludicrous nature of the objections raised: were the girls to play football, and the boys play with dolls? Were the girls to be caned? Would the boys dance all the time? Badley said that at first there should be fewer girls than boys because this strangeness always made it look as though there were more. This move, which seemed to take place almost haphazardly, and was certainly in line with Badley's desire to make his community more "real", has been attributed to him. But in fact it was due to his wife, Amy. A sweet and gentle character, she had also been a fervent supporter of women's rights and later supported the suffragettes. She had long been convinced that co-education was the only fair education and had refused to marry Badley until he promised he would bring this about.

I was twice told during my interviews, in all seriousness, that Maurice Bowra used to be taken to the reeds by the river at Bryanston so that he could watch the naked limbs of the bathers skim over him. Now it is true the boys bathed naked at Bryanston, but what Bowra is supposed to have done is quite impossible, unless he wore a diving suit. (Perhaps he did. It is a curious picture.) But the point is that progressive schools have always excited people in this way. The wildest fantasies, thinly disguised wishful thinking, spring up about the unrestrained sexual licence flourishing in them. They were, and are, sometimes relatively free, it is true; but they can be quite the reverse. The differences in sexual attitudes between progressive schools are typical of the sort of very wide differences that can exist between public schools, and the way these differences start is typical too.

I was first alerted to the situation at Bedales by a few lines of Badley's book, *Bedales*. Badley, from the photographs, had a kindly, rather eager face, with humorous eyes. His prose, however, is not particularly humorous (of all the progressive writers the only one you'd read for pleasure is A. S. Neill); Badley at best is calm and commonsensical, at worst boring. But about anything sexual he becomes instantly frigid—and also rather surprising. His view is that because boys and girls have each other as companions normal sexual attraction and behaviour can be postponed until adulthood. Or rather, any sexual behaviour or attraction other than platonic friendship is not normal, it is "silly". "Silliness" can be stopped, when it arises, by helpful talk; but it is best stopped if the community itself condemns "silliness", attempts to suppress "silliness", and if each member refrains from "silliness" him- or herself. And certainly this took place at Bedales from the start. Grant-Watson says that even before girls came, visitors were amazed at the "cleanliness" of the boys—even single sex was "silly". When girls came this was simply extended: "Love affairs were discouraged and held up to ridicule as sentimental and silly." And indeed the community, including the young masters, did try and seek out and stop any nascent sexuality.

And yet—what an odd attitude this is. You can think a great many different things about expressions of the sexual instinct—that they are disgusting, that they are delightful, that they are for adults only, or for anyone, that they are harmful, or beneficial, that they should be controlled or unrestrained; but it is rare to find someone thinking them "silly". The clue came from Mr. Moorsom, who put baldly what other people had hinted at. Badley had an extremely unhappy marriage. He had a cold and icy relationship with his wife, and hardly spoke to her. ("He was married to the school, not Amy," someone else said.) He used to sleep alone in a room next to one of the dormitories. He was therefore extremely frustrated, and this resulted in an intense and sublimated interest in the girls and concern for them. It also meant sex was completely suppressed. "Silliness" was, therefore, partly the calm "rational" way of expressing an attitude of disapproval towards sex that was common at the end of the 19th century, and partly due to his own repressed feelings.

It had a profound and long-term effect on Bedales. Someone who returned to the school in 1918 wrote, "When I knew Bedales as a boy, the dormitory life and life of the school generally was clean—now, it seemed to me, it was growing cleaner still." If a new boy proved "dirty in talk" he was reported by other boys, the matter being regarded as too important to be considered "sneaking". Jocelyn Brooke, at Bedales 1922–27, noted the tacitly anti-sexual atmosphere, the survival of "silliness". By 1936 sex had ceased to be silly and had become "a problem", but one, as we saw from Geoffrey Crump's advocacy, that could be solved by art. By 1945, when Sasha Young was there, the situation was much like that we've seen in certain public schools, where the staff were repressive and the pupils largely against complete physical expression but totally involved in passionate, intense romantic love affairs. "You could choose where you sat at lunch. You chose to be *near* the person you were keen on, never at the same table. You would look far too unattractive eating. You were too frightened to eat anyway. You wanted to look at him." The atmosphere was charged, full of intrigue and excitement.People acted as go-betweens. On St. Valentine's Day, Valentines were exchanged and, devoured by interest, people lounged against the pillars of the "quad", watching the reactions to their notes, their own reactions being watched.

This fraught, taut state ended if you agreed to "go with someone", or vice versa. This was a formal, recognised state. You sat together and did things together. "There was a lot of love-play, kissing and so on. But most people didn't make love; I didn't, nor any of my friends. We used to go and kiss for hours in haystacks. Even today the smell of hay is a romantic

Four examples of typical public school good looks, ranging from 1870 to 1955 (the Christ's Hospital boy was painted by his housemaster). Intense passions and "romantic friendships" consumed practically all public school boys.

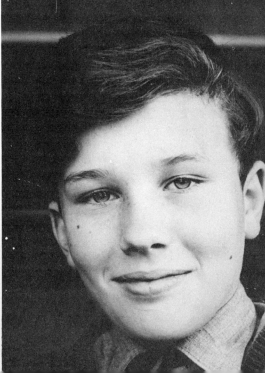

M. A. Douglas, Headmistress of Godolphin School, in 1890.

Miss Douglas transformed by twenty-nine years of power and adulation.

Miss Beale of Cheltenham Ladies' College, photographed in the 1860s.

Miss Buss of the North London Collegiate, from a photograph by Lambert, about 1857.

smell to me." A number of people, not a great many, did make love. "There was a boy called D—— who used to take one or two highly sexed girls into a boot cupboard"—(the romantic smell of boot polish).

We shall deal with other aspects of Bedales as they arise chronologically. But we can note that because of when it was started and because of Badley's temperament, it was always on the right wing of the progressive movement. The beneficial effects of co-education were diluted by the repressive anti-sex attitudes which he encouraged, because an anti-sex attitude spreads unconsciously to become, to the extent to which the two are joined, an anti-love attitude. He sought to make the most powerful and enriching of human instincts "silly" and therefore trivialised the whole infinite penumbra of emotions extending from it. Strong traces of this attitude can still be found at Bedales today.

Because Badley and Reddie were ex-public school boys, their progressive schools were public schools too and shared certain fundamental characteristics: their concern with character, for example, and the fact that they were boarding. The progressive school movement must be seen as a deviant off-shoot from, or advance guard of, the public school system. And of course many good public schoolmasters at this time—indeed at any time before and after—shared certain of their concerns on pragmatic grounds. The need for a wide curriculum, the enormous, indeed essential, educational value of interesting a pupil, the need for closer and more human relationships between masters/mistresses and pupils—Cory, for instance, exemplified all these. The difference is that the progressive schools were a *movement*, not examples of incidental enlightenment. This will become clearer as we proceed.

Another characteristic progressive schools shared with public schools is that they charged fees. That is, they were a middle-class development. They have often worried about this and some of them—Rendcomb, Dartington, the Quaker schools to an extent—have made valiant efforts to recruit from the lower classes but they have always been defeated by the necessity to pay their way. But it is more than this. There is a particular pressure—or temptation—at work which we could elevate into a psycho-economic law about public schools. An inspector at the Board of Education said in 1905, "The ambition of a successful school is not to do better the work it began with, but to pass on to work of a more ambitious character." The richer a school is the more teachers, equipment, class-rooms, games fields, telescopes, laboratories, theatres, billiard tables, etc., it can have. Teaching is more fun and more fulfilling and so is learning. There is a third aspect to this fee-dependency. It might have been thought that, in seeing themselves as communities which would represent a better society and so help to change society in their own image, progressive schools were reversing the more usual anthropological rôle of education—which is to extract and pass on the important accepted values, *mores* and social hierarchies existing in a society. But in practice the progressive schools did the same—only on behalf of a minute sub-society. They relied on people who approximately shared their views; that is to say elements in the larger society who had already changed. As these were rare, for many years they had to struggle, frequently depending on the children of cranks, and enrolling enthusiastic but inefficient amateurs to teach. However, early on they had a piece of luck. About this time, a Frenchman called M. Edmond Demolins wrote a book called *A Quoi Tient la Supériorité des Anglo-Saxons*? He traced this superiority to boarding public schools, but it so happened that the only ones he'd seen had been Abbotsholme and Bedales. The book was therefore read with some astonishment in England, but it was a godsend to Badley and Reddie. Hordes of foreigners—Dutch, Swedes and particularly Russians—rushed over and kept them going.

And that, finally, is the obvious but extremely important thing about Badley—he kept going. Where Abbotsholme disintegrated in a series of cataclysms, Bedales—with the aid of Oswald Powell—showed that Reddie's ideas could work, could last, could be successful. And the school was helped in this by both men living to an almost incredible age: Badley became a legend, dying in 1967, aged 102; Powell dying in the same year a few months before his hundredth birthday.

Indeed, to end this section on an irrelevance, I was repeatedly struck by this phenomenon as I read for this book: from Busby of Westminster in the 17th century aged ninety-eight, through Roberts still beating at eighty-three in the 18th century, dozens of old Eton masters in their eighties, tough nonagenarian schoolmistresses, moderately spry figures of 104 dug out of libraries or bungalows adjoining the games fields and detailed, leaning heavily on my arm, to show me round—their gift of longevity seemed equalled only by successful actresses, High Court judges and famous surgeons. And this may suggest the reason. These are all professions which provide an audience in perpetuity. I think it may be the promise of this, the continual little spurts of adrenalin driving round the blood, clearing the arteries, the drug of applause, that kept them alive so long.

4 Other progressive developments: 1900–1914

The second stage of progressive development—approximately 1890 to 1914—was a movement not so much of concerted action as of mutual knowledge and help and a strong feeling that shared ideas should spread. It resembles in this, though I think the progressives were more conscious of a crusade, the early years of public school reform with Arnold, Moberly, Wordsworth, Vaughan, etc. It consisted of five or six schools and two associated movements—Quaker and Theosophical.

Alexander Devine, the founder of Clayesmore, was a progressive in the bizarre Reddie tradition. Liable to bursts of manic and eccentric behaviour, he was extremely extravagant (his enemies said dishonest) and moved, or fled, through life in a perpetual cloud of debts. He was both an impresario and a snob, and enjoyed asking men of title and fame down to his school. In later years he took to living at Claridge's and in 1919 became Minister Plenipotentiary for Montenegro in London and awarded himself numerous decorations which he wore frequently.

His educational career was more tempered. He started by having a school for working-class offenders in Manchester, but soon ran into money troubles. He said he couldn't get money to expand; his supporters that he was being criminally extravagant. Next he moved to London and in the 1890s started a reformatory for expelled public school boys. He soon realised that it was the public school system that needed reforming and in 1896 he started Clayesmore, a school that was to be "a liberal democratic state, not a reactionary dictatorship".

Clayesmore in fact came somewhere between a conventional public school of the time and Bedales. Devine kept Eton jackets and top hats in the winter and straw boaters in the summer; there was fagging on a hierarchical basis; and there was ritual caning by the headmaster, often late at night. At the same time he knew Badley and Reddie and approved of their ideas. Lunatic athleticism was not allowed and work in the garden encouraged; the curriculum was wide up to age fifteen and then boys could concentrate on what they liked, so the classical restriction had gone; he also allowed a good deal of freedom for art, music and various hobbies.

A more radical school at this time was King Alfred's, a day public school started for Hampstead intellectuals in 1898 by Charles E. Rice, who had taught at Bedales. "He was the first of a dozen members of our staff," said Badley, "who have gone from their experience at Bedales to become heads of schools of their own and then helped to diffuse more widely the new educational ideal." It was a co-educational school with all the familiar features—wide curriculum, informal staff relations, wider freedom and so on. Pestalozzi was mentioned in the prospectus.

Clayesmore had a turbulent history under Devine. He was difficult to work with and masters left; salaries were frequently months in arrears and debtors besieged the euphoric headmaster while, laden with medals, he dined at Claridge's. Its most stable period was that between 1904 and 1914, when a bursar was responsible for the finances. Devine described this time as "my years of slavery". In the 1920s it really became a conventional public school again, and continues this today. King Alfred's, however, remained progressive. It still successfully serves the same North London clientele with that intimacy and informality which is so much easier for day schools—not subject to the fevers and exaggerations endemic in their total society, boarding companion schools.

But the significance of Clayesmore and King Alfred's at this period is that they were not yet further examples of flourishing and successful schools putting into practice new educational ideas.

Finally, let us look at the two associated movements—the Quaker and Theosophical societies. The first is an 18th-century movement; the second a 19th- and early-20th-century one.

Quakers are an interesting example of how, from the basic view of human nature, all else including educational practice flows. Friends believe that everyone has the capacity to understand and share spiritual experience. This experience—the Inner Light—is gained in direct, personal contacts with God. These personal messages from God can be passed on by anyone in the meetings regularly held for that purpose. And everyone, high or low, man or woman, has this power equally.

Now from these premises a number of positions, some with immediate educational consequences, can be deduced. Since all were in touch with God and all could pass on his message, English, the medium for communication, became of overwhelming importance. ("Plain speaking" was another consequence—God's message must not be overlaid or varnished in any way.) The importance of English was buttressed because many jobs were barred to Quakers. They did not necessarily condemn Latin and Greek, but they did reject the classical pagan authors—thus the universities and the law were impossible; they were pacifists, so could not join the army or navy; they clearly could not be clergy. In all that was left—medicine, teaching, trade and crafts—English was again the medium. English, therefore, and not the classics, was the basis of any Quaker curriculum.

Secondly, it was clear that nature was part of God's plan and therefore science, the study of nature, was important.

As far as sin went, with the bearing that had on punishment, Quakers believed in it but they did not think man was wholly sinful. How else, if there were not goodness too, could he listen to God, how else could God be in him? Their position therefore was midway between Rousseau and Arnold.

Men and women equally received the message; therefore men and women should both be taught.

Everyone receives the Inner Light, therefore everyone is equal and so is what they do. There is nothing degrading about labour.

Now for the late 18th century these ideas—English, not the classics, science, the "total sin" element removed from punishment, women's education, the dignity of labour and (theoretical) lack of class—all these are clearly revolutionary. And schools were set up to implement them: Ackworth (1779), Sidcot (1808), Saffron Walden (1811), Wigton (1815), Bootham (1822), The Mount (1831), Great Ayton (1841), Sibford (1842), Leighton Park (1890). Some were for girls only (Mount School for instance); but most were for boys and girls taught separately. All but two were started to teach the children of those not rich.

This is a very interesting development, but we must be careful not to overstate its radical nature nor overestimate its influence. The Quakers were a minority, numbering between 20,000 and 30,000. Knowledge about their schools, their influence, at first at any rate, was very much confined to the Quakers themselves. Nor were they in all respects as radical as they seem. As far as poorer pupils were concerned, the public school psycho-economic law soon began to operate. Fees were continually raised and most poor pupils were gradually squeezed out. Also Quakers are in some ways cautious and conservative people. It often took some time before they fully worked out the implications of their beliefs. Thus they did not abolish corporal punishment until the middle of the 19th century, and before that there are stories of cruelty equal to any we have already heard. Even after they had abolished it, acute public ridicule and solitary confinement were not uncommon. As far as the equality of women went it was not until 1907 that they were the equal of men in the Society's councils.

Nevertheless, in the end they did make real the implications of their beliefs, and as a result they were decades ahead of the public schools generally. By the end of the 19th century not only had they what we can now call a "conventionally" wide curriculum but also encouraged art, music and hobbies, and had craft and work shops and farms. By 1914 seven of them were properly co-educational, and the nine Quaker schools then, as now, formed the right wing of the progressive movement. They had also begun to let in pupils who were not Quakers, thus extending their influence beyond the minority.

Finally, the Theosophical schools. These grew out of a society founded by Mme. Elena Petrovna Blavatsky. Born near Odessa in 1831, she is supposed to have spent nearly a third of her life wandering round the Far East and Tibet, penetrating the mysteries of spiritualism and gathering the essence of various gnostic religions. Laden with all this she went to New York and, with Colonel H. S. Olcott, started the Theosophical Society in 1875.

The tenets of Theosophy need not concern us. It had no dogmas, no creeds, and the outlines of its mysticism were so broad that they caught in their blurred and generous folds the adherents of all faiths or those with none—asking only a vague and generalised agreement. (Even this—easy enough to give—they did not always get. The amorphous mass has sometimes split, as it did with Rudolf Steiner in 1913.)

But educationally it sponsored schools, like St. Christopher's (a day public school), which were run, if sometimes with a slightly cranky tinge, on progressive lines: co-education, wide curriculum, discipline but as mild as possible and no corporal punishment, freedom, democracy, and "awareness" of nature (much Theosophical work was done in the open air).

The progressive schools in England at this time were significant in two ways. From abroad it was clear that they constituted much more of a movement, and a much more important movement, than perhaps even its founders realised. The ideas on which it was based derived ultimately, as we have seen, from Continental thinkers—chiefly Rousseau, Pestalozzi and Fellenberg. But these ideas had been developed, significantly added to and implemented in England. The older public schools had imitators— half a dozen or so schools in South Africa, Rhodesia, Australia and India. But people flocked to Bedales, Abbotsholme and King Alfred's; Reddie and Badley and their followers started an entirely new line of country boarding schools in Germany, Switzerland, France, Holland and Belgium; schools like Wickensdorf, Bieberstein and the École des Roches. When America joined in in the 1920s these schools could be numbered in hundreds. The progressive schools have been infinitely more influential abroad than any other branch of the public school system.

But what of their influence at home? Now, in 1914, there were some fifteen successful, stable progressive schools, churning out pupils, passing exams, getting publicity, publishing articles and books, all proving that it was perfectly possible to educate adolescents in ways directly counter to the universally accepted and practised beliefs. You did not have to flog them, you did not need rigid hierarchical prefect systems, you did not need endless inducements and privileges, you could allow friendship between staff and pupils, you could let them act plays and have free time unsupervised, you did not only have to teach Latin, you could even—astounding thought!—educate boys and girls together without there being some sort of colossal orgasmic explosion. How did the public schools respond to all this? What indeed were they doing as we advance into the first fifty or so years of the 20th century? It is time to get back to the Monolith.

CHAPTER 13

The Conditions and Strength of the Monolith: 1900–1940/50

I never seriously thought of myself being brilliant enough to sit in that company, with those men, among any of them with their fresh complexions from their playing fields and all that, with their ringing effortless voice production and their quiet chambers, and tailors and mess bills and Oxford Colleges.

Bill Maitland in John Osborne's *Inadmissible Evidence*

The years around 1898, when Bedales first went co-educational, seemed to the majority of those living in them like some cosmic womb. It was the height of Victorian prosperity and calm. Year by year production, population and wealth increased like the growth of a beneficent pumpkin, bringing with it an increase in comfort, convenience and invention. The Empire was now not just accepted; it was expected to grow too:

> Wider still and wider shall thy bounds be set,
> God who made thee mighty, make thee mightier yet.

There had been no real war for over eighty years, there had been no one who could even threaten England since Napoleon. Disease, poverty, famine belonged to faraway places like China or India, and those unlucky lands were, in any case, bound to be all right soon because missionaries were hurrying out and, besides, the railway was about to arrive. It was a world we in Britain today can scarcely imagine, solid and certain, when in Alec Waugh's words, "the past was reverenced, the present accepted, the future awaited". Interest rates fell each year by minute but perceptible degrees and so, to earn money, money was invested abroad until eventually the whole world was in thrall to Britain, sending home each year its ten-fold tribute, a great river of golden coin. History, as Wells put it, was over; it had been superseded by the daily paper. The public schools, embedded now in 1,300 years of the past, certainly the beneficiaries of this enormous material and spiritual success, in their own view the architects of it, were the most self-satisfied and secure of the lot. If anyone had suggested they were in need of reform they would have considered he was raving mad.

The answer, therefore, to the question, what effect did the progressive movement we have just discussed have on the public school system in general is—absolutely none whatever. Very few of the masters in it were even aware it was taking place. Those that were, ridiculed it. Howson of Gresham's, himself in fact an educational, or at least disciplinary, innovator, said: "This is not the kind of school where, if a boy is not good at arithmetic, he is allowed to keep rabbits instead."

1 Little change in girls' schools

With girls' schools the story is still clear in our heads and in a number of cases I took the chronology into the 1920s and 30s. The picture is easily recalled. For example the schools entered heroically into the 1914–18 war, knitting, making crutches, entertaining wounded soldiers. In 1915 the whole of Roedean was received by Sir Robert Baden-Powell. But in a more general way women had shown they could do as well as men in many capacities. The result—particularly in the larger public schools—was to intensify that striving to be like men. The war had other effects. In quite a number of spheres it produced a mood of iconoclasm, a desire for new freedom and pleasure, for experiment and change. It might have been supposed that the schools (both boys' and girls'), responsive to such changes of attitude insofar as they found echoes in their clients, might have changed and become freer too. In fact, such movements are more complex. People will experiment with freedom, but they will also be frightened of it, particularly for their children. They may, in fact, expect schools to impose disciplines they are rejecting themselves or see society rejecting. We shall see this much more clearly in the late 1960s and 70s. But it happened in the 1920s. Miss L. M. Faithfull (apt name—Miss Beale's successor, 1907–1922) said that the changes and new freedoms of the 1920s "need discipline and steadfastness". Cheltenham grew stricter. (It is noticeable that over this period the study—that haven of freedom—never really developed in girls' schools, though it might have been expected to.) That spinsterly, often rather dykishly feverish atmosphere we were sometimes aware of continues. Elderly staff today swiftly explain the lack of married heads as due to the slaughter of the 1914–18 war. I think it is more likely that the profession attracted a proportion of spinsterly and (however much controlled) homosexually inclined women, just as happened with boys' schools. Also, much more significantly, the dichotomy between career and marriage remained just as strong. As a result (or concurrently) the fear of men remained powerful. When Professor Perkins from the Lansdowne Club first went to teach fencing at Roedean in 1925 he wasn't even allowed in the school. He had to have his lunch outside. And the traditions of dominant and autocratic headmistresses continued. Dame Emmeline Tanner, who took over Roedean in 1924 to start a twenty-three-year reign, was a masterful woman who frightened her staff. "One wouldn't have dared to contradict her." Drink was forbidden and nervous teachers sipped sherry in secret. And it is abundantly clear from my correspondence that in these respects, and many others, on the whole girls' public schools (particularly the larger ones) continued in the 1920s and 30s through into the 1940s, with their rigid routines, highly disciplined and even less susceptible to change than the boys' schools.

2 Growth; the war, the games madness continues

That the boys' schools resisted change will not surprise us. It is always easier and more reassuring to establish and maintain an authoritative régime than it is to relax it. And the importance they attached to tradition, the factors in all educational systems, but particularly in the public schools, intensifying that importance—all this we have seen again and again. But there were three special influences during this period that made change even less likely than usual.

The first was growth. Bamford makes surprisingly heavy weather over this. He notes that around 1900 the creation of public schools more or less stopped. What happened? Since population and wealth continued to increase, a stop in public school growth is really equivalent to a decline. Perhaps there was a loss of educational faith and ardour? Perhaps the 1902 and 1907 Acts which brought secondary education on grammar school (i.e., public school) lines siphoned off some of the market? He confesses himself at a loss.

Yet it is quite clear what took place. I chose seventy-eight schools at random from the 1939 *Public Schools Year Book*. Of these, only thirty-one were entered in 1900. Between 1900 and 1939 these thirty-one increased on average by over one-third, in terms of numbers and staff. And between 1900 and 1939 the remaining forty-seven "became" public schools. That is to say, there were in general two developments (with a proviso about the 1930s). First, during those years more and more schools (virtually all founded before 1900) grew in size and prestige until at last the esoteric "sensing" took place—"Does the school possess the Public School Spirit?"—and it was felt they could be admitted as public schools to the *Public Schools Year Book*. In 1900, ninety-six were admitted; in 1939, 190. Once in they continued to grow larger at the same rate as those already in, that is by about one-third over forty odd years. During the same period the number of pages devoted to prep schools in the *Year Book* increased from nine in 1900 to 116 in 1939. According to G. A. Lowndes, the number of pupils at all public and proprietary schools in 1935 was 30,000, compared to 120,000 at State secondary schools. This of course includes schools outside our scope, but it gives an approximate idea of number.

The fall in numbers was one of the major forces bringing about change in the 1820s and 30s. An institution enjoying such enormous success as the public schools did up to 1940 was under no such pressure. On the contrary.

The 1914–18 war was the second great influence against change. It operated in two ways. First, it produced a large number of new rich. Now the sons of barbed wire, bully beef, expanded metal and margarine, the heirs of fortunes built on dreadnoughts and tanks and shells and submarines had all to be educated. Their fathers wanted them to be like gentlemen before the war; clearly a public school rôle but not an influence for change.

Second, in the terrible slaughter of the war, in a war of great bravery, some of the bravest, among whom some of the worst of the slaughter took place, had been the young subalterns and captains just out from their public schools. So many were killed that it broke some of their head-masters—men like Howson of Gresham's, Holt—who had devoted their lives to their pupils. The schools were proud of these boys—and with justice. Why introduce changes when old ways had produced such heroes? It was illogical—after all, perhaps a type of education so effective in war might be ineffective, even dangerous, in peace—but understandable that our victory seemed to justify the entire system.

All these factors enormously strengthened the Monolith. The extent to which this was so is not always appreciated.

Take games. In his essay on athleticism in *The Victorian Public School* Norman Vance says that after the 1914 war it died away. This is nonsense. It is true that from about 1900 onwards some athletic energy got diverted into the Corps. There was criticism that games fanaticism was unpatriotic, for example in *The Loom of Youth* and Kipling's verse:

> Then ye returned to your trinkets; then ye contented your souls
> With the flannelled fools at the wicket or the muddied oafs at the goals.

After the war this carried on, and in most schools the OTC and ATC, even when nominally voluntary, were really compulsory. Armistice Day was religiously celebrated.

But the games mystique returned to most schools with nearly all its old vigour. It did not really die—though it gradually weakened—until the 1950s. Dr. Norwood made it the cornerstone of his educational theory. In 1928, in one of many ineffably silly remarks, he wrote: "[Cricket] has added a new conception of fairness and chivalry to the common stock of our national ideas, since everybody English knows at once what is meant by such statements as 'this is cricket' and 'that is not cricket'." Philip Toynbee, at Rugby in 1933, was known as "Dirt-eee Toyn-bee!" and was mercilessly bullied and teased and despised until he was seventeen, when suddenly his glands exploded into activity. Within weeks he was playing for the first fifteen. Almost instantaneously "it was necessary for my acquaintances to make a radical and awkward change in their attitude to me. The way in which they achieved this has always remained in my mind as a magnificent example of how to change with the wind and the tide." The elevation was indeed dizzying. Now, bedecked in colours, laden with privileges, a tasselled hat on his head, he walked almost arm in arm with M. M. Walford, captain of cricket and hockey, a rugger player who in two years would play for Oxford and, once, for England. Dirt-eee Toyn-bee became "Toyners". At Marlborough (1920s) there was a magazine satirising athleticism and the public school spirit—"upon Philistia I will triumph". Dr. Norwood, headmaster at the time, suppressed it and preached a sermon on intellectual arrogance. Exactly the same situation continued for years in the girls' schools. At St. Swithin's in the 1920s the games rivalry between the houses was ferocious. At Cheltenham Ladies' College and Roedean in the late 1930s they were out in the nets before breakfast, their bodies strengthened by conditions so tough that, at Cheltenham in winter, they had to hack off the sponges frozen to the washstands.

I could multiply these examples endlessly. Not only did all the old fanaticisms and shibboleths continue—at Lancing, for instance, in 1920, failures at games were contemptible and known simply as "wrecks", clear masturbatory language—but now permutations developed. We saw, for instance, how war and games had become almost synonymous. Now that the war to end wars had presumably done just that, some substitute had to be found. It was. Here is Buchan's Jim Maitland. The scene is Port Said and he suddenly leaves to follow a "dark-skinned man in European clothes" down a side street.

"Wait for me at the hotel," he said curtly, and there was a gleam in his eyes that had not been there before.

[An hour later, he comes back. He's off to Malta at once.]

"Care to come?"

"Somewhat sudden," I murmured mildly. "What's the game?"

"It's *the* game, Dick: the Great Game. The only game in the world worth playing. Sometimes I've been tempted to chuck up roving and take to it permanently. Do you know who that fellow was that I followed?"

"Some Egyptian of sorts, I suppose."

"That was Victor Head, of the Loamshire, temporarily seconded for service with the Government. He's officially A.D.C., I believe, to some General, and he's been on leave of absence for a year." Jim grinned. "That's the sort of General to have."

And suddenly it dawned on me.

"Secret Service work!" I cried.

Jim lifted a deprecating hand.

"Let us call it research amongst the native population," he murmured.

"You don't suppose, do you, old man, that the British Government runs five hundred million black men here and in India by distributing tracts to 'em?"

"But why Malta?" I cried, harking back. . . .

In this way, not only was another path opened, down which Ian Fleming, John le Carré and the almost innumerable other writers of the Secret Service *genre* were to crowd, but the spirit of public school athleticism was preserved in the popular consciousness.

3 How the Monolith survived

Similar permutations took place in other spheres. We saw that by 1900 games had become so dominant that, apart from the specialised sixth forms, public schools were really institutions for learning cricket, rugger, football and (occasionally) hockey. It followed that success at games was a perfectly legitimate qualification for a job. This was usual from then right through the 1920s and 30s. T. C. Worsley, for example, got a bad third in classics; however he had been in the eleven at Marlborough for three years, the fifteen in his last year, a good all-rounder at Cambridge, keeping wicket for the university against Yorkshire. It was these distinctions that got him his first job in 1929.

By the early 1930s it had even, paradoxically, become possible to get poems published if you were good at games (paradoxically because by this time games and any aesthetic pursuit were regarded as opposites). T. C. Worsley had sent a poem up to the London *Mercury*. To his delight it was accepted and the great editor J. C. Squire said that if there were any more he should "drop in" with them some day. He does this next holidays. I shall quote what follows from his *Flannelled Fool: A Slice of Life in the Thirties*. It is a marvellous book which deserves to be better known.

The great editor is sitting there, though Worsley is too nervous to notice what he looked like and is just aware of "an intensified public bar smell of smoke and drink".

"What did you say your name was?"

"Worsley."

"And the initials?"

"T.C."

He tried them over several times: T.C.Worsley, T. C. Worsley: and then something clicked.

"Not *the* T. C. Worsley?"

Heavens! Was I so well known already? If so, how had it come about? I had published nothing but this one sonnet in his magazine. Did this make me *the* T. C. Worsley? How amazing! Was it as good as that?

No it wasn't, as his next question showed.

"Let me see. Let me see," he rummaged through his memory. "I've got it!

Marlborough v. Rugby at Lord's three years running. Forty-three in the second innings of the second year. Perambulators against Etceteras, eighty-two. Fenners 1929. University v. Yorkshire same year. Am I right?"

He was, within a run or two, and was delighted to be told so.

"There you are. Of course I'll publish your poems. Leave them with us."

I have gone this far into games because there is some dispute as to how long the madness lasted. Other facets need not so long detain us. "Character", that vague and elusive ingredient whose fuzziness contributed to its importance, continued to be central; in the 1930s a master from Lancing, newly head of another school, had scholarships for "character". Sexual repression also continued unabated. T. C. Worsley describes "the unshakeable conviction of the Old Guard that any boy who was given a moment's leisure would inevitably get up to sexual mischief. The boys' days were organised down to the last minute of every hour. It was a most repressive and illiberal régime." The chief proponent of this was a master they called The Hun, who, assisted by five other aging housemasters, carried out continual Colditz-like anti-vice campaigns. Worsley's account of Wellington, where he taught for five years in the 1930s, tells how the terms were punctuated by squalid discoveries of petty sexual misdemeanours and their aftermath of desperate and terrified boys banished to sanatoriums, the locked boxes, weeping mothers, the expulsion. You still get *Eric* and Arnoldian overtones. Walking in Savernake Forest somewhere around 1920 a young master commented to the Headmaster of Marlborough on the beauty of the autumn leaves. The headmaster looked at him. "Yes, beautiful," he said, "beautiful outside but corrupt within, like the boys." My informant thought it was the headmaster before Norwood, but it has the authentic Norwood ring to me.

The whole edifice of privileges, colours, and hierarchies remained almost unchanged in most schools. At Eton in the 1930s the gradations were of an almost inconceivable complexity, with one-quarter and one-eighth colours, distinctions between one button, two buttons and three. Some simple reforms were suggested to the headmaster, Elliott. He agreed but, "You must persuade Pop." He wouldn't have dreamed of doing anything so revolutionary without their permission.

Public schools are extraordinary examples of how historical origins can both linger in, and continue to dictate aspects of, an institution long after the historical relevance, and even dynamism, have vanished. Auden noted in 1930 how by 1920, in fact long before, dogmatic religion, that is to say the Christian world-picture, had broken among schoolmasters and the culture generally. Yet the Christian religion continued to sustain the public schools, continued in some ill-defined way to be "central". When J. J. Christie was appointed Headmaster of Westminster in 1937 he was the first lay head since 1598. Although he was no such thing, when Roxburgh was appointed to Stowe in 1923, *The Queen* magazine automatically assumed he was a clergyman—The Reverend J. F. Roxburgh. And Miss M. E. Popham (Cheltenham 1937–53), was a rector's daughter and saw being a headmistress as in many ways a similar career. The girls' schools religion-related "honour and trust" also continued unabated through this period. And even though, as Auden also observes, "religion without dogma soon becomes, as it was at Holt, nothing but vague uplift as flat as an old bottle of soda water", the dreary hours of agnostic and atheist-producing religion continued in many schools, now with still less relevance, much as they had in the 19th century.

And this emphasis was a strong ingredient in the public schools' inability to change, and therefore in their growing irrelevance to English social and economic needs. In 1928, for example, in his *The English Tradition in Education*, Dr. Norwood devoted three whole chapters to religious teaching and ten pages to British technological backwardness and lack of trained managerial talent. He was unable to see the connection between what he pretended to deplore and his own emphasis. Cyril Norwood, incidentally, was in some respects a typical figure of the times. Because he became Headmaster of Marlborough in 1916 from a grammar school, he had some difficulty getting accepted by his snobbish pupils. And snobbish staff. One of my informants dated from those days, and his last energies—like a sudden sparkler in the dark—could still sometimes be ignited by class. I had heard from others how slack Harrow had become under Ford. "Rich and slack". The vice was incredible, not just ferocious buggery, "but whenever the police raided the Hypocrites Club", John Betjeman told me, "or the Coconut Club, the '43 or the Blue Lantern there would always be Harrovians there. They used to go down on the Metropolitan line. No one saw them. It got into the papers. Ford, by way of defence, said, 'Only seven out that night!'" Norwood was called in "to clean Harrow up". Forty were sacked in the first week. "But he failed," said my aged informer with considerable venom, "because he wasn't really a gentleman. His nickname here was 'Boots'—not quite-quite. He never got Harrow into his grip. He retreated to write his ridiculous book, to sit on Whitehall committees and eventually to St. John's College, where he made an even worse mess." He seems to have been a kindly but distant figure, not really interested either in teaching or boys, who enjoyed woolly discussions about educational theory (religion and games) and writing hymns.

The drive to conformity seems to have been nearly as strong at many schools as in those of the previous period. Brian Inglis, at Shrewsbury in the 1930s—where they had the full Monolithic structure, fagging, beating, sexual segregation, athleticism—says they were "as regimented as boys in a remand home". The prime need was to conform. John Carleton, in his lightweight but readable account of Westminster, of which he eventually became headmaster, cites Peter Ustinov as an example of one original writer he "failed to spot". The feeling is a boastful one—how easy it is, among so many talents in a great school, to miss one. Actually, Ustinov had been spotted at once. Carleton has simply re-arranged his attitude to accord with the times. In 1939 Ustinov's report read like this: "He shows great originality, which must be curbed at all costs."

Finally, violence—though it continued to decline—formed the background to much public school life, especially in the first two years or so, and was an almost universal (though not the only) method of punishment. At Westminster, in the 1940s, the "tanning poles" were long, vicious bamboos, six to eight feet long, with a string to fasten round the wrist. The beating scenes in the film *If . . .* were based on those at Tonbridge in 1949. Bullying. I think of Raymond Mortimer forced, at Malvern, to anticipate a scene in that same film, having his head thrust down into an unflushed lavatory bowl. Or a letter describing the terror of bullying in one particular house at Winchester in the 1920s, bullying so terrible that it led, in one case, to suicide at Oxford just after leaving. And the fear the writer felt even now. *"But please preserve my anonymity absolutely*—I have kept silence till now. . . ." He was aged seventy-two.

The strength of the schools aroused fear; fear perpetuated their strength. In 1895, virtually no Old Boy dared criticise them in print. In 1934 Graham Greene edited a collection of autobiographical accounts called *The Old School* . Many of them are critical, but nearly all show reluctance to criticise or apologise for it. "I am not one of those who regard the Old School and its institutions as fixed in a sacred unchangeableness," wrote William Plomer (at Rugby in 1914). The supposition behind that statement is that a lot of people still do regard the schools as unchangeable and, indeed, that a lot of people he knows will be shocked he is not one of them. In 1961 Brian Inglis edited *John Bull's Schooldays*, a similar collection. There are various differences, rather minor; but in the Inglis collection there is no air of apology. The fear has gone.

It was this strength and fear resisting the forces of change which establish the one dominant characteristic of the public school scene over the next forty to fifty years—that is, from 1900 to 1940/50. That characteristic is diversity. It becomes less and less possible to generalise about the system as a whole. They react at different times and in different ways to the same stimuli. The 1914 war, which in many places strengthened the *ancien régime*, at Rugby led to closer contact between boys and masters (this was partly the influence of a remarkable headmaster, Dr. A. A. David). Schools would become freer, and then suddenly change back under some "cleaning-up" headmaster like the new figure in *Lord Dismiss Us* (St. Columba's, late 1940s): "His hair was sandy, turning grey, and it had been cut high above the ears, to show that there was going to be no malingering." Nor were these reactionary headmasters necessarily old. At

Berkhamstead in the late 1920s and early 30s a liberal régime was gradually introduced by Graham Greene's father: rules were relaxed, there was little caning, the games fetish was crushed. Then a young headmaster, rebounding from school to university and back again, took over and restored the Monolith.

The continuing autonomy of houses (at Harrow they were still "owned" by their housemasters until 1948) meant that you could have the good fortune to be in a slack house. This happened to Anthony Powell, at Eton after the First World War. He was in a very "bad" house. Everyone agreed it was quite the worst house in the school. It had not survived the first round of the football ties for more than ten years; its only cup had been won for singing. It ran happily under an eccentric explosion of a housemaster "hurrying feverishly through the passages with some huge volume illustrating the history of footgear through the ages". And, being autonomous, houses too could change, and then change back. When Robin Denniston's election rose him to power in college at Westminster in 1944/5 they burnt the long tanning poles. A subsequent election restored them.

And this diversity is compounded—or at least a complicated picture is made more complicated—because as they approach modern times school histories become more and more anxious not to offend. From about 1920 (which is often when they see "modern times" beginning) they increasingly confine themselves to architectural developments or vague praise. Dame Emmeline Tanner was a best friend of Miss de Zouche and from 1924 the de Zouche history of Roedean really abandons any attempt at objective criticism and just proceeds in a series of paeans.

All this diversity, and the strength, obstinacy, fear and survival power which I have briefly tried to revive, will become much clearer as we proceed to examine the main elements struggling to bring about change.

CHAPTER 14

The Fight to Break the Monolith: Forces of Change

Out of Bounds is against Reaction, Militarism and Fascism in public schools. We attack not only the vast machinery of propaganda which forms the basis of the public school system, and makes them so useful in a vicious and obsolete form of society; we oppose not only the semi-compulsory nature of the OTC and the hypocritical bluff about "character-building". We oppose every one of the absurd restrictions and petty rules and regulations which would be more applicable to a kindergarten than to boys between the ages of fourteen and nineteen.

The manifesto of Esmond Romilly's magazine, *Out of Bounds*

1 *Books:* The Loom of Youth, The Harrovians, *etc.*

It may come as a surprise to learn that Alec Waugh's *The Loom of Youth*, which I have so far used exclusively to illustrate, quite unsatirically, various aspects of public school life, was in fact regarded when it was written in 1917 as a violent attack on the public school system. What was the essence of that attack?

In the first place, the book was regarded as the first "honest" public school book. Here is an example of its honesty—the captain of Gordon Carruthers' house (Carruthers is the hero) asks them to own up about who started a rumpus. "There was not a move. The idea that the public school boy's code of honour forces him to own up at once is entirely erroneous. Boys only own up when they are bound to be found out; they are not quixotic."

This seems mild enough. But to contemporaries—used to the sentimental fervour of *The Hill*, or the gallantries of the school-adventure stories where boys *were* quixotic—it came as a revelation.

The Loom was ostensibly an attack on athleticism and, to a certain extent, the classics. The degree to which these had become entrenched is indicated by the fact that these attacks constitute some of the major dramas of the book. A public debate takes place where a revolutionary master, Ferrers, argues that a classical education is all imitation. People should think for themselves. Therefore they must learn French, maths and science where you do think for yourself. Uproar. Even more daring, a debate is held against athleticism. Clarke: "If as a country we had only ourselves to think about, let us put up a god of sport. But we have not. We have to compete with the other nations of the world. And late cuts are precious little use in commerce. This athleticism is ruining the country." Rebellion is further fomented by reading a "modern" play.

In some ways *The Loom* is very like *Eric*. They are both moral tales. The out-of-control total society fervour, which had overheated games/classics and all the other public school spirits to such a degree, generated exactly the same exaggerated feelings in response. In *Eric,* "sin" (a few peccadillos stained with ghastly juices from Kibroth-Hathaavah) is conquered by Arnoldian religion pressed equally by God, a "good" master and "good" fellow pupil. In *The Loom,* "sin" is athleticism. This leads to anti-work, which leads to trivial minds, which leads to immoral behaviour. "No wonder the whole common room is repeatedly shocked by the discovery of some sordid scandal." Salvation lies in work, but in particular in work which has aesthetic value, literature, poetry, beauty. At the end of the book, Gordon's games ambitions collapse and beauty and literature triumph. As in *Eric* the transformation takes place with the help of a "good" master, Ferrers, and a "good" boy, Tester (Alec Waugh shares his brother's use of the symbolic name).

It seems almost unbelievable now, but all this was regarded as a savage and probably fatal attack. The book was a sensation. Partly it was an accident of the time. There was a boom in soldier-poets—Siegfried Sassoon, Robert Nichols and W. J. Turner had recently made their debuts. Now here was a soldier-novelist and one still in his teens. But the furore was caused by his "denunciation" of the public schools. Letters poured in on him, agreeing and violently disagreeing. H. G. Wells and Arnold Bennett wrote to his father. Many people saw it as the beginning of the end. One critic wrote: "[the book] builds up a merciless memorial of its evils and shortcomings." Another said it was "the *Uncle Tom's Cabin* of the public school system". Even Bennett admitted the possibility that the institution might not survive. Waugh was struck off the list of the Old Shirburnian Society.

There are of course other reasons for the book's success. Although in many ways absurd, it is extremely readable. It has great narrative drive. It was this that struck Bennett, who in fact was bored stiff by the public school problem. "What interests me," he wrote to Waugh's father, "is the very remarkable narrative gift of this man. . . ." There are deft and often amusing character sketches. Here is a portrait of a master:

> Mr. Finnemore was an oldish man, getting on for sixty, and his hair was quite white. He had a long moustache, his clothes carried the odour of stale tobacco, his legs seemed hung on to his body by hooks that every day seemed less likely to maintain the weight attached to them. He wore a continually sad smile on his face, a smile that was half self-deprecatory, as though uncertain of its right to be there. He was most mercilessly ragged.

He is, indeed, as Waugh describes, treated in incident after incident with complete disdain:

> On another occasion Betteridge walked quietly up to him, handed him a Shelley, and without any warning suddenly shrieked out: *"He hath outsoared the shadow of the night."*
>
> Finnemore looked at him sadly: "My dear Betteridge," he said, "and so early in the morning!"

He had started with high hopes, all dashed. "And then he realised that for the loss of youth there can be no compensation, and that in youth alone happiness can be found. And so he had decided to spend his life in company with high hopes and smiling faces."

But in fact, paradoxically for an "attack" on public schools, what comes across most strongly is Waugh's passion for school life. The involvement is total. The games—great epic, thrilling battles—form central peaks of narrative excitement. And in his autobiography, *The Early Years*, this passion surfaces again in swelling waves of nostalgia:

> How many pictures crowd my memory when I close my eyes. November rains dashing across the courts when one ran for the shelter of the cloisters; bland autumn mornings with the beeches browning on the slopes and a bite in the air that made one impatient for the football field; lazy summer afternoons, lying on a rug watching a cricket match, with a bag of cherries at one's side. . . .

The point is, he *loved* school, as he goes on to describe:

> I might well have seemed the very boy for whom the public school system was designed—gregarious, sociable, as keen on his work in the form as on his prowess on the field, a boy for whom the fifteen hours of the day seemed too narrow a casket for all that it contained.

It was his entire life. He came home each holidays to recuperate, then flung himself joyously back again.

At the same time, the autobiography reveals that he was furiously rebellious. He was enraged by authority and carried on a running battle with it in the shape of a master, G. M. Carey ("The Bull"). And then in his final term he was caught out in some undescribed sexual situation with a boy in, ironically, Carey's house. In the end, this boy, who was so passionate about his school, was humiliated by it and though not expelled left ignominiously and in disgrace.

This explains the intensity of the book; like all deep passions it was a fusion of love and hate. It was written in six and a half weeks when Waugh was seventeen and still obsessed. He was doing military training and used to get up at four-thirty to write, and then go on after parades. It is 115,000 words long and was printed exactly as written, unrevised. Waugh himself pin-points exactly what the book is:

It is in such a mood that a man at the end of a long and intense love affair writes to the mistress whom he still adores, but nonetheless holds largely responsible for the rupture. "Isn't it your fault," he cries, "here, and here and again here? We might be together still." Perhaps in the last analysis that is what *The Loom of Youth* is—a love letter to Sherborne.

The Loom, apart from the fact that it is an attack, is important for two other reasons. Waugh defines one area where conflict was to continue through the 1920s and into the 50s. Since games worship involved a philistine contempt of work, art, indeed intellectual pursuits of all kinds, aestheticism became the creed of those opposed to athleticism. Cyril Connolly therefore espoused aestheticism; at the same time, as a member of games-dominated Pop, he was racked by guilt and anxiety lest he should be betraying it, and also terrified in case as a result he lost popularity. He had secret, fifth-column meetings outside Pop. In secret, too, he read a pink album, *The Eton Candle*, circularising poems by, among others, the Sitwells.

One day Teddy Jessel introduced me to the editor, a boy in his house with a distinguished impertinent face, a sensual mouth and dark eyes with long lashes. He wrote to ask me to tea. I accepted, on Pop writing paper, and went round one summer afternoon to find *foie-gras* sandwiches, strawberries and cream and my postcard of acceptance prominently displayed on the mantelpiece. Seeing it up there for the world to know that Brian Howard had had a member of Pop to tea with him, I was miserable. I felt that once again I had let the Eton Society down. It was natural for Teddy Jessel to know Brian who was in the same house. The question was, *Who else did*? I swallowed down my tea like a lady who is offered a swig by a madman in a railway tunnel and bolted.

Later on, in the 1930s, as aestheticism to a certain degree and in certain schools became tolerated, a transposition achievable only by *simplicismus* sometimes took place. Since games had been a substitute for sex and aestheticism was a substitute for games, some masters came to the conclusion that aesthetic pursuits—plays, painting, music, literature—were therefore also substitutes for sex. We have seen this already with Geoffrey Crump at Bedales. Kurt Hahn of Gordonstoun is the most bizarre example.

Secondly, the fact that so mild an attack as *The Loom*—an attack which today reads more like a panegyric—should arouse furious opposition is yet further evidence of the incredible way the public school ethos had imposed itself. It is a tribute to those many forces involved—sociological, psychological, behavioural and so on—which we have already analysed. It is easy to forget how difficult it was for England to break loose from the great humbug embrace of the Victorian/Edwardian age, that it only happened by degrees and that it took courage to make the attempt. *The Loom of Youth, Sinister Street, Eminent Victorians* and others seem innocuous enough today but that, as Alec Waugh ends his comment on this episode of his life, is because "the situation is very different now, and my generation is responsible for the fact that it is different".

A similar book and one which caused a similar though smaller storm was *The Harrovians* by Arnold Lunn. It was written in 1913 and thus pre-dates *The Loom* as an "honest" account by four years. It was its honesty that caused the trouble: boys crib and cheat, some don't like games, they are cynical about the "public school spirit", beating is often unjust, they do talk about sex. (He means about girls. Neither he nor Waugh—though the latter has one or two trifling references—really dares refer to homosexuality.) The tone, too, is mildly ironic—"It is easy to exaggerate the harm caused by confirmation. The average boy . . . soon relapses into cheerful paganism." Yet once again there was uproar and Lunn had to resign from his five London clubs. (It seems more remarkable today that he should belong to five clubs than that he should resign from them. In fact it was quite normal. P. G. Wodehouse's Psmith belonged to six West End clubs.)

But reactions were more hysterical than a few Old Boy colonel figures exploding in White's. If harsh disciplines and restraints are imposed early and young and continuously, then many adults will grow up requiring a framework of outside-imposed discipline and restraint—by clubs, by conventions, by their jobs and so on—in order to function. They will be virtually incapable of self-regulation. Not only that; they will be terrified that if the disciplines and restraints are relaxed, then their personalities will collapse. They will expect the repressed desires and aggressions to pour out in a horrifying and uncontrollable flood; and, by extension, they will spread their terror of disintegration to the country, and even the world, at large. The two books we have discussed and similar, to us, mild criticism, some gentle reform we will come to, produced precisely this exaggerated and often ferocious response.

In 1914—at a time, remember, when most accounts of discipline in the public schools and elsewhere can still make one's hair stand on end—the Duty and Discipline Movement, whose aim was "to combat indiscipline in national life, especially in the home and in the school", produced its first series of tracts, *Essays on Duty and Discipline*. These had considerable success and were to appear for a good number of years (there were forty in all).

Some quotations will give the flavour. Sometimes the titles are enough.

Here are three: *The Value of a certain "HARDNESS" in Education*, by Mrs. Arthur Phillip; *Have we the "Grit" of our Forefathers?* by the Right Hon. the Earl of Meath, PC, KP; *The Discipline of Girls*, by Madame Cecilia (author of *Labourers in God's Vineyard*).

The texts more than live up to the promise of the titles. Here are two short extracts, the first from *Sentimental England*. The author, Raymond Blathwayt, starts with a challenging question—"Are we becoming degenerate through lack of discipline?" His answer is unequivocal.

> The backbone of steel has been removed from the national body, and one of putty has been placed in its stead. . . . Today the contemptible sentimentality of a certain degenerate section of the English people banishes the rod from the classroom. . . . They will not realise that a boy who cannot take a well-deserved thrashing without crying out about it is not worth calling a boy at all . . . emasculated and degenerate nation . . . great brutal murdering hooligans . . . discipline. . . .

Or from *Save the Boys*: ". . . that ingrained aversion from the discipline and control, unfettered licence in the specious cloak of Individual Liberty, which is fast rotting the heart out of the nation and drifting it towards a roaring Niagara of final disaster."

Clearly, people who felt like this—and many of what T. C. Worsley called the Old Guard certainly did—were not going to give way in the face of a few volumes of autobiography. People who believed that the schools should be freer, wider and less repressive places were going to have to fight. This is exactly what they did.

2 Battle is joined—boys and masters

From the start certain masters had viewed the rise of games with lack of interest and even distaste. Moss of Shrewsbury found them incomprehensible. "What time do they draw stumps?" he asked at a football match. As time passed distaste grew. Bell (Headmaster of Marlborough 1876–1903) could not contain his boredom. At speech day in 1900 he said ". . . it is time to say a word about games I suppose." His successor, Fletcher, was actively hostile, but the autonomy of the various departments and the momentum of the ideology meant that it was extremely difficult to eradicate. The struggle to reduce games was a feature at Marlborough, and many other schools, for the next thirty years.

The boys struggled too—usually much more aware of, and responsive to, the world outside than their older masters. When they had real power the struggle was (relatively) easy. This was, in fact, not always the case. Prefect rule has, both here and abroad, often been called self-government.

But usually it is not—it is self-administration, which is different. Someone else makes the rules. At Eton, however, there is a certain amount of self-government. In the years after the First World War, to give one example of the sort of thing that was now going on, Eton was swept by the same scepticism and revolutionary ardour that was abroad in England. Connolly and others of his election in college called themselves left wing or liberals, and after a great deal of argument—with Old Collegers interfering—they managed to introduce sweeping reforms: beating curtailed, less fagging, fewer games and so on. These struggles were duplicated elsewhere—even where the prefect system was one of administration. After all, in practical terms, a liberal *administration* of, say, beating, is much the same as an authoritative restriction of it. And both can be easily reversed. Connolly's election was followed by one dominated by the present Lord Hailsham and the reforms were swept away.

But the conflict was often far fiercer and more dramatic. Here is an example from Charterhouse in 1914. The debating society, run by sixth-form boys, constituted at that time what emasculated intellectual life survived at Charterhouse. It was held on Saturday nights and one decorous Saturday the debate was rudely interrupted by an invasion of bloods, fresh from a victory and probably drunk. They banged books and yelled and, after calling for order, Mansfield, the president, was forced to close the debate. Everyone thought that this was the end, that the thugs had had their pleasure. But suddenly a letter appeared in *The Carthusian* about the shocking behaviour of "certain first eleven babies". Signed—Mansfield, Waller, Taylor. The school was electrified. Would they be expelled? Beaten up? Let Robert Graves continue the story:

> The Captain of Football is said to have sworn that he'd chuck the three signatories into the fountain in Founder's Court. But somehow he did not. The fact was that this happened early in the autumn term and there were only two other first-eleven colours left over from the preceding year; new colours were only given gradually as the season progressed.

So, in fact, the other rowdies hadn't been bloods at all, only hopeful would-be bloods.

> ... It was a matter entirely between these three sixth-form intellectuals and the three colours of the first eleven. And the first eleven were uncomfortably aware that Mansfield was the heavy-weight boxing champion of the school, Waller the runner-up of the middle-weights

and Taylor a man of considerable physical strength. They did nothing. Now the sixth form pounced.

Choosing their ground with care, they moved deep into enemy territory. It was Sunday Chapel. Six hundred boys had come in and sat down. Then, the bloods came swaggering in and suddenly an extraordinary thing happened. The three sixth-formers walked up the aisle magnificent in grey flannel trousers, slit coats, first-eleven collars and with pink carnations in their buttonholes. It is impossible to describe the astonishment and terror that this spectacle caused. Everyone looked at the captain of the first eleven; he had gone quite white. But by this time the masters had come in, followed by the choir, and the opening hymn, though raggedly sung, ended the tension.

The school left chapel in form order and then went to gossip in the school library. To this Mansfield, Waller and Taylor hurried, having grabbed a talkative master, whom they kept talking with them all the way down to dinner, thus effectively paralysing the increasingly demoralised bloods. Thereafter, the two boxers and Taylor kept together. The school—long irritated by dress regulations—got behind them. Finally the captain of the eleven went in desperation to the headmaster. "The headmaster, who was a scholar and disliked the games tradition, refused his request. He said that the sixth form deserved as distinctive privileges as the first eleven." They would hold, therefore, what they had taken. From now on the prestige of the bloods declined greatly.

By such small steps—seeming enormous in those tiny communities—was liberty slowly won. The battle was still raging fiercely in the 1930s. And just as often it was the masters who fought, finding ranged against them figures like The Hun at Wellington. In the early years of that decade T. C. Worsley led a protracted war. The Old Guard, or Big Five, resisted any encroachment on their personal power in the name of tradition. They fought furiously to keep every petty restriction. There was, for instance, the battle of the school caps. For many years it had been customary for boys to wear caps, each slightly different according to his dormitory (at the college, houses were called dormitories). These got lost, got dirty, were the cause of minor bullying and persecution. They were in any case absurd. Worsley canvassed around and got a good number of colleagues to support him. He raised the matter at a masters' meeting. At once the Big Five rose solid in defence: there had always been caps, why no caps now? The whole character of the school would change. What would the Old Boys say?

In the passionate argument that developed, the master (that is, the head-master) as usual compromising and playing one side against the other, the progressives began to get rather incoherent and Worsley, realising they were losing, managed with great skill and subtlety to widen the issue and also at the same time involve the master personally.

Did the master, or any of us, fully understand why there was such strong opposition to abolishing those wretched caps? It wasn't tradition at all, or care for old customs. It was this ludicrous jealousy felt by the different tutors for each other's dormitories. For these caps denoted by the colour of the ribbons round them which dormitory every boy belonged to. As long as caps were still being worn any tutor could tell at any distance whether his boys were associating with someone else's. . . . Now, I went on, trailing my coat, as the master knew it was a rule that boys in different dormitories were not allowed to talk to one another and . . .

But here as I had hoped, the master burst in. He knew no such thing. What was this rule and where had it come from? And why had it been made and by whom?

T. C. Worsley goes on to explain that it has been made by the tutors. That's why they want the caps. It meant effectively that each boy could only speak to three or four contemporaries since he could also not speak to those above or below him.

At this the master explodes. There is no such rule, never has been, only an idiot would have such a rule. He wants the fullest possible association between the dormitories and is determined, as Worsley guessed, to show the tutors who is boss. He ends:

"Kindly understand, Worsley, that I have made no such rule. . . . There is no such rule or ruling. Is that clear?"

"Yes, master."

"And if that is what this ridiculous hubbub over caps is all about, if that is the misunderstanding on which the wearing of caps is based, we had better abolish them at once."

And with that he swept out of the meeting. . . .

One man's out-of-date tradition is someone else's power base. Worsley recounts many other such 1914-like advances across this sterile no-man's-land of dead custom. Every sort of sexual innuendo is employed against him. Finally, in a passage of breathtaking excitement, he persuades twenty out of fifty colleagues to sign a petition saying that unless The Hun (Mr. Hoffman) goes they will all resign. There is a dramatic meeting—"the master was as white as a sheet"—and Hoffman *does* go. It is true he is only suspended, but it is a major victory.

Wellington at this period does seem to have been even more obsessed with sex than public schools usually are—if that is possible. T. C. Worsley's position *vis-à-vis* the innuendos employed against him is somewhat weakened by the fact that he had discovered he was homosexual and found numbers of the boys extremely attractive. Weakened, but not fatally weakened because, as he says, he had no physical designs on any of them. At the same time he was much helped, and the Old Guard were much confused, by his athletic prowess. "It made them, with their traditional ideas, mistrust their own judgment. Could a young man capable of making a hundred against the school be wholly bad?"

The sexual obsession of the school made it natural, when one amiable but bumbling master became vaguely aware that winds of change were stirring, for him to think that this was a field where progress might be made. He asked a sexologist down to address the senior members of his dormitory. The sense of outrage in the college was prodigious. They were horrified. And among the Old Guard horror became hysterical when the sexologist arrived—and was a *woman*!

Not that Dr. Jameson was exactly a provocative figure herself. She was a sensible downright woman with spectacles who, naturally in her profession, prided herself on her plain speaking.

It was part of Scotty's arrangement that after the lecture she would make time for any boy or master who wanted to discuss their sexual problems with her, and for this purpose I took my place in the queue.

We walked round the garden together, and I tried to explain my problem, the difficulty being that I still had no language in which to pose it. I seemed to be gingerly confessing to being no more than over-fond of one of the boys. Dr. Jameson wasn't standing for any evasions of that kind.

"You mean you're in love with him?"

I still hadn't put it to myself in those terms, but faced with the question I supposed I was. Yes, that must be it.

"Well, then," she went on with her brash straightforward questioning, "how far has it got?"

It had "got" no distance at all, though this sounded, in front of so formidably progressive a woman, a feeble confession to have to make.

"You mean," she went on disbelievingly, "you haven't had his organ in your hand?"

"No, indeed not." I rejected both her suggestion and the idea.

"Oh, bad luck," she said encouragingly. "Bad luck. Never mind, that will be the next step, won't it?" And she briskly rounded off the interview.

The step is never taken. From sexual inhibition, caution, for whatever reason, Worsley never had any of his pupils. Indeed only one master was caught in this way, and ironically enough it was The Hun. It had always seemed likely that he beat boys for pleasure. There was no concrete evidence but it was somehow palpable—the colossal queues of boys outside his room waiting to be beaten, his excitement, the incessant vice-searches he instituted. In the end (he had now returned from his suspension) one boy complained. It was discovered that he made convulsive grabbings at the boys' genitals as he beat them—"It's odd how much boys will put up with, without complaining"—and he was sacked.

Worsley says that Wellington was thirty years behind the times. It was not alone in being like that—Shrewsbury, Malvern, Winchester and many other schools, as well as countless pockets of reaction in individual houses throughout the system were equally rigid. And as the 30s progressed this rigidity seemed ever more intolerable. It was the period of a second, and much more radical left-wing and pacifist movement among the English upper-class intelligentsia, fuelled partly by upper-class guilt exacerbated by the depression and General Strike and also delayed reactions to the war. The Spanish Civil War was only a few years away. And the fight had been going on for so long.

Since Waugh and Lunn, autobiographies had become more and more critical—and also numerous. Graham Greene's collection had just come out and Raymond Mortimer, in his review in *The New Statesman*, had given the public schools a brilliant and savage going over. Yet nothing changed. The schools seemed immovable. Then suddenly, in the early summer of 1934, the standard was raised against the entire system. War was declared.

3 Esmond Romilly and the public school revolt

A fifteen-year-old schoolboy, Esmond Romilly, ran away from Wellington and established himself in London. From there he issued a fiery revolutionary magazine called *Out of Bounds*. Its manifesto was the clarion call at the head of this chapter.

From all over the country boys wrote in and became agents of the rebellion. In Rugby, one figure was gloomily mooching about, dry tinder to the spark. Now that the rugger season was over, "Toyners" had lost his glory. His love, Simpson, had gone cold on him (he found out afterwards that he had recalled, belatedly, the awful warnings of his prep school headmaster). But Philip Toynbee had also been working in boys' clubs. He had become disgusted at the arrogant snobbishness of his fellow middle-class schoolboys, at the self-satisfied way in which they called all non-public school boys "Blogs". He wrote at once to the magazine's agent in Rugby. There followed a period of inaction. Toynbee grew more and more restless, the hot summer working in his veins, the image of the bold young Wellingtonian boy rebel in London becoming ever more intoxicating. Suddenly, one sultry afternoon, he could stand it no more. He wrote a defiant note and, terrified at what he had done, leapt onto the train to London. He went at once to the headquarters of the revolution in Parton Street; the goal now for revolutionaries all over England, as once Herzen's house in Hampstead had been for refugees from Europe:

> A boy was leaving the shop as my taxi drew up in Parton Street, a short, square, dirty figure with a square white face and sweaty hair. "I'm looking for Esmond Romilly," I said.
>
> "Yes?"
>
> He was instantly, dramatically, on his guard, conspiratorial, prepared for violent aggression or ingenious deceit. I thrilled and trembled more hysterically than ever.
>
> "I'm Toynbee," I said, "Toynbee of Rugby."
>
> Esmond looked sharply up and down the short street, then opened the shop

door and pushed me through it. That shop! the archetype of all the "People's Books", "Worker's Bookshops", "Popular Books" that I was to know so intimately in the next five years. The solemn red-backed classics of the Marx–Engels–Lenin Institute, the mauve and bright yellow pamphlets by Pollitt and Palme Dutt, the Soviet posters of the moonlit Yalta and sunlit tractors—the whole marvellous atmosphere of conspiracy and purpose. Now I could take better stock of my Herzen, my confederate, and, I already suspected, my pitiless leader.

Six months earlier he had run away from Wellington, established his headquarters in Parton Street and launched his astonishing assault on the whole entrenched world which he had left behind him. At this period he was at the height of his intolerant fanaticism, a bristling rebel against home, school, society . . . the world. . . . In 1934 Esmond was a terrifying figure. He was dirty and ill-dressed, immensely strong for his age and size; his flat face gave the impression of being deeply scarred, and his eyes flared and smouldered as he talked.

This was the figure I confronted in the Parton Street bookshop.

"I've run away," I said.

At once they were plunged deep in thrilling talk. Toynbee forgot his terror at running away and in the heat and excitement of that atmosphere quietly transformed it into a totally committed Communist revolt. His courage held for two heady days. But for Romilly and his supporters it lasted all that summer.

Delegates arrived at Parton Street from other public schools, and we interviewed them in our office behind the shop. "Ledward of Charterhouse— no bloody good." "Pilkington of Lancing—he's done some useful work." Esmond infected me with his apocalyptic faith in the imminent downfall of the citadel. The evidence was small enough but already a headmaster had lost his nerve and expelled an *Out of Bounds* agent, already three Eton boys had resigned in a body from the Officers' Training Corps, already an assistant master had promised an article.

Two more issues of *Out of Bounds* were printed, with explosive articles and news: "Headmaster's Expulsion Threat", "The Sex Question in Public Schools and Girls' Schools", "Dartmouth Royal Naval College Exposure". Money was pressing to the revolution. But Romilly's method of financing *Out of Bounds* was simple. After each issue he transferred his patronage to a new printer, leaving debts, threats and furious printers behind. But he was surviving and so was the magazine.

There was a curious, calm interlude in June and July when he spent, at its invitation, two months at Bedales. He liked it, its amiability and tolerance; but he was an anarchist, and did not want "comfort and security". Besides, it was not the enemy.

In late summer, he carried the war into the enemy camp. He paid visits to the great public schools, to inflame by his oratory and sell *Out of Bounds*. Once he went in the guise of a boy's uncle. The public schools fought back

furiously. Uniformed cadets were set on him; another time he was thrown
into a river by boys acting as hounds to a master's huntsman.

Few had Romilly's bravery. Toynbee fled back to Rugby after two
days. He was expelled, but so gracefully and kindly, allowed to say
goodbye to Simpson and his other friends—"Good luck, Toyners, good
luck"—that it scarcely hurt. Indeed, as he says in his fine book, *Friends
Apart*, from which I have taken these extracts, for him the end was
summed up by Evelyn Waugh's Captain Grimes. Some months later he
applied for a reference to an Oxford College, and received a glowing one.

"We consider," wrote the headmaster, "that the boy's action was in
many ways a fine one."

"They may kick you out," said Grimes, "but they never let you down."

The public schools could afford to be magnanimous. Romilly's rebellion posed no threat. Those "grim inscrutable forces in the red and brick
walls" remained intact. Nevertheless, personal, school-level struggles of
this sort—and there were hundreds of them, small and large, in all
schools, throughout this period, many of them successful—were one
definite strand in the forces bringing about change. It is now time to look
at a third—changes and experiments brought about officially by, or in
numbers of the public schools themselves.

4 Pockets of change in the public schools: Gresham's, Rugby, Rendcomb, Sanderson of Oundle

I said that if anyone around 1900 had suggested to the public schools that
they were in need of reform they would have thought he was raving mad.
This was an exaggeration—in fact there were at all times critics and
experimenters within the system itself. Rugby between 1914 and 1920, for
instance, was intensely preoccupied with the problems of greater freedom,
wider curriculum, more self-expression as opposed to the usual conservative line.

The autonomy—in houses, classrooms, and the many other sub-
departments of a public school—meant that always, but increasingly as the
20th century continues, little pockets of enlightenment or culture could
spring up, flourish and often perpetuate themselves even in the most
reactionary schools. It is clearly out of the question to chart so complex a
growth—it would be very boring for one thing. But a few examples will
show what I mean.

At Marlborough (where, oddly enough, William Morris was at
school), still violent, athletic and philistine in the 1920s, a marvellous art
department (art departments have frequently been oases of sanity and
freedom) developed under Anthony Blunt, Ellis Waterhouse and
Christopher Hughes. The last was not only an inspired teacher but "talked
to you as if you were his own age". The same sort of thing happened at

Haileybury in 1921. Robin McDouall, the distinguished writer on food, remembers being taken to his first Gauguin exhibition by his art master. Music has been strong at Winchester since Dyson was there (1924–37), a tradition strengthened by Watson.

Something of the same sort can sometimes be found in girls' schools, but the tradition of the all-powerful headmistress meant there were not small autonomous developments to nearly the same degree. Societies and hobbies became moderately numerous at Cheltenham in the 30s, but largely because they were encouraged by Miss B. M. Sparkes (1922–36).

Girls had another path to freedom. The accomplishment origin remained an influence, with its theoretical base that women should be educated to fill a special rôle. This affected the curriculum in public schools. There was always more music, art and so on, and many schools had special "girls'" courses—domestic science, botany, etc. But the accomplishment/academy side of girls' education was perpetuated by small private boarding schools which became extremely numerous in the 1920s and 30s, especially in the south of England. These were liable to abrupt and violent fluctuations in "tone". Neville Coghill, talking to Maurice Richardson, remembered one started in the late 1920s by two very old schoolmistresses who had been saving for years. It was forced to close in the middle of the second term when five in the sixth form were discovered to be pregnant (the bootboy). This is a path we cannot really explore, but it is relevant to our subject in that these schools contributed (and still do) an appreciable proportion of middle-class girls' education in England. They are therefore a reason there are not more girls' public schools.

But the Rugby of Dr. David (1909–1921) shows how radical some of the autonomous developments in boys' schools could be, running, if only for a while, directly counter to the accepted views. David was clearly an interesting man. William Plomer at fourteen remembered him lending his copy of Turgenev, and he enabled Plomer to avoid all games and certain classes. But his particular concern was the average or stupid boy, whose life was so boring. The autonomy of so many masters meant he could do little and on the whole Rugby was at this time a rigid philistine and unpleasant place, but it was also the setting for an experiment in progressive education such as we've so far only met in that movement itself.

J. H. Simpson had been much influenced by Homer Lane, the American educationalist, and he disliked the class bias of public schools; he also disliked the intense competitive stimulus. Simpson felt that the point about the competitive method—still widely used in public schools today—was that while it certainly spurred the best boys on to do better, it meant that two-thirds of the form had to fail. Said to be a method based on success it was actually one based on failure. This was a depressing atmosphere to learn in for most of a form (though not necessarily a depressing one to teach in). Third, Simpson disliked the imposed disciplines and rigidity and the lack of respect this showed.

He had been educated at Rugby, and he returned to teach there from 1913 to 1919. There was nothing he could do about the class bias at this time and in this setting. The other two, however, having a completely free hand in his classroom, he was able to affect. It consisted of boys from thirteen to sixteen who were probably typical: they were well behaved, friendly and easy to manage, and worked quite hard. They were, however, unspontaneous, unenquiring and completely subservient to convention. First of all Simpson introduced a system of self-government into the discipline and organisation of the class. Punctuality, tidiness, the general running were all handed over to the boys, who elected a chairman and various officers. This alone proved extremely stimulating, but it was not a large enough field. So Simpson introduced it into the work side.

He worked out a complex system whereby if the form *as a whole* achieved a certain standard over a certain time then it could win rewards—half days, expeditions and so on. Also, as far as possible, he let them correct, criticise and mark their own and each other's work. It was a success. Since the work of everyone, however slow or stupid, contributed to the general target and therefore to the rewards, the work improved rapidly. Freed from restrictions, the whole form became a far more exciting place to work in, with continuous and spontaneous discussion. Controlling each other and themselves, cheating stopped. Simpson also found it far more exhausting than conventional classroom methods.

It seems that he was only allowed to continue his experiment for a year or two. "I was transferred to other work," he says, rather enigmatically. But it is a tribute to Rugby and Dr. David that he was allowed to experiment to this degree at all. In the 20s he became headmaster of a completely progressive school, Rendcomb.

Now these pockets of advance and relaxation are interesting, but there were more substantial experiments within the system. Howson of Gresham's, Holt, is an example. He hated athleticism and encouraged work, but encouraged it on an individual basis (there was a magnificent library, where the boys could virtually teach themselves). He knew all his boys by name, and encouraged his housemasters to become friendly with their boys (all this was in 1900).

Howson was, thus far, successful. Auden, who was at the school in the early 1920s, said this about it: "I was—and in most respects still am (he is writing in 1933)—mentally precocious, physically backward, short-sighted, a rabbit at all games, very untidy and grubby, a nail biter, a physical coward, dishonest, sentimental, with no community sense whatever, in fact a typical little highbrow. . . ." Yet Auden was never bullied at Gresham's, could make friends with anyone he chose, could roam freely (there were virtually no bounds) and was, with one crucial exception, very happy there.

The exception was in the area of discipline where Howson made his most significant contribution. By 1900 a number of people were becoming sickened by the barbaric methods of punishment and violent disciplines. In an attempt to alter this, Howson abandoned corporal punishment and introduced what he called the "honour" system. Let Auden describe its operation in the 1920s, essentially the same as when it was started in the 1900s.

> About a week after he arrived every new boy was interviewed separately by his housemaster and the headmaster—half-watt hypnotism we used to call it—and was asked—I need hardly say how difficult it would have been to refuse—to promise on his honour three things. 1) Not to swear. 2) Not to smoke. 3) Not to say or do or condone anything indecent.

If you broke any of these promises you had to confess the breakage to your housemaster. Howson was also an enormously powerful personality. He managed to create the feeling in the school that it was for the good of the community that the honour system should be upheld.

The honour system worked. It also supposed, and sometimes produced, for that time, a new relationship between a boy and his housemaster. The idea was—if you tell me you have done wrong, I shan't punish you, I shall try to help you. A housemaster was someone you could consult. But at the same time it produced an extremely repressed community founded on guilt and fear—fear of informers, fear of "sin", guilt about breaking promises, or not reporting people who had broken theirs. The strain on some people was overwhelming. Auden compares Gresham's in this respect to a fascist state.

The point is that shame, the fear of what the community will think, the fact that what your peers think of you is what matters, are extremely potent forces. It has been discovered and used by many primitive cultures. The Manus, for instance, rely on it entirely to transform their adolescents, free and spontaneous after a care-free childhood, into property-, money- and prudery-obsessed adults. All public schools use it to some degree. We saw how Arnold used it in his elevation of the sixth form and reliance on his prefects. Howson was rather like Arnold in some ways. He had touches of the same mad fervour. The boys in his own house were to be "missionaries of his ideas". "In our prefects," he said, "we look for unflinching straightforwardness, desperate earnestness, and untarnished honour." His idea was not, as the progressives would have had it, to let character grow from within, but to change it from without, to mould it and stamp it. In effect he had taken the forces of moral guilt and community pressure and exaggerated them out of all proportion to bring this about.

There is always a danger that this will happen, especially when a school

J. H. Badley of Bedales.

A. S. Neill of Summerhill.

Robin Maugham while a
student at Eton.

Alec Waugh shortly after leaving Sherborne.

Esmond Romilly at fifteen, the
time of his rebellion.

Cyril Connolly while at Oxford;
on his way to be a tutor in the
West Indies.

abandons corporal punishment. But it can happen in schools where there is corporal punishment when, for whatever reason (at Gresham's it was the dominating personality of Howson), the official and unofficial sides of the school unite on the same "moral" goals. Simon Raven, writing with his customary wit, gives an example of how it happened to his house at Charterhouse in 1942. In the frenzied efforts to promote "keenness", "cleanness" and a "healthy atmosphere and a mass of cups", an informer system of the most totalitarian sort had developed. The code of not sneaking had vanished. Now it was called "showing up" and everyone did it. "Anything said or done that raised a moral issue, however piddling or remote, or that touched upon the tone or efficiency of the house, was suitable material for retailing to the authorities." He gives a number of odious examples:

> Chancing one day to be watching a cricket match, I was approached by a boy called Fisch:
> "Matron," said Fisch, "has asked me to tell you that your hair is too long and you must get it cut."
> "Tell matron," I said, "that I like it long and she can mind her own bloody business."
> And that, apparently, was what he did tell matron—verbatim. A summons from the head monitor followed fast.
> "What's this I hear about you telling matron to mind her own bloody business? She's complained."
> I explained the circumstances.
> "It never occurred to me," I said, "that Fisch would even dream of reporting my remark back to matron."
> "But," said the head monitor, "he was very properly showing you up to matron for taking an insolent tone behind her back."
> "I suppose you could look at it like that."
> "Any responsible person looks at it like that. ... . I shall beat you this evening."
> So I received four strokes of the cane, which I didn't care for, and a severe reminder, which I cared for even less, of what Cave-Watkins had told me the previous term. This reminder was the more sharp as Fisch was shortly afterwards appointed to some rudimentary office which carried authority over the first-year boys. He had scored some valuable points by reporting me and was now getting his reward.

The fact that this more usually happens (at any rate during the period up to about 1940 or so, though there are many examples even today) in schools which have abandoned corporal punishment is not an argument in favour of keeping that form of discipline. You might as well say that the bad effects of low wages in the Southern states of America were an argument for returning to slavery. There are arguments against slavery and corporal punishment quite independent of what took, or takes, their place. But we must bear in mind the excessive use of guilt and of community shame (with community support or not) when we come later to look, for instance, at Bedales again and at Bryanston or when we consider practically all girls' schools during this whole period. It is yet another area where total society fervour can get out of hand.

"The first truth a schoolmaster has to learn," wrote Auden—and he was for a time a master himself, and an inspired one—"is that if the fool would persist in his folly he would become wise. . . . There is far too much talk about ideals at all schools. Ideals are the conclusions drawn from a man of experience, not the data: they are essentially for the mature."

Education is often written about, but it is above all a practical art; it only exists when it is practised. It is about how to teach something to one person, how to teach it to another, how to stimulate, whom to encourage and when, whom to reprove, how to keep order and so on. The story of Sanderson, the last major figure in this chapter, is above all about the practical and changing progress, by trial and error, of a teacher and headmaster through this art.

When the governors of Oundle chose a new head in 1892 they felt vaguely that it was time for a new type of man. Even then, when conventional public schools were at the height of their conventionality, Oundle was regarded as extreme. It hadn't really changed for 500 years, except to add games obsession to Latin and beating. F. W. Sanderson was a young science master from Dulwich. He had not himself been to a public school and, with huge owlish spectacles, he was hopeless at games. He had no fixed ideas or plan of action like Reddie, but he had noticed three things: most boys were bored by the classics, whereas they were usually interested by the practical work of science; he didn't want any spectators, as many people as possible should participate in everything; he disliked, for the same sort of reasons as Simpson, the competitive method. With these rather vague aspirations, he set out to alter Oundle.

The result was extraordinary. It was as though he had tried to start a revolution (which of course he had). As one man, the school rose against him. The struggles of Worsley or Simpson were as nothing to those of Sanderson. Every imaginable weapon was used against him—he was "no sportsman", "no cricketer", "no scholar", "no gentleman". Classics-soaked prefects derided him behind his back, with scarcely veiled support from equally classics-soaked masters. To start a new school in the rigid years of the 1890s was tough enough; to alter an existing one, whose concrete had been hardening since the Middle Ages, must have seemed almost impossible. He had seven years of incessant opposition with almost the whole school united against him.

The climax came when the boys wrote a viciously satirical play, full of Latin tags and classical puns and allusions; many of the staff themselves contributed. It was a mock trial of an incendiary who had been found trying to burn down the new laboratories. Every speech, says an eye-witness, was full of "envenomed and insulting references both to the headmaster and all the things he was trying to do". Finally it was rehearsed before him. He sat brooding over it thoughtfully, as shaft after shaft was launched against him. "It did not seem so funny then," said the witness, "as it did when we had prepared it." The end was greeted with "ragged and unconvinced applause". Then "came a pause—a stillness that could be felt". The headmaster sat with downcast face, thinking. At last, after several minutes, he rose slowly to his feet. "Boys will regard this as the final performance," he said, and departed thoughtfully, with no more comment. He took no further action—neither punishing nor reproving—ignoring it with complete contempt.

But he had won. From then on the spirit of the school seemed to change in his favour. Sanderson was a scientist and his method of progress was that of a scientist—continuously experimenting, using trial and error, aided by sudden flashes of insight, then bit by bit discovering new ways of doing things, working out theory to support them, and then moving on and changing again. He never lost the adolescent ability to change. The way he changed Oundle, and to what, can perhaps best be introduced by describing how he changed his attitude to punishment.

The opposition and battles of the first years caused him frequently to lose his temper. He would be goaded far beyond a dignified silence and become furious with his pupils. He would seize them and thrash them in "a hail of swishing strokes that seemed almost to envelop them". The cuts fell everywhere and anywhere, on back, legs, fingers. It was the frustration of a man tried too far.

But gradually he beat less and less. During the last ten years there was no beating at all. By the end of his life he had come to think that all punishment was wrong—having passed through a stage during which he thought that prefects should punish: "Punishment, I declare from years of experience in this experiment, is a crime; not only a crime, a blunder." The ideal was this: "The community has so to arrange itself and adapt itself as to produce the reaction in the individual not to do objectionable things. . . ." This was not easy. It meant influencing by example, it meant instilling a sense of community and awakening loyalty. But as far as discipline went, Sanderson, by trial and error, had groped his way from a "white heat" of the 1840s type to what, in school terms, was a pacifist.

It is fascinating to trace his progress, similar in style, in the field of teaching itself. "When I became a headmaster"—this is an extract from his last speech—"I began by introducing engineering into the school—applied science. The first effect was that a large number of boys who could not do other things could do that. They began to like their work in school. They began to like school. That led to introducing a large number of other sciences, such as agricultural chemistry, horse-shoeing (if that is a science), metallurgical chemistry, biochemistry, agriculture. . . ." He built an observatory, a meteorological station, botanical gardens and an experimental farm, workshops, laboratories, metal and woodshops; a drawing office sprang up; halls for dynamos, motors and heat engines; a forge and a foundry—so effective, so *practical*, was this vulcan paradise that when the 1914 war came the workshops were easily converted and poured out munitions.

But now Sanderson moved on. Boys enjoyed the practicality of science, the doing of things; but he also noticed they did this better if they did it themselves and if they were given projects which extended over time. Furthermore, they enjoyed doing things in groups. Out of this grew the *science conversazione* each summer. These were group projects, done partly in school time and partly in their own time, to do with such things as building engines, working out experiments in geology or chemistry, setting up biological tests or programmes and so on. But the excitement and success of these projects—there were hundreds—extended themselves. Gradually group activity—as opposed to the sitting-in-forms lecture— became the basis of the mathematics, partly because this itself became a base for attacking the various problems arising in the laboratories and workshops.

Some years passed, and it suddenly occurred to Sanderson he could apply the same principles to literature. This at the time was largely the study of plays, and plays meant Shakespeare—the method was the annotated edition, books of criticism, the third-rate lecture (the method still in many schools). Sanderson said a play was to be acted and viewed. That was the only way to judge. So all plays were acted, viewed and judged. But since there were too many boys for one company, group companies formed. Thus there were three or four Othellos, five Desdemonas, four Iagos and so on. They all acted together, discussed together; discussed the business, the motivation, the interpretation of character and so on. Sometimes out of this a single definitive cast and interpretation would emerge and the play put on for the whole school. Sanderson made them read Shaw, Pirandello, Ibsen.

What could work for literature might work for history. It did. The school library took the place of a laboratory, and was as necessary. The official *Life* of Sanderson gives a typical scheme of a form studying the period 1783 to 1905. The subject was first divided into parts; let us say the *ancien régime* before the French Revolution; the French Revolution; the growth of the Industrial System; the effect of the Revolution on England; the railways, etc. The form was divided into groups and each group selected one of these parts. The object for a group was to provide, by the end of the term, a full report for the rest of the form, with maps, graphs, etc., on the section they had chosen. The master would give a general survey, and then each boy would set to on his sub-section of the part chosen by the group—reading, writing, discussing with the master and other members of the group. Then, gradually, the group would start to come together, discuss the report, draft it, prepare the material and eventually complete and present it. In some cases, or areas, where the group was in disagreement, there would be a minority report.

I have gone into all this in some detail, partly because education is a practical art. It is all very well talking about a "wider curriculum", "making work more interesting", "stimulating the pupil", and all the other phrases we have used about the progressive movement. Sanderson is a way of demonstrating them in action.

But also these methods and developments at Oundle had a number of interesting results. First, Sanderson himself became popular, then adored. He was a confused, abundant speaker, whose ideas poured out in a creative torrent. He was a brilliant classroom teacher who made science all-absorbing. His masters loved him and worked for practically nothing. Once, in the days when he was still beating, he caught a boy misbehaving in prayers. He seized him, rushed him out and beat him somewhere in the distance. The whole school waited in total petrified silence. "He could have got away with murder."

There were other effects. The group method involved all the boys. In the competitive method the star pupil (or pupils) shine; they even encourage the mediocre to slack because that lessens the competition. But in a group system each boy was essential and peer pressure proved an extremely effective way of getting everyone to work.

Secondly, it might have been thought that departmentalising subjects would lead to knowledge in pockets, to no concept of the whole. In fact, the opposite was true. Boys who have received the same lesson have nothing much to talk about, except the master's foibles and who's top. But a boy who has been preparing maps of Napoleon's military campaigns, say, may have a lot to discuss with a boy who has been studying the same period from the point of view of sea power. Indeed they would add depth (and impress the master) and introduce a new dimension to their report by doing so. And in fact there was intense inter-group discussion in the attempt to modify and improve their reports by including what the others had done. The final test was in examinations. Sanderson could not alter this system (there is no evidence he wanted to), and Oundle boys did very well in examinations. "The freedom at university was absolutely marvellous," I was told, "so I did absolutely nothing for three years. But then I'd been so well taught at Oundle I didn't need to do anything."

At the same time it would be a great mistake to suppose Oundle a straightforwardly progressive school. Sanderson could not alter the athleticism, which continued feverishly into the 1950s. Sexual misdemeanours were treated in an appalling way, and they were "rife". (But no one was sacked for sexual misbehaviour. Sanderson's theory was that a school should do its best for a boy. If he was bad material that was bad luck.) There was the whole hierarchical fagging and prefect system. There was a tremendous amount of old-fashioned compulsory "sermon-stunned" religion (five hours every Sunday). The discipline and routine were extremely strict and rigid (though completely free out of school). Wells, from whose brilliant account much of mine is taken, says that Sanderson gave up beating. This may be true of him personally, but my information is overwhelming that beating continued long after him. Not till the end of the 1930s did a prefect have to get permission from his housemaster before he could beat.

All these may be reasons why Professor Stewart leaves Sanderson out of his otherwise completely comprehensive survey of progressive education. He may be right. But I would have included him. Badley, Reddie, Curry wanted to found communities with common aims. They started with that ideal and with those aims already defined. Sanderson, stumbling on from the practical method of studying science, trying it on mathematics and finding it worked there, trying it on literature and then history and finding it worked there too, suddenly found that this combination of methods had one final effect, and most important of all—his community had an ever-increasing awareness of itself as a community with common aims and common characteristics. You feel the same pioneering excitement you get from Bedales but achieved, as it were, from the opposite end. And the characteristic they shared at Oundle under Sanderson was that they had discovered—although competition wasn't absent—that creativity and co-operation were far more exhilarating and far more worthwhile.

CHAPTER 15

The Monolith Starts to Crumble

The common assumption that good habits that have not been forced into us during early childhood can never develop in us later in life is an assumption we have been brought up on and which we unquestioningly accept merely because the idea has never been challenged. I deny this premise.

A. S. Neill, *Summerhill : A Radical Approach to Education*

The last wave of progressive experiment was influenced principally by two or three thinkers and by the war. Where the majority of the public schools regarded the war as confirming, almost sanctifying, the rigid structures and disciplines they had evolved during the 19th century, some people (notably Bertrand Russell) decided, on the contrary, that the war totally condemned exactly the type of education they stood for.

People educated to revere authority, to see themselves as graded powers in its hierarchy, humbly and gratefully fit their lives into an authoritarian society. Once this is done, they become ready to die for the ideals of their masters. They are therefore ready to die at the command of central authorities for causes which do not touch their real lives. If everyone on the German side, and on the French and English sides had *refused* to fight there would have been no war. War depends on an authoritarian government which in turn depends on an authoritarian education. An education which removed imposed authority and gradually allowed the individual to evolve his own self-regulating will—to be in effect his own authority— was the only way to ensure peace. (One might note that this argument is only partly logical. A self-regulating individual is not necessarily debarred thereby from choosing war. Therefore an electorate which had had a "non-authoritarian" form of upbringing could democratically elect a government with the authority to wage a war.)

To this particular reaction to the 1914 war was added the influence, apart from Russell, of Freud and the whole rapidly increasing psychoanalytical school of thought, and the work and ideas of Homer Lane.

1 Progressive developments 1920 onwards: Homer Lane; A. S. Neill and Summerhill

Homer Lane, who worked first in Detroit, was himself influenced by the Junior Republic set up in the late 1900s by W. R. George at the aptly named Freeville in New York. This was really a self-governing community (but for delinquent toughs) very like those we found in England in the 18th century, only with a miniature American constitution instead of an 18th-century English one.

Lane's ideas were altogether more radical—and exhausting. He believed that if you allowed children complete and total freedom they would learn from the resulting anarchy the need for law and order. He was invited to England in 1913 to advise, and soon run, the Little Commonwealth at Flower Farm near Dorchester. The result was little short of horrific. The children were often delinquent, and the aggression and chaos and general smashing were at first on a heroic scale.

The Commonwealth ended tragically in 1917 with Lane accused, wrongly, by two disturbed adolescent girls of making sexual passes at them. The home secretary pusillanimously said he could not stay. Lane had seen the next stage of his experiment as teaching, but in fact he didn't teach anything at all. After four years of racketing and smashing—when a sort of order was beginning to emerge—he was just about to get round to it when the Commonwealth was closed and he was in effect deported. But he was a fascinating man, who met and strongly influenced a number of people. J. H. Simpson met him and as a result started his experiments at Rugby and later Rendcomb.. And a young officer-cadet called A. S. Neill went from Tonbridge and sat up all night listening entranced as Lane spoke. It was through these two, but particularly Neill, that Lane's ideas spread.

By no stretch of the imagination could Summerhill, the school Neill started in 1924, first in Dorset and later at Leiston, Suffolk, fit into the Bamford definition of a public school. It takes a good deal of stretching to see it as a school at all. Consisting of about twenty-five boys and twenty girls, a good many of them foreign (usually American), who normally stayed till sixteen or so, it provided, for some, an education roughly up to what we would now call O-level. Nevertheless the school and Neill have had a very considerable influence. His ideas are widely known and respected. He was honoured in Japan and Scandinavia and America, given honorary degrees by universities and his books had enormous sales. Rightly. He is, as a writer, by far the most stimulating and intelligent of the progressive educationalists. He is also the most (the only) amusing one. It is important that we should have some idea of his flavour and what he did and thought.

A. S. Neill was born in Scotland in 1883, one of the large family of a schoolmaster. He was taught by his father, in the village school at Kingsmuir. "Payment by results" operated then—the teacher was paid only for those pupils who passed elementary tests in the three R's—and his father used to cuff him to drive the lessons home. (It is interesting, incidentally, that of all the main progressive reformers only Neill was unhappy at school. Reddie, Badley and Simpson at public schools, Curry at a grammar school, only criticised when they had left.) Neill seemed to have stumbled into teaching because no one could think of anything else for him to do. After his meeting with Lane he taught at King Alfred's School for two years, becoming increasingly irritated by what he regarded as the lack of freedom. In 1920 he resigned and went to work with refugee children in Germany. Here he met Wilhelm Stekel, a follower of Freud who had broken away from him. He underwent a long analysis with Stekel which he says he found little help. It was clearly of the utmost importance however. Freudian thought was central to Summerhill and many of Neill's insights could only have come from a man who had been thoroughly analysed. ("Death enters early into every child's fantasies." "The apparent remorse or tender love that a spanked child shows towards his parents is not real love. What the spanked child really feels is hatred which he must disguise in order not to feel guilty.")

> Freud showed that every neurosis is founded on sex repression. I said, "I'll have a school in which there will be no sex repression." Freud said that the unconscious was infinitely more important and more powerful than the conscious. I said, "In my school we won't censure, punish, moralise. We will allow every child to live according to his deep impulses." [The school magazine was called *Id*.]

At the same time, like all progressives, his basic view of human nature was Rousseauesque:

> My view is that a child is innately wise and realistic. If left to himself without adult suggestion of any kind, he will develop as far as he is capable of developing. Logically, Summerhill is a place in which people who have the innate ability and wish to be scholars will be scholars while those who are only fit to sweep the streets will sweep the streets. But we have not produced a street cleaner so far. Nor do I write this snobbishly, for I would rather see a school produce a happy street cleaner than a neurotic scholar.

The point of a school was to learn to live, to learn to be happy—"hearts not heads" (not hearts *and* heads). From these positions a number of things followed.

Since the aim of education was to learn to live, and since many of the pupils sent him were damaged, much of his time was spent in psychotherapy, which in early years he called Private Lessons.

Charlie, aged sixteen, felt much inferior to lads of his own age. I asked him when he felt most inferior, and he said when the kids were bathing, because his penis was much smaller than anybody else's. I explained to him how his fear came about. He was the youngest child in a family of six sisters, all much older than he. The household was a feminine one. The father was dead, and the big sisters did all the bossing. Hence, Charlie identified himself with the feminine in life, so that he, too, could have power.

After about ten Private Lessons, Charlie stopped coming to me. I asked him why. "Don't need Private Lessons now," he said cheerfully, "my tool is as big as Bert's now."

Charlie's case was also complicated by a lie about masturbation. Once this was cleared up, he was cured. What makes Neill's book so refreshing is that his examples are all drawn, like accounts of Sanderson, from the "practical art" of education and, in his case, the art of therapy. He later abandoned Private Lessons, concluding that children are best cured when they can act out their complexes in freedom. But his approach always remained partly that of a therapist.

Freedom—that was the keynote at Summerhill. Neill was the most extreme and radical of all the English progressives. Summerhill was more or less completely free. "Before the war we had certain out-of-bounds rules made by the staff. . . . The staff room was free from invasion. Gradually these . . . have disappeared. Gradually the staff room furniture goes the way of the pupils' sitting room furniture." There was no fear. "Children will say they have broken a window. They may have to pay for it. They won't be lectured or blamed or moralised. . . . Children make contact with strangers more easily when fear is unknown to them. English reserve is, at bottom, really fear." "Many people believe deep down: *If children have nothing to fear, how can they be good?* Goodness that depends on fear of hell or fear of the policeman or fear of punishment is not goodness at all—it is simply cowardice. Goodness that depends on hope of reward or hope of praise or hope of heaven depends on bribery."

To bring about this freedom, to prevent fear, the staff must clearly not use force. There was no distinction between staff and pupils in terms of privilege. "When Billy, aged five, told me to get out of his birthday party because I hadn't been invited, I went at once without hesitation—just as Billy gets out of my room when I don't want his company."

Misbehaviour and indiscipline are nearly always due to lack of love and too much discipline. The solution was less discipline and more love. At first, for several weeks or months new pupils would run amok, "working off" or "out" their anger. Then they'd settle down.

But this does not mean there were no rules at all. There were prohibitions over bathing, cycling, air guns, alcohol and sliding down the roofs. The school council met to discuss rules, make new ones—"The school that has no self-government should not be called a progressive school . . ."—

and punish with appropriate punishments: fines, missing the cinema, replacing broken property. On the votes taken about suggested rules, Neill's vote and that of the other staff were of the same value as that of each pupil. His own suggestions were frequently voted down.

As well as rules, freedom did not mean licence. If pupils need love, it would be worthless if it came from someone they did not respect. Neill shouts at a boy kicking at his door. Another master stops football in a corridor disturbing his work. Freedom stops being freedom when it interferes with someone else; it becomes imposition.

> Once a woman brought her child of seven to see me. "Mr. Neill," she said, "I have read every line you have written; and even before Daphne was born, I had decided to bring her up exactly along your lines."
> I glanced at Daphne who was standing on my grand piano with her heavy shoes on. She made a leap for the sofa and nearly went through the springs.
> "You see how natural she is," said the mother. "The Neillian child." I fear that I blushed.

Nor did freedom mean that there were no lessons; only that lessons were not compulsory. He found, at Summerhill, that pupils from other schools had lesson aversion and had to play about before recovering. "The recovery time is proportionate to the hatred their last school gave them. Our record case was a girl from a convent. She loafed for three years. The average period is three months." Neill is a bit vague sometimes. At another point he describes someone loafing for seven years—by which time his school life must have been almost over. But certainly pupils did attend lessons, and when it was proposed once at a school council that a culprit should be punished by being banned from lessons for a week, the children protested that the punishment was too severe.

And Neill is very good on what children are like. "It is taken for granted that every child should learn mathematics, history, geography, some science, a little art and certainly literature. . . . The average young child is not much interested in any of these subjects." He also points out something which cuts the ground from under one substantial pillar in a good many utopian progressive schools and communities, though I am sure he is correct—that is that from nine to eighteen adolescents dislike boring on-the-land work unless it is very close to their interests. He tried to get the pupils to help build a sanatorium at Summerhill. They refused, and the teachers and visitors built it:

> I once read about a school in America that was built by the pupils themselves. I used to think that this was the ideal way. It isn't. If children built their own school, you can be sure that some gentleman with a breezy, benevolent authority was standing by, lustily shouting encouragement. When such authority is not present, *children simply do not build schools*.

During his life Neill was subjected to a great deal of criticism and ridicule. It was said that he was uninterested in art or literature or pictures. But since beautiful things were eventually smashed and books ripped up, there was not much point in having them. Professor Stewart describes Neill talking "wistfully" of how he would have liked two schools—one full of libraries, gymnasia, workshops and beautiful things; another, close but apart, for children with a lot of aggression to work out. As it was he was too poor. The surroundings were drab and spartan, deafening with endless jazz records.

And perhaps one should always be careful of the idealistic statement of the master—and confront it as often as possible with the usually much less idealistic statement of the pupil. Badley's level but high-minded discipline with Mr. Moorsom's "ideal Badley type", his wife committing suicide outside his house; Carleton's blithe assumption that he somehow "missed" Ustinov's originality with the bleak assertion in the report. To the master, school is his life and lives need justification; to the pupil it can be just an institution.

I spoke to Mrs. Hall, a colourful and forthright character whose son had been to Summerhill:

Terrifying. Doors ripped off their hinges and replaced by blankets. Furniture destroyed by the little sods. A hoard of psychopaths—they stole everything. If you took in food you had to hide it. They'd kick in a box to get it. We went there on November 5th. There was a huge bonfire. No staff. We rescued several little kids from the flames. When I learnt they were going to build a swimming pool I pounced and took the children away.

At the same time, Mrs. Hall was almost too colourful. Neill was very old then, but she admitted that he had cured her daughter of bed-wetting in one interview. He said, "Why are you afraid of your parents?" In fact, Neill was the least cranky, in some ways the most practical of all progressive educationalists. And while it is true he kept no proper records or statistics, it is also true that he was remarkably successful. Summerhill produced a fair proportion of pupils who achieved intellectual and professional distinction—doctors, lawyers, soldiers, engineers, artists. And this judgment is corroborated by the report of the Inspectors from the Ministry of Education, in 1949, who, while criticising some of the teaching in the junior school, noted that in the upper school it was often extremely good. They observed that "it would be difficult to find a more natural, openfaced, unselfconscious collection of boys or girls. . . ." Their summing up was this: "What cannot be doubted is that a piece of fascinating and valuable educational research is going on here which it would do all educationalists good to see."

Neill's success is the more remarkable in that it was often achieved with very difficult children. With undisturbed and easier children it would undoubtedly have been far greater. And it was achieved because he was a remarkable man—gifted with great insight and capable of giving and arousing love and loyalty in his difficult pupils to an unusual degree. And it is this that is probably his significant achievement. He had to abandon the idea that he could change the world, and realised "that my primary job is not the reformation of society, but the bringing of happiness to some few children". And by example show everyone how they should bring up children and so perhaps, in the end, save the world after all. His final statement is moving and, surely—even if in a school it requires someone of Neill's stature to implement—in the last analysis true:

> ... The basic issue is ... to make the home more loving, the child free from inhibitions, the parents free from neurosis. The future of Summerhill itself may be of little importance. But the future of the Summerhill idea is of the greatest importance to humanity. . . . The bestowal of freedom is the bestowal of love. And only love can save the world.

Neill (he was called Neill by everyone) was fairly scathing about most other progressive schools at this time, most of which he regarded as barely progressive at all. He felt close to only one man working in this field and that was to William Burnlee Curry. Curry, with Neill himself, Badley and Reddie, is one of the great progressive headmasters.

2 Curry and Dartington

The school he was to transform, Dartington, was started in 1926 as an integral part of the Dartington Hall Trust Community set up on the Dartington estate near Totnes in Devon by Dorothy and Leonard Elmhirst. It was a practical venture, to be run on the liberal progressive co-educational lines with which we are familiar, to educate the children of Dorothy Elmhirst by a previous marriage, those of the Elmhirst butler, the children of those working on the estate and in the nurseries, craft centres, etc., associated with it. The start was erratic. There was no headmaster, no work to speak of, little discipline, the masters were amateurs, one of whom tried, unsuccessfully, to administer psychotherapy; the children became exhausted by the continuous discussion and consultation. And I might emphasise here something I have already noted. It is easier to run a conventional school than a progressive one. In a conventional school rules, customs, a set curriculum, the cane (if used), all buttress the weak, unimaginative and lazy teacher. A progressive school needs more masters, and more skilful and hardworking masters. Freedom—whether in marriage, politics or schools—may be more rewarding but it is harder. When Curry came in 1931 Dartington was on the point of foundering.

Curry had been educated at a grammar school and then been at Cambridge after the 1914 war where he had been much influenced by Russell's educationally libertarian ideas. He had taught at Gresham's School, Holt, and found Howson's "honour" system a detestable form of moral and emotional blackmail. After that he taught physics at Bedales from 1922 to 1926 and finally, before coming to Dartington, went to Philadelphia. He was an intellectual and looked like one, with a huge egg-shaped head, and a certain remoteness of feeling. Everything could be solved by reason, indeed had to be and therefore emotion, nakedly displayed, could irritate him. Once at a school council one of the girls burst in and embarked on a passionate speech. Curry interrupted angrily: "What are you doing? You don't represent anyone, you can't just burst out—representing no one. You're just a political faction, a Hitler, a caucus." The girl, astounded and bewildered, burst into tears and ran from the room. Ivan Moffat, who was a boy there at the time, remembers thinking, what an odd way to describe a lone girl—a political faction, a caucus.

Dartington, like Bedales, was an exciting place to be in those early days. The realisation that, after Summerhill, it was the most permissive school in the country, bound it together. "It gave one a sense of protection towards it, a sense of privilege. And you felt it was endangered from outside." They developed a strong feeling of being a group, and this was expressed literally—The Group—and became a community consensus, what those who had been there longest felt was right. Indeed, so strong was this feeling that it became the basis for the only real punishment, which was not being allowed to attend class. Newcomers would laugh, but soon, as well as anxious about work, they would find themselves drifting about the school alone, no longer part of "The Group".

Dartington on the whole allowed considerable freedom. There were no bounds and on Sundays the pupils could go anywhere. Smoking was allowed. (It still is. It is virtually Dartington's only tradition.) Curry believed in self-government, but in limited self-government. Complete self-government, he thought, imposed too great a burden on the pupil, unnecessarily removing the security which adult help gives. He thought it also resulted in harsher laws. (He may have been right. Neill did not find this, but then he was exceptional. In the Junior Republic in America they passed a rule that anyone who didn't work and was a "burden on the community" should be allowed to starve to death.) The organisation of the school council has altered over the years but basically it is a pupil law-making body tempered by adult co-operation and is a way of making student views known. Dartington has always had the minimum number of rules required to function with reasonable efficiency. It was and is (again apart from Summerhill) the most determinedly and consistently co-educational. The boys and girls have rooms next to each other and wash and live as mixed together as in a family (and often more mixed together).

Dartington was revolutionary in another way. It was one of the first schools where an effort was made to make the conditions of life comfortable and attractive. Single bed-sitting rooms are at least potentially individual and were always pleasant at Dartington; dormitories are almost invariably hideous. The food, too, was delicious, with masses of milk, cream, meat, bread and fresh produce from the estate. For many years this was organised by a series of lady dieticians, for some reason often eccentric. One was sacked after giving a Roman banquet of lavish proportions. She said she was introducing the pupils to the diets of other ages and cultures. But unfortunately she was eclectic, asking only eight people to the banquet. This both limited the benefits of the lesson and irritated The Group. Also the banquet was extremely expensive. And the fact that the eight, clad in togas, were all strikingly good-looking also, perhaps unfairly, weakened her case.

Curry realised that not all his pupils would want to work and even in 1956 the prospectus still says that there are some pupils "to whom pure scholarship is largely meaningless, and we foresee the possibility therefore that we may have to refuse in special cases to prepare children for examinations". Nevertheless, lessons were not voluntary and in the 1930s anyone falling behind was usually spoken to and given extra work. Standards at universities were much lower before the 1939 war, and a fair proportion of Dartingtonians passed school certificate and went to them.

One might note here that, first, the general principles of progressive education at this time were, not just that work should be exciting, but that it should be done as much as possible by the pupil himself because discovering knowledge in this way was more valuable and interesting ; and second, that it is important not to press too much too early. By allowing a child's interest to dictate what he studies, although he may fall behind for a time, he will catch up much faster later on and learn in two years the work required to pass exams for which an ordinarily disciplined child will need seven or eight years.

3 1920s–40s: Bedales and other progressive developments

Both Badley and Neill were agreed on these principles, but here as elsewhere Bedales in the 1920s and 30s arrived at a compromise between conventional public school education and extreme progressive. The teaching was partly conventional and partly do-it-yourself laboratory method —with a great deal of emphasis on art and music.

In fact the more radical progressive movements of this time sometimes show the more conventional aspect of Bedales up in a starker light. Sasha Young, for instance, who was there in 1945, remembers a Rimbaud figure, wild and unconventional, who took painting far too seriously and saw himself as Gauguin. He was, she and others felt, what Bedales was really about, the sort of person they should have approved of. Yet the staff were terrified of him. He had taught his dormitory to masturbate, and this was another mark against him. He was supposed to be a bad influence and eventually, after the usual confrontations, this unconventional but harmless figure, bringer of strange delights, one of the few original people there, was sacked. It seemed a betrayal of what Bedales was supposed to stand for. There was a degree of censorship and it was during this period that Neill's books, very widely read, were twice withdrawn—in 1937 and again in 1947. There was also a tendency to over-use community pressure. One of the (to an outsider) faintly embarrassing traditions at Bedales is "The Bedales Jaw". Each evening something not necessarily, indeed not normally, religious takes place—at this period it would be a reading from Tagore or Bridges' *Testament of Beauty*—and then the whole school files out and shakes hands with all the staff—"Goodnight, Alex, goodnight, Susan, goodnight, Indira. . . ." Sasha Young loathed this and wouldn't look at the staff when she shook hands. They decided to coerce her. She would walk out in front of the whole school and *not* shake hands. She (fortunately a day girl) retaliated by never going to a Bedales Jaw again. (One has only to shift the standard of reference back to the Monolith again, of course, for all this to seem very minor. Jocelyn Brooke gloried in the freedom of Bedales after running away from King's School, Canterbury, which, constricting as a suit of armour, was notorious for organised bullying during the early 1920s.)

We should note a number of independent developments over this period. There was Bembridge School on the Isle of Wight (1919); and in the same year Simpson finally escaped from Rugby and started his own school at Rendcomb. Rudolf Steiner founded Wynstones and, in 1925, Michael Hall. This year also saw Frensham Heights, Beacon Hill, started by Bertrand Russell and his wife, which ran from 1927 to 1943.

Many of these schools—far more inventive than anything that is being done today—would be extremely interesting to explore. Frensham Heights, for example, in effect a Theosophical school without the Theosophy, was extremely successful. Rendcomb, too, is interesting. Simpson points out that "self-government" is not an automatic opposite to anarchy. Advanced teachers sometimes seem to assume that, from chaos, adolescents will somehow spontaneously arrive at some form of 19th-century democracy. In fact, far more usually "pupils' government" is imposed; it is an artificial, planned, educational device introduced, like a particular type of history syllabus, to teach them, to bring them out. This is basically the same idea we found, in Cheam for example, in the 18th century and I think there is more to it than that, but certainly Simpson is illuminating on the practical effects and advantages of self-government as an educational device.

But to go into these schools in detail would involve a great deal of repetition of things with which we are now familiar. Also the ideas behind Steiner's Anthroposophy, for example, do not yield easily, if at all, to words. I think it is enough to appreciate that by 1940 or so the cumulative weight of progressive thought and practice (to which one should add the Montessori movement of the 1920s) had become, both numerically and, to a less extent, as regards popular intellectual awareness, very considerable. All this development was in the same middle-class area served by the public schools. It was, therefore, potentially at least, another powerful source of pressure on the Monolith to change.

It might be thought that there is virtually nothing in common between Neill and, say, one of the Latin masters at Harrow today (or at any time). But they are united, as Professor Stewart points out, in one fundamental way. A school education has to do with teachers, pupils, knowledge and the institution within which they exist. The reason they exist is to pass on knowledge. They can pass on experience, morals, values, develop character and a sense of community. But this is secondary; knowledge comes first. Without this function they would be something else—homes for the children of the divorced, therapeutic institutions for the disturbed or whatever it was. But they are schools. It follows that when they are set up, the position of the teacher has already been decided on—he is to instruct, and in order to do so he must lead, in that the pupils must follow his course of instruction and fulfil certain conditions in order that they and others can do so; silence, writing essays, and so on. He is not a "natural" leader because he has not arisen spontaneously from the group itself nor has he been chosen by them. Some sort of authority rests with him from his position, and friendly attitudes (or the reverse) and relationships spring up in a situation dominated by this fact. This unites a traditional public school master even with Neill. Because, although Neill will wait and allow the pupil's inner development finally to let him choose (or reject) the situation—the situation is still there, and if he accepts it, he accepts that Neill is a teacher who has something to give and which he, the pupil, must accept, and accept those conditions in which the teacher can give it.

Of course, the spread within this frame—the essence of which is allowing that a school is in some ways arbitrary, artificial and authoritarian (if authoritarian only in the sense that the teacher is the author of the knowledge, the person from whom the learning comes)—the spread inside this frame is colossal. The progressive teacher is essentially a guide, even a therapist, concerned with his relationship to the pupil, and accepting only the minimum of dominance freely granted in order to teach; the traditional teacher, even today, reverses this order in favour of imparting knowledge, to which end he is more concerned with dominance, hierarchy and the structure of control. But, at bottom, they are the same.

4 Gordonstoun, Bryanston, Stowe

Though the progressive movement was potentially a source of pressure on the public schools to change, in fact, so small was the experimental market, the pressure was minimal. But it was minimal for another reason too. Public schools had long inured themselves to outside influences, particularly if critical. Even today, going round them, I was fascinated how bored they were if I said what another school was doing—"Oh, really?" But if experiments or mild changes were made within the system (and as far as the public schools then were concerned progressive schools were very much not in the system), they would at least pay some attention. The more firmly within the system, the more attention. For that reason I should like to look briefly at three schools which, coming within the system as they did, are both evidence that change within the public schools' educational climate was taking place, and were themselves agents of change. Let us take them in ascending order of influence.

Gordonstoun was founded by Kurt Hahn when he was turned out of Germany by Hitler; it was founded on "Salem" lines, the school he had started in Germany, a school itself based on Hahn's ideas of what an English public school was supposed to be. At first sight it appears moderately progressive: a broad curriculum, with a good deal of art and craft, boys moving up academically at their own pace, athleticism curbed and replaced by estate work and, especially, coastguard and mountain rescue and fire service; cleanliness, religion and moral blackmail complete a familiar picture. But the closer one looks the odder Gordonstoun becomes. Stewart puts it in his book in a chapter called *The Slackening Tide*; the more I read about the school the more it seemed to me the tide had become more than slack. It had turned and started to flow quite fast in the reverse direction, or rather, in a series of strange directions, dictated by Hahn's obsessions.

Hahn himself, with his wide, full face and his large hats, was a man of overpowering and autocratic character, who gave off personality in thick waves. He pumped his energy into every corner of the school and its revival when he returned from propaganda or fund-raising trips was instantly noticeable. His masters worshipped him. In this way Gordonstoun resembled some of the schools we looked at in the 1840s and 50s, being entirely dependent on and dominated by one man—as Rugby was by Arnold or King's School, Canterbury, by Mitchinson.

It was old-fashioned in other ways. Hahn was obsessed by sex. But in combating it he managed to join a Farrar-like over excitement with the relatively new art-as-a-substitute in unique and bizarre combination. Puberty was a time of poisonous passions; these were the "loutish years" when sin stalked the unwary. But experience at Salem and Gordonstoun led Hahn to believe he had made a revolutionary discovery. Dismissing any possible objection from psychologists or psychiatrists—"We feel a certain missionary obligation to unmask the psychologists' dogma as the fallacy it is . . ."—he announces his revelation, ". . . what they consider a normal development during adolescence is in fact a grave and avoidable malady." "The so-called deformity of puberty," he wrote in 1957, "should not be regarded a decree of fate." Each child has a "guardian angel" who swoops to protect him during the dangerous period of sexual change and growth. But the school, too, aids this dramatic rescue work. Each child has a *grande passion* (it is interesting that he should use the language of love) which can, by a fortunate chance, grow powerful enough during the loutish years "to prevent the sexual impulses that well up during adolescence from absorbing the available emotional energy". These *grandes passions* are to be found in arts, crafts, drama, music, sculpture, painting, etc. The extension of the curriculum into these fields at Gordonstoun has, therefore, a very different root from that found in normal progressive schools. The idea of dramatic rescue increasingly appealed to Hahn and he was continually extending it from coastguard work to fire rescue to mountain-rescue teams and, eventually, to the whole Outward Bound concept.

Heckstall-Smith, an ex-public school master and head of two county grammar schools, who went to Gordonstoun in his fifties, noticed other capricious manifestations of Hahn's obsessions. The "Trust" system generated considerable tension; this combined with "rather emotional talks to the whole school in assembly" and a sudden, dramatic snakes and ladders system of promotion produced an atmosphere of mutual sympathy among the boys such as might be found in villagers living on the slopes of an active volcano. There was, too, Hahn's desire, which did not come to anything under him, of including a few girls in the school. "I got the impression," says Heckstall-Smith, "that Dr. Hahn regarded the girls as a gymnastic apparatus for improving the character of the boys (the ones who really mattered) by giving regular practice in chivalry."

The moral fervour which pervaded the denunciation of the loutish years spread out in the same way as the idea of dramatic rescue. Although the classical athleticism was absent, there was a tremendous cult of physical fitness, of training and drill routines to improve "character". There was (and is) a complex hierarchical system of monitors, colour-bearers and guardians which was extremely strict. And in one respect Gordonstoun was not unlike the Gresham's of Howson. "Character" was improved by a "Training Plan", which after a while a boy was "on his honour" to fill in. This was a series of routines a boy had to fulfil during the day (some of them, one suspects, aimed at the poisonous passions): a morning run, cold shower before breakfast and after afternoon activities and any other exertion, two cleanings of teeth, sixty skips, five press-ups, hair washed once a fortnight and so on. It is not entirely surprising that when

Heckstall-Smith moved on to teach at Dartington he found the change "like a dressing on a burn".

T. C. Worsley had several brushes with Hahn and describes them with his usual wit. He meets Hahn when he takes him one of his private pupils for an interview. Hahn likes him and, flooding him "with a powerful shot of his own force and will-power", persuades Worsley against his will (he really wants to get on with a novel) to come and write at Gordonstoun. He will, says Hahn, "absorb the atmosphere of the school" through his pores. "We find up there by the Firth of Moray that the sea breezes blow through you. They will invigorate, they will heal." At the end of the term he can decide, and if he likes stay on and teach.

Mesmerised, Worsley accepts. Almost at once, he begins to have doubts. He finds that Hahn cannot bear to lose at anything, even—or rather, especially—games. Tennis partners are chosen for him so that they will lose; if they are better they are instructed to let him win. I have already described the incident when Hahn sniffs and smells that "someone has been talking dirt in this room". There were other such incidents. He is taking Worsley to see the coastguard watchers.

As we walked towards it there came, trotting towards us away from it, one of the duty boys, dressed in the shirt and shorts which all Gordonstoun boys sensibly wore. The lad trotted by, and Hahn stopped me and in that familiar gesture of his gripped my arm:

"Did you notice that boy?"

I had noticed him only because he was well-known as the school tart; but I wasn't sure whether Hahn would have been aware of that so I replied non-committedly:

"Not particularly."

"You didn't," said Hahn, "notice his eyes?"

I admitted that I hadn't.

"Ah!" said Hahn sadly. "You should have noticed that. That's what coast-guard watching does for a boy. His eyes were crystalline and pure. You can only see such eyes in two kinds of people;" and with immense emphasis, "ze hunter home from ze hill and ze sailor home from ze sea."

This remark, and the other from the classroom seemed to me so ineffably, so Germanically silly that I couldn't take Hahn completely seriously from then on.

In fact the visit ended, in a minor way, disastrously. Worsley found the teaching to be bad (Hahn in fact did not care very much for scholastic attainments). Then he had a row over a boy not being allowed to play Hamlet because he spent a week with a prostitute in Edinburgh—an almost unparalleled explosion of the loutish years one would have thought, considering it was by someone deep in a *grande passion*. Finally, things came to a head over the Spanish Civil War, then raging. Hahn wanted to take a Spanish noble's son, because titles were very useful to a new public school in the 1930s. Worsley said that he shouldn't, because the Spanish noble was a fervent Franco supporter. Hahn argued that there would always be élites; the rôle of the educator was to train the élite to rule justly. This seemed to Worsley a compromise with a vicious system. He also thought the public school education provided training for a middle-class dictatorship and that Hahn's theories of education were close to Nazi-ism despite his high-flown rhetoric. He said all three things and Hahn flew into one of his rages.

"How dare you say such a thing after what I have suffered! You who have suffered nothing! Don't you know what happened to me at Salem?"

I knew, of course; the tale was often retold at Gordonstoun. But he told it again: how he had resisted the Nazi infiltration into his famous school for as long as he could, and when he couldn't any longer, and a Nazi Youth Group was formed, how he clung to the hope that he would be able to teach them the difference between good rule and bad; how he hoped to permeate this new élite with the Platonic Spirit; how, all the same, his dismissal was pronounced, and how—and this seemed to be the giveaway in his defence— he appealed to Hitler personally to be allowed to stay—and was refused. And he had to be smuggled out.

"So," I said triumphantly, blundering on without any thought of the pain I might be causing, "it was just for the accident of your being a Jew, that you finally had to leave? Otherwise you'd have been quite happy to stay?"

At this second, wholly unsubstantiated accusation, he flushed a deep red and instead of replying, picked up a large heavy book and flung it at my head. It missed. I picked up another and flung that at him, which ended not only that conversation but my association with Kurt Hahn and Gordonstoun.

That same slack tide, which carried Gordonstoun eccentrically spinning in its eddies, also bore Bryanston to the shore. As far as their history goes, the significance of Bryanston to the public schools is clear. By the mid-1930s the ideas we have discussed had gained sufficient ground for a basically conventional public school—with a hierarchical monitor system and moderately strict routine—to start up with a good many progressive features and not only for no one to be particularly surprised but for the school to be a success. Bryanston had no fagging, no ban on boys of different houses or ages mixing, a modified games ethic, a wide curriculum which encouraged art and—Coade's obsession—particularly the theatre. Caning was replaced by runs, free time was free, and the boys wore shorts to symbolise some vague aspiration towards the open air—a uniform which in later years was to make them look increasingly ridiculous. Coade, the second but really the founding headmaster, had a genius for choosing staff—among whom Wilfred Cowley, a brilliant teacher and delightful man, was outstanding. The most interesting thing about Bryanston, educationally, was its adherence to the Dalton Plan.

The Dalton Plan began in 1900, when Helen Parkhurst aged sixteen found herself teaching forty-eight pupils in a log cabin in Wisconsin. They were spread in age over eight grades (what we call forms) and the only way she could cope was to plan individual schemes of work and give them to the pupils to get on with while she taught the others. It worked, and Helen Parkhurst spent fifteen years developing it. In 1920 it was adopted for the State school of her home town, Dalton. Shortly after this it was brought to England and publicised in the *Times Educational Supplement.* Quickly, it became extremely fashionable and by 1926 over 2,000 schools were using it (and this too is a striking indication of how far we have come since 1900). But within fifteen years—largely because, like all progressive ideas, it made heavy demands on staff—it had died away. The schools returned to class teaching or various adulterated Dalton-type systems. Only Bryanston kept it—and continues to do so—pure and entire.

The essence of the system is that pupils increasingly work on their own. "Assignments" are set—let us say the French Revolution—and a time limit, say three weeks and so many forty-minute periods. Typed sheets are handed out with suggested reading, setting essays, pointing out topics, giving lists of questions to answer and so on. The pupils can come and discuss the subject with a master at various set times, and, of course, discuss it with each other. At the end of the three weeks the assignment is gone through, judged and marked. At the start of school the assignments are short and simple and there is a lot of class work. As the pupil moves up, the assignments become harder and more numerous until by the end he or she spends most of the time working alone.

With Stowe, started in 1923, we have almost returned to the Monolith —yet not quite. J. F. Roxburgh was an intriguing, in some ways enigmatic character whom it would be interesting to explore. There is time only for a brief sketch, but Noel Annan, whose account I follow, has written an excellent biography—*Roxburgh of Stowe.*

At first glance, Stowe seems completely conventional. Roxburgh always stated he wished to preserve the good qualities found in public schools—the loyalties, the scholarship, etc.—and in his eagerness to keep these he appears to have kept everything else: there was beating, fagging, a rigid prefect system and games. Roxburgh added nothing to the curriculum, to educational theory or to methods of organisation. He had wanted to abolish beating and fagging, but did not dare. He thought Stowe would be thought *outré* if he experimented with new methods of punishment— and thereby lose that class feeling which when Stowe started was essential for a successful public school. Class was where the money was, and this (though one cannot help feeling there was more than an element of snobbery in it) was why he pursued aristocrats. "To watch him with a countess," says Annan, "was a marvel: there was no hint of obsequiousness but he somehow managed to convey that, while to talk on terms other than that of equality would be odious, there was a subtle difference between her and the humanity round and about." Soon after he had opened the school at Stowe, the old home of the Dukes of Buckingham, the local hunt, the Grafton, began at his invitation to meet there again. He believed in a ruling class and that the duty of the public schools was to

> keep up the tradition of conduct, bearing and speech which marks off the well-bred Englishman from others. The first justification of an aristocracy is that it shall give leadership and service. But the second is that it shall maintain a standard of culture and refinement to which other classes can look—and eventually rise.

"We should all like," he said at another time, "to see the English nation a single nation. But it does not do any good to say that it is a single nation if it isn't." Certainly, he did not see it as his job to alter this state of affairs, and in later years there was always a special pleasure in his voice that so many old Stoics were doing well—"Some in the Arm-ah, some in the Nav-ah and some propping up the pound in the Cit-ah."

It may be wondered, with all this, how Roxburgh and Stowe can in any meaningful sense be described as agents of change. The answer lies in the character of Roxburgh himself. He was tall, extremely elegant, theatrical —"a bit like a noble, middle-aged *jeune premier*", said T. H. White—with a flamboyance, a sense of being larger than life which boys, in particular, like in a schoolmaster. He had a profusion of perfectly cut suits—"Another new suit, sir?" "Old as the hills, dear fellow"—from which he would produce huge coloured silk handkerchiefs (at the end of his life he was tested and six were found on him). He had a flow of talk and a light, almost camp humour. One day a heavy youth was reciting from Tennyson's *The Miller's Daughter* in a deep grating voice and an air of gloom:

> "And I would be the girdle
> About her dainty dainty waist."

The form began to titter. "Go on, my dear fellow—a very laudable ambition." He was also an inspired and incisive teacher. Even towards the end of his life he was still taking nineteen lessons a week.

Roland Oliver, who was taught by him in the late 1930s, wrote:

> What one chiefly remembers was the excitement of that wonderful period once a week when, whether it was Gothic architecture, or Virgil or Racine, one could be absolutely certain that there would be no boredom for forty minutes. There one was faced with the alertness of a lion tamer, the polish of a great actor and the tremendous communication of energy which is inseparable from great teaching.

His classical learning had taught him to value precision and clarity above all intellectual virtues; his self-disciplined Scots background to detest intellectual dishonesty. Evelyn Waugh, who was taught by him at Lancing (Roxburgh was there before being chosen Headmaster of Stowe), remembers one morning, after the school had sung Cowper's "God moves in a mysterious way", how Roxburgh launched into a devastating examination of the poem with his form:

A mine is a hole from which you extract something or else an explosive weapon. In neither case would you "treasure up" anything in it. And how, if his footsteps are on the sea, does God get into his mine? Is the "never failing skill" something God put there or found there? What is the use of the skill if it lies in "unfathomable depths"? If his "designs" are "treasured up" they are presumably not put into practice. How then does he work his sovereign will?

One can see the genesis, in part, of Waugh's sharp, pure, non-cant prose. But these sides of Roxburgh—his wit, his incredible energy, his brilliance as a teacher, his panache—are not the most important. He was, as Annan makes clear, a homosexual who succeeded in spreading and generalising his love so that it encompassed all his pupils and yet, paradoxically, at the same time allowed him to concentrate on each one as an individual.

His life was full of deep and genuine kindnesses. Here, from his Lancing days, is one of innumerable examples. One Friday, in chapel, as the Litany was ending, a boy leapt to his feet and scrambled along the chairs in front of the whole kneeling school and, having just got to the aisle, vomited. He then fled from the chapel. It was a boy called Rivers-Moore; a scholar, small for his age, short-sighted, spotty, devout, the son of an East End clergyman who was also a socialist. He was made for bullying, and he was bullied. Nobody noticed Roxburgh slip out of the chapel, but when the school poured out he could be seen in the chapel quad walking to and fro with his arm round Rivers-Moore. A witness wrote afterwards: ". . . it was his natural reaction. But it made an impression on me. I was one of Rivers-Moore's persecutors. . . ."

In fact, although Roxburgh loved intelligence and skill, grace, beauty and breeding, it was above all *need* he responded to, and he was thus as able, or even more able, to take in the scruffy and unprepossessing as he was the more obviously favoured. He always preferred the boys to the staff, and unmarried staff to married ones. (After the war he greeted the wife of a master who had just married and whom he had in fact already met three times with the words "At last we meet".) It was the elevation of individual attention to something that took place on a school-wide basis that distinguished him and Stowe. We have seen Cory's long reports, but detailed reports were still rare in the 1920s and Roxburgh's were both long and detailed. Howson at Gresham's had taken care to know all his pupils' names, and Gray at Bradfield had shown parents over the school before the First World War. But such concern for parents and pupils was still remarked on when Roxburgh showed it, which he did unfailingly. He not only knew his boys' names, he knew their nicknames often, their birthdays—he would give them presents, or, if they were prefects, dinners with "wine and Egyptian cigarettes". He concentrated on them. "He was extremely generous—a dinner at Hatchett's followed by Covent Garden to see Max Reinhardt's production of *Oedipus Rex* for six members of sixth form just before the spring term began." He seemed able to remember effortlessly and for ever the names, histories and parents of boys in a way which, even today, can tax the most diligent. Headmasters and headmistresses still try to emulate him—and sometimes it might be better if they didn't try so hard. One very senior mistress, a rather absent-minded but completely dedicated woman, went recently from Roedean to be Headmistress of King Edward's School for Girls in Birmingham. She got on a bus, rather tense with the burdens of her new post and, walking to the front, passed a strange man. She gave him, to his surprise, a strong, deliberate smile. Then she sat down some way ahead. Her stop was before his and on the way out she paused beside him and said, "I must apologise for smiling at you just now. I'm so sorry, but I thought for a moment you were the father of some of my children."

Roxburgh could never have made a mistake like that. And the concentration of his attention, his concern with each individual, was reflected in Stowe. He introduced individual games like tennis, fencing and golf; in the sixth, games ceased to be compulsory. Art and literature were as important as games. These were blows against athleticism. The evenings and weekends were completely free. There were no boy-made privileges —buttons done up, ways of carrying books, etc. It is impossible with Roxburgh—or indeed any master—to say how many boys he influenced. As Annan says, it is assumed that a "great" headmaster's virtues sink into boys by a sort of osmosis. This is not so. Many ignore him or are hidden in pockets round the school, out of reach. But his shifting of the emphasis onto the individual, his kindness, certainly affected a good number of people personally—at Oxford and Cambridge contemporaries found to their surprise that old Stoics had liked their school, where they had loathed their own. Stowe did bring pressure to bear on the Monolith, even if it was fairly mild—and it was the greater because it came from a school which the vast body of other public schools could quite clearly see was one of themselves.

5 The Cosy Years; cracks in the Monolith

This period from around 1914 to 1940 is in some ways the most difficult so far because it is the most diverse. The main picture to hold in the mind is still the Monolith: restrictive, snobbish; with classics (and to a certain extent, later, "arts" subjects like English and history) overwhelmingly important; incredibly and ridiculously hierarchical and conformist, with bullying and beating in the early years, the momentum of athleticism continuing and so on. But the processes we have been exploring, the increasing criticism and fury from those who had been at the schools, the more general criticism of writers like Strachey, Shaw, Wells, Compton Mackenzie, the battles that raged and which we exemplified by Worsley and had described by Graves and Toynbee, the attempts to find less oppressive methods of discipline (Howson), the development of ever more radical progressive schools and ideas, the consolidation and spread of old ones and the appearance of some of their ideas among conventional schools—in Bryanston particularly, Gordonstoun in bizarre form and Stowe very mildly—all these, many themselves evidence of change, did begin to have an effect. The *zeitgeist* of the 20s helped; even where the anarchy and freedom were often trivial and numerically minute—a sliver of upper-class boors being sick into one another's hatboxes. So too did the left-wing reactions of the 30s to the Depression and the Spanish Civil War. Upon the Monolith we must superimpose a mass of hairline cracks; chunks fall away, holes appear, more cracks.

For instance, games. It is true, as I said, that athleticism remained strong into the 1930s; but it was weakening steadily. At Eton a wet-bob who rowed could usually pass most of the time peacefully on the river developing, at up-stream pubs, a taste for beer. At Charterhouse (1917–23) you were given points for athletic activities: five for a run (along the top of the Hogs-back), five for a cricket or football match, three for rowing. You had to amass a certain number of points in a week, but could suggest alternative forms of exercise. This was fairly mild. Winchester has something of the sort now. Raymond Mortimer and John Betjeman (Malvern and Marlborough) were both hopeless at games. The doctor managed to find a heart condition for Raymond Mortimer (even now, at eighty-two, a man of enormous vitality) and he played golf all the time; at the end John Betjeman "somehow just didn't do anything". By 1932 some houses at Marlborough let games stop being compulsory at sixteen. By 1940 it was possible, but difficult, to avoid the games side at Oundle.

In the early 1920s a friend of Simpson asked a well-known headmaster (he gives no name; Simpson's criticism of the public schools is incredibly discreet) whether he should take an Educational Diploma—a Dip. Ed. "It can do no harm. And, after all, you need not tell people you have been trained." By the end of the 1930s an entirely new calibre of headmaster was appearing on the scene, with men like Robert Birley at Eton and Robert Longden at Wellington. We can trace the same upward movement among staff generally.

The schools had always supported great scholars, for instance H. G.

Dakyas at Clifton in 1900, or Page at Charterhouse, the editor of the great Loeb translation of the classics, or Coulton, the medieval historian who taught at several public schools. But these men were usually remote from teaching and spent all their time at the work which would eventually lift them to the universities. This tradition continues, only now the scholars start to get more involved. The Headmaster of Sherborne in Waugh's day, Wavell Charles Smith, was the leading Wordsworth scholar of his day and a very good teacher. But the figure who becomes more and more common is the gifted teacher, the man who did naturally what the progressives had set up as a stated aim: not to bludgeon in knowledge but to teach through excitement and stimulation. S. P. B. Mais, the novelist,

> hit Sherborne [wrote Waugh] like a whirlwind. Anything he taught became dramatic. In mathematics in the lower forms he awarded marks by the thousand. It caught the imagination of his pupils. They enjoyed announcing that as a result of the morning's work they had amassed 35,000 marks and the winner at the end of term proudly informed his parents that he had collected over ten million marks. The book-keeping of these arithmetic sums presented no problem for Mais; he knocked off the noughts and entered in his book Smith 35, James 33.

He was equally stimulating in literature. "Boys are partisans. They like championing a cause, they like adversaries. He encouraged debates on Byron v. Wordsworth, provided the boys had read the poets they despised or adulated." Mais taught at Rossall too, where, among others, he "discovered" J. R. Ackerley and Desmond Young, but he was best at inspiring average boys.

In this last, one might have thought laudable, skill Mais was helping create one of the grounds upon which public schools were later to be most violently attacked—and to find hardest to defend. We have seen how Simpson's concern at Rugby (and later Rendcomb) was the slower boy. During these years the public schools gradually perfected their skill at bringing precisely this kind of boy up to some sort of standard. Another example is A. C. Liddell of Westminster, a master there in the 1920s, who used to arrive early to coach the backward; or there was Dr. W. H. D. Rouse, the Headmaster of the Perse School, 1902–28. He pioneered the "Direct Method" of teaching languages, that is, you learn by speaking them, from which derive Berlitz, Linguaphone and indeed most teaching of languages in schools today ("pioneered" is actually incorrect; you will remember that this had already been discovered at Hazelwood in the early 19th century). He was also an inspiring teacher of English, teaching it with the aid of drama (Leavis went there; but less gifted pupils also benefited).

These two (in part related) processes—slowly rising calibre of the teachers, skill at teaching the stupid—were helped by the Depression. Several of my informants were dramatic about this; schools closed, houses were shut down, masters took salary cuts of twenty to twenty-five per cent. Many more schools—St. Bees in 1938 for instance—would have closed but for their Old Boys. I don't think it is as clear-cut as this. I took fifty-eight schools at random from the seventy-eight I analysed between 1900 and 1939 and analysed them much more closely, first between 1927 and 1939, second between 1930 and 1939. In the first instance, twenty-four grew larger, eleven stayed the same and nineteen shrank. In the second instance, eighteen grew, seventeen stayed the same and nineteen shrank.

There was not, therefore, a universal contraction. The most you can say is that during the 1930s the steady expansion, which characterises this period as a whole, stops for a while. Nevertheless some schools undoubtedly had a difficult time; there was also a surplus in the profession, as happens whenever a period of expansion falters (as now for instance); finally, since the same sort of thing was happening elsewhere, there were numbers of high-quality scientists, mathematicians, historians, etc., who became teachers because there were no other jobs for them to take. Both processes raised the calibre of teachers.

Certain developments in the curriculum accompanied this. The classics had established that the academic point of a school was to teach a relatively few scholars to a very high standard. This in turn meant the standards for a good classical honours degree at university were themselves high. As other subjects gradually achieved recognition—history, English, maths, science —the tradition continued; you had to be very good at your chosen subject; the standard for honours degrees remained very high and as a result there developed the English system of early specialisation. (The civic universities replaced colleges by faculties, but as they too were only concerned to see that boys knew their subject they also encouraged early specialisation.) At fifteen and a half or sixteen the abler boys abandoned all else to become brilliant at their subject. And masters encouraged this, partly because it gave the clever boys the "inestimable boon", as Annan puts it, of studying in depth for two or three years the subject they were good at ; and partly for their own pleasure—the pleasure and satisfaction of imparting all they knew to those capable of appreciating it.

The result was, amongst the clever, a very low standard of *general* education. But, because of a parallel development, it was low too amongst the less clever. As the calibre of masters improved more pupils were better educated; but there were still vast numbers of mediocre teachers, even vaster of stupid or lazy pupils, and this tradition also continued. To get into university these had only to pass the university exam ("Smalls and Little-go") or get five passes in the School Certificate (O-level GCE); the standard in both was low because it was designed to let in those who would only study for a pass degree not an honours one. And masters encouraged this also; it allowed them to teach boys of widely differing ability (unlike grammar schools). This sounds rather fashionable and contemporary—and certainly there was sometimes idealism there; but had they not done so three quarters of their market would have vanished and with it their jobs.

So the clever specialised early—or else, assured of getting to university, spent the last two years idling pleasantly along; and the stupid, too, could idle, or at some schools (Stowe, Oundle, Harrow) take special courses like geography or economics specially made for them. It was this situation, after two or three years, provided it was combined with a few of the chinks and cracks in the Monolith, with a "slack" house, or an area of change, or a pleasant master, and provided they either enjoyed or could escape games and were not irked by convention and avoided discipline, provided some at least of these conditions existed—and they did for a sizeable number of people—then for them these were the Cosy Years.

In 1915, when he was sixteen and a half, Alec Waugh was in the history sixth at Sherborne—and far freer than practically any sixth-form pupil at Bedales or Dartington today.

> I was allowed to do my reading in my study. I had a fireplace in my study; and the masters who were giving tuition to the specialists of the literature and history sixth used to take their classes there. How good it was on a late November afternoon, after a hard game of football, to come back to that study in which a fag had set the fire ablaze, to wait till the other specialists from the outhouses (houses lying distant from school house) came across. We would read our essays aloud to our special tutor and he would discuss them with us. I would be physically exhausted after football but mentally alert. The abbey clock would chime the hour. . . .

But Waugh soon abandoned even this pleasant and civilised course and devoted himself to poetry. His last year was spent entirely on a self-devised poetry course, reading it, writing it, and discussing it with his English master.

Anthony Powell, in his slack house, conveys the flavour of the Cosy Years, the reasonableness of Eton, the fun of the Corps, like a huge jolly game: "I used to enjoy field-days and once a boy in my company shot an umpire in the neck with a date-stone fired from a rifle." The comfortable melancholy nostalgia of:

> . . . those rare visits to out-of-bounds cinemas where the entertainment seemed so much better than any films seen since; while half a bottle of Graves for lunch at Henley lies deeper than mere sentiment, the first taste of those acid, savour-less vintages that fall to the lot of the indigent. I like to remember the melancholy fields that skirt the Sewage Farm across which we used to return from beagling, hoping that the boy we messed with had not forgotten to get the sausages for tea.

In some ways he was an ideal schoolboy, detached, an observer by nature, an enjoyer of gossip. Already you can hear the music of time starting to play in his head. Beatings "increased perceptibly during my middle period under a captain of games who had ideas about pulling the house together in the field of sport, a region in which he himself was fated to get into warm water later in life". Warm. The water in Powell is never hot.

At Eton during the same period Heywood Hill used to lower crumpets filled with ink from the low first-floor windows onto the mortar boards of passing masters and watch as, wobbling, the ink slowly brimmed over. At Mill Hill in the 1920s fagging was paid for at seven shillings and sixpence a term.

Cosy for some boys, cosy for the masters. It became a job for men of some private income, to which they added the £300–350 a year of the small but adequate salary in a prosperous school. (The average salary was much lower: £170 a year.) It was a job which everyone connected with it regarded as worthwhile and brought a strong sense of solidarity. A master could teach how he liked, and knew he would only be sacked if he was grossly incompetent or grossly immoral. It was a world of huge holidays (typically, as at Rugby for example, sixteen weeks), pleasant houses and gardens, uncompetitive, but where, on the whole, the ambitious man could get on.

Teaching therefore became the temporary shelter for many would-be writers: Evelyn Waugh, Auden, Aldous Huxley all taught. The critic and television director Julian Jebb says he can always tell the ex-teacher author by the didactic tone of his writing, and cites John Fowles, John le Carré and Anthony Burgess. Samuel Beckett taught at Campbell College. He hated it and soon left, to the astonishment of the headmaster. "But, Mr Beckett, don't you realise you're teaching the cream of Ulster?" "Yes," said Beckett, "rich and thick." On the whole writers resent anything that gets in the way of their writing, and public schools and prep schools got a bad press as a result—rather as advertising, which has taken their place as a Mæcenas, does now.

Several people told me to read *Their Prime of Life* by A. H. Trelawny Ross; "the best book ever written about public schools". It is not. Michael Campbell's *Lord Dismiss Us* is a far more evocative, accurate, penetrating and also amusing account. But *Their Prime of Life* is a distillation of cosiness and many people like to think that this is what public schools were really like, what their own adolescence was really like. We know that this is not the whole picture by any means, but it is an element it would be wrong to exclude.

6 *Some social effects*

With the schools as Mæcenas we move, in a somewhat marginal way, to their effects on British social life generally. During this period their

A housemaster and headmaster in the 1920s; the contortion of the housemaster is revealing.

Durham schoolboys in 1899. Another example of variety in articles of clothing, typical of the period.

The Conan Doyles see their sons off to school from Waterloo Station, 1923.

Public school activities. Bellowing for fags at Harrow (1951).

The Officers' Training Corps.

national importance was probably considered somewhat less than it had been in the late 19th century. There is less reporting of public school events in the press, public school matters are not raised in the House of Commons in the same way, the Eton and Harrow is not quite such an occasion and so on—but their impact, the amount they imposed themselves, were still considerable. The Southern Railway, for instance, had a series of School Class locomotives in the 1930s: "Sevenoaks", "Harrow", "Tonbridge", etc. But there are more significant effects in this general area that I would like to deal with here.

Brought up for generations and since a very early age in these rigid and usually ancient institutions it is hardly surprising that the English upper and middle classes by now tended to assume automatically that all major departments of public life were best run through institutions—that is that there should be some regular and fairly formal organisation to promote and direct such things, say, as the law, the Church, medicine, etc. The older they were, and if they could have some large and imposing building as a headquarters and an associated London club, so much the better. Now, it is possible this is the best way to run these areas of public life. One can argue whether it is or not. The point is that the products of public schools would seldom allow any argument about it. Not only was an institution the best way, it was the only way they could see themselves functioning. They depended on it. In this sense they had been "institutionalised".

Not only that, but these institutions were—and are still—run on public school lines by public school men. By this I mean two rather vague things —first, they have a prefect structure with a recognised order of seniority, and the laws by which they are run are internal ones and not imposed from outside; second, they depend on people's word being trusted, and this in turn depends on shared backgrounds and assumptions, on the fact that you can check up on people—"Well, he was my fag at school . . .". Nothing is defined exactly—but everyone involved *knows*. Take the City. This—the Stock Exchange, the Bank of England, the accepting houses, the merchant and clearing banks—is really a giant public school in which, even today, the Eton group is particularly strong. The take-over code is entirely dependent on voluntary following. The head of the school—the Governor of the Bank of England—has no legal power; he is obeyed because he is head of school. When things go wrong or someone steps out of line, as with Slater Walker recently for instance, then the offenders are quietly expelled—a senior prefect may move in for a while and take over (it is odd how often these offenders are *nouveau* figures, usually from some obscure State school). Bullies and cads are dealt with quietly in the old prefect-justice way. And the school will stand by lame ducks—as they did recently when a lot of secondary banks looked like collapsing. As a result the City is infinitely more efficient, flexible, and effective than any other financial centre in the world. Such a set-up would be impossible in any other country. The Bundesbank, the Bourse, Wall Street are all run by law. When Hersatt, a smallish German bank collapsed the other day, the Bundesbank hadn't the faintest idea what to do. It caused havoc. In London, the prefects would have moved quietly in, some of the richer boys would have stumped up, someone's bags would have been packed, his father phoned. . . . Millions of Deutschmarks and hundreds of people would have been saved.

If you are brought up in an institution—in particular in an institution part of whose aim is to teach you how to run it—then you are likely to be good at working in institutions all your life. You'd probably find it difficult to work outside one. Britain has a great many institutions like the City (Lloyd's is another) and they all work well for the same reasons— mutual trust and loyalty (transformed automatically from that engendered by house and school), flexibility, the fact that members think the same way about many things without realising they think the same, effective ways of dealing with wrong-doing and so on. Not only that, but these institutions—since their organisation and methods all spring ultimately from the same public school base—mesh in with one another efficiently. A prefect in the Civil Service can have a word with a prefect in the City; an Old Boy from Barings may one day find himself a new boy at the Treasury, but in fact he won't find it all that different from Barings; indeed not all that different, in essential respects, from Eton. All this is still to a considerable extent true today; during the period up to 1940, when many of these institutions were evolving under the hands of the ex-public school boys running them, it was even more so.

The second effect was on social order. Correlli Barnett notes that many of the disciplines inculcated by public schools—politeness, respect for authority and the law, standards of public honesty and trustfulness and service, loyalty to whatever job you find yourself in—all these are valuable and necessary social and civic virtues. We can appreciate them the more today as they appear in decline. They made Britain then a pleasant and civilised place in which to be (the fact that it is not necessary to embody these necessary social virtues in that particular form and with the attendant drawbacks is not relevant here). He goes on to say that as a result Britain was easy to govern, indeed almost self-governing at this time. I think this, too, is true; but the matter is more complex than he makes out. After all, it wasn't because public school boys behaved themselves that England was easy to govern. They were too small a minority—and were in any case doing the governing. The public schools could only have had so dramatic an effect on the social behaviour of the whole population in this simple direct way if the whole population had gone to a public school—which it manifestly had not.

We see here two things. The philistinism of the public schools, the curricula developments we have just discussed, meant relatively few schoolboys went to university and among these even fewer employed themselves in serious work. Since the universities charged fees and these fees were not alleviated by government grants the university population was small and virtually restricted to this, on the whole unintellectual, public school intake. State-run egalitarian systems naturally mean far more people go to university; they therefore almost invariably overproduce intellectuals. You get the European phenomenon of the unemployable graduate combined with a volatile mass student population—these form the culturally restless and politically hostile intellectual stratum which appears often to threaten revolution and which produces, through fear-filled reaction, authoritarian and illiberal government action. England did not develop this stratum. There was therefore no fear on the government's part and more freedom.

This situation also helps to explain—though the power of the schools is also directly concerned here, their authority—what Annan, actually writing on a related subject, described as the "paradox which has puzzled European and American observers of English life: the paradox of an intelligentsia which appears to conform rather than rebel against the rest of society".

The second thing we are seeing is yet another manifestation of the dominant way in which the idea of public school/upper- and middle-class leadership had imposed itself right down through the social strata. Not just down, but sideways too—even to the left. Laski, in the 1939 war, spoke (italics added) of the "pride every *citizen* of this country is bound to have in the amazing heroism and endurance of the *common people*". There was a huge reserve of acceptance, of that deference, as Anthony Sampson puts it, which could astonish foreigners and which castrated the working classes, making them unable to use their enormous power (you will recall Baldwin's "Now run along" to the Union leaders after the collapse of the General Strike). The schools perpetuated this by remaining the accepted avenue by which to rise in class and power. A revealing demonstration of this is the enormous success and sale of self-help and self-educate books in America during the 1930s and their relative failure among the lower middle and working classes here. The point is that in the US the idea was that you *could* better yourself; in England it was your children who would rise, not you; and the way they would rise would be through school.

7 Minor public schools; girls' schools

A final feature of the years up to 1940 is the minor public school. This was the cheap imitation, with small numbers, which would never have been invited to the Headmaster's Conference or got into the *Public Schools Year Book* but which became quite numerous during this period and which helped spread an often exaggerated version of "Public School Spirit" even further through the social strata. They could be more brutal, more restrictive, more snobbish than their originals—or simply, like the one brilliantly described by Kenneth Allsop in *John Bull's Schooldays*, decayed. Huge caps, a school song, a crest and motto, talk of "honour", athleticism, the classics, all hid a crumbling financial ruin: ". . . by the time I arrived there (in the 30s) the thin Greyfriars varnish had cracked and flaked, exposing the forlorn shanty-town structure beneath." The headmaster had had a distinguished academic record which must have been "dramatically wiped out in some personality earthquake, or it had been long since smothered beneath the anxiety and despair at his mismanagement of practical affairs".

The only time this intensely gloomy man—"a white-flecked auburn moustache dangled like a bunch of radishes beneath his nose; his eyes, which seldom met yours, were opaque with worry"—was at all happy was teaching Latin, when he would hide deep in the

convoluted tunnels of language . . . lapsing for long periods into a droning trance of introspective happiness. But if the self-hypnosis was disrupted by a boy's obtrusive stupidity, he would apparently go insane. Chin jerked out of collar, the radishes trembled and shook, the eyes swirled like stirred ponds. "Fool," he would say, at first quietly and levelly, and then, in a clattering of teeth and jawbones, as if a kitchen cabinet of pans had crashed over inside his mouth: "CRASS, INCOMPETENT FOO-UHL!" What was likely then to happen was a swinging blow from his large, bony hand which crashed upon the skull like a spray of knobkerries.

As far as staff went, these schools got the riff-raff:

. . . Cholly, cynical, debauched playboy in ginger plus-fours, who always tip-toed frailly into the classroom in the morning with a raging hangover. He spent the first twenty minutes slumped at his desk, head on arms, groaning melodramatically; having thus purged himself of the horrors, he would then revive and, propping up his gaily socked shanks, chatter nostalgically but amusingly about the hellraking times at Balliol that he had just had to relinquish. One morning a cheque had come, he jubilantly announced to the class, and at lunchtime he disappeared for ever.

They always left. Next came

a blatantly overt homosexual, a simpering, bottom-wagging old auntie who used eyebrow pencil. He also hastened away . . . after his affair with our rugger star had been exposed. In they came and out they went, a frayed, farouche, shuffling cavalcade, like a pedagogic police parade, on their uppers and down at heel, their references bad but their accents good, to linger a little while to bore us with facts that it bored them to repeat, and to tipple whisky behind the desk lid.

Lastly, I may have seemed to neglect girls' schools. This is partly because in a good number of instances I carried the story of those schools well into the 1920s and 30s in Chapter 10. But mainly it is because the same historical and psychological forces continued to operate. The girls' schools still tended to think that merely by existing at all they were doing something revolutionary. The autocracy of the headmistresses, at the expense of the other staff and the girls, continued unchecked. And girls themselves, and the schools as a whole, remained more ready to conform. As a result there were fewer pressures to change on the girls' schools and fewer significant changes. Furthermore, the growth of smallish private girls' schools, lineal descendants of the academies and the accomplishments, which were usually rather slack, meant that parents who wanted their children to have a freer, less restricted, if less academic, upbringing had an alternative choice.

CHAPTER 16

The Amorous Life of Adolescents

If . . . I tried to form a society in which adolescents would be free to have their own natural love life, I should be ruined if not imprisoned as an immoral seducer of youth.

A. S. Neill

The extent to which sex life is necessary and should be permitted to growing boys remains uncertain.

Cyril Connolly, *Enemies of Promise*

Before writing this book I had not thought it would be necessary to do more, as far as the sexual lives of adolescents were concerned, than describe what they were like at various schools at different periods of our history, to outline the social and moral ideas and attitudes which together produced those lives, to suggest certain ways all this might have affected the individuals concerned, and to do all this with brief references to the biological drives involved.

However, as I went round the schools and, among much else, discussed this subject, I realised that there were still deep-seated worries, doubts, fears and evasions about it. There was not only no consensus of opinion as to the sort of amorous life adolescents should lead; there were still pockets of reaction where even Farrar might have felt at home. Certainly Miss Beale would have had little to fear at Cheltenham. Furthermore, I had in my account sometimes directly or by implication criticised a number of attitudes, those of John Dancy, for example, or Badley, without committing myself to a view of my own. I therefore felt it would be both sensible and fair if I made one final exploration of the subject and tried to reach some conclusions.

Let me briefly recapitulate. We found that though it was not perhaps strictly and scientifically possible to say that sublimation was impossible, it was so rare and so difficult that out of a combined sample of nearly 13,000, and after diligent search, Kinsey found not a single clear-cut example. Its possibility is academic—and as far as public schools go irrelevant. It is no good just putting on endless performances of *Waiting for Godot* or *Hamlet* or buying another pottery wheel. And we might note here that the problem has become more acute and been thrown even more into the hands of the schools in that it starts earlier than it used to. As a result of improved diet, medicine and living conditions generally, puberty has arrived earlier in Western Europe and the United States by about one-third of a year every ten years. It now starts at about thirteen to thirteen and a quarter years on average; and there are vast individual differences. It is quite common for puberty not to start till fifteen or sixteen. In Fassbinder's film *Wildgame*, which from one angle was a drama of precocious development, the heroine was fourteen. But it also means that two per cent of ten-year-olds, and about ten per cent of eleven-year-olds will have already reached puberty.

Kinsey and later studies are clear as to the influence of early sexual life on future patterns. With boys (this is much less so with girls) who are brought up in single-sex institutions there is an increased likelihood of homosexual patterns and response developing. But, more importantly perhaps, the relationships between the sexes, particularly sexual relationships, are considerably impaired if entered on late. Both men and women have much greater difficulty in adjusting, more fears, more anxieties, less satisfaction. This is particularly so with girls—who find adjustment especially difficult as a result of the "tardy acceptance of heterosexual coitus". And again we might note that this is particularly important today. We have far greater expectations of married relationships, and particularly of sexual relationships. It is because these expectations are high that divorce is becoming more and more common. At the moment something like one in four marriages ends in divorce, and the rate is still climbing. (Among the middle classes it is in fact probably more like one in three; it has trebled in the last ten years.) By far the most common difficulties, particularly in first marriages, are sexual difficulties. Marjorie Proops, in her recent book about the problems she dealt with, said the overwhelming majority of them were sexual. And the source of these difficulties, as far as physical pattern and response go (we are not here discussing the matter psychoanalytically) is set in puberty and adolescence, in the years from eleven to seventeen. It is no academic exploration on which we are involved.

One of the first matters to resolve is the apparent difference in the rate and pattern of development between girls and boys. If they have such very different early patterns, then they must lead different sexual lives until the patterns coincide. There is very strong evidence, however, that in fact their patterns are not all that dissimilar; the evidence indeed is all the other way. Certainly *a priori* this is what one would expect. One can only guess at the reasons for early sexual development in man, but it is plain there was some strong evolutionary advantage. It is probable that the life of primitive man was, as a result of danger and disease, extremely short. The quicker, therefore, that he was able to reproduce the better; the more children and the earlier the larger and stronger the tribe. It has also been suggested that a strong sexual instinct was a cohesive force, compelling the early hunters to return and not abandon the tribe. On both counts a strong and early sexual appetite is at a premium. It would be extremely odd, however, if it had not developed in both sexes approximately equally. If the female was indifferent, and perhaps even antagonistic, to male advances, it would make the achievement of early reproduction much harder; nor would there be any incentive to hurry back. It is even odder that the female should reach her peak at a time—the late twenties, mid thirties—when one would suppose in the ordinary course of events in those remote and terrifying times that she would be dead. A similar rate of growth and development would be of greater evolutionary advantage. The fact that females are fully mature and able to bear children at around fifteen or sixteen is in line with this.

There are several speculative arguments of similar nature which can be advanced, but, in fact, the evidence clearly supports the supposition that the differences Kinsey found are culturally imposed. In the first place, pre-adolescent sex play—masturbation and so on—was the same in both sexes; in fact, girls were slightly more active than boys. It is at adolescence that the break occurs and this break is therefore crucial. Yet if you change the culture—or change the pattern imposed within a culture—the break vanishes and the two sexes develop in the same way. In cases where Kinsey found that there were no culturally imposed restrictions (and he found a substantial number, mostly among the lower and less inhibited segments of American society) then the pattern of activity carried on into adolescence with girls much as it did with boys. Observers of 19th-century life in London found the same thing. The author of *My Secret Life* wrote: ". . . nearly the whole of the girls of the lowest classes began copulating with boys of about their own age when about fourteen years old." Some people distrust this book, but on this fact he is corroborated by the studies of Mayhew and Acton. Dr. Fernando Henriques reports similar patterns appearing among teenagers in New York during the war in response to altering conventions and demands. Most primitive groups on which sexual data are available neither have this break nor such different patterns of development. In fact it is not found in any other mammal at all. It certainly seems to form part of that pattern which we have observed elsewhere—women are more sensitive to culturally imposed authority and restrictions and more influenced by them. And if their development was naturally more in line (exactitude is neither needed nor likely) with that of boys, as common sense and the evidence suggest, but has been artificially suppressed, it would help to explain why, as we noted, studies have shown that adolescence is a more disturbed and difficult time for girls than it is for boys.

We do not, however, have to be too specific about actual age at the moment. Let me put it like this: it is clear that at some point in the lives of all adolescents they are both ready and able to make love to each other. With some it will be when they are sixteen or seventeen or even eighteen; with others it will be fourteen or thirteen or even twelve. Suppose, for the sake of argument, they were allowed to do what they liked, when they liked, with no pressures either way; that their sexual lives, like those of adults, were left to them—what then?

What then indeed? To this question, which I sometimes put, I received a variety of answers and objections, many violent. If sexual freedom on this massive scale were allowed, I was told, there would be chaos; discipline would be impossible. It would make work impossible. Pupils would be so obsessed with their love life and sexuality generally that they would be able to concentrate on nothing else. There would be appalling promiscuity —they would never learn to associate sex with love, they would never, in later life, form stable sexual partnerships in marriage. There would be babies, abortions, miscarriages. Parents would never stand for it. The only answer I did not receive was that nothing would happen—it was plain that fear of the orgasmic explosion still haunted many of the speakers.

Now, there are answers to these objections. For instance, one might ask, are appetites and desires usually more obsessive when frustrated or when satisfied? Certainly, I find it quite impossible to imagine anything more sexually obsessed than a restrictive boys' public school in 1890 (or 1930 or 1960). And the fear that it would make people incapable of forming stable relationships later on, sexually or otherwise, is based on a misunderstanding of the psychological processes involved. Patterns of this sort, the abilities or disabilities associated, are set up much earlier, from the time of birth. Margaret Mead, in her study of Samoa, depicts a culture of extremely free sexual morality. Love affairs start very early and liaisons do seem much more casual. Adulteries are settled by an exchange of mats. "Love and hate, jealousy and revenge, sorrow and bereavement, are all a matter of weeks." But the reason for this is that babies in Samoa never form a strong relationship with either parent, they are brought up in common, passed from hand to hand among dozens of relations. Where you get an equal sexual freedom but a different form of early upbringing quite different patterns emerge (for a succinct account of the mechanisms of all this I refer you to *The Unnatural History of the Nanny*, in particular Chapters 4, 7 and 10). Also, one might note that to say children will not learn to associate sex and love unless somehow taught is really to assume that sex is disgusting unless it is associated with love. This is debatable. But I don't want to go fully into all the arguments put forward just now. I think the most sensible thing would be to find out exactly what does happen if you allow complete sexual freedom among adolescents.

Our culture has been, incidentally, unusual, indeed almost unique, in its non-acceptance (until very recently, at any rate) of pre-marital sexual

intercourse. Many societies defer marriage until its members are sufficiently mature to cope with the attendant responsibilities and emotional
stresses and intensities. But this has nothing to do with them freely allowing experimental pre-marital intercourse among adolescents. This has been
openly accepted among most other great civilisations of the world, in the
Orient, in the ancient world, in many European groups. It is universally
accepted among (so-called) primitive people throughout the world.
Today, we ourselves are moving towards it. Year by year the age of
consent in European countries is lowered (in Denmark it is fifteen, in
Sweden it is soon to be fourteen; the National Council for Civil Liberties
recently questioned whether the concept itself had any validity). I think a
large minority, perhaps even a majority, would accept that boys and girls
of university age should be able to have affairs. Certainly they do so. Even
ancient colleges at Oxford and Cambridge have gone co-educational and
the students there sleep together in the ordinary course of events. Yet even
this is years after the crucial processes of adolescence have taken place. It is
a very minor advance of freedom, far too late to affect development in any
radical way. To see what happens if you allow this sort of freedom at an
earlier age we have to turn to simpler cultures. Fortunately, one of the
classic studies of anthropology lies to hand in just this field—Dr. Bronislaw Malinowski's *The Sexual Life of Savages*. It is a detailed investigation
over four years of the natives of the Trobriand Islands in North-West
Melanesia. It was first published in 1929, but many times reprinted.

"In the 19th century," wrote Havelock Ellis, "the sexual behaviour of
savages seemed mostly unspeakable." It was not only their sexual
behaviour. The Victorians were strict with their children. The Trobrianders, although during the first six or seven years the children are close to
their mothers and fathers and live a family life, are extremely indulgent.
There is little discipline and they run fairly wild. As a result there forms a
sort of children's community in which, from the age of six to about twelve
or so, they spend more and more of their time. This community is
extremely independent. It often sets itself against the community of adults
—and wins. Dr. Malinowski noticed, for example, that if the children
decided they wanted to go away on a day's picnic not even the Chief
could stop them.

This independence extends to sexual matters. They are able to, and often
do, witness their parents making love—though they are expected to be
discreet and delicate about this and a child who is these things is praised.
They listen freely to adult talk however baldly sexual this may be and, as a
result, tiny children can often make sexual jokes which make their elders
laugh. As a result of all this, their sexual play is open and free from the
start. They begin from very early to explore and experience the functions
of their sexual organs—playing with each other, imitating their elders, and
watching and imitating the more advanced behaviour of older children;

the pattern and method, in fact, of all growth. By about eight in the case of girls, and ten to twelve in the case of boys, real intercourse can and does take place—"And from these times sexuality will gradually assume a greater and greater importance as life goes on, until it abates in the course of nature."

The adults of North-West Melanesia view these infantile experiments either with indifference or complacency; they find it natural and therefore see no reason to scold or interfere. Nothing but the degree of curiosity, and the differences between the sexual temperament of each child, determines how much or how little they indulge in such pastimes. But there is discretion here too. The games which involve all varieties of these experiments do not take place in the house but must be carried out in the bush or at the more distant beaches.

A change takes place at adolescence, but not the kind of change we are accustomed to. (It is significant, incidentally, that adolescence is not a "stage" in the Trobrianders' three-fold division of man and woman's life. This goes: childhood, maturity—*Ta'n* (men), *Vivila* (women)—and old age. Adolescence, starting between twelve and fourteen, is not separate but is the start of the main stage. The youth and the girl are now an embarrass-ment to adult love-making, and this leads to a partial break-up of the family. The girls go to live with an elderly aunt or similar relative; the boys go to a *Bukumatula*, or all-male bachelor house. This might sound like some distant relative of a public school. In fact, as we shall see, it is, in sexual terms, the exact opposite.

It is at this point that they start to learn how to take part in wider tribal activities, but this is a development we are not concerned with here. From our point of view, it is from now that sexual love becomes far more important, and they match, in the intensity of their absorption in it, the speed and strength with which they are now developing physically. They form temporary, and then less temporary but still not permanent liaisons. They feel free. They experiment, even though they expect (or pretend to expect) their semi-permanent partners to be faithful. They make love in a friend's house, or build hide-aways in the yam-house; they do not set up a permanent home yet. They go on picnics and make love on the beaches. It is a time of experiment, and so usually with a succession of, for a while, steady partners. Love is now passionate but free and adolescence marks the intermediate stage between childish experiment and stable adult marriage.

It is this, as time passes, that slowly begins to emerge. The liaisons last longer and the ties become stronger and more permanent. Gradually one love becomes stronger than all the others have been; perhaps because of a very powerful sexual affinity, or else a closeness and compatibility of character, or of both together. Now couples set up in open and almost permanent liaisons, sleeping together night after night, and indeed it is precisely this acknowledged and expected continuance which marks the transition and shows it to be a sort of engagement: *"La vivila mokita; imisiva yamburata yamburata"*—"his woman truly; he sleeps with her always, always." And now the *Bukumatula* comes into its own. It is a house in which four or five bachelors and their mistresses can sleep together (their cooking and eating are done in other households). The rules of life are strict, careful and decorous. They do not share partners or swap them. They make love when the other people are out or asleep (there are special silent techniques they practise, especially lying on the side); or else they agree not to watch when another couple are making love. As with all Trobriander sexual behaviour it is delicate, modest and straightforward. The liaison is still not legally binding, but is a test to see how much they like each other. If they split, the girl leaves to find another boy to sleep with and the boy goes and gets another girl. But it is one of these *Bukumatula* relationships which will lead to marriage.

What is the result of all this? How does it compare with our method of bringing up our adolescents in order that they may lead satisfactory marital, emotional and sexual lives (which is presumably what we want)? Let us look briefly at a few areas.

Trobriander marriages are stable, exclusive partnerships based firmly on strong mutual love. Adultery and infidelity are wrong. Their love and dependence, and the depth and complexity of that love, are just as varied and strong and mature as the relationships we value. Of course, human frailty is the same among the Trobrianders as it is among us. There are infidelities and divorces, unhappiness, jealousy, even suicide and murder over love; but the norms are strict, the hopes are high, and on the whole the marriages sound a great deal more secure than that institution is becoming here now.

What about all the illegitimate babies? The Trobrianders see no connection between sexual intercourse and procreation, there is therefore no contraception. But for some reason there are virtually no babies born before marriage, and in fact illegitimate babies are frowned on. Dr. Malinowski can't explain this, though he tries: there is for instance the physiological gap between the first menstrual period and the ability to conceive, known as the time of "adolescent sterility" (a later investigator, Robertson, has found it to be two years seven months). Could this, wonders Malinowski, in some way be extended in the Trobrianders? The lack of connection between intercourse and procreation is more easily explained. Conception is supposed to be by a spirit entering an open vagina and placing a potential baby in the mother's head. A technical virgin cannot therefore have a baby. But since intercourse starts so early and takes place so frequently with no apparent result it is hardly surprising they haven't connected the two. Indeed since there are no virgins among the Trobrianders it is rather surprising they've achieved even this vague link.

In fact, to digress a moment, unconscious psychological control of pregnancy is recognised today by many psychiatrists and psychologists. The mechanism is to close the fallopian tubes. You quite often find it in women in whose family there is some first-child difficulty—their mother's first child was born dead, or an eldest child was killed or committed suicide. These women frequently can't conceive; they adopt a child; then the tension goes and they can bear children. Another way round this unconscious block is to have the first child illegitimately. The rest can then be born normally in marriage. This is a common cause of illegitimate births.

As far as masturbation and homosexuality go, they of course exist among the Trobrianders. (There is a name for masturbation; *Isulomonic*—"he makes semen boil over".) It is regarded in a perfectly indulgent and amused way, but seen as something only done by someone who can't get a girl. It is seen as a product of frustration and is therefore very rare (since sexual frustration is very rare); it is a bit undignified, a sign of failure. At no particular *age* does anyone need to do it; or only when disfigured by age. Homosexuality, similarly, is scorned as a substitute for girls, and normal intercourse is so easy it is regarded as pointless. In fact they have strong feelings about excreta and these attach themselves to homosexuality. They often deny that it exists; but they have a word to describe it, so it can't be unknown.

There is no difference, as we would now expect, either between the libido (sexual energy) of men or women or of the times and rates at which their appetites start to grow. There are of course enormous differences between *individuals*—here Kinsey is completely confirmed—some need a great deal of love-making, some very little—but these differences are not gender based. (Nor has the rate of development of the girls anything to do with them being in a hot climate. The myth that girls in Southern climes mature earlier was destroyed some years ago in a large-scale study of the menarche or onset of menstruation; in Brazil, for example, it was 14·47, in Calcutta—14·12, whereas in North America at the time 14·2.)

Sexual difficulties—in "adjusting to heterosexual coitus", achieving orgasm, finding a compatible partner, female frigidity, early impotence, premature ejaculation, the whole desperate array of our tattered instinct—are virtually unknown ; as is sexual frustration. Although they protested the importance of physical beauty, Dr. Malinowski found that even repulsive old women could get youths to make love to them. This was proved once when the men in one of the villages contracted VD. The missionary doctor couldn't find the source, although he had twice tested all the girls and women in the village. There was, however, one really disgusting old woman whom he hadn't tested—he had left her out as being completely impossible. However, finally, with some distaste, he did test her—and found she was the carrier. A kindly people.

Now all this—the similarity between the sexes, the relatively early appearance of practice coinciding with early physical changes and appearance of desire, the early copying of adult behaviour, the getting closer and closer to it, finally experimenting with liaisons, testing appetite and need, *learning* about sexuality, and finally proceeding to marriage—all this seems much closer to what happens in other spheres of growth. It also seems a great deal more pleasant, humane, likely and sensible than Dr. Hadfield's mad gyrations. And as far as results go it seems, to put it mildly, to compare well with the "methods" we have evolved for bringing up our adolescents.

But we are talking about the running of *schools*, not South Sea islands. You might think, therefore, that this was all completely irrelevant. It is not. In the first place, here as elsewhere—indeed particularly here, where the effects are so far-reaching and important—it is essential to establish the right principle; the practice will follow. If it is beneficial to control and restrict the sexual instinct, then this must be established; the working out of this restriction will be fairly simple. If it is unnecessary and harmful to restrict it, then that too is capable of practical organisation in an institution. Because, and this is the second point, sexual freedom doesn't lead to anarchy. When Richard Bagley asked a recent Headmaster of Repton what he'd "done" about homosexuality, he said, "Well, I haven't made it compulsory yet, if that's what you mean." In fact it was clear to me that a great many masters in many boys' public schools today ignore physical relations between the boys, provided these are discreet and there is not some age exploitation. "Frankly, we don't feel it is our business," said one master. "Provided they don't actually do it at the back of the class, why on earth should I interfere?" said another. I won't give the names of the schools because, as with so many things in public schools, they preferred some unwritten, un-public code. But this freedom has, like others, always been true in pockets in public schools—it was true of college at Westminster in the late 1940s, and at St. Columba's at around the same time. It is simply a great deal more general now. (It also means that at practically every public school . . . the law is broken nightly. Under the Sexual Offences Act of 1967 behaviour of this sort is only allowed between consenting adults of twenty-one.)

But, for some reason, people now imagine it is much harder to allow such freedom in a co-educational school. It may be, but freedoms very roughly on Trobriand lines have been allowed (or perhaps more accurately have been taken) in co-educational schools without disaster.

Progressive school headmasters have always had to be careful in their pronouncements about any sexual freedom they allow. For one thing, there is the law. Even now, for instance, it is unlawful to have intercourse with a girl under sixteen (and such defences as exist are of little use to a school: for example, "a belief on reasonable grounds that the girl was the accused's wife"). It was even worse in the 1920s and 30s. It is clear that

Neill—as the quotation at the head of this chapter shows—would have liked to let adolescents do as they liked, only he feared the law. Even so, his statements are often ambiguous:

> Some years ago we had two pupils arrive at the same time: a boy of seventeen from a boys' private school and a girl of sixteen from a girls' private school. They fell in love with each other and were always together. I met them late one night and I stopped them. "I don't know what you two are doing," I said, "and morally I don't care, for it isn't a moral question at all. But economically I do care. If you, Kate, have a kid, my school will be ruined."
>
> I went on to expand on this theme. "You see," I said, "you have just come to Summerhill. To you it means freedom to do what you like. Naturally, you have no special feelings for the school. If you had been here from the age of seven, I'd never have had to mention the matter. You would have so strong an attachment to the school that you would think of the consequences to Summerhill." It was the only possible way to deal with the problem. Fortunately, I never had to speak to them again on the subject.

This could be taken as a plea for contraception. Certainly when Mrs. Hall went to Summerhill in the 1960s—"Something was said about the children not to be discouraged from making love. I can remember something being said about the pill." (But I'm not sure how reliable a witness Mrs. Hall was. She seemed to let fly in a rather wild way.) The same ambiguity can be found in some of Curry's replies. In 1936, W. K. Slater, a Director of Dartington Hall Ltd., sent a series of angry questions to Curry, among them one demanding to know whether the school actively encouraged sexual intercourse among the staff and pupils; does Curry condone it, encourage it or condemn it? Curry's reply is rather evasive: "Most English girls, brought up in the English climate, do not want complete sex relations while they are of school age." What of those who do?

But the situation at Dartington is clear enough. If you mix the pupils up, as they always have, and allow the conditions of privacy and freedom concomitant with progressive ideals, then a number of them are bound to sleep together. They have done so since the beginning. Ivan Moffat (there from 1932–36) said a sizeable minority did so. He remembered Curry taking him for a walk—"I understand you and X have been in each other's beds—you realise if anything happens the school might have to close down?" This too might be taken as an argument for contraception, and by 1953 Curry was giving regular advice to sixth formers on contraceptives. "The Group"—the consensus-creating core of those who had been there longest—in those early years also did not fully approve of sex, but they were not puritanical. One girl had an affair with a master and this was approved by the Group because it was felt that for her in particular—and at that moment—it would be good that she have a physical relation with someone she loved. And the fact that The Group was vaguely "against" sex is really what the position of the staff has always been—but "against" in circumstances and in a way that ensures that if anyone really wants to sleep with someone else they can. As to how many do, it is impossible to say. Robert Skidelsky, in a recent book on progressive schools, says it is not less than the national average for their age group, a statement that doesn't get one far as no such figure exists. My own impression—it is no more—is something like twenty-five to thirty per cent.

How do other co-educational schools cope? Skidelsky's own "solution" (how 19th century it begins to seem) is that schools are there to teach, but only partially to be complete communities—that is, boys and girls can mix there, but shouldn't sleep together there. The solution is long weekends away from school. Certainly I know of three co-educational schools where this is done with some success. But it really just palliates the situation. If you allow sex at weekends, no doubt you will find it taking place during the week—and your logical defence will have been much weakened. Second, why should schools be allowed to abdicate responsibility in this way over this one thing? A good many public school masters took the view "that this sort of thing isn't our business. It can be left to the holidays." This won't do. These are *boarding* schools, they are the temporary homes and families of the pupils at them (indeed, as far as time goes, it is the real homes and families which are temporary). That defines the extent of their responsibilities. Why is one of the most important aspects of their pupils' personal life suddenly "not their business" when every other aspect—the pastoral care for their happiness, their mental and physical health, their religious instruction to mention only three—is their business? The school is two-thirds of the pupils' lives; it sets the pattern for the rest, not the other way about. That is the source of all the patterns we have unravelled. It is not possible to suddenly exempt the sexual pattern.

The third course, which most co-educational schools struggle to follow, is to prevent any love affairs taking place at all. It is not surprising to find that Bedales is among this group. It is interesting to see at Bedales today—which I may say in every other way seemed to me a fascinating, stimulating and extremely successful school—how Badley's anxiety in this sphere still makes itself felt. You can sense it in the architecture. It is strangely open: common rooms open on to corridors, no real studies, just rooms for the sixth containing five or six people. It seemed impossible to be alone with someone—without it feeling secret. They have mixed-age same-sex dormitories of four or five, and these are clearly a valuable and cohesive force: the older look after the younger, they stop bullying, you can be with your friends, etc. Yet, was there not in the enthusiasm of the staff some element of relief that they were also so, well—safe? Certainly the staff are quite clear, and also worried. They dislike talking about it. It is not a moral issue exactly but if anyone is caught, then they must leave. The pupils on the other hand, or the half dozen or so I spoke to, did not seem particularly concerned. But they gave a more vivid picture of staff anxiety: "They panic easily, especially if there is drink about. They imagine *everyone* pregnant." One boy who had been caught but, exceptionally, not expelled—("The power of debate")—said they positively welcomed homosexuals. There are four or five known homosexuals, in mixed-age dormitories, who certainly wouldn't be expelled. They're "ill". I suddenly remembered Mr. Moorsom describing how he fell in love with a boy at Bedales in 1903 and walked about with his arms round him and no one minded. But I realised what was wrong when I wandered unheralded into the girls' dormitories one afternoon. I had wandered at will, and without difficulty, over girls' schools before now, and over other co-educational schools. Nothing had happened. But this afternoon—within two minutes of entering the building—I was pounced on almost simultaneously from two sides. In the distance a third figure was advancing at speed. It was like Colditz. In this area—central to the school's ideology as progressive, one of its earliest traditions—Bedales was, as it had been for many years, in the grip of total society fever.

The point is sexual behaviour is one of the hardest things on which to judge for other people. "The possibility," said Kinsey, commenting from experience, "of any individual engaging in sexual activity at a rate that is remarkably different from one's own, is one of the most difficult things for even professionally trained persons to understand." We have seen that individual variations are the norm—people start to develop at widely differing times, anything from nine to seventeen; variations of activity range from one orgasm a year to dozens a week. And all these differences are at their height in adolescence. To suppose that everyone can confine himself to one level of activity at any particular time is absurd; for some it is easy, for some difficult, for some impossible. And it seems impossible for even the most intelligent educators, when discussing this subject, to appreciate that they are legislating for some people whose needs are bound to be quite different from their own. They may advocate total freedom and indulgence; there will be some for whom it is a matter of complete indifference. They may insist on abstinence and self-denial; there will be some for whom it is intolerable.

And yet this is one area, perhaps the only area, where judgment and legislation are not needed (which is why, as far as adults go, we have virtually abandoned it). There is nothing intrinsic about the act of sex. It is not like a blow to the face, aggressive; nor like drinking or smoking too much, harmful to health. The only thing about it is that it gives pleasure. Studies by Kinsey and others have shown conclusively that even what some people regard as abhorrent acts—homosexual activity, animal intercourse, mouth genital contacts, etc.—are completely harmless *unless guilt is attached to them.* You can put almost any outside emotion on sex (guilt, love, even—as some prostitutes do—hate), but that is different. And this is true for sexual behaviour at any age—at eight or nine or fourteen, just as much as at twenty-five or forty. By denying, and therefore tacitly condemning as wrong, sexual expression until, say, the arbitrary age of sixteen, we impose guilt. Yet we have found that completely free heterosexual behaviour, allowed to develop without guilt from the earliest age, confers very real benefits. Why can't we allow it to our own children?

Of course there must be the most stringent precautions. There are already tough laws against assault, indecency and rape, and cases of force or pressure. There should probably be tougher laws relating to older people with younger, particularly giving protection to children in a position of dependence—on foster-parents, in families, with teachers and instructors. There are now so many methods of effective contraception that this should not prove a serious difficulty.

It seems easy enough to envisage with single couples: "My daughter aged fifteen has been sleeping with her boyfriend, also fifteen, in our small double bed. . . ." "Dear Worried Stiff, many adolescents are maturing early today and . . ." etc. But once they are together in schools, feverishness starts. It is as though they were like grains of gunpowder; two or three are safe, but a mass packed together and Bang!—the orgasmic explosion. I wonder what they imagine? Orgies in the classrooms? No one getting up in the mornings? The corridors echoing all night to the thunder of feet, the screech of springs, the screams of pleasure? But we have seen that a free adolescent love life can be "delicate, decorous and straightforward"—in fact more likely to be that because free. We have seen that in various schools (both boys' and co-educational) in various ways it can be allowed without chaos, disturbance or interference with the other aims of the school. I suspect that like so many other past things that were the results of total society fever—the need to separate the age groups, discipline depending on the cane, the ideology of games—once allowed, once the contending parties relaxed, if the schools ceased their long fight against this most powerful of instincts, they would find that the imagined difficulties, to their astonishment, had just silently and softly vanished away.

CHAPTER 17

1945–1977: The Academic Revolution and the Influence of the Public Schools Today

Educationally the average public school is superior to the average maintained grammar school. Public schools have a better quality among sixth-form masters. . . . On the average the public schools are educationally superior; they simply teach the children better.

Anthony Crosland in a speech of June 1961

It will have become noticeable, as we have drawn ever closer to the present day, that I have increasingly stressed the diversity and complexity of the picture before us.

This has so far been because that has indeed been the picture. The Victorian and Edwardian periods were in agreement about moral and social goals and standards in a way almost inconceivable to us now. The drive of the public schools to impose discipline was therefore a uniform one and produced uniformity. We could, by 1900, speak of the Monolith. The imposing of disciplined régimes is one thing; the replacing or mitigating of them quite another. It was to be expected that the schools, where they did alter, would do so at different speeds, different times and in different ways. Furthermore, the continuing reaction to the 19th and early 20th centuries meant an ever increasing number of different ideas and ideals seeking expression: one saw every shade of progressive public school, every variety of public school response. There is perhaps a general, Tolstoyan truth here: tyrannies are tyrannical in the same way; free societies, and societies becoming free, are always free in their own way.

But from 1945 or so on there is added an entirely new problem. We are faced with the notorious difficulty of interpreting contemporary history: the difficulty of deciding which trend is significant, which development temporary, what to select from a bewildering confusion of events and evidence. It might be thought there is a limit to what one person can discover—fortunately I was not alone. Royston Lambert and teams of researchers financed by grants from the Department of Education and Science and King's College, Cambridge, poured out sociological studies, often very large; other investigators followed suit. There is a survey of girls' schools by Mallory Wober, an amusing and penetrating book, except at the end where he becomes rather emotional about whether they should be abolished or not (he was one of only three boys at a girls' boarding school in India). The Headmasters' Conference commissioned a survey by Graham Kalton, published in 1966. There have been, and continue to be innumerable articles in newspapers and magazines. The schools themselves wrote to me.

Amidst all this I cannot pretend to anything like the same degree of certainty compared to what has gone before—and that was often tentative enough. The most I can do is outline briefly the four or five developments which seem most significant and interesting to me in the last thirty years, follow through some of our most important themes, and finally suggest what I think will happen in the future.

1 The economic background, the new academic thrust, the training of leaders

The immediate post-war years—1945 to 1949—were ones of relative gloom for headmasters and headmistresses. Labour governments are not friendly to public schools: there is talk of class and privilege and élites—the sword of abolition hangs in the air. Nor was there any money about. There were five years of building and repair to catch up on; many schools had nearly gone broke, with inadequate fees and often having to pay for bizarre if temporary accommodation in outlandish parts of the country. Westminster had to borrow a quarter of a million pounds from Lloyd's.

The 50s and 60s marked the change. Gradually, an unprecedented prosperity rolled over the country, a nation-wide prosperity, but Conservative-led, so that it benefited the middle and upper classes—and therefore the public schools—in particular. Fees could be paid by capital appreciation, or met by swiftly-rising salaries. From the late 50s on the results of those years in the early and mid-40s, when the nation appears to have ungirded its loins in a more than successful attempt to replace its dead, meant an ever-increasing number of public school candidates. It was boom time in the quadrangles of the West.

This, roughly, is the economic background until we reach the last two or three years (when the picture is, as far as the public schools go, surprisingly the same but for very different reasons).

Their reactions to these physical and economic pressures—apart from the almost universal expansion—were diverse and often contradictory; but as far as the academic side is concerned it is clear there were, within this general frame, two fundamental influences: the first was the rise of virtually free university education as a result of the government grant system, the second was the growth of science.

The provision of free university education when there were a limited number of places meant intense and open competition for them where the public schools came under increasing pressure, especially from the grammar schools. The result was an immediate and continuing intensification of the work orientation in the public schools; in girls' and progressive schools as much as in the boys' schools.

The sphere in which this took place most noticeably was in science. In 1955 a number of leading industrial firms set up the Industrial Fund for the Advancement of Science in Schools, which had the sole purpose of making independent schools produce more trained scientists. It had to dispense, initially, some three million pounds, with more to follow. But there was more to it than this. A fundamental and fascinating development during the last thirty years amongst the middle classes is the increasing concern and, it would seem, actual affection that they have felt for their children. My own feeling is that this is largely due to the collapse of the nanny system during and after the war and the growth of love consequent upon parents bringing up their own children. Certainly all schools are clear about the far deeper involvement of parents in the education and well-being of those at them. But in this sphere it perhaps hardly needs love to explain what happened. As the Colonial Services and the army and navy collapsed as sources of employment, so, in the nick of time, middle-class parents made industry and science acceptable (although industry came last and law, medicine, accountancy and the foreign and home Civil Service were the first choices). And both this and the work orientation generally were much reinforced by the steady but inexorable move towards egalitarianism. The working of all the various taxes directed against hereditary wealth, the increasing difficulty of accumulating and passing on capital, all meant that endowing their children with a good education gradually became one of the most certain ways of ensuring their future prosperity.

In the face of industry's lavish bribery, but more particularly spurred on by this last, traditionally the strongest of all pressures to which they could be subjected, pressures from their middle-class market, it is hardly surprising the schools responded with alacrity. The academic prejudices and obsessions of centuries dissolved in moments. Laboratories were built, science masters engaged, workshops and lathes and model furnaces became common. The richly endowed schools, and girls' schools—not eligible for grants—diverted funds and organised appeals. During the 1950s the science side at Roedean trebled (it had always been strong at Cheltenham and Cheltenham-influenced schools like St. Leonard's). Of course, there was resistance. The momentum of so many years didn't stop quite dead. At Winchester classics kept out English, for instance, till the late 1960s. One English master was introduced in the early 1950s, but he proved too exciting and was quietly moved out. A droning classicist, a local parson, was brought in to reduce English to its proper level. Eton still has more classics masters than it needs and there is always vague talk of this being adjusted. But in general, the change was swift and decisive. By 1968 a survey by the Public Schools Appointment Bureau showed the four top careers boys wanted to go into to be these:

1. Engineering   10·5%
2. Science   7·3%
3. Commerce or Industry   7·0%
4. Medicine, Dentistry, Veterinary   5·3%

It has so far proved impossible to check to what degree boys do what they say they would like to do—but there must be quite a close correlation. The trend revealed in 1968 continues. Here are the ten most popular careers of the 1974 and 1975 public school leavers. (Figures from Independent Schools Careers Organisation):

		1975	(1974)
1.	Engineering	9·85	(9·48)
2.	Science	8·01	(7·42)
3.	Economics	7·26	(5·94)
4.	Law	5·21	(5·95)
5.	Languages	4·84	(4·88)
6.	Medicine	4·57	(5·19)
7.	Accountancy	4·40	(4·21)
8.	Classics	3·88	(3·99)
9.	Agriculture, Forestry, Horticulture	3·83	(4·05)
10.	Services	3·25	(3·02)

At Winchester today, as with many public schools, more science is taught than any other single subject.

Both as a result of these two major moves (the increased orientation towards work and towards science) and also as a concurrent development, the last thirty years have seen a great surge of purely educational ideas and experiments. Mathematics, for example, has been entirely restructured from the base on a new system which originated in the University of Southampton, but was pioneered in practice by the public schools. There are the Nuffield Courses in science and classical languages: these are experiments to interest and stimulate the pupils, involving such things as the use of gadgets, self-devised experiments in science or package tours to Herculanaeum in the classics. In modern languages the move has been towards oral fluency—hence the language laboratory of tapes and play-back machines which is the photograph of every modern school—or of every modern school that can afford one. (They are very expensive. Winchester has a good one; so does Rugby.) It is possible this is an aspect of the general freeing and opening up of our society which is still taking place, this emphasis on communication. It is happening in a fairly small way even in English—a subject much less susceptible to change—with the

English Speaking Board Exams. A boy or girl chooses a subject, works on it; then talks on it and is cross-questioned. The point is what you say, how you say it, how quickly and effectively you can come back on the questioning. This is clearly a part of drama—or rather drama is an aspect of this subject, and so it impinges on art.

One might also note how often public schools now invent subjects or create their own syllabus. At Oundle, where they have a course in computer programming, the history syllabus at O-level is entirely the school's design. Or I think of David Butcher at Bedales. He is a fascinating and passionate man who sees that what is wrong with our education is its neglect of both the visual and the practical—the unfulfilled need to work with the hands. He senses that the current concern with the environment, ecology, the look of our cities and the objects we are creating—the concern, that is, with the mess we have made of our civilisation—springs from an awareness of this neglect. Almost single-handedly he has created an entirely new A-level course (and got it accepted by Oxford and Cambridge) covering this whole field at depth—"I more or less have to write my own textbooks sometimes"—in which both practical and theoretical work is produced. The practical " on course" work made during the year counts to the exam and adds zest to the task. Bedales hums with clean, powerful workshops, produces skilful carpenters and joiners reminiscent of Oundle in Sanderson's day, all led by this highly-effective visionary.

The needs both of the middle classes and of industry, the competition induced by free universities, the enthusiasm engendered by exciting curricular developments, have all generated an immense academic thrust in the public schools over the last thirty years, quite unprecedented so far in this history for its power, for the scope of its subjects, and for the degree to which it has spread throughout each individual school. And this thrust has been still further augmented by a number of other developments, some old, some new.

For one thing, the teaching in most public schools is still highly competitive—moving up and down is faster than in State schools, there are elaborate incentives, "fortnightly orders" and so on. In college at Eton, for example, privileges depend on your position in class. Eton, too, like a number of the older schools, has a great number of prizes for work— some worth trifling sums, others, like the Newcastle, worth several hundred pounds. At Winchester if you don't get your remove (that is, move up) within three terms you are in danger of expulsion. Every form of teaching—individual coaching and tutorials, seminars, what the Dalton Plan calls "assignment" work, classroom lectures—is employed to get pupils to learn; at the top the teaching is, as it has always been, close to that at university, both in standard and method.

The change to a general atmosphere of academic competition—so different from anything we have seen heretofore—can be demonstrated further by the fact that at three schools—Winchester, Westminster and Eton—where they still divide the scholars from the rest, a system which up till recently (this does not apply to Winchester) probably militated against a high level of general scholarship because it was felt that these little groups alone would provide sufficient academic distinction for the school's reputation, now operates in precisely the opposite way. Because the academic results of a scholar are usually better than their peers outside, with whom they are taught, their presence in a class is stimulating.

But more fundamental than conscious stimulation—rewards and prestige for learning, punishment for failing to do so—are the unconscious assumptions. The middle classes, as we have seen, have been sending their children away to prep schools and public schools for generations—in some cases for hundreds of years. From the moment they are born, they absorb ever-increasing indications of this background—a team photograph in the lavatory, say, or how fathers, grandfathers and great-grandfathers all went to the school they are destined for, how one was a wet-bob or the other won the history prize. They are taken to see the school before going to it— and there is their grandfather's name, squashed between two generals, in gold on some panel. That is to say by the time they arrive there the vast majority accept all the goals of the school, its values, activities and disciplines, at first without question. And, overwhelmingly today, a major goal is academic, and particularly examination, achievement.

It is this—to the middle classes themselves obvious—fact that strikes teachers who have moved over from the State system with such delight: the ease with which they can teach, the silence, *the assumption on the part of the pupils that they are there to learn.* I found this again and again, all over the country.

There are further contributory causes of the increased academic thrust, some connected with this willingness to learn. One which is partly so is that the standard of teachers has risen during this period. Several factors are involved. Low wages were the curse of the public school master in the 19th century. Ironically, it was the despised State system that started and then consolidated the change. In the middle of the 1914 war H. A. L. Fisher created a national system of pay and pension. Public schools now found that they would lose assistant masters if they did not equal these— but the figures were not generous. (In 1933 the average salary at a public school was still only £169 p.a.) It was not until a committee under Lord Burnham drew up a reasonable scale for State teachers in 1944, with appropriate differentials, that even small public schools provided a decent job. Since then every increase in the State scale has meant an increase in public schools—and an anguished flurry of raised fees. Today, salaries at public schools are usually higher than Burnham's scale, and the schools provide benefits like cheap accommodation and cheap schooling. Better wages have been accompanied by better training. Since the mid 1960s practically all public school teachers have acquired the Diploma of Education—on the whole it is now a necessary qualification, though headmasters and headmistresses can hire whom they choose.

Good masters are no longer attracted to public schools to the same extent by the superior facilities—though on the whole the facilities are better, just as the buildings and the surroundings are more attractive. But since the war the State spending on education has been colossal. In 1969-70 it overtook defence and has kept comfortably ahead ever since. In 1973–74 it was £7·263 million; 1974–75, £7·316 million; 1975–76, £7·493 million. (Defence, meanwhile, was £5·598 million in 1975–76.)*

One might note here that, as Dancy says, the widely held belief that public schools have huge endowments—great chunks of Birmingham or London dating from the 14th century, whose income piles privilege on privilege—is false. There are certainly some wealthy ones: Eton has property in Hendon, Finchley and Hampstead and from this and other sources derives about thirty per cent of its income; Winchester gets about twenty per cent from endowments; Rugby is well-off. But out of some 295 public schools, only about five—those I have mentioned, and Dulwich and Whitgift—rely on important contributions from this source. The rest have a good deal to spend—they charge enormous fees and they are certainly well equipped; but their wealth is not historical.

What is better is the standard of the pupils. The State must educate everybody; the public schools select. Of course they do not invariably select the clever. Progressive schools in particular try to choose so as to form a variety of types and backgrounds. Schools tend to boast that they have "mixed ability"—at Cheltenham Ladies' College I was told they went down to the State "D" stream. But in fact I would say they had very few at this level. A master from the State system, now at a public school, said of his predecessor at the school, "As for the intake—T. S. said they had mixed ability. *Mixed ability!* He'd no idea. Honestly—just because he had a few with an IQ of 102. I used to just laugh." In fact the vast majority of public schools select on the Common Entrance Examination results (they correct the papers themselves) and the standard—or potential—is high (though it is still often a good deal lower than the lowest accepted by the [old] grammar schools).

Finally, the recession over the last two years and the stabilising of the population have stopped an educational expansion which had been continuing for nearly thirty years. There are, therefore, as with the Depression in the 1930s, too many teachers seeking too few posts. The result, as then, will be to raise the standard.

The same ex-State teacher I quoted above said, "And I'm afraid the

*Figures, at 1976 Survey Prices, from the Government's Expenditure Plan, Command 6721–1.

calibre of the State is just not as good. They're dedicated, humdrum, run-of-the-mill teachers." I am not sure whether he is right; nor do I see how you can prove it either way. The fact that public schools get better examination results than the State system as a whole does not necessarily mean that the teachers themselves are better. The factors we have been considering—the new middle-class and public school impetus to learn, the willingness of the pupils to be taught, the high standard of equipment and of entry, the competitive position in the teacher market and so on—are quite sufficient to explain the differences. There are other complexities. Some of these factors—the standard of equipment, the teacher market—apply to both State and independent. As with so much in England, this situation is muddled by class. There are brilliant teachers in the State system who might leave to join the independent one but feel too embarrassed to do so; there are many more who wouldn't join it because they hate it, and wish to devote their lives to redressing what they see as the educational disadvantage of the rest of society. Nevertheless, these various things mean it is more satisfying, as a teacher pure and simple, to work in a public school. In most professions the likelihood must be that the best practitioners will go where the conditions of work are most rewarding. The probability is, therefore, that the standard of teachers is higher in the independent sector. At the least we can say that it is higher now than at any other time in this history. And, as far as comparisons with the State system go, I was repeatedly struck, when I did find teachers who had come over from comprehensive or grammar schools, by how they always seemed to be exceptionally talented. David Butcher, of Bedales, for example, was from the State system. And if some of the best State teachers are tempted into the public schools—who can blame them? I think of a remarkable ex-headmaster of a comprehensive school, who wished to remain anonymous, and who had sworn never to join the independent system. He was at another progressive public school, and had, while still in the State system, by chance read Curry, Reddie, Badley, Bertrand Russell and other figures with whom we are familiar.

I was amazed to find, expressed fifty, sixty, seventy years ago, many of the ideas I wanted to carry out in my own school. But it wasn't possible. They're just not conditioned to accept education as something valuable. I wanted to have good relationships between staff and pupils—but it's a bloody battle for survival in a State school. You've got to get your form under control. You haven't time for good relationships. . . . Then take another point. The parents here thank you. They are paying, therefore they've got to be right, therefore they thank you. In the State system, someone else is paying, someone else has employed you and they've made a mistake and therefore you're wrong. . . . Oh, it will change. But it will take three generations, seventy-five years. And I only have one life.

2 The training of leaders

In the *East Anglian Daily Times* one day in 1975 I read this report:

> Anthony John Summer, 17, who was expelled from an Essex public school for smoking cannabis, was told by Mr. Justice Thesiger, "I always doubt whether someone of a public school education gains much from Borstal training. He may even be a danger, through being regarded by others as a potential leader of escapes by virtue of his superior education."

We saw how during the 19th century, and indeed for many years afterwards, the public schools inculcated a fairly crude idea of social hierarchy and upper–class leadership, whose purest later expression was in the armed forces and Imperial Service, but which was implicit in any sphere an ex-public school boy (and later girl) might find him–or herself.

The point is that though there have been significant changes in the authority structure—fagging virtually gone, beating much less and usually non-existent, privileges minimal, punishments mild, and so on—the system of power and authority and such privileges as there are still extend from the headmaster or mistress, through the staff, to a fairly elaborate system of boy and girl power. The idea is to learn how to exercise authority over oneself and others, and so varied are the spheres—games, societies, dormitories, the organisation of the house, etc.—that there are few pupils who don't exercise *some* form of authority. There are great variations of this. For one thing, the word "authority" is seldom used. Masters talk—accurately—about self-confidence and raising self-esteem; about learning how to trust your own initiative, to think independently, about learning how to get on with other people, learning about the complexities of social life. Another favourite word—used to me by Michael McCrum of Eton and by John Dancy in his book—is "responsibility". Public schools "teach", or really encourage to develop, responsible behaviour; and if you find yourself in a position of authority in industry, say, then, "responsible" will mean consideration, consultation, willingness to compromise, the ability to get on with people and not antagonise a work force, as well as take decisions. From the mid–1950s on, industry began increasingly to recruit from the public schools, having shown, according to Dancy, some preference for the shop floor. The qualities they sought, as leading companies reported to the Acton Society Trust in 1962, were these: ability to get on with people, fifty-nine per cent; intelligence, thirty-one per cent; integrity, twenty-two per cent; leadership, eighteen per cent; initiative, sixteen per cent. But surely the significant fact is that they preferred to choose public school boys. Power is power, however tactfully you clothe it, and indeed, the very concept of "responsibility" presupposes the power to exercise that responsibility, and some sphere in which to do so. Ultimately, in this area, I think the premise behind a public school education—although a great deal more subtle and humane—is the same today as it has always been: it is to train the leaders of society. A few masters admitted this, indeed gloried in it. David Butcher at Bedales believes that only by fundamentally altering society's views towards labour and towards the visual will we be able to clear up the ecological and environmental mess in our industrial civilisation. But to do this, he must alter the people who are going to lead society. "The decision-makers of the future are here. I came from the State system, because here I can really achieve things. The head backs me, the governors back me. I can change the whole attitude to practical labouring work"—he held out his large tough hands—"even now, looked down on. The root of our troubles is that we are out of touch with the practical, the physical, the visual."

3 Exam pressure; academic achievement

Over the last thirty years the public schools have enjoyed a considerable amount of examination success. For example: in 1969 pupils from a public school were twenty per cent more likely to get two A-levels than pupils from State schools; Appendix I shows the league table of university awards from 1967–70 (ignore for the moment the striking success of the grammar schools) and Appendix J shows the most recent figures for A-level passes and university entrants, comparing the State and Maintained sector with the Independent and Direct Grant sector. These are average figures. Leading schools habitually do far better: from Westminster between eighty and eighty-five per cent of the boys go to university; Manchester Grammar School, seventy-six point one per cent; Winchester, seventy-five point two per cent; Dulwich, seventy point two per cent.

But there is another side to this success (Dancy is particularly good here). The freer, more open, more stimulating methods of teaching—such as are now represented, for example, by the Nuffield Courses—are most easily used and of the greatest benefit to the intelligent. It is they who can respond to the challenge and excitement and are best able to make use of the opportunities for research and discovery. The less intelligent find it harder. That is why progressive schools have had to have high staff-pupil ratios or, as with the Dalton Plan, have expected more of their staff, or have not cared over much for examination results. (An ironic, indeed tragic, corollary of this is that in choosing this type of teaching method the State comprehensives have adopted one which is likely to disadvantage still further the very pupils, the less able, they were hoping to help most.)

But the public schools evolved partly to teach the less intelligent members of the middle class—Beckett's "rich and thick"; their methods were designed for this purpose. This is still so. Although they don't have "mixed ability" to the degree that a comprehensive does, they still take boys of far lower IQ than the old grammar schools (see Appendix K)—

and do very well with these too. Dancy estimates (a rough estimate, taking Lancing as a model) that out of all those at public school who would have failed the old eleven-plus (that is, would not have gone to grammar school) ninety-three per cent get five or more O-levels and fifty per cent of these go on to get one or two A-levels and go to university. What has happened is that those standards of scholarship which, for centuries, we saw the public schools reserve for comparatively few have now, to whatever extent possible, become general.

This examination success has been gained at the expense of a good deal of relaxation. The schools, particularly for those in their last two years, are dominated by the need to pass exams in the same way as they once struggled to win matches—only these are single battles. You can sense the pressure immediately you visit them; and it reveals itself in numerous ways. John Sumption said that he'd noticed a new phenomenon in the teaching of art at Eton: boys came to take O- or A-level, and then never came to his art classes again. Cheltenham Ladies' College said the same. At progressive schools the problem is clearly particularly acute; at other public schools, what has happened is merely an extension of what was always part of their ethos; but such pressure is at variance with a fundamental aspect of the progressive ideal. The old ideal has had to shift. Bedales: "I've noticed things which might once have been important are being neglected. For example, we have an exchange with a comprehensive in Leicester; now, it's so difficult to reconcile with the time-table that nothing has been extended. Or drama say. It's not possible to do a lot of drama and games and work. You have to choose." It is seen in the efforts schools make to broaden the areas of study. It has often been a criticism of English education that it leads to early specialisation—a late result of the early classical impetus. Plainly, exam panic will intensify this. At Roedean, for example (all that I have said in this chapter applies equally to the girls' schools),the first-year sixth, aged fifteen and taking two A-levels, have five or six classes out of the thirty-five allotted to subsidiary courses—as on geology, say, or the history of art. At Rugby they are even bolder: out of thirty-five periods, seven are general studies (of which three are art and music) and there are four optional periods. Other schools have similar arrangements. Some of the top academic schools have always prided themselves on the purity of their scholarship—their best pupils study something for its own sake, for the love of knowledge. They pass examinations in the subject, as it were, incidentally and with ease. Specialisation hasn't bothered them. On the contrary. And if you study four or five subjects to A-level I'm not sure you can be said to be specialising exactly; you are in fact coming much nearer to the French system (that is eight or nine subjects—one of them physical education—studied over a seven-year course to reach approximately our A-level standard or higher by the time the Baccalaureat is taken). But even Winchester, the prime example of pure scholarship, has become far more exam-conscious recently; though they also give scientists six non-science lessons a week, and try, rather unsuccessfully, to get arts students to do a bit of science.

But, as far as examination results go, public schools are as effective as any other educational institution in the country. Many people would say that if you accept wider aspects of education as valuable—attitudes of mind, powers of discrimination, the ability to express diverse parts of the personality—then they give the best education. And this has posed a particular problem to socialist parents over the last thirty years. They too have thought as Anthony Crosland did in the quotation with which I headed this chapter, and the instinct to provide the best upbringing for your children is a violently powerful one; at the same time, they have disliked what they see as the dividing, privileged aspects of public schools. Instinct has often won. The prep and public school system has had few more savage critics than Orwell. In 1945 he wrote that the Labour government's first act must be "to abolish all titles, the House of Lords and the public schools". But he wanted to send his (adopted) son to Eton. Harold Wilson, Laski—a list of prominent socialists who have sent their children to public schools would cover pages. (Tony Benn entered his son, Simon, for Westminster, but when he failed the entrance exam he sent him to Holland Park Comprehensive—and has made a virtue ever since out of this "egalitarian" decision.)

4 Public schools and the foundation of an élite: the case of Eton

An élite means literally the choice part or flower of society; but like most current words it has gained and is used with a penumbra of associative meanings: an élite is a group, it enjoys the position of status and prestige, it is to a degree self-selecting and self-perpetuating, and there is sometimes a hint that it holds power. We have already seen how in the last century and deep into this one certain jobs and positions were open first on class grounds to people who shared middle- and upper–middle–class backgrounds, assumptions, values, accents and so on. Before even considering their qualifications it was just unthinkable that a barrister, say, would have been lower class. But even at the start, and increasingly during these years, academic and examination qualifications were also necessary for the professions, for doctors, solicitors, barristers, teachers, for posts in the Civil Service, the Foreign Office, to become officers in the army and navy and so on. Today the exam structure and career structure are almost parallel—the one precedes and dictates the other. One would suppose it axiomatic, therefore, that a class-based, or rather class-indoctrinating educational system—particularly one part of whose aim was and is to provide the leaders of society—which could also provide examination and academic success and which, in the educational picture of the country generally, had no rival, could not help but be the foundation of a social and probably political élite. And so, until quite recently, it has proved.

In 1950 Dr. N. Hans, in *Independent Schools and the Liberal Professions*, analysed the histories of 975 key Victorian figures. Sixty-six per cent came from sixty public schools—an amount totally disproportionate to their number in relation to the country generally. Between 1918 and 1935 forty-three per cent of all MPs came from public school. The Conservative Party were overwhelmingly public school, but they were significant, and growing, in the Labour Party (see Appendix L) and this was particularly so in Cabinet, where it is arguable that such power as MPs still retain exists. For instance there were four public school boys in Ramsey MacDonald's cabinet, while in Attlee's eleven out of thirty-four came from public schools, most from Winchester—Stafford Cripps, Hugh Gaitskell, Richard Crossman, Kenneth Younger, Douglas Jay. In the Liberal and Conservative parties what has been astonishing from 1884 almost until today, and often commented on, has been the extraordinary and long-lasting dominance of Eton—from 1901 to 1924 a quarter of all Cabinets were Old Etonians, in 1945 and 1950 one-tenth were Old Etonians; Macmillian was delighted to boast six Old Etonians in his Cabinet (during his day one-fifth of the Tory Party were Old Etonians) and before Heath the last three Conservative Prime Ministers had all been Etonians. Even in 1971 twenty-two per cent of the Government were Old Etonians, with three in the Cabinet and—an amazing number—sixty-five in Parliament. The same picture emerges from studies of other groups. W. L. Guttsman, in *The British Political Elite*, 1963 (it is odd how often we are investigated by foreigners), at the end of much tortuous analysis concluded: "Among the 339 persons in the group of the influential here analysed 151, or forty-five per cent, had received their pre-university education in public boarding schools—two-thirds of them in the twenty major public schools specially investigated." He went on. "There exists today in Britain a 'ruling class', if we mean by it a group which provides the majority of those who occupy positions of power, and who, in their turn, can materially assist *their* sons to reach similar positions." The position in 1971 was still substantially the same and Anthony Sampson in *The New Anatomy of Britain* was able to quote with confidence tables from the Newsom Report of 1968 (see Appendix M): this showed, for example, among much else, that seventy per cent of directors of big firms, eighty per cent of judges and seventy-seven per cent of directors of the Bank of England went to public schools.

But by 1971 changes which had started after the war and been gradually growing ever since now began to bulk large. The élite dominance of the public schools was at last declining. Sampson was able to write: "Whether the public schools will be able to maintain their confident position in the power structure of the 1980s must be very doubtful." He was able to write this for three reasons, the first of which, admittedly speculative, was that public schools would collapse because the middle classes would cease to be able to afford them.

The second reason has already been noted: the rise in importance of the new universities. In this area too they were becoming a dominating influence—it was there that contacts and friendships were being made, their degrees that counted. And the public school influence here was declining; in 1967/8 they still accounted for thirty-eight per cent of entrants to Oxford and Cambridge, but only for sixteen per cent of all university entrants.

This was because, the third reason for Sampson's statement, the grammar school successes were now very significant indeed:* in 1967/8 for instance forty-eight per cent of direct-grant pupils went to university and twenty-six per cent of maintained, as compared with thirty per cent of those from public schools (see also Appendix J). Nor, as Sampson noted, was there any resulting loss of confidence from going to a grammar school—or at least it was not evident in men like Roy Jenkins and Denis Healey. Michael McCrum said to me that the positions of power are still public school dominated because they reflect patterns operating twenty or twenty-five years ago. We must try to guess what would be the effect of the educational patterns operating now; it was plain to him that the already shrinking public school dominance would shrink still more. There is no doubt he was right: the enormous and increasing success of the grammar schools—acting as a bridge between the State system and the avenues of power—the continuing development of the new free universities, both these made it likely that during the 1980s the public schools would have had an influence much closer to the percentage of the school population with which they dealt.

But now—the bridge has been smashed. In 1975 the grammar schools began to be swept away. The Labour government decided to implement a decision taken in principle long ago in 1965. As I write nearly a hundred per cent of the old direct-grant grammar schools have decided to go fully independent; as have three or four of the old maintained grammar schools. In effect they will join the public schools. Many of them will find this quite in character. We saw before how steeped the grammar schools were in the public school ethos. Many of them, particularly the biggest direct-grant schools like Manchester, King Edward's, Birmingham, Bradford

---

*Grammar schools were of two sorts: the direct grant, which comprised most of the oldest and successful, and the maintained. The direct grant took a proportion of fee-paying pupils, and not less than a quarter, latterly sixty per cent from the State system. In return they received a direct grant from the Department of Education, and had to have local government people on their boards of governors. However, the local authorities did not really interfere with them as they did, in return for their grants, with the maintained grammar schools.

and Latymer Upper, rival the most successful public schools in their age, their traditions, their huge sixth forms and their entries into universities. If you stretch the in any case vague enough boundaries of the middle class they are, as the Dennison Report said in 1970, "predominantly middle-class institutions. . . . Three out of four pupils come from the homes of white-collar workers: three out of five have fathers in professional or managerial occupations. Only one out of thirteen comes from a semi-skilled or unskilled worker's family." They have come more and more to resemble the public schools with whose interests they have so much in common. It is even, on one technical ground, difficult to tell them apart. A definition of a public school is one whose headmaster is a member of the 226 strong Headmasters' Conference. Today this includes seventy-five direct grant schools—well over a quarter of the Conference. Now the identity is complete. It is very difficult to be entirely accurate about this, but public schools at present account for something between five per cent and eight per cent of the secondary school population (figures come from DES statistics and the Independent Schools Information Service); direct grant grammar schools account for about two per cent. If these are successful in their attempt to go fully independent (they seem fairly confident that they will be successful) then there will be a new middle class public school block on the road to a completely democratic form of education comprising some seven to ten per cent of children now at secondary schools. The position today, therefore, is that public schools continue to provide a very much larger number of people for the positions of comfort, status and (arguably) power than would be expected from the proportion they form of secondary schools; and that this will increase and not, as seemed likely only a short time ago, diminish.

"When an Etonian Cabinet minister comes into office he expects to find a Wykehamist civil servant running the department" (Lord Longford). I was given a great deal of such knowing stuff while writing this book. "What are truisms at Rugby are paradoxes at Harrow, and an Eton custom would prove a Marlborough revelation." "A lady wants a chair: the Wykehamist fetches it, the Etonian offers it, the Harrovian sits in it."

These uproarious in-joke sketches are of course usually rubbish. John Rodgers says Winchester has produced no great men, only men of influence, top civil servants, because "to a Wykehamist success is a sign of failure, since success demands qualities of thrusting, enthusiasm and ruthlessness contrary to the school tradition—which is summed up in the school motto, 'Manners Makyth Man'." How then did Manners makyth Gaitskell, Cecil King, Field Marshal Earl Wavell, A. P. Herbert, Oswald Mosley, Richard Crossman and dozens of other combative and often very successful men? You might as well say, as David Cecil used to, that people from Harrow all had black hair brushed back—soigné. He would point, for proof, to Cecil Beaton, Arthur Bryant, Terence Rattigan. There are sometimes differences between the products of various schools, no doubt—you could probably tell the difference between someone from Winchester and someone from Dartington say—but the differences imposed by different schools are not nearly so great as the uniformity imposed by them all; that was especially true in the past, but is true still.

Nevertheless the dominance exerted by Eton on the political life of this country from the 1880s until the 1960s is extraordinary. Is there anything special in the organisation of that school which might account for it? Hollis gives this search as one of the main reasons for his history and goes into it quite deeply; other writers have done the same.

The process began, in fact, in the 18th century. Although at the start Westminster dominated politics (Newcastle, Pelham, Pultney, Carteret and Hervey were all Westminsters), Eton was following it closely. Walpole, Townshend and others went to Eton. And this position was consolidated—as it was bound to be—since would-be politicians would be sent there to make powerful contacts, like Pitt, Bute, North, Fox and many others later in the century. By the end of it, Eton had overtaken Westminster. Clearly, family has a great deal to do with it. But Hollis and others have pinned down much more precise influences. There is, for instance, the tutor system, whereby someone, who may or may not be his housemaster, keeps an eye on his work through school—this is evidence, according to McCrum, of greater "personal contact". There is the rule of boys, library and Pop, and we saw with Connolly how real "political" battles were fought to change the conditions of their lives. Etonians are very keen on the lessons this teaches in democracy and also the depravity of man—Eton is the Eden of Original Cynicism. There is the fact that the headmaster is magistrate. "The unique feature of Eton life [Hollis speaking] is that the Headmaster's Court is the magistrate's court before which every offender against a regulation committed outside the boarding house or the school room has to appear. Offences far more trivial than at any other school are dealt with by the headmaster."

Seen from the close perspective of the initiate, these do indeed seem to be astounding differences. But I must confess to me, viewing from a position high above 200 schools, they seem trivial. Nor are they really unique. Rugby, Bryanston, UCS and other schools have had equivalent tutor systems for many years. In practice, as we saw, there is not a very important difference between prefect *administration*, and the prefect oligarchy and very limited law-making at Eton. We looked at equally relevant and ferocious battles at Charterhouse and Wellington. If it is concern with pupils and exercises in self-government that have made Eton successful politically then all progressive schools far surpass her; but in fact Eton is significantly different from other public schools here. As for cynicism—more cynical than Harrow? Than Westminster? I think all boys' public schools teach one to be fairly cynical. Most schools make the

Cricket at Roedean.

An Angela Brazil jacket.

Strictly speaking "The Tuck Shop" was usually on school premises; here, in the 1920s, girls are buying tuck at a local carrier and greengrocer.

Lord Faversham jumping at
an Eton fire practice.

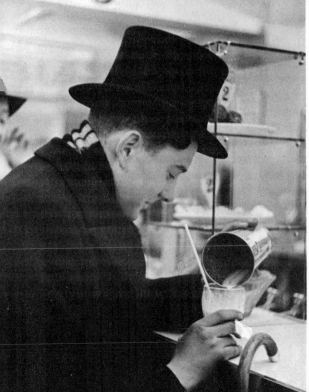

Westminster boy. Umbrellas
were traditional, as they
were at Eton and some other
schools, until comparatively
recently.

headmaster punish for certain offences; I don't see why making him punish for trivial ones does much more than waste his time (it does, however, allow him to affect the atmosphere of discipline in the school. You will remember Keate; and this fact was a source of trouble at Eton in recent years).

But actually this petty magistrate's rôle of Eton's headmaster does give us the clue to real differences. It is a factor imposing some uniformity on a very large school. Eton has always been enormous. In the 19th century, with, from 1855 on, 800–1,000 or so boys, it was two or three times as large as any other school (in the case of Westminster, ten times as large). Even today, with about 1,250 boys it is the largest. This has meant that the autonomy of the houses has been greater, if that were possible, than at other schools. Today, Eton housemasters are told at about the age of thirty that they are to get a house. For thirteen years they then "collect" its future members and assume command in their early forties. But this, as well as working to make Eton almost entirely consist of sons of Old Etonians (even today nearly seventy per cent are the sons of Old Etonians; it is like an hereditary club), gives far more control, a far greater sense of "ownership". Eton has always been rather like eleven or twelve (or whatever number of houses there are at the time) different schools. This, with the variety of influence it affords, together with the increased roulette chance of successful material that comes from large numbers, are probably significant factors. And numbers bring confidence. In a small school, ten eccentrics stand out. At Eton, they are lost. Until fairly recently, when they all started to relax, Eton does seem to have been more tolerant of intellectuals and nonconformists than most other public schools.

But an even greater source of confidence to Etonians than the size of the school (after all a lot of the old direct-grant grammar schools have been and are very large—Manchester has 1,400 boys at the moment) has been their class. Intellectuals and eccentrics were tolerated because if they were at Eton, they must be all right. Sociologists have shown (what everyone knew anyway) that the tendency to do the same sort of thing as your father and family have done before is extremely strong. In this respect, as in others, we know schools to be like families—if you went to Wellington (this into the 1950s) you would be surrounded by the sons of soldiers, as by the sons of doctors at Epsom; the idea of those careers would occur naturally to you. At Eton, the tradition of political families going there, the uniformity of upper-class boys going there—with their "right" to rule —was decisive. In the 1920s, Anthony Powell noted, there had been for years, centuries indeed, a sense that Etonians would rule. "The government of the country was somehow made almost a personal matter." In the early 1950s the ideal was still that of the aristocratic country gentleman. The pictures on the boys' walls were of hunting and shooting. The lower classes were to be paternally looked after, treated well—and governed. The overwhelming conclusion about Eton, against which all other considerations grow pale, is the obvious one: how colossal is the part that class, family, position and wealth have played in English politics until very recently; and in Conservative politics (seven Old Etonians in the Shadow Cabinet as I write) still play.

5 Class and the egalitarian revolution

England has always exhibited an extraordinarily complicated tangle of snobbery and equality, of subservience and independence. In the 1930s, following Orwell, I used comics—alongside much else—to demonstrate the extent to which the public school ethos had sunk through the social strata generally. Today the success of programmes like *Upstairs, Downstairs* or *The Duchess of Duke Street*, the continuing popularity of P. G. Wodehouse or Peter Wimsey might suggest that social rank of this Victorian and Edwardian sort still played a part in the English social scene, which it does not. No doubt there is some residual snobbery involved in the pleasure these entertainments provide, but it is very minor. Historical novels are also extremely popular, but that does not mean people still subscribe to the values of the 18th century; the obvious explanation is the true one. We watch and read these things because we want to escape; we want to return to a time of stability and social cohesion, a time of wealth and confidence when England was great.

For the last fifty or sixty years social barriers have been slowly but steadily altering and diminishing; and as they do we see the presumptions of the immediately preceding decades as intolerable. The 50s, 40s, and 30s now stand condemned. Roxburgh, it will be remembered, was quite openly, and to us unpleasantly, snobbish (he once congratulated the Headmaster of Canford that his "school list would soon resemble an extract from *Debrett*"). To what extent does this sort of thing continue in the public schools now?

Certainly, it has not vanished, even if it is now disguised. Sometimes it is barely disguised. Mallory Wober quoted a deputy head: "We try to get rid of accents; they are a lazy way of speaking." At another school a teacher, embattled in her bunker, her pocket of reaction, said to him, "I think there are still parents who would consider it an insult for their children to go to the same school as the butcher's children." I found the same sort of thing, though not as crude as this. Often attitudes to class revealed themselves unconsciously in the way the State system was spoken about. I spoke to a particularly obnoxious boy at one of the old great schools. He told me he didn't conform. A public school *taught* you not to conform. He went to deb dances, for instance, not to dance but to laugh at them. He was clever. He was at a clever school, which meant, he supposed, he must be clever. "There was this man who'd come here. He'd really come from rock bottom, picked himself up off the floor and made it to

Win. Coll." It turned out that "rock bottom" meant from a leading London grammar school. Similarly, Mallory Wober found that the heads of girls' schools would excuse themselves for not providing any contact with boys, because there were no other schools nearby from which they could come. In fact, there were often several schools in the area, but they were State schools.

But these were remnants. In fact, as far as I could judge, the movement, or attempted movement, in the public schools has been in precisely the opposite direction. They, like the rest of the country, have responded to the egalitarian trend of the last thirty years but, relative to their history, responded even more powerfully. And this move towards equality has been accompanied by, and is almost certainly related to, the move towards a freer and less authoritarian society—a move which has assumed such proportions to some people that they speak of a "crisis of authority" by which they mean a crisis of no authority. These two social movements have been so striking and have had such a powerful effect on our subject— underpinning as they do the second great change over the last thirty years, the liberalising of the public schools—that I think we should try to discover something of what caused them.

Both processes are in part 20th-century ones, they have been continuous throughout it and have their roots deep in the reactions to the 19th-century inequality and authoritarian social pattern. But the peculiar flavour and peculiar rapidity of these movements over the last thirty years began at the end of the war and it is tempting to look therefore in the war itself for possible causes. I said when we were discussing Correlli Barnett that the British reaction to the war—when we suddenly became "cannon hard" again—was at its very bottom a return to the hierarchical obedience of a feudal fighting machine, a structure which had been preserved over centuries in the class system. This was true; but at the same time we felt as a nation united in a way that was quite unique. Never before had *everyone* been united in waging a war like this. There was unity, of course, in 1914– 1918. But the actual fighting was out of sight. Now, the whole of the south of England watched as the public school boys from Biggin Hill brought enemy planes crashing to destruction on the Weald of Kent or the Sussex Downs. But, far more than this, the whole country fought too—in munitions factories, down mines, digging for victory, collecting for salvage, with ration books and under hails of bombs in London or Coventry. And since they were united against common danger people felt equal: you couldn't detect accent through a gas mask, a countess could be blown to bits as easily as a butcher's wife. And of all people women felt equal—equal to men. The war ensured they would never return to their cages. What they would return to would be a better society. The Phoenix myth is really a war myth. The dream that the fire and agony are worth it because they will result in something better. And since all were fighting equally, all should benefit equally; a mass war means mass reward. The egalitarian movement expressed in the exhilarating Labour legislation from 1945 onwards was a result of the equality engendered by the war and an attempt to make one, to continue as one, a hitherto divided nation melted together in the fierce heat of battle.

The war may have had other effects. Enormous and dramatic changes in status, living conditions, jobs, marriages and so on occurred to nearly everyone very quickly indeed. The possibility of quick change, in certain circumstances its desirability, was made clear, and indeed became customary. Voluntary change means freedom; people seldom seek servitude. And the very conditions of war—men leaving for the various fronts, perhaps to die, the long separations, the necessary abandoning of old customs in emergency, the influence of foreigners (the licentious American soldiery)—all resulted in less conventional and more spontaneous behaviour. I mentioned earlier the rather speculative idea put forward by my tutor Peter Laslett at Cambridge; that the break-up of vast but tightly knit armed forces is analogous to the break-up of a love affair and leads for a while to similarly anarchic and iconoclastic behaviour. On a par with this is a thesis put forward some years ago by Rattray Taylor in a fascinating book called *Sex in History*. His idea was that during wars men went off to fight and left the upbringing of children entirely to women. Women are more permissive than men and therefore children brought up during wars are freer and more independent and more likely to challenge convention. They have not had the male discipline which would have forced them to respect authority. This begs some questions and I don't think quite stands up to examination, but there is probably some truth in it.

Certainly in some quite profound ways our society is much freer than it was; but it is also possible to argue that we are not nearly as free as we think we are. Erich Fromm has argued that the decisive movements in the 20th century have been the growth of mass markets and mass democracies. Both have been persuaded that they want what they have been given: in politics by the mass vote; in consumption by advertising and the inculcation of the desire to consume more and more and "better" and "better" things. It has produced men who feel free, but who yet do what is expected, men who are led without leaders. Authority seems to have weakened, but it has just changed; instead of force, there is manipulation and suggestion. "In other words, in order to be adaptable, modern man is obliged to nourish the illusion that everything is done with his consent, even though . . . his consent is obtained, as it were, behind his back, or behind his consciousness." One might note that on this view, progressive education is really a similar trick—it is education by hidden persuasion and subtle coercion. It is not really free. It is a reflection of this particular aspect of social development. That is why both other public schools and the State system have finally adopted, quite uninfluenced either by the progressive writers or the progressive schools themselves, so many of its tenets. On this view, *One Flew Over the Cuckoo's Nest* is the accurate representation of public schools today where *If . . .* was of them in 1949. The engines of this social persuasion are many, but the media through which they work or are perceived are frequently the press, radio and television. That is why these have become so powerful and so feared. Alan Leigh, a master at Rugby with whom I discussed this, said that the "crisis of authority" was because the media were too powerful. Pressure groups had become adept at using them and could whip up such demagogic excitement that authority—that is the government—did not dare act. This fear of using authority became general and had infected the schools.

Finally, there is one recent development, so extraordinary, so massive, that it sometimes escapes comment by those facts alone. Over the last twenty-five years the *average* wealth in the country has quadrupled. This has never happened before, at any time in the history of the world, and is unlikely to happen again. It has been an astounding economic explosion, going off within a society whose structure was already altering because of the forces we have just outlined. It must inevitably have been one of the cardinal forces, probably the cardinal force, leading to change.

I would, rather tentatively, suggest five areas where this explosive economic force exerted itself. First, reinforcing the war, it showed that change in this most fundamental sphere was possible. Change was therefore possible anywhere; social hierarchies, social conventions were even less sacrosanct than before. Indeed change was desirable, any change—during the 60s the new, the fashion, change for change's sake became almost feverish.

Second, the whole country gradually became aware of wealth as never before, of its possibilities and its pleasures. More and more people went on package tours to places hitherto visited only by the wealthy. The fact that so much began to be in everyone's reach led to the idea that everything *should* be within everyone's reach; and so it appeared more monstrous than ever before that anything should be preserved exclusively for the rich. Privilege becomes even more unfair when you know what you are being denied. This is related to a third effect. Appetite grows by what it feeds on; given more, people have wanted still more and expected and dreamt about more even than that—higher wages, more cars, longer holidays, more television sets. Rising prosperity among the mass suddenly checked is the classic revolutionary situation. This has been the case in Britain for the last two years. It has not led to revolution; but it is scarcely surprising that it has led to a strong flow of egalitarian ideas, often, out of fear, embraced by the middle class, though this has not prevented them and the rich being made to suffer most economically compared to the rest of the nation. (These mini-revolutionary and egalitarian ideas have gained considerable energy because free universities have meant that we do now, finally, even if in rather a quiet way, share in that "European phenomenon —the culturally restless and politically hostile intellectual stratum, the left-wing undergraduate, and what he or she will soon become: the unemployable graduate".)

Fourth, greater wealth brings greater opportunities to enjoy; the more things there are to enjoy the freer you should be to enjoy them. Wealth brings a feeling of power, the power to be free, to ignore old authorities and conventions, to concentrate on the self. This was the more so because, the fifth area, for the first time in history (relative) wealth became available to the young. A new mass market of young people sprang up, to be catered for by industry and the world of entertainment, charmed by advertisers, a world whose music and heroes—pop stars, football players— became fashionable. This concentration on (some would say abdication to) the young reinforced that more general Freud-influenced and grow-ing consideration for children which has also been a mark of this century.

It is forces of this nature, great and complex movements in the social magma, interrelated and inter-acting, which alter societies—not Alan Leigh's dreaded media. They, like public schools, are just so much froth upon the surface, bubbles in the tides of change.

Public schools have been affected profoundly; it is possible to trace three different reactions. During the 1960s there was a conscious identifica-tion in public schools with the youth culture outside—hair was grown long, pop groups formed and there were other manifestations. (It is significant that, as the wealth explosion stops, so this particular reaction lessens.) But there was also—since the youth culture was a mass one— strong reaction against their own class. They adopted lower-class accents and manners. Their middle-class origin seemed almost a positive disad-vantage outside; it became shameful and disgusting. Many schools commented on this. Here's a master at one: "We give them an education which makes them think—as opposed to learn—so they think. Some of them are bound to feel guilty. They have doubts about what to do—to be a gardener instead of the Civil Service. They take on some proletarian features, a rougher voice—'yeah' instead of 'yes'." At Cheltenham Ladies' College they say they go to school at the C.L.C. or just in Gloucester; at Roedean they say Brighton. Class and the boarding situation were the two topics which always aroused the most furious discussion when I talked to boys and girls in the schools. There were many reactions—bafflement, consciousness of envy, secret pleasure, indifference; but it was clear that most did feel degrees of shame and guilt but did not see how they could help it or what they could do about it. And that is the damnable thing about class, as about colour. It is no one's fault. People don't ask to be born the child of middle-class parents any more than they do the child of lower-class ones; they do not ask to be black or white. Almost any sacrifice is worth making to eradicate that sort of basic social prejudice and condemnation, the condemnation that takes place before you are born. It can be enraging to be born disadvantaged and underprivileged and frustrated, but it is at least a clear and strong emotion. There is something crippling, something inner and twisted and undermining about guilt. It has always existed—we saw it in the 19th century. But I suspect it is as strong now, while some of the economic realities which underlay it rapidly disappear, as it has ever been. One of the psychiatrists I spoke to said that whenever he had middle-class patients, no matter if they were twenty or sixty, he was almost sure, whatever other problems they had, that he would find himself dealing with two things: their inability to express their feelings and their guilt about class.

The schools themselves, where once they preserved class distinctions, now fight to reduce them. Throughout the period they have struggled to break down the barriers between themselves and the State system. In 1942 R. A. Butler, President of the Board of Education, set up a committee under Lord Fleming

> to consider means whereby the association between the public schools (by which term is meant schools which are in membership of the Governing Bodies Association or Headmasters' Conference) and the general education system of this country could be developed and extended; also to consider how far any measure recommended in the case of boys' public schools could be applied to comparable schools for girls.

The conclusion was that the public school system should, by a system of grants, be gradually integrated into the State system—first taking a twenty-five per cent minimum of State pupils, later "to be completely accessible to all pupils". The report was instantly and unanimously accepted by the Headmasters' Conference.

Unfortunately, it had grave disadvantages. It was enormously cumbersome, potential pupils having to pass through sieve after sieve before acceptance. For another, the government was resolutely determined that, unlike the direct grant system, it was not going to supply the money that would pay for these twenty-five per cent—and finally perhaps, theoretically at any rate, a hundred per cent of State public school pupils. (In fact the State had demonstrated its reluctance to pay for State pupils at public schools as early as 1919, when the Headmasters of Charterhouse, Eton and Marlborough had offered to accept a percentage of elementary pupils if the government would subsidise them. H. A. L. Fisher, the then President of the Board of Education, refused.) Now, in 1942, the government said the Local Education Authorities must find the money from the rates, which they, in turn, were extremely reluctant to do. The scheme collapsed.

But in fact Dancy, in a paradoxically brilliant chapter, shows conclusively, by reference to the next twenty-year period, that the idea that either the government or the LEAs would or will submit boys from the State system is completely unworkable—unworkable in the sense that they will not try to make it work, not that it is impossible. They would not try even when the public schools offered quite generous sums to reduce the cost to the LEAs. Certainly the public schools were willing to try, and very occasionally—proving that it was possible—it happened. Here two places are taken up at Winchester by Hampshire, now, after Lancing has promised really large amounts of money to support ten places to five LEAs in 1960, only one (West Sussex) accepts; and these and many others were quite genuine, though, as time passed and it became quite clear that they would not be taken up, the schools were probably able to make their offers with more and more ease and abandon. By the end of twenty years scarce enough boys or girls had joined the 200 or so public schools to make a rugger team or fill a dormitory.

But if they failed here, not through want of trying, the schools made determined and in many cases successful efforts to break down the barriers between themselves and the outside world, to increase the range and type of contacts their pupils made, to make themselves relevant to the communities in which they lived. After 1945, two headmasters, L. C. Taylor and Dr. Hinton, made Sevenoaks a pioneer here. They organised exchange schools with Paris (and had an Anglo-French form); an international centre for the sixth form took two-thirds of its boys from overseas; today there is a voluntary unit, run with the State schools in Sevenoaks, which involves the boys in "the problems of the elderly, of young people in trouble, of the physically and mentally handicapped". It is this last that is the most impressive and widespread development among the schools in recent years. No doubt there is some small element of guilt about it, but it would be quite wrong to compare it to the distant and patronising sort of thing we saw with Roedean in 1900. I saw a good deal of this work and it was clear the pupils are extremely involved with what they do—and do a great deal. At Rugby, more than 300 boys (out of 720) coach educationally subnormal children, help immigrant children in the language laboratories, help local primary school drama classes, among a great deal of other community work. At Harrow some 200 boys (out of 700) are involved, particularly with old people and the handicapped. But it is invidious to pick on schools—Winchester, Shrewsbury, Solihull and dozens of others are engaged in this sort of thing.

These are interesting responses to the surging magma but they are, after all, fairly minor. It is time now to move on to the second major change (the first was educational) which has taken place over this last period—the liberalising of the public schools and the final dismantling of the Monolith.

CHAPTER 18

How the Public Schools Became (Relatively) Free; The Question of Their Survival

A history of the public schools? I imagine it's a valediction.
Present Master of the Scholars at Westminster, February 19th, 1976

We left the Monolith a mass of hairline cracks, which in pockets and chunks had crumbled away but which was still, essentially, intact. Royston Lambert, writing in 1966, said that changes in freedom, discipline and tradition, since they did not reflect on the academic record, had been fewer and less impressive. From his fairly close perspective that might have been true. From where we stand, able to see the sixty years it took to build those disciplines, restrict that freedom, to preserve (and invent) those traditions, and the further fifty odd years in which they were obstinately and ferociously defended, it is the way they came tumbling down that is impressive. In fifteen years, say from 1958 (an arbitrary choice), the edifice built and held over more than a century was transformed.

1 Last lumps of the Monolith

Nevertheless, it is true that great lumps of the Monolith persisted deep into our last thirty-year period. Partly, in contradiction to its more active influence for change, this was due to the war. Although teaching was a reserved occupation, many masters left to fight, leaving aged figures behind, and bringing still more aged ones hobbling from retirement. And, just as had happened after the First World War, Britain's victory seemed to justify the system. It is true that fewer boys died, but they were still killed in large numbers. Of 2,000 Old Stoics who served in the war, one in seven, nearly 300, lost his life. It broke Roxburgh's heart. To change seemed disloyal to their memory. For many years schools remained rabidly patriotic, with compulsory, or near compulsory, Corps, games like L'Attaque in the common rooms, Biggles on the shelves.

There were many other things we would recognise. Many girls' schools continued the tradition of all-powerful headmistresses. When Miss Tanner retired in 1947, Miss Horobin, a tough and withered spinster who terrified both staff and girls at Roedean, delayed progress for years. She ruled everything, refusing to delegate (she even acted as her own bursar). "Uplift" remained. "Work," carolled Miss Popham of Cheltenham in 1953, "grows into Joy!" And of course human nature remains a constant. There will always be murder in society; there will always be some bullying in schools. I was talking about the early public schools to one master. "I could match every single story you could give me from the end of the 18th century with one as bad from the last ten years. Only the other day we had a boy hung from a window by his ears." Throughout the 1950s many schools *felt* the same. This was largely because of traditions, but in particular traditional attitudes remained the same. A master at Harrow then remembers reading *The Hill* and thinking how relevant it still was. Wellington, in 1959, was still strongly army oriented ; the boys had to give a sort of finger salute to staff (and fags were still sent to the Rears—the lavatories—to warm the seats). At Eton in the early 60s a boy who said he'd decided to support Labour had his room painted red and slogans daubed over it in butter—he would have been all right had he said he'd vote Communist.(In a recent survey, Anthony Sampson told me, eighty-five per cent of Etonians supported the Tories. There were some Communists and no Labour.) At Cheltenham Ladies' College in the 1950s there was a parade of all 800 or so girls (many eighteen) in mid-winter in front of the headmistress. Rank after rank in turn had to lift their skirts to make sure they were all wearing green knickers, about which there had been some laxness at the time.

Cheltenham remains important for the same reason we found at the beginning of the century: it is a nursery for headmistresses. At this moment nineteen headmistresses—of which I note only two are married—are either Old Girls or ex-mistresses. There are fifteen recently retired headmistresses. So that in the last twenty years or so Cheltenham has supplied thirty-four headmistresses. The influence of this still fairly formal and academically distinguished school continues to be considerable. And so on. I could give dozens of other examples of old themes continuing. But the keynote of the period, the significance of it, is change.

2 How the schools changed

Aside from its rôle in what I called the social magma, the war was a more obvious and direct influence. It broke people and schools up, mixed them and moved them around, it forced them into improvisation and new intimacies. Occasionally boys moved singly. Euan Graham was at Eton and his parents were afraid he might be in danger from the proximity to Slough, so he was moved to Marlborough. There, however, he was machine gunned on the football pitch and blown out of bed by a bomb.

He returned to Eton the next term (he had found Marlborough much less strict and more relaxed than Eton). But the important movements were *en masse*. Roedean to Keswick in Cumberland, where piano lessons were given in neighbours' parlours, maths and geography taught in the station waiting room. Staff, as with other girls' schools, tended to be younger; to women, teaching was significant war work. CLS joined Marlborough and may, since as a day school it has always tended to be less intense than a boarding school, have contributed to that relative relaxation noticed by Euan Graham. Westminster went to Herefordshire, and the same sort of thing took place: working to repair houses, travelling several miles between classes, the tough exciting life drew them together. Masters and boys were on Christian-name terms, fagging in college almost disappeared (to return for a while after the war), beating stopped. Free time was no longer regulated—there was a boy who liked travelling to Crewe and back before breakfast on the train. A moment stands out in Carleton's history, when the school has come back to Westminster, and they hold the first post-war Greaze in the ruined roofless hall. Suddenly you sense the great feeling of strength that must have come to his staff and the school as the pancake whirled into the winter sky, that old tradition re-enacted once again, the same, just another year, another war.

Many schools had similar experiences (clothes rationing meant uniform relaxation for instance). And other changes took place in the war and during the 1950s. Athleticism, weakening as we saw in the 30s, now finally disappeared. It would be interesting to trace the actual mechanics of the decline. At Winchester, for example, there were old housemasters, Horace Arthur Jackson—"Jacker"—and H.S. Altham, who were, as regards games, virtually mad (a condition in "Jacker's" case exacerbated by shell-shock in the First World War). They spent months of the year roaming the prep schools of England and grabbing anyone promising for their houses. As a result they won all the cups. It was pointless other houses competing. So they lost interest. Then, when Jacker and Altham retired, they had created a climate, as it were, where the cult of games could die. It would take too long to follow the process in anything like the detail we did its growth. It could in any case never have survived the new emphasis on academic excellence. At girls' schools the reaction was extreme; the major games were actually unpopular for a while in the 60s at Roedean, and Mallory Wober found that, together with the desire to be a prefect, they came bottom of the aims girls held to be important at school. (In the 20s, of course, they would have come out top.) At the Eton and Harrow on July 12th, 1975, Lords—once thronged with carriages ten deep, dowagers fainting and cabinet ministers bellowing themselves hoarse—was practically empty. (A feature of the period has been the decline of cricket, as beleaguered in many schools as the classics.) I do not of course mean that no one is interested in games anymore. There is tremendous enthusiasm, and success: Ampleforth is renowned for rugger, Emmanuel and Eton for rowing, Bishop's Stortford for swimming. Sevenoaks took a rugger team to Australia this year and so on. I mean that games as a prime engine of education, as an ideology, vanished. They were no longer considered a method of instilling moral virtues, no longer a yardstick of a successful school career and therefore a passport to outside careers generally. Games have reverted to what they were at the schools up till about the late 1840s —just games. And so they are treated now. All schools have and encourage them; some sort of exercise must be taken; sometimes for a year or two the old major games are compulsory. Often not. There are dozens of individual pastimes and moderately energetic pursuits. But here, as elsewhere, the schools are sane again.

During the 1950s most schools instituted retirement for housemasters after fifteen years. As a method for allowing the advancement of the young and preventing the obstinate defiance of age this hardly needs pointing up.

But it was the 1960s that saw the most rapid change, when the Monolith was not so much dismantled as melted away. Now bounds were extended or ended, privileges cut back or abolished, traditions diluted or allowed to lapse; free time was allowed to be free, age groups and houses to mix, caps and tassels and colours disappeared or were reduced; headmistresses got married; a school which had produced one play a year in 1959, produced thirty in 1970; boys were called by their Christian names, then masters. It is extremely difficult, if not impossible (and not really necessary) to chart this exactly; to chart when this happened in one school, that in another. To compare school to school or house to house. My notes are full of evidence, in which the general pattern is absolutely clear, while individual ones are bewildering.

Let me give some examples of what was happening. In 1960, Bedales phased out uniforms for girls and stopped cold baths and early-morning runs for boys. Charterhouse slid into Christian names during the mid-60s. Rugby extended their mid-term exeat over this period. Rugby can serve as an example of how traditions continued but in diluted form. Arnold used his entire sixth form as prefects, a practice Rugby only gave up now. There remains, however, an academic bias among prefects. At Roedean, Mrs. Fort, a married woman with five children, steered through the liberating years: she stopped the singing of "Forty Years On" to stamping feet, the girls wore their own clothes in the afternoon, and could spend two weekends away from school a term. Today Roedean is run, rather than ruled, by John Hunt. At Cheltenham Ladies' College I had the impression that Miss Hampshire, dipping and shrewd, there since 1964, had more than kept her head in the mill race of change. "I think the school changed by degrees." Over fifty per cent of the staff, twelve of them men, were married (the girls saw it differently, as nearly fifty per cent unmarried

—"Have you *seen* the older ones—been here *years*").

Let us follow, for the last time, some old themes. At Westminster, personal fagging died out after the war. There was no trace of it in 1970. (Though, to show how impossible it is to chart these processes precisely, I know of at least one house at Marlborough where it was abolished in 1938.) At other schools it vanished during the 1960s and early 1970s; though remnants remain. Some of the Oppidan houses at Eton retain it; at Winchester you have a personal fag but you have to pay him three pounds a term. (Twenty-five pence a week in a twelve-week term. What I give my ten-year-old son.) Nor should it be thought these changes were easy. Many were made with misgiving—and understandably. In a complex and delicate community like a public school, whose interrelated organisation has been built up over years and years, each joint and dovetail fitting and working together, to disturb one is to send a tremor through the whole fabric and may necessitate a series of compensatory alterations throughout the structure. For example, Lambert found that in strict schools vertical communication was essential. It was necessary to mitigate and explain the imposition of rules which juniors had not framed and which had not been explained to them. Fagging had also been a system of vertical communication which knit a school together. Though it was abolished to benefit juniors, it in fact upset them. At Repton, as a method of bringing about integration, they have studies in which there is one boy from each year (compare with the Bedales mixed-year dormitories). In one of the houses at Rugby every single boy, whatever age, has a sphere of responsibility with appropriate authority—ranging from general tidiness, through light bulbs, the library, to elimination of mice (power over crumbs)—which achieves the same end.

Nothing is simple. Certainly not beating, next to the classics and religion our oldest theme. And perhaps one should note here that in this sphere the questions raised by Rousseau are still unresolved: is the essential character of man good or bad, how much discipline do children require and what sort of discipline? "A great number of people would not be in the dock if they had had corporal punishment when they were younger" (Judge King-Hamilton, QC, Central Criminal Court, February 4th, 1975). "Earlier," *The Times* report goes on, "defence counsel had asked for a psychiatric report on Mr. Foster. The judge said some people believed that for some offenders the best form of psychiatric treatment was best administered 'not to the head but to the backside'." The subject of beating can still raise violent feelings. Since 1840, we have seen in public schools that beating has been declining. How slow, how incredibly slow that "decline" has been! In the 1950s it was still the most common form of punishment. Eton still had the whole array of beatings—by Library, Pop ("Pop-tanned"), headmaster and so on—severe or mild depending on those involved. At Catholic schools the engine was a foot long, thought to be whalebone and covered in black leather. A boy at Belmont Abbey in 1953 can remember, aged thirteen, being given eight blows three nights running and going bloody to bed, unable to lie on his back. After thirteen, twelve blows were administered "usually by the headmaster, who I'm glad to say had a stroke and died soon after I'd left". In 1966, Graham Kalton carried out a survey for the Headmasters' Conference. Beating was still extremely common (see Appendix N); out of 134 schools, 124 allowed housemasters to beat, forty-four allowed other masters and three-quarters allowed boys to beat. The amounts were variable, but it was still possible to find schools where a great deal of beating went on. In 1968, Royston Lambert continued to find evidence that it was "usual", but he also said that it had started to decline fast and that some schools had abolished it. Certainly decline is the pattern. Take Marlborough: in 1927, all house prefects could beat; in 1935, only school prefects; in 1958, only the head of the house, and he beat perhaps ten boys a term. By 1965 Dancy found so many heads of houses reluctant to beat that he abolished boy beating boy. Now, only the headmaster and housemasters can beat, and they do so very occasionally. It seemed to me a good many people at Marlborough were rather ashamed of this. Many schools have abolished it; in still more it has simply fallen into disuse. No one has beaten at UCS for ten years. There has not, so far as I know, been another survey since Kalton's, but my impression was that beating is rare, hardly ever (I found only one school) done by boys—and at far the greater number of schools discipline is now mild and appropriate. That is, helping tidy up the school if you have messed it about, reporting early if you have been late and so on.

But, one might ask, why is there still any beating at all? We are in this respect an extraordinarily violent country. Poland abolished the beating of children 200 years ago. It became illegal to beat children in Holland in 1850, 1887 in France, 1890 in Finland, 1935 in Norway, 1958 in Sweden, and 1968 in Denmark. That same year we took a first tentative step by making it illegal to beat criminals. We still allow children to be beaten— and still beat them. In the State system it is widespread, on both sexes. But we have seen again and again in this history how beating is quite unneces- sary to the maintenance of discipline (a fact which has repeatedly been proved in surveys, for example that of the West Riding Education Committee carried out in 1961). The Plowden Report, after voluminous evidence, condemned it in 1967. All responsible psychological opinion condemns it. Yet, there are still public schools where beating goes on, there are still, though they are extremely rare, scandals of viciousness hushed up, and when STOPP—the Society of Teachers Opposed to Physical Punishment, which is primarily concerned with State schools— writes to these public schools it often receive letters (I have read them) of a violence or a pusillanimity scarcely to be believed. From the Monolith comes a last fear-filled flicker of rage, obstinacy and defiance.

In all else it has, relatively speaking (an important proviso), been transformed. Uniforms have been abandoned, or else have become approximations to what is worn outside. Only echoes of fancy dress remain. Many schools have pubs for their sixth formers. The architecture of freedom—the study and study-bedroom—is being continually extended: at Westminster two or three share a study-bedroom till the third year, then have one to themselves; at Marlborough, depending on house, they have bed-sitters at fifteen plus; at Wellington they are all in cubicle/bed-sitters. Girls' schools favour the sixth-form house, where the girls assume "student status" (Cheltenham seems to have pioneered this). I was interested with what ease and freedom I wandered the corridors at Roedean. At Bedales I would have been arrested.

And the concentration on the individual—or the permission to concentrate on the self—which a separate room symbolises, finds expression in the variety of activity which these transformed schools support—those humming evenings of gossip or computer war games or rehearsals for concerts or plays or pop concerts, or films or talks on child upbringing or, really, practically anything you can think of. They are enormously rich in possibilities for self-discovery and self-exploration.

As the barnacles dropped away, the schools, light as feathers, felt themselves rising ever faster, ever further into some heady ether of freedom; sometimes something like intoxication occurred. Mrs. Fort abolished prefects. There was considerable opposition from Old Girls, old staff and parents; the governors were "deeply worried"; "but the tide was with her". Dr. Rae was Headmaster of Taunton in 1960 and remembers abolishing cadet corps and having some voluntary chapel "more or less automatically". In other schools, games became voluntary, then disappeared. One or two progressive schools—Frensham Heights,for example—almost disintegrated. (Frensham Heights, incidentally, is an interesting example of how swiftly a school can respond to a new headmaster. Mr. Pattinson, after some vigorous initial changes, took three years to transform it. It is now becoming one of the most successful progressive schools in the country.) Nor was it just masters who became intoxicated. Soon a new smell was mingling with the decades of sour changing rooms, boiled cabbage, floor polish and boy: pungent, herbal, hallucinatory, the unmistakably fragrant scent of marijuana drifted under study doors and along the corridors of the public schools of England.

3 The reaction and other results

What were the results of all this? First, there was almost bound to be a reaction, and that has been taking place over the last two or three years. All the people I talked to were clear about this, and indeed it was visible, audible ("Mr. White's been tightening up"). I think it is surprising how mild, so far, the reaction has been. During the 60s the public schools were often in a state of confusion. Take games. One headmaster said to me: "It's all very well, but what do boys *do* on a wet afternoon in a deeply rural boarding school? People underestimate the adolescent's power to mooch. After all, games were originally introduced with a purpose." In a gentle way, they have often been introduced again. At Roedean, instead of prefects, Mrs. Fort made the whole sixth form responsible. It didn't work, because no one did anything. The head girl and the housemistresses ran the school. Everyone was "worried" but Mr. Hunt bided his time. Finally, the *girls* complained. So, after discussions with them, Roedean fixed on a system of government by a sixth-form committee elected by the sixth form—prefects under another name.

The culture public schools transmit is very largely based on the written and spoken word. Television seems (though in reality much of it is equally so based) completely antithetical to this. But masters also instinctively realise that television is not just a potent result of the forces of change; it is an engine of change itself. They therefore often loathe it and ban it. A housemaster of Winchester said, "Pop records and vice go together." He'd banned television, though a kindly matron let the starved boys watch. I had many similar examples, both of this and of a general internal pulling together. But of course, in this as in so much, public schools were also just mimicking the outside world. "We always act second-hand scenes among men," said the master at Westminster 150 years ago, explaining how the French Revolution had produced rebellion in the schools. So it is still. The pot that blew in scented wafts blew in from outside, from the pop culture and its city spread. The schools reacted, as did the outside authorities, with considerable ferocity. It became one of the most common reasons for expulsion. (One can imagine, therefore, the amazement of the tense and interested parents at a speech day of a local girls' school, when the pot panic, but also the period of rapid change, were both at their height. The headmistress seemed to be about to grasp this difficult and dangerous contemporary nettle. "Taking *pot*," she began. "We take enormous pains to get ah gels—all of them—to take pot. To take pot in the gym, on the games pitches, to take pot even in the dormitories." Mesmerised with horror, the parents listened to an endless, monstrous litany. It was complete capitulation. "To take pot on the stage, in concert, in the classrooms. To take pot joyously, together. . . ." The rising anger and louder protests were only stilled when the sense finally made it clear she meant *part*. The girls were to take part in as many activities as possible.) The drug problem in schools today has been largely cured by fashion and inflation together. It is less fashionable outside and it is far more expensive. Drink has taken its place.

But the responses to the outside have been more subtle and complicated

than this—just as the responses of the outside have been and are complicated. A factor in the reaction is that large sections of the middle classes
seem to have accepted the new freedom of the 60s for themselves, or
accepted them in principle—that is, in films or in print or among their
friends. They remain worried about them for their children. At the same
time, they have become confused about their authority; the instinct to
bring up your children as you were yourself brought up is very strong, but
this often seems to be contradicted by the need for a more relaxed type of
upbringing. They therefore rely on the schools to impose the discipline
they cannot impose themselves. Dancy said to John Betjeman in 1970,
"Parents no longer pay for good teaching. They pay for short hair." A
good many teachers at the more formal schools made the same point. The
middle classes have also reacted to the new freedom—to the emphasis on
individual exploration and satisfaction—by getting divorced; and
divorced in large and increasing numbers. From about 1960 on, more and
more schools saw they had a rôle providing a stable and secure background
for boys and girls from broken homes. It is another example of how
subtle and instant is their response to any basic need in their market. Dancy
is particularly good on the way public schools provide an often essential
second home; stimulating for the bored, safe for the distracted, release for
those under nuclear pressure. Finally—though here I'm guessing—I
suspect the schools may be part of a more general outside conservative
reaction. Certainly many masters said, with relief, that the 1975/6/7
generation were calmer and more conventional than their predecessors.
The element of student protest was absent.

But the major result, obviously, has been to open up and relax the
schools. In effect those tight little total societies—from whose totality, as
we saw, such an immense number of results flowed—have become less
total. There has been the enormous widening of the curriculum and of
outside activities, there are extensive contacts with the outside world;
there are few bounds, pupils go home far more; in the 50s most schools
still had a sanatorium, sometimes like their own little hospital. Now, they
rely on the outside (the sixth-form house at Roedean is the old sanatorium). Masters and mistresses have opened out too. Where before they
often had little more experience, and were therefore little different from,
those they taught ("So embarrassing when they suddenly break into the
slang," John Betjeman said), now they get married and divorced, have
outside friends. Even Auden could sit next to some of them without a
sinking heart. And it is fascinating to see, as the totality becomes less
intense, how some of the most extreme manifestations of it die away.
There is a little school literature about, but very little. As a *genre*, it is
finished. The fixated Old Boy or Old Girl is also rare, and it is clear from
the response I received from enquiries to schools that Old Boy and Girl
Societies have steadily weakened over the last thirty years. (Sometimes

their numbers have increased, but nearly always this is in fact a sign of their weakness. They have started a system of "opting out", and people leaving join and sign Banker's Orders automatically, bringing up numbers but being in fact completely inactive.)

Nevertheless, school does still supersede all other social systems—the family, outside society, the local community and so on. It is still technically total. Thus goals still get out of hand, you still get that "feverishness" on the part of authority; rebellion is still a method of growth; although to conform, to be the same, has ceased to be the ideology Harold Nicolson described, the pressure to conform in a total community is still strong; public schools still tend to impose that "romantic structure" on the personality for the same, if diminishing, reasons; and they generate the same group loyalty.

Public schools are very proud of how much they have changed. Skidelsky, in his short book on progressive schools, says that in fact the progressive movement has lost its function. It has been caught up with by other public schools. They are all progressive today. We, with our knowledge of their history—with the memory of the Monolith that so recently towered over us—can appreciate why the public schools have reason to be proud. But to someone outside, most of these changes don't seem all that marvellous. If told how recent they are and how numerous, then that person would just say they were obvious and long-overdue reforms to make the little communities more civilised.

It seemed to me that Rugby today, for example, in terms of freedom, the opportunity for outside activity and boy discipline, was approaching what Bryanston had been in 1950. At that time, aged seventeen, I thought it was a strict, conventional school with too many restrictions, too formal, although in my case saved by the presence of Wilfred Cowley. I realise now that, apart from my appreciation of my tutor, I was, *relatively speaking*, wrong. It was, for its time, an extremely free school; in many ways more liberal than Bedales, for example, at the same period. Girls came over from Cranborne Chase, a school which, where other girls' schools have traditions of academic excellence or lacrosse victories, has a tradition of beauty. It is impossible for any particular school to see its changes in absolute terms. If you have been a girl at a school where you can be hauled out on a winter's day, 800 of you, and have to lift up your skirt so that the headmistress can see whether or not you are wearing green knickers, then just to find yourself in a position where this won't happen is a vast improvement. All the changes we have discussed have been relative. Winchester still has forty-one colours for games; there used to be dozens more. Cheltenham Ladies' College still resists change in certain areas with the tenacity of the Monolith. A hundred years or so ago Miss Beale arranged that the school would always break up on a different day to the boys' school. Thus there would be no danger of the two sexes meeting and giving way to unbridled licence on the trains. It had just taken Miss Hampshire eighteen months of hard argument to get her council to agree they should break up—far more conveniently for the many parents with children at both schools—on the same day. In fact, many girls' schools are still secretly terrified of any contact with boys or indeed mention of sex. Mallory Wober had to argue tenaciously for an hour to get a question— "that the school should help girls learn to get on with the opposite sex"— put to the pupils. Finally it was allowed, for the sixth form only, like this: ". . . to prepare girls for the rôle of wife".

In researching this book, I grew adept at sensing, almost at once, whether or not a school was strict, excessively "total", restrictive; I could almost sense the form of punishment—"Mr.Y's getting quite a taste for beating". There was an instant increase in pressure, and I had forgotten how intense such communities could be. I can remember in one being seized by a group of sixteen-year-olds like an emissary from freedom, who might be shown and carry back the fearful truth. They rushed me down to the echoing damp dim baths where the tubs stood. We smoked. Then they raced me up to the dormitories; high rooms, freezing cold, without curtains, the woodwork chipped, feathers from a burst pillow blowing on the floor, the anxious alert faces of the thirteen-year-olds. One of my gang lifted the end of a bed high, as though to up-end it. "Mr. Y says would we treat our homes like this? But our homes don't look like this." Later, in a corridor, my wrist was held in a moist vice. Bulging slightly unbalanced eyes fixed on me, many times magnified by huge spectacles: "Tell them about the love and sex," he said, "tell them about *that*." It was not, really, so very different from some of the schools I was at that moment writing about, schools of forty and fifty years ago.

I suspect that prep schools have changed less than public schools and therefore go some considerable way to counteract the effect of the new freedoms. Some of Royston Lambert's findings in 1967 bear this out. He noted, for instance, that they were not at all concerned with their pupils' personal development, nor that the school should be "homely". They were obsessed with exam results. By ten, three-quarters of the boys had begun Latin and spent up to fifteen per cent of their time on it. Its value was entirely to impose self-discipline and accuracy, and make learning a "habit".

The changes in public schools, therefore, have been relative, and probably somewhat contracted by the lack of change in the prep schools. Nor have they abandoned their connection with the Church—the first and oldest of our themes. In this pagan country—embalming and continuing a dead faith—the Christian religion is still to most of them, in a way they often can't explain, "central". It has been so for so long they cannot imagine it otherwise. At Rugby, the masters—undoubtedly sincere —gave me that feeling the Church of England often does; of being busily engaged in "getting somewhere", in some cosy and completely irrelevant endeavour. Other masters find the routine soothing and aesthetically satisfying; it provides a structure to the week.

The progressive schools still try to develop the individual by removing pressure; they lay less stress on academic success (and are therefore less successful than, say, Westminster). The relations between staff and pupils are closer and informal. They still have fewer rules, less discipline, and a greater stress on creativity (though I don't think they are necessarily any more successful in their creative work). Just as I could always sense a formal school, so there was no doubt that progressive schools were more relaxed, their pupils more natural. (So were their staff. This was particularly so in answering letters. Some, like Dr. Royston Lambert, were so relaxed they didn't bother to answer letters at all.)

But today these are all differences of degree, not, as they once almost seemed, of kind. What it amounts to is that, due to all the factors we have considered among which the relativity of change is the key, the public schools now present an enormous variety of different institutions and types of discipline, training and upbringing. That is the great advantage and strength of the private sector. Among these the progressive schools represent, as they have always done, the left wing. Their rôle there is as valuable and important as ever.

4 The move to co-education in the boys' schools

The last great change in this thirty-year period has been the move to co-education. Towards the latter part of the 1960s the schools were coming to the end of the post-war bulge. Many of them had built up big sixth forms and these, with expensive equipment and highly paid staff requiring continual payment, are extremely sensitive to any drop in numbers. And a school is naturally reluctant to run down this apparatus. Quite apart from the time and care taken to build it up, it is, academically, its *raison d'être*; it is also what attracts high-grade staff; above all it is the source of scholarships and five A's exam success which in turn creates the school's outside reputation, its source of future support.

There was also at this time a rather vague stirring of interest in co-education for its own sake. It was realised that a good many parents would tolerate it, and might even welcome it. But that it was primarily an economic concern with numbers and to do with the sixth form is shown by the fact that most of those schools which embarked on this experiment in the late 1960s and early 1970s—Bryanston, Stowe and others—only took girls into their sixth forms. (At the moment forty-one Headmasters' Conference Schools take girls into the sixth form.) One headmaster was quite unabashed about this: "Don't quote me," he said gleefully, "but yes, they're pure profit. Say you have six boys doing Spanish. You can add three girls, and that's all. No extra overheads and it's still a very small class. Of course, it's not quite as simple as that. One of the girls may want to learn Russian. . . ."

Mr. Hunt of Roedean was extremely caustic about this movement. He said it was unsatisfactory for a number of reasons. These schools were far too much boy-oriented, and subjected the girls to a barrage of male-dominated influences, not the least of which was the intense pressure of male attraction. "You always hear, 'So good for the boys'." The surroundings were inadequate—not enough hair dryers or proper bathroom facilities. And girls need a particular pastoral system; that is, women to whom they can talk. Apart from that the movement was self-defeating. These partially co-ed schools were just hoovering girls up from the fifth-form top and so destroying the sixth. These small girls' schools will fold, schools like St. Mary's, Calne, and the source will be destroyed.

I saw some of the schools Mr. Hunt complained of. They did not agree, nor, on the whole, did the girls at them. As far as pastoral care went, at some schools (Bryanston for example) they build, or adapt, a special girls' wing or building and incorporate the necessary facilities; at others (Marlborough for instance), the girls sleep six or seven to a house, two together in their own room. They are only in married housemasters' houses and are the responsibility of his wife. In fact all the girls I spoke to, in several schools, agreed that the care taken of them and the interest shown in them by the staff were invariably higher than at the schools they had come from. This was true of day pupils as well—girls, for instance, at Westminster now who had come from St. Paul's. (In fact I have a strong suspicion, though I cannot prove it, that, contrary to what one might think, there is in many girls' schools a tradition of poor pastoral care as compared to boys' schools.) And so, far from being "good for the boys", it was equally good for the girls. "We give them self-confidence, we raise their self-esteem. They come not thinking they'll go to university, and then go. And they learn to have a better relationship, not just with boys, but with the adult staff."

As for hoovering up the fifth-form top—it wasn't entirely or even mostly that. At Marlborough I was told they took a lot of girls from those small south of England private schools, traditionally slack—the lineal descendants of the academies—and gave them a sixth-form training they would not otherwise have. But, yes, they did take from the little girls' public schools—St. Mary's, Calne, for example. (Actually St. Mary's, Calne, has a first-rate sixth form.)

All the girls agreed that the pressure of boy interest, the feeling of being on show was very strong indeed and exhausting. "You either go out with no one, in which case you are thought frigid; or you do go out with someone, in which case you're thought a tart." It was an enormous relief to escape and be alone with other girls sometimes. I was reminded of the war—seventy WRACs isolated in a brigade of three thousand ravenous soldiers. What effect would it have? Quite plain girls (though actually those I saw seemed all to be unusually attractive; some unconscious bias on the part of the masters selecting?) — but there must have been plain girls,—would be elevated to a position of desirability quite beyond reality. Would it give them a feeling of confidence and attractiveness useful in later life? Or, once the competition had widened, would they return to earth with a bump?

As to the more general beneficial effects, all schools who go co-educational are agreed.* The first thing that happens is that the homo-sexual charge vanishes. The gossip is all about the girls and where once it was the flower-like new boys who were scrutinised for their beauty, now it is the new girls. In an established co-educational school members of the opposite sex are viewed as people in their own right and not as sex objects or fantasy figures; and research like the Asherton Survey shows that the chances of a successful marriage are higher among those educated at mixed schools. This is true of Bedales, Frensham Heights or Dartington; it is not true yet, because of the heterosexual intensity, at the partially co-educational schools. The solution is for them to go wholly co-educational.

Boys are humanised by girls; girls become less petty and sentimental with boys. Girls are seen as mothers by new boys and often help them. The pressure to reduce or abolish corporal punishment becomes much stronger. The creative side of a school—particularly with plays and art—is enor-mously richer with girls. Bryanston and Marlborough have had traditional strength here, which has been enhanced; but it is evident now with schools like Stowe or Gordonstoun where you would not have expected it.

Michael McCrum of Eton said that if the major boys' schools went co-educational, then that was where the girls would go—not just for the advantage of co-education, but because it would be combined with academic excellence. "If I was the Headmistress of St. Mary's, Calne, I should be terrified." I began to feel sorry for St. Mary's, Calne. (In fact the girls' schools are fighting back. Some make parents sign an agreement to keep the girls at the school until their education is complete, so preventing a sixth-form transfer to a boys' school—or trying to prevent it.)

Will it happen? There is certainly a trend in that direction. Bryanston and Gordonstoun are in the process of going fully co-educational (in all, ten Headmasters' Conference Schools have now gone fully co-educa-tional). Marlborough and Stowe are increasing their intake. Dr. Rae said, "I can see how it is possible for a traditional boys' school, geared to a masculine atmosphere for centuries, to take girls into their sixth without major changes; but to go fully co-ed—fifty-fifty from eleven or thirteen—

*I am indebted to some notes about Bedales, whose experience is far more extensive and profound than these late economic converts, which were given to me by the relatively new headmaster, Mr. Nobes.

that most of them would find *very* difficult." Difficult, but I don't think insuperable. Many colleges at Oxford and Cambridge, geared for as many centuries to a masculine atmosphere, have managed it without difficulty—though the analogy is not exact; it is easier for them. But Rugby, as traditional and masculine as any, has watched with disapproval for six years. Now, it has been won round. Girls are starting this year, and Mr. Woodhouse, the headmaster, hopes the number will become substantial. (Conversely Roedean, once relentlessly feminine, now under Mr. Hunt with ten men on the staff where there was one when he arrived, is quite prepared to consider co-education as a possibility.) But of course the decisive influence will be economic. If the numbers of boys going to public schools start to drop then, by including girls, they immediately increase their market by a very considerable amount. If I were the headmaster of a public school, particularly a small one, I should start taking a few girls into the sixth form right away, to get my hand in and also gain a sort of reputation to put in the prospectus—come the deluge.

5 Will the public school survive?

What are the economic chances of survival for the public schools? Inflation has attacked them even more viciously than it has attacked everything else. This is because it has attacked from both ends. As the costs to the schools continue soaring their fees become astronomical and converging. In September 1974 the fees of twenty-eight leading boarding schools were £1,132 a year, by the following April they were £1,351. Shrewsbury's fees, to give another example, have leapt from £800 to £1,500 in two years. Soon many schools will cost £2,000 a year. At the same time, as we noted earlier, it is precisely those middle-class incomes on which they depend that have failed to keep pace with inflation. Nor is this the only threat. The policy of the present Labour government has been to allow the public schools to wither away, hoping that eventually just a very few schools—the nine "great schools" probably—would alone remain, the preserve of a few hundred rich boys; and some Arabs. A further twist will come when they are deprived of charitable status, through which they are exempt from rates and from income tax on endowments and donations, from which they benefit by some millions of pounds (exact figures are impossible to obtain).

The result of all this so far has been odd—the public schools are enjoying a boom such as they have scarcely known before. And this reverses a distinct trend in independent schools. In 1951, according to an article in *The Observer* of January 1976, there were 5,100 independent schools, in 1968 there were 3,120; but the numbers at Headmasters' Conference Schools rose by three point three per cent in 1973, a further one point eight per cent in 1974 and rose yet again in 1975. At the moment (January 1977) the Independent Schools Information Service tells me that public schools generally are heavily over-subscribed. Many of them have completed or are completing vast extensions. Rugby finished its school centre—art schools, bookshop, common room, careers library—in 1975. It remodelled its theatre and opened three new squash courts in the same year. Westminster now has 520 pupils, a situation unknown since the last time it reached a peak in the mid-18th century.

Can it possibly last? I think it can. The public schools are twisting like eels, showing a cunning and resource and a will to survive that we, who have seen them twist and survive before, will not find surprising. They, and their market, have become enormously flexible. One clue lies in that increase in independent pupils. In fact, according to Anthony Sampson, between 1960 and 1970 the number of boarding prep schools fell (from 506 to 472); but the number of pupils rose (from 55,513 to 62,354). The reason was that there were more and more day pupils. This is one small trend at the moment—even Winchester has started taking day boys—it could grow large. Then, a good many pupils are subsidised. The Foreign Office, the forces, most of the big companies pay for their employees' children to be educated at public schools when the parents are abroad. I tried to get reliable over-all figures for this but it proved extremely difficult (it is a sensitive area); for example the Foreign Office helps 1,879 children with their education; Shell something between 750 and 1,000. But you can get some idea when I say that two schools told me that one-quarter of their pupils' parents were abroad. Nor did this include the ever increasing number of foreigners who pay for their children to have an English public school education. Again, numbers are hard to get. But they must be quite large; *The Times* of May 30th, 1975, stated that in 1974 these pupils contributed £6·5 millions to Great Britain's foreign-currency earnings. But by far the most likely development, which has already begun to emerge, is increasing combinations of State and independent. For example, pupils can go to primary and comprehensive schools until they are thirteen, and then a public school until eighteen; or until sixteen and then into a sixth-form college. Or the senior public schools might become independent sixth-form colleges, while other public schools would become eleven to sixteen independent schools. Or, alternatively, parents would send their children to prep schools and hope the disciplines learnt there would carry them through a comprehensive. But the point would be to obtain, one way or another, two or three years of private education. And a good many schools—for instance Westminster, Haileybury and Shrewsbury—have prepared schemes along these lines. And behind all this, if it really comes to it, lies the great reserve of girls—eager to be tapped.

The point is that the schools and the middle class think they are fighting for their lives—or for the values and the money that made those lives worth living. And, paradoxically, that is why the assaults of inflation, the ever more direct assaults of an egalitarian government—on high incomes, on the accumulation and transmission of wealth—all of which so terrify men like the Master of the Scholars at Westminster, are precisely the forces which are, at the moment, working to save the public schools. If they cannot accumulate or pass on money the only way parents can benefit their children is by giving them a good education. Indeed, giving them a good academic education, or rather exam-passing education, is the only way to transmit wealth: a good education leads to a good job which leads to enough money to give your children a good education which . . . To achieve this, almost any sacrifices are worth making. And they are made. Aunts and uncles help pay; grandparents, like Royalists in the Civil War, sell the last of the gilt-edged. I had a letter from a ninety-two-year-old. Her father had been among the first boys at Malvern in 1863, and all his children and grandchildren had gone there. And now—the great-grandchildren would go. She described the determination and the sacrifices, and how the whole family was helping pay. "When the present government threatens to dispose of our public schools then I feel the end of England will indeed have come."

But most of the public schools have survived over a hundred years or more; some (if you stretch a point) have lasted over a thousand years. They will survive now.

6 Conclusion

In the final seventy-six years the public schools have once again reversed themselves. In 1900 they were a fiercely disciplined and restrictive Monolith, entirely obsessed with teaching games and, except for a select and brilliant few to whom they taught the classics, philistine to a degree, despising and ignoring, in particular, science; they were frenziedly repressive about sex, odiously class-conscious and shut off into tight, conventional, usually brutal little total communities.

Today—remembering the very considerable relative differences, a pattern indeed of enormous variety—they are academically excellent, barely acknowledging the classics and concentrating, if they concentrate on anything in an enormous range of possible subjects, on science; they are relaxed about games, fairly relaxed about sex, and moderate in discipline; they do their best to militate against class consciousness and to integrate themselves into the communities around them; in the freedom they allow their pupils, in the amount of individual activities open to them, they far more resemble an orderly version of what they were in 1800 rather than 1900; their creative renaissance, particularly in the theatre, resembles nothing that has gone before. I think they will survive. But, in a time of almost unprecedented growth and unprecedented danger, many of the schools are filled with gloom. There is a sense of lone scholars in a hostile world, keeping, as the darkness closes round them, and as did those tiny religious communities from which they sprang 1,300 years ago, a few glimmers of the sacred fire alight until the barbarian age has passed.

CHAPTER 19

Public Schools and Some Aspects of Social Justice

I am always afraid of determining on the side of envy or cruelty. The privileges of education may sometimes be improperly bestowed, but I shall always fear to withhold them, lest I should be yielding to the suggestion of pride, while I persuade myself that I am following the maxims of policy; and, under the appearance of salutary restraint, should be indulging the lust of dominion and that malevolence which delights in seeing others depressed.

Dr. Johnson

He is handling many themes at once: the subject bristles with difficult—perhaps insoluble—questions; and he is concerned to hold them up to the light rather than lay down dogmatic answers.

John Wain, in his biography, on Dr. Johnson's account of his journey to the Hebrides.

During the course of this history a number of subjects have arisen, a full discussion of which I have had to postpone. The first of these that I want to deal with is the most difficult: whether or not there is a case for abolishing public schools. It is a question at which, I need hardly say, my peers in the history class begin to look extremely shifty; shuffling their feet, beginning to search for non-existent India rubbers deep inside their desks, suddenly becoming drawn into their textbooks as though by an irresistible force. Bamford says the problem is outside the scope of his book. Why? Although his title is *The Rise of the Public Schools* —he does not deal at all thoroughly with the 20th century—one area, that of conferring privilege and creating an élite, he in fact covers in detail, almost up to the present day. Clearly a full discussion would be germane. Perhaps he means— beyond his own scope. However, he does give fairly broad hints that he reluctantly fears their existence may constitute something of a social injustice. Of the other writers, only Dancy, Wober and Hollis attempt the question. Dancy has dealt with himself. In the first part of his book he proves conclusively, from the results of Fleming, that the State sector simply won't contribute to sending State pupils to public schools. In the last part he offers this as a solution. He offers no reason why the State should change its mind for him.

Hollis, meanwhile, rises to his feet, crimson in the face, and launches into speech. But, for the only time in his excellent book, the mellifluous flow of his prose falters, his embarrassment revealed by his clumsy use of words: ". . . It undoubtedly is so that an Eton education does carry with it adventitious advantages in after-life." I don't really see that the advantages are all that accidental—they derive directly and deliberately from the education, the start being that it is a very good education. And this "after-life", as distinct from your life after school, your career; it must be almost the first time it has been claimed that Eton helps beyond the grave. He argues the difficulty of democratisation, and invents long conversations in which supposedly-lower-class parents say that if our son doesn't succeed he comes back all messed up class-wise—an argument somewhat contradicting the adventitious advantages. It is a rambling and inconclusive debate.

Come lads—surely we can do better than that. Let us set out in rough order the arguments to be raised in defence of public schools. In rough order because the case is not of a logical piece; it rests on two main but unconnected pillars, one pragmatic, the other idealistic, with a number of more or less unrelated but often scarcely less powerful considerations attending them.

1 *The case against abolition*

The language of the discussion is often loaded—or unloaded. For instance Mallory Wober, in his defence of the schools, speaks of an "economically dominant sub-culture", Royston Lambert of "patterns of social stratification in society", and the Registrar General's Groups I and II. Now, this sort of language may be sociologically more accurate, where to use the word"class"is both emotive and vague.I have used it throughout this book —and do so particularly in these last sections, even with the certainty that I will raise strong and often biased feelings—because it is just that vagueness and those emotions with which we have to deal. Ghosts they may be now, though still active, of the intense class conflict and antagonism that has bedevilled this country for decades, even centuries; but ghosts cannot be laid if they are not first raised. Other words have been affected. "Divisive" has become a knife-like word, somehow implying both rivalry and warfare. Yet its first meaning is something which separates, and not all separations are necessarily antagonistic. The generations are separate, in most countries; schools no doubt intensify this age-separateness a bit, but it is fairly mild and innocuous. It is arguable—on the lines we looked at when discussing total societies, where adolescents have to define themselves *against* something—that it is a necessary element in the growth to maturity. In certain respects public schools are cohesive—joining together. Wober says that this is true as regards regionalism versus nationalism; in fact it is also true in some of them, because of the close contacts they encourage between staff and pupils, as regards the divisions between generations.

But the pragmatic side of the discussion centres on the creation and perpetuation of an élite. The point here is that it is clear from a great deal of evidence that in Western industrial societies of our kind, not only are élites of the sort we have inevitable—*but it appears that they are inevitably and permanently filled, to an overwhelming degree, by the middle classes*. Take France. It has a far larger independent sector than we, though a diminishing one—almost forty per cent in 1957 according to *Schools of Europe* by Anthony Kerr; recent figures are seventeen per cent, obtained from the French Embassy. Most of these are private Catholic schools, attended by girls for reasons of religion and morality. They offer less attractive salaries to their teachers and therefore do not have such good ones. The best schools in France are the free State schools—the *Lycées* and the Colleges. From these, without going into details, through a series of fierce sieves, the French force their way upward, by merit and ferocious work, first to the universities or, better still, the *grandes écoles*; and there, if they are aiming for the top civil-service jobs, still more rigorously sieved, to the *grands corps*—of which three are particularly prestigious; the *Inspection des Finances*, the *Cour des Comptes* and the *Conseil d'État*. And this lofty pyramid is composed entirely of State institutions. It is natural to suppose, especially for us, that it is therefore democratic and egalitarian. It is not.

Not one person, for instance, whose father was either a skilled or unskilled worker has ever entered the *Inspection des Finances*. About sixty per cent of all top civil servants in France come from the prosperous upper-middle class. In one report of a group of 440 top civil servants, studied between 1946 and 1969, twenty-eight point four per cent—an astonishing figure—came from just three famous *Lycées* in expensive middle-class areas of Paris, as it might be from Westminster, St. Paul's and Dulwich.

In fact, only about twenty per cent of the French lower class go to the *Lycées*—the first rung. This is partly an expression of French lower class dislike of the *bourgeoisie* and the whole *lycée* system. But it is far more a result of the enormous initial advantage of being born into not just a richer and easier home, but particularly in this context into a home with those values—willingness to learn, appreciation of the academic aims and so on—which we saw were such an advantage here. And exactly the same picture emerges all over Europe and Scandinavia. It emerges in America. So much so that it has been found there, according to Illich, that the more public money that is given to schools the more the situation increases, because the children of the well-off benefit so much more from the money spent than the children of the poor.

There can be no doubt that if the public schools were abolished exactly the same thing would happen here; in fact it is clear that it is happening in a small way already. In *The New Anatomy of Britain*, 1971, Anthony Sampson wrote that all parties would agree on the need to democratise education, to rescue the near-illiterate failures but also to provide real opportunities for the clever. Yet as the process continues it grows more difficult and more complicated. Then, in an arresting image, he goes on: "The institutions which have upheld the class structure of Britain are beginning to be opened up; but as the first roots of the old system are unearthed and cut down, so much longer and thicker roots are revealed, deep underground." Destroy the grammar schools, and those comprehensives in the middle-class areas, pressed by interested and determined parents and filled with a majority of like-minded middle-class children, become new centres of privilege. Their huge sixth forms fed by careful streaming become the next forcing grounds for the universities, taking the place of the public and grammar schools. And of course the comprehensives assist the process. In an article in the *Sunday Times* in 1975, Miss Margaret Maden, Head of Islington Green Comprehensive, said quite frankly that she was in a highly competitive situation, engaged in a battle to get pupils, and get the best pupils. And the other side of the picture is the lower classes, still determinedly not pressing forward, still, as Sampson puts it, able to astonish other Europeans by their assumptions of deference and docility. And abolishing the public schools would probably add to this, rather than reduce it. Commentators have often pointed out that at public schools the cultured background of parents and pupils is roughly the same as that of the teachers; whereas the lower down the scale you get the greater the difference between the school background and the home background. The injection of a mass of new middle-class pupils would simply intensify this clash. This has been found in America, where the advantages of the richer, higher-status pupils put great stress on the lower-status pupils. There are tensions and humiliations. It is the main reason, according to Friedenberg, for the US school gangs.

It would seem, then, that the attempt to destroy the élite is a well-meaning, understandable but impossible dream. It is part of English romanticism. Not only that; it is not even possible in any serious way to alter the composition of the élite. All the evidence suggests that it will continue to be largely middle and upper-middle class whatever happens. This being so, what on earth is the point of destroying the method by which we, in England, partly arrive at our own élite now? It is efficient, if academic excellence is deemed a necessary ingredient; and it is efficient in the way it brings about unity of aim, of standards, of trust, of means of communication—the sort of efficiency we see exemplified by the City. It also inculcates some kindly, and necessary, social virtues and Christian principles. That it is wealth-based is an argument against hereditary wealth and/or against over-high financial rewards, both of which have other and quite simple solutions. It is not an argument against wholesale destruction of virtually the only educational system now left in this country that really works.

In any case, can the country afford to destroy this system? I don't mean literally—it is quite clear that in money terms no government at the moment could afford to buy out the public schools, as Reg Prentice, Education Secretary at the time, admitted in an interview with Ronald Butt (*The Times*, December 1975): "I think there will be an independent sector for a long time to come, whether we like it or not. We couldn't afford to take it over. . . ." Our discussion is in all senses academic; it is nevertheless essential to pursue it. The world has been changed by arguments which were once "academic". I mean, can the country at the moment afford to lose, for instance, the highly trained scientists and mathematicians being turned out by these schools? (I can find no figures to support this, but my clear impression was that more science and mathematics were being specialised in than any other single subject.) And I would repeat here what Alan Barker of UCS said. The public schools are subject to one irresistible force compelling their excellence—their very lives, figuratively speaking, depend on it. "We go to the wall if we don't produce results. If we start getting deplorable results, we soon empty." Miss Maden wants results too. She also wants a complete range of pupils, a "complete mix". She is fighting to get some of the "cream" hitherto skimmed by the grammar schools. But in the last analysis, if she fails to get them, either results or cream, she and her staff survive. The school will be filled. The last and sharpest point of the spur is missing. And this means that the public schools can act as something with which to challenge the comprehensives, something against which they can be judged; in exactly the same way ITV revitalised the BBC.

But this excellence is not just to do with learning. By some definitions the middle classes have disappeared or are rapidly disappearing. In crude Marxist terms, for instance, I imagine most of them are really working class; that is, they depend economically on the sale of their labour power (physical or mental), and neither own nor have any control over the processes and volume produced by the means of production. They are bossed or manipulated in some way by the directors and owners of the means of production. In financial terms, if the trends of the last few years continue, it seems clear that many more sections of the working class will receive wages as high or higher than many sections of the middle class— either because our society has decided that certain sorts (perhaps all sorts) of semi-skilled or unskilled labour deserve such reward; or because labour, united, is too powerful to resist.

But the middle classes are distinguished, also, because they are taught certain values. Moral values: honesty, thrift, the need for hard work, loyalty, the good of serving the community and so on. Cultural values: the worth of literature, music and art, of learning for its own sake, the need for reason, the importance of the individual, an appreciation of history, etc. It is all this that public schools enshrine and pass on; it was about this they became eloquent. I remember Michael McCrum of Eton, languid yet in some indefinable way powerful, suddenly becoming animated, his rather tired end-of-term face alive. Public schools don't teach their pupils that they are better in any way or that their education is better; that would be both arrogant and disgusting. But they teach them, or Eton tries to teach them, to think independently and creatively. They must become the creative leaven in society. And who can doubt, another master said, that if the schools were destroyed, much of this would be destroyed too? In some few favoured schools these attitudes might survive; but in far more the new middle-class entries would be a tiny minority. Even if there were, say, twenty per cent middle class they would be swamped by the other eighty per cent, swept away.

These pragmatic arguments against abolishing public schools are supported by even more important abstract ones. These have to do with the fundamental rights and liberties of the individual. It has long been considered that parents have a "prior right to choose the kind of education that shall be given to their children" (Universal Declaration of Human Rights). Freedom is an odd thing; when you have it, you hardly notice it. In this respect it is like some great natural element—water or air. In this country we can believe, say or write anything we like; no one tells us where to sit or walk or stops us leaving the country; we cannot be imprisoned without cause. Parliament makes laws but, if enough of us dislike them, we can make a new Parliament and new laws. We live in these and other freedoms as easily and unnoticingly as we breathe air; but take away air and we'd suffocate in two minutes. Remove our freedoms and we'd realise with astonishment how we valued them and needed them. Not that they are always easy. Someone may write something in the press of which you violently disapprove; or your daughter may meet a black man and marry him and you can't *stand* blacks. Yet you would be horrified if the government sent the police to smash up the presses and arrest the editor of the offending paper, as might happen in many countries; or passed a law forbidding marriages between blacks and whites because of their different colours, as has happened in South Africa. All these are truisms, no doubt; but truisms are no less true because obvious.

And among our freedoms is the freedom to spend our money in any way we like. There is controversy in this country at the moment over private medicine as well, but it is over whether private doctors should use National Health Service facilities. Nobody questions the right of private doctors to exist, provided they do not weaken the Health Service. If someone wants to spend vast sums on their health, they can. It's their money. Because you disapprove for whatever reason of private schools and don't like people spending their money on them you can't just forbid them to do it and destroy the schools, any more than you can forbid them to marry black people or from writing and printing what they believe. And this violence is somehow the more unpleasant because it would be exerted on the part of so many against so few. Why can't they leave us alone, said McCrum, we only teach seven per cent of the children now. Besides, as one of his predecessors said, "Exactly how is one to define the criminal offence which will be committed by a parent who spends some of his own money on the education of his children?" In fact the law required to abolish all independent schools and prevent any new ones would have to be as venomous and savage as the Conventicle Act of 1662, which forbade the religious meetings of Dissenters. At bottom the question of ending the public schools is a question of liberty.

2 *The case for abolition*

In looking at the case for abolition I do not intend to meet all the arguments I have just raised head-on. Indeed, in a sense the most fundamental argument—that of liberty—is unanswerable. The question of liberty is a question of principle, in the end a question of personal belief. I can try to persuade you that liberty should be tempered so far in the interests of equality; you can equally try to persuade me that to interfere that far would be wrong: in the end we will both take our stands firmly where we believe the right balance to lie—and both stands will be on the side of right because both liberty and equality are important social goals.

That is not to say that some of the other arguments are perhaps weaker than I may have made them seem. I think, for example, that Michael McCrum was being rather ingenuous when he complained that public schools teach "only seven per cent" of secondary school pupils. The point always has been, and still is, that from a minute proportion of the population we derive a large majority of our leaders, managers, and fill most of the wealth or comfort-giving jobs. In fact, the Institute of Practitioners in Advertising, who have good reasons to get these things right (their figures in any case correspond closely to those of the Registrar General), break the population down into five groups: A, B, C, D, and E. A and B are the upper middle and intermediate classes who fill precisely these positions, and comprise thirteen per cent of the population. Thus, on the old figures, over half these positions could come (and in fact did come) from the seven per cent public school population. Now, in fact, this population will total thirteen per cent of the whole. Theoretically all positions of this sort could be public school filled. The second point about numbers is that public schools, by being selective, not only remove a proportion of the most intelligent pupils from the common pool but more importantly a far larger share of the teachers—and, as we saw, the likelihood is that they are the best teachers. Again, the terror that "middle-class culture" would disappear is almost certainly unfounded. It has not disappeared on the Continent—indeed it is probably stronger in France than it is here. It is not permissible on the one hand to put forward the argument that there is no point in destroying the public schools because middle-class advantages will simply transfer themselves to the new educational set-up, and on the other hand argue that these advantages and qualities will disappear. Both can't be true. The point is that so long have our public schools done the broad job of inculcating moral, spiritual and cultural values that we now imagine this is the only way it can happen. But it is not. The family is just as efficient; indeed far more efficient. We had a complex and highly civilised culture, multi-layered as now, in the 16th, 17th and 18th centuries, which was passed on and evolved perfectly well long before public schools came on the scene in any large way. And it is equally absurd to suppose that many of our institutions—the Foreign Office, the City, for example— which we saw owed so much in their formation to public schools would collapse without them. They have long become institutions in their own right, capable of imposing their ways of behaviour on new entrants.

Nor am I impressed by arguments that dreams of equality are "Utopian" or an example of English romanticism or against "human nature"—"the weak must go to the wall". *All* improvements in the human condition have come because we are able to dream them first; and *all* improvements have been, when ideas, greeted with just these objections: these were the objections of the opponents to the abolition of slavery, of the opponents to extension of the franchise in 1832, of the opponents of change in the public schools in the 20s and 30s. It is because he can imagine a better world—able to throw the transparent image of his dream upon reality—and then struggle towards it, that man rises above the animals. Without that effort he remains with them. And for this reason, however Utopian—indeed precisely because Utopian—the imaginative effort must be made. Not that it is easy, either to dream, or, having done that, to implement the dream. Look at some of the concrete manifestations of our own contemporary expression of this force: as women became free so the figures of women's crime rise (indeed crime seems to rise generally with more generous social freedom); as people seek increasing self-fulfilment in marriage, divorces start rising. But this does not mean that women were not suppressed before or, alternatively, should be again, or that social freedoms are evil, or that people are wrong to seek fulfilment in marriage. It only means that freedom and fulfilment are difficult and we haven't yet learnt to cope with the first or attain the second.

Michael McCrum said that it would be arrogant and disgusting if public schools taught their pupils that either they or their education were "better". Yes—but surely in practice the attitudes taught are invariably and inevitably assumed to be superior. That is inherent in their being chosen and taught—why else teach them, if they are not better? Mallory Wober, pursuing the same argument as McCrum, also says that the "solution" is that the public schools should be allowed to continue passing on the middle-class culture; the economic and social privileges that go with it they should not pass on. But how on earth is this to be achieved?

Mallory Wober is silent.

Here surely is the nub. I was at pains to point out in the previous chapter that public schools give one of the best educations in England, that this education still leads to higher-paid jobs, sometimes to positions of power, always to more comfortable and pleasanter jobs. The ability to get this education depends largely on class and entirely on money, and is for this reason self-perpetuating, and, with the abolition of the grammar schools, instead of dwindling, this privileged sector of education is now becoming larger than ever before. I do not see how it is possible to deny that this system thus perpetuates and intensifies the class divisions in our country and that it is therefore unjust and wrong.

Clearly, we are not all born equal: some are clever, some stupid, some quick, some slow (I am not arguing here against the necessity to train the intelligent few). And let us allow for the moment that in our society unequal abilities will always tend to result in unequal financial rewards—since the chief good of our society is still money. But there is, within this, a fundamental sense of natural justice that people's abilities should be allowed to function equally and unburdened. Our "childhood" extends, in this context, to the age of sixteen to eighteen. As far as possible "childhood" should be equal, so that everyone should start life as an adult with an equal chance. Colour is not an ability—or a lack of it. Nor is class. Nor is your sex. Nor is wealth. They confer automatic advantages and disadvantages because of the structure of society. And that is why, in varying degrees, we remove both advantages and disadvantages. This is much more complicated in practice than this simple statement makes it seem. For example, wealth, as we have seen, confers advantages, but wealth is still the fundamental goal of society—it cannot therefore be totally removed without removing the goal. It can only be removed within limits, and it is in setting these limits that the discussion becomes difficult and fundamental. But however wide, in terms of that fundamental sense of what is just, to allow the erection and perpetuation of a totally different and superior system of education for the rich is outside these limits. So at any rate these arguments—and I must confess to a certain degree reluctantly—have compelled me to conclude.

What is to be done? How heal these divisions in our society? The solution, as a good many writers have noted, is to make the State system as good or better than the private. They remain vague as to how. Yet other countries—indeed most countries—manage it in one way or another. Why should it be beyond us? There are three courses. We can do nothing to the public schools but merely try to chivvy the State system. That is clearly not going to make any sudden difference; it is also, as we have seen, going to perpetuate the divisions (and in the light of current events exacerbate them). We can get the State to use the public school system and incorporate the two together in some way. But that, as Dancy showed, has never worked yet—and is still more unlikely to work at the moment. We can abolish the public schools and disperse them abroad into a new universal system of comprehensive State education. We would then have a situation which would parallel that in those countries where the State system is the best system—all the country's resources of brain, teaching power and parent power would be involved in it. Yet can we do this in such a way that we do not lose the very important qualities and excellencies the public schools seem able to pass on?

I think the best way to answer this is to look at Henry Morris.

3 Henry Morris and the village/community colleges

Henry Morris was an educationalist active in Cambridge during the 1920s and 30s. There were at that time a number of problems: the rural communities were declining as the clever and ambitious left for the towns and the schools declined with them. Somehow the clever, and with them the clever teachers, had to be lured back. There was the problem, then as now, of the educational drop-out. And there was the teaching itself—the need to pass exams leading to the stuffing in of too much information too quickly and too early.

Now these problems are analogous to our own, though there is no need to force the comparison. We have the problem of luring clever pupils and teachers to declining State schools; we are faced with a deficient sense of national community; I have spoken of the intense pressure brought about by the need to pass exams, and the attendant need for early specialisation and choice. And oddly enough a number of masters mentioned the restlessness that occurs in adolescents at the age of fifteen, sixteen or seventeen—it is perfectly clear in State schools that by fifteen many of them want to be free, to be earning and experimenting. But this is found in public schools. Mr. Mackichan of Marlborough said, "Is five years the right time? We have many boys who would like to change, to go, and who make that quite clear to the authorities. What adult, especially at first, stays in the same job for five years? And adolescence is the time of most aliveness, the strongest desire to experiment and change." The restlessness of the fourteen- to sixteen-year-old is well known at girls' schools; nor is this anything to do, or entirely to do, with the nascent desire to mix with boys because the same thing happens at co-educational schools. In most primitive cultures, in fact, it is at fourteen that boys and girls start to take part in the work of the tribe, and a number of anthropologists believe that the absence of adolescent "difficulties" in these cultures as compared to our own is because they are engaged in real tasks.

Morris solved all his problems with two, at that time, revolutionary ideas. The first was that people learn all the time—they do this automatically, whether they want to or not; therefore this fact must be used. They should be *able* to learn all the time. "We will lift the school-leaving age to ninety . . . education will be co-terminous with life." Once this was achieved, there would be no need for early specialisation: they would learn when they liked, when they wanted or needed to learn. It wouldn't matter if they dropped out at fifteen; they could come back at twenty-three or thirty-three. The second solution, and the one that, amongst much else, made the first practical, was his vision of the village and community college.

He saw that the essence of a community, whether urban or rural, was that it should be close—its pleasures enjoyed, its burden carried, shared, by all. And this must include education, which should become an integral part of its activities. Thus the facilities for the cultural and entertainment life of a region—theatre, cinema, bingo hall, athletic grounds, showers; for its politics—law court, council chamber; its medical facilities; its economic hub; its school or schools; everything, should all be grouped together and interact. In this way—by gathering the community together —Morris believed he could revitalise it. And since everything was grouped close it would be easy for adults to continue their education. There would be crèches for young mothers. And he envisaged the standard being extremely high—only thus could he attract the best teachers and pupils. Dons would come out to lecture from Cambridge; there would be recordings, films, the widest possible curriculum and range of courses, academic and technical—and of course primary, secondary and sixth-form education would all be in the same area.

Morris was a man of great eloquence, able to cast a spell on the hardened or bored farmers and tight-fisted councillors whom, in the early years, he had to convince.

> We ought to see our way to the organic provision of education for the whole adult community. We must do away with the insulated school. We must so organise the educational buildings of the towns and countryside that the schools of the young are either organically related to, or form part of, the institutions in which the ultimate goals of education are realised. We must associate with education all those activities which go to make a full life—art, literature, music, festivals, local government, politics. This is as important for the teaching of the young, as it is for the teachers themselves. It is only in a world where education is confined to infants and adolescents that the teacher is inclined to become a pundit or a tyrant.

Now all this sounds like a dream. The astonishing thing is that in six years Morris made it come true. It would not be relevant to describe the long and incredibly strenuous fight to realise his vision (there is a good account in the excellent *Life* of him by Harry Rée). He was an interesting and difficult character. He had enormous energy and drive, and almost

infinite resource. When councillors turned down his ideas as too expensive
he flew to America and raised most of the money there himself. He was a
homosexual who had, on the whole, to repress himself, and this became an
increasing strain, which he would vent on his colleagues and superiors. He
could be maddening. He was said to have driven his first boss in the
county education department of Cambridge, Austin Keen, into the grave.
It took him two years. Keen, said Morris contemptuously, was "insufferable, ignorant and intolerable". He was a dandy, who loved food, and a
witty conversationalist. Having asked for *insalata verde* in southern Italy
and being brought, not lettuce, but a bowl with some grass and dandelion
leaves floating in olive oil, he said to the Madame of the *albergo*: "Madame,
I am quite prepared to admire your countryside but don't expect me to eat
it." He was often devastatingly scornful, equally savage about British
capitalists "with faces like plates" and unrealistic British Communists—
"filleted" parsons and their fluting voices, or women dons; "their wombs
are stuffed with algebra".

Yet this complex man not only created his Utopia, but proved conclusively that all his ideas worked. By 1939 there were four colleges, the most
famous being at Impington, with its immense and marvellous building
designed by Gropius. Morris was vehement on the importance of art and
architecture—"the best means we have of instituting a compulsory
aesthetic education". He collected and commissioned works of art to
decorate his colleges—and flew into a rage if he saw reproductions put up.
Eventually, by 1960, there were twelve village colleges, covering the
county. The variety was enormous, some close to Morris's ideal, some not
so close. Early on, it was clear that he could in fact revive the communities
in this way, and that people responded. He wrote this account of Sawston
Village College after it had been going for some time:

> The senior school at the College is going well. All the children of the nine
> villages turn up daily without a hitch. The children cheer as they board their
> omnibus. . . .
>   The adult side is also going strong. The library is open every evening from
> seven till nine. An average of fifty readers and borrowers turn up nightly. The
> university extension course has a hundred students including young men and
> young women who cycle in from surrounding villages.

It was found that it stimulated adolescents and older people to work
together, the age barriers cracked; not only that, but discipline was
revolutionised. It is possible that indiscipline has something to do with the
fact that the teacher-pupil relationship is also that of adult-child; when
there are adults in the class this situation is changed—adults, being pupils,
are "one of us". The teacher can therefore be "one of us" too. A tension
relaxes. In any event, noisy classes became calm—it was both easier and
more stimulating for the teachers. This, therefore, is a different route to

achieve that middle class "willingness to learn" which is essential for academic achievement, and why the community school is a relevant context into which the public schools could merge. And the standards could be very high—up to those at university. Very good teachers indeed were attracted. The phenomenon of adolescents leaving at fifteen or sixteen for work or love continued; but was solved because they came back at nineteen or twenty-three or twenty-five—leaving their children, if they were wives, to be watched by pensioners reading in the library. Courses were taken up again. Exams were passed. The idea of lifelong learning was, for some, a reality. Nor was this success restricted to the country. Exactly the same results were obtained in urban areas with the community colleges.

How narrow, suddenly, for all their excellence, do public schools seem in the face of all this. This country could be one—the absurd class barriers, the stupid women afraid of butchers' daughters, the surly and arrogant antagonisms all vanished. There is something immature, for all its age, in a country in which the vast proportion of the people expect to be led. Maturity is leading yourself. Certainly, relaxing in the confidence that the élite would lead them out of it, the British people have been cushioned from, indeed ignored, the gathering reality of the last thirty years. And for the country to realise, perhaps for the first time in its history, that it could and should lead itself, to be freed at last from the clanking impedimenta of class, to revive the sense of community, would release great waves of energy. Rattray Taylor, in his book *Are Workers Human?*, estimated that this sort of change would mean, by itself alone, that Britain could expand her national income by half within five years without any additional capital investment, and reduce the cost of many manufactured goods by thirty per cent.

And schools, if that is the word for them, like those I have described, are one way of making such a change begin to happen. They are extremely flexible. For instance, it is clear that the intelligent and able few need special opportunities. In these complexes they could be taught separately. They could be separated to different and distant parts of this vastly expanded "school"; or just separated in adjacent classrooms. Or they could be taught with the rest. Or a mixture of both. Anything could be experimented with. Some way could be found, therefore, of both preserving and spreading the excellence of the abolished public schools. But the point is they would be part of the same community and the same school. Their separation—if it occurred—would not be because of class or money. Nor would they, indeed, be nearly as separate as would, say, a largely middle-class sixth form in a comprehensive. Children, adolescents and adults of all classes and incomes would be seen passing up if they were intelligent (and down if they failed); and passing by every day in the centre, taking part in its activities—and these would be community activities, not just school ones. It is here, at the bottom, at school when very young, that these changes must start—indeed it is unlikely that so profound a change in national character will be much affected by anything else.

4 The basic dichotomy between women's and men's education and their rôles in society

Bearing Henry Morris in mind, I want now to turn to a second problem raised earlier and left: the dichotomy between the education of women and their rôle in society. The most successful stream in girls' education has been that which as far as possible makes it resemble that given to boys. This got rather out of hand for a while. But for some years now the great English girls' public schools—Cheltenham, St. Leonard's, St. Paul's, Sherborne, Roedean and others—have been comparable to the boys' schools. No one's going to do any hoovering on *them*. But from the very start, implicit in this development, was the fact that sooner or later women, since they were being given the same education as men, would want to lead lives as fulfilling as men and be accepted as being as important as men. In the event, the change came later, quite recently. But society has not changed. There was and is therefore a fundamental dichotomy between the education given to girls and their rôle in society.

I find it difficult to gauge how serious, how widespread and how significant the various desires and efforts loosely characterised by the words "Women's Liberation" are. But as, and if, the co-educational trend in public schools continues, which I think it will, and as and if the standards of State education improve, then the liberation movement is likely to grow and become more significant. But it has not got very far in the past, and will get no further in the future for an obvious and simple reason. The economic division of labour and responsibility in Western society remains as it has always been: the home and the children are the woman's; the job of earning the family's way is the man's. You can fiddle about with this. You can insist on equal pay for the few jobs they do in common. You can provide crèches for little children. You can say that women will need a "gap" to bring up a family. But in practice in this sphere the decisive move must be economic. Men and women won't feel equal until they are equal economically. And, if society is serious about this development—if it believes that women should lead lives as various as their education fits them for—then it will require very fundamental changes indeed, particularly organisational. Men and women will *both* have to bring up the children, both wash up and shop and cook, and both go out and earn a living. The two basic animal obligations—to reproduce the species and to provide sufficient food and protection to survive—instead of being divided and given one to each sex will be shared; as they are, incidentally, in many other parts of the animal kingdom.

The vocational element, both in practice and discussion, entered girls' education because serious study of any sort seemed completely at variance with their rôle in society over centuries, millennia even. No such element has ever touched discussions on boys' education—certainly not as far as the middle and upper classes have been concerned anyway. Yet this is odd. At one point Correlli Barnett is discussing the remoteness of education from the jobs the country needs and which in any case many public school boys will do: technology, engineering, business and so on. His solution is to bring the education closer: to study science, economics, current affairs. But surely the logical end of this is to study directly and early for your vocation or job? Would a businessman not be better if he had studied business administration classes, the theory of office organisation, the theory of staggered working hours, management in theory and practice, investment and so on? It is all very well people calling glibly for scientists and public schools replying equally glibly that they are supplying them. They are supplying the wrong kind of scientists, pure scientists. What are needed are *applied* scientists, boys willing to be engineers and technologists, to grapple with the rough practice of science. Now of course there are objections to this. It would be far too narrow, it would result in far too early specialisation. But, as we have seen, to pass exams pupils are already concentrating on one, two or three subjects from fifteen or sixteen. Nor need vocational courses be narrow. Business and industrial sides would include British, European and American industrial history over the last 200 years, psychology, economics, political theory, the sociology and behaviour of groups and so on. But the real fact is that the classical and Arnoldian influences on all education in this country are far too strong. Vocational education is for after school—at the place of work or at a technical college or occasionally, and to a lesser extent than these two, at a university. School itself—both public and State—is, via the classical tradition, for academic learning, to achieve intellectual discrimination. The Arnoldian tradition, with its commitment to train the character, the "soul", has metamorphosed, with the passage of time and the changing *zeitgeist*, into a concern with individual development—hence, in part at least, the plays, the freedoms, the wide range of curriculum and outside activities.

This has had a curious result. There is an equal but different dichotomy, just as profound and powerful, between the education of men and their rôle—or rather rôles—in society as is the case with women. In fact, it applies equally to women in addition to their own problems. It is not quite the dichotomy we have just looked at above (though this does have some force I think) and it applies equally to State and public school education. It manifests itself in two ways; one obvious, the other more subtle.

State education has exactly the same aims as public school education—
even if at a less exalted level and achieved with less success at the moment.
But strenuous attempts are made to improve it. The school-leaving age is
raised. The supposition must be that it will eventually more closely
emulate that at the public schools. Yet what are enormous numbers, the
vast majority, of these children being educated for, for what are they being
encouraged to explore their individuality and discover their talents? To
join the ranks of the labouring working class, for jobs of appalling
monotony and waste, crude drudgery, lifelong slavery to assembly line on
factory and shop floor. It has been recognised for years and everywhere
how destructive this is; that this is the principal cause of industrial unrest
and dissatisfaction. It was what obsessed Sanderson during the last six
years of his life, and he died in the very act of preaching a solution in the
summer of 1922. It is a crime against man, a crime against the nation. The
solution then, as now, was simply to try to give more money and less
work; a solution which does not approach the cause and is both self-
increasing and insulting.

Sanderson's own solution was two-fold: first revolutionary changes in
industry: "It will lead to no less a thing than closing down certain
productions, certain classes of occupation, certain industries or processes."
Second, in some vague if exhilarating way which he did not make explicit,
these industrial processes must be made creative and exciting, just as he had
made science and other subjects at Oundle creative and exciting. I do not
think either of these solutions works. I do not see how you could close
down, say, the car-making industry and other assembly-line occupations
without producing economic collapse. Even theoretically and idealistically
(and it is on these levels we are arguing) that seems absurd. And how do
you make such occupations creative and exciting? Experiments in Sweden,
where for example a group of workers makes a whole car, haven't
succeeded. Nor does it really help to have even extreme forms of worker
democracy. It combats monotony to some extent to know you are helping
yourself, but the brute fact is still there: the job itself *remains the same*. You
can't make jobs like this creative and exciting because they are by their
nature destructive wasteful drudgery. You can't tinker. Far more fundamental changes are needed.

But there is more to it than this. Even if, by some such educational
mixing as I suggested, the class prejudices in Britain were dissipated still
further, the great disparity between the nature of jobs would tend to keep
it—does keep it—essentially the same. The white-collar worker, the
businessman, the man who works with his brain, can't help feeling different from the man who works with his hands. The likelihood is that he'll
feel superior; even if the worker with his hands despises him and himself
feels superior. Either way (and leaving for the moment the positive nature
of hand work, expressed by David Butcher) the same criticism applies to

many other labouring or semi-labouring jobs. We have, for example, on the whole abandoned the idea of a servant class in personal terms. But society itself has not abandoned the concept of servants at all. We have servants to clear up our rubbish, servants to deliver our milk, servants to deliver our letters: "Come, my good man, here is eight and a half pence— and I should like you to deliver this note to Moncrieff of that Ilk; I have indicated the address." I am not disputing the efficiency of this method; only that it often involves human beings spending their entire lives in ways which make no use of their potential talents or actual desires whatsoever.

So much is obvious, if in a hopeless way ignored. But it can be extended —and the fact that it is not is in large part a combination of desperate self-deception and an unconscious conspiracy of conceit on the part of the middle classes. For the last thirty years—but in part before that—they have been increasingly encouraged to extend their minds and explore their individual talents. Not only have they learnt the pleasures and excitements of intellectual and academic pursuit—studying the classics or literature or pure mathematics in depth, with additional and stimulating "broadening" courses on psychology or sociology—but they have found they can play the flute, are skilled at debating, enjoy metal work, or acting and writing plays. For a few short and vivid years vistas of what human nature, *their* human nature, is capable of stretch intoxicatingly ahead and then—crash! down comes the concrete curtain. People don't go into business, or if they do don't excel at it, because, compared to what might be, it is boring and trivial. If the truth were told, the vast majority of middle-class jobs—those jobs in boxes, in miles of offices, in the offices of Shell or ICI or the headquarters of British Steel, or those cells in the great slothful body of central and local bureaucracy sprawled lethargically across the land, staffed by initiative-sapped vegetables—all these and millions of other jobs are as stultifying and unrewarding and so ultimately as destructive, though far more physically comfortable, as are those of the workers upon whom they rest. Of course, there are satisfying jobs in line with the education—teachers, scientists in certain posts, sociologists, some of the professions, and satisfying positions near the top. (In 1966 a survey was conducted among 1,000 directors of British companies. Over seventy-five per cent said that their main ambition was to retire; over sixty-five per cent said that they felt their time at work was wasted. I wonder how different it would be today?) But for most people the first years in an office are torture as the mind is destroyed and ambitions vanish; then a grey apathy descends and they are carried ever more swiftly towards that longed for retirement, and death.

The fact is, the more stimulating and awakening public school (and State) education becomes, precisely to that degree does it make people less fit for the lives they will actually have to lead. They were probably doing this job better in 1920, as A. S. Neill noted. "By compelling our students' attention to subjects which hold no interest for them, we, in effect, condition them for jobs they will not enjoy."

5 The multi-rôle society—aspects of a solution

Two principles are clearly going to be involved in any solution to any of these problems: the first is flexibility, the second is rôle change. People are going to have to behave differently from the way they have behaved before. And I think the kind of flexibility and rôle change I have in mind is best demonstrated by considering the position of the labouring working class doing destructive drudgery on assembly line and shop floor.

We cannot abolish these industries. We should not expect people to spend their lives being engaged in them. It is clear to me that if our society depends on, and enjoys the results of these industrial processes—mass-produced cars, mass-produced cans of this and bottles of that—then society, the *whole* of society, should bear the burden of them. Clearly, this is not the place to work out exactly how this would be done. This is not an exercise in practical re-organisation, but an exercise in theory. Here I just want you to imagine the possibility of change, to catch a glimpse of what things could be like—to throw the transparent image of the dream upon reality. But if every single person in the country had to do for, let us say, one or two months a year, labouring work of this kind then I cannot believe it is beyond this technologically very well-equipped, easily governed and bureaucratically minded country to manage the logistics of it. What society wills, it achieves.

But this would only be a first step, though no doubt it would take some years to bring about. From there, the process would continue. Why should other people clear up our rubbish for us? Or deliver our letters? Or sweep our streets? If one week of that one or two months had to be devoted to community service, it would be comparatively simple to work out rosters and duties.

It should be noted that two basic principles underlie these changes. The first is that society should do its own dirty work. The second is that it is possible to combine two or even three rôles in one. In effect, although in most cases two of the rôles would be for a relatively short time, have three jobs. The first principle would revolutionise class attitudes in this country; the second would revolutionise attitudes to work.

For nearly twenty years, in order to write, I, like most writers, had to do other jobs. I did a great deal of free-lance advertising copywriting, I wrote book reviews, I did tutoring and so on. Often I did more than one of these. I remember one period of three or four months when I was working in a bookshop three mornings a week, tutoring three afternoons a week, doing one and a half days' copywriting and spending the other two and a half days writing a novel. These years taught me a good deal. I discovered that whereas I could work part of the week for months or even years on end and enjoy what I did,, when, as sometimes happened, I had to do it all the time, I gradually began to dislike it. I discovered things about myself I would not otherwise have discovered: I make a passable salesman, for instance; I could also be quite a good teacher. And, in an office situation especially, I could do in two days what it took my colleagues five to do. Anyone who works—whether in a factory, an office, a hospital, a hotel, no matter where—imagines he is busy. He would be amazed at what he could accomplish and, more importantly, leave out, if he had only two days in which to do what usually took him a week.

The glory of man is the multiplicity of his talents and his diversity; fulfilment comes from the development and use of as much of this diversity and as many of these talents as possible. In my view, it is some fundamental change on these lines that is now needed throughout Western society. I cannot listen when I hear Marxists or capitalists arguing; they sound like two groups in the same gang, squabbling about who's to have the most money. Greed and fear are, of course, powerful motives. I don't deny they work; only that cultures and societies which rely on them inevitably seem to evolve injustices. Public schools taught for years through fear of the rod and bribe of reward; gradually they found that interest and wide opportunity worked far better. Society would find the same.

Once the *principle* of a multi-rôle society is accepted then all the other problems fall into place; as in fact do many related problems of our time. It is a total solution. The great motive force of our Western society is money; and this is opposed in ideological warfare to the various, and superficially more attractive, Marxist/Communist goals. All you can really seek, if your goal is money, is more money; it therefore condemns us to continual expansion. For many centuries this was possible, even admirable. There was still plenty of stretch. Now we are impelled to swell until we burst. The multi-rôle society would have at its core— instead of, as today, as an occasionally hoped-for and usually abandoned adjunct—not money but the goal of personal fulfilment. As far as the class situation in Britain goes it would have a decisive effect: the city bankers' view of labour would change radically after a month on the assembly line at Ford's. I remember, when I was doing four things at once, that it gave me an unusual feeling of security. Everyone employed is afraid at some level of the sack. But a man with four jobs can face the loss of one with equanimity: as a result, the power both of management and the necessity for unions is at once diminished. Even economic depression becomes easier to bear, since the country is sharing its work load in an entirely new way. The rôle of women is resolved. Since husbands have jobs in series, so can wives; they can therefore share the children and the home. There is in fact strong evidence that taking up this sort of approach to life would lead to this anyway. Dan Miller, Professor of Psychology at Brunel University, has recently carried out research into how a man's working life affects his behaviour and attitude to his wife and children. He compared those in regimented, non-responsible, inflexible bureaucratic or assembly-line jobs with those in flexible, responsible, initiative-needing jobs. The research, and its result, cut across class lines: a professional craftsman or small shop-owner and the chairmen of big companies were both in initiative-needing jobs; the big-company salary slave and the assembly-line drudge were not. He found that the fathers in these slave jobs did not help in the home, never cooked or washed up, were less involved with their children and less fond of them—and generally flaccid and regimented. Whereas the reverse was true of those whose jobs in some way fulfilled them and demanded initiative; they took initiative at home too. Finally, space in work allows time for education. In the multi-rôle society there would be room for Henry Morris's dream—education could be "co-terminous with life".

I think that, in the interests of social justice, public schools should be abolished—but only in the context of a fundamental social revolution, such as I have outlined. A revolution in education, with a new State system radically altered along the Henry Morris Community College lines. A revolution in social organisation towards a multi-rôle society. If the schools were just abolished in vacuo there would be few profound benefits (particularly as regards class divisions) and much loss of excellence.

CHAPTER 20

The Power of the Public Schools Explained

We looked at this notice board to find which dormy we were in. Then my sister showed me where it was and left me to my fate.

... everything seemed strange, even the way we went into prayers and stood.
From Mallory Wober's, *English Girls' Boarding Schools*

I said early on that one of the most important things about public schools was that they were boarding schools. This also makes them comparatively rare, though they exist in countries which were once in the Empire. Australia, South Africa, Canada, India, and Rhodesia all have a small handful of select, expensive public schools very like our own. There is also a large boarding experiment in Russia with over a million pupils, but this is not like our system. But boarding schools are rare in America, Scandinavia and even more rare on the Continent. In France they are scorned and those in them pitied. All over the rest of the world—in India, China, Africa, as well, of course, as here in Britain—people go to school daily from home; the school is for academic learning and nothing else. That is, people go to school as to a job and in that sense it corresponds to what life will be like afterwards. "Natural" is a difficult word to use in this context, but on the surface this certainly seems more natural.

The fact that public schools are boarding has contributed enormously to the effects they have had, as we saw, for instance, in our discussion of them as total societies. There are other effects. Royston Lambert found that those who boarded, especially from an early age, tended to prize social rather than individual qualities in other people, and to prefer groups to single companions. They learnt, respected, then enjoyed, that is to say, how to get on in communities. Mallory Wober analyses the effects on family life in a rather confusing chapter in which the only certain conclusion is that boarders themselves thought it made them value family life more and therefore improved it. I wonder. No doubt absence makes the heart grow fonder; but I would think it almost impossible for children or adolescents to admit, at the time, that something so precious as family life and love was endangered. The effect is probably variable: sometimes it is enhanced (this is certainly so in the case of difficult family situations, the over-intense nuclear family, for example); but sometimes, especially if parents do not keep up contact, families do grow apart; sometimes, at a deep level, a child feels abandoned and unloved and the relationship is damaged. I doubt if it is an area that is really accessible to research. Wober also found that boarders have no more problems than day pupils; though day pupils were happier (just) at schools—the same schools—than boarders. Both he and Lambert discovered that boarders found it easier to talk to their friends about their problems than day pupils could talk either to friends or anyone else.

This is all interesting enough, though it is curiously unrevealing and bloodless in a way I find typical of sociologists' research. I think we will gain far more significant insights if we now move into that final area I want to look at. It is the area covered by anthropology.

1 Public schools considered anthropologically

People often doubt the relevance of studying life on, say, a South Pacific atoll and comparing it to that in London or New York. But in fact it is not that the set-up in New York is so different. Anthropology is the study of mankind. The difficulty is the size of New York, the diffuseness of its physical, social and psychological boundaries, the variety of cultures interacting within it; anthropological comparison is very difficult, though not impossible. But public schools are the ideal size. They are in fact the size of many villages or even small tribal communities. And they are also educational institutions. Now education, the leading of its younger members into adult life, is considered even more important in primitive communities than it is in ours. Many studies have been made of the aims, the methods and the results of the various forms of education that exist in cultures all over the world. We can expect a useful shift of perspective if we try to place public schools in this much larger context.

As well as the various authorities cited in the bibliography, I rely a good deal on Y. A. Cohen's *The Transition from Childhood to Adolescence*. I do not know how central he is in anthropological thinking today, but I did notice that he not so much differed from other writers on the subject as sometimes went further in his deductions. On the major issues, however, all anthropologists seem agreed. The purpose of education in all cultures is two-fold. First, to pass on the cultural heritage and assembled knowledge of the tribe, and this usually includes the religious knowledge. In most tribes, therefore, this activity is compulsive. It is, indeed, essential to the tribe's survival, both physically—without knowing how or where to hunt, for example, or how to cure sickness, they would rapidly die out; and spiritually—if they did not, say, pass on the knowledge of how to make sacrifices for dead souls their own souls would perish. These survival forces give to education the force and passion of an instinct. The second task is to place the individual on the social map and explain that map to him. This can be both simple and complex. In simple terms, it means moving a child

—a person on the fringes of society, a burden on it—into the position of an adult, where he takes his place in society and performs the various tasks suitable to his position in its hierarchy. And as well as necessary to society, the "placing" of an individual in this way is a vital part of forming his identity, since his view of himself, what he *is*, is very largely a social one; he is someone relative to all those around him. And to know this absolutely and securely, by removing confusion and uncertainty, releases energy. Often what has to be taught is complex. We saw, in discussing the importance of teachers, that who taught was of cardinal importance since that gave the clue as to the authority in a culture—if all the teaching is done by relatives of the father, then it is a patrilineal tribe and so on.

Education, therefore, is a social process in which the significant result is change—change from ignorance to knowledge, from a position of no social status to that of the correct status. The significant factor is time, the time it takes to bring about the change, but far more importantly, the time —or times—at which these changes are initiated. Now practically all cultures make their moves at one or two ages, and usually at both: eight to ten, and then again at puberty, that is around the age of thirteen. Cohen notes that these are both times of intense biochemical and hormonal change in the human body, when it undergoes a period of intense stress. The period between eight and ten is the most disturbing because it is not accompanied, as at puberty, by any physical change. The point is that these times of confusion are those when an individual is most receptive to cultural imprinting, and that is why a vast number of completely different societies choose these moments to impose their learning.

How are these changes brought about? In order to impress them indelibly on the minds of their children and adolescents many cultures have discovered the most effective means are sudden, physically forceful and often very painful events—the initiation rites, those *rites de passage* whose circumcisions, flagellations, slashings, as Wober notes, with their shrieks and agony and dramatic ceremonies so excite anthropologists. He also notes, with some satisfaction, that he didn't really find any initiation rites in his girls' schools. But he missed the point. The most painful and agonising of the initiation rites, the *sine qua non* of the most violent, the one most usual when there is no violence, discovered and used in various forms by dozens of cultures, is the most simple—*it is to remove the children from their families.* This alone is pain enough, this on its own has the violence necessary to drive home for ever the importance of what is being taught, to bring about the necessary change.

Cohen does not agree that British public schools are examples of "extrusion" (the technical term). He says it cannot be extrusion because they return in the holidays and sleep under their parents' roof. I would refute this. The first major reason for (or result of) extrusion is shock. And it is shock and terror that echo continually down the ages in practically every account I have used in this history—the cries of abandonment wrung from the lips of children ripped from their families at the age of seven or eight or nine.

> I felt like a waif before the wind
> Tossed on an ocean of shock and change.

So sang, and sing, the boys at Harrow. The long corridors, the bleak dormitories with their hard beds and snow swirling through the windows, the harsh games fields—it seems, in many of the early memoirs, the very landscape of loneliness and despair. Second, the fact that this was repeated three times a year does not weaken its effect; in behavioural terms, it reinforces it. Something painful is the more painful for being repeated, not less. Third, Cohen ignores the time involved. The tribes who practise extrusion do so for, and at, widely varying times. The Manus of New Guinea, for instance, do not separate boys until they are fifteen; the Didinga in Africa separate them at eight, at thirteen and again at eighteen —but only for three or four months at a time. And in most, even split up, the total time away is not more than one and a half to two years. English prep and public school children are away for two-thirds of the year. They are often away a total of seven or eight years in all. For all these reasons our system, so far from not being extrusion, or being an example of mild extrusion, is still one of the most extreme examples it is possible to find. In the mid-19th century and before, when children only came home for four to six weeks in the whole year, it was probably the most extreme form there has ever been.

It is now necessary to make a distinction in the cultural use of removing children from their families. Those societies who do it most forcefully and for longest are those that wish to impress that the central loyalty of the culture is not to the nuclear family but to something wider—to the tribe itself or to the mother's relations or whatever it is. Such cultures are, anthropologically speaking, ones of "sociological interdependence". Family estrangements are brought about in order to focus loyalty on these wider areas and so, in the end, to lead to a greater cohesion in society. Out of sixty-five societies which Cohen studied, twenty-eight were of this sort. For example, the Andaman Islanders in the Bay of Bengal transfer loyalty to the tribe by having children adopted by a family in a different band at around the age of ten; the Basuto of South Africa wish to transfer loyalty to the father's line, and children are therefore "usually" brought up by their father's kinsmen outside the family.

Tribes which do not want to transfer loyalties, but wish to keep nuclear families at the centre of the social organisation—that is to say societies which are a series of interactions between separate and powerful families (technically "sociological independence")—do not practice extrusion, at any rate not at the age of eight to ten. Examples might be the Chamorros on the Island of Guam or the Chenchis of Hyderabad in India. Cohen looked at thirty-six such tribes. The distinguishing mark was that children continued to live in their parents' house until schooling was finished.

The second stage of education occurs at puberty, and it is these stages which are most often accompanied by the *rites de passage*. These have a number of classic features: the rite must be presided over by older members of the tribe, it must involve processes of indoctrination into customs of the group, it must involve physical ordeals. To these well-known elements Cohen was able to add refinements: the elders are of the child's kin group, all members must undergo it, the opposite sex is excluded, the rite is conducted in the group.

It is at this point we might begin to note some rather striking parallels with public schools. The times at which the separations occur will have been obvious. But in fact, if you replace kin group by class group, every single one of the features above—with some provisos—apply to the initiation ceremonies we studied in public schools. The resemblances are often close. The Arunta have to lie on green boughs over an open fire—you will remember the crawling over very hot radiators at Marlborough in the 1920s. A major theme has been beating. The Hopi *rites de passage* involve a fairly lengthy period of severe and frequent whipping, as do those of the Didinga and other tribes. Some of the parallels are comic. The Arunta have a preliminary rite which is called "Throwing the Boy up in the Air". Boys of the right age are assembled and simply thrown into the air by their elders. A similar, and far more significant parallel, is that all *rites de passage* are accompanied by separation from the family—sometimes for a few hours, more usually several days, quite often a few months. Often, this alone is considered a sufficient enforcing agency. That is to say, both here and at the earlier time of imprinting, removal from the family is itself one of the most potent methods of initiation. (In fact out of twenty-eight societies studied, eighteen had *rites de passage* at puberty; far fewer had them at eight to ten. Oddly enough I found far more overt initiation—tossing in blankets, walking along beams, having books hurled at you by "elders", etc.—at public schools than I did at prep schools.)

It might be wondered why so much pain and violence are necessary. Partly this is because it demonstrates to the initiate the power of the elders and society and discourages future rebellion. Mainly, removal from the family helps re-direct loyalty to other groups. But one might think the arousal of such intense adverse emotions might set the initiate against those causing them. He might temporarily obey, but fundamentally hate those who had burnt him or removed him from his family. Cohen now suggests a further reason, and from our point of view a significant one, for stirring up such strong but often negative emotions—terror, abandonment, pain. He quotes a number of discoveries made fairly recently by experimental biologists and physiologists, in particular from J. P. Scott's *Critical Periods in Behavioural Development.*

> All the evidence indicates that any sort of strong emotion, whether hunger, fear, pain or loneliness, will speed up the process of socialisation. . . . We may also conclude that the speed of formation of a social bond is dependent upon the degree of emotional arousal irrespective of that arousal. . . . Fear responses thus have the . . . effect of facilitating the formation of the social bond during the critical period. . . .
>
> Evidence is accumulating [he goes on] . . . that given any kind of emotional arousal a young animal will become attached to any individual or object with which it is in contact for a sufficiently long time. . . . It should not be surprising that many kinds of emotional reactions contribute to a social relationship. The surprising thing is that emotions which we normally consider aversive should produce the same effect as those which appear to be rewarding . . . this concept leads to the somewhat alarming conclusion that an animal (and perhaps a person) of any age, exposed to certain individuals or physical surroundings for any length of time, will inevitably become attached to them, the rapidity of the process being governed by the degree of emotional arousal associated with them.

It is necessary to be careful here. These conclusions have been drawn from studies of animals, not human beings. Nonetheless the *physiology* of such a reaction would probably be the same. If true, it explains a number of curious phenomena. It explains, for example, the very strong relationship which often springs up between hostages and kidnappers. It certainly explains a good deal in the history of the public schools.

Here is the significance of that early history. It was because the first schools grew up round the early religious centres that they became boarding. They were so few and so far apart that the only way their pupils could continue at them was to board. Thus a tradition was established. And, since not obviously harmful, it continued: buildings grew up, lodgings, money was invested, fees sought, the practice of sending children away became the custom.

But it is clear that, in the boarding system, the public schools discovered, quite by accident, an immensely powerful instrument for bringing about social change and imposing the knowledge and *mores* of a culture. So far from being "unnatural", it is in fact the method adopted by many other cultures to bring about analogous changes. When the system was at its height in the 19th century—that is (though there were short holidays) when the extrusion was very rigid and public schools reinforced it with their harshness and often explicit initiation ceremonies—it was a time when quite subtle social re-alignments had to be performed (this is still relevant today). The public schools were producing leaders—that is to say loyalty had to be removed from the family and redirected to the community, in the form of the army, the squirearchy, business, Parliament, the Civil Service, Colonial or Imperial Service or whatever. At the same time, the family had to remain important—though not nearly so central as in many primitive cultures. What one might call the public school boarding system of extrusion was ideal for this. It brought about a profound realignment towards the school, and thereafter the country and community as a whole; but, with its holidays, allowed the family to remain strong.

It would seem that the more difficult the alignment or change, the stronger the force that has to be exerted. For the family to remain central is easy, to redirect loyalty elsewhere difficult; extrusion is therefore necessary for the second but not for the first.

In tribes, the elders inculcating the customs and the lore are also, usually, those responsible for the religious ceremonies. Thus they have a double power. And here too that process by which the public schools grew from the early religious centres, and which for centuries joined them to the Church, gave them this enormous sacerdotal strength as well. Its ancient magic hypnotises them still.

Our survey, brief as it was, casts light on other spheres. The fact that terror, strong emotion even if painful, pain itself, can arouse positive feelings of loyalty, and reliance, even love—if true—explains that fawning I noted at times towards the beating. It explains why Keate, for example, was not more hated—or at least why the reactions to savage masters and savage conditions were often ambivalent. Autobiographies often described conditions, particularly as juniors, equivalent to concentration camps and yet insisted that their authors loved their schooldays.

It is clear now how powerful are the rivets which bind the middle classes—they have been pounded together by the primitive force of extrusion. (It is this, of course, which makes nonsense of any attempt to break the class barriers by any method which continues—or extends—boarding schools for the élite, no matter what class they are drawn from. It was in this sense, also, I meant such an effort was "impossible".) Indeed, we see that Britain is literally two cultures in a profound anthropological sense: the lower classes go to school from home and are "sociologically independent"; the middle classes are subject to extrusion and are therefore "sociologically interdependent".

This boarding force can hardly be exaggerated. And it explains one last phenomenon—the power of the public schools over those who had been at them. I said that the bizarre figures—of the fixated Old Boy, *Sixteen—A Diary of the Teens by a Boy*, the Reverend E. E. Bradford's verse, Tuke's paintings, and all that—did not seem completely explained by Connolly's theory of permanent adolescence, or any other theory. It is clear now what had happened to those people. To a large extent public schools relied on boys to initiate the newcomer, and control him for two years or more. Taken from his home into the tribe of the school, it was boys who performed the ceremonies upon him. The "elders" were elder boys, whipping, beating, bullying to produce the pain that brought re-alignment. But they had roused up forces more powerful than they knew. A certain number of boys, at a deep level probably a good many, became, in an anthropological sense, permanently re-aligned on the school. A duck which is hatched while a football rolls past and becomes imprinted with it is not immature precisely; it just has the wrong terms of reference—football equals mother. These boys had been hatched as it were—we are dealing with forces nearly as primitive—while a public school rolled past. The school *was* the world and when they were turned out into the real world it was too late to change again—the process can only operate effectively at eight to ten or at puberty. They were trapped, sealed for ever in the amber of their vanished adolescence.

2 Conclusion

We have pursued these extraordinary institutions from their remote beginnings in the Dark Ages through the sinuous windings of nearly 1,400 years. We saw them grow in the Middle Ages until the first recognisable outlines of public schools appeared with Winchester and Eton; from the 15th to the 17th centuries we watched while fagging, the classics, boarding, beating and bullying became part of their established lore; we saw the decline in the 18th century when drunk masters staggered out of pubs and drunk boys out of brothels and fags shrieking with pain and terror were scalped in Long Chamber amidst scurrying rats, a period culminating in a number of colossal explosions, furious rebellions either thrashed into submission by men like Keate or put down by the militia; we saw the reaction as the schools multiplied in the 19th century, their gradual concentration into tight little, mostly country-house, communities, the rise of athleticism, the intensifying disciplines, the wire entanglements of the sexual obsession, the development of that rigid, uniform, totalitarian, Church-centred, class-creating, Empire-fuelling body we called the Monolith; girls' schools appeared and tried to turn girls into men; progressive schools came in successive waves; and we followed the intertwining reaction of all this through the Cosy Years, the battle with the Monolith until, eventually, too close to need reviving, we reached the present day—boom-time, or last flicker before the barbarian hordes crash in and the schools find themselves back in the Dark Ages where they came in.

For two hundred years or so nearly all our great men have come from the public schools. And, just as public schools set their stamp on these men, so, through them, have they set their stamp on the country. But if this were all, then we would indeed have just been studying that wafer of privilege I mentioned in the first chapter. And this would still be so, though very considerably extended as a history, even though we saw how, by 1900 and up till very recently, if not still, the public school ethos and ideals had penetrated right down to the very bottom of our society and spread to its remotest areas.

But their influence has been more peculiar than this. Many of the characteristics we studied are human ones—other countries, for instance, have eccentrics or people who are over-conscientious, or have men who like to congregate in clubs. But the point is that in no other country do, or did, people spend the years from eight to eighteen away from home locked in the intensifying atmosphere of a one-sexed school; nowhere else do they get so total a grip of their material when it is so young and so impressionable, when what is fixed is fixed permanently and fixed, as it were, with passion. That is why, although what we found can no doubt be paralleled in America or France, say, it will never be found, among the people studied, so completely, so universally and so rigidly.

But many of the characteristics we saw were not just human—they were those which we consider peculiarly British, ones which we all share, whatever our position, age or sex. "All classes of this island," Anthony Powell has written, "converse in under-statement and irony." Reticence about displays of feeling, that romanticism we noted, the English genius for friendship between men, our liking for tradition—these and others are *national*. And here I would like to add one last stone to our edifice. This book does not stand entirely on its own. It is the second volume in the study, the first of which I have referred to (with some restraint) only four times before — *The Unnatural History of the Nanny*. It is a fact that practically all public school boys and girls from 1840 to 1939 would also have been brought up by a nurse or a nanny. And the two methods interlock at many points, the public schools reinforcing the nanny in numerous and fascinating ways—but particularly in those areas which I have suggested above that we consider characteristically British. And one of the most important facts about nannies was that they were invariably labouring working class, and their methods of bringing up their charges were working-class ones. It is hardly surprising, therefore, if we find characteristics in common.

There is thus a combination of forces: the stamp from above by our great men; the spread of the public school ethos; the intensifying effect of the education working to reinforce tendencies (and here the circle joins) already started by nannies; and the fact that nannies were lower class. It is this combination, complex and inter-acting, which helps to explain the extraordinary cohesion of English society from, roughly, 1830/40 to 1940/50; and at the same time explains the peculiar tension within that society, which made it so strong in war and which, as time passed, made it begin to pull apart in peace.

I say "explain"; but that is perhaps too high a claim. There are many influences at work here. But the subject of our enquiry has allowed us to explore very different and often curious areas of English history; indeed I think that some of these areas are not really accessible unless this route is followed, just as—though the comparison is not exact—some areas of a human being are not really accessible without a knowledge of his child-hood and youth. And our exploration at this particular profound depth has been coupled with exploration in the depth of time: ". . . older even than the throne of the nation itself," intoned Leach. Our subject has allowed us to trace—as it has also helped to build—the great poles which, rigid and unchanged, rise up through an immense stretch of our history, holding (or marking) like scaffolding the fabric of our society, and ensuring that, whether they survive or not, the nation will long, perhaps always, show the influence of the public schools, for ever be half maddened and half enchanted by that golden-haired young god with his satyr-like enigmatic smile, for ever responding to his song:

> Jolly boating weather,
> And a hay harvest breeze,
> Blade on the feather,
> Shade off the trees;
> Swing, swing together,
> With your bodies between your knees.

> Rugby may be more clever,
> Harrow may make more row;
> But we'll row for ever,
> Steady from stroke to bow;
> And nothing in life shall sever
> The chain that is round us now.

> Others will fill our places,
> Dressed in the old light blue;
> We'll recollect our races,
> We'll to the flag be true;
> Youth will be still in our faces
> When we cheer for an Eton crew.

Appendixes

Appendix A

Comparative values of the pound

Comparing the purchasing power of the pound over long periods is notoriously difficult. Some rough idea can be got for the 19th century from these figures obtained from the Central Statistical Office, based on the value of the pound in 1974.

Comparative Purchasing Power of Pound Based on 1974

1830	£12.25	1880	£11.20	1930	£7.65
1835	£13.50	1885	£13.50	1935	£8.50
1840	£10.35	1890	£13.50	1940	no figures
1845	£12.25	1895	£15.00	1946	£4.60
1850	£12.25	1900	£13.50	1950	£3.80
1855	£9.60	1905	£13.50	1955	£3.00
1860	£11.20	1910	£12.25	1960	£2.70
1865	£11.20	1915	£9.80	1965	£2.30
1870	£11.20	1920	£4.90	1970	£1.85
1875	£11.20	1925	£6.90		

Appendix B

Public schools listed in the first *Public Schools Year Book*, 1889

Bedford	Glenalmond	Rossall
Boston G.S., Lincs.	Haileybury	Rugby
Bradfield	Harrow	St. Paul's
Brighton	Hereford Catholic School	Sherborne
Charterhouse	Ipswich	Shrewsbury
Cheltenham	Lancing	Stonyhurst
Clifton	Loretto	Tonbridge
Derby	Malvern	Uppingham
Dover	Marlborough	Wellington
Dulwich	Merchant Taylors', London	Westminster
Eton	Portsmouth G.S.	Winchester
Fettes	Radley	Wyggeston

Appendix C

The sixty-four leading public schools *c.* 1880–1902 according to Professor J. R. de S. Honey of the University of Rhodesia (taken from his article in *The Victorian Public School*, edited by Brian Simon and Ian Bradley).

On the grounds that a school would only associate with another it regarded as approximately equal, he has analysed who associated with whom in a number of activities, including rowing, gymnastic competitions at Aldershot, athletics, shooting at Bisley, Cadet Corps activities, and cricket, rugby, football, fencing and racquets matches.

The catagories below are the result. Although I think they are open to question in some respects—the distance between schools is a factor, for instance (Shrewsbury might therefore have been irritated by its category) —it does give an idea of the "Public School Community" in 1902.

Further details of the late Victorian community of schools and the method of determining it can be found in J. R. de S. Honey's *Tom Brown's Universe* (Millington, 1977).

GROUP I (22 schools)

Bedford (Grammar)	Glenalmond	St. Paul's
Bradfield	Haileybury	Sherborne
Charterhouse	Harrow	Tonbridge
Cheltenham	Malvern	Uppingham
Clifton	Marlborough	Wellington
Dulwich	Repton	Westminster
Eton	Rossall	Winchester
	Rugby	

GROUP II (8 schools)

Blair Lodge	Highgate	Lancing
Eastbourne	Hurstpierpoint	Merchant Taylors'
Felsted		Radley

GROUP III (20 schools)

Bath College	Cranleigh	Loretto
Bedford Modern	Edinburgh Academy	Merchiston
Berkhamsted	Epsom	Reading
Blundell's	Fettes	Shrewsbury
Brighton	Forest	University Coll. Sch.
Cambridge (The Leys)	Leatherhead (St. John's)	Weymouth
Canterbury (King's Sch.)		Whitgift

GROUP IV (14 schools)

Aldenham	Framlingham	South Eastern Coll.
Ardingly	Isle of Man (King	(St. Lawrence), Rams-
Chigwell	William's)	gate
City of London	King's Coll. Sch.	United Services Coll.
Derby	Oundle	(Westward Ho)
Dover	St. Edward's, Oxford	Warwick

Appendix D

School vocabularies

Here are two examples of school vocabularies. The first list is a selection from the 120-odd words in Winchester's *Notions*. New boys still have to learn the entire vocabulary. The second is a list of words currently in use at Cheltenham Ladies' College.

Winchester

Abroad—out of the sickroom
Battlings—weekly pocket money
Bogle—(n) bicycle
     (vb) to bicycle
Brock—(n) an act of cruelty or unfairness
     (vb) to tease; to bully; to treat unfairly
Cud—pretty
Cus—order of marks in division or set
Firk—to expel
Foricas—W.C.
Hour!—Time!
Impotens—off games sick
Jig—a clever man
Jockey—to steal; to appropriate
Junior—an inferior liable to be sweated
Man—a member of the school
Mugging—school work
Nail—to detect
Notion—any word, custom, person or place peculiar to Wykehamists
Oil up—ingratiate yourself
Purl—to dive
Pussy—long woollen scarf
Quill—a source of pleasure
Remedy, half—a half holiday

Suction—sweets
Sweat—(n) 1. fagging
          2. hard work
     (vb) to fag
Thoke—(n) a rest
     (vb) to be idle
Toll abs—to run away from school
Tother—a prep school
Tug—usual; dull; routine
Zephyr—a football jersey

Cheltenham Ladies' College

Blue dot week—use of language lab
Bundling—exam papers collected and tied in red tape
Bunny run—stairs for Lower College girls
Dragon duty—staff Saturday morning duty
Explans—explanations for girls who have been late
Field—games fields
Going over the top of the house—going to see the Principal
Grays—lavatories off grand staircase
Lines—the move to prayers in form/prefect lines
Merits—marks for good work
Mufti—non-uniform
Patch—to retake O-level in following January
Patchers—girls doing this
Prac—practising time in music; practical in chemistry or physics
Pre—prefect
Red tape—to tie exam papers
Rehearsal Day—when organising for next academic year is rehearsed –
          desks, classrooms, etc.
Repetition—a punishment (need not be something to be repeated)
Rush around—when pupils rush around and thank staff at end of academic
          year
Sack dump—where satchels are dumped and collected
Slab—cupboard where messages left
Slip field—miss games
Sop—Songs of Praise Hymn Book
Throne—large seat under portrait of Miss Beale in hall
VV book—book for marks done *viva voce* in class
VV paper—paper for quick tests

Appendix E

Victorian family networks

Taken from T. W. Bamford's *The Rise of the Public Schools*. Table 2 is also an example of public school incest at Eton.

TABLE 1: Brief outline of the George Butler family tree

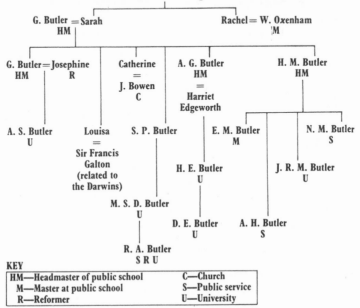

KEY

HM—Headmaster of public school	C—Church
M—Master at public school	S—Public service
R—Reformer	U—University

TABLE 2: Family network at Eton

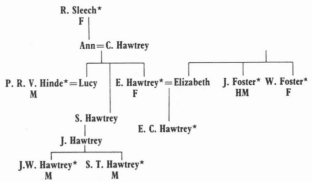

The names of men holding official posts at Eton are indicated by an asterisk(*).

P—Provost	VP—Vice-Provost
HM—Headmaster	F—Fellow
M—Assistant Master	

Appendix F

Church decline in the 19th century

Decline in the number of boys entering the Church during the 19th century. These figures from Rugby and Harrow are confirmed in detail by figures from Winchester over the century. Table from Bamford, *op. cit.*

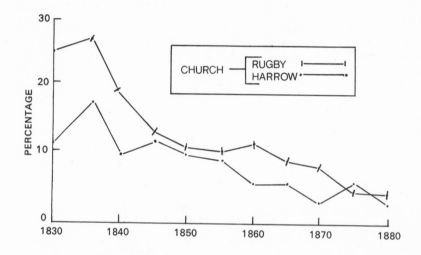

Appendix G

The future occupations of boys who entered Harrow and Rugby at five-yearly intervals from 1830 to 1880. From Bamford, *op. cit.*

Year	Armed forces	Church	Law	Administration and politics	Scholastics	Business	Overseas	Medicine	Science and Engineering	Other occupation	Died young	No information
RUGBY												
1830	9	28	13	12	3	3	3	1	0	0	1	40
1835	11	19	9	8	0	0	0	1	0	0	4	21
1840	21	22	9	11	4	5	3	0	1	0	4	39
1845	35	19	12	23	2	4	7	5	0	1	3	32
1850	38	15	15	16	5	5	9	2	0	4	10	28
1855	20	9	16	9	4	5	6	1	0	0	2	18
1860	26	16	27	7	5	9	14	2	3	3	3	28
1865	19	13	26	13	10	18	17	4	3	2	2	34
1870	18	11	19	8	2	34	11	3	4	5	5	21
1875	15	7	24	8	5	30	23	5	5	12	2	18
1880	8	5	22	5	6	26	11	7	6	2	3	13
HARROW												
1830	14	8	11	8	0	4	0	0	0	1	3	26
1835	7	6	3	10	0	2	1	0	0	0	0	8
1840	4	3	2	3	2	2	3	0	0	1	0	11
1845	14	9	10	16	2	6	2	0	1	2	4	9
1850	36	12	14	22	1	8	1	2	0	3	7	16
1855	42	13	25	23	1	9	3	0	1	0	0	22
1860	39	9	19	26	1	8	9	2	4	2	10	33
1865	26	9	13	19	1	24	16	1	2	4	5	38
1870	37	5	21	22	5	24	12	1	2	7	6	27
1875	32	9	22	21	2	23	13	3	1	9	1	23
1880	33	4	18	5	8	21	11	2	3	3	4	53
RUGBY AND HARROW COMBINED												
1830	23	36	24	20	3	7	3	1	0	1	4	66
1835	18	25	12	19	0	2	1	1	0	0	4	29
1840	25	25	11	15	6	7	6	0	1	1	4	50
1845	49	28	22	43	4	11	9	5	1	3	7	41
1850	74	27	29	39	6	13	10	4	0	7	17	44
1855	62	22	41	32	5	14	9	1	1	0	2	40
1860	65	25	46	33	6	17	23	4	7	5	13	61
1865	45	22	39	33	11	42	33	5	5	6	7	72
1870	55	16	40	30	7	58	23	4	6	12	11	48
1875	47	16	46	29	7	53	36	8	6	21	3	41
1880	41	9	40	10	14	47	22	9	9	5	7	66

Appendix H

Table showing which schools provided most officers in the Boer War and to which branches of the army. Taken from *The Victorian Public School, op. cit.*

School	Artillery (senior "departmental" service) Nos.
Cheltenham	84
Wellington	62
Harrow	43
Clifton	42

	Engineers
Wellington	26
Cheltenham	24
Clifton	16
Marlborough	15
Harrow	11

(Not a single Etonian in the Engineers!)

	Royal Army Medical Corps Nos.
Clifton	17
Edinburgh Academy	16
Dulwich	13
St. Paul's	13

(Epsom later became prominent here.)

	Infantry
Eton	610
Harrow	281
Wellington	280
Cheltenham	217
Charterhouse	191
Marlborough	191

Appendix I

Table taken from *The New Anatomy of Britain* by Anthony Sampson.

Public School League Table of Success in Winning Awards

School	Average sixth form	Total awards 1967–70	Percentage of sixth formers taking awards
Newcastle Royal Grammar	227	65	7·1
Dulwich	436	115	6·6
St. Paul's	359	95	6·6
Westminster	317	79	6·2
Winchester	366	88	6·0
Nottingham High	218	52	5·9
Christ's Hospital	272	61	5·6
Magdalen College School, Oxford	147	32	5·4
King Edward's, Birmingham	251	50	5·0
King's, Canterbury	357	70	4·9
Merchant Taylors', Northwood	278	55	4·9
King's College, Wimbledon	285	55	4·8
Manchester Grammar	537	101	4·7
St. Albans	193	36	4·7
Bradford Grammar	338	59	4·5
The Perse	122	21	4·3
City of London	252	42	4·2
Downside	285	47	4·1
Haberdashers' Aske's	283	47	4·1
Latymer Upper	311	49	4·0
Harrow	353	55	3·9
Clifton	352	47	3·8
Eltham College	143	22	3·8
University College, Hampstead	211	32	3·8
Highgate	237	35	3·7
Tiffin	241	36	3·7
Sherborne	305	44	3·6
Tonbridge	279	39	3·5
Rugby	415	56	3·4
Wyggeston	226	31	3·4
Eton	539	71	3·3
Sedbergh	199	25	3·1

Appendix J

These two tables, compiled from figures supplied by the DES (Department of Education and Science) and ISIS (Independent Schools Information Service), show the most recent successes of the Independent and Direct Grant Schools versus the State and Maintained sector. Clearly the State, since it teaches far greater numbers of pupils (81·05% of the total) gains numerically far more A-level passes. The significant point is that the Independent and Direct Grant schools teach *18·95%* of all pupils studying between 16 and 18. But they gain, both in A-level passes and in university entrants, far more than the 18·95% which, numerically, they should.

Table 1. A-Level Passes 1973

	2 As	3 As	4 As
State and Maintained	79·05%	71·82%	72·60%
Independent and Direct Grant	29·95%	28·17%	27·40%

Table 2. University Success 1974/76

	All Universities 74	Oxford 76	Cambridge 76
State and Maintained	52·3%	42·0%	40·0%
Direct Grant	15·1% } 25·8%	36·0% } 55·0%	35·0% } 53·0%
Independent	10·7%	19·0%	18·0%

Appendix K

Table from *The Public Schools and the Future* by J. C. Dancy.

Moray House IQ Distribution by Percentages in Public and Grammar Schools

Number of boys	Age	Dates	School	<104	105⁻⁹	110⁻⁴	115⁻⁹	120⁻⁴	125⁻⁹	130⁻⁴>	135
260	11	1945–52	Southern County G.S.	1	4	15	25	25	18	8	4
108	11	1949	Home Counties G.S.	1	7	11	18	23	21	16	3
188	11	1950–1	Northern County G.S.	—	1	7	16	22	27	21	6
72	11	1951	Highest of 3 London Area G.S.	—	—	—	7	32	25	15	21
640	13	1954–9	Lancing	4	7	19	23	16	14	5	12
548	13	1959–62	Marlborough	2	5	10	15	14	17	17	19

Appendix L

Educational background of MPs and Cabinet Ministers, 1918–55. From Bamford, *op. cit.* (after Guttsman).

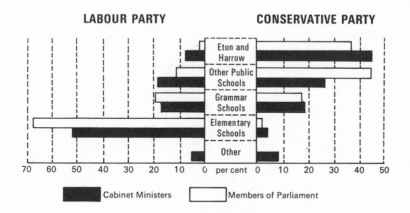

THE OLD SCHOOL TIE

Appendix M

Taken from Anthony Sampson, *op. cit.*

THE PROPORTIONS OF INDEPENDENT AND DIRECT GRANT SCHOOL PUPILS AT VARIOUS STAGES OF EDUCATION COMPARED WITH THE PROPORTIONS FROM THOSE SCHOOLS IN A SELECTION OF PROFESSIONS AND POSITIONS

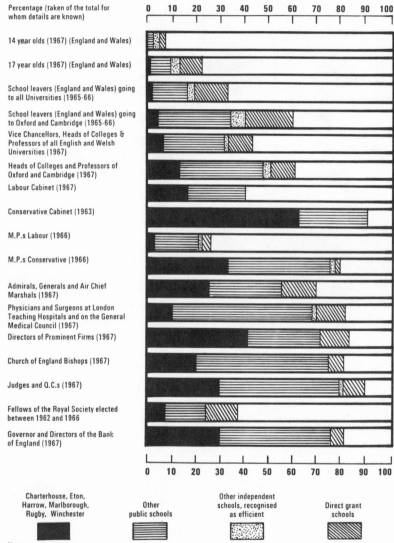

Percentage (taken of the total for whom details are known)

14 year olds (1967) (England and Wales)

17 year olds (1967) (England and Wales)

School leavers (England and Wales) going to all Universities (1965-66)

School leavers (England and Wales) going to Oxford and Cambridge (1965-66)

Vice Chancellors, Heads of Colleges & Professors of all English and Welsh Universities (1967)

Heads of Colleges and Professors of Oxford and Cambridge (1967)

Labour Cabinet (1967)

Conservative Cabinet (1963)

M.P.s Labour (1966)

M.P.s Conservative (1966)

Admirals, Generals and Air Chief Marshals (1967)

Physicians and Surgeons at London Teaching Hospitals and on the General Medical Council (1967)

Directors of Prominent Firms (1967)

Church of England Bishops (1967)

Judges and Q.C.s (1967)

Fellows of the Royal Society elected between 1962 and 1966

Governor and Directors of the Bank of England (1967)

Charterhouse, Eton, Harrow, Marlborough, Rugby, Winchester

Other public schools

Other independent schools, recognised as efficient

Direct grant schools

Notes
1. In these professions or positions former pupils of Scottish schools are included. Pupils at Scottish schools have not, however, been included in the totals of those at present receiving education because the categories of school in Scotland do not come within the same definitions as those in England and Wales. Inclusion of Scottish figures would not in any case significantly alter the diagram.

Appendix N

Table from *The Public Schools—A Factual Survey of Headmasters' Conference Schools in England and Wales* by Graham Kalton.

Authority of masters (other than headmaster and deputy headmaster) and boys to administer corporal punishment (1966)

Number of schools

Are any of the masters (other than the headmaster and deputy headmaster) allowed to administer corporal punishment?	Day	Mainly day	Mainly b'ding	B'ding	All survey schools
Yes	20	34	59	32	145
No	12	2	5	2	21
Total	32	36	64	34	166

Are any of the boys allowed to administer corporal punishment?	Day	Mainly day	Mainly b'ding	B'ding	All survey schools
Yes	13	19	44	27	103
No	19	17	20	7	63
Total	32	36	64	34	166

Bibliography

Allen, B. M. *Sir Robert Morant.* Toronto: Macmillan Co., 1934.

Annan, Noel, *Roxburgh of Stowe.* New York: Schocken Books, 1966.

Anon. *Sixteen—A Diary of the Teens by a Boy.* London, 1917.

Badley, J. H. *Bedales.* London: Methuen & Co., 1923.

Bamford, T. W. *Discipline at Rugby under Arnold.* Educational Review, Vol. X, No. 1.

———. *The Rise of the Public Schools.* Toronto: Nelson, Foster & Scott, 1967.

———. *Thomas Arnold.* London: Ambassador, 1960.

Barnard, H. C. *A History of English Education from 1760.* London: University of London, 1970.

Barnett, Correlli. *The Collapse of British Power.* New York: Morrow, 1972.

Betjeman, John. *Summoned by Bells.* Boston: Houghton Mifflin, 1960.

Birt, Dom Henry Norbert. *Downside.* London, 1902.

Blunden, E. *Christ's Hospital.* London: Christophers, 1928.

Bradley, A. G., *et al. A History of Marlborough College.* London, 1893.

Brown, Peter. *Augustine of Hippo.* Berkeley: University of California Press, 1967.

Buchan, John. *Pilgrim's Way: An Essay in Recollection.* Boston: Houghton Mifflin, 1940.

Bussy, Dorothy. *Olivia by Olivia.* New York: Sloane, 1949.

Campbell, Michael. *Lord Dismiss Us.* New York: Putnam, 1968.

Carleton, John. *Westminster School.* London: Hart-Davis, 1965.

Checkland, S. G. *The Gladstones.* New York: Cambridge University Press, 1971.

Churchill, Randolph S. *Winston S. Churchill, Vol. 1: Youth.* Boston: Houghton Mifflin, 1966.

Churchill, Winston S. *My Early Life.* New York: Scribner's, 1961.

Clarke, A. K. *A History of The Cheltenham Ladies' College.* London: Faber, 1953.

Coade, T. F. *The Burning Bow.* London: Allen and Unwin, 1966.

Cohen, Y. A. *The Transition from Childhood to Adolescence.* Chicago: Aldine, 1964.

Connolly, Cyril. *Enemies of Promise.* Boston: Little, Brown and Co., 1939.

Crump, Geoffrey. *Bedales Since the War.* London: Chapman and Hall, 1936.

Dancy, John. *The Public Schools and the Future.* New York: Humanities Press, 1967.

Disraeli, Benjamin. *Coningsby.* London: Dent, 1959 ed.

Douglas, M. A., and Ash, C. R., eds. *The Godolphin Schools, 1726-1926.* London: Longmans, 1928.

Doyle, A. Conan. *Memoirs and Adventures*. Boston: Little, Brown and Co., 1924.

Driberg, J. H. *At Home with Savages*. New York: Morrow, 1932.

Essays on Duty and Discipline. London: Cassell, 1914.

Evans-Pritchard, E. E. *The Nuer*. New York: Oxford University Press, 1968.

Farrar, Frederick W. *Eric, or Little by Little*. London: Hamish Hamilton, 1972 ed.

Firth, J. D'E. *Winchester College*. London: McDonald & Co., 1949.

Fortes, Mayer. *Time and Social Structure*. New York: Humanities Press, 1970.

Fraser, George Macdonald. *Flashman*. New York: World, 1969.

Freeman, Gillian. *The Schoolgirl Ethic: Life and Work of Angela Brazil*. London: Allen Lane, 1976.

Friedenberg, Edgar Z. *The Vanishing Adolescent*. Boston: Beacon Press, 1964.

Furse, Ralph. *Acuparius: Recollections of a Recruiting Officer*. New York: Oxford University Press, 1962.

Gardiner, Dorothy. *English Girlhood at School*. New York: Oxford University Press, 1929.

Gardner, Brian. *The Public Schools*. London: Hamish Hamilton, 1973.

Gathorne-Hardy, Jonathan. *The Unnatural History of the Nanny*. New York: Dial Press, 1973.

Glenday, N., and Price, Mary. *Reluctant Revolutionaries—A Century of Headmistresses, 1874-1974*. London: Pitman, 1975.

Goffman, Erving. *Asylums*. New York: Penguin, 1970.

Goulay, A. B. *A History of Sherborne School*. Winchester: Warren, 1951.

Graves, Robert. *Goodbye to All That*. Garden City, N. Y.: Doubleday, 1957.

Greene, Graham, ed. *The Old School*. London: Jonathan Cape, 1937.

Grier, Lynda. *Achievement in Education*. Toronto: Longmans Green, 1952.

Grosskurth, Phyllis. *The Woeful Victorian*. New York: Holt, Rinehart, 1965.

Hadfield, J. A. *Childhood and Adolescence*. New York: Penguin, 1970.

Hemmings, James. *Problems of Adolescent Girls*. London: Heinemann, 1960.

Henriques, Fernando. *Prostitution and Society*. New York: Grove Press, 1966.

Heussler, R. *Yesterday's Rulers: The Making of the British Colonial Service*. New York: Oxford University Press, 1963.

Hill, Rowland, *et al. Public Education: Plans . . . Hazelwood School*. 2nd ed., 1825.

Hollis, Christopher. *Eton: A History*. London: Hollis & Carter, 1960.

Holmes, Richard. *Shelley: The Pursuit*. New York: Dutton, 1975.

Hughes, Thomas. *Tom Brown's Schooldays*. London, 1857.

Illich, Ivan. *Deschooling Society*. New York: Harper & Row, 1971.

Inglis, Brian, ed. *John Bull's Schooldays*. London: Hutchinson, 1961.

James, Norman G. B. *History of Mill Hill*. London, 1909.

James, Robert Rhodes. *Rosebery*. New York: Macmillan, 1964.

Jameson, E. M. *Charterhouse*. Glasgow: Blackie, 1937.

Kalton, Graham. *The Public Schools: A Factual Survey*. Toronto: Longmans Green, 1966.

Kamm, Josephine. *Hope Deferred: Girls' Education in English History*. London: Methuen, 1965.

Kerr, Anthony. *Schools of Europe*. London: Bowes and Bowes, 1960.

King, Edmund J. *Other Schools and Ours*. New York: Henry Holt, 1958.

Kinsey, Alfred C., *et al*. *Sexual Behavior in the Human Female*. Philadelphia: W. B. Saunders; 1953.

———. *Sexual Behavior in the Human Male*. Philadelphia: W. B. Saunders, 1948.

Kipling, Rudyard. *Stalky & Co*. New York: Dell, 1968.

Lamb, G. F. *The Happiest Days*. Toronto: Collins, 1959.

Lambert, Royston. *The State and Boarding Education*. New York: Barnes & Noble, 1966.

———. *The Chance of a Lifetime?* London: Weidenfeld and Nicolson, 1968.

———. *The Hothouse Society*. New York: Penguin, 1974.

———. *A Manual to the Sociology of the School*. London: Weidenfeld and Nicolson, 1970.

———. *New Wine in Old Bottles?* London: G. Bell, 1968.

Lane, Homer. "The Age of Loyalty," from *Four Lectures on Childhood*. London: Allen and Unwin, 1928.

Leach, A. F. *History of Bradfield College*. London, 1900.

———. *Schools of Medieval England*. London, 1915.

———. *English Schools at the Reformation*. London, 1896.

———. *A History of Winchester College*. London: Duckworth, 1899.

Longford, Elizabeth. *The Years of the Sword*. New York: Harper & Row, 1969.

Lowndes, G. A. N. *The Silent Social Revolution*. New York: Oxford University Press, 1969.

Lunn, Arnold. *The Harrovians*. London: Methuen, 1913.

Mack, E. C. *Public Schools and British Opinion, 1780-1860*. London: Methuen, 1938.

———. *Public Schools and British Opinion Since 1860*. New York: Columbia University Press, 1941.

Malinowski, Bronislaw. *The Sexual Life of Savages*. New York: Liveright, 1929.

Marchand, Leslie A. *Byron*, Vol. 1. New York: Knopf, 1957.

Marshall, Bruce. *George Brown's Schooldays*. London: Constable, 1946.

Maugham, Robin. *Escape from the Shadows*. New York: McGraw-Hill, 1973.

Mead, Margaret. *Coming of Age in Samoa*. New York: Morrow, 1928.

Morgan, M. C. *Cheltenham College*. New York: Sadlier, 1968.

Morley, John. *Life of Gladstone*. New York: Macmillan, 1903.

National Foundation for Education Research. *A Survey of Rewards and Punishments in Schools*.

Neill, A. S. *Summerhill: A Radical Approach to Education*. New York: Hart, 1960.

Newell, Peter, ed. *A Last Resort? Corporal Punishment in Schools*. New York: Penguin, 1972.

Newsom, John. *The Education of Girls*. London: Faber, 1948.

Nicolson, Harold. *Some People*. London: Constable, 1958.

Ollerenshaw, Kathleen. *The Girls' Schools*. London: Faber & Faber, 1967.

Orwell, George. "Boys' Weeklies." Essay from *Inside the Whale*. London: Gollancz, 1940.

———. "Such, Such Were the Joys." Essay from *Collected Essays*. Toronto: British Book Service, 1962.

Orwell, Sonia, and Angus, Ian, eds. Journalism and Letters of GO, Vol. IV, *In Front of Your Nose*. New York: Harcourt Brace Jovanovich, 1968.

Percival, Alicia C. *Very Superior Men*. London: Charles Knight, 1975.

Pitt, Jeremy. *Square Peg*. London: Centaur Press, 1961.

Pryce-Jones, D., ed. *Evelyn Waugh and His World*. Boston: Little, Brown and Co. 1973.

Radcliffe-Brown, A. *The Andaman Islanders*. New York: Cambridge University Press, 1922.

Reé, Harry. *Educator Extraordinary—The Life and Achievement of Henry Morris*. Toronto: Longmans Green, 1973.

Rodgers, John. *The Old Public Schools of England*. New York: Scribners, 1938.

Rousseau, J. J. *Emile, or Education*. Trans. Barbara Foxley. Everyman, 1921.

Sadler, M. *Michael Ernest Sadler*. Toronto: Longmans Green, 1949.

Sampson, Anthony. *The New Anatomy of Britain*. New York: Stein & Day, 1972.

Sargent, John. *Annals of Westminster School*.

Simon, Brian, and Bradley, Ian, eds. *The Victorian Public School*. New York: Humanities Press, 1975.

Simpson, J. H. *Schoolmaster's Harvest*. London: Faber & Faber, 1965.

Skidelsky, Robert. *English Progressive Schools*. Baltimore: Penguin, 1969.

Stanley, A. P. *The Life and Correspondence of Thomas Arnold*, 2 vols. 1845.

Sterry, Wasey. *Annals of Eton College*. 1898.

Stewart, W. A. C. *Progressives and Radicals in English Education, 1750-1970*. New York: Kelly, 1972.

———. *Quakers and Education*. Port Washington, N. Y.: Kennikat, 1971.

Toynbee, Philip. *Friends Apart*. London: Macgibbon and Kee, 1954.

Trelawny-Ross, A. H. *Their Prime of Life*. Boston: Warren, 1956.

Usborne, Richard. *Clubland Heroes*. London: Barrie and Jenkins, 1975.

Vachell, Horace Annesley. *The Hill*. London: Murray, 1905.

Wakeford, John. *The Cloistered Elite*. New York: Praeger, 1969.

Walker, W. G. *A History of Oundle School*. Printed for The Grocer's Company, 1956.

Waugh, Alec. *The Early Years of Alec Waugh*. New York: Farrar, Straus, 1963.

————. *The Loom of Youth*. Ontario: Bles, 1955.

Waugh, Evelyn, *A Little Learning*. Boston: Little, Brown and Co., 1964.

Wells, H. G. *The Story of a Great Schoolmaster*. London: Chatto and Windus, 1924.

West, J. M. *Shrewsbury*. Salop, England: Wilding, 1934.

Wilson, James M. *Autobiography: 1836-1931*. London: Sedgwick and Jackson, 1932.

Wober, Mallory. *English Girls' Boarding Schools*. London: Allen Lane, 1971.

Wodehouse, P. G. *The Girl on the Boat*. New York: Simon & Schuster, 1956.

Woolf, L. *Sowing: An Autobiography of the Years 1880-1904*. New York: Harcourt Brace, 1960.

Worsley, T. C. *Flannelled Fool: A Slice of Life in the Thirties*. New York: Collins, 1967.

Zeller, Dom Hubert Van. *Downside By and Large*. New York: Sheed and Ward, 1954.

Zouche, Dorothy E. de. *Roedean—1885-1955*. Printed for private circulation.

Index

1 Lawrence Sheriff Street

2 Porch & Turret

3 Gate, High Street

4 The Cloisters

5 Hall